Teacher's Annotated Edition

Children
The Early Years

Dr. Celia A. Decker

Professor of Family and Consumer Sciences
Northwestern State University of Louisiana
Natchitoches, Louisiana

Publisher
The Goodheart-Willcox Company, Inc.
Tinley Park, Illinois

Contents

Introduction

Teaching Aids

Introduction

Children: The Early Years is a comprehensive text designed to help students understand children's physical, intellectual, and social-emotional development from the prenatal stage through the school-age years. In addition to the student text, the *Children: The Early Years* learning package includes the *Student Activity Guide, Teacher's Annotated Edition, Teacher's Resource Guide, Teacher's Resource Binder,* and *Test Creation Software*. Using these products can help you develop an effective child development program tailored to your students' unique needs.

● Using the Text

The text *Children: The Early Years* is designed to help your students learn about how children grow and develop. Students will learn basic information about meeting children's needs in each stage of development.

The text is divided into 7 parts with a total of 25 chapters. The material is organized and presented in a logical sequence of topics for the study of child development. Although the text was written to be studied in its entirety, individual chapters and sections are complete enough to be studied independently.

Children: The Early Years contains important components developed to support your curriculum and help you meet your students' needs. The text is thorough as well as easy to read. Hundreds of photographs, charts, and illustrations attract student interest and emphasize key concepts. The copy references all illustrations, which helps students associate the written material with the visual image and reinforces learning.

The text includes an expanded table of contents to give students an overview of the wide variety of topics they will be studying. The glossary helps students learn terms related to child development. A complete index helps them find information they want quickly and easily.

Each chapter includes several features designed to help students study effectively and review what they have learned.

Objectives. A set of behavioral objectives appears at the beginning of each chapter. These are performance goals that students will be expected to achieve after studying the chapter. Review the objectives in each chapter with students to help make them aware of the skills they will be building as they read the chapter material.

Terms. A list of vocabulary terms is also found at the beginning of each chapter. Terms are listed in alphabetical order. These terms are in bold italic type throughout the text so students can recognize them while reading. Discussing these words with students will help them learn concepts to which they are being introduced. To help students become familiar with these terms, you may want to ask them to

- ☐ look up, define, and explain each term.
- ☐ relate each term to the topic being studied.
- ☐ match terms with their definitions.
- ☐ find examples of how the terms are used in current newspapers and magazines, reference books, and other related materials.

Summary. A chapter summary is located at the end of each chapter. This section is a review of the major concepts covered in the entire chapter.

To Review. The review questions at the end of each chapter cover the basic information presented. This section consists of a variety of true/false, completion, multiple choice, and short essay questions. It is designed to help students recall, organize, and use the information presented in the text. Answers to these questions appear in the front section of the *Teacher's Annotated Edition* as well as in the *Teacher's Resource Guide* and the *Teacher's Resource Binder.*

To Do. The activities in this section offer students opportunities to increase knowledge through firsthand experiences. These activities encourage students to apply many of the concepts learned in the chapter to real-life situations. Suggestions for both individual and group work are provided in varying degrees of difficulty. Therefore, you may choose and assign activities according to students' interests and abilities.

To Observe. The observations in this section are intended to expand student thinking and follow up on the content in each chapter. The observations are meant to be thought-provoking exercises that reinforce chapter content with real-life examples. They should motivate students to seek further information and to exchange their thoughts and opinions with other class members.

To Think Critically. These activities at the end of each chapter encourage critical thinking. Thought-provoking questions require students to apply chapter material to their own lives. The use of imagination and problem-solving techniques are promoted.

● Using the *Student Activity Guide*

The *Student Activity Guide* designed for use with *Children: The Early Years* helps students recall and review material presented in the text. It also helps them think critically about chapter content and form their own conclusions.

The activities in the guide are divided into chapters that correspond to the chapters in the text. The text provides the information students will need to complete many of the activities. Other activities will require creative thinking and research beyond the textbook.

You may want to use the exercises in the *Student Activity Guide* that are directly related to textual material as introductory, review, or evaluation tools. Ask students to do the exercises without looking in the book. Then they can use the text to check their answers and to answer

questions they could not complete. The pages of the *Student Activity Guide* are perforated so students can easily turn completed activities in to you for evaluation.

The *Student Activity Guide* includes different types of activities. Some have specific answers related to text material. Students can use these activities to review as they study for tests and quizzes. Answers to these activities appear in the *Teacher's Resource Guide* and *Teacher's Resource Binder.*

Other activities ask for students' thoughts or opinions. Answers to these activities cannot be judged as right or wrong. These activities allow students to form their own ideas by considering alternatives and evaluating situations thoughtfully. These thought-provoking exercises can often be used as a basis for classroom discussion by asking students to justify their answers and conclusions.

The use of each activity in the *Student Activity Guide* is described in the *Teacher's Resource Guide* and *Teacher's Resource Binder* as a teaching strategy under the related instructional concept. Activities are identified by name and letter.

● Using the *Teacher's Annotated Edition*

The *Teacher's Annotated Edition* for *Children: The Early Years* is a special edition of the student text. It is designed to help you more effectively coordinate materials in the *Student Activity Guide* with text concepts. It also provides you with additional suggestions to help you add variety to your classroom teaching.

Annotations are located throughout the text. Numbers are placed in the right and left side margins that correspond with annotations located at the bottom of each page. The following chart details the annotations used in the annotated edition.

Annotation Term	Annotation Description
Vocabulary	Suggests vocabulary reinforcement activities such as defining terms, using terms in sentences, looking up terms in the glossary, or comparing important new terms.
Discuss	Discussion questions to reteach or reinforce learning. Questions may also relate to charts in the chapters.
Reflect	Questions to ask students to think about regarding the concepts presented, often by applying the content to their own lives. These questions are often more personal than the discussion questions are.
Activity	Activities related to the chapter that would reteach and reinforce concepts.
Note	Additional points the instructor might want to make regarding the chapter, or to spark student interest in the discussion. Points might include statistics, interesting facts, or historical notes. These may also be notes to the instructor regarding the subject matter.
Example	An example to use in illustrating an important point in the chapter material.
Enrich	Activities that relate to the concept, but are more involved and challenging for students. Examples include role-playing, research topics, debates, surveys, bulletin boards, field trips, or guest speakers.
Resource	An activity from the *Student Activity Guide* that is appropriate for use with this section of the chapter.
Answers	These annotations indicate where answers to questions may be found.

In addition to annotations placed throughout the student text, the *Teacher's Annotated Edition* includes a special front section. It begins with a detailed introduction explaining how to use the various components in the teaching package for *Children: The Early Years.* This section also contains several features designed to help you prepare meaningful lessons for your students.

▶ Teaching Suggestions

A number of suggestions are given to help you increase the effectiveness of your classroom teaching. This information includes suggestions for teaching students of varying abilities, evaluating students, communicating with students, and promoting your program.

▶ Correlation of National Standards for Human Development with *Children: The Early Years*

In 1998, the National Standards for Family and Consumer Sciences Education were finalized. This comprehensive guide provides family and consumer sciences educators with a structure for identifying what learners should be able to do. This structure is based on knowledge and skills needed for work life and family life, as well as family and consumer sciences careers. The National Standards Components include 16 areas of study, each with a comprehensive standard that describes the overall content of the area. Each comprehensive standard is then broken down into content standards that describe what is expected of the learner. Competencies further define the knowledge, skills, and practices of the content standards and provide the basis for measurement criteria.

By studying the text *Children: The Early Years,* students will be prepared to master the competencies listed for the area of study called *Human Development.* To help you see how this can be accomplished, a *Correlation of National Standards for Human Development with Children: The Early Years* has been included in the *Teacher's Annotated Edition, Teacher's Resource Guide,* and *Teacher's Resource Binder.* If you want to make sure you prepare students to meet the National Standards for Family and Consumer Sciences Education, this chart should be of interest to you.

▶ Scope and Sequence Chart

A *Scope and Sequence Chart,* located at the end of the introduction, identifies the major concepts presented in each chapter of the text. This special resource is provided to help you select for study those topics that meet your curriculum needs.

▶ Teaching Aids

The last item in the front section of the annotated text is a chapter-by-chapter teaching aids resource. It is designed to assist you in developing lesson plans and evaluating student learning. The following aids are included for each chapter of the text:

Chapter Outline. An outline of the chapter's main points is provided to give you an overview of the content and organization of chapter material.

Suggested Observations. A listing of suggested observations for the chapter is provided. Use this resource to help you make any advance arrangements necessary for your students to observe various aspects of child development.

Answer Key. Answers for the "To Review" questions at the end of each chapter are supplied to assist you in clarifying student understanding of chapter concepts.

● Using the *Teacher's Resource Guide*

The *Teacher's Resource Guide* for *Children: The Early Years* suggests many methods of presenting the concepts in the text to students. It begins with some of the same helpful information found in the *Teacher's Annotated Edition,* including teaching suggestions, the *Correlation of National Standards for Human Development with Children: The Early Years*, and a *Scope and Sequence Chart.*

▶ Basic Skills Chart

Another feature of the *Teacher's Resource Guide* is a *Basic Skills Chart.* This chart has been included to identify those activities that encourage the development of the following basic skills: verbal, reading, writing, mathematical, scientific, and analytical. (Analytical skills involve the higher-order thinking skills of analysis, synthesis, and evaluation in problem-solving situations.) The chart includes activities from the "To Do" section of the text, activities from the *Student Activity Guide,* and strategies from the *Teacher's Resource Guide/Binder.* Incorporating a variety of these activities into your daily lesson plans will provide your students with vital practice in the development of basic skills. Also, if you find that students in your classes are weak in a specific basic skill, you can select activities to strengthen that particular skill area.

▶ Chapter-by-Chapter Resources

Like the *Student Activity Guide,* the *Teacher's Resource Guide* is divided into chapters that match the chapters in the text. Each chapter contains the following features:

Objectives. These are the objectives that students will be able to accomplish after reading the chapter and completing the suggested activities.

Bulletin Board Ideas. Bulletin board ideas are described for each chapter. Many of these ideas are illustrated for you. Putting up bulletin board displays can often be a stimulating student activity.

Teaching Materials. A list of materials available to supplement each chapter in the text is provided. The list includes the names of all the activities contained in the *Student Activity Guide* and all the masters contained in the *Teacher's Resource Guide/Binder.*

Introductory Activities. These motivational exercises are designed to stimulate your students' interest in the chapter they will be studying. The activities help create a sense of curiosity that students will want to satisfy by reading the chapter.

Strategies to Reteach, Reinforce, Enrich, and Extend Text Concepts. A variety of student learning strategies are described for teaching each of the major concepts discussed in the text. Each major concept appears in the guide in bold type. The student learning experiences for each concept follow. Activities from the *Student Activity Guide* are identified for your convenience in planning daily lessons. They are identified with the letters SAG following the title and letter of the activity. (*Bedtime Rituals,* Activity A, SAG.)

The number of each learning strategy is followed by a code in bold type. These codes identify the teaching goals each strategy is designed to accomplish. The following codes have been used:

RT identifies activities designed to help you *reteach* concepts. These strategies present the chapter concepts in a different way to allow students additional learning opportunities.

RF identifies activities designed to *reinforce* concepts to students. These strategies present techniques and activities to help clarify facts, terms, principles, and concepts, making it easier for students to understand.

ER identifies activities designed to *enrich* learning. These strategies help students learn more about the concepts presented by involving them more fully in the material. Enrichment strategies include diverse experiences, such as demonstrations, field trips, guest speakers, panels, and surveys.

EX identifies activities designed to *extend* learning. These strategies promote thinking skills, such as critical thinking, creative thinking, problem solving, and decision making. Students must analyze, synthesize, and evaluate in order to complete these activities.

Answer Key. This section provides answers for review questions at the end of each chapter in the text, for activities in the *Student Activity Guide,* for the reproducible masters in the *Teacher's Resource Guide/Binder,* and for the chapter tests.

Reproducible Masters. Several reproducible masters are included for each chapter. These masters are designed to enhance the presentation of concepts in the text. Some also provide related material beyond the scope of the text that you may want students to know. Some of the masters are designated as *transparency masters* for use with an overhead projector. These are often charts or graphs that can serve as a basis for class discussion of important concepts. They can also be used as student handouts. Other masters are activities designed to be copied and given to students to encourage creative and critical thinking.

Chapter Test Masters. Individual tests with clear, specific questions that cover all the chapter topics are provided. True/false, multiple choice, and matching questions are used to measure student learning about facts and definitions. Essay questions are also provided in the chapter tests. Some of these require students to list information, while others encourage students to express their opinions and creativity. You may wish to modify the tests and tailor the questions to your classroom needs.

● Using the *Teacher's Resource Binder*

The *Teacher's Resource Binder* for *Children: The Early Years combines the Teacher's Resource Guide* with color transparencies. These transparencies add variety to your classroom lecture as you discuss topics included in the text with your students. You will find some transparencies useful in illustrating and reinforcing information presented in the text. Others will provide you with an opportunity to extend learning beyond the scope of the text. Attractive colors are visually appealing and hold students' attention. Suggestions for how the transparencies can be used in the classroom are included.

All the materials are included in a convenient three-ring binder. Reproducible materials can be removed easily. Handy dividers included with the binder help you organize materials so you can quickly find the items you need.

● Using the *Test Creation Software*

In addition to the printed supplements designed to support *Children: The Early Years, Test Creation Software* is available. The database for this software package includes all the test master questions from the *Teacher's Resource Guide/Binder* plus an additional 25 percent new questions prepared just for this product. You can opt to choose specific questions from the database and, if you wish, add your own questions to create customized tests to meet your classroom needs. You may want to make different versions of the same test to use during different class periods. Answer keys are generated automatically to simplify grading.

● Teaching Techniques

You can make the study of child development exciting and relevant by using a variety of teaching techniques. Some principles that will help you choose and use different teaching techniques in your classroom are the following:

☐ Make learning stimulating. One way to do this is to involve students in lesson planning. When possible, allow them to select the modes of learning they enjoy most. For example, some students will do well with oral reports; others prefer written assignments. Some learn well through group projects; others do better working independently. You can also make courses more interesting by presenting a variety of learning activities and projects from which students may choose to fulfill their work requirement.

☐ Make learning realistic. You can do this by relating the subject matter to issues that concern young people. Students gain the most from learning when they can apply it to real-life situations. Case studies, role plays, and stories of personal experiences all make learning more realistic and relevant.

☐ Make learning varied. Try using several different techniques to teach the same concept. Use outside resources and accounts of current events as they apply to material being presented in class. Students learn through their senses of sight, hearing, touch, taste, and smell. The more senses they use, the easier it will be for them to retain information. Bulletin boards, films, tapes, and transparencies all appeal to the senses.

☐ Make learning success oriented. Experiencing success increases self-esteem and confidence. Guarantee success for your students by presenting a variety of learning activities. Key these activities to different ability levels so each student can enjoy both success and challenge. You will also want to allow for individual learning styles and talents. For example, creative students may excel at designing projects, while analytical students may be more proficient at organizing details. Build in opportunities for individual students to work in ways that let them succeed and shine.

☐ Make learning personal. Young people become more personally involved in learning if you establish a comfortable rapport with them. Work toward a relaxed classroom atmosphere in which students can feel at ease when sharing their feelings and ideas in group discussions and activities.

Following are descriptions of various teaching techniques you may want to try. Keep in mind that not all methods work equally well in all classrooms. A technique that works beautifully with one group of students may not be successful with another. The techniques you choose will depend on the topic, your teaching goals, and the needs of your students.

One final consideration concerns students' right to privacy. Some activities, such as autobiographies, diaries, and opinion papers, may invade students' privacy. You can maintain a level of confidentiality by letting students turn in unsigned papers in these situations. You may also encourage students to pursue some of these activities at home for personal enlightenment without fear of evaluation or judgment.

▶ Helping Students Gain Basic Information

Many teaching techniques can be grouped according to different goals you may have for your students. One group of techniques is designed to convey information to students. Two of the most common techniques in this group are reading and lecture. Using a number of variations can make these techniques seem less common and more interesting. For instance, students may enjoy taking turns reading aloud as a change of pace from silent reading. Lectures can be energized by the use of flip charts, overhead transparencies, and other visual materials. Classroom discussions of different aspects of the material being presented get students involved and help impart information.

Other ways to present basic information include the use of outside resources. Guest speakers, whether speaking individually or as part of a panel, can bring a new outlook to classroom material. Guest lectures can be videotaped to show again to other classes or to use for review. In addition to videotapes, students also enjoy related films and filmstrips.

▶ Helping Students Question and Evaluate

A second group of teaching techniques helps students develop analytic and judgmental skills. These techniques help your students go beyond what they see on the surface. As you employ these techniques, encourage students to think about points raised by others. Ask them to evaluate how new ideas relate to their attitudes about various subjects.

Discussion is an excellent technique for helping students consider an issue from a new point of view. To be effective, discussion sessions require a great deal of advance planning and preparation. Consider the size of the discussion group and the physical arrangement. Because many students are reluctant to contribute in a large group, you may want to divide the class into smaller groups for discussion sessions. Participation will also be enhanced if the room is arranged so students can see each other.

Discussion can take a number of forms. Generally it is a good idea to reserve group discussions involving the entire class for smaller classes. Buzz groups consisting of two to six students offer a way to get willing participation from students who are not naturally outgoing. They discuss an issue among themselves and then appoint a spokesperson to report back to the entire class.

Debate is an excellent way to explore opposite sides of an issue. You may want to divide the class into two groups, each taking an opposing side of the issue. You can also ask students to work in smaller groups and explore opposing sides of different issues. Each group can select members to present points for their side.

▶ Helping Students Participate

Another group of teaching techniques is designed to promote student participation in classroom activities and discussion. There are many ways to involve students and encourage them to interact. Case studies, surveys, opinionnaires, stories, and pictures can all boost classroom participation. These techniques allow students to react to or evaluate situations in which they are not directly involved. Open-ended sentences often stimulate discussion. However, it is wise to steer away from overly personal or confidential matters when selecting sentences for completion. Students may be reluctant to deal with confidential issues in front of classmates.

The "fishbowl" can be a good way to stimulate class discussion. An interactive group of five to eight students is encircled by a larger observation group. The encircled students discuss a given topic while the others listen. Observers may not talk or interrupt. Positions can be reversed at the end of a fishbowl session to allow some observers to participate.

One of the most effective forms of small group discussion is the **cooperative learning group**. The teacher has a particular goal or task in mind. Small groups of learners are matched for the purpose of completing the task or goal, and each person in the group is assigned a role. The success of the group is measured not only in terms of outcome but also in the successful performance of each member in his or her role.

In cooperative learning groups, students learn to work together toward a group goal. Each member depends on others for the outcome. This interdependence is a basic component of any cooperative learning group. The value of each group member is affirmed as learners work toward their goal.

The success of the group depends on individual performance. Groups should be mixed in terms of abilities and talents so there are opportunities for the students to learn from one another. Also, as groups work together over time, the roles should be rotated so everyone has an opportunity to practice and develop different skills.

The interaction of students in a cooperative learning group creates a tutoring relationship. While cooperative learning groups may involve more than just group discussion, discussion is always part of the process by which cooperative learning groups function.

▶ Helping Students Apply Learning

Some techniques are particularly good for helping students use what they have learned. Simulation games and role-playing allow students to practice solving problems and making decisions under nonthreatening circumstances. Role-playing enables students to examine others' feelings as well as their own. It can help them learn effective ways to react or cope when confronted with similar situations in real life.

Role-plays can be structured, with student "actors" following written scripts. Role-plays may also be improvised in response to a classroom discussion. Students may act out roles as they would respond to a situation, or they may act as they presume a person in that position would behave. Roles are not rehearsed and lines are composed on the spot. The follow-up discussion should focus on the feelings and emotions participants felt and the manner in which the problem was resolved. Role-playing helps students consider how they would behave in similar situations in their lives.

▶ Helping Students Develop Creativity

Some techniques can be used to help students generate new ideas. For example, brainstorming encourages students to exchange and pool their ideas and to come up with new thoughts and solutions to problems. No evaluation or criticism of ideas is allowed. The format of spontaneously expressing any opinions or reactions that come to mind lets students be creative without fear of judgment.

You can also promote creativity by letting students choose from a variety of assignments related to the same material. For example, suppose you wanted students to know what to look for when selecting toys for children. You could ask them to contact a government agency to find out what the law requires in terms of toy safety. You might give them the choice of writing a short story about a child who was given a toy that was not age-appropriate. Designing a toy that meets standards for selection or collecting pictures of a variety of toys and making a display would be options, too. Any teaching techniques you use to encourage students to develop their own ideas will foster their creativity.

▶ Helping Students Review Information

Certain techniques aid students in recalling and retaining knowledge. Games can be effective for drills on vocabulary and factual information. Crossword puzzles can make the review of vocabulary terms more interesting. Structured outlines of subject matter can also be effective review tools. Open-book quizzes, bulletin board displays, and problem-solving sessions all offer ways to review and apply material presented in the classroom.

● Teaching Students of Varying Abilities

The students in your classroom represent a wide range of ability levels. Students with special needs who are mainstreamed require unique teaching strategies. Students who are gifted must not be overlooked. They need to be challenged to their potential. The needs of students in between must also be considered. Often you will be asked to meet the needs of all these students in the same classroom setting. It is a challenge to adapt daily lessons to meet the demands of all students.

To tailor your teaching to mainstreamed and lower-ability students, consider the following strategies:

☐ Before assigning a chapter in the text, discuss and define the key words that appear at the beginning of each chapter. These terms are defined in the text's glossary. Ask students to write out the definitions and define the terms in their own words. You might invite students to guess the meaning of the words before they look up the definitions. Students can also use new words in sentences and find sentences in the text where new terms are used.

☐ When introducing a new chapter, review previously learned information students need to know before they can understand the new material. Review previously learned vocabulary terms they will encounter again.

☐ Utilize the "Introductory Activities" section in the *Teacher's Resource Guide/Binder* for each chapter. Students who have difficulty reading need a compelling reason to read the material. These introductory activities can provide the necessary motivation. Students will want to read the text to satisfy their curiosity.

☐ Break the chapters into smaller parts and assign only one section at a time. Define the terms, answer the "To Review" questions, and discuss the concepts presented in each section before proceeding to the next. It often helps to rephrase questions and problems in simple language and to repeat important concepts in different ways. Assign activities in the *Student Activity Guide* that relate to each section in the book. These reinforce the concepts presented. In addition, many of these activities are designed to improve reading comprehension.

☐ Ask students, individually or in pairs, to answer the "To Review" questions at the end of each chapter in the text. This will help them focus on the essential information contained in the chapter.

☐ Use the buddy system. Pair nonreaders with those who read well. Ask students who have mastered the material to work with those who need assistance. It may also be possible to find a parent volunteer who can provide individual attention where needed.

☐ Select a variety of educational experiences to reinforce the learning of each concept. Look for activities that will help reluctant learners relate information to real-life situations. It helps to draw on the experiences of students at home, in school, and in the community.

☐ Give directions orally as well as in writing. You will need to explain assignments as thoroughly and simply as possible. Ask questions to be certain students understand what they are to do. Encourage them to ask for help if they need it. You will also want to follow up as assignments proceed to be sure no one is falling behind on required work.

☐ Use the overhead projector and the transparency masters included in the *Teacher's Resource Guide/Binder*. A visual presentation of concepts will increase students' ability to comprehend the material. You may want to develop your own transparencies to use in reviewing key points covered in each chapter.

If you have advanced or gifted students in your class, you will need to find ways to challenge them. These students require assignments that involve critical thinking and problem solving. Because advanced students are more capable of independent work, they can use the library and outside resources to research topics in depth. Learning experiences listed in the *Basic Skills Chart* that involve analytical skills are appropriate for gifted students. You may be able to draw on the talents of advanced students in developing case studies and learning activities to use with the entire class.

● Evaluation Techniques

A variety of evaluation tools can be used to assess student achievement. Try using the reproducible forms "Evaluating Individual Participation," "Evaluating Individual Reports," and "Evaluating Group Participation" included with the introductory material in the front of the *Teacher's Resource Guide/Binder.* These rating scales allow you to observe a student's performance and rank it along a continuum. This lets students see what levels they have surpassed and what levels they can still strive to reach.

In some situations, it is worthwhile to allow students to evaluate their own work. When evaluating an independent study project, for example, students may be the best judge of whether or not they met the objectives they set for themselves. Students can think about what they have learned and see how they have improved. They can analyze their strengths and weaknesses.

You may ask students to evaluate their peers from time to time. This gives the student performing the evaluation an opportunity to practice giving constructive criticism. It also gives the student being evaluated the opportunity to accept criticism from his or her peers.

Tests and quizzes are also effective evaluation tools. These may be given in either written or oral form. In either case, however, both objective and subjective questions should be used to help you adequately assess student knowledge and understanding of class material.

● Communicating with Students

Communicating with students involves not only sending clear messages but also receiving and interpreting feedback. The following are some suggestions for productive communication with your students:

☐ Recognize the importance of body language and nonverbal communication, both in presenting material and interpreting student responses. Eye contact, a relaxed but attentive body position, natural gestures, and an alert facial expression all command attention. The same positive nonverbal cues from students are an indication of their response and reactions. Your tone of voice is also an important nonverbal communicator. Cultivating a warm, lively, enthusiastic speaking voice will make classroom presentations more interesting. By your tone, you can convey a sense of acceptance and expectation to which your students will respond.

☐ Use humor whenever possible. Humor is not only good medicine, it opens doors and teaches lasting lessons. Laughter and amusement will reduce tension, make points in a nonthreatening and memorable way, increase the fun and pleasure in classroom learning, and break down stubborn barriers. Relevant cartoons, quotations, jokes, and funny stories all bring a light touch to the classroom.

☐ Ask questions that promote recall, discussion, and thought. Good questions are tools that open the door to communication. Open-ended inquiries that ask what, where, why, when, and how will stimulate thoughtful answers. You can draw out students by asking for their opinions and conclusions. Questions with yes or no answers tend to discourage rather than promote further communication. Avoid inquiries that are too personal or that might put students on the spot.

☐ Rephrase students' responses to be sure both you and they understand what has been said. Paraphrasing information students give is a great way to clarify, refine, and reinforce material and ideas under discussion. For example, you might say "This is what I hear you saying "...correct me if I'm wrong." Positive acknowledgment of student contributions, insights, and successes encourages more active participation and open communication. Comments such as "That's a good point. I hadn't thought of it that way before" or "What a great idea!" will encourage students to express themselves.

☐ Listen for what students say, what they mean, and what they do not say. Really listening may be the single most important step you can take to promote open communication. As students answer questions and express their ideas and concerns, try not only to hear what they say but to understand what they mean. What they do not say can also be important. During discussion sessions, make room for silence, time to think, and time to reflect.

☐ Share your feelings and experiences. The measure of what students communicate to you will depend in part on what you are willing to share with them. Express your personal experiences, ideas, and feelings when they are relevant. Don't forget to tell them about a few of your mistakes. Sharing will give students a sense of exchange and relationship.

☐ Lead discussion sessions to rational conclusions. Whether with an entire class or with individual students, it is important to identify and resolve conflicting thoughts and contradictions. This will help students think clearly and logically. For example, when discussing the decision to become a parent, a student may express a desire to cuddle a baby but may not want to change a baby's diaper. Pointing out and discussing the inconsistency in these two positions will lead students to more logically consider the responsibilities of parenthood.

☐ Create a nonjudgmental atmosphere. Students will only communicate freely and openly in a comfortable environment. You can make them comfortable by respecting their ideas, accepting them for who they are, and honoring their confidences. It is also important to avoid criticizing a student or discussing personal matters in front of others.

☐ Use written communication effectively. The more ways you approach students, the more likely you are to reach them on different levels. Very often, the written word can be an excellent way to connect. Written messages can take different forms—a notice on the chalkboard, a note attached to homework, a memo to parents (with good news as well as bad), or a letter exchange involving class members.

☐ Be open and available for private discussions of personal or disciplinary problems. It is important to let students know they can come to you with personal concerns as well as questions regarding course material. Be careful not to violate students' trust by discussing confidential matters outside a professional setting.

● Promoting Your Program

You can make child development one of the most important course offerings in your school. Because you cover material that every student and teacher can use, it pays to make the student body and faculty aware of your program. With good public relations, you can increase your enrollment, gain support from administrators and other teachers, and achieve recognition in the community. The following are some ways to promote your program:

☐ Create visibility. It is important to let people know what is going on in child development classes. Some ways to do this include announcing projects and activities at faculty meetings and in school bulletins or newspapers, creating displays in school showcases or on bulletin boards, and writing articles and press releases for school and community newspapers. Talk about your program with administrators, other teachers, and students. Invite them to visit your classes.

☐ Interact within the school. Child development is related to many fields of learning. You can strengthen your program and contribute to other disciplines by cooperating with other teachers. For example, you can work with the health teacher to present information on childhood diseases, the physical education teacher to cover muscular development, or a science teacher to discuss the biology of heredity. The more interaction you can generate, the more you promote your child development class.

☐ Contribute to the educational objectives of the school. If your school follows stated educational objectives and strives to strengthen specific skills, include these overall goals in your teaching. For example, if students need special help in developing verbal or writing skills, select projects and assignments that will help them in these areas. The *Basic Skills Chart* in the *Teacher's Resource Guide/Binder* will give you ideas for activities that strengthen specific skills. Show administrators examples of work that indicate student improvement in needed skills.

☐ Serve as a resource center. Child development information is of practical use and interest to almost everyone. You can sell your program by making your department a resource center of child development materials to meet the needs of anyone who interacts with children. Invite faculty members, students, and parents to tap into the wealth of child development information available in your classroom.

☐ Generate involvement and activity in the community. You are teaching concepts students can apply in their everyday lives. You can involve students in community life and bring the community into your classroom through field trips, interviews with businesspeople and community leaders, surveys, and presentations from guest speakers. You may be able to set up cooperative projects between the school and community organizations around a variety of topics.

☐ Connect with parents. If you can get them involved, parents may be your best allies in teaching child development. Let parents know when their children have done good work. Moms and dads have had experiences related to many of the issues you discuss in class. They have cared for newborns, made decisions about substitute child care, and handled children with developmental differences. Call on them to share individually or as part of a panel addressing a specific topic. Parents can be a rich source of real-life experience. Keep them informed about classroom activities and invite them to participate as they are able.

☐ Establish a student sales staff. Enthusiastic students will be your best salespeople. Encourage them to tell their parents and friends what they are learning in your classes. You might create bulletin boards or write letters to parents that focus on what students are learning in your classes. Ask students to put together a newsletter highlighting their experiences in child development class. Students could write a column from your department for the school paper.

We appreciate the contributions of the following Goodheart-Willcox authors to this introduction: "Teaching Techniques" from *Changes and Choices*, by Ruth E. Bragg; and "Evaluation Techniques" from *Contemporary Living*, by Verdene Ryder.

Correlation of National Standards for Human Development with *Children: The Early Years*

In planning your program, you may want to use the correlation chart below. This chart correlates the Family and Consumer Sciences Education National Standards with the content of *Children: The Early Years.* It lists the competencies for each of the content standards for Human Development. It also identifies the major text concepts that relate to each competency. Bold numbers indicate chapters in which concepts are found.

After studying the content of this text, students will be able to achieve the following comprehensive standard:

12.0 Analyze factors that impact human growth and development.

Content Standard 12.1 Analyze principles of human growth and development across the life span.	
Competencies	**Text Concepts**
12.1.1 Examine physical, emotional, social, and intellectual development.	**1:** What is child development?; individual life cycle; factors that influence growth and development; differences in the rate of growth and development; principles of growth and development; Havighurst's theory of developmental tasks; Maslow's theory of human needs; observation techniques **4:** Conception; stages in prenatal development **5:** Factors that affect the baby's health; health habits during pregnancy; health hazards to avoid; birth defects; bonding **6:** Care for premature babies; physical traits of a newborn; reflexes; meeting the newborn's physical needs; meeting the newborn's intellectual needs; meeting the newborn's social-emotional needs **7:** Skeletal growth of infants; motor development; differences in physical development of infants **8:** Perception; cognition; perceptual concepts; beginnings of language development in infants **9:** Temperamental differences in infants; the infant's growing social world; learning to trust; showing attachment; infants express emotions **10:** Physical needs of infants; intellectual needs; social-emotional needs; recognizing developmental delays **11:** Body growth and development of toddlers; motor development **12:** How and what toddlers learn; beginning of thought; language abilities **13:** Self-awareness of toddlers; extending social relations; emotions **14:** Physical needs of toddlers; intellectual needs; social-emotional needs; recognizing developmental delays of toddlers **15:** Body growth and development of preschoolers; motor development **16:** How preschool children learn; what preschool children learn **17:** Developing social awareness during the preschool years; feeling and controlling emotions **18:** Physical needs of preschoolers; intellectual needs; social-emotional needs; recognizing developmental delays

	19: Physical development of school-age children; intellectual development of school-age children; helping school-age children meet their intellectual needs; social-emotional development of school-age children; helping school-age children with their social-emotional needs; recognizing developmental delays **20:** Children and their world of play; stages of play; types of play; providing enrichment activities for children; books and literature **21:** Protecting children from disease and illness; accident prevention; caring for an ill or injured child; caring for a terminally ill child **24:** Sibling relationships **25:** Children with developmental differences; children who are exceptional; exceptional children need special help
12.1.2 Examine interrelationships among physical, emotional, social, and intellectual aspects of human growth and development.	**1:** Growth and development have interrelated parts **6:** Meeting the newborn's physical needs; meeting the newborn's intellectual needs; meeting the newborn's social-emotional needs **10:** Physical needs of infants; intellectual needs of infants; social-emotional needs of infants; recognizing developmental delays **14:** Physical needs of toddlers; intellectual needs of toddlers; learning through play; social-emotional needs of toddlers; recognizing developmental delays **18:** Physical needs of preschoolers; intellectual needs of preschoolers; social-emotional needs of preschoolers; recognizing developmental delays **19:** Physical development of school-age children; intellectual development of school-age children; helping school-age children meet their intellectual needs; social-emotional development of school-age children; helping school-age children with their social-emotional needs; recognizing developmental delays

Content Standard 12.2 Analyze conditions that influence human growth and development.

12.2.1 Investigate the impact of heredity and environment on human growth and development.	**1:** Factors that influence growth and development; heredity; environment; heredity and environment combined **2:** Roles of parents; parenting styles; characteristics of healthy families **4:** How heredity works; multiple pregnancy
12.2.2 Determine the impact of social, economic, and technological forces on individual growth and development.	**3:** Sharing parenting responsibilities; managing finances; managing careers **5:** Medical care; ultrasound; chorionic villus sampling; amniocentesis **6:** Medical care and testing; care for premature babies **17:** Developing social awareness **18:** Learning through observing; television **19:** Peer groups **24:** Sibling relationships; parental employment; balancing family and work; family moves
12.2.3 Examine the effects of gender, ethnicity, and culture on individual development.	**1:** To pass down culture **17:** Learning gender roles; cultural factors **18:** Aiding gender role learning **19:** Extending gender role

(continued)

Competencies	Text Concepts
12.2.4 Examine the effects of life events on individuals' physical and emotional development.	**2:** Changes affecting families today; changes in family roles; family types; adoption; the family life cycle **24:** Parental employment; balancing family and work; children in self-care; family moves; death; divorce; single parenting; remarriage and stepparenting; teens as parents; child abuse and neglect **25:** Children with developmental differences; children who are exceptional; exceptional children need special help

Content Standard 12.3 Analyze strategies that promote growth and development across the life span.

12.3.1 Examine the role of nurturance on human growth and development.	**1:** To be a responsible parent; to protect children's rights **2:** Roles of parents; nurturance; guidance and discipline; parenting styles **3:** Learning parenting skills **6:** Meeting the newborn's social-emotional needs **9:** Separation anxiety; the infant's growing social world; learning to trust; showing attachment; infants express emotions **10:** Social-emotional needs of infants **13:** Self-awareness of toddlers; extending social relations; emotions **14:** Social-emotional needs of toddlers; recognizing developmental delays **17:** Developing social awareness during the preschool years; feeling and controlling emotions **18:** Social-emotional needs of preschoolers; recognizing developmental delays **19:** Social-emotional development of school-age children; helping school-age children with their social-emotional needs; recognizing developmental delays **20:** Children and their world of play; stages of play; types of play; providing enrichment activities for children **24:** Sibling relationships
12.3.2 Examine the role of communication on human growth and development.	**8:** Beginnings of language development; how babies communicate; passive versus active vocabulary **11:** Language abilities of toddlers; learning spoken language; different rates of learning to talk **14:** Language activities for toddlers **16:** Language abilities of preschoolers increase; articulation of preschool children; vocabulary of preschool children; grammar of preschool children **18:** Preschoolers use symbols in language; learning through language **19:** Language is mastered by school-age children **20:** Language-logic play; books and literature
12.3.3 Examine the role of support systems in meeting human growth and development needs.	**21:** Preparing a child for routine and hospital care; caring for an ill or injured child; caring for a terminally ill child **22:** Types of child care programs; choosing a group program; effects of group care on children; helping children adjust to group care **24:** Resources for children in crises **25:** Exceptional children need special help

Scope and Sequence

In planning your program, you may want to use the Scope and Sequence Chart below. This chart identifies the major concepts presented in each chapter of the text. Refer to the chart to find the material that meets your curriculum needs. Bold numbers indicate chapters in which concepts are found.

Part 1 Children in Today's World

Parenthood

1: Why study children? To understand yourself; To be a responsible parent; To pass down culture; To protect children's rights

2: Changes affecting families today; Changes in family roles; Family types; The family life cycle; Roles of parents; Nurturance; Guidance and discipline; Parenting styles; Characteristics of healthy families

3: Why is it hard to be a good parent? Learning parenting skills; Deciding about parenthood; Reasons for choosing parenthood; Reasons for not choosing parenthood; How children affect relationships; Sharing responsibilities; Managing finances; Managing careers; Family planning

---

Principles of Growth and Development

1: Why study children? To be a responsible parent; To protect children's rights; Factors that influence growth and development; Heredity and environment combined; Differences in the rate of growth and development; Principles of growth and development; Growth and development are constant; Growth and development are gradual and continuous; Growth and devel-opment happen in sequenced steps; Growth and development happen at different rates; Growth and development have interrelated parts; Theories of growth and development; Havighurst's theory of developmental tasks; Maslow's theory of human needs; Why observe children?

Physical Growth

1: To be a responsible parent; Observing children

Intellectual Growth

1: To be a responsible parent; To work with children; Observing growth

---

Social-Emotional Growth

1: Why study children? To understand yourself; To be a responsible parent; Observing growth

---

Caring for and Guiding Children

1: To be a responsible parent

2: Changes affecting families today; Changes in family roles; Family types; The family life cycle; Roles of parents; Nurturance; Guidance and discipline; Parenting styles; Characteristics of healthy families

3: Why is it hard to be a good parent? Learning parenting skills; Deciding about parenthood; Reasons for choosing parenthood; How children affect relationships; Sharing responsibilities

---

Family Relationships

1: To be a responsible parent; To pass down culture; Individual life cycle

2: Changes affecting families today; Changes in family roles; Family types; Two-parent families; Single-parent families; Blended families; Extended families; Families with adopted children; The family life cycle;

Characteristics of healthy families

3: Why is it hard to be a good parent? Learning parenting skills; How children affect relationships; Sharing responsibilities; Managing finances; Managing careers; Family planning

Safety and Health

1: To be a responsible parent

3: Why is it hard to be a good parent? Learning parenting skills; Infertility; Sterility

Exceptional Children

1: Why study children? To protect children's rights; To work with children

Leadership and Careers

1: Why study children? To work with children

3: Managing finances; Managing careers

Part 2: Prenatal Development and the Newborn

Parenthood

5: Bonding

6: Meeting newborns' physical needs; Clothing and dressing; Diapering; Scheduling; How can parents help their children learn? Meeting parents' needs; Need for rest; Organize tasks; Time to be with adults

Prenatal and Postnatal Care and Development

4: Stages in prenatal development; Germinal stage; Embryonic stage; Fetal stage

5: Signs of pregnancy; Medical care; Factors that affect the baby's health; Mother's age; Mother's weight; Mother's emotional health; Health habits during pregnancy; Nutrition; Weight gain; Hygiene practices; Rest and sleep; Physical activities and exercise; Health hazards to avoid; Diseases or illnesses in mother; Monitoring the baby's development; Ultrasound; Chorionic villus sampling; Amniocentesis; Family decisions concerning childbirth; Time to be born

6: Medical care and testing; Care for premature babies; Apgar test; Neonatal assessment scales; Other hospital care; Meeting newborns' physical needs

Principles of Growth and Development

5: Bonding

6: What can newborns do?

Physical Growth

5: Factors that affect the baby's health; Mother's age; Mother's weight; Health habits during pregnancy; Nutrition; Weight gain; Birth defects; Monitoring the baby's development; Time to be born; Bonding

6: Medical care and testing; Care for premature babies; Physical traits of a newborn; Reflexes; Meeting the newborn's physical needs; Feeding; Clothing and dressing; Bathing, Sleeping; Exercising; Scheduling

Intellectual Growth

5: The role of the family; Family involvement; Bonding

6: Meeting the newborn's intellectual needs; What can newborns do? How can parents help their babies learn?

Social-Emotional Growth

5: Factors that affect the baby's health; Mother's emotional health; The role of the family; Family involvement; Bonding

6: Meeting the newborn's social-emotional needs; Alertness of newborns; Soothing a fussy baby

Caring for and Guiding Children

5: The role of the family; Family involvement; Bonding

6: Meeting the newborn's physical needs; Meeting the newborn's social-emotional needs

Family Relationships

5: The role of the family; Family involvement; Bonding

6: Meeting the parent's needs

Safety and Health

4: How heredity works; Chromosomes and genes; Inheriting unique traits; Dominant and recessive traits; Sex chromosomes; Multiple pregnancy; Fraternal births; Identical births; Mixed types; Conception

5: Signs of pregnancy; Medical care; The first appointment; Factors that affect the baby's health; Mother's age; Mother's weight; Rh factor; Mother's emotional health; Health habits during pregnancy; Nutrition; Weight gain; Hygiene practices; Rest and sleep; Physical activities and exercise; Health hazards to avoid; Diseases or illnesses in mother; Drugs; Radiation exposure; Environmental pollution; Birth defects; Spontaneous abortion; Monitoring the baby's development; Chorionic villus samplings; Ultrasound; Amniocentesis; Family decisions concerning childbirth; Time to be born; The last weeks of pregnancy; Stages of labor; Instrument methods of birth; Cesarean births; Hospital care; Bonding; Postnatal maternal care; Postpartum blues

6: Medical care and testing; Care for premature babies; Apgar test; Neonatal assessment scales; Other hospital care; Meeting the newborn's physical needs; Feeding; Bathing; Exercising

Part 3: Infants

Parenthood

10: Physical needs; Establishing routines; Intellectual needs; Social-emotional needs; Baby-adult interaction; Handling special problems; Recognizing developmental delays

Principles of Growth and Development

10: Recognizing developmental delays

Physical Growth

7: Skeletal growth; Length and weight; Body proportions; Bones and teeth; Motor development; Head-to-foot development; Center-to-extremities development; Differences in physical development

10: Physical needs; Feeding; Weaning; Recognizing developmental delays

Intellectual Growth

8: How infants learn; Perception; Cognition; What infants learn; Perceptual concepts; Beginnings of language development; How babies communicate; Passive versus active vocabulary

10: Intellectual needs; Activities to stimulate the senses; Problem-solving activities; Language activities; Recognizing developmental delays

Social-Emotional Growth

9: Temperamental differences in infants; Infants' growing social world; Interacting with others; Learning to trust; Showing attachment; Infants express emotions; Love; Fear; Anxiety; Anger

10: Social-emotional needs; Baby-adult interaction; Helping babies develop their self-awareness; Handling special problems; Recognizing developmental delays

Caring for and Guiding Children

10: Physical needs; Feeding; Weaning; Clothing; Diapering a baby; Tub bathing; Establishing routines; Intellectual needs; Activities to stimulate the senses;

Problem-solving activities; Motor activities; Language activities; Social-emotional needs; Handling special problems; Recognizing developmental delays

Safety and Health

10: Physical needs; Rest and sleep; Sudden Infant Death Syndrome; Recognizing developmental delays

Part 4: Toddlers

Parenthood

14: Physical needs; Intellectual needs; Social-emotional needs; Recognizing developmental delays

Principles of Growth and Development

13: Achieving autonomy

14: Recognizing developmental delays

Physical Growth

11: Body growth and development; Height and weight; Other body changes; Motor development

14: Recognizing developmental delays

Intellectual Growth

12: How and what toddlers learn; Discovering new ways to solve problems; Beginning of thought; Language abilities; Learning spoken language; Different rates of learning to talk

14: Intellectual needs; Learning through activities; Learning through play; Sensory stimulation activities; Problem-solving activities; Motor activities; Language activities; Recognizing developmental delays

Social-Emotional Growth

13: Self-awareness; Achieving autonomy; Extending social relations; Emotions; Affection; Fears; Anxiety; Anger

14: Social-emotional needs; Discipline; Guidance: Helping children control their emotions; Planning self-awareness activities; Recognizing developmental delays

Caring for and Guiding Children

14: Physical needs; Feeding; Clothing; Rest and sleep; Hygiene; Toilet training; Intellectual needs; Learning through activities; Learning through play; Sensory stimulation activities; Problem-solving activi- ties; Motor activities; Language activities; Discipline; Guidance: Helping toddlers control their emotions; Planning self-awareness activities; Recognizing developmental delays

Safety and Health

14: Hygiene; Toilet training; Recognizing developmental delays

Part 5: Preschoolers

Parenthood

18: Physical needs; Handling sleep and toileting problems; Intellectual needs; Discipline: Helping with initiative and mistakes; Sharing responsibility; Aiding gender role learning; Providing time for friendships; Helping children with emotional control; Recognizing developmental delays

Principles of Growth and Development

16: How preschool children learn; What preschool children learn; Concepts children learn; Language abilities increase

17: Developing social awareness

18: Recognizing developmental delays

Physical Growth

15: Body growth and development; Height and weight; Body changes; Motor development; Large-muscle development; Small-muscle development

18: Physical needs; Recognizing developmental delays

Intellectual Growth

16: How preschool children learn; Obstacles to logical thinking; New abilities emerge; What preschool children learn; Language abilities increase; Articulation of preschool children; Vocabulary of preschool children, Grammar of preschool children

18: Intellectual needs; Learning through observing; Learning through problem solving; Learning through symbolizing; Learning through motor skills; Learning through language; Recognizing developmental delays

Social-Emotional Growth

17: Developing social awareness; Taking the initiative; Showing responsibility; Learning gender roles; Extending social relations; Feeling and controlling emotions; Dependency; Fear and anxiety; Anger and aggression; Jealousy

18: Social-emotional needs; Recognizing developmental delays

Caring for and Guiding Children

18: Physical needs; Selecting the right clothes; Handling sleep and toileting problems; Intellectual needs; Discipline: Helping with initiative and mistakes; Sharing responsibility; Aiding gender role learning; Providing time for friendships; Helping children with emotional control; Recognizing developmental delays

Family Relationships

17: Learning gender roles; How does gender role develop? Cultural factors

Safety and Health

18: Physical needs; Meeting nutritional needs; Recognizing developmental delays

Part 6: Guiding and Caring for Children

Parenthood

19: Helping school-age children meet their intellectual needs; Helping school-age children with their social-emotional needs; Guiding and modeling behavior; Helping children control their emotions; Helping children improve their self-concept; Recognizing developmental delays

20: Adult role in children's play; Providing enrichment activities for children; Adult's role in stimulating art experiences

21: Protecting children from disease and illness; Accident prevention; Safety devices and safety measures; Safety lessons

22: Helping children adjust to group care

Principles of Growth and Development

19: How school-age children think; Using reversibility logic; Using deductive and inductive reasoning; Physical knowledge concepts; Logical thinking concepts; Recognizing developmental delays

20: Children and their world of play; Importance of play; Stages of play; Providing enrichment activities for children; Stages of development in visual arts; Manipulative stage; Representation stage

Physical Growth

19: Physical development of school-age children; Body growth and development; Recognizing developmental delays

20: Play and physical development; Active-physical play; Manipulative-constructive play

Intellectual Growth

19: Intellectual development of school-age children; How school-age children think; What school-age children learn; Language is mastered; Helping school-age children meet their intellectual needs; Recognizing developmental delays

20: Play and mental development; Imitative-imaginative play; Books and literature; Benefits to children

Social-Emotional Growth

19: Social-emotional development of school-age children; Self-concept; Showing social awareness; Controlling emotions; Providing time for friendships; Helping children control their emotions; Recognizing developmental delays

20: Children and their world of play; Importance of play; Stages of play

22: Effects of group care on children; Effects on social development

Caring for and Guiding Children

19: Helping school-age children meet their intellectual needs; Guiding intellectual growth; Helping school-age children with their social-emotional needs; Guiding and modeling behavior; Helping children control their emotions; Helping children improve their self-concept; Recognizing developmental delays

20: Adult's role in children's play; Providing enrichment activities for children; Adult's role in stimulating art experiences

21: Protecting children from disease and illness; Childhood diseases and allergies; Accident prevention; How do accidents happen? Anticipating possible hazards; Helping children meet goals in a safe way; Childproofing the environment; Safety lessons; Preparing a child for routine and hospital care; Caring for an ill or injured child; Caring for a terminally ill child; Helping the ill child cope; Helping the family cope

22: Choosing a group program; Program activities; Quality of group programs; Helping children adjust to group care

Family Relationships

19: Enjoying family ties

20: Adults' role in children's play; Providing enrichment activities for children

Safety and Health

19: Encouraging health and safety practices; Recognizing developmental delays

sures; Safety lessons; Preparing a child for routine and hospital care

21: Nutrition, rest, cleanliness, and exercise; Medical and dental care; Immunization; Medical attention during illness; Childhood diseases and allergies; Accident prevention; Safety devices and safety mea-

22: Choosing a group program; Regulations; Housing and equipment; Effects of group care on children; Effects on health; Effects on mental development

Leadership and Careers

22: Types of group programs; Child care programs; Kindergartens; Nursery schools; Montessori schools; Head Start; Staff

23: Types of careers in child-related fields; Health and protective services; Care and education; Entertainment; Design; Advertising, marketing, and management; Entrepreneurship; Research and con-

sulting; Heading toward a career; Personal qualifications; Professional qualifications; Job search skills; Making a wise career choice by getting involved; Study children's development; Involve yourself with children; Join professional organizations; Consider the future; Make wise career moves

Part 7: Special Concerns

Parenthood

24: Lifestyle changes

Caring for and Guiding Children

24: Financial concerns; Lifestyle changes; How can adults protect children from neglect and abuse? Resources for children in crises

Family Relationships

24: Sibling relationships; Sibling interactions; Birth order and development; Children of multiple births; Parental employment; Effects on children; Effects on parents; Balancing family and work; Children in self-care; Coping with family moves; Coping with death;

Helping children cope with grief; Coping with divorce; Effects of divorce; Single parenting; Problems single parents face; Remarriage and stepparenting; Teens as parents

Safety and Health

24: Health risks for the teen mother and baby; Child neglect and abuse; Who is abused? Who abuses and neglects children?

Exceptional Children

25: Children are more alike than different; Children who are exceptional; Children who are gifted and talented; Children with physical disabilities; Speech disorders; Children with mental disabilities; Learning dis-

abilities; Behavioral disorders; Exceptional children need special help; How many children are exceptional? What kinds of help do exceptional children need?

Teaching Aids

● **Part 1**
Children in Today's World

▶ Chapter 1
Learning About Children

Chapter Outline

I. Why Study Children?
   A. To Understand Yourself
   B. To Be a Responsible Parent
   C. To Pass Down Culture
   D. To Protect Children's Rights
   E. To Work with Children

II. What Is Child Development?

III. Individual Life Cycle

IV. Factors that Influence Growth and Development
   A. Heredity
   B. Environment
   C. Heredity and Environment Combined

V. Differences in the Rate of Growth and Development

VI. Principles of Growth and Development
   A. Growth and Development Are Constant
   B. Growth and Development Are Gradual and Continuous
   C. Growth and Development Happen in Sequenced Steps
   D. Growth and Development Happen at Different Rates
   E. Growth and Development Have Interrelated Parts

VII. Theories of Growth and Development
   A. Havighurst's Theory of Developmental Tasks
   B. Maslow's Theory of Human Needs

VIII. Observing Children
   A. Why Observe Children?
      1. What Do Researchers Want to Know?
   B. Ways to Observe
      1. Direct Observations
      2. Indirect Observations
   C. Guidelines for Observing

Suggested Observations

You may want your students to conduct the following observations:

1. Observe examples of culture that have been handed down from one generation to another. Examples of culture include language, attitudes, values, rituals, and skills. What cultural characteristics have you seen passed along to children?

2. Observe a person working with children in a child-related career, such as a child care teacher or care provider. What characteristics does this person exhibit when working with children?

3. Observe characteristics in others that are due to heredity. What are some of these characteristics?

4. Observe some characteristics in others that are due to their environment. What are some of these characteristics?

Answer Key

Answer key for "To Review" questions in the text, page 35

1. false

2. (List five:) to understand yourself, to be a responsible parent, to pass down culture, to protect children's rights, to work with children

3. the scientific study of children from conception to adolescence

4. prenatal stage, neonatal stage, infancy stage, toddler stage, preschool stage, school-age stage

5. heredity, environment, heredity and environment combined

6. false

7. does

8. Developmental acceleration is when a child is performing like an older child. Developmental delay is when a child is performing like a younger child.

9. (Student response.)

10. c. The order of the steps in growth and development is about the same for most children.

11. physical growth: b; social pressures: a; inner pressures: c

12. (Student response.)

13. (List five:) Know your objectives, obtain permission to observe, know what to do at the site, observations should not distract children from their regular activities, observe carefully and objectively, record accurately, protect the rights of all observed.

▶ Chapter 2
Families Today

Chapter Outline

Suggested Observations

You may want your students to conduct the following observations:

1. Observe how couples with young children share their responsibilities. What techniques do they use to help them meet their obligations?

2. Observe families in informal settings, such as shopping malls and parks. Do the couples seem comfortable in their roles as parents? What behaviors help form your opinion?

Answer Key

Answer key for "To Review" questions in the text, pages 50-51

1. (Student response.)

2. b, d

3. nurturance, guidance, and discipline

4. democratic

5. (Student response.)

6. Children in these families learn to interact with people of all ages: a; Children may not learn new skills from many people: b; Many family members are there to help during stressful times: a; Transition to parenthood may be too quick: c; Older family members hand down family culture and family history to younger members: a; Children see only one parent as a role model: c; Children often may have to adjust to two sets of rules: d

7. Children are taught and guided by others: c; Other people are becoming important to children: c; Children may still need guidance and help: d; Parents may feel they are no longer needed: e; This time is used to get to know each other better: a; Time for new interests and hobbies: f; New people come into children's lives: e; Perhaps the most confusing and difficult period: d; Diapers, bottles, and new routines are part of this stage: b

8. These include shared values, a mutual commitment to family life, shared responsibilities, and good communication.

▶ # Chapter 3
Preparing for Parenting

Chapter Outline

I. Why Is It Hard to Be a Good Parent?
  A. Learning Parenting Skills
II. Deciding About Parenthood
  A. Reasons for Choosing Parenthood
    1. "We want to share our love with a child."
    2. "Wouldn't it be nice to have a cute little baby?"
    3. "Our parents want grandchildren."
    4. "Our older child needs a brother or sister."
    5. "A child can make us proud."
    6. "Others will see me as a stable, reliable person."
    7. "A child will comfort us in our old age."
    8. "A child will make us love each other."
  B. Reasons for Not Choosing Parenthood
    1. "We're not ready for a child."
    2. "A baby costs a lot."
    3. "A child will tie us down."
    4. "A child will interfere with our careers."
    5. "Our child could be sick or disabled."
    6. "Our marriage could fail, and I don't want to be a single parent."
III. Factors to Consider
  A. How Children Affect Relationships
    1. Children and the Couple
    2. Children and Relatives and Friends
  B. Sharing Responsibilities
  C. Managing Finances
  D. Managing Careers
    1. Maternity and Paternity Leave
    2. Problems with Work and Family
IV. Family Planning
V. Infertility
  A. Sterility

Suggested Observations

You may want your students to conduct the following observations:

1. In an informal setting, observe parents who are having a difficult time with a child. What parenting skills might they need to help them with their children? For example, do they need to know more about appropriate developmental tasks for the child's age, discipline methods, or how to childproof their home?

2. Observe examples of literature and professional services for parents in your local school and community.

3. Observe how dual-career families share responsibilities for home and child care.

4. Observe how an employer in your community helps parents meet their work and family obligations. For example, does the employer offer maternity leave, paternity leave, child care programs, and/or flexible work schedules?

Answer Key

Answer key for "To Review" questions in the text, page 71

1. false
2. (List three:) We want to share our love with a child. Wouldn't it be nice to have a cute little baby? Our parents want grandchildren. Our older child needs a brother or sister. A child can make us proud. Others will see me as a stable, reliable person. A child will comfort us in our old age.
3. d
4. having enough time and energy for both, finding good child care services
5. financial; career
6. (Student response.)
7. Maternity leave is the time off from work before and after the baby is born.
8. Family planning affects how many children and when a couple will have children.
9. false
10. (Student response.)

● PART 2
Prenatal Development and the Newborn

▶ Chapter 4
Pregnancy

Chapter Outline

    I.   How Heredity Works
        A. Heredity and Steve
            1. Chromosomes and Genes
            2. Inheriting Unique Traits
            3. Dominant and Recessive Traits
            4. Sex Chromosomes
   II. Multiple Pregnancy
        A. Fraternal Births
        B. Identical Births
        C. Mixed Types
  III. Conception
  IV. Stages in Prenatal Development
        A. Germinal Stage
        B. Embryonic Stage
        C. Fetal Stage

Suggested Observations

    You may want your students to conduct the following observations:

1.   Observe your physical features. Which features seem to come from your mother? Which come from your father? Which features do you share with other relatives?

2.   Observe brothers and sisters. Which characteristics do they share? How are they different?

3.   Observe identical twins. Which of their characteristics are most alike? Which are similar but somewhat different? Which are dissimilar?

Answer Key

    Answer key for "To Review" questions in the text, page 88

1.   23
2.   false
3.   b
4.   twins, triplets, and quadruplets
5.   fraternal
6.   false
7.   b
8.   false
9.   bones
10.   c

▶ Chapter 5
Prenatal Care

Chapter Outline

    I.   Signs of Pregnancy
   II. Medical Care
        A. The First Appointment
  III. Factors that Affect the Baby's Health
        A. Mother's Age
        B. Mother's Weight
        C. Rh Factor
        D. Mother's Emotional Health
  IV. Health Habits During Pregnancy
        A. Nutrition
        B. Weight Gain
        C. Hygiene Practices
        D. Rest and Sleep
        E. Physical Activities and Exercises
   V. Health Hazards to Avoid
        A. Diseases or Illnesses in the Mother
            1. Diabetes and High Blood Pressure
            2. Rubella and Other Childhood Diseases
            3. Sexually Transmitted Diseases (STDs)
        B. Drugs
            1. Medication
            2. Alcohol
            3. Nicotine
            4. Illegal Drugs
        C. Radiation Exposure
        D. Environmental Pollution
  VI. Birth Defects
 VII. Spontaneous Abortion
VIII. Monitoring the Baby's Development
        A. Ultrasound
        B. Chorionic Villus Sampling
        C. Amniocentesis

IX. The Role of the Family
   A. Family Involvement
      1. Today's Fathers-to-Be
   B. Family Decisions Concerning Childbirth
      1. Home or Hospital Delivery
      2. Choosing a Method of Delivery
X. Time to Be Born
   A. The Last Weeks of Pregnancy
      1. Contractions
      2. Other Signs of Labor
   B. Stages of Labor
      1. Stage One—Dilation of the Cervix
      2. Stage Two—Expulsion of the Baby
      3. Stage Three—Expulsion of the Placenta
   D. Instrument Methods of Birth
   E. Cesarean Births
XI. Hospital Care
   A. Rooming-In
XII. Bonding
XIII. Postnatal Maternal Care
   A. Postpartum Blues

Suggested Observations

You may want your students to conduct the following observations:

1. Observe pregnant women in informal settings. Which activities (behaviors) do you see as unhealthy?
2. Observe advertisements by local hospitals or health programs. What services do they offer for prenatal care, preparation for delivery, and labor and delivery? What options are there in your community (delivery versus birthing room, delivery by obstetrician or trained midwife)?
3. Observe families preparing for a new baby. How is each family member helping with this preparation? How is an older child reacting to the upcoming birth of a baby?
4. Observe a sonogram photo. Which features of the baby can you see?

Answer Key

Answer key for "To Review" questions in the text, pages 116-117

1. b
2. b
3. false
4. false
5. true
6. d
7. (Student response.)
8. the show: b; dilation of the cervix: c; birth of the baby: a; cutting of the umbilical cord: e; expelling the placenta: d
9. false
10. a
11. true
12. postnatal

▶ Chapter 6
The Newborn

Chapter Outline

I. Medical Care and Testing
   A. Care for Premature Babies
   B. The Apgar Test
   C. The Neonatal Assessment Scales
II. Other Hospital Care
   A. Well-Baby Checkup
III. Physical Traits of a Newborn
IV. Reflexes
V. Meeting the Newborn's Physical Needs
   A. Feeding
      1. Breast-Feeding
      2. Formula-Feeding
   B. Clothing and Dressing
   C. Diapering
   D. Bathing
   E. Sleeping
   F. Exercising
   G. Scheduling
VI. Meeting the Newborn's Intellectual Needs
   A. What Can Newborns Do?
   B. How Can Parents Help Their Babies Learn?

VII.   Meeting the Newborn's Social-Emotional Needs
    A.   Alertness of Newborns
    B.   Soothing a Fussy Baby

VIII.   Meeting the Parent's Needs
    A.   The Need for Rest
    B.   Organize Tasks
    C.   Time to Be with Adults

Suggested Observations

You may want your students to conduct the following observations:

1.   Observe a newborn. Compare the newborn's physical characteristics with those in chart 6-8.

2.   Observe a newborn's movements. What reflexes did you observe?

3.   Observe a parent caring for a newborn. How much time does each task take? Which tasks seem easy? Which tasks seem more difficult?

4.   Observe a newborn being dressed. Which clothing features made dressing the baby easy? Which made dressing the baby difficult? Did the clothes look comfortable on the baby? Why or why not?

Answer Key

Answer key for "To Review" questions in the text, page 140

1.   d

2.   A reflex is an involuntary reaction that occurs in response to a certain stimulus, such as a touch, light, or sound. Voluntary movements are movements that a person makes at will. (Students may describe any of the reflexes discussed in the text.)

3.   vernix caseosa: b; fontaneles: c; lanugo: a; stork bites: d

4.   (Student response.)

5.   Formula: 2-2.5 oz. × weight of child in pounds (10) ÷ number of feedings per day (6) = 20-25 oz. of formula per day, or 3.3-4.1 oz. per feeding

6.   false

7.   (Student response.)

● PART 3
Infants

▶ Chapter 7
Physical Development of the Infant

Chapter Outline

I.   Skeletal Growth
    A.   Length and Weight
    B.   Body Proportions
    C.   Bones and Teeth

II.   Motor Development
    A.   Head-to-Foot Development
        1.   Head and Neck Control
        2.   Trunk Control
        3.   Leg Control
    B.   Center-to-Extremities Development

III.   Differences in Physical Development

Suggested Observations

You may want your students to conduct the following observations:

1.   Observe three infants who differ by two or three months in age. How do they differ in their physical maturity? How do they differ in their motor skills?

2.   Observe two infants who are the same age. How do they differ in their physical maturity? How do they differ in their motor skills? Does one infant have a lag in maturity or skills? If so, did the parent say anything that explains the lag, such as low birth weight or serious illness?

3.   Observe how several babies move toward a toy. Describe exactly how the baby moves toward the toy. (Often babies use more than one motor skill to reach a toy.)

Answer Key

Answer key for "To Review" questions in the text, page 152

1.   Add 1/2

2.   true

3.   false

4.   increase in length of bones, ossification begins to happen, changes in number of bones

5. false
6. true
7. d
8. sits without support with back straight: 3; raises head while on abdomen: 1; creeps: 4; walks: 6 or 7; rolls over from front to back: 2; stands without help: 5; picks up object with thumb used in opposition to finger: 6 or 7
9. unlearned; learned

▶ Chapter 8
Intellectual Development of the Infant

Chapter Outline

I. How Infants Learn
    A. Perception
        1. Perceptual Learning
        2. Cognition
        3. The Sensorimotor Stage

II. What Infants Learn
    A. Perceptual Concepts
        1. Object Constancy or Sameness
        2. Object Concept
        3. Depth Perception

III. Beginnings of Language Development
    A. How Babies Communicate
        1. Crying and Cooing
        2. Babbling
        3. First Words
    B. Passive versus Active Vocabulary

Suggested Observations

You may want your students to conduct the following observations:

1. Observe infants as they play. What concepts are they learning?
2. Observe infants as they see, hear, or touch objects in their environments. Compare your observations with information given in chart 8-5.
3. Observe objects at a baby's crawling and walking height. Describe how the objects look from these views.
4. Observe a baby trying to "talk." Describe how cooing is different from babbling. What might the baby have been "saying" in babble language?

Answer Key

Answer key for "To Review" questions in the text, pages 166-167

1. false
2. the baby's physical development (mainly brain growth) and the environment
3. b
4. a. 3-D objects
    b. solid-colored cards
    c. patterned cards
    d. human face
    e. curved lines
    f. new objects
5. true
6. false
7. true
8. a
9. Babies change some of their reflex skills, such as opening and closing their hands: 2; Babies hit their hands on the high chair tray and realize they made the sound: 3; Babies exercise inborn reflexes: 1; Babies can pick up a rubber duck, place it in the water, and give it a big push: 5; Babies look for objects they have dropped: 4
10. Maria: c; Joe: a; Tyrone: b
11. 1. crying: 2. cooing: 3. babbling: 4. reduplication babbling: 5. first words

▶ Chapter 9
Social-Emotional Development of the Infant

Chapter Outline

I. Temperamental Differences in Infants
II. The Infant's Growing Social World
    A. Interacting with Others
        1. Interacting with Adults
        2. Interacting with Other Children
    B. Learning to Trust
    C. Showing Attachment
III. Infants Express Emotions
    A. Love
    B. Fear
    C. Anxiety
    D. Anger

Suggested Observations

You may want your students to conduct the following observations:

1. Observe a group of infants. Note differences in temperament. Do some infants seem easygoing? Do other infants seem more difficult?

2. Observe an infant with a parent or regular caregiver. How does the baby show attachment? How does the adult encourage attachment (for instance, by soothing the baby or showing affection)?

3. Observe a baby showing fear, anxiety, or anger. What seemed to trigger the infant's reactions?

Answer Key

Answer key for "To Review" questions in the text, page 178

1. true
2. (Name two:) heredity, prenatal conditions, ease of birth, environment after birth
3. cries, coos, and smiles
4. true
5. false
6. e
7. (List two:) trying to stay close to the adult, following the adult, clinging to the adult, smiling at the adult, crying for the adult, calling to the adult
8. false
9. d
10. false
11. comes from good physical care: a; is often taught by hearing adults say "No! That will hurt you!" b; is seen as a reaction to being held against their will: d; is similar to attachment: a; in its early form may be the startle reflex: b; is not seen as a response to unknown children: b; is closely related to fear: c; may be a reaction to an adult trying to distract a hungry or tired baby: d

▶ ## Chapter 10
Providing for the Infant's Developmental Needs

Chapter Outline

I. Physical Needs
   A. Feeding
      1. Feeding During the First Year
      2. Baby Foods
   B. Weaning
      1. Weaning to a Cup
      2. Weaning from the Breast
      3. Spoon Feeding
   C. Clothing
      1. Style and Color
      2. Shoes
      3. Good Consumer Sense
      4. Caring for Baby Clothes
   D. Diapering a Baby
   E. Tub Bathing
   F. Establishing Routines
   G. Rest and Sleep
   H. Sudden Infant Death Syndrome
   I. Places for Sleep and Play
II. Intellectual Needs
   A. Activities to Stimulate the Senses
   B. Problem-Solving Activities
   C. Motor Activities
   D. Language Activities
III. Social-Emotional Needs
   A. Baby-Adult Interaction
   B. Helping Babies Develop Their Self-Awareness
   C. Handling Special Problems
IV. Recognizing Developmental Delays

Suggested Observations

You may want your students to conduct the following observations:

1. Observe a baby trying to drink from a cup or handle a spoon. What problems does the baby experience? How are these problems related to messiness?

2. Observe several babies wearing different types of outfits. Describe the outfits and list the advantages or disadvantages of each.

3. Observe a baby (6- to 12-months-old) at home. If this were your baby and home, what childproofing would you need?

4. Observe a baby playing. What senses are being stimulated? Which motor and language skills are being developed?

5. Observe a baby playing. How does the parent or caregiver encourage a positive relationship?

Answer Key

Answer key for "To Review" questions in the text, pages 204-205

1. physical

2. (List three): A baby cannot digest complex nutrients found in solids. Starting solids too early may cause allergy problems. Some solids have too much sodium. Solids may be too high in calories. Jaw and throat muscles must develop before swallowing solids is easy and safe. During spoon feeding, a baby cannot be held and given the warm feeling of physical closeness that he or she receives during bottle- or breast-feeding. Babies do not need solids for nutritional reasons in the first half year.

3. a, c

4. false

5. (Student response.)

6. true

7. b. watching for signs of each baby's interest in certain experiences

   a. repeating games many times over several months

   b. letting babies try things for themselves

8. false

9. true

10. (List two:) Talk to a baby. Ask questions as you talk. Pronounce words correctly. Talk about baby's everyday world as babies begin to understand their world.

11. (Student response.)

● PART 4
Toddlers

▶ Chapter 11
Physical Development of the Toddler

Chapter Outline

I. Body Growth and Development
   A. Height and Weight
      1. Years One and Two
      2. After Year Two
   B. Other Body Changes
      1. Bones
      2. The Brain
      3. Fat Tissues

II. Motor Development
   A. Large-Muscle Development
      1. Walking
      2. Running
      3. Jumping
      4. Climbing
      5. Throwing and Catching
   B. Small-Muscle Development

Suggested Observations

You may want your students to conduct the following observations:

1. Observe the height of several 24-month-olds. Do the taller toddlers have taller parents? Do the shorter toddlers have shorter parents?

2. Observe infants and toddlers. How do they look different?

3. Observe a toddler just beginning to walk and a toddler who is just three years old. How are their upright posture and walk different?

4. Observe a toddler while playing catch with a soft rubber ball. What does the toddler do with his or her arms and hands as you begin to toss the ball? What does the toddler watch—you or the ball? How does the toddler pick up a missed ball? How does the toddler throw the ball—overhand or underhand, with one or two hands? How close to you (the target) does the ball come?

5. Observe toddlers with materials that require fine-motor skills. How do the toddlers grip pencils, crayons, or markers? How messy is their self-feeding? Are breads and puzzle pieces hard to manage?

Answer Key

Answer key for "To Review" questions in the text, pages 218-219

1. heredity; environment
2. true
3. true
4. b
5. false
6. (List two:) Some children are not physically ready to walk but want to so much that they fall when they try. Children who creep quickly may not walk early because creeping gets them where they need to be. Girls often begin to walk before boys. Lighter babies may walk earlier than heavier babies.
7. Toddlers must visually monitor their foot placement to keep from falling. If they are distracted from their monitoring task, they are apt to fall.
8; walking: f; running: b; jumping: a; climbing: d; throwing: e; catching: c
9. false
10. false

▶ Chapter 12
Intellectual Development of the Toddler

Chapter Outline

I. How and What Toddlers Learn
    A. Discovering New Ways to Solve Problems
        1. Working Toward a Goal
    B. Beginning of Thought
        1. Thinking and Imitation
        2. Thinking and Goals
        3. Thinking and Hiding Games
        4. Thinking and Shape, Size, Color, and Texture
        5. Thinking and Object Exploration
        6. Thinking and Language

II. Language Abilities
    A. Learning Spoken Language
        1. Learning to Articulate
        2. Learning Meanings
    B. Different Rates of Learning to Talk

Suggested Observations

You may want your students to conduct the following observations:

1. Observe a toddler playing with an object. Which senses did the toddler use? How did the toddler handle the object (shake, hit, or squeeze it)? What might the toddler have learned about the object (color, texture, rolls when dropped, soft when squeezed)?
2. Observe a toddler. List words the toddler says. Did the toddler seem to understand each word's meaning or incorrectly name some items? What type of words did the toddler mainly use (nouns, verbs, adjectives)?
3. Observe two or more toddlers of the same age. After listening to them talk, compare their vocabularies, articulation skills, and abilities to speak in sentences (versus words or phrases).

Answer Key

Answer key for "To Review" questions in the text, page 230

1. e
2. true
3. c
4. true
5. (Student response.)
6. *Articulation* means to make the sounds of language.
7. common
8. false
9. a, b
10. (List three): hearing loss, greater interest in motor skills than in learning to talk, mental handicap, getting what one wants or needs without speech, living in an environment that is not interesting or having little or no freedom to explore one's environment, being a boy

► **Chapter 13**
Social-Emotional Development of the Toddler

Chapter Outline

I. Self-Awareness
  A. Achieving Autonomy
    1. Promoting a Toddler's Autonomy
  B. Extending Social Relations
    1. Getting Along with Other Children
    2. Self-Esteem
II. Emotions
  A. Affection
  B. Fear
  C. Anxiety
  D. Anger

Suggested Observations

You may want your students to conduct the following observations:

1. Observe two or three toddlers of the same age. How do they show their attachments to several people? How do the strengths of these attachments differ for a parent versus a babysitter?

2. Observe several toddlers playing together. Are they possessive about toys? How do they reclaim a special toy from another child? How does the child react once the toy is claimed by the first toddler? How do adults settle toddlers' disputes?

3. Observe several toddlers playing. Describe actions that would show positive self-esteem. Describe actions that would show the toddler doesn't feel good about himself or herself. What did the adults do to promote positive self-esteem in toddlers?

4. Observe a toddler showing affection, fear, anxiety, or anger. What seemed to trigger the emotion? Compare what you noted with your text.

Answer Key

Answer key for "To Review" questions in the text, pages 240-241

1. false
2. true
3. true
4. a. Autonomy often happens during routines.
   b. Autonomy often involves trying to work beyond the ability level.
5. (Student response. See chart 13-4 in the text.)
6. false
7. c
8. does
9. physical
10. Toddlers react to a wider range of stimuli. Toddlers can better read emotions in others. Toddlers have a wider range of responses to feelings. Toddlers' abilities to think, and thus imagine, increase the number of emotions that are difficult to handle.
11. (List three:) imagined creatures, animals, darkness, nightmares, bad people, injury, gestures or noises made to frighten toddlers.
12. Adults should stay calm and not give too much attention to the tantrum. After the tantrum, adults should be loving and reassuring to the toddler.

► **Chapter 14**
Providing for the Toddler's Developmental Needs

Chapter Outline

I. Physical Needs
  A. Feeding
    1. The Eating Style of Toddlers
    2. Meeting Nutritional Needs
    3. Preventing Feeding Problems
  B. Clothing
    1. Choosing Garments
    2. Fitting Shoes
    3. Rest and Sleep

C. Hygiene
   1. Water Play
   2. Dental Care
D. Toilet Training
   1. Physical and Emotional Factors
   2. Procedure for Toilet Training
   3. When the Toddler Is Ready
   4. Once Training Begins
   5. Accidents
E. Indoor and Outdoor Spaces

II. Intellectual Needs
A. Learning Through Activities
B. Learning Through Play
C. Sensory Stimulation Activities
D. Problem-Solving Activities
E. Motor Activities
F. Language Activities
   1. Toddlers Need to Hear Language
   2. Clear and Simple Speech
   3. Choosing Books for Toddlers

III. Social-Emotional Needs
A. Discipline
   1. Balancing Self-Assertion and Obedience
B. Guidance: Helping Toddlers Control Their Emotions
   1. Contrariness
   2. Temper
   3. Fears and Anxieties
C. Planning Self-Awareness Activities

IV. Recognizing Developmental Delays

Suggested Observations

You may want your students to conduct the following observations:

1. Observe a toddler at home or in a child care setting. How does the toddler show his or her independence? In what ways does the toddler depend on adults?

2. Observe a toddler in his or her bedroom or playroom. What decorations seem to have been chosen with a toddler in mind? What things seem to especially fit this toddler?

3. Observe a toddler playing. What type of learning(s) does the play activity involve (sensory problem solving, motor, language, and/or self-awareness)?

4. Observe a toddler while reading a story. Which features of the book did the toddler like? Was there anything about the book that didn't seem fit for toddlers? Explain.

5. Observe adults caring for toddlers who are having a hard day. What actions seem to work best? Why? What adult actions do not seem to work? Why?

Answer Key

Answer key for "To Review" questions in the text, pages 268-269

1. true
2. b, e
3. taking off
4. false
5. (List four:) Have a definite hour for bedtime and use a neutral stimulus to signal the hour. Set up a ritual that is relaxing. Choose a comfortable place for sleep. Tell toddlers who resist that they do not have to sleep right away, just stay in bed. If toddlers show fear, tell them where you'll be while they sleep, provide a night light, give them a stuffed toy or doll to take to bed, tell them that you will check on them often to see that they are all right, and follow through with checks every 10 to 15 minutes until they are asleep.
6. b
7. false
8. b
9. (List two:) Tell the toddler what is going to happen five minutes in advance. Play a pretend game of obedience. Allow the toddler to make a few decisions when the results are not harmful.
10. (List three:) Reduce or avoid demands when the toddler is tired. Make requests in a pleasant tone of voice. Remove difficult toys or play equipment that seems to frustrate. Have enough toys to prevent boredom. Offer help when the toddler seems to need it. Give in on small demands. Praise the toddler for signs of control.
11. false

● PART 5
Preschoolers

▶ Chapter 15
Physical Development of the Preschooler

Chapter Outline

I.   Body Growth and Development
   A.   Height and Weight
   B.   Other Body Changes
      1.   Bones
      2.   Organs
      3.   Fat Tissues

II.   Motor Development
   A.   Large-Muscle Development
   B.   Small-Muscle Development
      1.   Age Three
      2.   Age Four
      3.   Age Five

Suggested Observations

You may want your students to conduct the following observations:

1.   Observe a group of preschoolers playing. What motor skills have they developed? What motor skills need improvement?

2.   Observe three-year-olds and five-year-olds doing fine-motor activities. What differences in the skill levels did you observe? Were there exceptions in either group?

Answer Key

Answer key for "To Review" questions in the text, pages 281-282

1.   false
2.   c
3.   true
4.   b
5.   true
6.   false
7.   false
8.   walking: d; running: c; jumping: a; throwing: b; balancing: e
9.   (Student response.)
10.   false

▶ Chapter 16
Intellectual Development of the Preschooler

Chapter Outline

I.   How Preschool Children Learn
   A.   Obstacles to Logical Thinking
   B.   New Abilities Emerge
      1.   Symbolic Play
      2.   Drawing
      3.   Language

II.   What Preschool Children Learn
   A.   Concepts Children Learn
      1.   Logical Thinking
      2.   Cause and Effect

III.   Language Abilities Increase
   A.   Articulation of Preschool Children
   B.   Vocabulary of Preschool Children
   C.   Grammar of Preschool Children
      1.   Grammar at Age Three
      2.   Grammar at Ages Four and Five
      3.   Grammar Problems

Suggested Observations

You may want your students to conduct the following observations:

1.   Observe a group of three- and four-year-old children. As they play and talk, note what they do or say that shows they still do not think logically. Which concepts seem difficult for these children (time, classification, and cause and effect)?

2.   Observe a group of preschoolers in a child care program. As children make up symbols, list them. Share these in class.

3.   Observe a three- or four-year-old. Note errors in articulation and grammar. Compare your findings with charts 16-13 and 16-14.

Answer Key

Answer key for "To Review" questions in the text, pages 295-296

1.   a
2.   false
3.   true
4.   b

5. is a step between symbolic play and mental images: b; is made up of the most abstract symbols: d; are symbols stored in the mind: c; children use ideas from their real world, dreams, and imagination: a

6. (Student response.)

7. true

8. true

9. false

10. a. "Mommy fixed my toy."

    b. "I'm never going no more to your house."

    c. "I like food. I like apples best."

▶ # Chapter 17
Social-Emotional Development of the Preschooler

Chapter Outline

I. Developing Social Awareness
   A. Taking the Initiative
   B. Showing Responsibility
   C. Learning about Gender Roles
      1. How Does Gender Role Develop?
      2. Cultural Factors
   D. Extending Social Relations
      1. Adults Are Still Important
      2. Other Children Become More Important
      3. Making Friends
      4. Learnings from Play Groups

II. Feeling and Controlling Emotions
   A. Dependency
   B. Fear and Anxiety
   C. Anger and Aggression
      1. Causes of Anger and Aggression
   D. Jealousy

Suggested Observations

You may want your students to conduct the following observations:

1. Observe a preschooler at home or in a group program. What tasks was the child asked to do? How did the adult explain the task? Was the child able to do it, and why or why not? Did the child seem to feel successful?

2. Observe preschoolers in a group program. What emotions were expressed? How did the adult handle the intense emotions? Did the adult help the children find more acceptable ways of expressing feelings?

Answer Key

Answer key for "To Review" questions in the text, pages 306-307

1. false

2. true

3. false

4. false

5. true

6. false

7. c

8. Peers make play experiences richer. Children are taught how to behave by peers. Children become less egocentric in peer groups. Children see friends as fun.

9. b, c, f

10. false

11. known

12. true

▶ # Chapter 18
Providing for the Preschooler's Developmental Needs

Chapter Outline

I. Physical Needs
   A. Meeting Nutritional Needs
      1. You Are What You Eat
      2. Basic Food Choices
      3. Food Attitudes Are Learned
      4. Preventing Eating Problems
      5. Making Meals Fun
   B. Selecting the Right Clothes
      1. Fit
      2. Fabric and Construction Features
      3. Self-Dressing Features
      4. Shoes and Socks
      5. Clothes and Self-Concept
   C. Handling Sleep and Toileting Problems
      1. Providing Needed Space and Furnishings
      2. Learning Responsibility

II. Intellectual Needs
    A. Learning Through Observing
        1. Television Viewing
        2. Learning Through Problem Solving
        3. How Adults Can Help Preschoolers Solve Problems
    B. Learning Through Symbolizing
        1. Using Symbols in Art
        2. Using Symbols in Language
    C. Learning Through Motor Skills
    D. Learning Through Language
        1. Television and Reading

III. Social-Emotional Needs
    A. Discipline: Helping with Initiative and Mistakes
        1. Limits
        2. Honest Communication
    B. Sharing Responsibility
    C. Aiding Gender Role Learning
    D. Providing Time for Friendships
        1. Helping Children's Social Relations
        2. Reducing Conflicts
    E. Helping Children with Emotional Control
        1. Dependency
        2. Fear and Anxiety
        3. Anger and Aggression
        4. Jealousy over a New Baby

IV. Recognizing Developmental Delays

Suggested Observations

You may want your students to conduct the following observations:

1. Observe preschoolers in a child care program eating lunch or a snack. What foods are they provided? Did they seem to like the foods or reject some? Why do you think a certain food was rejected? How did the adult encourage eating?

2. Observe preschoolers in a group program. How do the space and furnishings meet preschoolers' needs? Which features could or should be used in the home?

3. Observe preschoolers playing in a group program. Which materials help them solve problems (classify, put things in order, and symbolize)? Which materials help their motor skills?

4. Observe two or more preschoolers playing. What examples did you see of self-assertion? What conflicts occurred? Why did these conflicts occur? How were they resolved? What examples did you see of cooperation? Why do you think the children were cooperative (ages of children or enough play materials)?

Answer Key

Answer key for "To Review" questions in the text, pages 336-337

1. b, c
2. true
3. c, d, e
4. (List three:) long shoelaces; no reflective tape on clothes worn after dark; nondetachable hoods; floppy headwear and/or pant legs; long, wide sleeves; drawstring ties; long scarves and sashes; too large clothes
5. true
6. a, c, d, f
7. (List two:) Restrict bedtime liquids. Remind children to use the toilet when they wake up, before they go to bed, and before they leave the house. Make certain children's clothes are easy to put on and take off.
8. false
9. adults
10. should not
11. (List two:) Give positive statements when children are successful. Give children the freedom to try things on their own. Give children reasonable limits. Admit their own mistakes to children.
12. true
13. (List two:) Teach children that they do not always have to share any more than adults do. Model concern for the hurt rather than shame the aggressor. Explain feelings of both children wanting the same toy or wanting to do the same thing.
14. false

● **Part 6**
Guiding and Caring for Children

▶ **Chapter 19**
School-Age Children

Chapter Outline

I. Physical Development of School-Age Children
   A. Body Growth and Development
      1. Height and Weight
      2. Body Proportions
      3. Bone Growth
      4. Muscle Growth
   B. Motor Development
      1. Skill Performance
      2. Providing for School-Age Children's Physical Needs
   C. Encouraging Health and Safety Practices
      1. A Healthful Diet
      2. Exercise and Other Health Practices
      3. Safety Practices
      4. Selecting the Right Clothing
   D. Providing Needed Space and Furnishings

II. Intellectual Development of School-Age Children
   A. How School-Age Children Think
      1. Seeing from the Viewpoint of Others
      2. Focusing on More Than One Part
      3. Noting Transformations
      4. Using Reversibility Logic
      5. Using Deductive and Inductive Reasoning
   B. What School-Age Children Learn
      1. Physical Knowledge Concepts
      2. Logical Thinking Concepts
   C. Language Is Mastered
      1. Vocabulary
      2. Articulation
      3. Grammar

III. Helping School-Age Children Meet Their Intellectual Needs
   A. Guiding Intellectual Growth
      1. Preparing the Child to Enter School
      2. Reinforcing School Tasks

IV. Social-Emotional Development of School-Age Children
   A. Self-Concept
   B. Showing Social Awareness
      1. Sense of Work Being Industrious
      2. Peers Become Important
   C. Controlling Emotions
      1. Love
      2. Fear and Anxiety
      3. Anger and Aggression

V. Helping School-Age Children with Their Social-Emotional Needs
   A. Guiding and Modeling Behavior
      1. Balance Dependence with Independence
      2. Extend Gender Role
      3. Encourage Work and Industry
      4. Expand Children's Horizons
      5. Keep Family Communication Open
   B. Enjoying Family Ties
   C. Providing Time for Friendship
      1. Loss of Friendship
   D. Helping Children Control Their Emotions
   E. Helping Children Improve Their Self-Concept

VI. Recognizing Developmental Delays

Suggested Observations

You may want your class to conduct the following observations:

1. Observe school-age children eating their school lunches and choosing snack foods. How nutritious are the foods they eat (not just buy)? What problems do you see with their diets in terms of sugars, fats, etc.? What physical problems, if any, can you observe?

2. Observe school-age children playing a table game like checkers, chess, or cards. What evidence of the use of logic (strategy) do you see? How would this be different for a five-year-old attempting to play the game?

3. Observe a group of school-age children. What "rules" are being set for acceptance in the group? Which aspects of development are being the most critically judged by peers (body appearance, physical skills, intellectual abilities, or socialization skills)? Explain your answer. What is happening to children on the fringe of the group?

4. Observe school-age children in the classroom. Which emotion or emotions seem the hardest to control? Give examples of how displays of anger, aggression, fear, or anxiety may be a way of saying "I need love." Explain your answer.

Answer Key

Answer key for "To Review" questions in the text, page 369

1. false
2. false
3. An adequate diet is needed to meet growth needs. Foods are needed to meet the great energy demands caused by school-age children's physical activities. Proper diets help children resist infections. School-age children must store nutrients for the rapid growth of the teen
4. possibly wrong
5. true
6. (Student response.)
7. Goals for kindergarten and first grade are unlike the goals of preschool programs, and children must learn independently, follow directions, stay on one task, and put a teacher's desires ahead of their own wishes. There is a switch from the home and preschool program of learning about real objects through direct experiences and some symbolic play to the school program of learning abstract symbol systems. Children must cope with peers for many hours.
8. social

9. to do their best
10. Close friendships are formed from peer groups. Friendships with peers provide school-age children the chance to join rather formal groups, such as 4-H. Peers help children become less dependent on adults. Peers provide emotional support. Peers share information with each other. Peers affect each child's self-concept.
11. b, c

▶ Chapter 20
Teaching Through Play

Chapter Outline

I. Children and Their World of Play
    A. Importance of Play
        1. Play and Physical Development
        2. Play and Mental Development
        3. Play and Social-Emotional Development
    B. Stages of Play
    C. Types of Play
        1. Active-Physical Play
        2. Manipulative-Constructive Play
        3. Imitative-Imaginative Play
        4. Language-Logic Play
    D. Adult Role in Children's Play
        1. Allow Freedom to Play
        2. Allow Time to Explore
        3. Display the Right Attitude Toward Play
        4. Select Toys with Care

II. Providing Enrichment Activities for Children
    A. Art
        1. Stages of Development in Visual Arts
        2. Manipulative Stage
        3. Representation Stage
        4. Reacting to Children's Art
    B. Music
        1. Benefits of Music Experiences
        2. The Adult's Role in Guiding Music Experiences
    C. Science
        1. What Is Science?
        2. How Adults Can Encourage Science Activities
        3. Focus of Science Activities

D. Books and Literature
　　1. Benefits to Children
　　2. Selecting Books and Literature
　　　for Children

Suggested Observations

You may want your students to conduct the following observations:

1. Observe children of different ages at play. Using chart 20-4 as a reference, identify the stage of play you are observing. Explain your answer. Also identify the type or types of play involved.

2. Observe a teacher encouraging children's creative development in visual arts or music. How is the teacher guiding the children's development? How are the children reacting? What skills are children developing? Are the children learning to enjoy the experiences? Explain your answer.

3. Observe children as they select books in a preschool center. Listen to the children talk with each other about the books. Describe the types of books that interest young children. (Note subject matter; illustrations; novelty items, such as "pop-up" pictures; or fun language, such as rhymes.)

Answer Key

Answer key for "To Review" questions in the text, page 394

1. d
2. active-physical play: c; manipulative-constructive play: b; imitative-imaginative play: a; language-logic play: d
3. true
4. false
5. false
6. true
7. false
8. can
9. true
10. false
11. true
12. (Student response.)

▶ **Chapter 21**
Protecting Children's Health and Safety

Chapter Outline

I. Protecting Children from Disease and Illness
　　A. Nutrition, Rest, Cleanliness, and Exercise
　　B. Medical and Dental Care
　　C. Immunization
　　D. Medical Attention During Illness
　　E. Childhood Diseases and Allergies

II. Accident Prevention
　　A. How Do Accidents Happen?
　　　1. Creating a Safe Environment
　　B. Anticipating Possible Hazards
　　C. Helping Children Meet Goals in a Safe Way
　　D. Childproofing the Environment
　　　1. Indoor Safety
　　　2. Outdoor Safety
　　　3. Traffic Safety
　　　4. Baby Items and Toy Safety
　　　5. Pet Safety
　　E. Safety Devices and Safety Measures
　　F. Safety Lessons

III. Preparing Children for Routine and Hospital Care
　　A. Preparing Children for Routine Care
　　　1. Helping the Child during the Examination
　　B. Preparing Children for Hospital Care
　　　1. Easing the Stress of Hospital Care
　　　2. During the Hospital Stay

IV. Caring for an Ill or Injured Child
　　A. Giving Medication and Proper Care

V. Caring for a Terminally Ill Child
　　A. Helping the Ill Child Cope
　　B. Helping the Family Cope

Suggested Observations

You may want your students to conduct the following observations:

1. Observe a group of toddlers or preschoolers at play. What traits of this age group make them prone to accidents? Give specific examples. How did adult actions or the environment prevent or lessen potential accidents?

2. Observe toddlers or preschoolers in a doctor's waiting room. What environmental factors increase the stress? How did parents increase or decrease stress in children?

Answer Key

Answer key for "To Review" questions in the text, pages 427-428

1. true
2. b, e
3. true
4. The adult's ability to supervise changes with the time of day. For instance, more accidents happen when adults are busy with supper or other tasks in the late afternoon and early evening hours.
5. c
6. true
7. d
8. A baby sharing a seat belt with an adult is likely to be crushed by the adult's force in an auto crash, even at a rather slow speed.
9. (List four:) Select a physician or dentist with care. Take along books, toys, and clothing changes (if necessary) in case you must wait. Be prepared with information or questions to save time. If the child feels sick, reassure the child it is all right to feel sick. Explain just a little about procedures and relate them as much as possible to everyday life. During the examination, stay in view of the child, use a soft, soothing voice, hold the child as the doctor requests, do not say things will not hurt, and do not distract the child by making sounds. Never threaten a child with a doctor's visit or a shot.

10. (List three:) Hospitals, in general, may be seen as a place where people experience separation from loved ones, pain, and even death. Hospitals may seem large and impersonal. Parents are no longer in charge of the care of their children. Parents are often asked to assist with painful tests and treatments. Parents or other adults may feel guilty about the cause for the needed hospital care.
11. false
12. (Student response.)

▶ Chapter 22
Child Care in Group Settings

Chapter Outline

I. Types of Group Programs
    A. Child Care Programs
        1. Historical Overview
        2. Types of Child Care Programs
    B. Kindergartens
        1. Background of Kindergartens
    C. Nursery Schools
        1. The Origin of Nursery Schools
        2. Today's Programs
    D. Montessori Schools
    E. Head Start

II. Choosing a Group Program
    A. Regulations
    B. Housing and Equipment
    C. Staff
    D. Program Activities
    E. Other Considerations
    F. Quality of Group Programs

III. Effects of Group Care on Children
    A. Effects on Health
    B. Effects on Mental Development
    C. Effects on Social Development

IV. Helping Children Adjust to Group Care

Suggested Observations

You may want your students to conduct the following observations:

1. Observe activities in two types of group programs for children. How were the programs similar? What differences did you notice?

2. After carefully studying chart 22-22, observe a child care program. Use the checklist to rate the program. Explain why you would or would not enroll a child in this program.

Answer Key

Answer key for "To Review" questions in the text, page 448

1. number; type

2. false

3. businesses may operate these for their employees' children: a; based on the methods used to help mentally handicapped children: d; the oldest types of group programs: a; funded by government monies to help children from low-income families overcome some of their problems: e; based on the idea "play is the highest level of child development": b; stresses that children absorb from their world as they work at tasks: d; have served as a laboratory setting for the study of children: c; today, most are operated on a for-profit basis: a; have a focus on sensory learnings and daily living tasks: d; part of the public education system in the United States: b

4. (Student response.)

5. true

6. (Name two:) costs of transportation, supplies, and disposable diapers and formula for babies; money that may be added from a second income; money saved in the cost of utilities and food for at-home care; child care tax credits

7. false

8. (List three:) Make the adjustment seem casual. Realize that adults can be anxious as well as children. Show that you are sure of the child's ability to adjust. About one month before enrolling a preschool child in a group program, explain what the new program is like and visit the program if possible.

► **Chapter 23**
Careers in Child-Related Fields

Chapter Outline

I. Types of Careers in Child-Related Fields
   A. Health and Protective Services
   B. Care and Education
   C. Entertainment
   D. Design
   E. Advertising, Marketing, and Management
   F. Research and Consulting
   G. Entrepreneurship

II. Heading Toward a Career
   A. Personal Qualifications
      1. Concern for Children
      2. Flexibility
      3. Leadership Skills
   B. Professional Qualifications
      1. Job Training
   C. Job Search Skills
      1. Step One
      2. Step Two
      3. Step Three
      4. Step Four
      5. Step Five

III. Make a Wise Career Choice by Getting Involved
   A. Study a Child's Development
   B. Join Professional Organizations
   C. Consider the Future
   D. Make Wise Career Moves

Suggested Observations

You may want your students to conduct the following observations:

1. Observe a person working in a child-related career field. What skills does he or she use? What aspects of the child's development (physical, mental, and/or social and emotional) does he or she especially need to know for this career?

2. Observe your friends as they become involved with children in different settings. What skills are they developing? Would these skills be helpful in parenting?

Answer Key

Answer key for "To Review" questions in the text, pages 464-465

1. increasing
2. false
3. consultants
4. (List three:) toys; clothing; furniture; tapes, records, and films; educational materials
5. health and protective services: a, e, g, j; care and education: b, d, i; entertainment: h; design: f; advertising, marketing, and management: l; research and consulting: c, k
6. true
7. d
8. (List three:) Be in good physical health. Be kind and patient with children and their families. Be able to cope with children's noise and activity. Enjoy children's physical, mental, and social worlds. Feel comfortable in helping young children with physical needs. Be very adaptable. Be a good leader.
9. taught
10. false
11. child development

Part 7
Special Concerns

▶ Chapter 24
Concerns of Children and Families

Chapter Outline

VIII. Teens as Parents
    A. Health Risks for the Teen Mother and Baby
    B. Financial Concerns
    C. Lifestyle Changes
       1. Life with Mom and Dad
       2. Social Life Changes

IX. Child Neglect and Abuse
    A. Neglect
    B. Abuse
    C. Who Is Abused?
    D. Who Abuses and Neglects Children?
    E. How Can Adults Protect Children from Neglect and Abuse?

X. Resources for Children in Crises

Suggested Observations

You may want your students to conduct the following observations:

1. Observe older siblings with their younger siblings. In what ways, either directly or indirectly, do older siblings influence their younger brothers and sisters?

2. Observe a family in which the parent or parents work outside the home. What advantages do you see for the child or children? What disadvantages do you see? Do you feel the parent or parents show any role strain? Explain.

3. Observe a child who has recently experienced the stress of a move, death, or a family divorce. What seems to be the child's greatest stressor? (For example, if there was a divorce, does the main stressor seem to be missing the noncustodial parent? fearing being left by the custodial parent?) How is the child coping? How are parents, teachers, friends of the family, peers, or others helping the child cope?

Answer Key

Answer key for "To Review" questions in the text, pages 497-498

1. playmates, teachers and learners, protectors, rivals
2. false
3. false
4. (List four:) Children live in more structured homes with more clear-cut rules. Children miss fewer days of school. Children are often seen as good children by teachers and neighbors. Children help around the house, thus learning more home care tasks. Because mothers are models of people who can do a good job both in and outside the home, children have broader gender-role concepts. Children show more self-esteem because they learn to do more for themselves and for their families. Children interact more with people other than their mothers.
5. false
6. Life can stop. Death is forever. People and pets cannot come back to life, even if they really want to.
7. false
8. (Student response.)
9. false
10. Neglect is a failure to properly meet the physical, mental, or emotional needs of the child. Abuse is intended hurtful actions to the child. These can be physical, emotional, or sexual.
11. true
12. false

▶ ## Chapter 25
Children with Developmental Differences

Chapter Outline

  I.   Children are More Alike than Different
  II. Children Who Are Exceptional
      A. Gifted and Talented Children
      B. Children with Physical Disabilities
      C. Speech Disorders
      D. Children with Mental Disabilities
      E. Learning Disabilities
          1. Causes of Learning Disabilities
      F. Disorders
  III. Exceptional Children Need Special Help
      A. How Many Children Are Exceptional?
      B. What Kind of Help Do Exceptional Children Need?

Suggested Observations

You may want your students to conduct the following observations:

1. Observe a classroom for children with disabilities or a classroom in which children with disabilities have been mainstreamed. Explain how all the children are more alike than different.

2. Observe exceptional children in a group setting. List all the ways you note the children received special help.

3. Observe an exceptional child in any setting. What special challenges do you think the parent of this child would face?

Answer Key

Answer key for "To Review" questions in the text, pages 511-512

1. are; may not
2. true
3. speed; degree
4. (List three:) general mental ability (high IQ), specific academic aptitude, creative or productive thinking, leadership ability, visual or performing arts ability, psychomotor ability
5; asks many complex questions at a young age: a; watches others' faces very closely: c; uses one sound for another sound: d; shows poor distance judgment: b; writes *saw* for *was:* f; likes repetition: e; can't identify right and left: f; uses a large vocabulary: a; hits without being provoked: g; has many interests: a; has a poor self-concept: g; at an early age, plays a musical instrument with much skill: a; has delayed motor skills and finds complex ideas hard to grasp: e
6. (Student response.)
7. testing: 2; writing an IEP: 4; referral for testing: 1; finding a suitable program to help the child: 3; retesting and writing a new IEP from time to time: 5

Children
The Early Years

Dr. Celia A. Decker
Professor of Family and Consumer Sciences
Northwestern State University of Louisiana
Natchitoches, Louisiana

Publisher
The Goodheart-Willcox Company, Inc.
Tinley Park, Illinois

Library of Congress Catalog Card Number 98-53654
International Standard Book Number 1-56637-559-2

2 3 4 5 6 7 8 9 10 00 03 02 01 00

Library of Congress Cataloging-in-Publication Data

Decker, Celia Anita.
Children: the early years / Celia A. Decker.
    p.cm.
ISBN 1-56637-559-2
1. Child development. 2. Child psychology. I. Title.
HQ767.9.D43 1999   98-53654
305.231—dc21   CIP

Cover photo provided by The Little Tikes Company

Introduction

Children: The Early Years helps you understand how to work with and care for children as they grow. It explains how children develop physically, intellectually, socially, and emotionally. *Children: The Early Years* also helps you apply what you've learned to meet children's needs in the best possible ways.

Children are different from adults. You need to know how children grow in order to work with them effectively. This text begins by explaining the study of children. It helps you understand why studying child development is important—whether you become a parent, work in a child-related field, or just spend time with children. The text also discusses the choices and preparation involved in becoming a parent.

This text takes you from the prenatal stage through the child's school-age stage of development. The text presents the facts and theories about the child's development. It also uses many examples to help you apply this information when working with children of all ages.

Children: The Early Years helps you explore how family situations affect children. It explores the special needs and concerns of children with developmental differences. This book also presents ways to care for children, including play activities, ways to keep children healthy and safe, group programs, and child-related careers.

About the Author

Celia A. Decker is currently serving as a professor in the Department of Family and Consumer Sciences at Northwestern State University of Louisiana. She teaches courses in early childhood education, child development, and family relations. She is also the coordinator of graduate studies in early childhood education. In addition to writing this text, she and her husband, Dr. John R. Decker, wrote *Planning and Administering Early Childhood Programs.* Dr. Decker has also published numerous chapters in books and articles. She presents papers at the national and state annual meetings of professional associations, such as the National Association for the Education of Young Children, Southern Early Childhood Association, Association for Childhood Education International, National Association of Early Childhood Teacher Educators, and the Society for Research in Child Development. She does extensive consultant work for Head Start, Even Start, and local school systems.

During her years of teaching, Dr. Decker has been named to Who's Who in Child Development Professionals, Who's Who in Personalities of the South, Who's Who in American Women, and the World's Who's Who in Education. In 1994, she was selected as the Outstanding Professor at Northwestern State University.

Table of Contents

▶ ## Chapter 6   The Newborn   120

Part 1

Children in Today's World

Until recently, people thought training in child development was unnecessary. They thought the knowledge and skills adults need for child-related careers—including parenting—come naturally. Many felt just being raised in a family teaches adults all they need to know about children and child care skills.

Today, experts know that understanding children requires careful study. Changes that are taking place in society and in today's families require people to know more about child development than what they observed in their own family.

In **chapter 1,** you will learn many reasons for studying children. You also will study the basic concepts of a child's growth and development. Finally, you will learn more about children through observation. By studying **chapter 2,** you will learn about the family's role in a child's development. You will read about the many family types in which children are raised, the family life cycle, and parenting styles. **Chapter 3** will introduce you to the roles of parents and the questions adults should consider before they have children.

Chapter 1

Learning About Children

Children are an important part of society. By studying them, you can learn how to help children grow and develop into happy, healthy adults.

After studying this chapter, you will be able to

- [ ] list reasons for learning about children.
- [ ] define the term *child development*.
- [ ] describe the individual life cycle.
- [ ] describe three factors that promote growth and development.
- [ ] identify differences in the rate of growth and development
- [ ] explain and give examples of some major principles and theories of growth and development.
- [ ] develop observation skills.

After studying this chapter, you will be able to define

character
child development
child-centered society
culture
development
developmental acceleration
developmental delay
developmental tasks
direct observation
environment
heredity
indirect observation
individual life cycle
principles of growth and development
sequenced steps
teachable moment

Child development is one of the most fascinating subjects you can study. Children are constantly changing and discovering. They are also curious and creative. Who else would use a cardboard box for a house, a race car, or a submarine? If you have spent any time with children, you know they can be lovable and challenging.

How will studying children help you? Whether you are interested in caring for children or being a parent someday, learning about children will help you better understand them as well as yourself. As you learn, you will see that children go through many stages of growth and development. This book emphasizes their early years because these years help shape children's lives.

Studying children will also help you learn positive ways to care for them. People like to think they live in a **child-centered society**—a society that sees children as important and works for their good. However, some children also experience a great deal of harm through abuse and neglect. Children need safe environments. They need homes, schools, and other places where they can develop to their best potential, 1-1. All children should have the chance to grow in a place that will further their health and well-being. By studying children, you will learn how to provide these safe places.

● Why Study Children?

Knowing how to meet children's needs is not easy. Before studying how adults can help children develop and learn, you must understand why you should study children.

▶ To Understand Yourself

Studying how children grow and develop can help you grow, too. It can help you appreciate all that goes into taking a first step or saying a first word. When you help a child overcome a fear or learn a skill, you feel good. Adults often enjoy just being with children, 1-2. Their awe of beauty, their frankness, and their world of magic please adults.

1-1   Activities that are fun and challenging encourage mental and social development.

© John Shaw

1—*Activity:* Write phrases to describe a favorite child. How is the child creative? How is the child challenging? How could studying child development help you?

2—*Enrich:* Ask exchange students to discuss how people in their country value children (in terms of housing, schools, and children's services). Compare to your community. Discuss child abuse and neglect.

3—*Note:* Summarize the benefits of studying children on the blackboard or a transparency.

4—*Discuss:* Describe an interaction with a child that made you feel good or special.

© John Shaw

1-2   Just being around children is a happy experience for many adults.

Children can share gifts that, sadly, adults often outgrow. Many times, adults are not fully aware that the people they are today are a result of the children they were. As you study children, you can gain insight into your own growth, development, and value system. You can also understand how your values affect your feelings about, and reactions to, children. This knowledge can help you serve children in better ways.

▶To Be a Responsible Parent

By studying children, parents know their children's needs at each stage of development. They also know the best ways to respond to those needs. Parenting is a mind-boggling task! How much adults know about children, however, can determine the kind of parents they become.

Studying children also helps parents have realistic expectations for their parenting abilities. They are responsible for meeting all of their children's needs, such as

☐   **physical needs**. Children need the right diet to nourish their growing, active bodies. They need well-fitting clothes that also promote self-esteem. They need shelter and physical protection, 1-3. Parents must provide for these needs.

☐   **intellectual needs**. Parents need to provide good experiences for their children, 1-4. Experiences can help children learn and develop skills they need to survive. Parents must also meet children's creative needs, 1-5.

☐   **social needs**. It's important for parents to enable children to be with other children. This helps children learn how to respond to others. Part of a parent's responsibility is helping a child develop character. ***Character*** is an inward force that guides a person's conduct. It helps people make choices that meet acceptable standards of right and wrong. As you read this book, you will learn about ways to guide children's social development. These methods will help develop a child's character.

☐   **trust needs**. Children need to feel they can cope with demands of family, friends, and society. Trusting parents helps them gain confidence. Trust begins early in life when parents meet children's needs. It continues to grow when parents allow children the freedom to develop.

☐   **love/discipline needs**. Parents and children need each other's love. In loving children, parents must listen to their children, set limits, and share their reasons for limits, 1-6. Through love and discipline, parents help children grow into self-directed adults.

▶ To Pass Down Culture

Both children and adults are part of a culture. ***Culture*** is the way of life for a group of people. It includes a group's language, attitudes, values, rituals, and skills, 1-7. What a culture

1—*Reflect:* How do you feel when you are around children?

2—*Activity:* Provide copies from a section of a developmental scale chart. Discuss how knowing what is typical at a certain age helps parents interact more positively with children.

3—*Resource: Parents Aid Children's Growth and Development,* SAG.

Fisher-Price

1-4   Adults need to provide the right learning experiences for a child's stage of development.

1-5   Children grow intellectually through creative experiences.

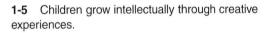

1-3   Infants and young children have many safety needs.

Photo provided by and reproduced with permission of Binney & Smith

© John Shaw

1-6 Setting limits is part of loving and disciplining children.

1-7 Learning family rituals is part of a child's culture.

© John Shaw

1—*Activity:* Clip pictures of individuals from different cultures. Discuss how their language, attitudes, values, family and cultural rituals, and skills vary.

expects of its members is handed down from adult to child. Children make it possible for a culture to continue. The future of a society is determined by its children.

▶ To Protect Children's Rights

Children are easily hurt because they are physically weaker than adults and because they cannot reason as adults. Society must protect them.

Recently, the Convention on the Rights of the Child (United Nations International Children's Education Fund) wrote 54 articles that set out the rights of every child in the world. These rights can be given under 11 major rights. Children have the right to:

☐ **an identity** (government should protect children's name, family ties, nationality)

☐ **a family** (children should be able to live with their parents unless this is not in the children's best interest, and parents have the responsibility for raising children with government support)

☐ **express themselves and have access to information** (children have the right: to express their views; to freedom of thought, conscience, and religion; and to obtain information)

☐ **a safe and healthy life** (children have the right to life, and the government should do everything it can to make sure that children survive and develop; children should have access to medical services and to a decent standard of living)

☐ **special protection in times of war** (children who are refugees are entitled to special protection; children who are under 15 should not take part in armed conflict)

☐ **an education** (primary education should be free and required of all children; secondary education should be accessible to all children)

☐ **special care for the disabled** (children who are disabled have the right to special care, education, and training)

2—*Resource: Children's Bill of Rights,* SAG.

☐ **protection from discrimination** (all rights apply to all children; children have the right to practice their own culture, religion, and language)

☐ **protection from abuse** (children shall be protected against abuse and neglect; government shall be involved with laws and programs concerned with abuse)

☐ **protection from harmful work** (children have the right to rest, leisure, play, and participation in cultural and artistic activities; children have the right to be protected from having to participate in work that threatens their health, education, and development)

☐ **special treatment if arrested** (children are entitled to assistance and treatment that respects their rights)

In the United States, parents have the rights of guardianship and determine their children's upbringing. For example, they control the children's level of financial support. They also control religious and moral teachings, the kind and extent of education, and health care choices. The state can come between a parent and child when courts feel the child needs more protection. For example, the state may require foster care.

Each state can make laws and policies to protect children. For example, school attendance laws, child labor laws, and laws against selling drugs to minors help protect children and society. State laws protect children from the results of their own lack of judgment. For example, young children are not responsible legally for their contracts. They are not treated in the same way in the courts. The state can also make laws to develop child welfare services. For instance, the state office checks on the quality of child care programs.

Children have gained rights, too. For example, they have gained the rights of due process and fair treatment in the juvenile courts and schools. In some states, children may receive medical help without parental consent.

Locally, state laws are enforced. Additional local laws may be enacted, too, such as curfews. Citizen groups at the local level often become advocates of children's rights by attempting to get

needed laws passed and by notifying the appropriate persons when any child's rights seem to be violated.

4

▶ To Work with Children

Adults with child-related careers must study children. (See chapter 23 to read about these careers.) Most careers focus on only some of children's needs. A school cook, for instance, is concerned with children's nutritional needs. A teacher is more concerned with their intellectual needs. However, the child is a whole person. Anyone in a child-related field should know about all aspects of children's growth and development, 1-8.

5

1-8 Classroom teachers are mainly prepared to meet the mental needs of children. They must also be aware of children's other needs and how these affect mental growth.

Radio Shack, A Div. of Tandy Corp.

What Is Child Development?

1

Development is the process that turns babies into adults. The process has many stages, such as infancy, childhood, adolescence, and adulthood, 1-9. Development takes place from the time you are conceived until you die.

How children grow and develop is based on scientific studies. *Child development* is the scientific study of children from conception to adolescence.

2

Child development focuses on changes that occur in children. This includes the way children's bodies grow and develop and the way children think and learn. Child development also focuses on the way children feel about themselves and interact with others.

1-9   Between infancy and adulthood, children go through many stages of development.

By doing research, experts in medicine, education, sociology, and family and consumer sciences help gather knowledge about children. People then use these facts to learn about children. Child development is not just for experts, though. Anyone who is around children can use this knowledge. Child development teaches people how to care for children.

Individual Life Cycle

The *individual life* cycle is a description of how people change through the years. For the purpose of understanding, we cluster certain age-related changes in growth and in the common behaviors of people and refer to this as a "stage." Although a given person may go through these stages at different ages, we usually name these stages in terms of the ages in which they occur in most people. The age ranges are placed on the stages to provide an idea when a stage first appears and when it ends for children. Six stages are described in this book.

☐   The **prenatal stage** begins at conception and ends about nine months later at birth. The prenatal stage is the time of the fastest growth. The child grows from a single cell to a complete organism.

☐   The **neonatal stage** extends from birth through the second week. During this period, the baby physically adapts to life outside of the mother's body.

☐   The **infancy stage** begins at two weeks and continues through the twelfth month. The infant develops the foundation for motor skills, thinking, and language skills and begins to interact with others.

☐   The **toddler stage** begins at one year and ends at 36 months (when the child celebrates his or her third birthday). In the toddler stage, the child makes great strides in motor, thinking, and language skills and begins to test his or her dependence on adults.

☐ The **preschool stage** begins at three years and ends at 72 months (when the child celebrates his or her sixth birthday). During this stage, the child becomes very self-sufficient, spends many hours in play exploring the physical and social world, and develops a rather stable self-concept.

☐ The **school-age stage** or middle childhood begins at 6 years and ends at 12 years. This stage corresponds to the typical ages of children in the elementary school years. Achievement is the central goal of these years as children master the basics of reading, writing, and arithmetic and are exposed to many other "school learnings." Because of the increased contact with peers and group instruction in the schools, self-control must be learned.

● Factors that Influence Growth and Development

Why is each child different? The differences are due to each child's unique, inborn traits as well as the environment. The way the traits and the environment affect each other also make children different.

Heredity and environment are the factors that influence growth and development. *Heredity* includes all the traits from blood relatives that are passed down to a child. *Environment* includes all the conditions and situations that affect a child. To understand the effects of heredity and environment on children, experts have carried out many studies. They have learned a lot about how these factors influence growth and development, but unanswered questions still exist.

▶ Heredity

Heredity is passed on through genes. Genes carry the inborn instructions that help make a person what he or she is. They are found in a person's cells. Genes affect your growth and development in many ways.

1—*Activity:* Students list hereditary and environmental factors that make them unique.

☐ The genes' instructions are lifelong. For example, the same genes determine hair color for life. A person may be born with dark hair that later turns blond, then brown, and finally gray. Although the hair color changes, the genes do not.

☐ Genes affect some parts of growth and development more than others. For instance, genes determine body features like blood type, facial structure, and color of hair, eyes, and skin, 1-10. However, genes and environment affect mental ability and social-emotional traits.

1-10   Brothers and sisters may look alike in many ways because they both inherit genes from their parents.

☐ Some genes determine whether or not a person has a trait. For instance, a person either is or is not an *albino*. (An albino is a person with white skin, almost white hair, and pink eyes.)

☐ Other genes affect the range of a trait. Traits like height (very short to very tall) and athletic ability (almost no ability to greatness) come from these genes. These genes determine a trait's highest *potential*. (Potential is the greatest amount or level possible.) Whether a person will show or use that trait to its highest potential depends on the person's life. For instance, good diets will help children grow in height.

2

2—*Reflect:* What traits were passed on to you that genes determined?

Once they reach their potential, however, they cannot grow taller. On the other hand, children with poor diets may not achieve their full potential.

▶ Environment

The environment also affects growth and development. The environment includes physical conditions, such as food and rest. It includes first-hand experiences from which children learn, 1-11. What children hear or read is also part of their environment, as are their relationships with others. All of these factors affect the way a child grows and develops.

Some factors in the environment affect physical traits. For instance, diet can affect height and health. Most factors in the environment affect mental and social-emotional traits, 1-12. For example, studies show that babies do not learn as quickly when no one holds or talks to them. Children who are given attention and the chance to read, hear music, and play games often learn more easily than other children.

Lakeshore Learning Materials, Carson, Calif.

1-12   An environment with appropriate play materials encourages much concentration and learning during play.

1-11   Children learn through firsthand experiences.

© John Shaw

▶ Heredity and Environment Combined

For years, people argued about what affected growth and development more—heredity or environment. Now, experts agree they work together.

Genes, for instance, control how quickly a baby's muscles and bones grow (heredity). A proper diet is needed for the baby to grow (environment). However, a better diet does not make bones and muscles bigger than heredity allows (heredity and environment).

Going one step further, parents can exercise their baby to help muscles become stronger (environment). Nevertheless, the baby cannot

1—*Discuss:* What do children learn from playing in the mud? with play dough?

2—*Discuss:* How do some television shows, movies, and books affect children's intellectual and social development? Discuss both negative and positive effects.

3—*Discuss:* Name some environmental factors that decrease the effect of hereditary factors.

4—*Resource: Heredity or Environment?* SAG.

walk until muscles and bones are ready (hered-ity). When the baby's body is ready, parents can help the baby walk as soon as possible through exercise and encouragement (heredity and environment).

Differences in the Rate of Growth and Development

All people change with time. They grow and they develop certain skills and behaviors in the expected sequence we call "stages." As you just read, many factors influence growth and develop-ment. These factors make each person unique in his or her own rate of development.

Some people go through the stages earlier and some later than the typical ages. **Developmental acceleration** is when a child is performing like an older child. For example, a 30-month-old child who speaks in long, complex sentences is developmentally accelerated in lan-guage. On the other hand, **developmental delay** is when a child is performing like a younger child. For example, a three-year-old who speaks in two-word sentences is developmentally delayed in language. Usually, children with delays catch up with other children.

People do not always move forward in all developmental areas at the same rate. For exam-ple, a child may be developing at a fast rate in motor skills and at a slow rate in language usage. Such a child would be considered developmen-tally accelerated in motor skills, but developmen-tally delayed in language skills. Some children, however, seem to have such an overall favorable heredity and environment that they may be devel-opmentally accelerated in most, if not all, areas of growth and development. Sometimes, too, major unfavorable conditions may delay most areas of development. For example, a child born very early may be developmentally delayed in most ways for several years.

1—*Activity:* Clip ads for baby formulas and foods. Highlight parts that emphasize growth and development. Are these ads credible?

2—*Resource: A Look at Tomorrow,* SAG.

3—*Discuss:* What are some examples of constancy in your growth and development?

Principles of Growth and Development

Each person is unique, yet people are more alike than different. Experts study these like-nesses to find a pattern of growth and develop-ment. These patterns, or **principles of growth and development**, do not fit every person exactly. However, they are true enough that we can use them as a guide when learning about children. The following describes important pat-terns or principles of growth and development.

▶ Growth and Development Are Constant

There are many unchanging aspects of a person's growth and development. This is called *constancy*. What a child is today is a good hint—but not proof—of what he or she will be tomorrow. For example, tall two-year-olds tend to be tall adults. Children who are good students in ele-mentary school are likely to be good students in high school. Happy, secure children tend to be cheerful, confident adults.

Why is this so? There are two reasons for constancy in growth and development. First, traits controlled by heredity do not change. Second, people often live in the same environment for years. In order for major changes to take place in growth and development, however, major changes must take place in the environment.

▶ Growth and Development Are Gradual and Continuous

Growth and development are gradual and continuous because changes that take place hap-pen in little, unbroken steps. A child does not grow or develop overnight. A baby takes those first steps on a certain date, for example, but each day before walking the baby grew, the body matured, and the baby practiced motor skills, such as crawling and pulling up. All of this led to the baby's first steps, 1-13.

4—*Discuss:* Compare a baby's motor skills at birth to the motor skills of a baby animal. (An animal is able to walk almost at birth; a baby takes almost one year.)

Photographs courtesy of Carter's; Photography by Bruce Plotkin

1-13   Children must practice many motor skills before they take their first steps. Before walking, children pull themselves mainly by their arms (A), creep on all fours (B), pull themselves onto their feet (C), stand without support (D), and try standing on one foot (E).

In a positive way, the principle suggests that good development does not reverse overnight. A few mistakes or stresses usually do not cause severe problems. As an example, a one-day junk food binge does not seriously harm a healthy person.

The principle also suggests that if people do not grow or develop when they are supposed to, they can make up that learning later in life. For instance, if children are not taught to read at age six, they can learn a few years later without too many problems. (One exception involves changes in the body. Once growth and change are complete in places such as the bones and brain, therapy cannot help.)

On the negative side, the principle suggests that poor growth and development is not easily reversed. For example, consider a child with poor health due to a long-term poor diet. The child may need to eat from a carefully planned diet for many months to restore health. This means the principle can work to a person's advantage or disadvantage.

1—*Discuss:* Compare how a one-day grapefruit diet and a three-week grapefruit diet each affect a person's health. Compare to a child who does not eat a well-balanced diet for a long period of time.

▶ Growth and Development Happen in Sequenced Steps

In order for growth and development to be continuous, change must build on what children have already learned. For instance, writing comes from making marks that are not letters. The steps in growth and development follow one another in a certain order called **sequenced steps**. Think about the changes that happen in children in ranked stages—one stage always occurs before another stage.

A **teachable moment** is a time when a person can learn a new task. It occurs when the body is physically ready, when caregivers encourage and support the child, and when the child feels a strong desire to learn. If a child has not reached the teachable moment, he or she will feel stressed when trying to master a task or skill. Waiting too long after the teachable moment occurs may cause problems, too. For example, a child who was ready to ride a bicycle but did not have the chance to learn may have trouble learning the skill as an adult.

▶ Growth and Development Happen at Different Rates

Growth and development happen at different rates throughout life and for different people. Experts know when fast and slow periods of growth and development occur. Height and weight increases are fast in infancy, for example. The increases are moderate in preschool, slow in elementary school, and fast again in junior and senior high school.

Rates of growth and development vary from one child to another. Some children develop quickly and others slowly. Although the sequence of growth and development is similar for all children, the rates of change differ. Why do these rates differ? Children grow and develop at different rates because of heredity, environment, and motivation.

Heredity determines different growth rates. For example, girl's bones and organs are more mature than boy's at all ages because of heredity.

A good environment is something children need to grow at the best rate. If the environment lacks proper nutrition, for example, *lags* or delays in growth and development occur. Does this mean that trying to speed up development is good? No—an adult's attempts to hurry growth and development may cause a child harmful stress.

Motivation, which is a child's desire to achieve, also makes growth and development rates vary. Some children are eager to achieve and others are more poorly motivated.

▶ Growth and Development Have Interrelated Parts

In this book, the physical, mental, and social-emotional aspects of growth and development are often discussed in separate sections or chapters. This is so you can better understand each aspect. In reality, however, all aspects interact with each other in complex ways. For instance, as children's bodies grow and mature, their motor skills improve. These motor skills, in turn, help their social skills, 1-14. As social skills improve, children talk to more people and learn about new ideas. This helps their mental skills. As mental skills improve, children can play in more complex sports, which helps their motor skills.

People who work with children must understand how different parts of growth and development affect each other. For instance, a teacher's job is to improve children's intellectual growth. However, the way a teacher treats children also affects their social-emotional growth. Understanding these interrelationships improves the way people work with children.

● **Theories of Growth and Development**

Robert J. Havighurst and Abraham Maslow are two researchers who have studied children. Their research led them to the following theories about growth and development.

4

5

1—*Discuss:* List the steps of making a cheese omelet. Discuss or demonstrate why the order could not be reversed (such as beating the eggs before cracking them). Compare to a baby's need to roll over before crawling. Define sequence in your own words.

2—*Reflect:* Do you recall a time when you were forced to learn something for which you were not ready (a mental, physical, or social skill)? Discuss your feelings. Discuss a teachable moment for you or for a child you know.

3—*Activity:* Provide group pictures of different grade levels, from preschool through elementary school. Observe differences in physical development.

4—*Discuss:* What could happen if a child is overfed or underfed to speed or retard physical development? What could happen if a child is pushed to develop social skills too early, such as with early dating? What could happen if a child is pushed to learn reading, writing, or math skills too soon?

5—*Resource: The Wholeness of Growth and Development,* SAG.

1-14 Becoming mature enough to jump rope brings lots of fun with friends.

▶ Havighurst's Theory of Developmental Tasks

Each child masters skills and activities that fit his or her level of growth and development. In all cultures, children are expected to learn skills like crawling, self-feeding, and dressing at a time that is right for them. These are called *developmental tasks*, or tasks that should be mastered at a certain stage in life.

Havighurst, a well-known educator and behavioral scientist, believed achieving developmental tasks leads to happiness and success with later tasks, 1-15. Failure to achieve tasks leads to unhappiness and problems with later tasks.

Havighurst identified the developmental tasks of children as coming from the following three sources:

☐   physical growth. A baby comes into the world as a helpless being. As its body matures, the child is able to learn many new skills, such as walking and reading.

1—*Enrich:* Provide examples of developmental tasks for adolescents. (An example is dating to learn about desirable qualities in a future mate or trying different jobs to learn about a future career.)

☐   social pressures. Society (family, friends, teachers, etc.) pressures the child, through rewards and penalties, to master important tasks. Developmental tasks may differ from culture to culture, because different groups value different skills. For instance, playing in order to win has no value to Hopi Indian

Courtesy of the Perfection Learning Corporation

1-15   Mastering school tasks is needed for success in later life.

children. However, most other American children feel that winning is important. Tasks differ from region to region, too, 1-16. Over time, the tasks also change to reflect changes in society, 1-17.

☐   inner pressures. The actual push to achieve comes from within children. In the end, the child is responsible for mastering each task. Children will work harder to learn tasks they like, 1-18.

Louisiana Department of Wildlife and Fisheries

1-16   Children in southern states learn how to catch crawfish (crayfish).

1-17   Learning computer skills is a developmental task that is needed because of changes in technology.

© John Shaw

▶ Maslow's Theory of Human Needs

Maslow, a noted psychologist, believed development comes from meeting personal needs. According to Maslow, all humans work to fulfill basic needs and higher-level needs.

Basic needs are both physiological (organic, or related to the body) and psychological (related to feelings). Maslow divides basic needs into four categories. One category includes all physiological needs. The other three categories are the psychological categories of safety, belonging and love, and esteem. Higher-level needs include the category Maslow labeled "aesthetic and cognitive and self-actualization," 1-19.

Maslow places basic needs and higher-level needs in a ranked order called the *hierarchy of human needs*. In other words, basic needs are lower-level needs that must be fulfilled to a reasonable extent before the higher-level needs can be met.

Understanding Maslow's hierarchy of human needs is important for all adults who want to study about and care for children. Maslow's work implies that the further up the hierarchy of needs a person can go, the more growth and fulfillment he or she seeks. Maslow sees humans as driven by the need to become.

Adults need to learn and practice ways to help children meet their needs. The first step is to help children meet their basic needs. For instance, adults help children meet these needs by offering them nutritious foods. Once adults satisfy children's basic needs, they can meet their higher-level needs. For example, well-fed children can turn their attentions away from eating to psychological needs. These might include enjoying pretty scenery or a group of friends. Higher-level skills help children to realize their full potential as adults, which is called *self-actualization*.

3

4

1—*Enrich:* Invite exchange students to discuss cultural values and skill expectations in their country.

2—*Reflect:* What tasks motivate you to achieve because you like to perform and learn them?

3—*Activity:* Provide a hierarchy sketch on a transparency, poster, or blackboard. Label each level, placing examples of each need on the diagram. Why do infants start out at the lowest level? Which levels must caregivers meet?

4—*Resource: Children Fulfill Their Needs,* SAG.

Developmental Task	
Sources of Developmental Tasks	**Examples**
	Area: Motor Task **Task for middle childhood:** Learning physical skills needed for common games **Example of task:** Learning skills needed to play ball
Physical growth	Child needs bone and muscle growth; eyes and hands must work smoothly together.
Social pressures	Other children reward skillful players (accept them as friends) and punish failures (tease or reject them as friends). Parents and school coaches may also expect children to master the skill.
Inner pressures	Child desires to be admired by other children, parents, and coaches.
Must see new possibilities for behavior	Child sees older children playing ball.
Must form new concept of self	Child thinks, "I can be a player."
Must cope with conflicting demands	Child thinks, "I can get hit with a ball and I can be teased for striking out. But if I do not play, the other kids will make fun of me and my parents and coaches will not consider me grown-up."
Wants to achieve the next step in development enough to work for it	Child now spends hours in practice.

1-18 Children master developmental tasks when their body is ready, when others place pressure on them, and when they want to learn a new skill.

● Observing Children

Observations are the oldest, most often used, and best ways to learn about human behavior, including the behavior of children. As humans, we enter the world with our own observation equipment—our senses.

Sometimes the senses are all we need for observations. For example, we react quickly to a sudden movement or loud noise. This instinctive observation and response helps protect us.

At other times, we are unaware when we observe and learn. We learn by imitating others. This is how we learn speech and our gestures. Because so many of our skills are learned

through imitation, this type of observation is important.

For the most part, observation skills must be learned. These skills come with knowledge and practice. For example, pretend you are looking at an X-ray with your doctor. You only see shadows and lines, but your doctor sees a bone fracture. Why does your doctor see more? Because of knowledge and practice, your doctor sees meaning in images you may not notice or consider to be important.

If you have ever cared for or worked with children, you might have used this method of observation. At times, you may give an unthinking response to an observation. For instance, you

1—*Activity:* Close your eyes and listen for sounds that could be used in an observation. Tape additional, more specific sounds.

2—*Activity:* Show students a prenatal sonogram. What do we recognize in the image? Why does a doctor see more?

Maslow's Needs	
Categories	**Examples**
Basic Needs	
■ physiological	■ food, water, air, shelter, and clothing
■ safety	■ avoidance of illness, danger, and disruption; security
■ belonging and love	■ affiliation (belonging to groups such as family), acceptance, and love
■ esteem	■ mastery, adequacy, achievement, competence, and recognition
Higher-Level Needs	
■ aesthetic and cognitive and self-actualization	■ knowledge and appreciation of beauty, goodness, freedom, and a realistic view and acceptance of self and others

1-19   Maslow sees two kinds of needs in all humans: basic needs and higher-level needs.

react immediately when you see a child in danger. You also learn many skills by imitation. For example, you may observe a teacher sitting on the floor working with children. Later, you may sit on the floor when you work with them.

You will learn more about children when you use your mind to "see" more. For instance, observing children will help you understand what you read in this book and what you hear about children. At the same time, what you learn as you read will help you "see" more when you observe, 1-20.

1—*Reflect:* What have you learned through observation? Recall the instance and who you observed.

© John Shaw

1-20   Each time this student observes and takes notes, she is learning to "see" more.

▶ Why Observe Children?

How do researchers know so much about children? They have been observing and writing about children for many years. As you observe, you will behave like a researcher, too.

Usually, a researcher has a question, then observes children to learn the answer. What you observe will depend on the purpose of your observation. Because this book looks at the sequence of children's growth and development, you will consider these principles when you observe. Your teacher will assign you a task from the book. As you observe, you will look for answers to each task.

What Do Researchers Want to Know?

Sometimes researchers, while observing, think of another idea to study. You, too, will notice behaviors that were not part of your assigned work. You will want to ask questions about what you see. This is how researchers learn.

Other times, researchers want to know more about a behavior and decide to observe further. For example, you may hear three-year-olds reciting numbers to 10. Does this mean they can count objects to 10, also? To find out, you may need to observe behavior more closely.

Researchers may also look for causes that affect behavior, such as factors that cause a child to feel secure. You may also try to understand the behaviors of children or note why a certain game worked well with children.

2—*Discuss:* List some specific observation topics, such as sharing toys, participating during group time, and performing certain large-motor skills.

Another reason to observe children is to help you better interact with children in your care. You can learn this by observing how others work with children and how the children react to them.

▶ Ways to Observe

There are many ways to observe children. The best way is to observe children directly. However, many observations are done indirectly.

Direct Observations

A ***direct observation*** means that you watch children in their natural environments. These environments include home, play groups, child care programs, schools, and public places, such as shopping centers, parks, and restaurants, 1-21.

Researchers often observe in special laboratory settings where they can study what they do not often see in the natural environment. They may need to see, for example, how a baby reacts when the mother leaves the room and a stranger

1-21 Researchers carefully observe and record many aspects of children's development.

John Shaw

enters. Researchers also use special laboratory observations to speed up the observation process. Suppose researchers want to observe a child's balancing skills. If they go to a park with a balance beam, they may wait hours before enough children walk on the beam. In a laboratory, however, children arrive at the setting, walk the beam, and leave. Researchers also use laboratory settings when special equipment is needed.

Observations set in laboratories cannot answer all questions. For instance, it would be hard for researchers to know if children really like playing on a balance beam. Although some information in this book comes from research done in the laboratory setting, you will not observe this way. You will begin observing in the natural setting, as all researchers do.

Indirect Observation

Although, direct observation is the main way to learn about children. Researchers also use other observation methods to study something in more detail or check direct observations. ***Indirect observation*** is also important when observing children. This may include asking questions of parents, teachers, or children. Indirect observation also includes observing products children make, such as artwork or stories children dictate or write.

You can learn a lot from children's products. You can learn even more when you observe children making these products. For example, it is easy to look at a drawing and tell that a child colored outside the lines. How can you tell if this is due to motor control, a damaged crayon, or a rushed coloring job? Only direct observation will tell you.

▶ Guidelines for Observing

Anyone observing children should follow certain guidelines, 1-22. These guidelines are important for several reasons. First, they protect the rights of the subject and the observer. They also list proper behaviors you should follow when visiting a child care center. Finally, they will help you make meaningful and accurate observations.

1—*Note:* Observing others at work can be equated to job shadowing. This can help you decide whether or not you really like a job.

2—*Resource: Observation: Children at Play,* SAG.

3—*Note:* These research examples are used to develop child development theories and to help students in child development courses.

4—*Note:* In these observations, children are not directly performing an activity. Researchers observe artwork or interview caregivers for comments about children.

5—*Discuss:* Why do you think direct observation is the main way to learn about children?

Guidelines for Observations

Guidelines	Details About Guidelines
Know your objectives.	Objectives tell us ■ what age children to observe ■ what type of activity to observe ■ where to observe (in some cases) ■ how much time to spend observing ■ what type of records to keep
Obtain permission to observe.	In public places (a park or shopping center), you may observe children without permission. Parents or other adults are more cooperative, however, when they know what you are doing. Explain that you are learning about, not judging, children and their skills. In addition, explain that you will not be using the children's names. Private places (homes or child care programs) require prior approval before granting you permission to observe. Find out whether you or your teacher will receive this approval. Observe only on approved dates and at approved times. If observing in a home, call the day before to be sure the time is still convenient for the parent.
Know what to do at the site.	Remember, you are an invited guest. ■ Always introduce yourself and state your purpose. ■ Try not to distract children or adults from their activities. Move quietly, and do not talk unless you are working with children. ■ Thank the parent or teacher when leaving. ■ Leave promptly when you have completed your work or at a break between activities. ■ If you moved a chair, return it to the original spot. Sites also have different procedures. At some sites, you observe in an observation room looking through a one-way mirror. At other sites, you may help with the children. In still other sites, you sit away from the children. Find out in advance what you will be expected to do.
Be sure observations do not distract children from regular activities.	Try not to add anything new to the setting. Some general guidelines are the following: ■ Get acquainted with the children and the setting before observing. Children learn to ignore observers if frequently observed. ■ Unless asked to help, do not position yourself any closer to the children than necessary. (When making language observations, however, you must be close.) ■ Do not smile at children or wear jewelry or clothing that especially appeals to them. If children come to you, answer them briefly but encourage them to return to their activities. ■ Avoid talking directly to children, including giving hints about how to do an activity. (Laboratory observations may require you to talk to children, but natural observations do not.) ■ Your objectives should never interfere with the program objectives. Do not, for example, request certain activities. <div align="right">(continued)</div>

1-22 Care must be taken when doing observations.

1—*Activity:* List observation guidelines on a transparency, a poster, or a blackboard. Add extra suggestions and post in the observation room.

2—*Note:* Be careful to follow through on these statements.

3—*Note:* Record only those observations that coincide with the program objectives.

Guidelines for Observations (continued)	
Guidelines	**Details About Guidelines**
Observe carefully and objectively.	Observations require intense mental activity. Observing children is like having a meaningful conversation. The observation should be so intense that you can remember it vividly. Many situations can affect objectivity, such as distractions, fatigue, or discomfort. Biases also affect objectivity. For these reasons, observers should not study their own children or children of close friends or relatives.
Record accurately.	Humans are not cameras or tape recorders. Anything that affects observations will affect note taking. The following three errors occur when recording information: ■ The observer leaves out information that may help him or her understand the situation. Naturally, behavior cannot stop while you record. Try to write the entire sequence of behavior. Write in complete sentences. After you finish the observation, go back and check your spelling and other details. ■ The observer records behaviors that did not occur. This happens when the observer does not pay close attention or relies on memory to complete notes. Sometimes biases cause the observer to use inaccurate words. Avoid using too many adjectives in your descriptions. ■ The observer finds the notes out of sequence. Control this by writing the time in your notes every three to five minutes.
Protect the rights of all observed.	Observers know information about children, parents, and teachers for learning purposes. People have privacy rights we must protect in the following ways: ■ Never discuss a child in front of that child or an adult except the child's teacher. Talk about observations only in the classroom or privately with the child's teacher. ■ Change the child's real name or use the child's first name only during class discussions. (Researchers often use letters or numbers to identify children.) ■ Respect parents' rights to refuse your request to observe. ■ Keep information confidential. Take notes discretely so others cannot read them as you write. File notes in a secure place when you are not using them. ■ Use the same care when discussing information other observers share as you would with your own observations. ■ Destroy all notes carefully when they are no longer useful. This applies to the original notes; handwritten, typed, or word processed notes; and notes on disks as well as hard copies. (If notes placed in the trash are easy to read, they are not destroyed.)

1

2

3

1—*Note:* You may need to develop your own codes for speed writing. This will help you avoid errors and record all the information you need.

2—*Note:* It is best to record any final touches on your notes as soon as possible after the observation. This will help you avoid errors.

3—*Note:* Be sure to stress the importance of confidentiality.

Summary

The scientific study of children is called child development. Children's growth and development depends on three factors—heredity, environment, and the way heredity and environment work together. Children follow similar patterns, or principles, of growth and development.

Researchers have formed a number of theories about how children grow and develop. Havighurst and Maslow are two researchers with such theories.

The best way to learn about the behavior of children is by observing them. Child observations are done to answer questions, to get new ideas, and to look for causes that affect behavior.

To Review

1

Write your answers on a separate sheet of paper.
1. True or false. Only people who will be parents someday need to know how to care for and guide children.
2. List five reasons why people study children.
3. Define the term *child development*.
4. List the six stages of the individual life cycle for children.
5. What are the three factors that promote growth and development?
6. True or false. Genes affect the physical, mental, and social aspects of development to the same degree.
7. The environment _____ (does, does not) greatly affect growth and development.
8. Explain the difference between developmental acceleration and developmental delay.
9. Explain one principle of growth and development and provide an example.
10. Which of the following statements is most true about child growth and development?
    a. The order of the steps and the rate of change in growth and development are about the same for most children.
    b. The rate of change in growth and development is about the same for most children.
    c. The order of the steps in growth and development is about the same for most children.
11. Match each source of mastering developmental tasks with the correct example.
    ___ physical growth
    ___ social pressures
    ___ inner pressures
    a. The child's teacher says learning math skills is important.
    b. The child's brain cells are developed.
    c. The child has read about space industry careers and feels that such a career would be fun.
12. Explain Maslow's hierarchy of human needs.
13. List five guidelines for observing children.

1—*Answers:* Answers to review questions can be found in the front section of this TAE.

To Do

1. Make a display called "Children in Our Society." In the display, use newspaper clippings, magazine articles, and other information on children and products for children.
2. Ask your school or local librarian to help you find information on child labor laws. Share with your class how the needs of children led to these laws.
3. Read all or some of the chapters from the Laura Ingalls Wilder books *Little House in the Big Woods* or *Farmer Boy*. Share with your class examples of the skills and personal priorities that parents handed down to children in the stories.
4. Interview a person over 60 years of age. Ask the person to describe developmental tasks (chores, hobbies, games, etc.) he or she mastered that people seldom master today.
5. Read about the life of a famous person in any career. Write a paper giving examples of constancy in the person's growth and development. How did this consistency lead to fame in their career?
6. Divide into groups and discuss how aspects of development are interrelated. Each group should trace the effects of a different problem—poor nutrition or lack of affection—on all aspects of development.

To Observe

1. Observe examples of culture that have been handed down from one generation to another. Examples of culture include language, attitudes, values, rituals, and skills. What cultural characteristics have you seen passed along to children?
2. Observe a person working with children in a child-related career such as a child care teacher or care provider. What characteristics does this person exhibit when working with children?
3. Observe characteristics in others that are due to heredity. What are some of these characteristics?
4. Observe some characteristics in others that are due to their environment. What are some of these characteristics?

To Think Critically

1. With a group of classmates, make lists of some of the ways our society is child-centered and some of the ways our society is adult-centered. Discuss your lists. Can a society find a solution to opposing interests? How can a new family resolve these differences for a happier family life?
2. If you were asked to recruit other students in your school to take a course in child development, what would you say or do to convince them that child development is a worthwhile subject? Be specific and explain "the why" behind your idea(s).
3. Havighurst said that one source for developmental tasks comes from social pressures. Given the situations in our society today, what developmental tasks do you believe will be important for future children? Why?

Learning about children will help you to understand the basic concepts of a child's growth and development.

Chapter 2

Families Today

After studying this chapter, you will be able to

☐ describe changes affecting families today.

☐ explain the role of families in today's society.

☐ list the main advantages and disadvantages of living in different types of families.

☐ explain changes that take place during the life cycle of a family.

☐ describe the major roles of parents.

☐ define three parenting styles.

☐ list characteristics of healthy families.

After studying this chapter, you will be able to define

adoption
adoption agency
authoritarian
blended family
closed adoption
democratic
discipline
extended family
family culture
family history
family life cycle
foster home
guidance
illegal market adoption
independent adoption
induction
joint custody
love-withdrawal
nurturance
open adoption
permissive
power-assertion
single-parent family
stepfamilies
two-parent family

Families are the main force in shaping a child's physical, intellectual, and social-emotional growth.

The family is the oldest known social group. Why did it come into being? Experts do not know exactly. Most believe people began living in families for children's well-being. Throughout history, families have held different ideas about children's needs. These changing ideas have changed the roles of parents and family structures. However, families continue to be the basic unit of society.

Changes Affecting Families Today

Changes in society have caused major changes in the family. Before the Industrial Revolution, most families lived on farms. Farm families met most of their own needs. They were producers who built their own homes, made their own clothing, and grew their own food. During the Industrial Revolution, many families moved off the farms and into the cities to work in factories, leaving relatives and friends behind. In the cities, families began to depend on others outside the family to produce most of the needed goods and services. City families became consumers. Earning an income, rather than making things, was most important.

Without extended family, families looked within their own small family groups for companionship and emotional support. The family became more important for love and security. When these needs were not met within families, divorce rates increased.

Today, these changes are affecting families:

- ☐ The age of first marriages has increased. (More than one-third of all men and one-fourth of all women are not married by 30 years of age. In fact, the overall rate of marriage has declined.)

- ☐ Birthrates and family size have decreased.

- ☐ More women are working for economic reasons and personal fulfillment. (Over 61 percent of women with children under the age of six are employed and are earning incomes almost equal to those of men.)

- ☐ Divorce and remarriage rates have increased. (Over 40 percent of all children experience family divorce, and 10 percent will deal with two or more divorces. Almost half of the children of divorce will have to make the adjustment of parents remarrying.)

- ☐ The rate of single-parent families is increasing due to more people raising children outside of marriage and due to rising divorce rates. (About one in three children are born to single mothers, and about one in two children will live with a single parent at some point in childhood.)

- ☐ Poverty is on the rise and particularly affects uneducated, single-parent families. (One in three children live below the poverty level.)

Changes in Family Roles

The roles of family members have changed through the years. Up until the 1700s, parents were the only ones to meet children's physical needs of food, clothing, shelter, and safety. They expected children between the ages of four and seven to work long days in factories or on farms.

As adults learned more about children's needs, parent-child roles changed. Today, adults still must meet children's physical needs. They also see childhood as a special time in each person's life. A child's "job" is to learn about the world. Families serve as a support system where children can learn and be as free from stress as possible. Most people believe children's needs are best met first in a loving family and later by other social groups.

Family Types

There are many types of families in the world. For example, some of your friends may live with a mother and father, others with a mother, and others with parents and a grandparent.

1

2

3

1—*Enrich:* Research family life in other cultures. How are children's needs met? What is a typical parent-child role? What is the purpose of childhood?

2—*Note:* The family is the first socialization influence on a child. It is important that this first exposure is nurturing and supportive.

3—*Resource: Family Types,* SAG.

Why do so many types of families exist? Family types result from the ways that people best solve their problems and meet their needs. In turn, family types that fit society's norm receive more support from that society. In the United States, children are members of many types of families. The main types are two-parent, single-parent, blended, extended, and families with adopted children.

▶ Two-Parent Families

A father, a mother, and their biological child or children make up a **two-parent family**. This type of family exists in most societies. In two-parent families, grown children leave home when they become adults. When these children marry, they begin their own family away from their parents.

When you think of the "typical family," what type of family comes to mind? Many think of the two-parent type, with a working father and a mother who cares for children at home. Is this type of family really typical in the United States? No—actually, only a small number of American families are the two-parent type. Even fewer families have mothers who stay home with children.

Compared to other types of families, two-parent families have some disadvantages. For instance, children may not learn to get along with many types of people, including the elderly. Also, they may not learn new skills from different people because they do not live with relatives. Finally, the family may not be near enough to relatives to rely on them for support in times of stress. On the other hand, two-parent families have some advantages. Adults and children may have their needs met more easily because family members can share responsibilities. Children may be apt to learn more flexible home and child care roles in the two-parent family. Adults often share these tasks, and children who see role sharing may be better prepared for the future.

▶ Single-Parent Families

Single-parent families are families headed by one adult. One parent heads the family when one parent dies, parents divorce or separate, or single parents adopt children. One parent also may head the family if a parent deserts a family or if parents have children outside of marriage.

The numbers of single parents are growing. Much of this is due to the increase of divorce. In addition, more unwed parents are choosing to keep their babies. Women usually head single-family households. However, there is an increase in the number of fathers gaining custody and raising their children, 2-1.

Raising children alone is hard. Single parents face the responsibility of providing care, supervision, and financial security for their children. Single parents must spend a lot of time and effort building a secure family unit. However,

2-1 More single men are opting to raise their children.

© Nancy P. Alexander

1—*Activity:* List advantages and disadvantages of two-parent families—one with a working father and stay-at-home mother and the other with two working parents.

2—*Discuss:* What is flexibility? How would flexibility be important in a recently established single-parent family? How would the roles of each family member change? What stresses might result?

children raised in well-adjusted single-parent homes are more stable than children raised in unhappy two-parent homes.

When possible, both parents should help raise the children even if they don't live in the same home. *Joint custody*, or coparenting, occurs when both parents make decisions that affect children's lives. Joint custody is becoming more common. Children usually are happier when both parents spend time with them.

▶ Blended Families

Blended families are families that merge when at least one single parent marries another person. A blended family may also result when two single parents marry. You may know blended families that are called *stepfamilies*. Many children live in blended families. Other children have stepfamilies with whom they do not live. These numbers continue to rise.

Adjusting to life in a blended family is different than moving from a two-parent family to a single-parent family. Studies show that family members in blended families face different types of problems. All family members find themselves in instant relationships—stepparents must relate with stepchildren and stepchildren must relate with each other. As in all marriages, parents must work out the husband-wife role, as well. In addition to all of this, children must work out relationships with family members from the previous marriage(s).

Children may have problems adjusting to a new family. Many children are asked to adjust to two sets of rules. This can be a major problem for school-age children, who are weighing family and peer priorities in search of self-identity. Dealing with two families may further confuse their self-identity.

One study reported that, although they do face problems, almost two-thirds of blended families have good relationships. In this study, both mothers and children tended to rate stepfathers as good parents—just as good as biological fathers. Some special effort, however, is needed to help families blend smoothly.

▶ Extended Families

In an *extended family*, several generations of one family live together. In the past, the extended family was most often made up of an older couple with their children, in-laws, and grandchildren. Today, many other family groups may form an extended family.

Sometimes the extended family lives in one home. Each family unit may have some space to call its own. However, extended family members might cook and eat together. In extended families, members may live together because they run a family business. They often share housework and child care. Each member does a certain task, and family members usually do not change roles with others often. For instance, the same person may cook each day.

In the United States, extended families are not as common as they once were. Fewer family businesses and less economic need for large families are reasons for the decline. However, sometimes an extended family forms temporarily. For instance, young adults may move back home while trying to establish their careers. A divorced family member may need a temporary residence while trying to save money. Aging family members may need temporary care.

There are some problems that members of extended families experience more than members of other kinds of families. Sometimes children and even adults find they must deal with too many people. Also, members make decisions for the good of the entire family rather than the special needs of each person.

These families also have many advantages. Children learn to interact with many people of all ages because young and old members are in daily contact. This helps family members know about and respect each other. Extended families are good at handing down *family culture* (what a family believes and does) and *family history* (stories of a family's past), 2-2. Because there are so many members, extended families can perform more duties than small family groups. For instance, some family members can care for the children of working parents. Also, when stressful events, such as death, happen in extended families, many others are there to help both children and adults.

4

5

1—*Note:* It is important for parents to keep relations with each other as cordial as possible.

2—*Note:* It is best for a couple to agree on discipline and other family-related issues before marriage. Children also should be included in these discussions when a new baby is expected.

3—*Reflect:* What problems could occur in a blended family? What adjustments need to be made?

4—*Discuss:* Name some extended family situations that are common today.

5—*Discuss:* How do grandparents hand down family culture and history?

© John Shaw

2-2 Grandfathers often take pride in handing down family culture and history.

▶ **Families with Adopted Children**

Adoption occurs when a child of one pair of parents legally becomes the child of other parents. Adoption legally ends the rights and responsibilities between a child and the birthparents (biological parents). The adoptive parents are then granted these rights. Adoption gives the child a new family.

People want to adopt for a number of reasons. Among them are the following:

☐   The couple cannot give birth or can give birth, but with great difficulty.

☐   The couple may want to add to their own family.

☐   The couple know a child who needs a home.

☐   A single person wants children.

There often are not many children, especially babies, who are of the same background as the adoptive parents and available for adoption. For this reason, people are adopting more foreign-born children, older children, children with special needs, children who have been in group or foster homes, and children who are *biracial* (whose natural parents are of two different races).

Adoption Agencies and Independent Adoptions

Most parents who have adopted children have spent much effort finding them. There are two ways to adopt children legally—through an adoption agency and through an independent source.

An ***adoption agency*** is an agency licensed by the state to handle adoptions. It is either state funded (such as the agency that also handles foster home care) or private (managed by a church or organization). The agency works out the details between the birthparents (biological parents) and the adoptive parents. Final legal aspects of the adoption are handled in state courts.

In an ***independent adoption***, a person, such as a lawyer or physician, works out the details between the birthparents and the adoptive parents. In some independent adoptions, fewer details must be worked out. Such cases include adoption of relatives or stepchildren. All independent adoptions are handled in state courts and thus follow state laws. Foreign adoptions can be either agency or independent adoptions. The pros and cons of each type of adoption are presented in 2-3.

Adoption Options and Rights

The laws of each state govern adoption options and rights. In all states, when people pay money that exceeds medical and legal costs to an agency, independent source, or birthparents, they are "buying" a child. This is called an ***illegal market adoption.***

Adoption options include open and closed adoptions. Agency and independent adoptions can be either closed or open.

In a ***closed adoption*** the identity of the birthparents and of the adopting family are not revealed to each other. In closed adoptions, the

1—*Enrich:* Contact adoption agencies for information. Arrange for a speaker from an agency.

2—*Enrich:* Research how long adoptions take.

3—*Enrich:* Research illegal market adoptions.

Types of Adoption		
Type	**Pros**	**Cons**
Agency	☐ Legal aspects are handled in a correct manner. ☐ Children can be matched with adoptive parents on the basis of physical appearance and educational level. ☐ Birthparents can request certain types of families for their children. They may request certain religious backgrounds and interests. ☐ Adoptive parents can choose a child of a certain sex, the child's age, and the child's family background. ☐ Adoptive parents receive information about children. (Information may not identify birthparents.) ☐ Birthparents may receive information about adoptive parents. (Information may not identify adoptive parents.) ☐ Social workers counsel both birthparents and adoptive parents. ☐ Adoptive families are supervised from the time children are placed until the adoption is final. ☐ Adoption is usually less expensive than independent adoptions. In addition, adoptive parents who have more income may pay more. Adoptive parents who have less income may pay somewhat less.	☐ Concern for children is emphasized before concern for those wanting children. Thus, when there is a shortage of children, many suitable homes may be turned down for homes that seem better in some ways to the agency. ☐ Adoptive parents often must meet many requirements. These requirements may include age, years of marriage, religious beliefs, income, type of housing (apartment, house, etc.), and residence. ☐ The study of adoptive families is extremely detailed and goes into all aspects of each person's personal and married life. ☐ Long waiting periods are common when fewer children are waiting to be adopted.
Independent	☐ There are no stated qualifications for adoptive parents. Thus, older persons, single persons, remarried couples, and couples married less than three to five years may adopt children. ☐ Birthparents are allowed to know the adoptive families if they wish. ☐ Waiting lists are not as long as those at an agency.	☐ Legal safeguards may not be met. (Adoptive parents should hire lawyers who handle adoption cases.) ☐ Records of the birthparents and the adoptive parents may not be kept private. ☐ The child may not receive careful medical checks. ☐ Matching the child with the adoptive family is seldom done. ☐ Adoptive parents may know little about the child's background. ☐ The child is placed in a home before the adoptive family is studied. Thus, the child may be placed in an unsuitable home. (Some study is done before adoption becomes final.) ☐ Fees may be higher than those charged by an agency. (Some adoptive couples may find themselves involved in an illegal market adoption without knowing it.)

2-3   Both types of legal adoptions have some advantages and disadvantages that adoptive parents should consider.

1—*Discuss:* Why might both natural parents and adoptive parents need counseling?

2—*Discuss:* Why is this detailed study important?

agency, attorney, or physician works out all the details of the adoption. Once the birthparent(s) have signed the adoption papers in keeping with state laws and a period of time has lapsed for these papers to become final, the child is placed in the home of the adoptive family. Only nonidentifying information is exchanged by the birthparent(s) and the adopting family through the agency or person handling the adoption process. The adoptive family and the child have a right to know the medical and social backgrounds of the birthparents. The birthparents have a right to know about the type of family in which the child will be placed. Sometimes, too, the birthparent(s) may write a letter to the child that will be given to the child when he or she is old enough to understand the contents. (This letter would be signed with a non-identifying signature, such as "Your Birthmom.") The laws of each state govern whether identifying information can be made available to anyone, including an adopted adult seeking the information, if the adoption is closed.

Fewer closed adoptions are now occurring. Open adoptions are becoming more common. An **open adoption** is an adoption that involves some degree of communication between birthparent(s) and adoptive family. The *openness* of the adoption refers to how much information is exchanged and how much contact occurs between the birthparents and the adoptive family. An open adoption can mean that the birthparent(s) can meet and choose the adoptive parents or that the birthparent(s) can choose the adoptive parents from resumes and/or photographs. Open adoptions have become more common in the last 20 years. The birthparents feel they have more choice in the decision. Adopting families will not think of the adoption process as something "secret" and will also have the information and support to best parent their children. Children benefit from knowing their adoptions were loving decisions and communication took place to help them. Open adoptions usually make all adoption records accessible to adopted children when they become adults.

Adoption rights protect those involved in adoption. In most states, the birthfather has legal rights. State laws may permit him to deny paternity (being the birthfather), give all rights to the birthmother, or give permission along with the birthmother for the child to be adopted. In some states, if the father cannot be found, he may be considered to have abandoned the child and his rights to make any decisions about the child are ended.

Foster Homes

Some adopted children come from group homes (children's homes) or foster homes. In **foster homes**, families take care of, but do not adopt, children who cannot live with their birthparents. Children in foster homes must adapt to different living situations much like children who live in blended families. When it appears doubtful that these children can ever have safe and secure lives with their birthparents, the state ends the rights of birthparents and assumes permanent custody. The children can then be adopted. Sometimes they are adopted by foster parents or they may be adopted by nonfoster parents. Some states are making decisions about foster children more quickly so these children can experience family stability earlier in their lives.

Adoption Issues

Children who are adopted generally have stable, happy home lives. This is because their adopted families wanted them very much, 2-4. Some problems can exist, however. Parents who

2-4 Adoption is often a happy situation for both parents and children.

© John Shaw

1—*Activity:* Contact social services for foster home information. Review the literature in groups and report to the class.

do not experience nine months of pregnancy must make the transition to parenthood very quickly. Persons wanting to adopt may be on a waiting list for many years. Then, one day, the adoption agency may call and announce that a child will be ready for them the next day! Also, adoptive parents may not know many facts about the child they adopt, such as medical history.

Other problems may arise related to the adopted child's birthparents, especially if the adoption is closed. Birthparents may want to see the child. There is a chance they may want to become part of the child's life. Children who are adopted as babies or young children often ask questions about their adoption. They may want to know about—or even want to meet—their birthparents. Older children who have lived with their birthparents and are then adopted by a new family need to adjust to their new parents.

Adoptive parents should answer their children's questions about adoption in direct and honest ways. Adopted children should be told from the very beginning that they are adopted. The fact that a child was adopted should not be a secret. Most parents create a loving family life that overcomes any stress adopted children may feel.

● The Family Life Cycle

Families, just as individuals, change through the years. Most families change in similar ways, or stages, that are called the **family life cycle**. The family life cycle can be divided into the following stages:

- ☐ Establishment stage—a couple gets to know each other and thinks about having children.
- ☐ Childbearing stage—the couple begins having children.
- ☐ School years stage—the couple's children begin entering school.
- ☐ Adolescent stage—the couple's children are teenagers.
- ☐ Launching stage—the couple's children begin leaving home.

- ☐ Postparental stage—the couple's children have left home and the couple may become grandparents.

Just as children go through different stages as they grow and develop, which we call the individual life cycle, so do families. Couples should be prepared for the changes that take place at each new stage.

In the *establishment stage*, the couple is a family of two. During this time, they get to know each other better. They also decide whether or not they want to become parents.

Most new parents give much thought to the *childbearing stage*. They understand their roles in caring for and guiding children through their earliest years. As parents enter later stages, their roles will continue to change.

As children enter the *school years stage*, parents must realize other people will be teaching and guiding their children. Children begin to learn more from teachers and peers. Parents need to stay involved with their children's growth. They also must realize that other people are becoming important to their children.

Children's adolescent years, the *adolescent stage*, can be confusing for both parents and children. Adolescents are striving to become more independent. They are not always ready to handle as much responsibility as they want to, however. Adolescents may want more privacy, but they still need to know they can talk to their parents. At this stage, parents need to begin treating their children as adults. They also need to know when to provide guidance and help.

The *launching stage* brings new feelings for parents. As children leave home, parents may feel lonely. They may also feel their children no longer need them. They must acknowledge the fact that their children are adults. Now their relationships may be more equal. Parents may continue to be an important part of their children's lives.

In the *postparental stage*, parents may find more time for themselves than they did when their children were home. They may devote more time to new interests or hobbies. Keeping in touch with their children will still be important. They may be involved with their grandchildren. Health problems may cause them to need help from their own children. During this stage, all family members may need to make many adjustments.

6

1—*Activity:* Summarize these problems. Add additional ones.

2—*Reflect:* Would you rather be adopted as a newborn or as a two-year-old? Why?

3—*Reflect:* How would you feel if you found out today that you were adopted as an infant? What would you do?

4—*Note:* Prepare a "Family Life Cycle" bulletin board, poster, or transparency listing the six stages. Prepare illustrations to accompany each stage.

5—*Resource: The Family Life Cycle,* SAG.

6—*Note:* This is also known as the empty-nest syndrome.

A new challenge for families occurs when grown children return home after the launching stage. Economic troubles, divorce, or other situations may cause them to move back home again. Parents may have to learn new ways to relate to these children. They may have adjusted to the fact that their children are now adults. Now, however, they may not know how to treat them as adults when they are all living in the same home. Likewise, children may not know what parents expect of them. Family members need to communicate openly in order to make sure that family members continue to get along.

● Roles of Parents

Parents are responsible for the good of their children. In American society, parents' roles mainly involve nurturance, guidance, and discipline. Children thrive in a nurturing environment and need guidance and discipline to learn right from wrong.

Playskool, Inc., Chicago, Ill.

2-5 Fathers are now seen as highly important in the nurturance of their children.

▶ Nurturance

Nurturance, in a narrow sense, includes the physical aspects of child care, such as feeding, dressing, and bathing children. In a broad sense, nurturance also includes meeting emotional and social needs, such as helping children feel secure and loved. Studies in child development show that physical care, love, and concern are important for children's healthy growth. Both mothers and fathers play an important role in nurturing their children, 2-5.

▶ Guidance and Discipline

Child guidance and discipline are important responsibilities of parenthood. Parents provide **guidance** for their children in their daily interactions with them. The words and actions parents use influence their child's behavior. For instance, when parents face frustrations, but react calmly,

they are guiding their children to do the same. By showing children they are not upset when they don't get their way, parents are modeling good behavior. Guiding children in a positive way is an important parental role.

Discipline is part of guidance. **Discipline** is using different methods and techniques to help teach children self-control. Through discipline, children learn to act in ways that society finds acceptable.

The goal of guidance and discipline is to teach children behaviors that will help them guide themselves. Guidance and discipline teach children to think and act in safe and acceptable ways. There are many different ways to help children learn this, and some are more effective than others.

▪ Types of Discipline

Probably every parent would like to find the perfect method for handling children's unpleasant

1—*Activity:* Draw a tree with five branches. Label each branch with a parental role. Share in class.

2—*Discuss:* How do these aspects of nurturance relate to Maslow's Hierarchy of Needs?

3—*Discuss:* Compare and contrast the nurturance of mothers versus the nurturance of fathers.

4—*Reflect:* How does a person model positive words and actions when dealing with children? Describe positive actions caregivers or teachers have modeled for you.

5—*Activity:* List differences between guidance and discipline.

6—*Resource: Types of Discipline,* SAG.

or disruptive behaviors. What is the goal of discipline? Most parents agree discipline should teach children self-control. This is because parents will not always be able to guide children, especially as they become older. Studies have found that parents and other adults use three types of discipline—power-assertion, love-withdrawal, and induction.

Power-Assertion

Power-assertion occurs when parents use or threaten to use some form of physical punishment. Severe or frequent physical punishment can harm children. Certainly, many people can name children who were occasionally spanked and are now healthy, normal adults. Some adults even claim spankings were good for them. If this is true, why are most parenting experts against power-assertive techniques?

There are several reasons why power-assertive techniques are not healthy forms of discipline. First, power-assertion works because the child fears the adult. As the child grows physically, however, fear lessens and the technique no longer works. Even for young children, fear is based on being caught and punished. Many power-assertive adults will threaten, "Don't let me *catch* you doing that again!" Thus, the child weighs the chances of being caught and the likely punishment. The child is not being guided by what is right or wrong.

Another reason why power-assertion techniques are poor is because, to children, being physically punished for an act of aggression such as hitting another child seems like a double standard. The child may think, "You are hitting me; why can't I hit others?"

In addition, power-assertive techniques are often used when parents are angry. If parents are prone to losing their tempers, their intended light physical punishment could become abusive when done during anger.

Finally, all discipline techniques are imitated or modeled by children. Children disciplined through power-assertiveness are more apt to use that technique when they become parents. If their parents lose control, children may become violent during the teen years or abusive when they marry or become parents.

Love-Withdrawal

Love-withdrawal, another discipline technique, is a discipline technique in which parents threaten children or suggest some form of parent/child separation. An extreme example is parents telling children they do not want or love them. Some parents even tell their children they are going to give them away. Milder forms of love-withdrawal include ignoring the child or giving the child the "silent treatment." Experts consider love-withdrawal, in its extreme forms, to be psychological or mental abuse. Even in its milder forms, the technique creates stress and prevents the expression of feelings.

Induction

The third technique, *induction*, happens when parents discipline by reasoning and explaining. Adults, as older and wiser people, explain why children should or should not do certain behaviors. Children disciplined by this technique tend to show better self-control, display more concern for others, and take responsibility for their own failures.

Different discipline techniques seem to work better with some age groups than with others, 2-6. These techniques are discussed in more detail in later chapters on meeting children's needs.

● Parenting Styles

Most parents want to raise their children so they will become responsible, well-mannered adults. They realize guidance and discipline are important. New parents need to give some thought to the style they will use to guide and discipline their children. Parenting styles can be grouped into three main categories: authoritarian, permissive, and democratic.

3

4

1—*Reflect:* Recall a time when you were spanked. What emotions did you feel? What type of discipline would have been more successful with you?

2—*Enrich:* Write one-half of a page on the phrase "Don't let me catch you doing that again!"

3—*Discuss:* Describe disadvantages in the love-withdrawal method.

4—*Discuss:* How does induction (reasoning and explaining) help a child to develop self-control?

| Examples of Specific Discipline Techniques ||
Age	Effective Discipline
0 – 3 months	None. Parents try to soothe babies with routines.
3 – 6 months	None. Parents try to interact with babies as much as possible.
6 – 12 months	None. Parents still try to interact with babies and to make houses childproof.
12 – 18 months	None. Parents provide a secure base for normal exploration and childproof their houses and yards.
18 – 36 months	Parents should remove children from dangerous situations. They should say no and give a one- or two-word explanation, such as "Hot!" or "Hurt baby." Parents should also keep houses childproof.
3 – 4 years	Parents should explain why children cannot do or continue to do something. After the first offense, take or send children to a quiet place where they are alone but not afraid. Children should remain alone for three or four minutes.
4 years – school age	Parents should use the induction method. Adjust reasons to the child's age. Some good techniques include the following: <ul><li>Listen to the child's story.</li><li>Acknowledge the child's feelings with statements like "know you feel angry."</li><li>Express your feelings about the consequences and your expectations with statements like, "I was furious that you left your wagon outside to rust in the rain. The wagon goes in the garage each day."</li><li>Avoid attacking a child's character. For example, do not call the child stupid.</li><li>Allow the child to make amends.</li><li>Give the child a choice of meeting a standard or losing a privilege. For example, "If you cannot wash your dishes, I cannot let you eat a snack."</li></ul> Parents may need to send some children to a quiet, safe place for about one minute per age.

2-6   Discipline needs to be based on love and understanding.

▶ Authoritarian

Some parents use an *authoritarian* parenting style, a style in which the main objective is to make children completely obedient. These parents think obedience is the most important behavior their children should learn. They expect children to respect their authority with little or no explanation as to why children should obey. Such parents are likely to use physical punishment when children are not "good." They seldom reward good behavior.

Authoritarian parenting may teach children to obey their parents. However, these children may not understand why they should act as their parents wish. They may not be able to develop self-control. They may also fear their parents and even rebel against them when they become older. Most parents do not practice this style of parenting any longer.

1—*Discuss:* Why is it as important to reward good behavior as it is to punish negative behavior?

2—*Discuss:* How does authoritative parenting ignore the goal of discipline?

▶ Permissive

Permissive parents give children almost no guidelines or rules. They feel children should make their own decisions about right and wrong. They may think children will feel unhappy or unloved if they set limits for their children. The truth is, these children may feel lost without guidelines. They may have trouble getting along with others later in life because they have never needed to follow rules.

▶ Democratic

Most parents find a compromise between these two styles of parenting. They use a *democratic* style, a parenting style in which parents set some rules but allow children some freedom. When these parents set rules, they explain to children why the rules are needed. Children may even be allowed to help set some rules and decide some punishments. These children learn self-discipline in a positive, encouraging setting.

● Characteristics of Healthy Families

Families, like individuals, may be healthy or unhealthy. At one time the health of a family was measured mainly by durability (family staying together for many years). Often, durability and a healthy family life do go together. Sometimes, however, people are "families" in name only.

There is no magic recipe to create a healthy family. Families can be very different and yet healthy. Some characteristics are often seen in healthy families. The most common characteristic is that the couple enter marriage with shared values. They use these values to decide on goals throughout their marriage and to guide them in rearing their children.

Closely tied to these shared values is the belief that family members are individuals. These families accept the fact that even individuals who share many values will be somewhat different. They also realize that life itself can cause changes in goals. Healthy families are willing to adjust as needed.

Healthy families seem to have a mutual commitment to family life. They want their marriages to succeed and their parenting to be successful. Part of the commitment involves growth—becoming more loving, caring, and understanding. They also want to do many things as a family unit.

Healthy families seem to be made up of individuals who have healthy personalities. In healthy families, each family member lives by the idea that they should help each other and cannot be self-centered. They share responsibilities. Although the division of tasks may differ from family to family, healthy families seem to happily follow their own choices about duties. Individuals within the family can depend on each other to keep promises, fulfill commitments, and be honest.

Healthy families communicate. They are polite and consider each other's feelings. They talk about everything, including problems, and use problem-solving skills to work on problems rather than trying to change others. Above all, they support each other's efforts within the family and express appreciation through mutual affection.

1—*Reflect:* Recall a family that uses permissive parenting. How is this reflected in the children's behavior?

2—*Discuss:* Compare democratic parenting to the induction method of discipline.

3—*Resource: Parenting Styles,* SAG.

Summary

The family is the oldest known social group and remains the basic unit of society. Many changes affect families today. Different family types result from the different ways people choose to meet their needs and solve their problems. The main family types are two-parent, single-parent, blended, extended, and families with adopted children. Each family type has its advantages and disadvantages.

Many changes occur during the various stages of the family life cycle. From the establishment stage through the childbearing, adolescent, launching, and postparental stages, the family grows and develops.

Parents have many responsibilities with respect to their children. They have parental roles to fulfill. Discipline takes many forms. Some are more appropriate and effective for children than others. Children best learn self-control through the induction technique of discipline. When parents use a democratic style of parenting, children learn self-discipline in a more positive way.

Several factors contribute to the health of a family. These include shared values, a mutual commitment to family life, shared responsibilities, and good communication.

To Review

Write your answers on a separate sheet of paper.

1. Describe the role of families in today's society.
2. Circle the statement(s) that are most correct.
   a. In our society, children are expected to take on major tasks at an early age.
   b. Children's needs are best met in a caring, loving family and later by other social groups.
   c. Children's needs are best met in a society where child care providers care for children.
   d. The family serves as the support system for children.
3. Being responsible for their children's welfare involves the parental roles of _____, _____, and _____.
4. The _____ parenting style of discipline allows some freedom but sets rules.
5. Describe three types of discipline and their effects on children.
6. Match a family type with the advantage or disadvantage it best fits.
   a. extended families
   b. two-parent families
   c. single-parent families
   d. blended families
   e. families with adopted children

1

_____ Children in these families learn to interact with people of all ages.
_____ Children may not learn new skills from many people.
_____ Many family members are there to help during stressful times.
_____ Transition to parenthood may be too quick.
_____ Older family members hand down family culture and family history to younger family members.
_____ Children see only one parent as a role model.
_____ Children often may have to adjust to two sets of rules.

7. Match the family life cycle to the description it best fits.
   a. establishment stage
   b. childbearing stage
   c. school years stage
   d. adolescent stage
   e. launching stage
   f. postparental stage
   _____ Children are taught and guided by others.
   _____ Other people are becoming important to children.
   _____ Children may still need guidance and help.
   _____ Parents may feel they are no longer needed.
   _____ This time is used to get to know each other better.
   _____ Time for new interests and hobbies.
   _____ New people come into children's lives.
   _____ Perhaps the most confusing and difficult period.
   _____ Diapers, bottles, and new routines are part of this stage.
8. List factors that contribute to the health of a family.

To Do

1. In small groups, play the roles of family members in various stages of their family life cycle. Emphasize the changes that take place in each family cycle.
2. Arrange a panel discussion on changes that happen in family life because of children.
3. Interview parents in the postparental stage of the family life cycle. Ask how their roles as parents changed throughout different stages. Write a paper on your findings.
4. Write a fiction story entitled, "The Joys and Trials of . . ." (Living in an Extended Family, Living in a Single-Parent Family, Living in a Blended Family).
5. Ask an elementary school librarian for children's books about divorce and/or blended families. Give the bibliographical information, the age for which the book was written, and a few statements about the main ideas the book conveys.
6. Read reference material about disciplining children. Write a short paper on new findings from your reading.

To Observe

1. Observe how couples with young children share their responsibilities. What techniques do they use to help them meet their obligations?
2. Observe families in informal settings, such as shopping malls and parks. Do the couples seem comfortable in their roles as parents? What behaviors help form your opinion?

To Think Critically

1. What are some of the advantages and disadvantages of joint custody over single-parent custody for parents? For children?
2. What are some possible benefits and problems of open adoption for the birthmother? The adopting family? The child? Whose benefit should take priority? Why?
3. Many adults know that reasoning rather than power-assertion is a better form of discipline, yet many adults still use threats to discipline children. Why do adults use threats? Can threats be justified? Why or why not?

The family is the basic unit of society.

Chapter 3

Preparing for Parenting

Baby showers help parents prepare for a new baby.

After studying this chapter, you will be able to

☐ explain why parenting is more difficult than other jobs.

☐ analyze some of the motivations for and against parenthood.

☐ identify factors to consider before becoming a parent.

☐ describe effects of family planning.

☐ list birth control options.

☐ explain physical and psychological problems of infertility.

☐ describe fertility methods.

After studying this chapter, you will be able to define

abstinence
artificial insemination
birth control methods
family planning
fertility counseling
foregone income
GIFT
in vitro fertilization
indirect costs
infertile
involuntary infertility
maternity leave
paternity leave
sterile
surrogate mother

Parenting is a rewarding and difficult task. Many people invest more money, time, and emotions in their children than they do in any investment in their life. Most parents hope their children will inherit all their strengths and avoid their weaknesses. They also hope their children will have opportunities they did not have.

Before having a child, a couple must seriously consider all aspects of parenting. This chapter discusses some of the important decisions they must make to prepare for parenting.

Why Is It Hard to Be a Good Parent?

Parenting skills are not automatic; a person does not just become a good parent. Just because a person is biologically able to reproduce, that does not mean he or she will be a good parent. If a person has long, agile fingers, does that mean he or she can automatically play the piano well?

Becoming a good parent is harder than becoming a good pianist for a few reasons. First, parenting involves relationships with people. In a good relationship, each person wants what's best for the other. They support each other. Sometimes, because of people's individual differences, this is hard. In addition, the parent-child relationship is difficult because it is more one-sided than other relationships. For many years, parents are the "givers" and children are the "takers," 3-1.

Parenting also is hard because training to become a parent is not nearly as clear as training for most jobs. Parents probably have studied and trained more for their careers than for their roles as parents. Their job skills may be better than their child care skills, for which they have had little or no training.

Another reason parenting is difficult is that, years ago, children could see their parents handling younger brothers and sisters. They even may have helped care for them. Families are becoming smaller these days, however, and

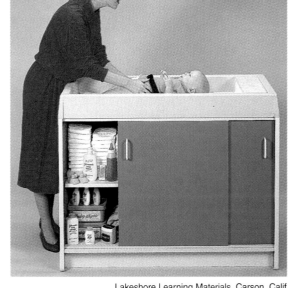

Lakeshore Learning Materials, Carson, Calif.

3-1 Children require much care in their first years. They are not able to give much in return.

many children do not have this chance. Families also are located farther apart. For years, most young parents turned to relatives for parenting help. However, in the United States today, there are fewer extended families. Mobility also has placed many miles between young parents and their relatives.

Although being a good parent is hard, being a good parent is most parents' greatest wish. Because of this desire, couples are becoming better informed about parenting skills and child development. A parent can best measure success by rearing a child who can say as an adult, "If I could have chosen my parents, I would have chosen you."

Learning Parenting Skills

Many couples feel they need help learning how to become good parents. They want to find the following resources that can help them learn about child care and development:

☐ professionals and/or successful parents to give advice

☐ literature (books, magazines, etc.) that is accurate, practical, and available

☐ available child care classes (Community colleges and local American Red Cross chapters may offer such classes.)

☐ families with infants and young children (Spending time with children by baby-sitting and volunteering in schools and churches can help you understand what it is like to care for children, 3-2.)

© John Shaw

3-2   A couple can learn about children by baby-sitting for the child of a friend.

New parents also should realize there is not one right way to parent. Although some methods may be more respected than others, many factors influence parenting. The culture in which a child is raised affects how parents raise children. The personalities of parents and children also affect parenting. The ways couples have seen their parents or friends care for children influences how they care for their own. All these factors are important to think about when learning child care skills.

● Deciding About Parenthood

Deciding whether or not to have children is a personal choice. For the sake of the couple and the future child, the husband and wife should agree on the decision. Hopefully, the couple discussed their feelings about parenthood before they married.

The decision to parent is unlike many life decisions in two ways. First, the decision to parent is a permanent choice. Once a child is born, he or she is part of that person's life forever. A person can choose to change careers, for example, but having a child is different. Once a parent, always a parent.

Second, a decision not to parent is not permanent. People must make many life choices within a limited amount of time. For example, if a person wants a career in ballet, he or she must begin studying as a youngster and continue for many years. Couples have a longer period of time to decide whether or not to become parents. Young couples have 15 or more safe childbearing years. The option of adopting a child may increase this time by a few years. Thus, some couples may want to be parents, but may choose to wait until a better time. Other couples may not be sure about parenthood and may wait to decide. Even couples who decide they never want children can change their minds later.

Couples have different motivations for and against parenthood. Some of these are discussed below. In the end, each couple must make the choice by respecting their feelings and needs.

▶ Reasons for Choosing Parenthood

Couples have various reasons for choosing parenthood. Although they may not always be able to explain why, they see children as part of their life. The following are reasons couples give for wanting to become parents. Some are better reasons than others.

"We want to share our love with a child."

This is perhaps the most important reason for wanting a child. A couple's desire to share their love and time with a child is the best reason for parenthood, 3-3. Parents should want a child with "no strings attached." If parents hope a child will fulfill other needs or goals, the parent-child relationship may not be healthy.

3-3   Parenting involves sharing knowledge and love with a child.

"Wouldn't it be nice to have a cute, little baby?"

When some couples see others with babies, they think it would be nice to have a "cute, little baby" too. It's good for couples to think positively about babies. The problem is, babies aren't always cute. All babies are sick, fussy, and cranky at times. In addition, they do not stay babies long.

"Our parents want grandchildren."

Some couples want to fulfill their parents' wishes to be grandparents. It is fine for a child's parents to want a grandchild. Grandparents can give a child much love. It is more important, however, for parents to want and love a child.

"Our older child needs a brother or sister."

When a couple wants a playmate for an older child, the parents are fulfilling someone else's needs, not their own. This reason is similar to having a baby because parents want

grandchildren. Although a child might enjoy a brother or sister, there are other ways to meet the only child's needs for playmates.

"A child can make us proud."

Some couples see children as sources of pride. They want children to carry on the family name and customs, inherit the family business or money, or achieve certain goals. It is good for parents to be proud of their children and want them to achieve. They must be careful, however, that their hopes do not stifle their children's goals. Parenthood is not a good choice if a child is wanted only to boost the parents' ego or to meet their unfulfilled goals.

Parent-child relationships suffer when children cannot meet their parents' goals. Not meeting parents' goals can make children feel inadequate. The relationship also suffers when children can meet the parents' goals, but feel that they can't be themselves. This often leads children to resent their parents.

"Others will see me as a stable, reliable person."

A few couples see having children as giving them the image of stable community members and reliable employees. Fortunately, such ideas are beginning to break down. People are judged more today on their own merits and not on family status. Parents should not want children simply to help them create an image or fulfill their goals.

"A child will comfort us in our old age."

Sometimes couples think of children as sources of help in their old age. It is natural for people to think about being helpless or lonely when they grow old. However, an aging parent cannot count on a child's help. In fact, parents may outlive their children.

"A child will make us love each other."

Some couples hope that a child will save a failing marriage. Children may enrich family life for stable couples. Unstable couples may find that children make their problems worse. Studies show that couples with children often argue about child rearing practices—especially discipline. Children also add a financial burden. Usually, these problems add to the instability of marriages.

1—*Discuss:* List other negative characteristics about babies.

2—*Discuss:* List ways to meet an only child's needs for playmates.

3—*Discuss:* What problems could occur if children are unable to meet parents' goals?

4—*Discuss:* What problems may occur when a couple has a child to re-establish love? List possible end results.

5—*Resource: Is This a Good Reason for Choosing Parenthood?* SAG.

Couples who stay together "because of the children" may always be unhappy. Sadly, their children often feel responsible for the home problems.

▶ Reasons for Not Choosing Parenthood

Some couples decide to postpone parenthood. Three to five percent of all couples plan to be childless permanently. These couples feel parenthood does not suit them—at least at the present time. Even couples who want children should think about how children will change their lives.

■ "We're not ready for a child."

When couples say they're not ready for children, they usually mean they need to mature. They may want to pursue their interests before caring for a child. They may feel they need more time as a couple for their marriage to mature. They may need more time for education or job maturity. Some jobs take many years of education or training, 3-4. Many people want to spend time establishing themselves in a career before becoming parents.

■ "A baby costs a lot."

Babies do cost a lot. At one time, large families were an economic asset because children helped with the work. Today, children cannot contribute a great deal, if anything, to family income. (Later in this chapter, you will look more closely at the cost of having a child.)

■ "A child will tie us down."

With children comes endless responsibility. Unlike many other responsibilities, child rearing cannot be put off until later. It cannot be ignored while on vacation. Even with the best babysitters in charge, parents cannot completely forget their roles. They are always called if children are hurt, ill, or need help. However, the couple can arrange to have personal time with a little planning.

■ "A child will interfere with our careers."

Both children and careers require time and attention. When tending to both their career and children, parents face two common problems. First, it is hard for parents to have enough time and energy for both raising children and succeeding at work. Second, it is difficult to find good child care services.

3-4 One of the problems of parenting is having enough time and energy to devote to both parenthood and career.

1—*Enrich:* Interview a couple who chooses not to have children. What are their reasons? Do they think they will be happy with this decision at age 40 and beyond?

2—*Enrich:* Interview grandparents or great-grandparents. Ask questions about their family size, family income, family vacations and events, schooling, jobs away from home, and peer relationships. Compare to today's trends.

3—*Discuss:* Analyze television programs or movies that address these themes.

Some careers make parenting easier than others. For example, school teachers have hours and vacation times similar to those of their children. Other careers make parenting more difficult. For example, they may require parents to work long hours, night shifts, or at irregular times. Other examples include jobs that make parents feel stressed, demand parents to travel, or ask families to move often. Jobs that require families to live in areas that are unsafe or don't have schools are also hard for parents. Couples who combine these types of jobs with parenting must plan carefully.

"Our child could be sick or disabled."

There are no guarantees that a child will be perfect once he or she is born, 3-5. Babies can be disabled or become seriously ill or injured. Good medical care before and after birth reduces—but doesn't eliminate—these risks. Disabled, ill, or injured children have special needs that healthy children may not. However, most parents feel that raising disabled children is highly rewarding.

"Our marriage could fail, and I don't want to be a single parent."

Couples whose marriages are unstable may feel this way. Couples with marital problems may want to solve them before having children. Being a single parent is hard. Single parents may lack money, help with household and child care tasks, and the support of a spouse. Without these resources, the single parent can't always take part in adult activities like other adults do. However, many single parents can solve such problems.

● Factors to Consider

Parenthood happens quickly. When a child is born or placed (during adoption), the mother and father instantly become parents. Few, if any, other jobs give a beginner such responsibility. No wonder most people refer to their first child as the "experimental child." To prepare for parenthood, couples need to know how children will change their lives.

3-5   A child with a disability needs special care. However, rearing such a child can be highly rewarding.

Courtesy of GameTime, Fort Payne, Ala., U.S.A.

1—*Reflect:* Do you think a couple with secure feelings for each other would consider this reason to remain childless? Discuss the issue.

▶ How Children Affect Relationships

People who think about having children must look at their lives. They should look at the strengths and weaknesses of their present relationships. Couples should remember that, for children's healthy growth, their strengths should balance each other, 3-6. In addition, the couple should think about other changes parenthood will bring.

3-6   When couples have happy, sharing relationships and want children, their children have the best chance for growth and development.

▪ Children and the Couple

Couples should begin looking at their relationships by asking questions about their feelings for others. These kinds of questions relate directly to parenting. For starters, couples might ask themselves the following:

☐   Are we loving and sensitive to others' needs?

☐   Are we careful not to judge people and ideas?

☐   Can we recognize and respect others' rights?

☐   Are we self-disciplined?

☐   Do we relate well with others?

☐   Are we flexible enough to accept changes?

☐   Are we brave about challenges?

☐   Can we be honest about our feelings for others?

After answering these questions, couples should think about how their relationship with their partner would change if they were parents. The following questions may help:

☐   Do we have the time and energy to give to children?

☐   Do we want to share some of our time together with children?

☐   Are we doing in our daily lives what we want our children to do? (Children model parents' behavior.)

Couples can't set up a "formula" for successful parenting. They must realize that children bring extra work to a marriage. Children usually do not strengthen a weak marriage. However, if a couple can answer most of these questions positively, their relationship is probably strong enough for parenthood.

▪ Children and Relatives and Friends

Couples also must look at their present relationships with relatives and friends. Good relationships with others are positive for the couple and for possible children. Couples might want to ask themselves certain questions about their relationships with others.

☐   Do our relatives and friends share our basic values?

☐   Can we ignore small differences in beliefs?

☐   Can we ask for advice and also use our own judgment?

☐   Can we tell others about our needs and accept the help they offer?

☐   Can we recognize others' needs and offer our help?

☐   Can we avoid abusing others' generosity, including time and money?

☐   Can we share fun times with others?

1—*Reflect:* Do you think a couple who answered no to at least half of these questions would make good parents?

2—*Activity:* Make up a weekly schedule for a working couple with one infant. Make up another weekly schedule for a couple with one working and one at-home parent of an infant.

3—*Resource: Couple Relationships Affect Parenthood,* SAG.

4—*Reflect:* Without providing names, write about someone who is too proud to ask for another's advice or help. How do you feel about that?

If couples can answer most of these questions positively, having a child should not cause problems in relationships outside the family. When couples enjoy their relationships with relatives and friends before parenthood, 3-7, these relationships can include children.

Couples must also think about how their relationships with others can affect their children. There are at least three advantages to children's relationships with others. First, relatives and friends provide children with their first link to the outside world. Second, grandparents and older relatives can teach children about the past. Third, when many relatives and friends care for children, they feel more rooted to their family. Since each relative and friend is unique, children learn to understand that people are different. They also learn to accept people's unique traits. This interaction will help children get along well with others as they grow.

▶ Sharing Responsibilities

Couples should examine how they feel about home care responsibilities. Some couples practice more traditional roles. For example, the husband brings home the paycheck and the wife cares for the home.

Today, many wives work (for reasons of economics or self-fulfillment). When wives work outside the home, husbands may help with home and child care tasks more than they would in traditional roles, 3-8. Many men enjoy this. Sometimes, husbands and wives switch traditional roles. For example, the wife may work outside the home and the husband may care for the home and children. Couples need to ask themselves the following questions:

☐ Are we happy with the way we share responsibilities?

☐ Do we appreciate each other's help?

☐ Do we feel equally important in efforts to reach our goals?

Next, the couple must consider how children will affect how they share responsibilities.

☐ If we become parents, will there be major changes in the way we share responsibilities?

☐ Can we agree on how to divide home and child care tasks?

2

3-7   Couples who have fun with other adults may find they also will enjoy children.

© John Shaw

1—*Reflect:* Do you agree or disagree that couples who enjoy being with other adults also will enjoy being with children? Explain.

2—*Note:* Emphasize that couples should discuss all of these questions before marriage. Couples may discover they have strong, conflicting attitudes that would produce great conflict after a child is born.

© John Shaw

3-8 Dividing tasks saves time and allows a parent to spend time alone with children.

If one of us works outside the home and the other cares for children, will we feel that we are contributing to our goals equally? How will the full-time employee develop a close relationship with the children?

Couples who want to share responsibilities should answer these questions. How they choose to divide tasks can depend on each person's needs. If couples plan carefully and try all ideas, they can divide tasks so both partners are happy.

▶ Managing Finances

Couples must realize that children cost a lot. The first year is expensive, and expenses grow as the child grows.

The first baby is often the most expensive. Later children may use some of the firstborn's supplies. However, each extra child increases the

costs. A second child usually doubles costs. Couples should think about finances before becoming parents.

☐ How do we earn and spend our money now?

☐ Are we happy with our budget?

☐ Do we have regular savings we could use to meet child-related expenses? If not, can we adjust our budget to meet such expenses?

☐ Can we expect more income or lower expenses during the next few years to help offset child-related costs?

☐ What type of savings goals do we need for a child?

☐ What is an estimate of child-related expenses for the first and next several years?

☐ What are the indirect costs of having a child? *Indirect costs* are not actual expenses. They are resources parents use to meet child care costs that they could have used to meet other goals.

Couples must think about many factors when they estimate the direct and indirect costs of parenting. This is because each family is different. These differences show in the way families spend their money.

Indirect costs also depend on each couple's needs. Some couples may have relatives who will baby-sit free of charge. The time they give up is an indirect cost for that couple. Other couples may lose earnings because one parent stays home to raise the child. This is called *foregone income*. Foregone income is greater for the person who would earn a higher salary than for the person who would earn less. If the person is not employable, there is no foregone income. Also, foregone income is greater per child when a parent stays home with one child than with more than one child.

Another indirect cost is the impact that time out of the labor force will have on career opportunities. This cost is the most difficult to calculate.

Carefully planning financial resources is important for everyone, 3-9. In some ways, financial planning becomes more important when

1—*Enrich:* Working together provides a common bond and social time. For example, a father and preschool-aged child can work together to empty the dishwasher and set the table for dinner while the mother prepares the food. Working together provides a common bond and social time. Discuss other examples.

2—*Discuss:* Why is foregone income greater for a one-child family than for a two-child or three-child family?

3—*Discuss:* What careers would require retraining if a person stayed out of the labor market more than three years?

1

© John Shaw

3-9   Parents must carefully budget their income to meet the high costs of having a baby.

couples begin to think about children. This is because children rely on their parents for financial support for many years. Parents are also models of either good or poor consumers for their children.

▶ Managing Careers

Couples must decide whether they will both work or whether one will care for children at home. Some fathers do choose to stay home while mothers work, but this is not as common as the reverse situation. Usually mothers decide whether to stay home with children or to work outside the home, 3-10.

Today, because most women work, child care decisions are extremely important. Parents must decide who will care for the baby, as well as how much time they will take from work when the baby is born.

Maternity and Paternity Leave

The mother-to-be generally takes time off from work before and after the baby is born. This

is called **maternity leave**. Federal law requires companies to grant maternity leave according to their medical disability policies. The amount of time off the woman takes varies from company to company. Some companies grant the mother six weeks off with benefits and a percentage of her salary. Others may grant a longer leave. Some companies even allow several months or a year off. A recent survey shows that pregnant women are more likely to stay on the job until just before the baby is born. They usually return within three months of the birth, although many would prefer more time off. Most mothers do not take more leave for financial or career reasons.

Maternity leave allows the new mother time to regain her strength and get to know her newborn. The first few weeks after the baby is born are usually hectic and exhausting. The mother needs time to rest and adjust to her new role. This time also helps her to bond with the baby.

Some employers grant paternity leave to fathers. **Paternity leave** is like maternity leave without sick pay. It is usually an unpaid leave for a certain period of time after a child's birth. At the end of the leave, the company must offer the father a job and salary comparable to the one he left. A few companies pay for the leave.

3-10   Working mothers often have dual pleasures and dual responsibilites.

© John Shaw

1

There are some problems with paternity leave. These include economic hardships during the time without pay. Some fathers also complain that companies do not give salary raises and promotions to men who chose this option. These problems may change if more men take paternity leave. Even with the problems, fathers who have taken paternity leave value sharing this special time with their baby and wife.

Problems with Work and Family

Working parents often encounter several problems as they strive to do well at their jobs and care for their family. Couples will need to answer the following questions:

- ☐ Can we find good child care during working hours?

- ☐ Can we balance job demands and children's needs? For instance, will we be able to give complete or only partial attention to our children after work?

- ☐ Can we work out mutual responsibilities for child and home care tasks?

- ☐ Can we make enough time for ourselves as individuals and as a couple free of other concerns?

- ☐ Can we be organized? Can we be flexible and meet changes in our schedules? For instance, what will we do to meet the needs of a sick child? What will we do when job demands are heavy for a short time?

- ☐ If any of the above are answered negatively, what are other options for us?

Parents worry about how their children will be affected when both of them work outside the home. Studies show that, if children have good care, being separated from parents during work hours does not harm them. However, the mother's attitude about work seems to be most important. The happiest children come from homes where the mother wanted to work and did or wanted to stay home and could. If the mother is happy about her situation, children benefit from her attitude. Children may suffer if their mother's attitude about her situation is negative.

1—*Discuss:* What advantages does paternity leave provide for the family? for the baby?

● Family Planning

After considering all these factors, many couples practice family planning. *Family planning* happens when a couple decides how many children they want and when to have them. Couples who want to plan their families need to discuss different birth control methods with their physicians. *Birth control methods* are methods couples use to control the conception of children. Family planning is more successful today than ever before because many birth control methods are available. Physicians can explain each method in terms of:

- ☐ how the method prevents pregnancy or helps the couple know when to conceive, if they want children.

- ☐ how successfully the method prevents unwanted pregnancies.

- ☐ the method's possible side effects and the people more likely to have these effects.

- ☐ the method's cost.

Many birth control methods are available. The only completely successful way to avoid unwanted pregnancies and sexually transmitted diseases (STDs) is abstinence. *Abstinence* is choosing not to have sexual intercourse. More people are choosing to say, "no" for many reasons. Most realize they have the right to say "no"

- ☐ to unwanted pregnancies that will forever change their lives.

- ☐ to unplanned children who may have to be placed for adoption or raised in less than the best situations.

- ☐ to STDs that may result in sterility and even death.

- ☐ to emotional scars that may follow a broken relationship.

- ☐ to conflicts with parents and other adults who care for them and with their own consciences over moral values.

Although there are several ways to classify birth control methods, the methods in this text are classified as:

2—*Note:* Emphasize the fact that an individual or a couple need to be mature enough and responsible enough to use the contraception effectively.

☐ hormones that keep eggs from being released by the ovaries.

☐ devices that block the sperm from reaching the eggs and chemicals that kill the sperm. (These are often used in combination with each other.)

☐ the intrauterine device (IUD) that prevents the zygote from implanting in the uterus.

☐ sterilization or surgical procedures that are permanent ways to prevent sperm from reaching eggs.

☐ natural planning that involves temporary abstinence during the woman's fertile period.

For couples, such as married couples, who decide not to practice abstinence, several birth control options exist. See 3-11.

Before giving medical advice, the doctor will look at the couple's health history and give them a complete checkup. The couple should think about which birth control method they prefer. This will depend on their religious beliefs and their likes and dislikes of certain methods.

2

3-11   Many birth control options are now available.

Birth Control Options			
Option	Effectiveness	Advantages	Possible Problems
Hormones			
The Pill Also called birth control pill and oral contraceptive Hormones are estrogen and progestin, or progestin	97% No protection against STDs	More comfortable Less acne Less iron deficiency Fewer tubal pregnancies	Must be taken daily Temporary irregular bleeding Increased risk of heart attacks and strokes for women over 35 years
Implants Match-size, soft plastic tubes are placed under the skin in the upper arm. These are inserted and removed through a small incision	99.9% No protection against STDs	Effective for up to 5 years; can be removed at any time	Irregular periods and spotting
Injections Injection (shot) given in the arm or buttock every 12 weeks	99.7% No protection against STDs	Effective for 12 weeks	Irregular bleeding Weight gain Headaches Depression Abdominal pain (continued)

1—*Enrich:* Research various birth control methods to discover side effects.

2—*Enrich:* Invite a doctor to speak to the class about birth control methods, effectiveness, side effects, and costs.

Birth Control Options (continued)			
Option	**Effectiveness**	**Advantages**	**Possible Problems**
Mechanical Devices			
Diaphragm or cervical cap Diaphragm is a round latex dome that is inserted in the vagina and covers the cervix Cervical cap is a thimble-shaped latex cap that fits over the cervix Often combined with spermicide for greater protection	Diaphragm—82% Cervical cap for women who have had children (64%) Cervical cap for women who have not had children (82%) No protection against STDs	Can last several years, but must be inserted each time	Messy Allergies to latex and spermicides can develop Cannot be used during vaginal bleeding or infection May be difficult to fit and difficult to use Diaphragm increases risk of bladder infection
Male condom Condom is a sheath made of latex or animal membrane worn over the penis	88% Latex condoms are effective against STDs Can increase effectiveness if used with spermicides	Easy to purchase Can help relieve premature ejaculation	Allergies to latex (or to spermicides Loss of sensation Breakage or condom slips off in the vagina
Female condom Latex pouch that lines the vagina	79% No protection against STDs		Allergies to latex
Intrauterine device			
IUD (Intrauterine device) Small plastic device inserted into the uterus for up to 10 years. The IUD contains hormones or copper	98% (with hormones) 99.2% (with copper) Increased risk of STDs; more problems with STDs if infected	Effective for up to 10 years IUDs with hormones may reduce menstrual cramps	Temporary increase in in cramps Spotting between periods Heavier and longer periods Increased chance of tubal infections Usually not recommended for women who have not had children due to the size of the uterus

(continued)

Birth Control Options (continued)			
Option	**Effectiveness**	**Advantages**	**Possible Problems**
Sterilization			
Tubal ligation Fallopian tubes (tubes that carry the eggs to the uterus after released by ovaries) are cut and permanently closed under general anesthesia	99.6% No protection against STDs	Permanent	Difficult, if not impossible to reverse
Vasectomy Vas deferens (tubes that carry the sperm) are cut and permanently closed under local anesthesia	99.85% No protection against STDs	Permanent	Difficult, if not impossible to reverse
Natural Planning			
Natural planning Also called Periodic Abstinence, Rhythm Method, and Fertility Awareness Avoiding sex near time of ovulation by noting: (1) changes in cervical mucus; (2) changes in body temperature (3) changes in both above—called sympto-thermal; and (4) counting days in which ovulation should occur	80% No protection against STDs	Easy to get equipment No medical or hormonal side effects Accepted by most religions	Uncooperative partner Taking risks during "unsafe days" Illness or stress can cause changes in ovulation Not effective with irregular cycles Vaginal infections or douches change mucus

Family planning is a couple's personal choice. There are some points that couples should keep in mind as they plan families. First, to protect the mother's health, doctors advise a year or more between pregnancies. After several pregnancies, mothers may need even more time. A woman should consult a doctor about her health before becoming pregnant.

In addition, there is often less jealousy between children with three-year differences between them. This is because older children can help with the new baby and feel needed. Also, some research shows that children born three years apart may develop better. The spacing gives parents time to work with each child alone before they must divide their attention.

Not all couples feel they can handle another child right away. These feelings depend on their finances, emotional and physical energy, career, age, and lifestyle. Couples should not feel guilty if they want only one child. They should realize that an only child is not necessarily spoiled or lonely. The most important reason for wanting another child is the same reason for wanting the first. If a couple wants to share their love and time with another child, they should have one.

Infertility

About one-third of all couples have some difficulty reproducing. However, only 10 to 20 percent of all couples are **infertile**, or unable to reproduce. The number of infertile couples is unknown because those using birth control do not know whether they are infertile. In addition, other infertile couples never seek medical help.

The inability to reproduce after one year of trying to become pregnant is called **involuntary infertility**. The problem of involuntary infertility occurs in males 40 to 50 percent of the time. It occurs in females 30 to 40 percent of the time. Sometimes infertility occurs in both partners. When both partners have a minor problem, their chances of having a baby are much lower than when only one partner does.

Doctors look for causes of infertility in males and females, 3-12. Some infertility problems may be caused by drugs, chemicals, radiation, sexually transmitted diseases, and smoking. Excessive exercise coupled with low weight and increased age also can cause infertility. Sometimes doctors can correct these causes of infertility and help couples have biological children. Other times the causes of infertility are unknown and couples never conceive.

▶ Sterility

While infertile couples eventually may be able to conceive naturally, couples who cannot are considered **sterile**. Couples who decide they would like to pursue having biological children can go to physicians to receive fertility counseling. **Fertility counseling** consists of determining the reasons for sterility and the fertility options available.

Even with the various options, 3-13, many sterile couples are never able to have biological children. The methods are very expensive, too. Various issues are sometimes raised concerning these methods. For example, using a **surrogate mother** who bears, and sometimes both conceives and bears, a child for the couple can raise both moral and legal issues. Using a surrogate mother can raise the moral issue of whether someone other than the couple wanting the child should be involved in the pregnancy.

3-12 There are many causes of involuntary infertility and sterility. Some are unknown.

Major Causes of Infertility and Sterility	
Women	**Men**
lack of ovulation	low sperm count
hormone deficiencies	hormone deficiencies
irregular ovulation	inability of sperm to move
damage to reproductive organs	damage to reproductive organs

1—*Discuss:* Why should a woman consult a doctor before becoming pregnant?

2—*Reflect:* How do you feel about the spacing of children?

3—*Enrich:* Research causes of infertility. Report to the class.

Fertility Methods		
Method	**Used to...**	**Problems**
Artificial insemination	Increase sperm count for conception in biological mother Impregnate surrogate mother	Slight risk of infection If sperm is not husband's, moral issues and legal issues (legitimacy and biological father's rights) are raised
Hormone therapy (fertility drugs)	Stimulate ovaries to function properly	Multiple pregnancies Possible increased risk for female cancers
Microsurgery	Attempt to open the fallopian tubes	Risks of surgery such as anesthetic and infection risks
In vitro fertilization (called "test-tube" babies)	Allow a woman with permanently blocked fallopian tubes to have her eggs surgically removed and fertilized with her husband's sperm in a laboratory dish. After a few days, the fertilized eggs are implanted in the mother's uterus Impregnate surrogate mother	Risks of surgery Multiple births
Gamate Intra-Fallopian Transfer (GIFT)	Increased chances of conception if men have a low sperm count or women have problems ovulating. (Several eggs are surgically placed in the fallopian tubes; sperm are also placed directly in the fallopian tubes.)	Risks of surgery Multiple births
Surrogate mother	Replace the sterile couple's role in bearing a child. (Surrogate mother (a) may bear a child who is the sterile couple's biological child conceived by in vitro fertilization, (b) may bear a child with her egg and the husband's sperm (of the sterile couple) that were introduced to the surrogate mother through artificial insemination, or (c) may bear a child not biologically related to the sterile couple by using her own eggs and donor sperm introduced through artificial insemination.	Moral issues Legal issues

3-13   Sterile couples now have many options for having children.

1—*Enrich:* Research (in groups) the topics of artificial insemination, in vitro fertilization, and GIFT, including ethical and legal issues and approximate costs. A hospital or a medical clinic may provide information or a speaker.

Legal issues are raised concerning any fee and what happens if the oral or written agreement is broken. For example: Who pays if the surrogate mother's and/or the newborn's medical fees are much higher than the contract fee? What happens if the surrogate mother decides she wants to keep the baby who may be biologically her child? What happens if the couple decides they do not want this child because they have conceived in the meantime or because the child has a birth defect?

Artificial insemination occurs when the sperm is introduced into the uterus by a medical procedure rather than by sexual relations.

In vitro fertilization occurs when the mother's egg(s) ovum or ova are surgically removed and fertilized with the husband's sperm in a laboratory dish. After a few days, the fertilized egg is reintroduced and implanted into the mother's uterus. This is then often referred to as a test-tube baby.

A *GIFT* (gamete intra-fallopian transfer) occurs when the sperm is introduced into the woman's fallopian tubes, where several ova also have been placed by surgery. Using several ova helps insure conception but often results in a multiple pregnancy. Couples may also use other methods in which babies are not related to both or either partner. These methods involve ethical and legal questions.

Involuntary infertility and sterility are painful for couples in a psychological sense. Some couples feel helpless about their life plans. This feeling is often most severe for women who are used to setting goals and obtaining them. The partner who is found to have the problem may feel damaged, defective, or guilty. Couples who seek treatment will find it expensive and perhaps disappointing. Unless couples resolve these problems, they may have a crisis because they feel that two purposes of marriage are unfulfilled—having children and raising them.

Summary

Parenting is more difficult than other tasks because it involves relationships. Parents usually are not trained to be parents. Most jobs require training, but parenting, one of the most important jobs of all, is often undertaken without preparation. With fewer extended families today and more mobility, having supportive relationships is more difficult.

Those considering parenting need to find out what resources are available to them. They should learn as much about children as possible. These resources include professionals, successful parents, books, magazines, or child care classes. Spending time with other infants and children also will increase a couple's knowledge of children. The way the couple was raised will also affect their parenting roles.

Couples have different reasons for wanting or not wanting children. There are a number of factors couples must think about when deciding on a family. They must consider how having a baby will change their relationships with each other, relatives, and friends. Couples should also think about how children will affect their shared responsibilities at home. In addition, they should also understand how children will affect their finances and career.

Many couples today practice family planning. A number of birth control methods are available that make family planning more successful. Some couples who plan for children find they are infertile for a time or even sterile, due to a number of causes. Some of these causes are unknown. New methods can treat infertility. These methods include artificial insemination, in vitro fertilization, and GIFT. Sometimes, however, these methods do not work and couples must adjust to being childless.

1—*Discuss:* What are some feelings or events that could occur if one partner or both partners are infertile or sterile?

To Review

Write your answers on a separate sheet of paper.

1. True or false. For most couples, parenting is a natural, automatic response that follows a baby's birth.
2. List three poor reasons people give for wanting to become parents.
3. Which is the best reason for wanting to have a baby?
   a. Our parents want to be grandparents.
   b. Babies are so cute.
   c. We need a child to carry on the family business.
   d. We want to share our life and love with a child.
   e. A child will give us a reason to love each other again.
4. What are the most common problems of meeting both career and parenthood demands?
5. Most women keep their job after the birth of their children for _____ and _____ reasons.
6. Define foregone income.
7. What is maternity leave?
8. How does family planning affect children?
9. True or false. All women who want babies can become pregnant.
10. Explain the effects of infertility on parents.

To Do

1. Write a short paper giving your views on the kinds of maturity couples should have before becoming parents.
2. Construct a poster or collage showing different parenting responsibilities.
3. Interview several young couples about the parenting skills they had to learn after having their children. Ask them to share some funny stories about trying to care for their children.
4. Invite a child care professional to speak about parenting programs. Ask him or her to explain the importance of the programs, topics covered, costs, and number of sessions available. Invite the person to demonstrate a parenting skill, as well.
5. Collect some books, magazines, and pamphlets about child care. Write the title of the publication, name and address of publisher, topics covered, age of children discussed, and other important information on index cards.
6. Invite a couple with a full-time homemaker and a couple who both work outside the home to class. Ask them to discuss how they share home and child care tasks.

To Observe

1. In an informal setting, observe parents who are having a difficult time with a child. What parenting skills might they need to help them with their children? For example, do they need to know more about appropriate developmental tasks for the child's age, discipline methods, or how to childproof their home?
2. Observe examples of literature and professional services for parents in your local school and community.
3. Observe how dual-career families share responsibilities for home and child care.
4. Observe how an employer in your community helps parents to meet their work and family obligations. For example, does the employer offer maternity leave, paternity leave, child care programs, and/or flexible work schedules?

To Think Critically

1. If a married couple chooses not to have children or wants to wait longer before having a child, what can they say to their parents who want grandchildren? Why do older people often want grandchildren? Besides having grandchildren, what are some ways older people can fulfill their needs to be with younger children?
2. What are some specific ways a dual-career couple can equally share home care tasks so that both partners are happy? What could be done to make the sharing of home tasks fair if the demands of one person's job involves travel or work that does not permit time at home daily, very long work hours in comparison to the partner's work hours, or bringing work "home from the office"?
3. Why might companies choose to offer paternity leave to their employees? Why might companies choose not to offer paternity leave to its employees?

Parenting is an important job. People must consider the responsibilites as well as joys before becoming parents.

Part 2

© Nancy P. Alexander

Prenatal Development and the Newborn

Pregnancy is a special time for a new family. The feelings of parents range from great excitement to anxiety. However, when a couple want children, they adjust to parenthood rather easily.

The prenatal period, which lasts about 280 days, is the shortest stage in the life span. This formative stage also is the most critical time for a child's development. For this reason, proper prenatal care is crucial for all mothers-to-be.

The baby is called a neonate for the first two weeks following birth. During this period, the neonate adjusts to life outside the mother's body. Parents adjust during this time, too, by adapting to the first challenges and demands of parenthood.

In **chapters 4** and **5,** you will learn about pregnancy and prenatal care. **Chapter 6** will introduce you to the new baby.

Chapter 4

Pregnancy

Children inherit traits from their parents.

After studying this chapter, you will be able to

☐ describe how a person inherits traits through genes.

☐ list the three different types of multiple pregnancies.

☐ describe the three main stages of prenatal development.

After studying this chapter, you will be able to define

age of viability
amnion
cartilage
cell
chorion
chromosomes
conception
dominant
embryonic stage
fallopian tubes
fetal stage
fetus
fraternal twins
genes
germ cells
germinal stage
identical twins
multiple pregnancy
ovum
placenta
prenatal development
quickening
recessive
sperm
umbilical cord
uterus
zygote

1

1—*Activity:* Locate pictures of you as a baby with a parent or parents. Identify ways in which you looked alike then. Do you still bear the same resemblances? Discuss in class.

A baby begins to grow and develop about nine months before birth. This development begins when an **ovum** (the egg or female sex cell) and a **sperm** (the male sex cell) unite. However, before the baby actually is born, many complex changes must take place.

Many factors help the fertilized egg cell develop. One factor is a baby's genes. Genes determine a lot about a person's looks, personality, and physical size. A baby's genes come from both the mother and the father, 4-1. These genes control how babies grow and develop before they are ever born.

● How Heredity Works

Life begins when the ovum and sperm unite. This beginning is called **conception**. At conception, every person is just one cell. A **cell** is the smallest unit of life that is able to reproduce itself. The cell grows into a human being that is different from any other person. What causes each person to be so different? Heredity does, and it works in complex ways. You may understand heredity better by reading about Steve.

4-1 Even as an infant, this baby resembles his father. Genes are responsible for their physical similarities.

Nancy Konopasek

1—*Discuss:* Why is Steve different from his older brother Chris if they have the same parents?

▶ Heredity and Steve

Steve is a five-year-old boy. Like many other children his age, Steve asks many questions, enjoys pretend games, and shows interest in letters and numbers. Although Steve shares many traits of other five-year-olds, he is uniquely Steve—not Kate, Peter, Susan, or even his older brother Chris. How did Steve become the person he is?

Like all people, Steve began life as a single cell. The *nucleus*, or center, of the fertilized egg cell contains a set of instructions to build a living thing. These instructions determine whether the living thing will be a person, an animal, or a plant. The instructions are written in what scientists call a *genetic code*.

Where does nature keep this important genetic code? The genetic code is stored in DNA (deoxyribonucleic acid). DNA is a chemical compound. It is found in thread-like structures called **chromosomes**, which carry genes in living cells. Chromosomes contain the information nature needs to make Steve a human.

▪ Chromosomes and Genes

All living organisms have a certain number of chromosomes. Each human baby receives a total of 46 chromosomes, or 23 pairs. The sperm and egg cells contain 23 chromosomes each. Twenty three of the baby's chromosomes come from the mother's ovum and 23 come from the father's sperm, 4-2.

Each chromosome contains many genes. **Genes** are sections of the DNA molecule. They determine the individual traits each person will have. Each human cell contains about one million genes. There are about 20,000 genes in each chromosome. Sometimes, one gene determines one trait. Other times, a group of genes determines one trait.

Steve's genes have determined that he has blue eyes; light brown hair with a reddish tinge; and fair, freckled skin. Steve's genes give him Rh positive blood, type O. They also give him a better-than-average chance of getting high blood pressure. Because of his genes, Steve learns quickly. This is only part of Steve's genetic

1

2

2—*Enrich:* Obtain a DNA poster to explain its composition. Have students research and report on current applications of DNA testing, such as declaring paternity, matching hair and blood samples in criminal cases, and determining diseases or disabilities.

The Hereditary Process

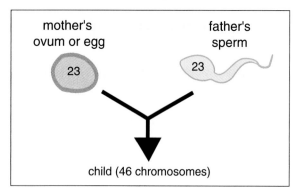

child (46 chromosomes)

4-2 Every child inherits 23 chromosomes from the mother's ovum and 23 chromosomes from the father's sperm.

information. The sum of Steve's genes, along with his environment, makes him Steve and no one else.

Inheriting Unique Traits

Steve doesn't look exactly like anyone in his family. Some of his features look like his father's and others look like his mother's. Some of his features don't look like either of his parents'. For instance, Steve's hair is the same color as his mother's. His body is built like his father's. Even though both of his parents have brown eyes, Steve's eyes are blue.

Steve's traits were passed on to him through germ cells. **Germ cells** are the sperm and ovum. How did they get this name? The sperm and ovum are called germ cells because they are the basis for growth. Their purpose is the same as a germinating seed that is the basis of growth for a flower.

Each germ cell contains 23 chromosomes. "Chance" determines the particular chromosomes found in each sperm and each ovum. When the sperm and ovum unite, a fertilized egg cell with 46 chromosomes is formed. As the fertilized egg cell (called a **zygote**) divides, each cell formed will have 23 pairs of chromosomes, or a total of 46. One chromosome from each pair originated from the father. The other chromosome originated from

the mother. During the course of nine months, the zygote will develop and grow into a baby. The traits the baby has depends on the final combination of chromosomes.

Each chromosome contains many genes. Genes occur in pairs. In each gene pair, one gene originates from the father and one originates from the mother. The genes from each parent work together to determine the appearance of each trait in a child.

Dominant and Recessive Traits

You read before that Steve's eyes are blue and his parents both have brown eyes. You may wonder how Steve's parents could pass on this trait even though neither has blue eyes.

People can pass on traits that don't show up in them. This is because some traits are dominant and some are recessive. **Dominant** traits show in a person even if only one gene in a gene pair is for that trait. **Recessive** traits do not show if only one gene is present. Both genes in the pair must be the same for a recessive trait to show.

Genes for tallness and shortness are examples of dominant and recessive genes. Tallness is dominant and shortness is recessive, 4-3. There were both tall and short relatives in Steve's mother's family—possibly even several generations back. Because of this, Steve's mother inherited one gene for tallness and one for shortness, so she is tall. Steve's father also had tall and short relatives. He is a tall man but also has one gene for tallness and one for shortness. When the chromosomes in Steve's mother split to make germ cells, some ova were for tallness and some for shortness. In like manner, some sperm from Steve's father were for tallness and some for shortness. Steve received an ovum and a sperm both for shortness (just like the child on the right in 4-3). Steve's brothers and sisters could be short like Steve or tall like the other child in 4-3.

Sex Chromosomes

Of the 23 pairs of chromosomes, 22 are alike in both males and females. These 22 pairs provide genetic information for both males and females, such as height and eye color. The chromosomes that make up the twenty-third pair

1—*Discuss:* Do you know individuals who do not look like anyone in their family? Do you know others who look very much like a parent, sibling, grandparent, or other relative?

2—*Note:* Diagram this example for students so they can see the combination that produced Steve's trait for tallness.

1

Dominant and Recessive Traits

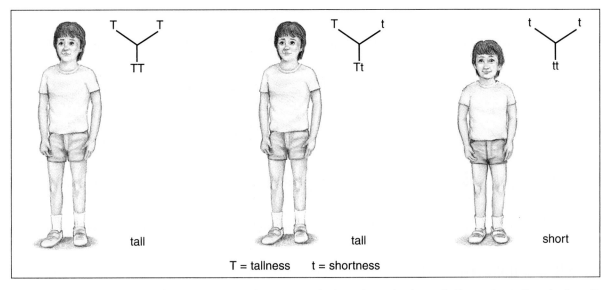

T = tallness   t = shortness

4-3   A dominant trait shows if both genes or only one gene in the pair are for that trait. Recessive traits only show if both genes are for that trait.

are different for females and males. This pair is called the *sex chromosomes*. Height and eye color are determined by only one or a few gene pairs. The sex of the child, however, is determined by the entire chromosome pair.

Females have the chromosome pair called *XX* (because the pair viewed with a microscope looks somewhat like the letters *X* and *X*). When a female's chromosome pair splits to form germ cells (ova), all ova will be X because each chromosome pair was XX.

Males have the chromosome pair called *XY* (because the pair viewed with a microscope looks somewhat like the letters *X* and *Y*). When a male's chromosome pair splits to form germ cells (sperm), unlike females some of these germ cells will be X and some will be Y because each chromosome pair was XY.

If the mother's egg cell, which always carries the X chromosome, is fertilized by a sperm carrying an X chromosome, the child is female (XX). If the sperm cell is carrying a Y chromosome, the child is male (XY). Because the mother contributes only X chromosomes and

the father can contribute either an X or Y chromosome for the twenty-third pair, the sperm always determines the sex of the child, 4-4.

4-4   The father's sperm determines whether a child will be a boy or a girl.

Union of Sperm and Ovum

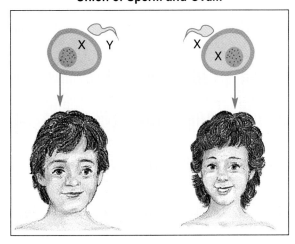

1—*Note:* Relate this illustration to similar ones that often appear in secondary school biology texts, Gregor Mendel's tall and short peas.

2—*Activity:* Diagram the example of the female X chromosome combining with the male X chromosome. Diagram another example combining the female X chromosome with

the male Y chromosome.

3—*Note:* Emphasize that the father is the determiner of the child's sex.

4—*Resource: Biology of Heredity Review,* SAG.

5—*Resource: Inheriting Unique Traits,* SAG.

Multiple Pregnancy

Sometimes, two or more babies develop in the same pregnancy. This is called a **multiple pregnancy**. Multiple pregnancies are not as common as single pregnancies. Likewise, twins are more common than triplets, and triplets are more common than quadruplets.

In the United States, the frequency of having twins is one in 73 births of black babies. The frequency is one in 93 births of white babies. The likeliness of having triplets is one in 10,000. Only one in 620,000 births is of quadruplets. These statistics vary in different parts of the world.

In the future, multiple pregnancies may become more common. This is because more women who have trouble conceiving are using drugs to help them become pregnant. Many of these drugs increase the chances of multiple pregnancy.

A common multiple pregnancy occurs when twins develop. There are two types of twins—fraternal twins and identical twins.

Fraternal Births

The most common multiple pregnancy is when twins develop from two or more ova. Each ova is fertilized with a different sperm, 4-5. Each child has different genetic makeups, so they are as much alike and different as any other brothers and sisters, 4-6. These children are often called **fraternal twins**, triplets, etc. ("Fraternal" comes from a Latin word meaning "brother.")

Fraternal Births

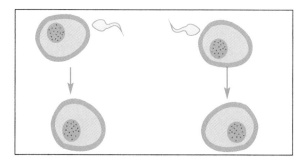

4-5   Fraternal twins grow from two separate zygotes. Each zygote carries different genetic codes from the same parents.

4-6   One of these fraternal twins looks more like his older brother than his twin.

© John Shaw

1—*Discuss:* Why would these statistics vary in different parts of the world? Discuss in terms of technology, medical practices, and methods of assisting infertile couples (from chapter 3).

2—*Discuss:* How are these fraternal twins different?

Fraternal children may or may not be the same sex. They look different at birth and show greater differences as they mature. Children of fraternal births each have a chorion, 4-7. The **chorion** is a membrane that surrounds the baby in the uterus.

▶ Identical Births

In identical births, children develop from a single ovum that was fertilized with a single sperm. During the early days of the pregnancy, the ovum splits to produce two or more children, 4-8. Scientists do not know why the ovum splits.

If the ovum does not completely split, the babies will be *conjoined twins* (*Siamese twins*). These twins are joined in one or more places. Some may even share internal organs, such as a stomach.

Babies from an identical birth have the same genetic makeup. This is because they came from one fertilized ovum. These babies are usually called **identical twins**, triplets, etc.

Identical children are very similar in appearance. They are often confused by family members, 4-9. However, except for their genes, identical children are not exactly alike. Their fingerprints, palm prints, and footprints are similar but not exactly the same. Also, environment makes identical children different. For instance, one child may be larger because of better nourishment, even before birth.

4-7   All fraternal twins have separate chorions.

Fraternal Twins

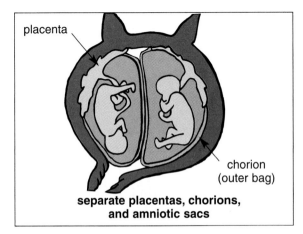

placenta

chorion (outer bag)

separate placentas, chorions, and amniotic sacs

Identical Twins

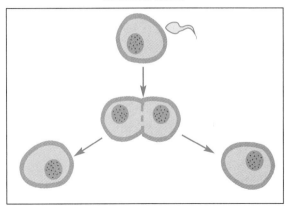

4-8   Identical twins grow from a single zygote that splits into two cells carrying the same genetic code.

4-9   These identical twins have the same genetic makeup.

Some identical twins are *mirror twins*. They look the way you and your mirror image would appear. For instance, one may have a birthmark on the right shoulder and the other may have one on the left shoulder. One may be right-handed and the other left-handed.

Sometimes it is difficult to tell if children are identical. At the time of birth, a physician may be able to tell. Blood tests also can be used for

6

7

1—*Discuss:* Describe fraternal twins that you know. How are they different? How are they similar?

2—*Activity:* Diagram the process that produces identical twins and fraternal twins to visualize the process for the students.

3—*Enrich:* Use the library to research cases of conjoined twins. Write a report and report findings to the class.

4—*Discuss:* What are other environmental conditions that would make identical twins different?

5—*Note:* If identical twins were separated at birth, this would produce the maximum influence of environmental conditions.

6—*Discuss:* Describe identical twins you know. How are they different? How are they similar?

7—*Reflect*: How would you react to the news that you were having twins? What difference would it make if this were your first pregnancy or your second pregnancy?

positive proof, as well as skin grafting. Identical children must be of the same sex. Unlike fraternal children, they usually share one chorion, 4-10. However, identical children may each have their own chorions.

▶ Mixed Types

Multiple pregnancies may be both identical and fraternal if three or more children are born. In mixed types of pregnancies, two or more ova are fertilized by separate sperm (fraternal). Then, one or more of the fertilized ova may split (identical).

Triplets are not mixed pregnancies if all children are identical or if all children are fraternal. However, it is common for triplets to be from a mixed pregnancy, with two children identical and one fraternal, 4-11.

In like manner, quadruplets also may be all identical or all fraternal. However, quadruplets often are a mixed pregnancy type. With quadruplets there could be several types of mixed pregnancy combinations. Three children could be identical and one fraternal, or two could be identical with the other two fraternal. There could even be two identical pairs, but so far as anyone knows, there has never been such a case.

Production of Triplets

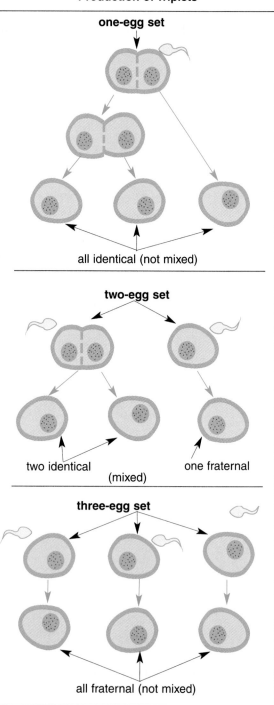

4-11 Depending on the number of zygotes, triplets may be all identical, two identical and one fraternal, or all fraternal.

Most Identical Twins

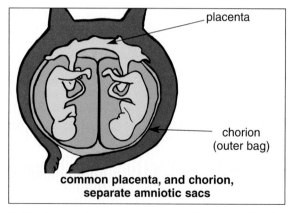

common placenta, and chorion, separate amniotic sacs

4-10 Twins who share a common chorion are identical. Identical twins, however, also may have their own chorions.

1—*Activity:* Add this situation to your diagram of fraternal and identical twins.

2—*Discuss:* Explain what occurs to cause various combinations of identical and fraternal siblings in a multiple pregnancy.

3—*Resource: Multiple Births,* SAG.

● Conception

As you read earlier in the chapter, each person is produced by the union of *one ovum* with one sperm. Each ovum is stored in a small sac inside the ovary called a *follicle*. Hormones cause some follicles to grow and fill with fluid each month. Around the middle of the menstrual cycle, one ovum is released from the follicle, and the other follicles become inactive. (Sometimes more than one ovum is released—as in a fraternal twin pregnancy.)

The **fallopian tubes** are two hollow tubes extending from the right and left sides of the uterus. One end of each tube is connected to the uterus. The other end of each tube, with its finger-like projections, lies near but is not attached to the ovary. The projections from the tube help gather the ovum as it emerges from the ovary. Once inside the fallopian tube, the ovum moves very slowly down the tube.

At the time the egg is released, hormones help the fallopian tube move to gather the egg. They also prepare the uterus for the arrival of the fertilized egg. The **uterus** is the organ in which the baby develops and is protected until birth.

Over 100 million sperm enter the woman's body during intercourse. These sperm begin a journey to the ovum that lasts around 10 minutes. Many sperm do not survive. Only a few hundred reach the fallopian tube.

Sperm may meet the ovum at any point. Conception usually happens when the ovum has moved no further than one-third of the way down the fallopian tube. Conception after that point is unlikely because the ovum begins to die about 24 hours after ovulation.

About a dozen sperm approach the ovum and try to break through its surface. Only one sperm successfully enters, or fertilizes the egg. Once one sperm is accepted, no other sperm can enter the ovum. This is the point of conception.

● Stages in Prenatal Development

Many changes happen between conception and birth. The development that takes place during that time is called **prenatal development**, 4-12. Prenatal development is divided into the germinal stage, the embryonic stage, and the fetal stage. See 4-13.

4-12   Cell division results in the beginnings of a baby and in a life-support system between the mother and baby. The amnion, chorion, and placenta develop at the end of the germinal stage. They protect and nourish the baby until it is born.

Fetus in the Uterus

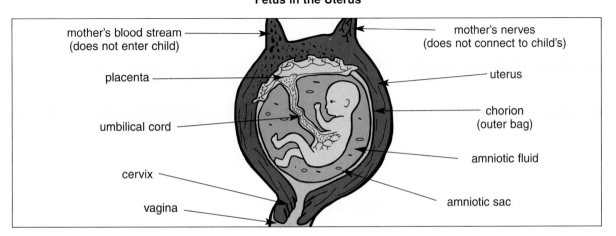

1—*Enrich:* With a chart or transparency, illustrate the female reproductive system. Show students what occurs during conception.

2—*Note:* Explain that an infertile male may not produce enough sperm or may produce sperm that do not have enough activity and die before reaching the ovum.

Prenatal Development by Week

1

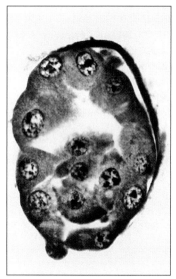

Carnegie Institute of Washington, Dept. of
Embryology, Davis Div.

4-day-old zygote

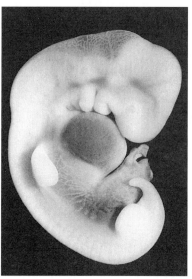

Carnegie Institute of Washington, Dept. of
Embryology, Davis Div.

4 1/2 weeks

The Germinal Stage	
Time Frame	**Development**
conception through 2 weeks	☐ cell divisions occuring ☐ fertilized egg embedding in the wall of the uterus ☐ amnion, placenta, and umbilical cord beginning

The Embryonic Stage	
Time Frame	**Development**
2 weeks through 8 weeks	☐ internal organs (heart, liver, digestive system, brain, and lungs) developing ☐ tissue segments (future vertebrae in a spinal column forming ☐ limb buds (future arms and legs) appearing ☐ ears and eyes beginning

4-13   Prenatal development occurs throughout three major stages.

1—*Resource: Development in the Unborn,* SAG

Prenatal Development by Week

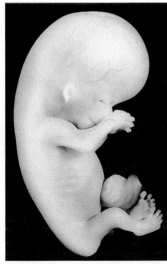

Carnegie Institute of Washington, Dept. of Embryology, Davis Div.

9 weeks

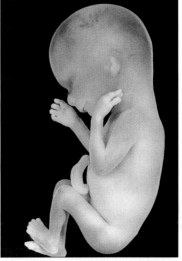

Carnegie Institute of Washington, Dept. of Embryology, Davis Div.

12 weeks

The Fetal Stage	
Time Frame	**Development**
9 weeks	☐ facial features forming ☐ limbs, hands, feet, fingers and toes developing
12 weeks	☐ 3" long; weight 1 oz. ☐ muscles forming ☐ teeth and vocal cords developing ☐ eyelids and nails appearing
16 weeks	☐ 6-8" long; weight 5-6 oz. ☐ lanugo (cottony growth) appearing ☐ heartbeat audible through a stethoscope ☐ eyebrows and eyelashes growing
20 weeks	☐ 10-12" long; weight 1 lb. ☐ sweat glands forming ☐ head hair appearing ☐ vernix caseosa (cheesy material) covering body ☐ skin developing
24 weeks	☐ 14" long; weight 2 lbs. ☐ eye maturing ☐ taste buds developing
28-38 weeks	☐ rapid growth ☐ lanugo disappearing ☐ fatty tissue forming under skin ☐ body organs maturing

1—*Enrich:* Obtain an anonymous sonogram and try to identify body parts. (A labeled picture will help.) Discuss or research the ultrasound's purpose and timing.

2—*Enrich:* Use a ruler to show students the different prenatal lengths.

3—*Note:* Emphasize the importance of good nutrition and health habits throughout a pregnancy.

▶ Germinal Stage

The first stage of prenatal development is called the **germinal stage**. Conception marks the beginning of the germinal stage. This stage covers about two weeks of the pregnancy.

The fertilized egg, or zygote, remains a single cell for about a day and a half. After that time, it begins to divide. On the third day, an egg with 32 cells enters the uterus. Cell division continues at a rapid pace for about three days. During this time, the egg floats freely in the uterus.

About one week after conception, the ovum begins to embed in the wall of the uterus. The cells continue to divide. The chorion and **amnion** (a fluid-filled sac) begin to form. They surround the cells and protect the baby until birth. The **placenta**, an organ filled with blood vessels, begins to develop against the wall of the uterus. The umbilical cord grows out from the developing child, at the site of the future navel, and connects with the placenta. Refer once again to 4-12. The **umbilical cord** contains three blood vessels that connect the child with the placenta. The placenta nourishes the baby, removes its wastes, serves as a gas exchange mechanism, and provides it with needed hormones. When the baby can receive nourishment from the mother, the germinal stage has ended.

▶ Embryonic Stage

The second stage of prenatal development is the **embryonic stage**. Experts say this is the most critical stage of pregnancy. That is because, at this time, almost all body systems develop. The embryonic stage lasts about six weeks.

In this stage changes happen so quickly that, when it ends, the embryo looks like a small human being. The embryo has tiny arms, legs, fingers, toes, and a face. It does not yet have solid bones, so cartilage supports the body. (**Cartilage** is soft, gristle-like tissue that is structural, such as bones, but more flexible. Cartilage is the tissue found in the tip of your nose.) The embryo also has a beating heart, a brain, lungs, and all the other major organs.

The baby now receives both good and harmful substances from the mother's placenta through the umbilical cord. Because the baby's body parts are developing so quickly, passing harmful substances to the child can affect him or her for life. That is why the mother's health habits become very important during this stage. She should eat a balanced diet so the baby receives nutrients. She should also avoid substances like alcohol, drugs, excess caffeine, smoke, and X rays that may harm the baby. By taking care of herself, a woman does her part to help her baby be healthy and normal when it is born.

▶ Fetal Stage

When bone cells start to replace cartilage, the baby enters the **fetal stage** of development. This stage begins about nine weeks after conception. From this point until birth, a baby is known medically as a **fetus**.

During the fetal stage, all parts of the body mature, and overall size increases quickly. Major changes happen in the fetus. By the fourth month, the fetus has usually grown enough for the mother to look pregnant.

Two milestones happen during the fetal stage. Between the fourth and fifth months, a mother begins to feel her baby move. Amazingly, the baby can turn, swallow, and even suck its thumb. The baby also can move its head and push with the hands, feet, and limbs. When the mother feels these movements, it is called **quickening**. The mother should tell her doctor when she first feels movement. This will help the doctor tell how old the baby is and when the child may be born. After quickening, the mother can usually hear the baby's heartbeat for the first time by listening with the doctor's stethoscope.

1

2

A second milestone is reached when the fetus is seven months, or 28 weeks, old. This is the age at which most babies could survive if they were born. By this time, the baby's brain has more control over the body systems than it ever had before. The seventh month after conception is called the ***age of viability***. Most babies born at this time would need some intensive care in hospitals. A few babies born before seven months have survived with special care.

Even though a baby born at seven months can survive, it has a better chance of surviving the closer it gets to nine months. (This is true unless earlier delivery is needed for medical reasons.) In the last two months of pregnancy, the baby's lungs become stronger and the baby becomes larger.

In the ninth month of pregnancy, the fetus receives immunities from the mother. These help prevent the baby from catching some diseases after it is born. The baby also turns to a head-down position (in most cases) to prepare for birth.

Summary

The development of the child begins with the union of an ovum and a sperm at conception. The nucleus of this single cell contains the genetic code for that person. The genetic code is found in DNA molecules, which compose the chromosomes. Humans have 23 pairs of chromosomes. An equal number of chromosomes are received from the mother and father. Each chromosome contains genes that determine individual traits. Sometimes one gene pair determines a trait, and at other times, groups of genes determine one trait.

The way in which genes from the two parents interact determines individual traits. Some traits show up in a person and are dominant. Other traits may be masked by the dominant gene and are recessive.

The sex of the child is controlled by the twenty-third pair of chromosomes called the *sex chromosomes*. The male's X or Y sex chromosome determines the child's sex.

Multiple pregnancies occur when one or more eggs are fertilized by one or more sperm. Fraternal twins occur when two different eggs are fertilized by two different sperm. Each twin has a different genetic makeup. Identical twins are products of a single egg fertilized by a single sperm, but at an early stage the embryo divides. These two halves carry the same genetic makeup. Multiple pregnancies may include combinations of identicals and fraternals.

Prenatal development is divided into the germinal stage, the embryonic stage, and the fetal stage. During the germinal stage, the zygote floats freely in the uterus before becoming embedded in the wall of the uterus. Cells continue to divide. Almost all body systems develop during the embryonic stage. The fetal stage lasts from about nine weeks until birth. During this stage, the fetus continues to grow and body systems mature, until the ninth month of pregnancy. At the ninth month, the baby is ready to be born.

1

1—*Enrich:* Visit a hospital nursery to view and learn about the different arrangements for delivery, the birth process, babies, and the nursery.

To Review

Write your answers on a separate sheet of paper.

1. Germ cells have _____ (23, 46) chromosomes.
2. True or false. Because Susan looks just like her mother, she inherited more traits from her mother than her father.
3. Paul and Emily both have blue eyes. They are expecting a baby. Their baby's eyes will be
    a. brown, because both of Emily's parents and Paul's father have brown eyes.
    b. blue, because neither Paul nor Emily carry traits for brown eyes.
    c. blue or brown, because Emily inherited a trait for brown eyes from her mother.
4. List the three different kinds of multiple pregnancies.
5. Patty and Patrick—who look almost alike in size, coloring, and facial features—are _____ (identical, fraternal) twins.
6. True or false. In the germinal stage, the zygote receives nutrients through the placenta.
7. The stage in which the baby's body systems and organs start to appear is the
    a. fetal stage.
    b. embryonic stage.
    c. germinal stage.
8. True or false. The mother's nutrition doesn't matter during the embryonic stage because the baby has not developed enough.
9. During the fetal stage, the baby's limbs are supported by _____ (cartilage, bones).
10. By the fourth or fifth month of pregnancy, the baby begins to
    a. develop vital organs.
    b. receive nutrients from the mother.
    c. turn and kick.

1

To Do

1. You have heard that "Jane" has her mother's smile and her uncle's artistic ability. Because our blood relatives have common ancestors, family members share common traits. Make a list of some traits of someone you know. Include physical, mental, and personality traits as well as interests and talents. Beside each trait, write the relative(s) with whom that person shares a trait.
2. Collect pictures of identical and fraternal twins, triplets, etc., and note how alike or different they are. Try to find pictures of the same people that have been taken over a period of several years.
3. On a bulletin board or poster, show how quadruplets can be all identical, three identical and one fraternal, two identical and two fraternal, two identical pairs, and all four fraternal.
4. Design a poster on the theme, "Be Good to Your Baby Before He or She Is Born."

To Observe

1. Observe your physical features. Which features seem to come from your mother? Which come from your father? Which features do you share with other relatives?
2. Observe brothers and sisters. Which characteristics do they share? How are they different?
3. Observe identical twins. Which of their characteristics are most alike? Which are similar but somewhat different? Which are dissimilar?

To Think Critically

1. Sometimes conception is referred to as the "miracle of life." Biologically, why can conception indeed be thought of as a "miracle"?
2. How do the stages in prenatal development follow the principles of growth and development (that is, growth and development are constant, happen in sequenced steps, happen at different rates, and have interrelated parts)? Give specific examples as part of your explanation.
3. Identical births have exactly the same heredity. What are some of the biological advantages of having an identical sibling?

Chapter 5

Prenatal Care and Childbirth

After studying this chapter, you will be able to

☐ describe the early signs of pregnancy.

☐ explain the relationship between the health of the mother and the health of the baby.

☐ describe how diseases, drugs, radiation, environmental pollutants, and birth defects can harm the fetus.

☐ list ways family members can be involved during pregnancy.

☐ describe the birth process.

☐ describe physical and emotional changes in the mother during the postnatal period.

After studying this chapter, you will be able to define

acquired immuno-deficiency syndrome (AIDS)	forceps
	labor
adrenaline	Lamaze method
afterbirth	Leboyer method
amniocentesis	lightening
birth defect	Lyme disease
birthing room	natural childbirth
bonding	obese
breech birth	obstetrician
certified nurse midwives (CNM)	postnatal care
	postpartum care
chorionic villus sampling (CVS)	postpartum blues
	premature
cesarean section	Rh factor
diabetes	rooming-in
dilation	rubella
eclampsia	sexually transmitted diseases (STDs)
episiotomy	sonogram
expulsion	spontaneous abortion
false labor	stillborn
fetal alcohol effect (FAE)	the show
fetal alcohol syndrome (FAS)	toxemia
	toxoplasmosis
Fifth disease	ultrasound

The prenatal period is full of preparations for the new baby, such as getting the nursery ready. A mother's body is preparing for birth, too.

1

1—*Discuss:* What are some other preparations that would have to be made?

At no other time are two people closer than a mother and baby during the prenatal period. Even before the mother knows she is pregnant, the baby affects her life. The mother's body changes to prepare for nine months of growth. The baby continues to affect the mother's body through delivery.

The mother has a great effect on her baby's body, too. The mother gives the baby a safe "home" in her uterus. She eats, breathes, and gets rid of wastes for them both, and she helps bring the baby into the world.

Before a baby is born, all family members need to be close. Family members should help each other adjust to life with a baby. Couples who are close during the prenatal stage can actually have better marriages. Family closeness also can ensure better parenting through each stage in the child's development.

The March of Dimes urges mothers to "Be good to your baby before it is born." Parents-to-be should take this slogan seriously. Because experts know more about pregnancy, childbirth, and infant care than ever before, parents-to-be can take many steps to keep mother and baby healthy and safe.

Women should start taking care of themselves before they become pregnant. Good health habits during childhood and adolescence help prepare a woman for childbearing. As soon as a woman believes she is pregnant she should seek prenatal care. A woman always needs good medical care, whether it is her first, second, or a later pregnancy.

● Signs of Pregnancy

A woman cannot feel the sperm and egg unite. She cannot feel cells divide as the baby begins to develop. Nevertheless, her body immediately begins to nourish and protect the new life. Hormones trigger changes in some of the woman's organs. The signs of pregnancy help a woman recognize these changes.

The signs of pregnancy are not signs of an illness. Pregnancy is a normal process. If a woman is healthy and happy about having a child, she may even feel better than before she became pregnant. The signs of pregnancy are divided into presumptive signs and positive signs, 5-1. The *presumptive signs* could be signs of pregnancy or something else. Doctors must determine their cause. However, doctors identify *positive signs* as definitely being caused by pregnancy.

● Medical Care

The best way to make childbearing safe and successful is with medical care. Many women choose to visit **obstetricians,** or doctors who specialize in pregnancy and birth.

Ideally, a woman should have a complete checkup before she becomes pregnant. Some health problems can be corrected before pregnancy. Once a woman believes she is pregnant, she should make an appointment with a doctor.

▶ The First Appointment

The first appointment prepares soon-to-be parents for the pregnancy. It is a good idea for the couple to go together. The doctor's exam will include the following:

- ☐ The doctor usually gathers general information (employment, age, address). He or she finds out the couple's health history.

- ☐ The doctor asks for information about the woman's menstrual cycle and other pregnancies. He or she also asks the date of her last menstrual period to estimate the time of birth.

- ☐ The doctor will weigh the woman and take her pulse, blood pressure, and respiration rates, 5-2.

- ☐ The woman's breasts and abdomen are checked. Her pelvis is measured to make sure it is large enough to allow the baby's head to pass through.

3

1—*Note:* Many medical experts recommend a twelve-month pregnancy period. They advocate a healthy lifestyle three months before conception.

2—*Discuss:* Why is good prenatal care so important?

3—*Note:* Having a complete checkup prior to becoming pregnant coincides with the twelve-month pregnancy period. If a woman has a definite health problem, it would be wise to delay pregnancy.

Signs of Pregnancy

Presumptive Signs

☐ **Amenorrhea** (menstruation stops)—If the woman is usually regular in her menstrual cycle, a delay of 10 or more days is a sign.

☐ **Nausea**—Nausea is present in about 1/2 to 2/3 of all pregnancies. Because it often occurs in the morning hours, it is called "morning sickness." Nausea may happen at any time of the day or evening. Nausea occurring at the same time daily through the fourth to twelfth week is a sign.

☐ **Tiredness**—Many women feel tired during the first few months of pregnancy.

☐ **Frequency of urination**—The growing uterus puts pressure on the bladder. Hormones may also cause more frequent urination.

☐ **Swelling and tenderness of the breasts**—This is often the first sign women note.

☐ **Skin discoloration**—Red marks may be seen as the breasts and abdomen enlarge. Darkening of skin may occur on the face and nipples.

☐ **Internal changes**—Doctors often note softening of the cervix (Goodell's sign). There also may be a softening of the lower part of the uterus (Hegar's sign) and a bluish tinge to the vagina and cervix due to circulatory congestion (Chadwick's sign). The uterus is also enlarged with irregular areas of firmness and softness (Piskacek's sign).

☐ **Other signs**—Other symptoms include backache, groin pains, faintness, abdominal swelling, leg cramps, varicose veins, and indigestion.

Positive Signs

☐ **HCG (Human Chorionic Gonadatrophin)**—HCG is a hormone found in the blood and urine of pregnant women. Lab tests may detect the hormone's presence as early as the first two weeks of pregnancy.

☐ **Fetal heartbeat**—This can be heard through a stethoscope at 16 weeks.

☐ **Fetal movement**—Spontaneous movement begins at 11 weeks but is not felt until 16 to 18 weeks.

☐ **Fetal image**—This may be seen on X-ray film or with ultrasound scanning.

☐ **Fetal shape**—The baby's shape may be felt through the abdominal wall.

☐ **Uterine contractions**—A doctor may note these painless contractions.

5-1   Presumptive signs could be signs of pregnancy. Other conditions may cause them also. Positive signs, however, are definitely caused by pregnancy.

☐ The doctor will test the woman's overall health by analyzing her urine and testing her blood. The blood test checks for her blood type, anemia (a condition caused by lack of iron), and diseases that can harm an unborn child.

☐ The doctor also checks the woman's eyes, ears, nose, throat, teeth, heart, and lungs.

Following the check-up, the obstetrician will give an estimated due date for the baby's birth. Babies are usually born about nine months and one week after the beginning of the last period. The doctor will discuss the woman's prenatal diet and exercise habits.

Couples then choose the date for the next appointment. Usually the doctor sees a pregnant woman once a month during the first six months of pregnancy. The visits increase to twice a month during the seventh and eighth months. During the ninth month, visits increase to once a week or more.

1

2

1—*Note:* If a woman has a history of irregular menstrual periods, it could be hard to calculate her due date. Ultrasound at a later stage of pregnancy will help to determine the due date and check the earlier calculation.

2—*Math Activity:* If the date of a woman's last menstrual period was February 8, calculate the approximate birth date for her baby. Use a calendar for the calculation.

On the calendar, mark dates for her medical visits to figure out how many times she would see a doctor on a regular basis prior to delivery.

© John Shaw

5-2   Checking weight is a routine part of a mother-to-be's checkup.

Factors that Affect the Baby's Health

An unborn baby depends on the mother for a healthy start. Mothers with good health habits usually have healthy babies. The habits help them have problem-free pregnancies. These women often share certain qualities. Women who do not have these qualities are often called *high-risk* mothers-to-be. The qualities include age, weight, Rh factor, and emotional stability.

▶ Mother's Age

The ideal time for a woman to have a baby is between the ages of 21 and 28. Teens and women over 36 are high-risk mothers-to-be.

Because teenage mothers are still growing themselves, their bodies cannot always meet the needs of babies. Teens tend to have *premature* babies (babies born too soon or small), *stillborn* babies (babies born dead), and malformed babies. Women over age 36 tend to have more babies with birth defects, 5-3.

▶ Mother's Weight

To have a healthy pregnancy, it is vital for a woman to be the proper weight for her age, height, and body type. A woman whose nonpregnant weight is below 85 percent of her proper weight could endanger her and her child's health. The same is true for a woman whose nonpregnant weight is above 120 percent of her proper weight.

2

5-3   Down syndrome is a birth defect that occurs more often in children born to older women than to younger women.

© Nancy P. Alexander

3

1—*Reflect:* What would be your ideal age to be a first-time parent? Explain your reasons.

2—*Math Activity:* Calculate the weight boundaries (upper and lower) for a woman whose proper weight is 120 pounds. Use 85 percent for the lower boundary and 120 percent for the upper boundary. What type of recommendation would you give her if she is below or above the boundary weights?

3—*Reflect:* Do you know someone with Down syndrome? Describe the individual. How have family members learned to cope with the situation?

The mother's body meets her dietary needs before it meets the needs of her baby. For instance, an underweight woman's body will first use her food intake to correct her own vitamin deficiencies. Her body will pass fewer nutrients to the baby. Therefore, the baby will not get enough nourishment. Underweight women often have low-birthweight infants. A *low-birthweight* baby weighs less than 5 1/2 pounds at birth.

Compared with an ideal-weight woman, an **obese** (extremely overweight) woman uses a greater proportion of her food intake for energy. High blood pressure, diabetes, and delivery problems are more likely. (**Diabetes** is a disease caused by the body's inability to utilize sugar. This happens when the body does not produce or use insulin properly.)

A mother should reach her ideal weight before becoming pregnant. Most doctors do not try to make major changes in the mother's weight during pregnancy. If a pregnant woman eats less, she may not eat enough nutrients to help the baby grow properly. A pregnant woman should carefully follow her doctor's recommended diet.

▶ Rh Factor

The **Rh factor** is a protein substance found in the red blood cells of about 85 percent of the population. (The substance was discovered and first tested in the Rhesus monkey. This is why it is named Rh factor.) People who have the substance are called Rh positive (Rh+), and those who do not are called Rh negative (Rh−).

When a father is Rh+ and a mother is Rh−, the combination can cause the baby problems. This combination occurs in 12 percent of all marriages. If the baby inherits the Rh+ blood type from the father, the baby may be a victim of Rh disease. *Rh disease* is a type of anemia that destroys the baby's red blood cells.

Rh disease does not affect the first Rh+ unborn. However, during any pregnancy, some of the baby's Rh+ cells may enter the mother's bloodstream during birth. This happens in about four percent of the cases. These cells are foreign to the mother's Rh− system. The mother's body fights these Rh+ cells by making antibodies. This then makes the mother immune to the blood cells of future Rh+ babies. In the next pregnancy, these antibodies cross the placenta. If the baby has Rh+ blood, the antibodies destroy the baby's red blood cells.

In the past, parents who had this problem had to limit their family size. This is because once the Rh problem begins, the effects worsen with each pregnancy. In 1968 a vaccine, *anti-Rh-immune globulin,* was approved that has greatly reduced this danger. The Rh− mother is given the vaccine within 72 hours after the birth of each Rh+ baby. The vaccine blocks the growth of antibodies. The vaccine must also be given after a miscarriage or abortion of an Rh+ baby. If an Rh− female receives Rh+ blood during a transfusion, she should receive the vaccine, also. The vaccine is almost 100 percent effective, unless she has already become sensitized to Rh+ cells.

▶ Mother's Emotional Health

Positive thoughts and feelings are important for a woman to have a healthy baby. Feelings stimulate the nervous system and the flow of adrenaline. (**Adrenaline** is a hormone that prepares the body to cope with stress. It can make a person feel more energetic.) Both the nervous system and adrenaline control heart rate, breathing, and muscle tension.

When a mother is happy and relaxed, her adrenaline level is low, her heartbeat and breathing are slow, and her muscles are relaxed, 5-4. When the mother is under stress, adrenaline crosses the placenta to the baby, carrying stress signals. The mother's stress increases her heartbeat and muscle tension as well as the baby's. Later in the pregnancy, the baby not only receives the adrenaline signal but also hears changes in the mother's heartbeat and breathing.

Can stress harm the unborn baby? The unborn baby can handle some stress. However, if the stress is long lasting, severe, or frequent, the mother may have a more difficult delivery. The baby may be smaller, fussy, or quite active. Thus, emotional support during pregnancy is good for both mother and baby.

1—*Note:* This ideal weight recommendation goes along with the twelve-month pregnancy theory.

2—*Activity:* Do you know someone who has had difficulty with the Rh factor? Interview the person to discover what was done to eliminate problems.

3—*Note:* The release of adrenaline can make an athlete perform better.

4—*Discuss:* Name other types of familiar hormones. How do they affect the body?

5—*Note:* Everyone has times of stress. Prolonged, frequent, and severe stress, however, causes concern.

6—*Discuss:* What types of emotional support would a pregnant woman find most helpful? least helpful?

Adrian Demery

5-4   Staying relaxed and content is important to the baby's health.

Health Habits During Pregnancy

Health habits for pregnant women are similar to good health habits for all people. Good health habits are always important. However, when a woman is pregnant, health habits have an even greater effect on her health and her baby's health.

During pregnancy, certain health habits do change. For instance, a pregnant woman may have to eat more of some foods. She may have to take vitamins. A pregnant woman may also need to be more cautious. For instance, during the last few weeks of pregnancy, the mother gains more weight and feels more tired. This may require her to give up active sports, such as tennis.

Every pregnant woman should take care of herself. Because every pregnancy is different, the mother-to-be should ask her doctor for health guidelines to follow.

▶ Nutrition

The old saying that mothers-to-be are "eating for two" (or maybe more) is correct. During the first week, the baby is fed entirely on the contents of the ovum's yolk sac. After embedding, the fertilized egg feeds on mucous tissues that line the womb. By the 12th week, the yolk sac is used, and the baby completely depends on the mother for food.

"Eating for two" does not mean a woman should double or greatly increase the number of calories she eats. After all, the unborn baby is tiny. The mother needs to eat foods that are more nutritious than what she usually may eat. This will help the baby grow.

Scientists now feel that a woman needs essential nutrients throughout her life to prepare for motherhood. Providing for her own needs and those of her baby puts a nutritional strain on the woman's body. Pregnant girls under 17 years of age have more nutritional problems because they are still growing. Women should continue good nutritional habits after the baby is born. Parents are responsible for shaping the eating patterns of their families. There is a direct link between what a pregnant woman eats and the following factors:

☐   her weight gain

☐   the unborn's weight gain

☐   the infant's growth

☐   the infant's mental capacity

☐   the infant's physical performance

Thus, a well-balanced diet is essential. For cells to grow normally, they need proteins, fats, carbohydrates, minerals, and vitamins. Diets rich in nutrients include all these, 5-5. Diets for pregnant and nursing mothers provide more calcium, iron, folic acid, and protein than diets for nonpregnant women.

1

2

3

4

Basic Daily Diet for Pregnant Women

Food Group	Number of Servings	Typical Servings	Special Notes
Bread Group	9	1 slice bread 1 biscuit, muffin, or roll 1 ounce ready-to-eat cereal 1/2 to 3/4 cup cooked cereal, grits, rice, or pasta	Look for whole grain or enriched breads and cereals.
Vegetable Group	4	1/2 cup vegetable, cooked, or chopped, raw 1 cup of raw, leafy vegetables 3/4 cup vegetable juice	Eat at least one good source of vitamin A and vitamin C daily. Good sources of vitamin A include dark green and deep yellow vegetables and fruits, such as spinach, carrots, sweet potatoes, and cantaloupe. Good sources of vitamin C include citrus fruits, tomatoes, strawberries, broccoli, and brussels sprouts.
Fruit Group	3	1/2 cup fruit 3/4 cup juice 1/2 large grapefruit 1 medium fruit (apple, orange, banana) 1/2 cup chopped, cooked, or canned fruit	

Milk Group	3	1 cup whole or skim milk
		To equal the calcium content of 1 cup of milk it would take
		   1 cup plain yogurt
		   3-inch cube Cheddar cheese
		   1 1/2 slices American processed cheese
		   2 cups cottage cheese
		   1 3/4 cups ice cream
			Remember that 1 3/4 cups of ice cream have the same amount of calcium as 1 cup of milk, but the ice cream has many more calories.

Meat Group	6 ounces	2-3 ounces of cooked, lean meat, poultry, or fish
		The following count as 1 ounce of lean meat:
		   1/2 cup cooked dry beans
		   1 egg
		   2 tablespoons peanut butter
			Eat a variety of protein foods from both animal and vegetable sources.

5-5 Pregnant women should consult their doctors about diets suited to their special needs. The Food Guide Pyramid shows the number of servings a person needs to eat a day from each group.

1—Resource: Menu for a Mother-to-Be, SAG.

2—Note: Remember that skim milk has the same amount of calcium as whole milk, but it has fewer calories. Yogurt also is an excellent source of calcium.

Food Guide Pyramid

A Guide to Daily Food Choices

Fats, Oils, and Sweets
USE SPARINGLY

Milk, Yogurt, and Cheese Group
2-3 SERVINGS

Meat, Poultry, Fish, Dry Beans, Eggs, and Nuts Group
2-3 SERVINGS

Vegetable Group
3-5 SERVINGS

Fruit Group
2-4 SERVINGS

Bread, Cereal, Rice, and Pasta Group
6-11 SERVINGS

▶ Weight Gain

Mothers-to-be and their doctors are concerned about weight gain. Experts suggest pregnant women gain between 25 and 35 pounds, depending on the woman's height and nonpregnant weight. To do this, pregnant women need to eat 200 to 300 extra calories per day. Weight gain during pregnancy is not all stored as fat, 5-6.

Doctors carefully watch how much weight pregnant women gain. They do not want them to

1—*Discuss:* Why do doctors watch how much weight pregnant women gain?

1

Weight Gained During Pregnancy	
Portion of Added Weight	Weight Gain in Pounds
Baby	7.5
Uterus	2.0
Placenta	1.5
Amniotic fluid	2.0
Increased maternal blood volume	3.5
Increased maternal breast mass	1.5
Increased maternal stored fat and protein	4.0
Increased maternal fluid retention	4.0
Total weight gain = 26.0	

5-6   Pregnancy adds to normal weight.

gain too much. This puts extra strain on the heart and makes the woman uncomfortable. Doctors also watch for sudden weight gain and unusual swelling. These conditions are serious and require prompt medical attention.

A woman should gain a healthy amount of weight during certain times in her pregnancy. The following amounts are common:

☐   From one to three months—about five pounds total.

☐   From four to eight months—about two to three pounds per month.

☐   During the ninth month—about one pound per week.

▶ Hygiene Practices

Women should continue their normal grooming and body care habits during pregnancy. Paying attention to appearance may help the mother-to-be feel better during physical discomfort or emotional stress, 5-7.

Many doctors suggest pregnant women do the following:

☐   Have a dental check-up.

☐   Avoid very cold or very hot baths.

☐   Replace tub baths with showers or sponge baths during the last four to six weeks of pregnancy. (This helps to prevent internal infection. It also helps to prevent possible falls due to the woman's larger body size.)

▶ Rest and Sleep

A mother-to-be needs much rest and sleep. Many doctors advise eight hours of sleep at night. In addition, pregnant women need at least one 15-30 minute rest (with or without sleep) during the day. Most women feel tired during the first few months and last weeks of pregnancy. Exhaustion

5-7   Wearing comfortable and attractive clothing and being carefully groomed helps the mother have a good attitude through pregnancy.

© John Shaw

1—*Enrich:* Determine what problems could result from sudden weight gain and unusual swelling.

2—*Discuss:* Why would these desired gains in weight be designated for each of these three time intervals?

3—*Note:* It is important for a pregnant woman to tell her dentist that she is pregnant before a visit. This keeps the woman from being subjected to X rays that may harm the unborn baby.

is never good, especially in pregnancy. However, a sleepless night is not dangerous. If a woman has problems sleeping, she should never take drugs unless her doctor prescribes them.

▶ Physical Activities and Exercise

Unless advised by her doctor to limit physical activity, a pregnant woman can and should be active. Exercise is always important. It helps keep weight within normal limits, strengthens muscles women use in delivery, increases energy, and relieves tensions.

Many doctors do advise that mothers-to-be avoid contact sports, sports that jolt the pelvic region, and sports that could result in falls. On the other hand, doctors often advise women to walk during pregnancy.

Special exercises are often taught in childbirth classes. These exercises are used to relieve back and leg strain of later pregnancy. They also prepare her muscles for delivery. She can do other special exercises after delivery. They help the uterus contract and strengthen the stretched abdominal muscles.

● Health Hazards to Avoid

Many birth defects can be prevented if the mother protects herself before and during pregnancy. Only about 20 percent of all birth defects are strictly inherited. Most are caused by outside factors, such as diseases, drugs, radiation, and environmental pollutants. There are many hazards that can harm the fetus, 5-8. Experts may add others to the list as research continues.

Many harmful substances enter the mother's body, then pass through the placenta to the baby. Other substances are passed from the mother to the baby during the birth process. Any substance may be harmful if passed to an unborn child at a critical time during growth.

In most cases, the strength of the disease or drug is not as important as when it reaches the baby. For instance, thalidomide is a tranquilizer.

Women in Europe used it in the early l960s to control morning sickness. The drug caused birth defects in babies whose mothers took it. Mothers who took many tablets between the 27th and 40th days of pregnancy had children with birth defects. However, mothers who took just one tablet during that crucial time also had children with birth defects.

▶ Diseases or Illnesses in the Mother

Maternal illnesses may exist prior to pregnancy. They may also develop during pregnancy. Some illnesses have few effects on the fetus, while others affect the baby severely.

▪ Diabetes and High Blood Pressure

A mother with diabetes usually has a large baby that often weighs 10 to 12 pounds at birth. A large baby is a risk to the mother during delivery. In addition, half of these babies will be obese as children.

High blood pressure, called **eclampsia** (formerly called **toxemia),** occurs later in pregnancy. The condition is dangerous because the mother retains fluid and cannot rid her body of the baby's wastes. Doctors watch this condition carefully.

▪ Rubella and Other Childhood Diseases

Rubella (formerly called *German measles)* is a virus that crosses the placenta and affects the baby during the first three months of pregnancy. For the mother, this disease is mild. Infected babies, however, may be born blind and deaf, have a mental disability, or have heart defects.

Doctors are also concerned about chicken pox, mumps, and measles. The only way to protect babies is to prevent mothers from catching these diseases. Mothers should have received vaccinations for all of them, except chicken pox, during childhood. Many adults have a natural immunity to chicken pox, which they developed when they had the disease as a child. (A vaccine for chicken pox called the varicella vaaccine is now available.)

1—*Note:* It is extremely important not to take ANY drugs or medicine during pregnancy. If a pregnant woman becomes ill, she should see her doctor immediately and only take medication the doctor has recommended.

2—*Enrich:* Investigate exercises that are recommended during pregnancy.

1

Effects of Harmful Substances	
Name of Substance	**Possible Effects on Fetus or Newborn**
Drugs	
Hormones used for birth control or treatment of reproductive disorders	Limb malformations
Aspirin	Prolonged labor Bleeding in mother and baby
Tranquilizers	Decreased activity Cleft palate
Narcotics	Delivery complications Reduced growth rate Respiration (breathing) problems Withdrawal symptoms
Drugs given for pain reduction in labor/delivery (especially a general anesthetic)	Respiration problems
Steroids (such as Cortisone)	Cleft palate
Nicotine (tobacco products)	Fetal distress (abnormally high and low heart rate) Low birth weight Spontaneous abortion Stillbirth Death during first few weeks of life Lasting effects like smaller physical size, poor reading skills, and poor school adjustment
Alcoholic beverages	Low birth weight Heart, joint, and eye defects Mild to moderate developmental disabilities Very active (nervous) Stillbirth Lasting effects like smaller physical size and poor development
Tetracycline (antibiotic)	Teeth and bone problems
Sulfa	Liver function problems

Vitamins (excessive)
  K
 	
  D
  B$_6$
	
	Severe anemia with possible brain damage or death
	Circulatory damage
	Convulsions

	(continued)

5-8   These substances are considered harmful to the baby, although any substance could be dangerous.

1—*Resource: Drugs and Diseases in Mothers-to-Be,* SAG.   2—*Note:* Stillbirth refers to the birth of a dead fetus. Explain and discuss in class.

Effects of Harmful Substances (continued)	
Diseases	
Rubella	Cataracts Deafness Heart problems Dental deformities
Diabetes	Increased chance of toxemia Delivery complications due to large baby Stillbirth Spontaneous abortion
Anemia	Anemia
Toxoplasmosis (common infection caused by microscopic worms found in raw meat or in fecal matter, including dust inhaled while dumping kitty litter.)	Developmental disabilities Deafness Blindness
Other Substances	
Radiation (X rays)	Slow growth Developmental disabilities Sterility Possible cancers in later life
Inadequate maternal diet	Developmental disabilities Physical disabilities Lowered resistance to infection
Changes in maternal hormones due to stress (repeated or prolonged)	Spontaneous abortion Delivery complications Irritability

Fifth disease causes dangerous anemia in the unborn any time during pregnancy. **Lyme disease,** spread by the deer tick, can cause heart defects in the unborn and result in premature birth or stillbirth.

Toxoplasmosis is caused by a parasite that can damage an unborn's nervous system. Because the parasite primarily infects cats, pregnant women should avoid contact with cats. They should not garden, be near soil used by cats, or change the cat litter box.

▓ **Sexually Transmitted Diseases (STDs)**
Sexually Transmitted Diseases (STDs) are infectious diseases, transmitted primarily through sexual intercourse. They can cause infections in the blood stream of the mother, then cross the placenta to the unborn. Some STDs cause infections in the mother's reproductive tract that the baby can get during the birth process. All STDs are dangerous to the baby, 5-9. They are a growing problem.

Acquired immunodeficiency syndrome (AIDS) is a disease that attacks the body's immune system. The mother gets it through sexual relations and through blood or other body fluids. Infected mothers can give the virus to their babies. Infected babies generally do not live more than two years. There is about a 30 to 50 percent chance that the baby will get the virus during the birth process. This happens when the umbilical cord separates from the placenta. Scientists continue to work on a cure for AIDS.

2

1—*Enrich:* Research (individually or in groups) the following conditions that cause birth defects: thalidomide; diabetes; high blood pressure; rubella; chicken pox, mumps, and measles; fifth disease; lyme disease; toxoplasmosis. Describe the condition or disease, problems that could occur in the baby, and safe methods used to correct the situation.

2—*Enrich:* Research types of sexually transmitted diseases and AIDS. How can they be prevented? How are they treated during pregnancy? What types of problems do they cause for the mother and baby?

STDs and Their Effects on the Unborn/Newborn		
Syphilis	Contracted by mother through sexual activity. Crosses the placenta beginning in the eighteenth week of pregnancy.	Effects prevented if treated before the sixteenth week. Untreated infection causes deafness, brain damage, skin lesions, bone and facial deformities, and fetal death.
Cytomegalovirus (CMV)	Transmitted by respiratory contact or sexual activity. CMV crosses the placenta.	Fatal for embryo or young fetus. Brain, liver, and blood defects common in surviving fetuses. No treatment or means of prevention.
Herpes Simplex ("genital warts")	Contracted primarily by sexual relations. Transmitted to baby at or shortly before delivery by baby's contact with infected secretions.	Newborns develop skin lesions and brain damage, and 50 percent die. No treatment available. C-sections may prevent contact with secretions.
Gonorrhea	Contracted by sexual relations. Transmitted to baby at or shortly before delivery by baby's contact with reproductive tract infection.	Blindness if untreated. Treatment includes placing silver nitrate in the infant's eyes and treating baby with antibiotics.
Chlamydia	Transmitted through sexual relations. (Twice as common as gonorrhea.) Women rarely experience symptoms. May lead to sterility.	Miscarriage, low birth weight, and death of infants due to lung disorders.
Acquired Immunodeficiency Syndrome (AIDS)	Acquired through sexual relations and blood or other body fluids. Infected mothers transmit the virus in 30 to 50 percent of the births. (Women who are pregnant usually have HIV only with full-blown AIDS following pregnancy.)	Death of child within two years. Treatment of symptoms. No cure.

5-9   STDs have serious effects on the unborn.

▶ Drugs

The term "drugs" includes medications, alcohol, nicotine (from cigarettes), and illegal drugs. All of these drugs cross the placenta and reach the baby. Some drugs harm the baby in the early months of pregnancy, and many harm the baby throughout pregnancy. Some drugs, such as aspirin, are more hazardous near delivery.

1—*Note:* Due to lack of or minimal symptoms, many cases of chlamydia go undetected.

Medication

People sometimes say that women never should take drugs during pregnancy. A woman's doctor should carefully monitor any drugs she takes. If a woman is severely ill, her doctor must weigh the risks of taking drugs against their benefits for the mother. Most doctors prescribe some pain killers during delivery.

2—*Discuss:* List over-the-counter drugs that students, peers, or family members regularly use. What alternatives can a pregnant woman safely use?

Over-the-counter drugs are more common than prescribed drugs. One nationwide study showed that women take at least four drugs during pregnancy, not including vitamins. Women should discuss all medications with their doctors.

Alcohol

Doctors advise women not to drink alcohol during pregnancy. Any alcoholic drink, whether beer, wine, or hard liquor, can harm the baby. Taking even one drink may cause the baby to be abnormal.

Almost three babies in every 1,000 are born with a condition called **fetal alcohol syndrome (FAS).** This happens when mothers drink heavily or excessively during their pregnancies. FAS babies are shorter and weigh less than other babies. Their growth and development is slow. Their small heads and unusual facial features are distinctive. They may also have heart defects, poor motor development, and developmental disabilities. **Fetal alcohol effect (FAE),** a term used to describe less severe damage, causes children to have serious learning problems.

Nicotine

When a pregnant woman smokes, her baby feels the effects. Babies of smokers are usually smaller than average or premature. Nicotine raises the mother's heart rate, blood pressure, and breathing rate and reduces the flow of blood. While a mother is smoking, the baby's oxygen is greatly reduced. Babies need oxygen as they grow, especially during the prenatal period. Smoking, particularly after 16 weeks, is extremely risky.

Smoking also causes the baby's brain to develop abnormally. This makes these children have learning problems in school. It is also linked to children's hyperactivity and poor attention spans. Smoking increases a woman's chance to miscarry. Secondhand smoke affects an unborn baby's health in similar ways.

Illegal Drugs

Illegal drugs, such as cocaine, crack, heroin, and marijuana, all cross the placenta quickly and reach the baby. If a woman is hooked on drugs, chances are her baby is, too. In large urban areas, up to 10 percent of all babies born have been exposed to cocaine before birth.

Pregnant women who use drugs often have low-birthweight and premature babies. One of the greatest problems for these babies happens after they are born. Because they no longer are receiving the drugs (as they cross the placenta), they actually go through withdrawal. This causes the baby great stress. Symptoms of the baby's withdrawal include a high-pitched cry, shaking, poor feeding, and fever.

Babies affected by cocaine grow slowly. They may have malformed urinary and intestinal tracts and poor attention spans. These babies' behaviors worsen by the first month rather than improve.

Pregnant women who heavily use illegal drugs often neglect their own health. In many cases, these women also eat poorly, smoke, or abuse alcohol. Some never see a doctor during pregnancy. For these reasons, babies whose mothers use drugs have a slim chance of living a healthy life.

▶ Radiation Exposure

X rays are not too dangerous to the fetus if several precautions are taken. To be safe, X rays must be low in intensity, taken away from the fetus, and done only when the lower abdomen is protected by a safety drape. X rays aimed toward the fetus increase the likelihood of childhood cancer.

▶ Environmental Pollution

Parents should determine whether their home and workplace are safe. Lead, chemicals, pesticides, and herbicides all pose risks to the unborn baby. Pregnant women should check to be sure that their environments do not harm their babies.

1—*Enrich:* Research fetal alcohol syndrome and fetal alcohol effect. Why are these serious problems today?

2—*Activity:* Design a public service announcement that promotes healthy habits during pregnancy. Critique these in class. Make corrections and submit them to local television and radio stations for viewing or airing.

3—*Enrich:* Do research on radiation exposure and environmental pollution. Present information to the class.

4—*Resource: Mothers-to-Be Affect the Health of Their Unborns,* SAG.

Birth Defects

A ***birth defect*** is a physical or biochemical defect that is present at birth and may be inherited or caused by environmental factors. Birth defects and diseases occur with varying degrees of severity. Several birth defects and diseases are described in 5-10.

Spontaneous Abortion

A ***spontaneous abortion*** is the ***expulsion*** (or forcing out) of the baby from the mother's body before it can survive. A spontaneous abortion can be due to natural causes. It can also happen if a woman is in an accident. The common term for spontaneous abortion is *miscarriage*. *Induced abortions* are planned abortions caused by an outside factor (saline solution or suction).

5-10   Birth defects have various symptoms, causes, and treatments.

Birth Defects and Diseases			
Defect/Disease	**Symptoms**	**Cause**	**Treatment**
Cleft lip/palate	Noticeable at birth. A cleft lip occurs when the two sides of the upper lip fail to grow together properly. A cleft palate occurs when an opening remains in the roof of the mouth. This creates problems in breathing, talking, hearing, and eating.	Variable; often caused by a number of factors working together.	Corrective surgery and speech therapy.
Cystic fibrosis	A chemical failure affects lungs and pancreas. Thick sticky mucus forms in the lungs, causing breathing problems. Reduced amounts of digestive juices cause poor digestion of food. An excess amount of salt is excreted in perspiration.	Recessive gene.	Physical therapy, synthetic digestive enzymes, salt tablets, and antibodies can lessen the effect of the symptoms. However, there is no known cure. These people usually have shorter-than-normal life spans because they are highly susceptible to respiratory diseases.
Diabetes	Metabolic disorders cause high blood sugar. The patient feels, thirsty, hungry, and weak and usually loses weight.	A number of factors working together.	The disease can be controlled by insulin injections and careful diet and exercise. It cannot be cured.
Down syndrome	Distinct physical features are evident. Slanting eyes; large, misshapen forehead; oversized tongue; single crease across palm of each hand; and varying degrees of mental retardation are typical.	Chromosome abnormality. More likely to occur when mother is over age 35.	Special education. Life span may be nearly normal.

(continued)

1—*Enrich:* Present information about the three types of induced abortions and abortion alternatives.

2—*Enrich:* Ask a speaker to talk about the types of induced abortions.

Birth Defects and Diseases (continued)			
Defect/Disease	**Symptoms**	**Cause**	**Treatment**
Huntington's chorea	The brain and central nervous system gradually deteriorate when the person is between 30 and 40 years old. This causes involuntary jerking, loss of mental abilities, insanity, depression, and finally death.	Dominant gene	None.
Hydrocephalus	Extra fluid is trapped in the brain. The person's head is larger than normal.	A number of factors working together.	Surgical removal of excess fluid. Without treatment, children rarely survive.
Muscular dystrophy	A group of disorders which damage muscles. They cause progressive weakness and finally death.	Often sex-linked.	There is no cure, but therapy and braces offer some relief.
Phenylketonuria (PKU)	An enzyme defieiency makes the person unable to digest a certain amino acid. The baby appears normal at birth, but slowly develops mental retardation because the amino acid builds up in the body and causes brain damage.	Recessive gene.	A carefully prescribed diet that balances the enzyme deficiency. The effects of the disease can usually be avoided if treatment begins within the first six weeks of birth.
Sickle-cell anemia	Red blood cells are sickle-shaped rather than round. They cannot carry oxygen efficiently throughout the body. People become pale, tired, and short of breath. They have occasional pains and low resistance to infection. Their life span is often shorter than normal.	Recessive gene.	There is no cure. Various treatments relieve some symptoms, and blood transfusions are needed occasionally.
Spina bifida	A condition that causes partial paralysis due to an incompletely formed spinal cord.	Heredity and environmental factors.	Corrective surgery and physical therapy.
Tay-Sachs Disease	A lack of a specific chemical in the blood resulting in an inabilitiy to process and use fats. Leads to severe brain damage and death, often by the age of two or three.	Recessive gene.	None.

Miscarriages end about one third of all pregnancies. Many complications in the mother can cause a miscarriage. For instance, the baby may be developing in the fallopian tube instead of the uterus. Sometimes the placenta is not working properly or detaches from the wall of the uterus. Major falls and car accidents may cause a woman to miscarry, also.

Miscarriages may occur more frequently with certain diseases as well as when the mother smokes, drinks, or uses drugs. Miscarriages frequently occur for unknown reasons. Women who miscarry for reasons other than accidents are at high risk to miscarry again. However, many women who miscarry go on to have successful pregnancies.

● Monitoring the Baby's Development

Monitoring the baby helps doctors determine the baby's health and exact age. Monitoring also indicates the size and sex of the baby. It will show if there is one or more than one baby in the mother's uterus. It will also indicate the baby's position before delivery.

▶ Ultrasound

One of the first tests to be developed was the ultrasound. The **ultrasound** is a test in which sound waves bounce off the fetus to produce an image of the fetus inside the womb. The picture of the fetus the ultrasound produces is called a **sonogram.**

The technician holds a *transducer* over the mother's abdomen. The transducer emits sound waves. The waves are deflected or absorbed at different rates, depending on whether they hit bone, organ tissue, blood, or water. These differences are changed into electrical impulses. This produces a visual image of the fetus on a television screen, 5-11.

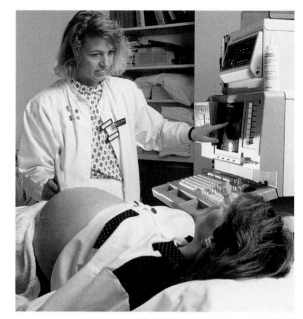

"Child Development: Prenatal to Birth," Meridian Education Corp.

5-11 An ultrasound is a safe way for obstetricians to check on fetal health.

Because ultrasounds are considered safe, they are used routinely. Ultrasounds provide information much like X rays but without radiation risks.

Chorionic Villus Sampling

Chorionic villus sampling (CVS) is a procedure for finding abnormalities in the unborn by testing a small sample of the chorion, which later develops into the placenta. CVS is used between the eighth and 12th weeks of pregnancy. Serious problems can thus be detected early in the pregnancy.

A hollow tube is inserted through the vagina into the uterus and guided to the chorion (a tissue layer surrounding the unborn). Chorionic villi projections from the chorion transport nutrients to, and wastes from, the unborn. A small section of the villi is painlessly suctioned off and then analyzed for birth defects. CVS has a slight risk of infection which can result in a miscarriage.

1—*Note:* This is called a tubal pregnancy.

2—*Reflect:* What emotions might a miscarriage cause you to experience? What resources could help you?

▶ Amniocentesis

Amniocentesis is a prenatal test used to check for the presence of over 100 birth defects. Usually it checks for Down syndrome, Tay-Sachs disease, and sickle-cell anemia.

To perform the test, a medical specialist inserts a needle through the abdominal wall into the uterus. Ultrasound is done at the same time to position the needle. The specialist draws a small amount of fluid from the amniotic sac.

Why does this fluid give so much information? Cells cast off by the fetus float in the fluid. These cells are cultivated in a lab for three to five weeks and are then checked for birth defects.

Amniocentesis cannot be done until the fetus is 14 to 16 weeks old. At that time there is enough fluid. Due to the lab time required, the woman will be 20 to 21 weeks pregnant when she learns the results.

Amniocentesis is a rather safe procedure. In less than one percent of the cases there is risk to the fetus. Miscarriages or premature births may also occur. Because there are some risks, amniocentesis is not a routine procedure.

● The Role of the Family

Pregnancy should be a family affair. Studies show that fathers-to-be who become involved with pregnancy and childbirth later become more involved in rearing their children. Children enjoy preparing for the new arrival. Children who help prepare for the new baby are not as jealous of a new sister or brother.

▶ Family Involvement

Long ago, when mothers delivered their babies at home, some fathers became involved. However, women relatives and friends usually helped the new mother. When hospital deliveries became common, fathers were further detached from the birthing process. It was the father's duty to call the doctor and bring his wife to the hospital. Once in the hospital, he was sent to the "pacing room" to pace the floor, nap, compare notes with other fathers, and watch the clock. When the baby was born, the father handed out cigars and smiled at his baby through the nursery window.

Today's Fathers-to-Be

Today, many fathers-to-be are taking a more active role during pregnancy and delivery. Their role changes throughout the pregnancy and birth. During the first few months, many mothers are concerned about their health and that of their babies. Husbands need to reassure their wives. Husbands can also help select a doctor and decide other aspects about delivery.

The middle part of pregnancy is often the most pleasant for the entire family. Mothers-to-be often feel their best. Husbands and family members are more aware of the baby because they can see the mother's stomach grow. They can also feel the baby move. The couple may decorate a nursery and gather items needed for the baby. At this time, young children are often told about the baby. Parents should include them in baby preparations as much as possible.

The final months are an exciting and trying period. Mothers-to-be are often concerned about their health and safety in delivery. They may also feel more tired as the due date approaches. Husbands should support their wives. Couples often become educated about childbirth by reading books and attending classes, 5-12.

Today, more than 50 percent of fathers see their babies being born. When fathers are involved in childbirth, there are many benefits. Some research shows that it is good for mothers to have helpers during labor. (***Labor*** is the process that moves the baby out of the mother's body.) Mothers with helpers have shorter and more problem-free labors. This is because helpers have a calming effect on the mothers. Anxiety changes the blood chemistry. This decreases contractions and causes a longer labor. These changes in the blood chemistry also decrease the flow of blood to the baby, which could harm the child. Husbands who help with labor and delivery often have closer relationships with their children.

1—*Enrich:* Research Down syndrome, Tay-Sacks disease, and sickle-cell anemia. Report symptoms associated with each disease and how amniocentesis is used to detect each.

2—*Activity:* Interview several people who are parents and grandparents to find out how fathers were involved in delivery. Report findings to the class.

3—*Discuss:* What are some other ways to involve the father and plan for the baby together?

4—*Resource: The Role of the Father-to-Be in Pregnancy,* SAG.

© John Shaw

5-12 Husbands can support their wives through pregnancy by attending childbirth classes.

▶ Family Decisions Concerning Childbirth

Parents have many decisions to make before the baby is born. They must choose where the birth will take place (a hospital or at home). Parents also need to choose a method of delivering the baby. The delivery method should mainly depend on the condition of the mother and baby. Parents should base their choices on their doctor's advice as well as their own preferences.

Home or Hospital Delivery

Parents-to-be may choose between home and hospital deliveries. Home deliveries were the norm 50 years ago. Hospital deliveries became more common because women wanted relief from pain and safer conditions, which hospitals provided.

Doctors have taken a stand against home births. They pose too much risk to the mother and baby in cases of emergency. About 10 to 15 percent of deliveries need special medical help. The infant death rate is higher for home births than for hospital births.

Those who favor home births believe parents should have more control over their children's births. To them, hospital deliveries tend to treat childbirth as an illness rather than a natural process. They think hospitals lack family warmth and support. To make home births safer, some parents use **certified nurse midwives (CNM)**. These nurses have special training in delivering babies during normal pregnancies. CNMs do not handle high-risk pregnancies. Many CNMs work out of hospitals where they can call for help if an emergency arises.

More hospitals are offering parents the choice of a home-like birthing room rather than a standard delivery room. The **birthing room** is furnished like a bedroom. It is used for both labor and delivery. Family members and/or a few close friends stay with the mother-to-be throughout labor and delivery. In most hospitals, a nurse attends the labor. The nurse calls a doctor just before delivery. The birthing room provides a home-like setting with family support and hospital safety.

Choosing a Method of Delivery

Parents may choose between many methods of delivery. All methods try to make labor and delivery safer and more comfortable for the mother and baby. Labor is hard work. It requires the use of many muscles. Some of these muscles are seldom used except during labor. Pain is a part of labor, but if muscles are tense, the mother has even more pain.

Some mothers hope to be totally awake and alert through delivery. They cope with pain by using breathing and relaxation techniques. Other mothers prefer some drugs to help them cope with pain. A few mothers ask to be asleep through delivery.

Using drugs to relieve pain was common from the mid 1800s through the mid 1900s. Since then, doctors have moved away from using drugs. Most doctors like the mother to stay awake and alert through delivery. An awake mother can help bring the baby into the world. Also, any drugs used can cross the placenta and affect the baby. Drugs used to put the mother to sleep can make the baby sluggish.

Natural Childbirth. One method of delivery without drugs is called **natural childbirth.** This method was developed in the 1930s by Dr. Grantly Dick-Read, an English physician.

Dr. Dick-Read questioned the regular use of drugs when one of his patients chose not to use them. The woman felt little pain during labor. The case made Dr. Dick-Read decide that part of the pain from labor was due to fear.

In natural childbirth, the woman has the birth process explained to her so that she knows what to expect. She is also trained to breathe and relax in a way that helps the birth process. With this training, the woman can deliver without drugs. The father usually plays an active role in prenatal study and delivery with this method.

Lamaze Method. Another method similar to natural childbirth is called the **Lamaze method.** It is named for Dr. Fernand Lamaze, the French doctor who made the approach popular. The idea behind the Lamaze method is that women are conditioned to fear childbirth. In Lamaze training, the mother is taught to focus on something other than pain, like an injured athlete who thinks about the competition rather than a painful injury.

In this type of delivery, the mother uses breathing patterns (such as deep breathing or panting) to keep her mind off the pain. The pregnant woman and her "coach," usually the father, attend Lamaze preparation classes. The classes help prepare her mentally and physically, using instruction and practice. The following features describe the Lamaze method:

☐ The woman's coach—the father or another person—learns the breathing patterns and helps the mother-to-be through labor. The doctor usually delivers the baby.

☐ The woman receives medication when necessary. Not all women can deliver without drugs, even when they are informed about childbirth. Women usually need drugs when there are complications. A woman may also use drugs if she becomes too afraid.

☐ Training in childbirth is given in small classes—usually no more than 10 women and their coaches. Classes are held weekly for 8 to 12 weeks before the delivery date. The instructor provides

factual information about childbirth. He or she teaches physical exercises to tone the body for delivery. The instructor also teaches breathing patterns to use in labor and delivery and encourages couples to talk about their feelings.

When a father is not able to share in the birth of his baby, a mother using the Lamaze method must choose someone else as a birth attendant. These mothers often choose other family members or close friends. Some of the factors to consider when choosing a birth attendant include:

☐ Someone with whom the mother has a good relationship. The mother must feel comfortable both physically and emotionally with the attendant.

☐ A person who will be available at the time of the birth and who can complete the entire course of training.

☐ A person who is emotionally prepared to cope with the process of delivery. For example, a grandmother, an aunt, or an older friend who has had children may be better able to handle the situation than a teenage sister.

Many parents who have used this approach say that childbirth was both comfortable and rewarding. Mothers were more alert and felt better without using many drugs. There was also no concern about the effects of drugs on the baby. Through this method, the mother and father shared the experience. Both parents were present and ready to welcome their newborn, 5-13.

Leboyer Method. Frederick Leboyer, a French doctor, developed the **Leboyer method** of delivery. This method focuses on the comfort of the baby during delivery as well as the safety of the baby and mother. The Leboyer method assumes that delivery is painful for the baby as well as the mother. This method does not use bright delivery room lights. It also does not place the newborn on a hard, flat table to be weighed and measured. These techniques are thought to add to the baby's discomfort.

1—*Reflect:* Do you think using drugs during delivery would affect the happiness associated with the birth?

2—*Activity:* Interview young parents about Lamaze classes. Did they attend? Who attended? What did they learn each week? Was it helpful during the delivery? Who was the coach? Did he or she find the training was beneficial?

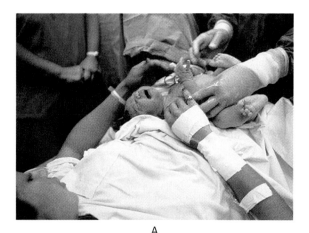

A

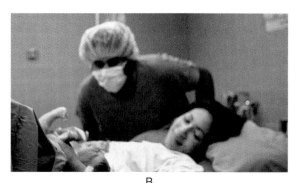

B

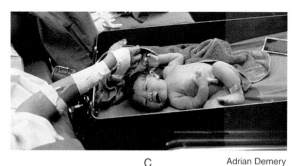

C   Adrian Demery

5-13 Childbirth is a shared experience for this family. As the awake mother holds her newborn (A), the father proudly shares his daughter's birth (B), and the baby gazes at her parents (C).

The Leboyer method calls for the lights in the delivery room to be cut to the minimum needed for delivery. Noise is also low, because everyone in the delivery room talks in quiet tones. The doctor supports the baby after the head appears.

After birth, the baby rests on the mother's body as she cuddles her newborn. The umbilical cord is cut after it stops functioning. Thus, the baby begins breathing on his or her own. A few minutes after birth the baby is lowered into water that has been heated to near body temperature. The supported baby can kick and move about in a way similar to that before birth. Finally, the baby is dressed and wrapped in a warm blanket.

Of course, babies can't say how they feel. Certainly, though, the environment before and after birth is different. Some studies show that babies delivered using this method are less fussy than babies delivered using standard methods. The Leboyer method may also have a calming effect on the mother.

● Time to Be Born

The months of waiting and excitement during pregnancy come to an end sooner than expected. Friends and relatives often give celebrations like baby showers. Parents may put the final touches on the nursery. Boy and girl names are often chosen. If parents are planning a hospital delivery, they pack a suitcase for the hospital. Arrangements with employers are made. Babysitters are secured for young children.

Final natural preparations are taking place, too. The mother's body is making hormonal changes needed for labor to begin. The baby is moving into position for birth. The doctor checks these preparations and keeps the parents informed.

Labor takes most parents by surprise. It may begin any time and any place—even in the middle of sleep. The first contractions are usually so mild that many parents still wonder if the time has really come. Once begun, labor and delivery are completed within hours. Following childbirth, there is a period of readjustment for the mother to a nonpregnant condition. The father (and other children) also must adjust to changes the new baby brings.

1

2

1—Reflect: How would this change if the father were not part of the birth experience or family?

2—Enrich: Consult an encyclopedia for pictures and additional information about the Leboyer method.

3—Resource: Choices for Delivery, SAG.

▶ The Last Weeks of Pregnancy

Birth occurs about 270 days after conception. How does this baby enter the world? A series of contractions in the uterine muscles move the baby out of the mother's body. These contractions are involuntary. In other words, the mother cannot make these contractions happen. Natural signals from the body control when they begin, how long they last, and how strong they are. Contractions happen in intervals. They are separated by periods of time that allow the mother's muscles to relax.

▪ Contractions

The nature of contractions changes throughout labor. In early labor, contractions may last about 30 seconds. Gradually, their length increases to 1 minute. The strength of the contractions increases until the baby is born. The intervals of relaxation begin at 15 to 20 minutes and decrease to about 2 minutes.

During the last few weeks of pregnancy, especially for a first baby, the mother experiences *lightening.* Lightening is a change in the baby's position. The uterus settles downward and forward, and the baby descends lower into the pelvis. In most cases, the baby's body rotates so the head is toward the birth canal. In about two percent of the cases, the baby gets into a buttocks-first position. This is called *breech birth* position. When lightening happens, the mother is able to breathe easier. However, she may have leg cramps and may need to urinate more often due to the increased pressure on her bladder.

Because the mother's body is preparing for labor during lightening, the mother may have a few irregular contractions. These irregular contractions are known as *false labor.* The contractions are real, but true labor has not begun. Some parents-to-be have gone to the hospital only to find out that the contractions were false labor. (Most doctors prefer the mother go to the hospital if she is not sure. They don't want a mother who planned a hospital delivery to end up having the baby at home.) Mothers should carefully time the intervals between several contractions to tell whether she is really in labor.

▪ Other Signs of Labor

Besides regular contractions, there are several other signs of the coming labor. One sign is that the mother may feel a burst of energy due to increased adrenaline. Mothers shouldn't use the energy to do strenuous tasks. They should save the energy for labor.

Another sign is that the mucous plug in the cervix will become loose. The small amount of blood in the mucous is called *the show.* It means labor should happen within 24 hours.

A third sign is that part of the amniotic sac (sometimes called the *bag of waters)* may break before labor begins. (Often the sac breaks after labor begins.) If the mucous plug becomes dislodged or the amniotic sac breaks, the mother should not bathe. Once contractions begin, the mother should not eat food or drink liquids.

▶ Stages of Labor

In medical terms, labor is divided into these three stages: (1) *dilation,* or opening, of the cervix; (2) expulsion, or birth of the baby; and (3) expulsion of the placenta, 5-14.

▪ Stage One—Dilation of the Cervix

In the early part of labor, contractions come every 15 or 20 minutes and last about 30 seconds. The uterus narrows. This straightens the baby's body and presses the baby's head (or buttocks) against the cervix. As the baby pushes against the cervix, the cervix flattens and opens (dilates).

If the amniotic sac has not broken, the doctor will break it when the cervix has dilated four inches. The fluid in the sac lubricates the birth canal. When the cervix has opened 4 1/2 to 5 inches in width, the first stage of labor ends. The length of time varies a great deal, but the average length of labor in the first stage for first pregnancies is eight hours.

▪ Stage Two—Expulsion of the Baby

During the expulsion stage, the baby's head enters the birth canal. The mother's muscles push to move the baby down. The walls of the upper part of the birth canal are elastic.

2

1—*Enrich:* Show pictures of the normal position, breech birth position, and transverse birth position. Discuss why breech and transverse positions are difficult.

2—*Activity:* How does a pregnant woman know she's in labor? Interview a mother about her signs of labor.

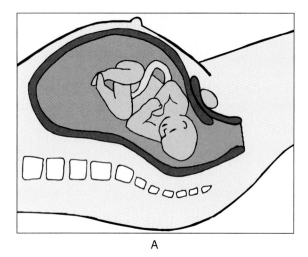

A

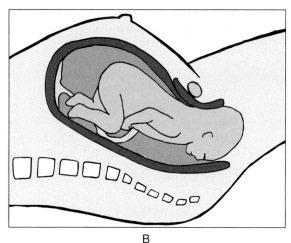

B

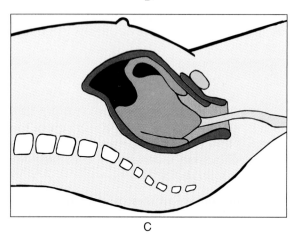

C

5-14   The three stages of labor are (A), the dilation of the cervix, (B) the birth of the baby, and (C) the expulsion of the placenta.

1—*Activity:* Provide a ruler to show students the width of 4¹/₂ to 5 inches so they can understand the need for the epi-siotomy. Compare the size of a newborn to the width of the opening.

2—*Resource: Stages of Labor*, SAG.

However, the arrangement of muscles in the lower part of the canal causes resistance. The resistance causes the mother pain. Many doctors inject the mother with medication to prevent pain in the lower part of the canal. They may also have the mother use natural techniques, such as breathing, to reduce pain. Often, an incision (called an *episiotomy)* is made from the vagina to the anus to prevent tearing. After delivery, doctors close the incision.

The baby changes position during birth. The baby faces downward as the head emerges. Then the head rotates to the side, and the shoulders, abdomen, and legs follow. The remaining fluid from the amniotic sac is expelled. The doctor helps the baby by holding and turning the baby as needed. The doctor uses instruments to suck out fluid from the baby's mouth and helps the baby take his or her first breath.

The second stage ends when the baby is free of the mother's body. This stage usually lasts from 30 to 90 minutes. The doctor cuts the umbilical cord before the third stage begins.

Stage Three—Expulsion of the Placenta

About 20 minutes after birth, the mother has a few irregular contractions. These cause the placenta to completely detach from the uterus and descend. The placenta and fetal membrane that are expelled following the birth of a baby are called the *afterbirth.* As the third stage ends, mothers feel a little cold and physically tired. They also feel emotionally relieved and overjoyed.

▶ Instrument Methods of Birth

Sometimes the unborn baby appears to be in danger due to a prolonged labor, too much pressure on the head, or lack of oxygen. The doctor may use forceps to speed up the birth. *Forceps* are steel tongs that fit the shape of a baby's head. Doctors use them to grip the baby's head and gently pull or turn the baby.

▶ Cesarean Births

In some cases, the traditional methods of delivery would be unsafe or unwise. About 25 percent of children born in the United States are born by the cesarean section (or C-section) method. In the **cesarean section,** the mother's abdomen and uterus are surgically opened and the baby is removed. The incisions are then closed as with any other surgery. (The method was named for Emperor Julius Caesar who, it has been incorrectly said, was born that way.) Doctors use C-section deliveries for the following reasons:

- ☐ The mother's pelvis is small or not shaped correctly for an easy birth.
- ☐ The baby or the mother are at medical risk.
- ☐ The baby's head is large.
- ☐ Contractions are weak or absent.
- ☐ The baby is in an incorrect position for birth.
- ☐ The doctor feels that previous cesarean scar(s) could rupture during labor (one cesarean birth does not mean that all later births must be C-sections, too).

Some couples have planned for a Lamaze method of delivery but found that a C-section was necessary. To help these couples share the childbirth experience, some hospitals use drugs that permit the mother to be awake but feel no pain during the surgery. They allow the father in the room. These couples are able to experience the same benefits and joys as couples who used the Lamaze method.

● Hospital Care

Nurses care for babies in nurseries. These nurses are on duty at all times. The contact the mother is allowed to have with her baby varies. Some hospitals hire a person who is not a nurse to rock and help feed the babies in the nursery. The father (who must wear a hospital gown) is often encouraged to be with the mother and baby in the mother's room. Other family members may be allowed to see the baby through the nursery windows during certain hours. Brothers and sisters under 12 years of age may not be able to see the baby until the mother and baby are home. Jealousy over the new baby may be partly

caused by not being a part of the baby's first days. For this reason, more hospitals are beginning to allow sibling visits, 5-15.

2

▶ Rooming-In

Some hospitals provide a **rooming-in** arrangement. If the baby is healthy, he or she is placed in a bassinet in the room with the mother. Sometimes the father stays in the room, too. Nurses help the parents learn to feed, change, clean, dress, and soothe the baby. Nurses encourage parents to take over these responsibilities before leaving the hospital. (If the mother needs extra rest, the nurse will care for the baby.)

3

Rooming-in helps parents develop a warm feeling for their new baby. This arrangement offers the best of both home and hospital care for the baby and parents.

● Bonding

Bonding, or developing an attachment (feeling of affection), is important for parents and

5-15   Many hospitals encourage the whole family to spend time together with the new baby.

© John Shaw

1—*Activity:* Interview a young mother who has had a C-section. Why was this necessary? Has the woman had any normal deliveries or other C-sections? Was the woman awake during delivery? Was recovery difficult?

2—*Discuss:* What are some other ways to minimize jealousy of older siblings?

3—*Discuss:* What are some advantages and disadvantages of rooming-in? Would you choose this method if your insurance provided coverage? Why or why not?

their baby. The first hour after birth is perhaps the most sensitive bonding time. The newborn will watch, hear, and respond to the body movements, voice, and touch of the mother and father. Bonding continues during the next few weeks as mothers and fathers become more and more attached to their babies, 5-16 and 5-17.

Bonding helps both infants and parents, 5-18. Because bonding is so helpful, many hospitals have changed their rules regarding premature or ill infants. These new policies allow mothers and fathers to visit the intensive care nursery and feed, touch, talk, and sing to babies.

Postnatal Maternal Care

Postnatal care is the care the mother receives during the six to eight weeks following the birth of her baby. (The medical term for postnatal care is *postpartum care.*) The six- to

© John Shaw

5-17   Fathers need to bond with their newborns, too.

5-16   Bonding occurs as a mother cuddles and looks at her newborn.

© John Shaw

1—*Reflect:* Do you think as much bonding occurs if an infant is adopted three to four days after birth?

5-18   Bonding helps both infants and parents. It is the first step toward a healthy parent-child relationship.

Benefits of Bonding
To Infant
☐ increased chance of survival ☐ better weight gain ☐ less crying, more smiles and laughter ☐ fewer infections ☐ possibly higher IQ ☐ better language development
To Parents
☐ less incidence of child abuse ☐ faster recovery from delivery ☐ longer breast-feeding ☐ more self-confidence as a parent ☐ less "depression" after delivery

eight-week period is the time when the mother's body returns to its prepregnancy state. For nursing mothers, the complete return to the prepregnancy state requires more time.

The first hour after birth is a critical time for restoring body stability. Vital signs (pulse, respiration, and other body functions) are measured every few minutes just as they are following surgery. Doctors pay special attention to make sure the uterus contracts properly.

In order to regain their strength and avoid health problems, women are encouraged to get out of bed within 24 hours of delivery. Many women walk much sooner.

After a few days, certain exercises, done with the doctor's approval, help tone the abdominal muscles. These exercises are done slowly and gradually for safety and best results. Most mothers also want to lose some of the extra weight from pregnancy. On the average, a woman loses 11 pounds during birth and another 7 pounds during the few weeks after birth. The remaining weight must be lost through diet and/or exercise.

A woman should check with her doctor about dieting. A well-balanced diet is essential for everyone, especially a new mother as her body returns to normal. For nursing mothers, the final pounds are usually shed after weaning.

Rest is also important. For a couple of days after delivery, many mothers seem to need a great deal of sleep. Doctors often advise a day nap and 8 to 10 hours of sleep at night. New mothers can get some needed rest by planning ways to lessen their workload. A mother can take the following timesaving steps:

☐ Ask a friend to watch the baby so the mother can take a nap.

☐ Put away nonessential items that add to housekeeping time.

☐ Prepare and freeze meals before baby comes to use after the baby is born.

☐ Use disposable diapers, plates, and cups for a few days or weeks.

If the mother must return to work before the end of the postnatal period, she should get special guidance from nurses and doctors. The key to complete recovery, whether the mother is at home or on the job, is to go slow with activity. Too much activity slows the reversal process.

▶ Postpartum Blues

Closely linked to physical changes are emotional changes. Emotional changes may be due to changes in the hormones. Some women experience a down feeling within a few days after birth. This feeling is called **postpartum blues.** It is caused by hormonal changes that began at conception. Hormone levels do not return to normal until 3 to 10 weeks after delivery, and later for nursing mothers.

The blues may also happen because of the around-the-clock care a new baby requires. After birth, the mother tires quickly. She may feel overwhelmed with the work involved in caring for the baby.

The blues usually pass quickly. The following suggestions seem to help most new mothers:

☐ Get enough rest.

☐ Improve appearance. She may try new cosmetics, get an easy-care hair style, or buy new clothes.

☐ Develop some outside interests. Plan an evening out without the baby, or buy a new book or magazine.

☐ Talk to others who have had babies.

Doctors are concerned about their patients' emotional well-being and physical health. Mothers who have intense or prolonged postpartum blues should discuss the problem with a doctor.

By the third month, most women are in good shape. No two women, however, are alike. A new mother should be patient with her body and give it all the time needed after having the baby.

3

4

Summary

As soon as the signs of pregnancy are detected, a woman should seek medical care. The health of the baby depends on the health of the mother.

Good health habits need to be practiced during pregnancy. Doctors recommend that women gain between 25 to 35 pounds. Mothers-to-be should rest when they feel tired. They also should remain active during pregnancy.

Many diseases or illnesses in the mother can harm the baby. The health of the fetus is also endangered through drug use. Radiation exposure and environmental pollution can create possible harmful effects. Birth defects can occur for various reasons and occur in varying levels of severity.

Sometimes spontaneous abortions take place when mothers have complications. Sometimes they occur because the mother smokes, drinks, uses drugs, or has contracted certain diseases. They may also occur for unknown reasons. The ultrasound and amniocentesis are two tests that monitor the health of the fetus.

Family decisions to be made before the birth include where the baby will be born and which method of delivery will be used. When a mother-to-be is about to deliver, she goes into labor. If a birth appears to be too difficult the natural way, the doctor may perform a C-section.

Most babies born in the hospital are cared for in the nursery. Rooming-in is an arrangement whereby the baby stays in the room with the mother.

During the postnatal period, the mother's body needs to return to normal. She will need to rest, exercise, and eat well-balanced meals. Getting the postpartum blues is common. This is due to hormonal changes that affect emotions. Although no two women are alike, after the third month a mother's body should return to normal.

1

To Review

Write your answers on a separate sheet of paper.
1. Which is not a sign of pregnancy?
   a. enlarged and sore breasts
   b. cravings for pickles and ice cream
   c. missed menstrual cycle
   d. morning sickness
2. The best age for a woman to have a baby is between
   a. 17 and 20 years
   b. 21 and 28 years
   c. 36 and 40 years

2

1—*Activity:* Invite several mothers with new babies to visit class. Prepare a list of questions to ask them. Send the mothers these questions prior to the visit. Ask the mothers to be prepared for spontaneous questions also.

2—*Answers:* Answers to review questions can be found in the front section of this TAE.

3. True or false. The unborn baby is able to take whatever nutrients it needs for its own development, even if the mother's diet lacks these nutrients.

4. True or false. During pregnancy it is safer to take over-the-counter drugs like cough medicine and aspirin than stronger prescription drugs.

5. True or false. Crying and feeling sad are quite normal a few days after giving birth.

6. Name the statement that is most true about a normal pregnancy.
    a. Pregnant women should limit physical activities to protect the baby.
    b. Most women feel tired and uncomfortable during the entire pregnancy.
    c. After they have a baby, women usually do not return to their prepregnant weight.
    d. Good health practices are almost the same during pregnancy as they are before pregnancy.

7. List two ways a father can take an active role during pregnancy and childbirth.

8. Place the following steps of labor in proper order:
    a. birth of the baby
    b. the show
    c. dilation of the cervix
    d. expelling the placenta
    e. cutting of the umbilical cord

9. True or false. False labor pains are not real pains. The mother imagines them.

10. Which of the following is the most accurate statement about delivery?
    a. The delivery method should mainly depend upon the condition of the mother and her baby.
    b. Natural childbirth is best because drugs can harm the baby.
    c. Cesarean sections are best because the mother and baby can avoid a long and uncomfortable labor.
    d. Being put to sleep is best, because fear of pain makes labor longer and more difficult.
    e. The method of delivery should be only the mother's choice, because it is her body.

11. True or false. The birthing room and the rooming-in arrangements are designed to provide the best of home and hospital delivery and care.

12. _____ care is essential for a healthy return to a nonpregnant state.

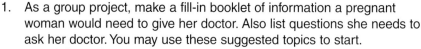

To Do

1. As a group project, make a fill-in booklet of information a pregnant woman would need to give her doctor. Also list questions she needs to ask her doctor. You may use these suggested topics to start.
   a. Information the doctor needs:
      family health history
      history of menstrual cycle
      history of any serious or chronic diseases or conditions
      history of other pregnancies
      date of last menstrual period
      current use of drugs, including over-the-counter drugs.
      (Add your own.)
   b. Information the mother-to-be needs:
      due date
      present weight and amount of weight gain
      recommended diet, exercise, rest
      treatment of any disease or condition
      information on giving birth (place, types of delivery, and arrangement for care of newborn)
      fees and insurance
      appointment dates and how to contact doctor in an emergency
      (Add your own.)

   Placing the booklet in a folder with pockets is often helpful, because many doctors give their patients charts and pamphlets.
2. Interview two women who had their children two or three generations apart. Then write an article summarizing the interviews entitled, "Pregnancy and Childbirth Yesterday and Today."
3. Invite a health care worker to speak to your class about childbirth classes for parents-to-be.
4. Arrange to visit a local hospital's facilities for giving birth and caring for the newborn.
5. Invite a certified nurse midwife to discuss the advantages of a home versus hospital delivery, the type of training required of a CNM, and the type of deliveries the CNM handles.
6. Create a bulletin board on the theme "Eating for Two Requires Careful Planning." The bulletin board might contain one week of sample menus for a pregnant woman. Pictures and/or a list of some potentially fattening, nonessential foods might be used on the bulletin board, too.
7. Give a class report on one birth defect.
8. Write a paragraph on the importance of bonding for both the infant and the parents.

1—*Note:* Include birth difficulties and genetic birth defects in the immediate family.

2—*Note:* Include current use of caffeine and nicotine.

To Observe

1. Observe pregnant women in informal settings. Which activities (behaviors) do you see as healthy? Which activities (behaviors) do you see as unhealthy?
2. Observe advertisements by local hospitals or health programs. What services do they offer for prenatal care, preparation for delivery, and labor and delivery? What options are there in your community (delivery versus birthing room, delivery by obstetrician or trained midwife)?
3. Observe families preparing for a new baby. How is each family member helping with this preparation? How is an older child reacting to the upcoming birth of a baby?
4. Observe a sonogram photo. Which features of the baby can you see?

To Think Critically

1. Some of the most severe birth defects are recessive traits. Based on this statement, why is it biologically not best for closely related blood relatives to marry? Explain your answer.
2. At one time pregnancy and childbirth were considered a "woman's affair." Now this event is thought of as a whole family affair. How can various family members be involved? Make a list.
3. Years ago pregnancy could not be confirmed for several weeks. Today's tests can confirm pregnancy within days of conception. What advantages occur as a result of early confirmation?
4. You are friends with a couple who have just had a premature baby who will likely remain hospitalized for several weeks. What problems might they face concerning bonding? What are some things their family and friends might do to help the couple bond with the baby?

1—*Reflect:* If you see someone engaging in an unhealthy activity, would you intervene? If yes, how would you proceed to intervene?

2—*Reflect:* When do you think an older child should be informed that he or she will have a new sibling? How does the age of the child affect when you would tell him or her?

Chapter 6

The Newborn

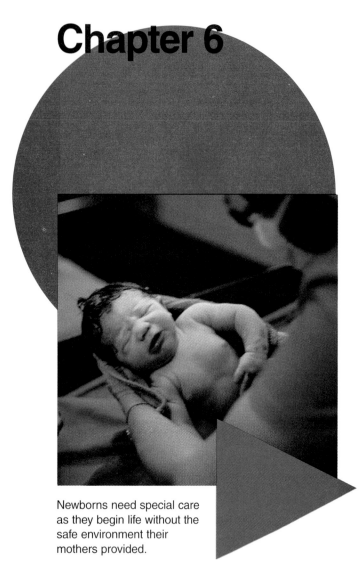

Newborns need special care as they begin life without the safe environment their mothers provided.

After studying this chapter, you will be able to

☐   describe the characteristics of a newborn.

☐   identify a newborn's physical, intellectual, and social-emotional needs.

☐   explain how parents of newborns can meet their own needs.

After studying this chapter, you will be able to define

anemia
Apgar test
Brazelton scale
colic
cradle cap
fontanels
intensive care nursery (ICN)
neonatal intensive care units (NICU)
neonate
neonatology
pediatrician
PKU
reflexes
rooting reflex
well-baby checkup

When the doctor cuts the umbilical cord, a baby's life begins. The official time of birth happens when the baby is clear of the mother's body. From birth to the age of one month, the baby is medically known as a **neonate.** (Neonate is from the Latin words *neo*, meaning new, and *natus*, meaning born.)

Great changes happen in the *neonatal* (or newborn) period of growth and development. Newborns come from a world that was dark and quiet. They lived in a home of warm, comfortable water. They received food and oxygen easily and without waiting. The water's support helped them move easily and cushioned them from shock.

At the moment of birth, babies enter a more exciting world. They are exposed to light and noise. The newborn's life support system— the placenta and umbilical cord—stops functioning minutes after birth. The newborn's air passage is drained of water. The lungs expand and the baby takes his or her first breath. Now the baby must search for a nipple and suck when hungry. The baby's body feels different because gravity hinders movement. Suddenly the head and trunk seem heavy to the baby. This new world is different and sometimes frustrating.

The time of birth also turns a man and woman into parents. They must adjust to a different world, too. Parents can enjoy this time of adjustment if they do the following:

☐ Plan carefully.

☐ Accept the responsibility of parenthood.

☐ Love and communicate with each other.

☐ Live one day at a time.

☐ Realize that, in time, frustrations such as sleepless nights will decrease and the joys of parenthood will increase.

● Medical Care and Testing

Good prenatal care gives the baby the best chance for a healthy start. All newborns also need medical care for healthy development. Of course,

a sick or tiny newborn needs medical care. However, healthy newborns must also go through a few simple procedures.

In hospitals, doctors and nurses care for the baby from the time of birth until the baby leaves. After delivery, the baby is often held head downward. Then the doctor applies suction to the nostrils and mouth with a syringe. The mother may hold the baby on her abdomen until the cord is clamped and cut. The nurse then takes the baby to a special table that has a heater above it. The nurse dries the newborn with warm towels, 6-1.

▶ Care for Premature Babies

Some babies are born too small or too soon. Some are born with problems, such as heart, digestive tract, spine, or brain defects. These babies need immediate, intensive care. They are often placed in an **intensive care nursery** (ICN). The ICN can save these newborns' lives or keep them from further damage, 6-2. Newborns that need intensive care live in **neonatal intensive care units (NICUs)**. Neonatal intensive care units are heated,

4

6-1 This healthy newborn is being wiped dry with a warm towel.

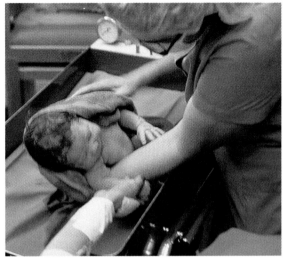

Adrian Demery

1—*Enrich:* Attach a cord to a doll and illustrate the cutting of the cord. Use pictures from medical books or encyclopedias as visual images.

2—*Resource: Newborns and Parents Adapt,* SAG.

3—*Reflect:* Write a short paragraph discussing how you would or would not be ready for parenthood based on the suggestions for enjoyable parenting.

4—*Discuss:* About what other birth defects or health problems have you heard or read?

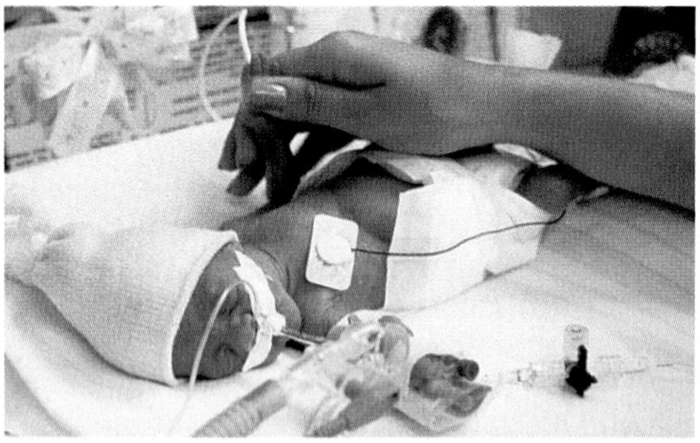

March of Dimes Birth Defects Foundation

6-2 The neonatal intensive care unit (NICU) protects babies who were born too soon.

completely enclosed beds. They have two doors (which are slightly larger than an arm) that open and close to permit care. NICUs are equipped with devices for giving oxygen and for monitoring breathing and heart rate. The doctors and nurses who work in ICN's have special training in neonatology. **Neonatology** is a branch of medicine concerned with the care, development, and diseases of newborns.

▶ The Apgar Test

In most hospitals, the newborn's physical shape is checked using the **Apgar test.** This test checks the baby's chance of survival. The baby scores a 0, 1, or 2 in each of five areas, 6-3. The best total score possible is a 10.

The Apgar test checks the baby's pulse, breathing, muscle tone, responsiveness, and skin color. The baby's heart rate and breathing are most important. The skin color, which is a sign of circulation, is least important. The test is given one minute and five minutes after delivery. (Usually the cord has not been cut for the first scoring. It usually has for the second.) The five-minute score should be higher.

Most normal babies score 6 or 7 at 1 minute, then 8 to 10 at 5 minutes. If a baby scores 7 or less at 5 minutes, the infant is tested

1

2

6-3 A newborn's condition may be quickly determined by the Apgar test.

Apgar Test			
	Scores		
Sign	0	1	2
Heart rate	Absent.	Slow; fewer than 100 beats per minute.	More than 100 beats per minute.
Respiratory effort	Absent.	Weak cry; hyperventilation.	Good; strong cry.
Muscle tone	Limp.	Some flexing and bending of extremities.	Well flexed.
Reflex irritability	No response.	Some motion.	Cry.
Color	Blue; pale.	Body pink; extremities blue.	Completely pink.

1—Enrich: Have students investigate whether other countries use this test for infants.

2—Activity: Take your own pulse and compare it to the score of two on the Apgar Test.

again at 10 minutes after birth. A low score means the baby needs special medical care.

After the first test, the baby is weighed and measured. Drops of silver nitrate are put into the eyes to prevent infection. Before the baby is taken from the delivery room, footprints are made, 6-4. Also, name bands are placed around the baby's wrists and/or ankles for identification purposes, 6-5.

▶ The Neonatal Assessment Scales

Some doctors use the *Neonatal Behavioral Assessment Scales.* This test is commonly called the **Brazelton scale.** It helps doctors spot any problems as early as possible. (This differs from the Apgar test, which predicts the chances of survival and helps newborns with low scores.) The Brazelton scale tests if the baby is normal in the following four areas:

☐ interaction with the environment—tests the baby's alertness; attention to sound, light, and other factors; and cuddliness

☐ motor processes—tests the baby's general activity level and reflex behavior

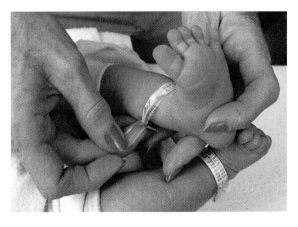

6-5   Bands on the wrists and/or ankles, labeled with the family name, help identify the baby.

☐ control of physical state—tests self-quieting behaviors and levels of excitement and irritability

☐ response to stress—tests the newborn's response to stress. Responses may include startle reactions and trembling

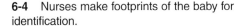

6-4   Nurses make footprints of the baby for identification.

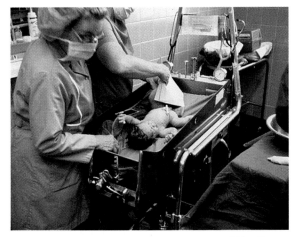

Adrian Demery

⬤ Other Hospital Care

Pediatricians run other tests to determine the newborn's health. (A **pediatrician** is a doctor who cares for infants and children.) Blood tests are run to rule out anemia. **Anemia** is a low level of oxygen-carrying substances in the blood. These tests also check the presence of **PKU** (phenylketonuria), which is a disease that can cause mental retardation if left untreated by diet.

Another condition that requires special care is jaundice. *Jaundice* is a condition that occurs in newborns that makes their skin, tissues, and body fluids look yellow. Jaundice happens because some babies' livers are immature. Doctors treat jaundice by placing the baby under bright lights, 6-6.

1

2

3

4

1—*Vocabulary:* Compare and contrast the Apgar test and the Brazelton scale. Are they mandatory? How many times are they done normally? How would each test help parents learn more about children?

2—*Enrich:* Divide the class into three groups. Do short-term research on anemia, phenylketonuria, and jaundice. Report results to the class.

3—*Activity:* Use the doll to illustrate how a pediatrician or nurse conducts the blood test for PKU.

4—*Enrich:* Predict what might happen if a baby remains in the hospital after his or her mother is discharged. Consider physical, social, and emotional implications for mother and baby.

© Nancy P. Alexander

6-6   Jaundice is a common problem with newborns. Placing the baby under special lights helps to reduce the skin's yellow color. A blindfold protects this baby's eyes.

Well-Baby Checkup

Before the newborn leaves the hospital, the pediatrician will ask the parents to make an appointment for a well-baby checkup. (A **well-baby checkup** is a checkup doctors give babies and children, even when they appear healthy.) The checkup will take place within a month (or less if the baby is small or sick). During the well-baby checkup, the pediatrician will examine the baby, answer questions, and make recommendations, 6-7. If the doctor is different from the doctor used during pregnancy, the pediatrician will ask for the family health history. The nurse will weigh and measure the baby's length, head, and chest. Parents then schedule their baby's next checkup.

● Physical Traits of a Newborn

The songwriter who said, "You must have been a beautiful baby," was not talking about newborns. The plump, cute babies you see in advertisements are usually several months old. What does a newborn look like? Their physical traits are described in 6-8.

Newborns possess other physical traits that sometimes worry parents. They cough and sneeze to clear mucus from their air passages and lungs. They breathe unevenly, about 46 times per minute, from the diaphragm in the abdominal area. (Adults breathe about 18 times per minute, usually from the chest.) Newborns' heart rates are often between 120 and 150 beats per minute. (Adults' heart rates are about 70 beats per minute.)

● Reflexes

All people have built-in behaviors that they did not learn. For instance, your knee jerks when tapped with a mallet. These automatic, unlearned behaviors are called **reflexes.** Newborns enter the world with many reflexes. Some are triggered by an outside stimulus (light, touch, sound) that is directed to a body area (hands, feet, cheeks, eyes, and ears).

For newborns, reflexes are important.

6-7   This pediatrician enjoys examining the newborn in a well-baby checkup.

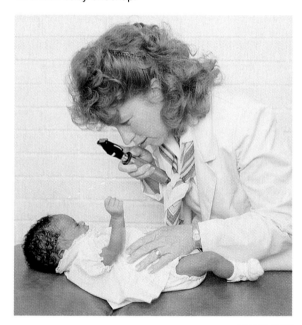

© John Shaw

1—*Enrich:* Contact a clinic for a complete list of well-baby checkup exams, vaccinations, and costs.

2—*Activity:* Locate pictures of newborns. Compare and contrast their appearance with chart descriptions.

3—*Discuss:* How does an infant's breathing and heart rate differ from an adult's?

4—*Example:* To illustrate a reflex, ask one student to leave the room. Throw a paper ball at the student when he or she returns, and watch for reactions. Discuss reflexes most adults have retained.

What Do Newborns Look Like?

Feature	Description
Size	☐ Most full-term babies weigh slightly over seven pounds and are about 20 inches long. Boys are slightly larger than girls. ☐ Newborns will lose weight after birth, then regain birth weight within 10 days. ☐ They will grow about 1 1/2 pounds and one inch during the first month. ☐ Newborns look thin because they have little body fat.
Body Proportions	☐ Newborns look out of proportion. ☐ The head is 1/4 of total length. An adult's heads is 1/10 of total length. ☐ The chest is rounded. ☐ The stomach protrudes, and the pelvis and hips are narrow. ☐ The legs are drawn up and appear to bow because of their position before birth. ☐ The legs are short compared to the arms. ☐ Newborns have almost no neck.
Face	☐ Newborns have a broad, flat nose. ☐ They have a tiny jaw and chin. ☐ These features help them suck more easily.
Cranium 	☐ Newborns have **fontanels** (called soft spots) where the skull is not closed. Fontanels allow the skull and brain to grow. ☐ The fontanels fill with bone as the skull grows. The skull completely closes between one and two years of age, when brain growth has slowed. ☐ The membrane that covers the fontanels moves in and out as the baby breathes. It may be seen in a baby with little hair. ☐ The bones of the skull are soft and may be molded into an egg shape during birth. This makes birth easier. The molded shape of the head will disappear in a couple of weeks.
Skin 	☐ Newborns have thin, dry skin. ☐ The skin may look blotchy and ruddy. You may see the blood vessels. ☐ The skin of the feet is loose and wrinkly. ☐ The wrists have deep, bracelet-like creases. ☐ The scalp skin is also loose. ☐ At birth, newborns have protective, cheese-like coverings called the *vernix caseosa*. ☐ Down (called *languno*) on the ears, shoulders, back, forehead, and cheeks frequently appears on premature babies. ☐ Babies often develop a rash one or two days after birth. This should disappear in one week. (continued)

6-8   A newborn looks different from older children or adults.

1—*Math Activity:* Find out your birth length and weight and record on a chart. Add the total birth lengths and weights of all students and calculate average length and weight for the class.

2—*Note:* The fontanels consist of six soft spots. The skull bones are not fused together, allowing the head to flex as the baby travels through the birth canal. They are covered by a tough membrane, which needs to be protected from bumps and falls until the bones are completely fused at one to two years of age.

What Do Newborns Look Like? (continued)

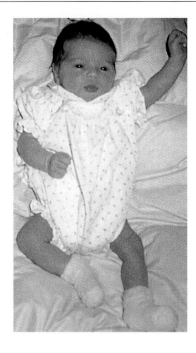

☐ Some newborns have pinkish marks on the forehead, eyelids, and the back of the neck. These are called stork bites. They fade within a year. The name comes from the mythical stork who delivered babies. However, the blotches are from a collection of small blood vessels.

☐ Newborns of African, Mediterranean, and Asian decent may have greenish-blue spots on the back. These are called *Mongolian spots.*

☐ Many newborns look yellow because of jaundice.

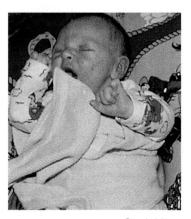

Stork bites

Eyes

☐ Newborns' eyes appear small.

☐ Their eye color is usually a dull gray-blue due to lack of pigmentation. Eye color develops around six months of age.

☐ Red spots may appear in the white of the eyes.

☐ Babies do not produce tears until three months. Their eyes may drain from the side effect of silver nitrate, however.

☐ A newborn's eyes may cross at times. Eyes usually work together at about six months.

Mouth

☐ Newborns have puffy cheeks. This is because they have sucking pads on the inside of the cheeks.

☐ The tongue is short and cannot be extended beyond the gums.

☐ The lining of the lips will peel.

☐ Most newborns are toothless, but some are born with one or more teeth.

1

☐ Reflexes are a clue to the health and maturity of the nervous system. The absence or weakness of a reflex may mean prematurity or a birth defect. For instance, newborns jerk or withdraw their legs when the soles of their feet are pricked. This reaction is called the *with-* *drawal reflex.* The reflex continues throughout life, and its absence may be a sign of brain damage. However, some reflexes should disappear at a certain time. If these reflexes do not disappear, it may be a sign of brain damage.

1—*Resource: Reflexes of the Newborn,* SAG.
2—*Note:* Emphasize that it is important for all reflexes to be present, but that it is also important for them to disappear at specified times. This indicates the brain is developing properly and there is no brain damage.

☐ Babies need some reflexes for survival. For instance, when you touch a newborn's cheeks or skin around the mouth, the baby searches for food. The head turns and the mouth moves. This is called the ***rooting reflex***. After finding an object with the mouth, the baby begins to suck. This reflex should vanish in three to four months.

☐ Some reflexes lead to voluntary, learned behaviors. The knee jerk does not lead to a learned behavior. It always remains the same. On the other hand, the sucking reflex leads to learned sucking. The newborn learns to vary sucking strength with the softness of the object.

☐ Using reflexes may give the newborn the practice needed to develop voluntary behaviors such as sitting, walking, and climbing. These behaviors are essential for development.

There are many reflexes, and researchers are observing and describing more. Several are illustrated in 6-9.

● Meeting the Newborn's Physical Needs

Newborns are completely helpless. They depend on adults to meet their physical needs. They even look small and helpless. Because newborns are so dependent and fragile, it's no wonder people are nervous to take care of them at first.

▶ Feeding

People need nutrients to grow and stay healthy. Because newborns grow quickly, their nutritional needs are especially important. Parents meet these needs by either breast-feeding or formula-feeding babies. The choice is a personal one. The mother and father should compare the advantages of each, 6-10. They should feel good about their choice. Some parents find they have many of the advantages of both types of feeding by bottle-feeding breast milk.

▦ Breast-Feeding

Mothers who breast-feed their babies should do the following:

☐ Eat a balanced diet. The quality of breast milk varies only slightly from mother to mother. Even malnourished women provide high-quality milk, but their own bodies suffer. Nursing mothers should eat about 200 more calories than pregnant women. The foods they choose should be nutritious, because they need more vitamins and minerals at this time.

☐ Drink plenty of liquids.

☐ Check with a pediatrician about giving the baby a supplementary source of iron and vitamin D.

☐ Realize that certain foods may upset the baby. These include coffee, tea, chocolate, cola, cocoa, herbal teas, and artificial sweeteners. The baby's intestinal tract may be irritated by foods the mother has eaten such as broccoli, asparagus, eggplant, onions, tomatoes, garlic, and spices. The mother may need to stop eating some of these foods while she is nursing.

☐ Tell doctors and dentists when nursing. Also, the mother should talk to her physician before taking over-the-counter drugs. Any drug could affect her milk and the baby.

☐ Rest and avoid stress. Milk can "dry up" when mothers are tired or under stress.

☐ Consult with a doctor or nurse for help with breast-feeding.

☐ Use breast-feeding time to bond with the baby. As they breast-feed, mothers should smile at, sing to, talk with, and cuddle their newborns, 6-11.

▦ Formula-Feeding

If parents prefer formula-feeding, they should do the following:

☐ Consult with a doctor about the type of formula to use. Most parents purchase commercially-prepared formula in powdered, concentrated liquid, or ready-to-feed form.

1—*Discuss:* How does the rooting reflex lead to the sucking reflex? At what age should the reflexes disappear?

2—*Note:* Describe a voluntary behavior. List some types of voluntary behaviors.

3—*Activity:* Display two green plants, one that is healthy and another that is almost dead. Discuss differences in how each plant was cared for physically. Compare to a newborn. List

other components of an infant's care, such as social, emotional, and mental stimulation.

4—*Discuss:* If a mother is malnourished, how will this affect her baby?

5—*Discuss:* What are other results of a mother's stress on a baby and family?

1

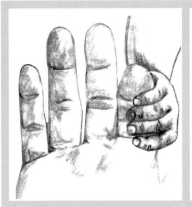 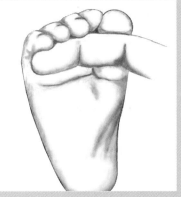 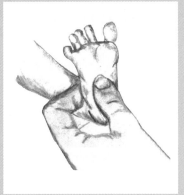

Palmar (grasping) Reflex
Newborns' fingers tighten around any object placed in the palm. Grasp is strong enough to lift them into a sitting position.

Plantar (grasping) Reflex
Newborns' toes tighten around any object when the ball of the foot is stroked. This reflex disappears between 8 and 15 months of age.

Babinski Reflex
Newborns' toes fan out if the outside of the sole is stroked from heel to toe. Reflex ends at about one year of age.

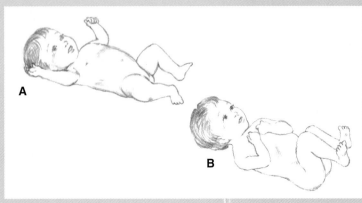 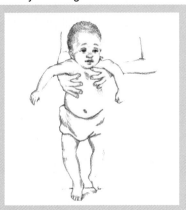

Moro Reflex
The reflex consists of two movements. Newborns fling arms and legs out (A) and pull them back again (B) when they are startled.

Walking Reflex
When babies' feet touch a solid surface, alternating steps are taken as in walking. This reflex disappears in three or four months.

Thomas J. Roberts

6-9   Some major reflexes help infants survive and learn.

☐   Do not feed the baby whole milk before the baby is six months old. Cow's milk has too much salt and protein for newborns. It may cause irritation, bleeding, pain, and eventually anemia.

☐   Feed newborns the right amount of milk. Two to 2 1/2 ounces per pound of body weight in a 24-hour period is correct.

☐   Refrigerate ingredients used to make formula. Keep utensils, bottles, and nipples completely clean.

1—*Activity:* Using the doll, demonstrate each reflex. If students have difficulty remembering, they may associate some word or letter cues with each reflex.

2

Advantages of Breast-Feeding and Formula-Feeding

Breast-Feeding	Formula-Feeding
☐ Breast milk contains the right proportions of proteins, carbohydrates, fats, vitamins, minerals, and water.	☐ Formulas are similar to breast milk.
☐ Breast milk is easy to digest.	☐ Formulas have iron; breast milk is low in iron. Iron-fortified foods must be added to a breast-fed baby's diet after the baby triples his or her birth weight.
☐ Breast milk is ready immediately.	
☐ Mother does not overfeed.	☐ Formula-feeding makes it easier to be away from home.
☐ Babies fed entirely on breast milk are seldom constipated.	☐ Because nonnursing mothers do not need as many calories, it is quicker for them to return to a prepregnancy size.
☐ Breast-fed babies have fewer digestive upsets and disorders, skin disorders, and respiratory infections.	☐ Mothers need no nursing pads or brassieres.
☐ Vigorous sucking required for breast-feeding usually satisfies the need for sucking and promotes good development of facial structures.	☐ There are no worries about an inadequate supply of milk.
	☐ Formula is not affected by the mother's diet, illnesses, or medications.
☐ Mother's immunities to certain diseases are passed to the baby.	☐ Anyone can help feed the baby. Feeding may help fathers and others develop a good relationship with the baby.
☐ Nursing stimulates hormones to be released that help the uterus contract to normal size.	
☐ Mother and baby easily develop a warm relationship because of touch and eye contact.	

6-10   Breast-feeding or formula-feeding is a personal choice. Parents should discuss the advantages and disadvantages of each before deciding.

☐ Check nipples. Large or clogged holes cause feeding problems. Pieces bitten off of worn nipples could cause the baby to choke.

☐ Babies do not always finish their bottles. Throw away all unfinished formula.

☐ Hold and cuddle the baby during feeding. Parents may want to take turns feeding the baby. This helps them both to bond with the baby, 6-12.

☐ Avoid propping the bottle. Babies can choke while feeding. (If a baby chokes, parents should turn the baby on his or her side or abdomen, then pat on the back.)

Burping the Baby.   Whether breast-fed or formula-fed, babies must be burped. This is because they swallow air while sucking or crying. Burping rids the body of this air. To burp a newborn, do the following:

1—*Enrich:* How would you react to an individual who disagreed with your choice of feeding your baby?

2—*Enrich:* Organize a nursing versus formula-feeding debate. Emphasize the physical, social, emotional, and mental aspects; parental bonding issues; adaptations for working parents; costs; and psychological implications for the mother if she is physically unable to nurse.

Gerber Products

6-11   Breast-feeding helps a mother and baby bond.

ties, buttons, or snaps are also good choices. Be sure that clothes are flame-retardant and that fasteners and decorative items are secure. Because babies kick off their blankets, they need warm clothes. However, do not overdress them.

Because baby clothes are so cute, it is easy to make unwise choices. Babies outgrow their clothes quickly, so they don't need too many. Parents can stay within their clothing budget by watching for sales. They can also save money by borrowing baby clothes from friends and relatives. Choosing clothes suitable for either boys or girls (and storing for the next child) is smart, too. Another smart idea is for parents to buy or make clothes the baby can "grow into." Clothes should be easy to launder, also. Clothes that must be hand-washed or washed with like colors are not practical. See 6-13 for a newborn's basic clothing needs.

6-12   Formula-feeding helps a father develop a good relationship with his baby.

1
- ☐ Place the baby in a sitting position with a hand on the collar bone and under the chin.
- ☐ Laying the baby face down across your lap is another way to burp him or her. (You may burp a newborn on your shoulder, but the shoulder position is easier when the baby is larger.)
- ☐ Lightly pat the baby's back once he or she is in position. Pat the baby below the ribs for two or three minutes, unless the baby burps sooner.

2
- ☐ Burp a baby before, midway, and/or after feeding.

▶ Clothing and Dressing

Babies' clothing should be comfortable, easy to put on and take off, suitable for weather and temperature, and safe. What clothes do babies find comfortable? Loose-fitting clothes are easy to move in, and clothes without too many

© John Shaw

1—*Activity:* Explain three ways to burp a baby, and demonstrate with the doll. Discuss when and why burping is necessary.

2—*Enrich:* Research how infants are fed in other cultures. What are your reactions to these methods?

3—*Enrich:* Find pictures of desirable and undesirable baby clothing.

4—*Enrich:* Evaluate a high-cost item versus a low-cost item. Compare the length of time the items will be worn, how often, and if they might be used as planned hand-me-downs.

5—*Discuss:* How can parents save money on children's clothing?

Basic Clothing Needs for the Newborn
☐ 3-4 cotton knit nightgowns or kimonos
☐ 3-4 cotton knit shirts
☐ 2-3 sweaters or sweatshirts
☐ 1 knit cap.
☐ 3-6 dozen cloth diapers or several boxes of disposal diapers
☐ 1 dozen cloth diapers (for burping, protection of bedding, etc.)
☐ 3 plastic pants, if using cloth diapers
☐ 3-4 pairs of socks
☐ 4-6 bibs
☐ 1 dressy outfit for outings and pictures

6-13 Parents usually receive these basic baby clothes as gifts shortly before and after the baby is born.

Remember, dressing time is a chance to talk with newborns. Newborns talk with their body movements, eyes, and sounds. Tell babies what you're doing as you dress them. ("I'm snapping your shirt . . . snap . . . snap . . . snap.")

Newborns are easier to dress than older babies because they do not squirm as much. The following suggestions should make dressing easy and safe.

☐ Pull out the baby's clothes before you begin. Undo any buttons or snaps before you get the baby.

☐ Support the baby's head as you lift him or her.

☐ Pull the baby's arms and legs through the openings. Newborns can't push.

☐ Cuddle fretful babies before continuing to dress them.

▶ Diapering

Parents can use either disposable or cloth diapers for babies. There are many different brands and sizes of disposable diapers. They all have waterproof outer layers and are easy and convenient to use. Some babies wear cloth diapers, with plastic pants over them, most of the time. Then when they are traveling or during emergencies they use disposable ones. See 6-14 on how to diaper a baby.

There are advantages and disadvantages to using either cloth or disposable diapers. Parents must consider cost and convenience. They must also consider how much time they have to wash diapers. In some places, a parent has the option of using a diaper service that picks up soiled diapers and delivers sterilized cloth ones.

Parents can prevent most diaper rashes by changing the baby's diapers regularly. Diaper rashes may develop from the constant use of plastic pants or from the outer layer of disposable diapers. Bacteria builds up on the warm, moist, and air-free skin, causing diaper rash. Most babies develop diaper rashes at one time or another. The most common treatment is to wash

2

6-14 If you unfasten a disposable diaper and find the baby does not need to be changed, refasten the diaper with tape or diaper pins.

How to Diaper a Baby
1. Gather diapering material before you get the baby.
2. Place the baby on a safe, firm surface. Unfasten and remove soiled diaper.
3. Clean the diaper area thoroughly.
4. With one hand, grasp the baby's ankles and slide a fresh diaper under the baby's bottom. Then pull the front of the diaper up between the baby's legs.
5. When using disposable diapers, the tape fastens from the front to the back. With cloth diapers, protect the baby from the pin by slipping two of your fingers between the baby and the diaper. (Diaper pins that have been pushed into a bar of soap will glide easily through a cloth diaper.)

3

2—*Math Activity:* Determine how many times parents change diapers during an average day. Using newspaper ads, catalogs, and a telephone book, determine costs of using cloth and disposable diapers for a week.

3—*Activity:* Demonstrate diapering and dressing a doll.

the area with soap and water after each change, expose the area without ointment to air, and use petroleum jelly or a rash ointment before diapering. If the rash persists following several days of treatment, parents should consult a pediatrician.

▶ Bathing

Newborns don't get too dirty except for their faces, necks, and diaper areas. These areas must be kept clean.

Sponge baths are recommended until the navel has completely healed—up to three weeks after birth. (Leave the cord alone until it becomes dry and loose. Then wipe with a cotton swab dipped in 70 percent rubbing alcohol four or five times per day.) See 6-15 on how to give a sponge bath to a baby.

▶ Sleeping

Newborns average about 17 hours of sleep per day. This means they can sleep as little as 11 hours to as much as 23 hours. There is no relationship between sleep requirements and good health.

Newborns do not sleep quietly between feedings. They usually take seven or eight naps in which they suck, wheeze, and gurgle. This pattern of light sleep continues for the first half year. Newborns adjust to regular household sounds, so it isn't necessary to whisper or tiptoe while they are sleeping.

Place the baby on a firm mattress in a bed that has sides to prevent the baby from falling. Pillows and stuffed toys should only be used after the baby is six months of age. Until a baby can change sleep positions easily, a pillow or stuffed toy could hamper breathing. It may be best never to place pillows and stuffed toys in a baby's bed. Once he or she can stand on these items, the baby can climb over the railing.

Until the age of one, babies should be placed on their backs to reduce the risk of Sudden Infant Death Syndrome (SIDS). If infants are placed on their sides, they can roll over onto their stomachs. This position increases the risk of SIDS. Because babies' skulls are soft, sleeping in one position may slightly, but permanently, flatten the head in one place. However, this is not

How to Give a Baby a Sponge Bath

1. Collect all supplies. You will need the following:
   - ☐ Towel or sponge for baby to lie on.
   - ☐ Baby soap.
   - ☐ Cotton balls.
   - ☐ Washcloth, towel, and wrapper (a hooded cape or a hooded, front-opening "robe" to wrap around baby), or another large towel.
   - ☐ Bath oil and lotion.
   - ☐ Baby powder.
   - ☐ Manicure scissors (made for babies).
   - ☐ Hair brush and comb (made for babies).
2. Place supplies within the adult's reach but out of the baby's reach.
3. Place the baby on a towel or a baby-sized sponge placed on a cabinet or on a bathing table. Never leave the baby unattended—even for a second!
4. Wash the baby's face with a washcloth dipped in clear water and squeezed out.
5. Clean eyes, ears, and nose with fresh cotton balls dipped in clear water and squeezed out.
6. Lightly soap the rest of the baby's body and rinse with a wet washcloth. Pat the baby dry as you wash each area. Keep the baby covered with a wrapper or an extra towel.
7. If using powder on newborns, don't let it get into the baby's nose or eyes. Also, don't let it collect in folds of the baby's skin.
8. Moisten the baby's skin with baby oil or lotion.
9. Shampoo the scalp once or twice a week with soap to prevent scaling, called **cradle cap.** Use oil (not lotion) on scalp.
10. Brush and comb hair after you have dressed the baby.
11. Cut the baby's nails when necessary.

6-15　Gather and organize all bath supplies before placing the baby on a towel.

1—*Activity:* Using the doll, demonstrate how to give a baby a bath. List safety precautions.

2—*Activity:* Present pictures of different types of baby bathtubs and bath devices. Discuss costs.

3—*Activity:* Demonstrate how to position a baby for sleeping.

serious. The flat spot does not affect the brain, and hair will make the flattened area unnoticeable.

Bedding equipment and supplies are simple for newborns. The basic items needed are listed in 6-16.

6-16   The bedding needs of newborns are simple.

Bedding Equipment and Supplies

Bed

☐ Bassinets, cradles, or baby beds are all fine beds.

☐ A baby bed should be high and stable enough to prevent young children or pets from tipping it over.

☐ If a cradle or bed with slats is used, the slats should be no further apart than 2 3/8 inches. This prevents babies from wiggling feet first through the slats until their heads are caught. This could cause serious injury or death.

Bumper pads

☐ Use bumper pads in cradles or beds with slats.

☐ Do not use bumper pads until babies can lift their heads. This prevents suffocation.

☐ Remove bumper pads when the baby can stand. This prevents the baby from using these as climbing devices.

Large pieces of flannelette sheeting

☐ Cover the mattress or pad with two or three pieces of 25 by 30 inch waterproof flannelette sheeting.

☐ Put the sheet over these pieces. (Large pieces are important once the baby begins to move around in bed.)

☐ Use the sheeting until the child is toilet trained at night.

Small pieces of flannelette sheeting

☐ Place four to six 18-inch squares of waterproof flannelette sheeting on top of the baby's sheet.

☐ Use the sheeting to catch overflows from a diaper or from spitting up.

Sheets

☐ Three or four sheets are needed. Fitted bottom sheets are the easiest to use.

☐ Sheets come in various sizes to fit bassinets, standard-size cribs, and cradles.

Blankets

☐ Three or four cotton flannel blankets may be needed.

☐ Receiving blankets (about 30 by 40 inches) are often used.

☐ Crib blankets (36 by 50 inches) may be more economical. Babies soon outgrow the smaller blankets.

☐ Sleepwear that keeps the baby warm is essential. Babies kick off their blankets while they sleep. Warm sleepwear has drawstring bottoms, tube feet, and cuffs that convert to mittens.

☐ Sleepwear includes drawstring-bottom gowns and sleep-and-play suits.

☐ Sleepwear should be "roomy" and warm.

1—*Discuss:* Discuss implications and adjustments in small homes where the baby will have to sleep in the same room with several other family members. Expand your discussion to include societies with small or one-room homes as well as with extended families.

2—*Note:* Make sure bumper pads are tied securely to the slats. Check this on a regular basis.

▶ Exercising

Movement is a large part of life—before birth and in the newborn stage. Watch the constant movement of newborns lying awake on their backs. Exercise is important for muscle development, coordination, and even relaxation. Exercising newborns will not cause them to crawl or walk sooner. It may help the general development of the muscles. To help the baby exercise, see 6-17.

Exercising a baby has added bonuses. Exercising, if started early in life, may become a daily, lifelong habit. Exercise is also a way to have fun with babies and develop a warm relationship. Many families find exercise-related activities to be great family fun for years.

6-17 Exercising is good for the baby. It also gives the parents and baby time to "talk."

Suggestions for Helping Babies Exercise

☐ Place the baby on a foam pad or bed where he or she is comfortable and safe.

☐ The baby should wear nonrestrictive clothing while exercising so he or she can move easily.

☐ Select a good time. The baby should exercise for 10 to 15 minutes. Choose a time when the baby is alert but not fussy. Watch a baby's schedule for several days before selecting a time. (Just before or after a feeding time is not a good time.)

☐ Move the baby gently. If the baby shows resistance, stop.

☐ Talk or sing to the baby during exercise.

☐ Try the following exercises for a newborn. Be creative and use others, too.

    a. With the baby on his or her back, lift arms above the head, straighten them from the shoulders (in the form of a cross), and down to the sides.

    b. Draw the palms of the hands together as in clapping.

    c. Alternately move one knee up to the chest and then the other.

    d. Straighten the knees by holding the legs together with one hand under the calves and the other hand gently pushing the knees flat.

▶ Scheduling

Babies don't come into the world knowing anything about a schedule. The age-old question is:

Q *Should parents try to figure out when their baby is "telling them" that he or she is hungry or sleepy, or should parents try to teach babies to adopt a schedule for eating or sleeping?*

A One answer that works well for parents is to watch their baby for a few days. Then they can work out a schedule based on their baby's needs as well as their own. They should try to keep within a few minutes of the schedule.

In time, babies will adopt the schedule as long as it closely parallels their needs. There is evidence that babies fed on schedule are less fussy. Parents should keep in mind that the needs of babies change. For instance, three-hour feedings eventually change to four-hour feedings. Also, parents may need to change the schedule for their own convenience. Parents need to remember that scheduling is one way to show consistency. Babies learn to trust the world (and show less fear and anxiety) when their environment is consistent.

● Meeting the Newborn's Intellectual Needs

For years people thought newborns were sleepy, helpless, and unable to understand the world around them. The more people study children's learning, the more they realize that learning begins right after birth. In fact, the brain and some of the senses are active before birth. Because learning begins so early, parents are a child's first teachers.

The *sense organs* (eyes, ears, nose, skin, tongue) transmit information from the environment to the brain. All of our sense organs are functioning at birth. (Dogs and cats are born "blind.") Thus, newborns have a great ability for learning.

1—*Enrich:* Develop a chart headed with the categories "Flexible Scheduling" and "Rigid Scheduling." List characteristics under each category. Then make two headings under each category, "Advantages" and "Disadvantages." Compare lists.

2—*Discuss:* How does an infant have an early advantage over a cat at birth? Refer to their sensory development at birth.

3—*Resource: Learning Through the Senses,* SAG.

▶ What Can Newborns Do?

Newborns can tell the difference between human speech and other sounds. Some studies found that babies in the delivery room responded to human speech by looking in the direction of the sound. The same babies ignored other sounds. Babies between 12 and 24 hours old can move arms and legs rhythmically to human speech.

During the first few hours after birth, babies can tell the difference between a click and a tone sound. They know whether to turn their heads right or left for a reward of sugar water. Within a week, newborns become even better at distinguishing sounds. For example, newborns will cry in response to another baby's cry, but not to a fake cry. By three weeks, babies can distinguish between a parent's and a stranger's voice.

During the first few weeks of life, babies begin to learn about space. If babies see a moving object approaching them on a collision course, they will turn their heads or pull away as much as possible. If the object is not on a collision course, babies will not defend themselves.

Imitation is a common way humans learn. Until recently, experts thought babies didn't imitate until they were at least eight months old. Now they know newborns can imitate adults' facial and hand gestures. The baby's ability to imitate develops quickly. Within a year, infants can imitate some child care tasks. For instance, they can give a doll a bottle.

Newborns show that they're learning by their behavior. When presented with a stimulus such as your face, an object, or a sound, they respond by becoming quiet and looking. Their heart rate increases. Newborns also show learning because they can remember for a short period of time. If you show newborns a stuffed dog a few times and then show them the same stuffed dog and a stuffed duck, they will look at the duck. Thus, you know they remembered the older stimulus (the dog) and were more interested in the newer stimulus (the duck).

▶ How Can Parents Help Their Babies Learn?

As you can see, newborns are learners. Just as parents need to meet the newborn's physical needs, they need to meet the newborn's intellectual needs. Parents must take time to stimulate newborns.

Most parents ask, "When and how do I stimulate my newborn?" Babies learn in their waking, alert state. Their eyes are open and shiny, and they look around. When they are over-stimulated or bored, they either become more active and fretful or go to sleep. (Adults behave in much the same way.) Because newborns can't walk or crawl, experiences must be taken to them. Newborns learn through their senses.

Most of the stimulation comes from being near parents and other caregivers. Newborns are fascinated at seeing faces, hearing sounds, and feeling warm and loved when cuddled, 6-18. Warm and expressive talk stimulates newborns. Newborns love to hear singing (and they are an uncritical audience).

Newborns enjoy looking at objects, 6-19. Because their distance vision is limited for three or four weeks, mobiles hung above the beds are almost useless. Newborns are often placed on their stomachs. They can see objects in the corners of their bed as they turn their heads left and right. (Because newborns tilt their heads back, they see objects placed in the corners of the bed more easily than objects placed on the sides.) Objects should be changed frequently. Newborns get bored, too.

Grasping objects during the newborn stage is a reflex action. For added safety, objects should be securely fastened, nontoxic, and too large to swallow.

Other ways to stimulate the newborn include using colorful bed bumper pads. A wind chime, a music box, or some lullabies or soothing music are other good sensory experiences for newborns.

3

1—*Discuss:* Give examples of ways you have noticed imitation occurring in infants. Do you think a negative role model would influence babies under eight months of age?

2—*Activity:* Use two stuffed animals to illustrate the older and newer stimulus.

3—*Enrich:* Discuss overstimulation of infants with the following case study. Jorge is now three months old. His father is very excited about changes in Jorge's alertness and new learnings, so he rushes home every night to play aggressively with his son. Jorge reacts by becoming very fussy and tired. What suggestions would you give Jorge's father?

6-18   Babies need to be cuddled.

● Meeting the Newborn's Social-Emotional Needs

Each baby is born with an individuality. Some babies are more active. Some like to be cuddled. Some cry a lot, and others seem happy. This individuality influences the parents' response to the baby, just like a person's personality affects the way you respond to them. In this section, you will examine the individuality of babies. You also will learn ways parents can meet their babies' social-emotional needs.

▶ Alertness of Newborns

Babies seem to learn best when they are in the alert inactive state. At this time, babies are quiet but alert. In this state, babies also seem to develop warm relationships with others. Newborns are not much fun if they are always asleep or fussy. Parents often refer to alert-inactive babies as "good" babies and fussy babies as "difficult" ones.

6-19   Newborns' first toys are objects to see, and they already show toys they prefer.

Newborn Toys

Designs and Patterns	Objects that Move	Circular-Shaped Objects	Other Objects
Newborns like bold, black and white patterns. They prefer horizontal and diagonal designs to vertical ones. Babies like spiral patterns and concentric circles more than solid-colored circles.	Helium-inflated mylar balloons and plastic lids with designs painted on them flutter with the bed's movement.	Newborns enjoy balls made from aluminum foil and bright-colored yarn. Rings are also a favorite.	Pictures of faces are favorites. Newborns also enjoy bright-colored bows and ribbons, artificial flowers, and mirrors.

1—*Resource: Toys for Newborns,* SAG.

2—*Discuss:* How would the Brazelton scale help parents predict a difficult baby, develop strategies for relieving their stress, and make the baby more content?

Babies differ in alertness because of their individuality and age when they were born. (Premature babies are often not as alert.) Also, babies differ in the amount of time they are alert. There seems to be a general pattern in the development of alertness. Unless affected by the drugs used in delivery, newborns are usually alert for a while after their birth. Then newborns tend to sleep a lot during the next few days. With each passing week, newborns spend more time in the alert-inactive stage. They average 11 hours the first week and 22 hours the fourth week.

Parents can establish a good relationship early in the newborn's life, even if the baby is sleepy or fussy most of the time. Time takes care of the sleepiness of healthy newborns. Parents should take advantage of their alert states by cuddling and playing with them. Parents can enjoy fussy newborns in their alert quiet times and attempt to soothe them when fussy.

▶ Soothing a Fussy Baby

All newborns cry. Some babies cry $\frac{1}{6}$ to $\frac{1}{4}$ of each day, even when nothing is wrong. Parents need to understand that crying is not related to their parenting abilities. Some babies just cry more and are harder to soothe than others.

Newborns cry for almost any reason, because crying is the way they "talk." They may cry because they are tired, hungry, lonely, or uncomfortable. Too, they may cry to relax from tension. Colic is a major reason babies cry, especially during the first three months. **Colic** is a condition (not a disease) in which the baby has intense abdominal pain. There are many causes of colic, such as allergies, tension, swallowing air when sucking, and hunger. Medication may be prescribed in severe cases, but soothing often works.

Parents should try to soothe newborns. Until the baby is about six months old, parents will not spoil the baby by answering cries. To soothe a newborn, try to interpret the cry, then respond. Chart 6-20 describes three distinct cries and how to respond to them. Some ways to soothe a baby are the following:

☐ Rock the baby in a vertical (over your shoulder) position. Put your hand behind the baby's head and rock quickly.

☐ Carry the baby around the house or yard.

2

3

6-20   Newborns communicate with their cries.

The Meanings of Cries		
Cause	**Sound of Cry**	**Ways to Respond**
Pain	Cycle begins with shrill scream, followed by silence, and ends with short gasps. Cycle is repeated.	Ease pain if possible. Cuddle baby to calm.
Hunger or Boredom	Slow cries that become louder and rhythmic.	Feed if near feeding time. OR Entertain by giving baby a tour of the house or yard.
Upset	Fussy, rather quiet cry. Cry sounds a bit forced.	Cuddle or entertain.

1—*Math Activity:* Calculate how many hours a baby would cry if he or she normally cried $\frac{1}{6}$ to $\frac{1}{4}$ of each 24-hour day.

2—*Discuss:* In the above example, if you were a working parent and your baby picked your togetherness time as his or her crying time, how might you feel and react? What could you do about this crying situation?

3—*Enrich:* Interview new parents you know (or a teacher at your school with a young child) about what they have done for extreme fussiness. Compare the responses.

☐ Sing and play music. Babies like the quiet tones of lullabies or even a steady tone. Dr. Hajime Murooka recorded the sounds a baby hears before birth—the mother's breathing and heartbeat. He found that these sounds soothe the newborn. The recording is now sold as *"Lullaby from the Womb."*

☐ Take the baby for a car ride.

Crying causes tension in parents. Relief from tension is good for family relationships. Using a baby-sitter for an hour or so each day, or even an entire afternoon, may help reduce tensions.

● Meeting the Parents' Needs

Parenting skills do not come automatically. They are learned. Even experienced parents find they must learn new things with each child. Each parent learns to cope in a different way. Because learning takes time, the first few weeks are especially difficult ones.

Parents shouldn't forget about their own needs while learning to care for newborns. Even though their sleep and rest will be disrupted by demands of newborns, parents still need to rest. They need to organize their tasks. They need adult companionship.

▶ The Need for Rest

Getting enough rest is always important, and it is even more important for new parents. Newborns can tire parents. This is hard on their physical health. It can also lead to irritability and depression. Thus, it is important for parents to rest when possible. Parents of newborns need to put off unnecessary chores, such as cooking difficult dishes or doing extra cleaning. They should sleep or rest while babies sleep. Parents who formula-feed babies can take turns feeding. This will help both parents get more rest.

▶ Organize Tasks

Parents need to organize their households. Valuable time is wasted looking for misplaced items. New parents need to find a place for baby gear. If parents travel with babies, additional places such as the car have to be organized. Parents need to be mentally organized, too. A bulletin board used for posting doctors' recommendations, appointments, shopping lists, and other reminders may help.

▶ Time to Be with Adults

Parents need to have time to spend with other adults—especially each other. Mothers and fathers need attention, too. Spending some time with adults each day restores their energy. Parents should plan for extra time for each other and other adults.

Parents need to get out of the house with and without newborns, 6-21. Spending too much time in the house often gives parents the feeling that they are living in a baby's world. Going out, even for a short walk, restores physical and mental energy. It can make both babies and parents feel better. Parents also need to have competent baby-sitters for some outings without babies.

6-21   New parents need to spend time away from their baby to help restore mental energy.

© John Shaw

1—*Activity:* Demonstrate the methods listed for soothing a baby.

2—*Reflect:* Write a short paragraph listing ways you would relieve your stress from a fussy baby.

3—*Discuss:* How could a parenting class or support group help parents learn coping and parenting strategies? How

would it help them to recognize differences among children?

4—*Discuss:* Recall a time when you were very tired. How did you compensate? Would this work for a parent?

5—*Enrich:* Assume that you are starting a new semester in school and a new job. How would you organize your time? What techniques could help parents of newborns?

New parents can learn a lot from sharing with other parents. Many first-time parents find it helpful to call special friends for advice. In fact, studies show that many parents who found having children an unhappy experience were isolated from family or friends.

The successful development of newborns depends on the parent-child relationship. When parents have their needs met, newborns have a good chance of having their physical, intellectual, and social-emotional needs met. Babies whose needs are met by loving parents are off to a good start, 6-22.

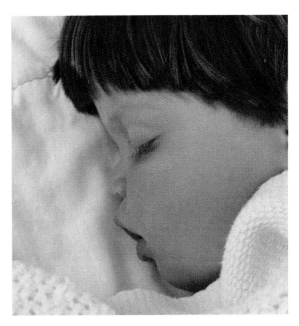

6-22   Babies whose needs are met by loving parents are off to a good start.

Summary

Newborn babies undergo a number of tests to determine whether they are healthy. Among these are the Apgar test, the Brazelton scale, and the test for PKU.

Newborns are not always the pretty babies shown in advertisements. Their body looks out of proportion to their head. Their skin may be wrinkled, blotchy, and reddish in color.

Babies have a number of automatic, unlearned behaviors called *reflexes*. How babies respond to these helps determine the health and maturity of their nervous system.

Parents must decide whether newborns will be formula-fed or breast-fed. Nursing mothers need to eat a well-balanced diet.

Newborns' clothing should be comfortable, safe, easy to put on and take off. They should also be appropriate for the temperature and easy to launder. Using disposable or cloth diapers is a decision parents make based on expense and convenience.

Stimulation meets the intellectual needs of newborns. Most of this comes from being near parents and other caregivers. Hearing and seeing others talk and looking at and feeling objects helps their sensory awareness. Parents meet the social-emotional needs of children by enjoying babies' alert quiet times and soothing them when they are fussy.

Parents must respond to their own needs. Caring for babies is time-consuming and can be exhausting.

1—*Activity:* Divide into four groups representing parents with full-time jobs; a father with a full-time job and mother with a part-time job; a mother with a full-time job and a father who stays home; and a working single parent. Describe your needs to get out of the house (with or without the child). List activities you could do with and without the child. Discuss the need to spend time with adults.

2—*Resource: Meeting New Parents' Needs,* SAG.

To Review

Write your answers on a separate sheet of paper.

1. Which of the following is not included in the Apgar test:
   a. breathing effort
   b. heart rate
   c. muscle tone
   d. eye movements
   e. skin color
   f. responsiveness

2. Explain the difference between reflexes and voluntary movements. Describe two reflexes seen in the newborn.

3. Match the following descriptions of a newborn's appearance with their definitions.
   _____ vernix caseosa
   _____ fontaneles
   _____ lanugo
   _____ stork bites
   a. soft, downy hair on ears, shoulders, back, and face
   b. whitish, cheese-like covering on skin
   c. "soft spots" on skull
   d. pink blotches on forehead, eyelids, and back of neck

4. List three advantages of breast-feeding and three advantages of formula-feeding.

5. Chris is a newborn who is formula-fed every 4 hours during a 24-hour period. He weighs 10 pounds. Calculate the minimum ounces of formula Chris needs for each feeding. (Add a little extra, because Chris may want more or less than the minimum at feeding.)

6. True or false. Newborns who cry a lot are just spoiled. The way to stop the crying is to let them cry it out.

7. Explain how parents may meet their own needs for the following:
   a. rest
   b. time spent with each other
   c. organizing their household
   d. getting out of the house

To Do

1. Look through current magazines and find pictures of infants. Explain how you can tell whether or not the baby is a newborn.

2. Divide the class into groups. Make a shopping list of items needed for the following:
   a. clothing and diapering
   b. formula-feeding (bottles, nipples, sterilizer, formula, etc.)
   c. bedding
   d. bathing
   Do some comparison shopping to find the range of prices for each item. Design a bulletin board entitled "Big Needs for the Little One."

3. Make some safe, interesting objects for an infant's crib (see 6-19).
4. Assist a mother of a newborn with the routine tasks of feeding, bathing, diapering, and dressing.
5. Ask a pediatrician to talk with your class about the care of a newborn and the importance of well-baby checkups.
6. Arrange to tour a local hospital. Focus the tour on the following:
    a. appearance and activity of newborns
    b. nurses' care of newborns
    c. pediatricians checking newborns
    d. facilities for care of newborns
    e. arrangements for mothers and fathers to spend time with their newborns

To Observe

1. Observe a newborn. Compare the newborn's physical characteristics with those in 6-8.
2. Observe a newborn's movements. What reflexes did you observe?
3. Observe a parent caring for a newborn. How much time does each task take? Which tasks seem easy? Which tasks seem more difficult?
4. Observe a newborn being dressed. Which clothing features made dressing the baby easy? Which made dressing the baby difficult? Did the clothes look comfortable on the baby? Why or why not?

To Think Critically

1. Some new parents have never been near newborns. How do you think advertisements posing older babies as newborns affect their perceptions of their newborn babies?
2. Child development experts often advise parents to "follow the baby's lead." Brainstorm with classmates how you can follow a baby's lead in meeting his or her needs. Are there times when newborns should follow their parents' lead? Why or why not?
3. Sometimes a spouse becomes unhappy when the other spouse spends so much time with the baby. How can a spouse tell when this is a reasonable complaint? What are some specific ways parents can have some time to meet each other's needs?

Part 3

Infants

Infancy is defined as the period of life between two weeks and one year following birth. Children's development during this time is exciting, because they grow and learn new skills each day.

By studying **chapter 7,** you will learn how quickly an infant's size and body proportions change. You also will see how motor skills follow growth patterns. This means they proceed, in an organized way, from reflexes to the first wobbly steps.

As you read **chapter 8,** you will learn how babies actively master their worlds. Their well-worked senses are becoming more refined and coordinated. Babies are interested in hearing others speak. This helps them learn, and by the end of their first year, babies reach the stage of beginning speech.

Special bonds are as important for the infant as they are for you. In **chapter 9,** you will see how babies' tools for interaction change throughout the first year. These interactions help babies form secure attachments, develop self-awareness, and become more independent.

Chapter 10 will teach you how to care for babies during their first year. Babies depend on adults for physical care. In addition, they need support for their mental and social development.

Chapter 7

Physical Development of the Infant

Children change a lot physically during their first year.

After studying this chapter, you will be able to

☐ describe how an infant develops physically during the first year.

☐ describe the order in which an infant's motor skills develop.

After studying this chapter, you will be able to define

age norm
body proportions
crawl
crawling
creeping
cruising
deciduous teeth
failure to thrive
large-motor skills
locomotion
motor development
ossification
sequence
skeletal system
small-motor skills
teething
voluntary grasping

With the help and care of others, babies develop physically during the first year. A human's physical growth is completed at 20 or 21 years. This growth period is longer than that of any living creature. During much of this time, others must care for the human.

Just as babies grow quickly during the prenatal and neonatal stages, they grow quickly during their first year of life. It is fun to watch a small infant grow into a chubby baby. Good physical development is important during this time. A healthy baby keeps growing and developing in all areas.

Skeletal Growth

The **skeletal system** is made up of bones and teeth. *Skeletal growth* refers to the changes in height and weight and the appearance of teeth.

▶ Length and Weight

The baby's length and weight changes quickly during the first year. (The term *length* is used for the first year because the baby does not stand. After the first year, the term *height* is used.) Changes happen so quickly that even people who see the baby daily are amazed at how fast he or she grows. They can see the baby change.

All children grow at their own rate. Most normal infants, however, grow $\frac{1}{2}$ (9 or 10 inches) of their birth length (20 to 21 inches) during the first year. They double their birth weight in four or five months. They triple their birth weight in one year.

The baby's rate of growth is more important than the actual length and weight. The baby's length increases about 20 percent in the first three months, 7-1. It increases about 50 percent in the first year. Weight doubles by five months. From 6 to 12 months, weight increases about one pound per month. Usually boys are slightly longer and heavier than girls (by about $\frac{3}{4}$ of an inch and $1\frac{1}{2}$ pounds).

By about nine months, the infant becomes chubby. This change happens because fat tissues under the skin have increased. After this time, fat tissues begin to decrease. Even at this early age, boys have more muscle length and thickness while girls have more fat.

Sometimes babies experience a **failure to thrive**. This is a failure to grow, which is diagnosed as a drop in growth percentiles over time. For example, if you were looking at a growth chart, a baby who drops from the 25th percentile to the 10th percentile would be diagnosed as a "failure to thrive." Some of the causes include:

☐ Diseases that prevent all or some nutrients from being absorbed or that cause nutrients to be quickly expelled from the body

☐ Maternal milk is not good due to maternal illness, malnutrition, etc. or diluted formula

☐ Baby is not given enough time for feeding

☐ Night feedings are skipped, or many feedings are skipped due to neglect or abuse

▶ Body Proportions

Infants do not look like small adults. Even their body proportions are different. (**Body proportions** are the relative size of body parts.) For instance, the head is about $\frac{1}{4}$ of the infant's total length. It is $\frac{1}{10}$ of the adult's height. Unlike the

3

7-1 A baby's length and weight increase quickly during the first year.

4

Average Length and Weight During First Year		
Age in Months	Length in Inches	Weight in Pounds
Birth	20	$7\frac{1}{2}$
3	$23\frac{3}{4}$	$12\frac{1}{2}$
6	26	$16\frac{3}{4}$
9	28	20
12	$29\frac{1}{2}$	$22\frac{1}{4}$

1—*Activity:* Display pictures of different full-grown animals with labels telling their age. Compare to humans at ages 20 or 21.

2—*Math Activity:* If your weight at birth was 7.5 pounds, calculate what it would be at 16 if it multiplied at the same rate as during the first year. If your length at birth was 21 inches, calculate what your height would be at 16 if it multiplied at the same rate as during the first year.

3—*Activity:* Examine a closeup picture of a newborn, pointing out some typical physical traits.

4—*Note:* Point out that length is hard to measure because neonates maintain the fetal position after birth.

adult, an infant's forehead is wider than the chin. The jaw is smaller and slopes backward. This is commonly called the "baby look."

From birth until six months, the infant's head is larger than the *thorax* (chest). In normal six-month-old children, the thorax becomes larger. The difference in the distance around the thorax as compared to the head continues to increase with age.

Besides having a large head, an infant has a long trunk, a "pot-bellied" abdomen, and short legs. The baby grows longer during the first year because the trunk, not the legs, grow. The abdomen sticks out because the internal organs are large for the baby's small body. Because the center of gravity is high on the baby's body, the result is poor balance. No wonder babies "toddle" rather than walk.

▶ Bones and Teeth

The infant skeleton is mainly made up of cartilage. That is why infants' bones do not break easily. There are large spaces between their "bones" to help the joints bend easily without breaking. They can suck their toes without any trouble, but sitting or standing are impossible because the skeleton is not sturdy. An infant's bones can become misshapen due to their softness. That is why it is a good idea to change the position of babies when they sleep. Always lying on the same side can make their head flat in one place.

Three changes occur in a baby's bones.

- ☐ First, the length of the bones increases.
- ☐ Second, **ossification** (the depositing of the minerals calcium and phosphorus) begins to occur. Ossification helps the skeletal frame become sturdy. This helps the infant sit and eventually walk.
- ☐ Third, the number of bones changes. For example, the hand and wrist of a one-year-old infant has only three bones, but there are 28 bones in the adult's hand and wrist. Also, ossification in the skull results in several bones becoming one skull bone. This growth is completed in about two years.

Teeth, a part of the skeletal system, begin forming in the sixth week of fetal life. By birth, all 20 **deciduous teeth** (nonpermanent teeth) and a few permanent teeth are developing deep in the jaw. Babies usually begin **teething,** or cutting teeth, during the second half of the first year, 7-2. The **sequence,** or order, that teeth appear is easier to predict than *when* teeth appear. In fact, a few babies are born with one or more teeth. Other children do not get any until after the first year.

⬤ Motor Development

Motor development is the use and control of muscles that direct body movements. Learning to use and control large muscles helps babies to crawl and walk. These abilities are called **large-motor skills**. Being able to control small objects, hands, and fingers uses small muscles. These abilities are called **small-motor skills.** Having control over the body is a sign of the babies' growth and development.

The baby's motor skills develop in three main patterns. This order of motor development builds upon the order of brain development. The following list shows the pattern of motor development.

7-2 Deciduous (nonpermanent) teeth appear in a predictable pattern.

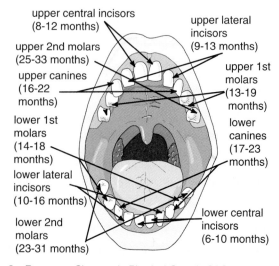

upper central incisors (8-12 months)

upper lateral incisors (9-13 months)

upper 2nd molars (25-33 months)

upper 1st molars (13-19 months)

upper canines (16-22 months)

lower canines (17-23 months)

lower 1st molars (14-18 months)

lower lateral incisors (10-16 months)

lower 2nd molars (23-31 months)

lower central incisors (6-10 months)

1. Babies move slowly because they must think as they move.
2. Babies' reactions develop from general to specific. At first, babies show general reactions to what they see and hear. Later in the first year, babies give more specific reactions. For instance, if young infants see something they want, they wiggle all over. Older infants smile and reach for the object.
3. Motor development occurs in two directions. The first is from the head out to the foot. The second is from the center out to the extremities (trunk out to the hands and feet).

▶ Head-to-Foot Development

Head-to-foot development begins before birth. The fetus develops a head, then arm buds, then leg buds. At birth, babies have developed facial muscles but not leg muscles. This is why babies can suck but cannot walk.

Drawing 7-3 shows the sequence in which babies can control their head, neck, and trunk muscles. This order describes milestones in the infant's motor development. The order of these steps is more important than how fast the baby actually does them. How do experts know that babies develop at these ages? Some babies develop when they are older, others when they are younger. Experts use the average of this range of ages, called an **age norm,** to know when babies develop.

Head and Neck Control

Newborns need to have their head supported because their muscles are not strong enough to do so. Some babies can raise their unsteady head briefly when lying on their stomach. By two months, most babies spend a great deal of time with their head and chest raised. Between three and four months, eye muscles are well developed, permitting them to focus on objects in any direction. They can smile when they want to and make some sounds with the lips. Head control is almost complete when babies are about six months old. By this time, babies can raise their head while lying on their back. They can also hold their head while sitting.

Trunk Control

Control of the trunk develops more slowly than control of the head. Babies placed on their stomach can lift their head before they can lift both head and chest, 7-4. Trunk control permits babies to achieve two major milestones in motor control—rolling over and sitting.

Rolling Over.   Often between the second and fifth month, babies learn to roll over. Usually they will roll from front to back. A month later, they usually roll from back to front. It is easier for babies to lift the head and trunk when they are on the abdomen than the back.

Sitting.   Learning to sit takes several months. The baby first must gain strength in the neck and back. The baby also must be able to control the head.

Babies can sit briefly with support (being held or with pillows placed at their back) at three or four months of age. Three or four months later they can sit for a short time without support. Older infants often lean forward and support themselves with their arms and legs, 7-5. They may even topple over if distracted. Progress in sitting is rapid in the next few months. By nine months, most babies can sit without support.

Leg Control

Leg control is the last phase of head-to-foot development. With leg control, locomotion really begins. (**Locomotion** is the ability to move from place to place.) Babies usually go through the stages of crawling, creeping, standing, and walking.

Crawling.   **Crawling** is one of the first steps toward walking. How can you tell when a baby is gaining leg control? When the hands and feet work together smoothly, this shows leg control. Babies play with their own feet and toes at about seven months. They begin to crawl at the same time, 7-6. Babies **crawl** by pulling with the arms. They do not lift the abdomen from the floor.

Creeping.   Babies may begin **creeping** between six and eight months. They begin by

4

5

1—*Activity:* Point out head-to-foot development on a chart that illustrates the growth of the fetus.

2—*Note:* For survival, babies must suck immediately. Walking is not necessary for survival.

3—*Note:* Age norms are interesting for comparisons, but caregivers should not worry if children develop slowly.

Development is sequential, but the rate is individual.

4—*Activity:* Use the older doll to demonstrate first attempts at sitting, showing how a caregiver can help the infant learn to sit without support.

5—*Activity:* Demonstrate crawling and creeping with the doll. Point out that many people reverse the definitions of these terms.

2 months (chin up)

3 months
(chest up—arm
support)

4 months
(sits with support)

5 months
(sits on lap—
grasps object)

6 months
(sits on high chair,
grasps dangling
object)

7 months
(sits without
support)

8 months
(stands with help)

9 months
(stands holding
furniture)

10 months (creeps)

11 months
(walks when led)

12 months
(pulls to stand by
furniture)

14 months
(stands alone)

15 months
(walks alone)

Thomas J. Roberts

7-3   Babies gain control over their head and neck, then their leg muscles.

1—*Discuss:* Review the order of development pictured.

7-4   This baby can raise his head and chest high for rather long periods of time.

American Guidance Service, Inc.

7-5   Until back muscles are strong, leaning forward helps babies to sit unaided.

7-6   Playing with toes is a sign of the leg control needed for crawling.

lifting their abdomen and hips off the floor alternately. The movement may become a rhythmical, rocking motion. Within a couple of months, many babies can move forward or backward on hands and knees, or on hands and feet, with their abdomen off the floor, 7-7.

Standing and Walking.   Six-month-old babies enjoy standing when supported under the arms. They push with their feet and bounce on adults' laps. A few months later, babies can pull up into a standing position. When babies stand alone, they often enjoy *cruising,* or walking with the support of an adult.

At first babies stand with support, holding on to a stable object. As they develop, babies stand further away from objects. They use them for balance by holding on with one hand. They also take a few cautious steps between objects and people, 7-8. Most babies stand alone between 12 and 14 months and begin walking a few weeks later.

© John Shaw

7-7   To creep, this baby must raise the trunk of her body and coordinate the movements of her arms and legs.

▶ Center-to-Extremities Development

In center-to-extremities development, control begins with the trunk, then arms, hands, and fingers. This control extends to the hips, then legs, feet, and toes. Children can crawl and walk before they are able to use good hand and finger control necessary, for example, to stack blocks. As you can see, the ability to control the body begins with the center, or the trunk, of the body and moves outward.

As you read earlier, the baby comes into the world with a grasping reflex (Palmar reflex), which disappears at about four months of age. The grasping reflex is replaced by *voluntary grasping,* 7-9. Voluntary grasping is well developed by five or six months. Arm, hand, and finger control develops in stages, 7-10.

7-8   With adults ready to "catch," a baby who is almost ready to walk will take a few steps.

© John Shaw

1—*Discuss:* Compare this walking to the stepping reflex that is typical shortly after birth.

2—*Resource: Motor Skills Develop Rapidly,* SAG.

3—*Resource: Observation: Babies Use Motor Skills in Play,* SAG.

Grasping Ability

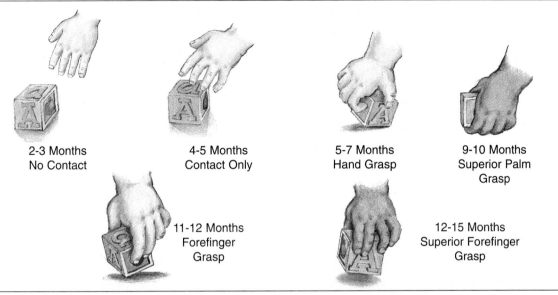

2-3 Months
No Contact

4-5 Months
Contact Only

5-7 Months
Hand Grasp

9-10 Months
Superior Palm
Grasp

11-12 Months
Forefinger
Grasp

12-15 Months
Superior Forefinger
Grasp

Thomas J. Roberts

7-9   A baby's grasping ability goes through stages. In the beginning, a baby has a rather clumsy grasp, using the fingers to press an object to the palm. Later the baby is able to grasp precisely, using the index finger and thumb.

7-10   Babies develop complex grasping skills during the first year.

Arm and Hand Control	
Approximate Age	**Skills**
2 months	☐ Babies can swipe at objects with either hand.
4-5 months	☐ Babies can reach and grasp a stationary object.
	☐ The body sways, so babies may need support to successfully grasp.
5-6 months	☐ Babies accept one object handed to them.
	☐ Babies can reach for and grasp dangling objects.
6-7 months	☐ Babies carry objects grasped to the mouth.
7 months	☐ Babies accept two objects handed to them.
8-9 months	☐ Babies pick up objects with thumb used in opposition to fingers.
10 months	☐ Babies accept three objects handed to them.

● Differences in Physical Development

With few exceptions, the order of physical development is the same for every child. However, every child develops at his or her own rate. The rate is affected by heredity, nutrition, illnesses, and activity. Some infants develop quickly; others lag behind. Some develop quickly in one area but slower in another.

If development seems to be much slower than the norms, parents should talk to a doctor. Giving infants regular medical care is the best way to find and treat problems.

2

3

Summary

A baby's physical development is rapid during the first year. The length and weight increase quickly. The baby's body proportions soon change. The bones begin to develop. Teeth begin to appear in a certain order.

Motor development is the ability to have small and large muscle control. Walking, crawling, and using arms, hands, and fingers are motor skills. This development helps the child control body movements.

Control over the body comes in a slow, predictable pattern. Babies' reactions to things they see and hear are general at first, then become more specific. Control of the body begins from head to foot and also goes from the trunk outward. There is a sequence to babies' motor development.

All children develop physically in much the same way. The rate may vary because it is affected by heredity, nutrition, illnesses, and activity.

To Review

Write your answers on a separate sheet of paper.

1

1. Babies _____ (add half, double, triple) their birth weight during the first year.
2. True or false. The rate of growth over the months is more important than total growth.
3. True or false. In the first year, the baby gets longer because the legs grow.
4. What are three changes that occur in the bones during development?
5. True or false. Motor development is the way children learn how to play with others and share their toys that develop motor skills.
6. True or false. There is a pattern to children's physical development.
7. Which best describes the motor skill development of infants?
   a. Infants develop the same motor skills at the same time.
   b. Infants develop rapidly and slowly in the same areas.
   c. Infants learn at the same rate but the sequence of skills varies.
   d. Infants learn in the same sequence but the rate varies.
8. The baby gains body control in a certain order. Number the following motor skills in order of occurrence.
   _____ sits without support with back straight
   _____ raises the head while on abdomen
   _____ creeps
   _____ walks
   _____ rolls over from front to back
   _____ stands without help
   _____ picks up object with thumb used in opposition to finger
9. Reflexes are _____ (learned, unlearned). Voluntary movements are _____ (learned, unlearned).

1—*Answers:* Answers to review questions can be found in the front section of this TAE.

To Do

1.   Observe a doctor giving a well-baby exam. Ask the doctor to explain each procedure. Note measurements of weight and length, and head and thorax. Also note heart and breathing rates and reflexive and voluntary movement. How does the baby's progress compare to age norms? Check progress the baby has made since the last checkup.
2.   Ask four or five mothers who have infants to bring them to class. You may visit a child care program to watch infants there. (The infants should be of different ages such as 2, 4, 6, 8, and 11 months.) Compare the babies' abilities to sit, move about, and grasp objects.
3.   As a group or class project, write a one- or two-page brochure that explains at what age parents can expect their children to learn certain motor skills. You may also find pictures or drawings to illustrate the various skills. The brochure could be checked by a physician before making copies. Find out whether copies could be given to new parents at the hospital, posted in medical offices, or printed in a local paper.
4.   Observe two or three infants who are between 6 and 12 months perform the following motor skills: crawling and creeping, getting into a sitting position, pulling up to a standing position, returning to a sitting position, walking while holding on, and other skills. Note the babies' ages and levels of skill.

To Observe

1.   Observe three infants who differ by two or three months in age. How do they differ in their physical maturity? In their motor skills?
2.   Observe two infants who are the same age. How do they differ in their physical maturity? How do they differ in their motor skills? Does one infant have a lag in maturity or skills? If so, did the parent say anything that explains the lag, such as low birthweight or serious illness?
3.   Observe how several babies move toward a toy. Describe exactly how each baby moves toward the toy. (Often babies use more than one motor skill to reach a toy.)

1—*Activity:* Also observe reflexes, head and neck control, trunk control, creeping, and crawling. Ask each mother questions about her baby's development.

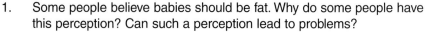

To Think Critically

1. Some people believe babies should be fat. Why do some people have this perception? Can such a perception lead to problems?
2. Parents sometimes "push" their babies to walk early. How can this be harmful to babies?
3. As you read, the grasping reflex is not highly developed until almost one year of age. Can parents assume that small objects on the floor cannot be grasped by a baby and inserted in the mouth, nose, or ears? Why or why not?

Crawling is one of the first steps toward walking.

Chapter 8

During their first year of life, babies learn a lot about the world around them.

Intellectual Development of the Infant

After studying this chapter, you will be able to

☐ describe how and what infants learn.

☐ explain how infants express what they know through language.

☐ identify the order in which infants learn.

After studying this chapter, you will be able to define

active vocabulary
babble
cognition
concept
coo
depth perception
imitating
inflections
intellectual development
monotone
object concept
object constancy
object identity
object permanence
passive vocabulary
perception
perceptual learning
reduplication babbling
sensorimotor stage
stimuli
vocabulary

Intellectual development is how you learn, what you learn, and how you express what you know through language. (It also is called *mental development* or *cognitive development.*) During the baby's first year, intellectual development happens as quickly as physical development.

Babies come into the world using all of their sense organs. They react to **stimuli** (sound, light, and others) with certain reflexes. Within 12 months, infants have highly developed sense organs and motor skills. They use these to learn about people, objects, places, and events in their world. At birth, the main sound babies make is crying. By the end of the first year, they know many words. Some can even say a few words.

● How Infants Learn

For many years, people have wondered how infants learn. A baby's brain and sense organs mature a lot during the first year. This helps babies learn. As motor skills develop, infants are able to move toward many sights, sounds, and other learning experiences.

Learning involves more than physical development. Most researchers in child development believe babies *want* to learn. Each month infants exert more and more effort to explore their world, 8-1. Instead of just seeing, hearing, and touching, babies try to make sense of people, objects, sounds, and events. Experiences that are repeated or like others reinforce a baby's learning. New experiences help expand a baby's knowledge.

8-1 Each month, infants exert more and more effort to explore their world.

1—*Discuss:* What are other senses through which babies learn? What types of stimuli result from all of these senses?

© Nancy P. Alexander

8-2   Common experiences—even a trip to the back-yard—provide a rich mental diet for the infant.

Babies don't just try to figure out what is happening. They also try to cause things to happen, like making their cradle gym bounce or making a ball roll. Babies like to repeat and vary these events, too.

The following two factors seem to affect the rate of mental development:

☐   the baby's physical development (mainly brain growth)

☐   the baby's environment

Just as an infant needs good nutrition for physical growth, he or she also needs a good mental diet. Interesting things to see, hear, and touch are "food for thought." Because the world is brand-new to the infant, common objects and experiences provide a rich mental diet. The adult's face, a cardboard box, some old pans, or a trip in the yard can provide good learning experiences, 8-2.

Babies Choose One Object over Another

You have noticed that babies seem to prefer some toys or objects over others. Babies have certain preferences. They prefer to play or interact more with one object than another. Researchers feel that infants have inborn abilities to choose the stimuli that will most help them learn. Studies show the following changes in preferences, or choices, they make:

☐ **Preferences change from parts of objects to complete objects.**

At first, infants react to, or study, parts of objects. Later, they pay more attention to the entire object. For instance, at two months they smile at eyes drawn on a blank background. At three months, they study a picture that has eyes and a nose. By five months they smile only at the picture of the full face. They prefer the complete objects rather than parts of objects.

☐ **Preferences change from simple to complex objects.**

Until babies are almost two months old, they do not prefer one object over another. After that, babies prefer more complex objects. For example, babies prefer 3-D objects over 2-D pictures. They prefer patterned or textured cards over plain white or solid-colored cards. Babies also prefer a drawn human face over any other drawn pattern or solid-colored card. Other preferences include slow-moving objects over nonmoving objects and curved lines over straight lines. They may show little or no reaction to complex stimuli because they can not understand it.

☐ **Preferences change from familiar to new objects.**

After two months of age, babies begin to explore things that are new to them. They ignore objects that are too different because they may not understand them.

8-3   Infants change their preferences for certain objects.

1—*Discuss:* What are some other common experiences that increase mental development?

2—*Reflect:* How does repetition help you learn? What could you repeat for infants to help them learn?

3—*Discuss:* What are some inexpensive or no-cost items that could vary an infant's environment and result in greater learning?

4—*Discuss:* How does this apply to a real person or regular caregiver?

▶ Perception

Perception involves organizing information that comes through your senses. This is a major step in learning. You perceive by noting how things are alike and different in size, color, shape, and texture. Perceptions come through the senses about form, space, weight, and numbers.

Perception also involves how fast you organize the information. For instance, a mature reader can tell the difference between a "b" and a "d" faster than a beginning reader.

Finally, perception involves the way you react to different sensory experiences. For instance, a child in a room crowded with strangers may run to his or her mother. However, if the child is alone with the mother, he or she may play with a toy and ignore her.

Perceptual Learning

The process of developing perception is called **perceptual learning**. Perceptual learning happens because the sense organs mature and preferences for certain stimuli change.

The sense organs develop at rapid rates. At birth, infants can hear differences between high-pitched and low-pitched sounds. They can move their bodies to the rhythm of adult speech. By

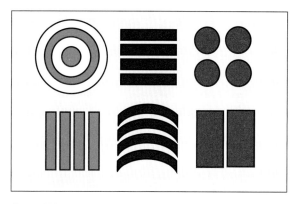

8-5   When shown each of these pairs of lines, infants liked the curved lines more than the straight lines. (Frantz's study.)

three months, babies can tell the difference in the sounds of words like "daddy" and "mama." Their vision improves as their eye muscles become strong enough to focus on objects.

Changes in Preferences.   From the time of birth, babies are bombarded with all types of stimuli. In order to learn, infants must choose among stimuli. See 8-3 through 8-6 to see why babies tend to choose some things over others.

▶ Cognition

Cognition is the act or process of knowing or understanding. Cognition gives meaning to perceptions. The baby's brain begins to piece together perceptions to form a picture in the mind.

Jean Piaget (pya-zhā), a Swiss psychologist, described how humans learn. He believed people learn by exploring on their own in a stimulating environment. Because of reflexes such as sucking and grasping, people begin to explore the world from birth. As reflexes disappear, voluntary movement and sense perceptions help infants explore.

The Sensorimotor Stage

Because infants explore with their senses and their motor actions, Piaget called the first stage of mental development the **sensorimotor stage.** The stage begins at birth, and most

8-4   When shown each of these figures, babies' preferences (from most to least liked) were—circle with face, circle with words, concentric circles, red circle, yellow circle, and white circle. (Frantz's study.)

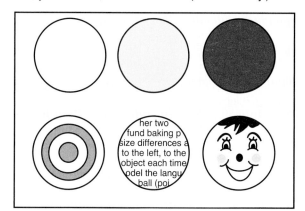

1—*Activity:* Provide an infant toy for each student. Report how perception is involved in an infant's learning. Include similarities and differences in size, shape, color, texture, weight, and number.

2—*Enrich:* Research perceptual learning. Report to the class.

3—*Resource: Toys to Stimulate a Baby's Perception,* SAG.

3

Infants' Preferences for Experiences			
Approximate Age	**Seeing**	**Hearing**	**Touching**
Birth to 3 months	☐ Follows slow-moving objects with eyes. ☐ Looks when held to shoulder. ☐ Looks at hairline part of face at 1 month. ☐ Looks at eyes, nose, and mouth at 2 months. Often smiles. ☐ Prefers patterns to solids. ☐ Follows the gaze of an adult to look where the adult is looking at 2 months.	☐ Reacts physically to sounds by opening eyes widely or startling, etc. ☐ Is calmed by gentle voice. ☐ Connects voices with faces at 1 month.	☐ Lessens reflexive grasping and begins voluntary grasping between 6 weeks and 3 months. ☐ Holds objects less than 1 minute. ☐ Swipes at objects suspended overhead at 2-3 months.
3-6 months	☐ Prefers red and blue to green and yellow. ☐ Enjoys mirrors but does not know his or her own image until after 1 year of age. ☐ Grasps what is seen. ☐ Enjoys small objects. ☐ Imitates facial expressions.	☐ Learns the meaning of familiar sounds, such as making food and a nearby parent. ☐ Reacts to differences in tones of voices. ☐ Tries to locate source of sounds. ☐ Repeats own sounds. ☐ Tells differences in sounds, such as "ba," and "pa."	☐ Grasps with both hands and often clasps hands when object is out of reach at 3-4 months. ☐ Takes 1 object at a time. ☐ Plays with hands at 4 months. ☐ Plays with toes at 5 or 6 months. ☐ Mouths all objects; opens mouth well in advance of approaching objects. ☐ Opens hands wider for larger objects than for smaller objects. ☐ Uses arms and hands

8-6 Babies change their seeing, hearing, and touching preferences as they try to learn about their new worlds.

Infants' Preferences for Experiences...Continued			
6-9 months	☐ Examines objects with eyes and hands. ☐ Recognizes drop-offs (but not safe from falls). ☐ Looks for hidden (covered) toys.	☐ Learns noises different toys make. ☐ Notes differences between questions and statements by changes in pitch. ☐ Enjoys hearing singing and tries to sing along.	☐ Handles objects by turning, shaking, etc. ☐ Enjoys toys with moving parts such as dials and wheels. ☐ Holds own bottle. ☐ Uses 1 object to work another, such as hitting a drum with a stick. ☐ Transfers objects from 1 hand to the other.
9-12 months	☐ Shows less interest in faces except to quickly identify the familiar face and the strange face. ☐ Looks where crawling. ☐ Watches dropped objects with interest to see whether they roll, break, etc. ☐ Enjoys hiding games, such as hide and seek.	☐ Imitates sounds. ☐ Enjoys hearing own name. ☐ Makes sounds of some animals. ☐ Knows meaning of many words and may respond to requests.	☐ Predicts weight of objects with correct arm tension. ☐ Enjoys self-feeding. ☐ Shows held objects to others. ☐ Enjoys dropping objects into pails and boxes. ☐ Enjoys stacking blocks and knocking them down. ☐ Takes lids off objects. ☐ Pulls and pushes roll toys. ☐ Turns knobs and switches. ☐ Nests (puts smaller into larger) objects.

children complete it in two years. During this stage, infants use their senses and motor skills to learn and communicate. Learning at this time is important because it is the basis for all future mental growth.

Piaget described the learnings of the sensorimotor stage through a series of processes that become more and more complex. He found that children solved problems by working through a certain order, 8-7.

Practicing Reflexes and Repeating New Learnings. Piaget observed how infants go from the stage of practicing reflexes they already know, such as sucking, grasping, and crying, to changing some of their reflex skills. For instance, they may suck their thumbs or open and close their hands. They repeat their actions often.

Beginning to Control. Infants then begin to control their world by making a connection between what they do and what happens. If they

1

1—*Discuss:* What are some other actions infants do because of connections or cause and effect?

1

Paiget's Stages **of Cognitive Development**

Stage 1: Sensorimotor Stage (Birth to 2 years)
  a. Substage I: Practicing Reflexes (birth to 1 month)
  b. Substage II: Repeating New Learnings (1 to 4 months)
  c. Substage III: Beginning to Control Their World (4 to 8 months)
  d. Substage IV: Applying Learnings to Solve Complex Problems (8 to 12 months)
  e. Substage V: Discovering New Ways to Solve Problems (12 to 18 months)
  f. Substage VI: Beginning of Thought (18 months to 2 years)
Stage 2: Preoperational Stage (2 to 7 years)
Stage 3: Concrete Operations Stage (7 to 11 years)
Stage 4: Formal Operations Stage (11 years on)

8-7 Piaget described how infants use their senses and motor skills to learn. Infants are in the sensorimotor stage.

kick the cradle gym, the bells ring and the characters move. When they cry, a parent comes to see what they want. Infants try many new actions during this time. They also realize that objects exist even when they can't see them. For example, they look to see where something has been dropped.

Solving Problems. By the time babies are a year old, Piaget believed they applied all of their learnings to solve other kinds of problems. They may mouth an object like a teething ring. They may squeeze, hit, turn, and shake an object to see what it will do. By combining several actions, they discover new ways to solve problems. For example, they may push away a box in order to grasp a toy.

Imitating. Children also learn by *imitating* others. This is an important way to learn. Before this stage, babies could imitate simple things that they could see themselves doing. For instance, they might bang their hands on a table after seeing an

adult do this action. In this stage they can imitate more complex actions that they cannot see themselves do, such as making faces.

● What Infants Learn

As babies explore their world, they learn many concepts. A *concept* is an idea formed by combining what you know about a person, object, place, quality, or event. Thinking is organized through concepts. For instance, if you see an animal you believe is a cat, you immediately think of all you know about cats. Then you note how this animal is like or different from other cats you recall. Children must learn to understand the ideas of cats, then animals, and finally living creatures, 8-8.

Concepts change as the child's brain matures and experiences increase. Concepts change from simple to complex. A child understands the word "chair" before knowing about the many types of chairs. Concepts also change from concrete to abstract. For example, children can draw themselves and their parents (concrete) before they can draw other people (abstract).

8-8 Children must learn to understand the concepts of cats, then animals, and finally living creatures.

1—*Enrich:* Do research on the Sensorimotor Stage of Piaget's Cognitive Development Theory. Report findings to the class.

2—*Resource: Mental Advances in the First Year*, SAG.

3—*Discuss:* Define *concrete* and *abstract*. Give examples of each.

4—*Reflect:* Why is the concept of "dog" confusing? How can you help a child to understand dogs, animals, and living creatures?

8-9 Babies begin to make order out of what they see, hear, smell, taste, and touch.

As children grow, their concepts change from incorrect to correct. First, a child may call all men "daddy." Later, they understand the concept of men.

Concepts are different for each person, too. No two people have exactly the same experiences. Not only do experiences differ, but many concepts involve our emotions. For example, the concept of school may be pleasant for one person but not for another person.

During the first year, infants form many concepts. These concepts help infants make sense of their world. The concepts learned further their mental development.

▶ Perceptual Concepts

Information comes to infants through their senses. At this time, babies begin to make order out of what they see, hear, smell, taste, and touch, 8-9. They begin to perceive, or organize, this information. The following are the major perceptual concepts children learn in the first year:

▪ Object Constancy or Sameness
Object constancy is the ability to learn that objects remain the same even if they seem different. For example, a child may see a big airplane take off and then look small in the sky. Children learn that, although it may look different in size, shape, or color, it is still the same plane, 8-10. Object constancy begins during the first year. It is not fully developed until the second or third year.

1

8-10   Seeing a chair from different views while crawling (A and B) and later while walking (C and D) helps a baby learn object constancy.

2

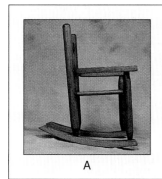

| A | B | C | D |

© John Shaw

1—*Discuss:* Give an example of object constancy.

2—*Discuss:* Summarize positive aspects of crawling.

Object Concept

Object concept is the ability to understand an object. Parents are often the first "objects" with which babies relate. People they know and objects with which they are familiar have permanence. They can relate to them. This must happen before they can think about all people and objects in a general sense.

Object concept has two parts—object identity and object permanence. A child who has **object identity** knows that an object stays the same from one time to the next. For example, a toy bear is the same bear each time the child sees it.

Object permanence begins to develop after two months. The child understands that people, objects, and places still exist even when they are no longer seen, felt, or heard. Baby may know that mother is in the house, even though he or she does not see her in the room. Children will search for a hidden toy they know is there by the age of 8 to 12 months.

Depth Perception

Depth perception is the ability to tell how far away something is. It is needed for safety purposes, to keep a person from stepping off an object far from the ground. It is also used to judge how far something is so that a person can reach it. Depth perception is rather well developed by seven to nine months of age. However, children are not safe from falls for many years.

● Beginnings of Language Development

Language is closely related to mental development. As people understand more concepts, their vocabularies tend to grow. (Your **vocabulary** consists of the words you understand and use.)

Since language and mental growth are closely related, vocabulary words are often thought to measure mental growth. However, this is not always true. People can do and understand more than they can explain. This is especially true

for infants. Their speaking vocabularies lag behind what they understand. In addition, people sometimes use words they don't understand.

There is a relationship between language and social and emotional growth. Language is used to express feelings or emotions. Before infants develop language, they show feelings by crying, laughing, clinging, and other physical signs. Even young children express more of their feelings physically than do other children. They express these feelings with temper tantrums, snatching a toy from another child, and hitting. As children grow older, they learn to express more of their feelings in words. Through language, children learn to make friends and get along with others.

▶ How Babies Communicate

From the time infants are born, they are communicating. Through the sounds they make, others learn to understand their language.

Crying and Cooing

Newborns do not have control over the sounds they make. They make many while eating and sleeping. They swallow noisily, smack, burp, yawn, and sigh. During the first month, babies communicate by crying. Parents can quickly learn what their baby's cries mean.

Between the sixth and eighth week, most babies begin to **coo** (make a light, happy sound). Babies coo more when others talk to, smile at, and touch them.

Babbling

Between the fourth and fifth month, babies begin to babble. Babies **babble** by making a series of vowel sounds with consonant sounds slowly added to form syllables, such as "be," "da," and "gi."

Babbling is an important pretalking skill. When babbling begins, babies practice all the sounds of all the world's languages. Babies are ready to learn any language or languages they hear, 8-11. Around one year, however, they can make only the sounds needed to speak the language they hear.

1—*Resource: Object Identity,* SAG.

2—*Reflect:* Explain in your own words why vocabulary words may not measure mental growth.

3—*Discuss:* How does language relate to mental growth? Social and emotional growth?

4—*Discuss:* Why do you think older children (two or three years old) express anger by hitting, kicking, biting, or other physical means rather than yelling or talking?

5—*Activity:* Observe an infant while he or she is sleeping and awake. What sounds does the infant make? Describe and share with the class.

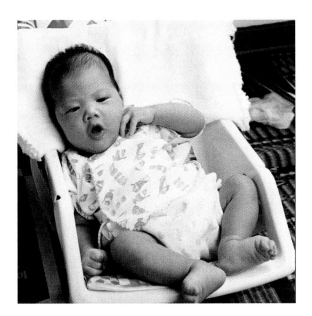

8-11   A baby babbles all the sounds of all languages.

Babbling is not **monotone** (at a single pitch). Babies babble with **inflections** (changes of pitch) to express happiness, requests, commands, and questions. Often a baby babbles with so much feeling you can almost guess what he or she is saying!

First Words

Babies may begin talking during the last three months of the first year. Many start talking later. Most experts state that in order to count sounds as a word, the same sounds must be used each time to refer to a specific person, object, place, or event.

No wonder many babies do not talk during the first year! Before talking, babies must do the following:

- ☐ understand object permanence
- ☐ understand that people, objects, places, and events have names
- ☐ remember words that go with people, objects, places, and events
- ☐ have the ability to make the sounds
- ☐ realize that talking is important

2

Reduplication Babbling.   Often, first words come from babbling. Babies do **reduplication babbling.** They repeat the same syllable over and over, such as "da-da-da-da." An adult that hears da-da-da-da or ma-ma-ma-ma may say, "That's right, 'dada.'" The adult may point to daddy. The daddy may pick up the baby, smile and nod, and call himself "dada." After a time, the baby makes the connection between the sound, which was already mastered, and the person.

3

The number of words that babies learn varies a great deal. Most studies show that babies only say about three words by the end of the first year. Spoken vocabulary does not begin to increase quickly until later in the second year.

▶ Passive versus Active Vocabulary

Although babies can say only a few words, they understand many, many more. The words people understand but don't say are called their **passive vocabulary.   Active vocabulary** includes the words used in talking or writing.

4

Babies' passive vocabulary far exceeds their active vocabulary. Once babies get the idea that the objects in their world have names, they learn these names quickly. They even understand sentences that refer to part of their daily routines such as, "Time for breakfast." Soon their favorite spoken word may be "whaddat" as they begin to learn language.

5

1—*Discuss:* When talking to infants, why should you use the same sounds or words to refer to an item?

2—*Resource: Learning to Talk—A Complex Skill,* SAG.

3—*Activity:* Have students give examples of reduplication babbling.

4—*Vocabulary:* Compare and contrast *active vocabulary* and *passive vocabulary.*

5—*Reflect:* What are some words or phrases that babies you know use as passive vocabulary?

Summary

Intellectual development includes how babies learn, what they learn, and how they communicate. The rate of development is affected by the child's physical development and the environment.

Organizing information that comes through the senses is a major step in infant learning. Babies perceive whether things are alike or different in size, color, shape, and texture. They develop perceptions of form, space, weight, and number. They begin to piece this information together and give meaning to their perceptions.

In addition to their senses, children use their motor development to know and understand their world. As inborn reflexes give way to voluntary movement and sense perceptions, children learn. Piaget called this first stage of mental development the sensorimotor stage. He found that children go through a series of more difficult processes before they discover new ways to solve problems.

Through children's early experiences, they form ideas, or concepts, about the world around them. As their brain matures and experiences increase, they learn various perceptual concepts. These include object constancy or sameness, object identity and permanence, and depth perception.

Language and mental development are closely related. Vocabulary tends to increase as more concepts are understood. Learning to express themselves helps children in their social and emotional development.

Crying is the baby's first communication method. Before first words are said, often between nine months and one year of age, cooing and babbling occur. Babies have a much more extensive passive vocabulary than active vocabulary.

To Review

Write your answers on a separate sheet of paper.

1

1. True or false. A baby's intellectual development is slow compared to physical development during the first year.
2. What are two factors that affect the rate of intellectual development?
3. Which of the following is an example of perception?
   a. tasting a sugar cube
   b. telling the difference between a mother's face and the faces of other women
   c. calling mother "mama"
4. Which member of the pair do infants like better?
   a. 2-D pictures or 3-D objects
   b. plain white cards or solid-colored cards
   c. patterned cards or solid-colored cards
   d. human face or other patterns
   e. straight lines or curved lines
   f. new objects or familiar objects

5. True or false. Babies first study parts of an object before they pay attention to the whole object.
6. True or false. Babies would rather play with an old familiar toy than try a new toy.
7. True or false. Babies can make all the sounds needed to speak any language.
8. Which statement would Piaget support?
   a. Children learn more by exploring on their own in a stimulating environment.
   b. Children learn more when adults sit down and teach them.
   c. Children learn the same amount, whether they explore on their own or are taught by adults.
9. The baby gains knowledge in a certain order according to Piaget. Place the intellectual skills in the proper order of occurrence.
   _____ Babies change some of their reflex skills, such as opening and closing their hands.
   _____ Babies hit their hands on the high chair tray and realize they made the sound.
   _____ Babies exercise inborn reflexes.
   _____ Babies can pick up a rubber duck, place it in the water, and give it a big push.
   _____ Babies look for objects they have dropped.
10. Match the incidents with the perceptual concepts.
    a. depth perception
    b. object permanence
    c. object constancy
    _____ Maria is looking from the back door and sees her mother in the garden. She happily exclaims, "Mamma!"
    _____ Joe is being carried in a department store by his father, who is shopping. When the father stops at one counter, Joe quickly picks up a toy car without knocking over a sign in front of the toys.
    _____ Tyrone wakes up and looks around. His mother is not in the room. He begins to cry loudly so his mother will know that he is awake.
11. Pretalking skills begin at birth. Place the following skills in their proper order of occurrence.
    _____ cooing
    _____ crying
    _____ reduplication babbling
    _____ babbling
    _____ first words

To Do

1. For one week, keep a record of an infant exploring his or her world for 30 minutes per day. What senses were used at the time? What were some of the possible learnings?

2. Have your teacher or one student give a common word such as blue, school, music, or food. Each student should write a few phrases about what they think when they hear the word. Compare the perceptions of class members. Discuss your experiences and emotions associated with your perceptions of that word.

3. Make a poster using words and/or drawings to describe the baby's learnings during the first year as stated by Piaget.

4. Try an object permanence experiment on babies who are four, six, and eight months old. To do the experiment follow these steps.
   a. Place a toy in front of the baby. Let the baby play with the object.
   b. Take the toy and use a small baby blanket or towel to partly cover the toy. If the baby gets the toy, continue to (c).
   c. Take the toy and completely cover with a blanket or towel. If the baby gets the toy, continue to (d).
   d. Take the toy and cover with a box. If the baby gets the toy, continue to (e).
   e. Take the toy, place it in a small box, and place that box in a large box.

   Note the ages of the babies and the number of steps they can do.

5. Listen to a recording of the sounds of babies who are 2, 4, 6, 8, 10, and 12 months old. Try to distinguish cooing from babbling. Listen for babbling sounds that are similar to words.

6. Interview the parents of young children about the first words their babies said and the age the babies began to talk. Share your findings with the class, then compare them. Note the similarities and differences in the beginning spoken language.

To Observe

1. Observe infants as they play. What concepts are they learning?

2. Observe infants as they see, hear, or touch objects in their environments. Compare your observations with information given in Chart 8-5.

3. Observe objects at a baby's crawling and walking height. Describe how the objects look from these views.

4. Observe a baby trying to "talk." Describe how cooing is different from babbling. What might the baby have been "saying" in babble language?

1—*Note:* Practice these steps in class before doing the experiment.

2—*Activity:* Consult your baby books to learn about your language development.

To Think Critically

1. Bring in several toys designed for infants. What do you think would be appealing about each toy? Make a list. What suggestions would you make to improve the appeal?
2. Hold up a given object (such as a colored cube or cylinder). How could that object look different in size? Color? Shape? Be specific in your explanation.
3. A friend of yours remarked that it isn't important for adults to talk to babies until babies begin to talk. Do you agree or disagree? Why? What should parents do?

Chapter 9

Social-Emotional Development of the Infant

Each infant has a unique temperament and level of emotions. These affect the infant's social-emotional development.

After studying this chapter, you will be able to

☐ identify temperamental differences in babies.

☐ describe the infant's major first-year social tasks.

☐ explain the roots of four emotions—love, fear, anxiety, and anger.

After studying this chapter, you will be able to define

age-appropriate behaviors
anxiety
attachment
attachment behaviors
dependence
disposition
emotions
initiate
separation anxiety
siblings
social-emotional development
temperament

Social-emotional development is an important part of development. It has three main parts. The first part is a person's **disposition** or mood. Some people have a more cheerful disposition, and others are more moody. The second part is learning to interact with people and social groups. These may include family members, schools, and clubs. The third part includes the ways people show feelings through emotions of love, fear, anxiety, and anger. (Social-emotional development is also called *affective development*.)

Social-emotional development happens as quickly during the first year as physical and intellectual development. Babies enter the world with some unique traits. These traits are the root of their later personality. By the end of the first year, the traits show even more. As a baby's social world expands, the infant forms ideas about whether or not the world is a friendly place. The baby begins to express feelings with different emotions.

Temperamental Differences in Infants

Temperament is the tendency to react in a certain way, such as in a cheery way or a grumpy way. Sometimes the word "disposition" also defines the ways people react. Experts think temperament is partly inherited. They also think a person's temperament may be due to prenatal conditions and ease of birth. These factors, along with environment, shape a person's personality. A baby's temperament often shows by two or three months. In many children, but not all, temperament stays the same for years.

Some experts rate characteristics of a baby's temperament. These ratings place most babies in one of three groups. These groups are called *easy, slow to warm up*, and *difficult*.

☐ *Easy*—Easy babies have regular habits (eating, sleeping, and others). They respond quickly to a new situation. They are cheerful.

☐ *Slow to warm up*—These babies take more time to adapt to new situations.

☐ *Difficult*—Difficult babies are irregular in their habits. They often withdraw or protest—even scream—when facing new situations.

Researchers found that 4 in 10 babies are easy. One in 10 babies are slow to warm up, and 1 in 10 are difficult. A few babies cannot be grouped because their temperaments vary from day to day.

Easy babies usually get off to a good start with their parents. Difficult babies often get off to a rough start. This may be because many parents feel they are doing something wrong since the baby is unhappy. If the parents are stressed, this may cause increased stress in the child. Good, constant care of difficult babies, including extra holding, cuddling, and soothing, may make babies happier.

The Infant's Growing Social World

Infants are not truly social at birth. *Social* refers to a relationship between two or more people. Social development is shaped by how other people affect the baby and how the baby affects other people. By the end of the first year, social development is well underway. This section will focus on three aspects of social development in the first year. These three aspects are (A) interacting with others, (B) learning to trust, and (C) showing attachment.

▶ Interacting with Others

Babies are born with tools for social development. At birth, babies can turn in the direction of the human voice. They move their bodies in the rhythm of human speech. They like to look at other people's faces.

Babies understand social messages by the way others talk to, look at, or hold them. Babies send signals to others through their cries, coos,

1—*Reflect:* How do you feel about people who usually are grumpy, whiny, cheerful, quiet, and talkative?

2—*Note:* Review the Brazelton scales. This is an attempt to inform a parent of a child's temperament.

3—*Reflect:* Identify a baby you know. Classify the baby into one of these three groups. Why did you select this group?

4—*Math Activity:* Poll students to count how many babies were in each group. Compare results with statistics. If there are differences, what could account for them?

5—*Resource: Difficult Babies Make Parenting Stressful,* SAG.

1

and smiles. These begin as early as two weeks after birth. Smiles with expressive eyes begin around the fifth or sixth week, 9-1.

From the third to the sixth month, babies become even better at understanding and sending social signals. They also begin to distinguish between those who care for them and strangers.

Once babies are able to creep easily and have better arm and hand control, they *initiate* (begin) social contact. For instance, they may follow others around the house. They reach with their arms to signal, "pick me up."

Interacting with Adults

Babies thrive most when they are held, talked to, cuddled, and comforted. They are often happier babies, crying less than those who receive little attention. Parents and caregivers help their baby's mental development as well as their social development by providing lots of loving care.

2

Grandparents, friends, baby-sitters, and others are helpful to babies' total development. When they care for and show an interest in them, babies learn to understand and trust others. This helps expand babies' social environment.

9-1   Babies communicate happiness and love with their smiles.

© John Shaw

9-2   Babies and their older brothers and sisters learn from each other.

Interacting with Other Children

Babies enjoy being around *siblings* (brothers and sisters) and other children. Babies tend to watch and follow children. They like to play with the toys of older children. Infants learn from older children. From infants, older children learn lessons in loving and caring for others. All children benefit in these relationships, 9-2.

▶ Learning to Trust

Trust is an important part of social development. The amount a person trusts (or doesn't trust) others affects how he or she interacts with others.

One psychologist, Erik Erikson, thinks learning to trust others is the first, most basic stage of social-emotional development. He believes people can trust versus mistrust by having their basic needs met. When basic needs are met, people feel the world is reliable.

1—*Discuss:* Do you think a baby will smile less and at a later time if his or her caregiver does not smile and talk to the baby? How does imitation help to explain this?

2—*Reflect:* Darrell and Samantha are six months old. Darrell's caregiver spends a lot of time with him, cuddling, talking, smiling, and socializing him with adults who interact

similarly. Samantha's caregiver is reserved and self-conscious, experiencing discomfort cuddling, talking to, and smiling at her. Samantha is rarely around other people. How do you think the caregivers have affected and will affect the social-emotional development of these babies?

3—*Discuss:* What do they learn?

Cycles of Trust and Mistrust

9-3   When a baby's needs are met, both baby and parent are happy.

Babies' basic needs include food, clothing, warmth, sleep, cleanliness, cuddling, playing, communicating with others, etc. If these physical and psychological needs are met, then babies feel the world is a good and happy place. This helps them learn to trust others and adapt to their world. If needs are not met, or only partly met, babies feel helpless and confused. They develop mistrust. Feelings of trust or mistrust are the basis for later positive or negative feelings toward others.

When adults meet babies' needs, a relationship of trust develops. If needs are not met, the babies develop mistrust for others. Figure 9-3 shows the cycle of how parents affect babies and babies, in turn, affect parents. The cycle shows that meeting babies needs is helpful to adults as well as babies.

▶ Showing Attachment

Attachment is closeness between people that remains over a period of time. In chapter 5, you learned about a special type of attachment called bonding. *Bonding* is the feeling of love parents have for their baby that often begins soon after birth. During the first year, babies come to care for their parents, too. This is called *attachment*, 9-4.

Babies develop an attachment to those who care for them. They show this in a number of ways. **Attachment behaviors** are actions one person demonstrates to another person to show closeness to that person. Attachment behaviors include trying to stay close to, following, or clinging to the adult. Smiling, crying, or calling are other attachment behaviors. However, babies who cry loudest are not always the ones with the strongest attachment. For instance, a strongly attached baby who is sure of the parent's return may not cry much when left. Attachment often develops in a certain order, 9-5.

4

5

1—*Discuss:* Many parents do not meet babies' basic or emotional needs because they fear they will spoil babies. Research shows it is important to meet these needs. How will spoiling occur? Not occur?

2—*Reflect:* If mistrust develops, how does it surface in adult life?

3—*Resource: Building a Trusting Relationship,* SAG.

4—*Reflect:* Compare bonding and attachment. List three comparisons and three contrasts.

5—*Discuss:* List attachment behaviors, both positive and negative. Identify as strong or weak attachments.

Bonding and Attachment	
Relationship	**Term Used**
Parents come to love their babies soon after birth. parents ———▶ baby	bonding
Babies whose needs are met come to love their parents. Children realize this tie after six months of age. baby ———▶ parents	attachment

9-4 *Bonding* and *attachment* are terms used for two loving relationships between parents and babies.

9-5 Attachment behaviors are closely related to the baby's mental development.

Development of Attachment Behaviors	
Approximate Age	**Attachment Behaviors**
1 month	Baby can recognize familiar and unfamiliar voices.
2 weeks to 2 months	Baby smiles.
5 months	Baby gives joyful movements, such as kicks, coos, and gurgles. Baby may even laugh.
4 to 5 months	Baby becomes still and breathing becomes shallow when unknown people are close.
7 to 8 months	Baby cries when a stranger is nearby or when the baby is left alone.

Attachment is closely related to fear of strangers and fear of being left alone. These emotions are described in the next section.

Attachment can be good. For healthy social-emotional development, attachment is important. Everyone needs to be loved and to love. Attachment also helps mental development. Attached babies tend to explore their worlds through play more than babies who are not attached to others.

● **Infants Express Emotions**

During the first three or four months, babies have two basic responses to their worlds. The first is distress, shown by crying and muscle tension. The second is excitement, shown by smiling, cooing, and wiggling the body. By the end of the first year, babies can express love, fear, anxiety, anger, jealousy, joy, and sadness. Babies who express a range of emotions, from happy to unhappy, show healthy development.

Emotions are thoughts and feelings that cause changes in the body. For example, if you are angry (a feeling), you are angry at someone or something (a thought). You then may have an increased heart rate (change in your body). In emotions, thoughts cause the feelings.

Because thinking changes, the situations that cause emotions change over the years. Four-year-olds may fear monsters in their rooms at night, but older children do not. As people mature, the way they respond because of emotions changes, too. For instance, a two-year-old may throw a temper tantrum when angry. Adults show their anger in more mature ways. When people act their age, they use *age-appropriate behaviors.* These are proper or normal ways to express emotions at certain ages.

1—*Reflect:* Why is it important to have strong attachment?

2—Resource: *Observation: Attachment Behaviors,* SAG.

3—*Discuss:* List ways children show anger. Next list ways adults express anger. Label each way as either positive or negative. What can you do about your negative reactions to anger? Define *age-appropriate behaviors.*

▶ Love

It takes time for babies to know that other people make them feel full, clean, and comforted. As they become attached to their caregivers, they begin to feel and show love and affection, 9-6. Not only do babies show love to important adults, but to children who keep them company as well.

Besides loving people, babies become attached to objects, including pacifiers, stuffed toys, and even blankets. Babies seem to need these objects when they are upset or afraid. They also seem to need them when routines change. Sometimes adults worry about children's love for these objects. However, such attachments tend to give babies security and are important to them. Children will give up these objects in time.

▶ Fear

At birth, babies become startled when they hear loud sounds or do not have support for their bodies. By four or five months, some babies fear adult strangers. They may even fear adults they know if they have new hairstyles, hats, sunglasses, or other such changes. Babies do not seem to fear young children they do not know.

Fear as an emotion occurs at around six months. To be fearful, babies must know they can be hurt. The following are the two kinds of fear:

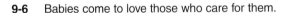

9-6   Babies come to love those who care for them.

Adrian Demery

9-7   The unknown, such as these pine needles, causes fear.

- ☐ Fear of the unknown, 9-7. Infants fear adult strangers, a new bed, or a sudden movement. They also fear different sounds, such as the crack of thunder or a screaming siren.
- ☐ Fear learned from direct experiences or teachings. Infants may fear getting soap in their eyes, a doctor's office, or a snapping dog because of a negative past experience. They also fear hot stoves and bad dogs because of an adult's constant warning.

What adults say and how they act affect babies' fears. Adults who act or look fearful in a storm, for instance, will cause children to be fearful. Adults who tell babies that many situations can hurt them teach children to fear. Of course, some fear is good. However, too much fear is not healthy. Fear affects motor and mental growth because fearful babies often will not welcome new experiences.

▶ Anxiety

Anxiety is fear of a possible future event. Sometimes the words "worry" or "concern" are used to mean anxiety.

1—*Discuss:* Have you ever seen a baby become excited when an older child comes near?

2—*Discuss:* What objects were attachments for you? How long did the attachment last? What would you do if your child persisted in an attachment at age five?

3—*Note:* This is the Moro or startle reflex.

4—*Discuss:* What are some other fears in each category?

5—*Note:* Ridicule is inappropriate when a child expresses a fear. Talk about the fear and help the child work through it.

Anxiety is seen in babies most often between the 10th and 12th months. This anxiety is called **separation anxiety,** 9-8. During this time, babies become anxious when those adults whom they love leave for work, shopping, etc. The anxiety is more intense when strangers, such as baby-sitters, are near.

Most two-year-olds do not show as much separation anxiety as younger babies do. Separation anxiety in babies younger than two years may be due to the following points:

☐ Babies younger than two cannot understand why parents must leave.

☐ Unlike two-year-olds who remember their parents have returned after each seperation, babies do not have the memory or the experiences of events.

☐ During the first year, babies need someone to fulfill their needs. (Relying on someone else to meet your needs is called **dependence.**) Two-year-olds are more independent (want to do things for themselves).

9-8 Even when parents are out of sight for only a moment, babies who are near 12-months-old may feel separation anxiety.

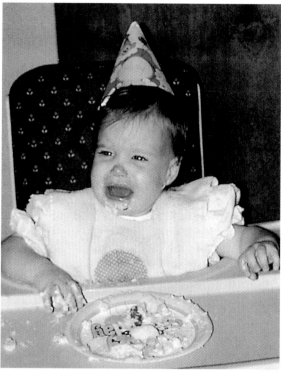

© Nancy P. Alexander

9-9   Angry babies may turn red and cry loudly.

☐ Two-year-olds can express their needs better. Young babies cannot express their needs to others well, especially to those adults they do not know.

▶ Anger

Almost from birth, babies get angry at times. Angry infants may swing their arms and legs excitedly, turn red, and cry loudly, 9-9.

By 8 to 10 months, babies direct their anger toward a certain person or object. Babies express anger in physical ways. They may try to get away from a person holding them. They also may grab, shake, or hit an object. Babies often show anger when

☐ they are held against their will. They may be angered if held when they want to be down. They also may be angered if being diapered or dressed when they don't want

1—*Reflect:* Write about an example of separation anxiety that has been especially difficult for you in a child care situation. How did you handle it? Did it work? How might you handle it better next time?

2—*Note:* They have learned object permanence.

3—*Resource: Helping to Ease Separation Anxiety,* SAG.

to be. In addition, being left in a playpen when they want to be out makes them angry, too.

☐ toys are being taken from them. Babies show anger when they cannot reach a toy that they want.

☐ they are being distracted when they want their needs met. For example, showing a crying, hungry baby a toy may cause the baby to cry louder and push the toy away.

Babies vary in their amount and strength of anger. Some babies whose dispositions are calm seem to show little anger during the first year. Babies whose moods are more negative may show much more anger. Meeting the baby's needs quickly often prevents anger. Staying calm by talking in a quiet voice and not looking upset helps children see how to control their anger. Parents can reduce anger by restraining, or holding back, babies but only when needed and for a short time.

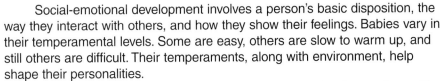

Summary

Social-emotional development involves a person's basic disposition, the way they interact with others, and how they show their feelings. Babies vary in their temperamental levels. Some are easy, others are slow to warm up, and still others are difficult. Their temperaments, along with environment, help shape their personalities.

An infant's social development is affected by his or her interactions with others, learning to trust, and showing attachment. Babies interact with others at an early age through crying, cooing, and smiling. They need the loving care provided by parents and other caregivers. Others in their life provide them with needed attention.

Babies learn trust by having their basic needs met. These basic needs include physical needs of food, clothing, warmth, sleep, and cleanliness. Psychological needs such as cuddling, loving, playing, and being talked to are also important in their development. Having the baby's needs met makes the baby happier, which makes parents happier, too.

Many babies develop an attachment for their parents and others who are close to them. These attachments are important for healthy development. Babies who form attachments tend to reach out and want to explore their world.

Emotions of love, fear, anxiety, and anger arise in all children. These emotions consist of thoughts and feelings that cause changes in the body. It is healthy for babies to express a wide range of emotions, from unhappy to happy. Emotions are handled differently throughout life.

1—*Discuss:* Describe situations you have experienced.

1

To Review

Write your answers on a separate sheet of paper.

1. True or false. Babies enter the world with unique traits.
2. Name two factors that affect a baby's temperament.
3. What are three pretalking social signals babies can send to the parents?
4. True or false. Giving babies love and care helps their mental and social development.
5. True or false. Meeting an unhappy baby's needs by soothing his or her cries will spoil the child.
6. Adults can help a baby develop trust by
   a. meeting the baby's needs as soon as possible
   b. changing all of the baby's toys once a week so the baby doesn't get bored
   c. comforting babies when they get hurt
   d. both a and b
   e. both a and c
7. Give two examples of attachment behaviors.
8. True or false. Babies who cry loudly when parents leave them are more strongly attached to their parents than babies who do not.
9. Which statements about emotions are true?
   a. Feelings occur before thoughts.
   b. Over the years, the situations that cause emotions remain the same.
   c. Over the years, the ways a person expresses emotions remain the same.
   d. Over the years, the situations that cause emotions and the ways one expresses emotions both change.
10. True or false. Babies are as afraid of children they do not know as they are of adult strangers.
11. Identify the emotion that completes each sentence.
    a. Love
    b. Fear
    c. Anxiety
    d. Anger
    _____ comes from good physical care.
    _____ is often taught by hearing adults say, "No! That will hurt you!"
    _____ is seen as a reaction to being held against their will.
    _____ is similar to attachment.
    _____ in its early form may be the startle reflex.
    _____ is not seen as a response to unknown children.
    _____ is closely related to fear.
    _____ may be a reaction to an adult trying to distract a hungry or tired baby.

To Do

1. Write a one- or two-page brochure about the importance of trust in the infant's life. Explain how adults can help promote trust in the infant.
2. Interview one or more parents about the expanding social world of their baby. (Plan interview questions in advance.) Use these for starters.
    a. Who were the first people (not including hospital staff) to see your baby? hold your baby? feed, dress, and change your baby?
    b. Besides the baby's parents, who are other important people in your baby's life?
    c. How did your baby react to siblings and other children? How did siblings and other children react to your baby?
    d. Did your baby become attached to an object? What object?
3. Try this attachment experiment. Have the mother or father of a 3-month-old, 6-month-old, 9-month-old, and 12-month-old visit the classroom. Follow this routine with each baby.
    1. Hand the baby to two different students. Have each hold the baby for two or three minutes unless the baby protests. Then hand the baby back to the parent. (The baby should see the parent.)
    2. Hand the baby to another student. After student holds the baby for two or three minutes, the parent should leave the room. (The baby should not be able to see the parent.)
    3. Record each baby's reaction. Did babies over six months react more than the baby under six months? What types of reactions did the babies show? Discuss attachment with the parents. Perhaps the parents can talk about attachment behaviors seen in their babies at other times.
4. Have a class discussion on how emotions are useful. Compare this to how emotions can hinder abilities to work and play to the fullest.
5. People's expression of emotions should change as they mature. Each stage of life has age-appropriate behaviors. List behaviors that would be considered immature for a high school student.

To Observe

1. Observe a group of infants. Note differences in temperament. Do some infants seem easygoing? Do other infants seem more difficult?
2. Observe an infant with a parent or regular caregiver. How does the baby show attachment? How does the adult encourage attachment (for instance, by soothing the baby or showing affection)?
3. Observe a baby showing fear, anxiety, or anger. What seemed to trigger the infant's reactions?

1—*Activity:* Use the computer to prepare the brochure.
Distribute the brochure (with permission) to local preschools,
child care centers, and medical centers.

2—*Note:* Practice the routine in class prior to the parent-child
visit.

To Think Critically

1. Babies' temperaments seem to shape their personalities. How would you describe your temperament? Have you had this (these) characteristics for a long time? Do others in your family (grandparent, parent, cousin, etc.) have the same temperament?
2. Some parents believe that you can spoil babies by holding them when they do not have physical needs. Do you agree with this idea? Why or why not?
3. Your friend has a cute baby you'd like to hold. As you approach the baby, you see obvious signs of stranger anxiety. What are some things you can do to lessen the baby's anxiety?

By soothing a fussy baby, a parent helps a baby develop a relationship of trust.

Chapter 10

Providing for the Infant's Developmental Needs

As infants grow, adults must meet their basic needs, such as the need for food.

After studying this chapter, you will be able to

☐ plan ways to meet the developmental needs of babies in their first year.

☐ care for babies' physical needs.

☐ stimulate babies' mental development.

☐ enhance babies' growing awareness of themselves.

After studying this chapter, you will be able to define

coordination
depressants
enriched environment
fine-motor skills
gross-motor skills
intolerance
nutrients
sensory stimulation
solids
stimulants
weaning

Babies develop so fast their first year that they have many needs. To meet their physical needs, adults must understand babies and respond to their signals. To meet their social-emotional needs, parents must touch, hold, and look at babies lovingly. Adults also must meet baby's mental needs with activities that help infants learn and develop.

Babies develop best when they feel the love and joy of their caregivers. By meeting a baby's needs promptly, adults help the baby develop trust. From learning to trust others, the baby becomes more aware of his or her own abilities.

● Physical Needs

Babies, unlike other people, need others to meet all their physical needs. *Physical needs* are the most basic needs of humans, like the needs for food and sleep. When people are hungry, tired, or sick, they suffer in physical, mental, social, and emotional ways. For instance, a baby who is fed a little late may not want to play and explore. The baby may also act fussy.

▶ Feeding

The need for food is the baby's most basic physical need. This is because a baby's body grows so quickly in the first year. In fact, the body grows three times faster in the first year than in the second or third years. The baby also is busy exploring and developing. A proper diet gives the baby the nutrients he or she needs to grow, explore, and develop. **Nutrients** are the substances in food that give babies energy and help them grow.

Food also comforts babies. As adults feed the baby, they should show warmth and concern, 10-1. Babies who are fed by gentle, loving adults are more likely to learn what Erikson calls "basic trust."

Cosco Peterson

10-1 Parents can use feeding time as a time to build a baby's trust.

4

▪ Feeding During the First Year

How much food does a baby need? It all depends. Every baby has different needs. These needs depend on the baby's size and how fast he or she is growing. The baby's health, heredity, and level of activity also affect his or her food needs. A pediatrician can help parents learn what and how much to feed a baby.

5

First Foods. Most babies begin "eating" an all-liquid diet of milk (either breast milk or formula). Between six months and one year, the baby begins to eat fruits, vegetables, meats, and breads. These foods are called **solids.** Most doctors recommend babies wait until at least six months before eating solids. (See chart 10-2 for a basic first-year feeding plan.) Doctors do not suggest solids for the first six months for the following reasons:

Basic Feeding Plan for Baby's First Year

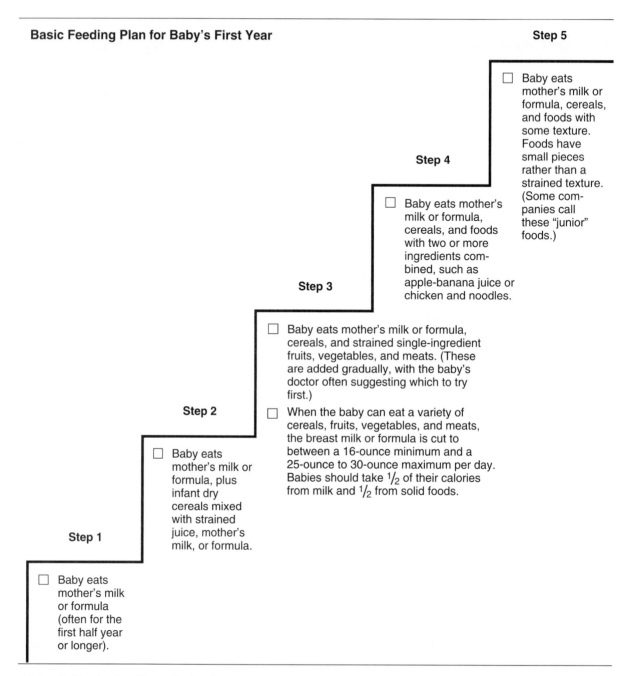

Step 5

☐ Baby eats mother's milk or formula, cereals, and foods with some texture. Foods have small pieces rather than a strained texture. (Some companies call these "junior" foods.)

Step 4

☐ Baby eats mother's milk or formula, cereals, and foods with two or more ingredients combined, such as apple-banana juice or chicken and noodles.

Step 3

☐ Baby eats mother's milk or formula, cereals, and strained single-ingredient fruits, vegetables, and meats. (These are added gradually, with the baby's doctor often suggesting which to try first.)

☐ When the baby can eat a variety of cereals, fruits, vegetables, and meats, the breast milk or formula is cut to between a 16-ounce minimum and a 25-ounce to 30-ounce maximum per day. Babies should take $1/2$ of their calories from milk and $1/2$ from solid foods.

Step 2

☐ Baby eats mother's milk or formula, plus infant dry cereals mixed with strained juice, mother's milk, or formula.

Step 1

☐ Baby eats mother's milk or formula (often for the first half year or longer).

10-2 Babies begin with a milk diet. Gradually, other foods are added to the diet.

1—*Discuss:* Why are other foods added gradually?

□   A baby cannot digest complex nutrients found in solids.

□   Starting solids too early may cause allergy problems.

□   Some solids have too much sodium. This may increase the baby's chance of high blood pressure as an adult.

□   Solids may be too high in calories. This may make the baby gain weight too quickly.

□   Babies are not born with the ability to swallow solids. Their jaw and throat muscles must develop before swallowing is easy and safe.

□   Holding a baby close while formula- or breast-feeding gives the baby a warm feeling of physical closeness. Spoon feeding does not do the same.

□   Babies do not need solids for nutritional reasons in the first half year.

Introducing New Foods.   When babies are ready for solids, parents should introduce one food at a time, 10-3. They should feed the new food in small amounts, such as a bite or two.

Parents should not add another new food for at least four or five days. This helps the parent see if the baby has an intolerance for the food. *Intolerance* is a negative reaction that eating a certain food can cause. A food may cause fussiness, a rash, or an upset stomach. Intolerance often shows in one to four days. Many doctors suggest waiting until after the first birthday to try these foods again. If babies react to many foods, doctors can test the baby and give him or her a special diet.

Foods to Avoid.   Babies should not eat some foods, 10-4. For instance, small foods like berries may cause the baby to choke. Foods like cake, crackers, and soft drinks may have too much sugar, sodium, or artificial flavors. Unpasteurized yogurt and foods that contain yeast are hard for babies to digest. Also, stimulants like coffee and depressants like alcohol may harm babies. (*Stimulants* are substances that speed up the

functions of organs, like the heart, and the nervous system. *Depressants* are substances that slow the functions of organs and the nervous system.)

The Feeding Schedule.   The daily feeding schedule should fit the baby's needs. Some babies like smaller, more frequent meals. Others eat more food less often. When the baby's growth rate slows during the end of the first year, his or her appetite will decrease, 10-5. Most babies will establish an eating pattern, but some days they will be hungrier than others.

■   **Baby Foods**
Parents today can choose from a variety of commercially prepared baby foods in the grocery store. Still, many prefer to make the baby's food at home for health or economic reasons. See 10-6 and 10-7 for advantages to both methods.

3

4

5

10-3   When babies are ready for solid foods, parents should introduce them one at a time.

1—*Note:* This is an emotional need.

2—*Note:* An intolerance could be caused by an upset stomach or allergy.

3—*Resource: Foods Babies Should Not Eat,* SAG.

4—*Note:* When preparing baby food at home, make sure you do not add salt. It also is important to prepare smaller amounts because the food contains no preservatives. Store the food in the refrigerator for no longer than two days.

5—*Resource: Choices in Baby Foods,* SAG.

1

Foods Babies Should Not Eat	
Food	**Reason to Avoid**
☐ berries ☐ small candy ☐ raw carrots ☐ whole kernel corn ☐ grapes ☐ hot dogs sliced in rounds 　(rounds should be quartered) ☐ nuts ☐ peanut butter ☐ popcorn	☐ choking
☐ cake, in excess ☐ candy, in excess ☐ cookies, in excess	☐ too much sugar
☐ crackers, in excess	☐ too much sodium
☐ artificially flavored fruit drinks ☐ soft drinks	☐ little to no nutritional value ☐ usually high in calories ☐ too much sugar ☐ artificial flavors and colors
☐ yeast or unpasteurized yogurt	☐ hard to digest
☐ coffee ☐ tea ☐ soft drinks with caffeine ☐ cocoa	☐ stimulants
☐ alcohol	☐ depressant

2

10-4 Some foods are not good for a baby's health.

1—*Note:* Emphasize the foods on the choking list.

2—*Note:* Avoid spicy foods because babies' stomachs are not developed enough to digest them.

First-Year Daily Feeding Schedule	
Months	**Hours between Feedings**
1 to 3*	3 to 4
3 to 5	5**
6	6**

*Often sleeps through the night in about 3 months. Babies are given a late evening feeding (about 11:00 p.m.). They sleep until early morning (5:30 or 6:00 a.m.).

**Nutritious snacks of their regular baby food (fruit juice, fruit, etc.) or milk and water should be offered about halfway between feedings (2½ to 3 hours after each feeding) if the baby is awake.

10-5 A baby's feeding schedule changes during the first year.

Feeding a Baby. When buying commercially prepared baby food, check for freshness. Look at the date on the cap or the side of the container. This date is the last date the store should sell the product. (You can still safely use the food for a few days after this date.) Make sure food containers are sealed properly. Caps on jars should be concave to show that the jar is still vacuum-sealed. Boxes of food should be unopened.

When you are giving the baby store-bought food, spoon out the amount of food you need. Do not feed the baby from the jar. Saliva from the baby's spoon can harm the food. Most babies like food at room temperature. If the food needs to be heated, test the temperature by putting a small drop on your wrist before serving. After baby food

3

Advantages of Commercially Prepared Baby Food
☐ Food is easy to buy and use. In fact, commercially prepared foods were first introduced as "convenience foods."
☐ The food may be more economical than homemade food if the cost of ingredients, gas or electricity, and time used to prepare the food are considered.
☐ Many foods are available in all four seasons. (Some fruits and vegetables may not be available year-round for preparing homemade foods.)
☐ Foods can be bought with the right texture for the baby's age.
☐ Foods are sterile until opened.
☐ Unopened foods can be stored without refrigeration for a long time before they lose quality.
☐ Foods, except dry cereals, are packaged in small amounts for one or two servings.
☐ Possibly harmful additives have been removed or reduced.

10-6 Commercially prepared baby foods may have many advantages.

Advantages of Homemade Baby Food
☐ Possibly harmful additives are not used.
☐ Food is usually less expensive to prepare.
☐ Food can be prepared while making foods for other family members.
☐ No special appliances are needed to prepare baby food.
☐ Making your own food saves storage space required for baby food products.
☐ If the baby has allergies, it may be necessary to prepare special food.
☐ Recipe books are available with many tasty recipes.
☐ A creative cook is not limited to commercially prepared foods.
☐ Making food brings a sense of satisfaction to those who like to cook.

10-7 Parents may choose to make their own baby food for many reasons.

1—*Reflect:* Do you think the schedule should be flexible or fixed? Why?

2—*Reflect:* Would you use commercially prepared or homemade baby food? Why? What factors would influence your decision?

3—*Discuss:* Summarize safety practices for using commercially prepared foods.

jars have been opened, store them in the refrigerator. Use the leftover baby food within two or three days.

▶ Weaning

Weaning is the process of taking a baby off the bottle or breast. The process should be gradual, since the baby must learn a new way to drink. The process also takes time. Allow the baby to get used to this change.

When do you start to wean a baby? The age to start weaning is different for each infant. Some begin at about 9 months, or when the baby begins to show less interest in drinking from the bottle or breast. Often the baby is completely weaned by 18 months. Older babies who drink only milk and eat small amounts of solids can become *anemic* (do not have enough iron).

■ Weaning to a Cup

Some babies learn to drink from a cup by imitating others. Parents often teach babies to drink from a cup in the following ways:

☐ Give the baby a special baby cup. The cup may have two handles and be weighted to keep it from tipping.

☐ Praise the baby when he or she tries to handle the cup. Parents should not expect this to be an easy task until about 18 months. Even after that age, many accidents will occur.

☐ Give the baby a few sips (about one tablespoon in the bottom of a cup) at about six months. The small amount is less scary if it splashes against the baby's nose. It also is less messy if spilled.

☐ Let the baby drink small amounts of milk at one feeding. Choose a feeding at which the baby already drinks small amounts of juice or water. A baby should work up to at least four ounces of milk at one feeding.

☐ Gradually replace other bottle feedings in the same way. The night bottle is often the last to be replaced.

■ Weaning from the Breast

When a nursing mother decides to wean her baby, she must reduce her fluid intake. The mother should nurse her baby only when she feels uncomfortable. Mothers often go through the following steps:

☐ Begin offering formula as part of one feeding. (The 6:00 p.m. feeding is usually best, because there is less breast milk then.) Increase the amount of formula at this feeding until the baby has taken an entire feeding by bottle for several days.

☐ Apply the same steps to another feeding until the baby is weaned to a bottle. (The early morning breast feeding is often the last one to stop.) Often, breast-fed babies accept a cup sooner than bottle-fed babies.

■ Spoon Feeding

When babies are ready to use their throat and tongue muscles to eat, they are ready to eat solids, 10-8. Solids should not be mixed with liquids and fed from a bottle because it may cause babies to choke.

10-8   A grandfather's smile makes spoon-feeding pleasant.

Fisher-Price

2—*Reflect:* When do you think a nursing mother should wean her baby? Why?

3—*Note:* Grandparents also need chances to bond with the baby.

For the first spoon feedings, the baby should be held in the adult's lap in an almost upright position. Use a small spoon with a long handle (an ice tea spoon) to make feeding easier. Place a small amount of food on the tip of the spoon. Two or three bites is enough for first feedings. Later, parents can feed babies from high chairs.

During the first few spoon feedings, babies often push the spoon and the food out of their mouths. This is a natural response to having strange objects in the mouth.

Self-Feeding.   Self-feeding with a spoon begins in the second year. Younger babies may want to help adults by grabbing the spoon. Adults can often solve this problem by giving the baby a spoon to hold as they feed. They may even hold a spoon in each hand. Some parents then let the baby use the spoon on the last few bites. The spoon rarely reaches the mouth, but this is good practice for later self-feeding.

Mealtimes should be pleasant for the baby. Caregivers should always be calm regardless of what or how much the baby accepts or rejects. If the adult is unpleasant when the baby rejects a food, the baby is more likely to refuse the same food next time. Kindness makes foods easier to accept.

▶ ## Clothing

Infants grow quickly during the first year and outgrow their clothing. Because babies grow at different rates, infant clothing must be bought by size, not age. (Sewing patterns should be bought by size, also.) Chart 10-9 shows the common sizing used for infants.

From three months to the end of the first year, babies move more with each passing week, 10-10. Clothing should be easy to move in. The basic points given in 10-11 can be used to select baby clothing.

10-9   Baby clothes should be purchased by size, not age.

Typical First-Year Clothing Sizes			
Sizes for Clothes Other Than Sleepwear			
	Newborn	**Small**	**Medium**
Length	to 24 in.	24½-28 in.	28½-32 in.
Weight	to 14 lbs.	15-20 lbs.	21-26 lbs.
Sizes for Sleepwear			
	NB	**1B**	**2B**	**3B**
Length	to 23 in.	23½-26 in.	26½-29 in.	29½-32 in.
Weight	to 13 lbs.	14-17 lbs.	18-22 lbs.	23-26 lbs.

1—*Note:* Holding the baby for the first spoon feedings also will foster emotional closeness between caregiver and baby.

2—*Discuss:* Have you ever had a baby try to "help" you feed him or her? How did you solve any resulting problems?

3—*Discuss:* What should a caregiver do when a baby rejects squash two feedings in a row?

4—*Discuss:* Why should clothing be purchased by size instead of age? How do you feel when your clothing is too tight or too big?

© John Shaw

10-10 Babies move more with each passing week. Their clothing should make moving easy.

Style and Color

The style and color of baby clothes is a personal choice. Almost any style has its advantages and disadvantages. For instance, two-piece outfits (tops and bottoms) often can be worn longer because they do not get as tight in the crotch as one-piece outfits. Two-piece outfits make changing the diaper easy, too. One-piece outfits, such as jumpsuits and overalls, look neater on crawlers because they do not separate. These outfits are warmer, too.

Shoes

Shoes are not needed until a baby begins to walk outdoors. Shoes protect and cushion the feet from outside dangers. Indoors, babies should walk without shoes to prevent flat-footed walking. Most shoes worn in the first year are for decoration. These shoes have soft, cloth soles. Babies need socks or footed clothing in cool weather to keep their feet warm.

Good Consumer Sense

Because babies quickly outgrow clothing, good consumer sense is important. Adults should shop for quality and compare prices. They should follow these tips:

☐ Buy garments a size or two larger than needed. These may be worn longer because the baby grows quickly.

☐ Look for built-in growth features. These include a double row of snaps or buttons at the waistline to lengthen the garment from shoulder to crotch. Two buttons on straps used for lengthening is a good feature. Also look for stretch waists and stretch leg and arm openings.

☐ Choose more stretch knit garments than woven garments. Babies can wear these longer.

☐ Look for flame-retardant finishes on clothing.

Caring for Baby Clothes

Parents can care for baby clothes properly by following these practices:

☐ Before cleaning clothes, read labels and tags. Follow directions. Pretreat stains before washing to prevent them from setting. Also, mend tears before washing to prevent them from getting larger.

☐ Infants' and children's clothes often need to go through more rinses than other clothing. Extra rinses help remove detergent from clothes. Babies' skin is more sensitive than adults', and detergent residue may cause skin rashes.

1

1—Reflect: How do you feel about designating certain colors for boys or girls?

2—Discuss: What can you do to make sure babies can wear clothes longer?

Points to Consider When Choosing Baby Clothes	
Feature	**Examples**
Safety	☐ fire retardant ☐ not tight or binding ☐ no loose buttons or other fasteners ☐ no loose trim ☐ antibacterial (labeled *Sani-guard* or *Sanitized*)
Comfort	☐ soft (made of knitted fabric) ☐ nonirritating clothes (flat seams and fasteners) ☐ garments without too much extra fabric, so that baby does not rest on the bulk ☐ no fuzzy trims that tickle ☐ neck openings large enough for easy dressing ☐ right weight for needed warmth (Several layers of lightweight clothes, such as an undershirt, a T-shirt, and a sweater are warmer and more comfortable in warm weather than one heavy garment.) ☐ roomy for active body movements ☐ antistatic ☐ absorbent (manufactured fibers, such as polyester or nylon, should be blended with cotton to increase absorbency)
Easy care	☐ machine washable ☐ can be washed with other clothes ☐ soil-release finish (to make stain removal easier) ☐ shrinkage control ☐ little or no ironing needed ☐ easy to mend

10-11   Babies need clothes that meet their special needs.

☐ Many parents store baby clothes for future children or as keepsakes. Before storing, clean the clothes. Soiled spots change over time, and then stains cannot be removed. When clothes are clean and dry, they are ready to be stored. Do not use plastic bags. Fabrics need air to maintain their strength and oils. Store light and dark clothes separately to prevent the transfer of dyes. All clothing should be stored away from damp areas. Dampness promotes mildew and insect damage.

▶ ## Diapering a Baby

Diapering is the same as described in chapter 6. When using disposables, the baby will need larger diapers as he or she grows. Cloth diapers can be folded differently for older babies.

3

4

1—*Note:* It is a good idea to wash new baby clothes before the clothing is worn. Some babies react negatively to special finishes on fabrics.

2—*Resource: Wise Clothing Choices,* SAG. Catalogs or store advertisements may be used.

3—*Activity:* List special finishes that are desirable and explain why each is needed.

4—*Activity:* Obtain one diaper from as many different brands as possible. Include types of cloth and disposable diapers. Practice diapering the doll. Which diaper was easiest to use?

Older babies wiggle more and may even protest when diapered. Adults may find the task harder. Because diapering requires a few minutes several times a day, it is a good time to talk to and play with the baby.

Adults must keep diaper changing areas very clean! This is crucial. Also, caregivers should wash their hands each time they change a baby.

▶ Tub Bathing

Tub bathing can begin as soon as the baby's navel has healed. When preparing for a tub bath, the steps are the same as those used for sponge bathing listed in chapter 6. The only difference is that a small tub is filled with about three inches of water. The water should be comfortably warm. Test the water with your wrist or elbow. See the steps for tub bathing in 10-12.

Bathing, like diapering, is a good time to play with babies. As babies are bathed, they enjoy parents who talk, sing, cuddle, and smile, 10-13. Babies often respond well because warm water is relaxing. As babies get older, they enjoy kicking in the water as their parents hold them. Kicking in the water is good for baby's motor skills. It also is fun.

▶ Establishing Routines

Routines help children feel secure because they learn what to expect. Although babies do not know clock time, they do develop a sense of rhythm in their lives from routine care. Schedules also help adults get their baby-care tasks done with greater ease. A schedule is important, but remember to change it as needed.

Routines should fit babies' and adults' needs. Schedules also should change as babies mature. Feedings are more widely spaced, daytime naps grow shorter, and more playtime is needed.

▶ Rest and Sleep

Rest and sleep are important to the baby's health. Babies, like older people, vary in the amount of rest and sleep they need. Many babies begin sleeping through the night at six weeks, but some sleep less hours for many months. Adults may get some relief by rearranging babies' schedules. They may awaken babies after four hours of sleep in the day to help the baby sleep at night. Parents should not awaken a daytime sleeper who sleeps at night.

Some babies who have slept through the night may begin to awaken and cry during the night. This often happens between five and eight months. Hunger often is not the reason for crying. Sleep is lonely. These babies awaken, know parents are nearby, and signal to them. Parents should check on their babies, comfort them for a few minutes, then put them down again. Playing with a baby during the night is not a good habit to form.

Many babies take both long morning and long afternoon naps until five or six months. At this age, babies often take a short morning nap and a long afternoon nap. Most babies drop their morning nap between 9 and 15 months. They may continue to take an afternoon nap until three to five years of age.

▶ Sudden Infant Death Syndrome

Sudden Infant Death Syndrome (SIDS) kills many infants during their first year of life. Like the name suggests, this syndrome happens suddenly. It strikes babies who seem healthy in their sleep. In many cases, the infants simply stop breathing. SIDS strikes about 2 out of every 1,000 infants. The most common age for SIDS to strike is between two and four months. In the United States, thousands of infants die of SIDS each year.

The cause of SIDS is still unknown. Experts think the cause may be a virus. This virus attacks the brain stem (where breathing is controlled) before or shortly after birth. Studies also suggest that soft bedding may cause up to 25 percent of deaths. Soft bedding could form a pocket around the infant's face, trapping air the baby exhales. The cloth absorbs exhaled carbon dioxide, which the baby then breathes back into the lungs. Parents are encouraged to use only flat, firm mattresses and sheets under infants.

1—*Discuss:* Why should a baby be bathed in only three inches of tub water?

2—*Note:* This will help a baby's social-emotional development.

3—*Discuss:* Why are routines and schedules important for babies? How should they change with age?

4—*Discuss:* List ways to extend a baby's sleep time at night without interfering with trust.

5—*Note:* Do not allow a baby to sleep on a water bed. The baby could smother in the same way.

How to Give a Tub Bath

Doctors usually recommend tub baths as soon as the baby's navel and circumcision are healed. Fill the tub (often a large dishpan) with about three inches of comfortably warm water. Test the water temperature with your elbow or wrist. Also, place a towel on the bottom of the tub to keep the baby from slipping.

Step 1: On the Table
Undress the baby, except for the diaper. Cleanse the eyes, nose, ears, and face as you would in a sponge bath. Apply liquid baby bath to head with hand, or use washcloth after about first two months. Note: When the baby is older and has more hair, use a liquid baby shampoo that will not irritate the eyes.

Step 2: Into the Tub
After removing the baby's diaper, you can place the child in the tub. Use a safety hold—slip your right hand under the baby's shoulders. Place your thumb over the right shoulder and your fingers under the right armpit. Support the buttocks with your left hand, grasping the right thigh with your thumb and fingers. Lower the baby into the tub feet first, keeping the head out of the water. With your left hand, rinse the head, letting water run back into the tub.

Step 3: Bathing the Body
Soap the front of the baby's body, being careful to wash inside all the skin folds and creases, then rinse. Reverse your hold to soap and rinse the baby's back. It is not necessary to turn the baby over. Clean the genital area during the bath, just like the rest of the baby. In the external folds of a baby girl, a white substance may gather. If it remains after bathing, gently wipe it away with a washcloth or with a cotton ball dipped in baby oil. Be sure to wipe from front to back. When cleansing a baby boy who has not been circumcised, do not push back the foreskin unless your doctor tells you to. If your baby has been circumcised, he may be immersed in a tub as soon as the area has healed, or sooner, on your doctor's advice.

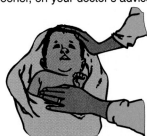

Step 4: Out of the Tub
Use the same safety hold to lift your baby onto a warm, dry surface. Cover the baby with a towel and pat dry, paying special attention to folds and creases.

Step 5: Diaper Area Care
To keep the diaper area dry, use baby cornstarch to help prevent irritation and redness.

Step 6: General Skin Care
Moisten fingers on a cotton ball dipped in baby oil or baby lotion. Apply it to all tiny creases, such as around the neck, armpits, arms, hands, legs, and feet. Use a little baby oil on a cotton ball to help remove "cradle cap." Apply baby cream to any irritated part. Sprinkle baby powder on your hand and pat lightly over large areas of the body.

Johnson & Johnson Baby Products Co.

10-12 Tub bathing should be done carefully and quickly for the baby's comfort and safety.

2

1—*Activity:* Practice the safety hold with the doll.
2—*Enrich:* Do research on circumcision. Report to the class.

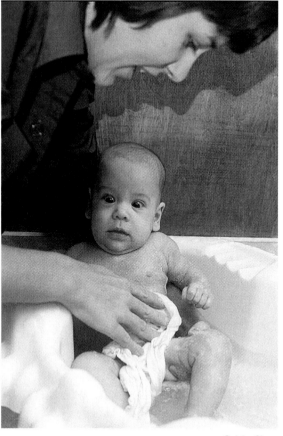

© John Shaw

10-13   When babies are bathed, they like parents to talk to and smile at them.

Research continues for the cause and prevention of SIDS. Several groups are considered at risk for SIDS, 10-14. The highest at-risk group is babies whose mothers took cocaine during pregnancy. Some risks, such as smoking and drug use, can be prevented. Good prenatal care also lessens the chance of babies being born premature and having a low birth weight.

▶ Places for Sleep and Play

Where do babies sleep and play? Planning space for sleep and play is based on a family's lifestyle and housing. However, a few guidelines are important.

Babies should sleep away from major activities. Some parents screen off a small section in their bedroom. They also may ask another child to share a bedroom with the baby. Other parents provide their baby with a separate bedroom or bedroom/playroom.

The space for sleeping should be large enough for a full-size crib and other furnishings. Children often sleep in a crib until four years of age. Many parents like to have space for a dressing table. Dressing tables can be purchased. You may also make one by attaching a vinyl-covered pad and safety belt to a dresser. An adult-size rocker nearby is convenient. Parents also need space for clothing and baby products.

If adults plan a playroom, they should not expect a baby to stay there all the time. Children like to be near others. During the first year, babies need places to play and toys in several rooms where household activities take place. A portable playpen may be used for short periods of time, especially when babies need a safe place to play.

When choosing play spaces for babies, adults should keep the following points in mind:
☐   Babies are messy by adult standards.
   Spaces for children should be washable.

10-14   Certain conditions put infants at a high risk for SIDS.

High Risk Infants for Sudden Infant Death Syndrome (SIDS)
☐ infants born to mothers younger than age 20
☐ infants born to mothers who smoke or use illegal drugs, especially cocaine
☐ infants of multiple birth
☐ infants born more than two weeks before the due date
☐ infants born at term who weigh less than five pounds
☐ infants with a sibling who was a SIDS victim
☐ male infants who have some of the above risk factors

☐ All spaces must be safe. A house must be childproofed by the time a baby can crawl around. (This is discussed in chapter 21.)

☐ Decorate children's rooms with their tastes in mind. Rooms should be bright and cheerful. Place pictures and wall hangings at eye level. Floor coverings should allow play with blocks and toys with wheels.

☐ Babies grow quickly. Spaces should be planned for easy and economical changes as babies' needs change.

● Intellectual Needs

Babies need more than good physical care to grow. Experts know that babies are born with the ability to learn many things. They also know that babies need an environment that gives them a chance to learn. This is called an **enriched environment,** 10-15. One study found that babies whose caregivers expected them to learn at an early age developed more quickly than other babies. Maybe this is because adults who expect more provide more activities to help babies learn.

10-15   Babies can learn about the world around them when taken on a trip in a stroller.

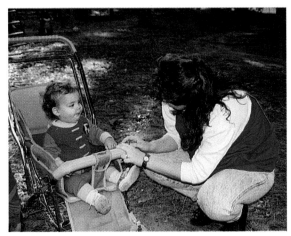

© Nancy P. Alexander

Adults can provide learning experiences for babies soon after birth. In fact, the sooner adults provide activities, the more babies want to learn. Adults shouldn't forget, however, that babies learn at different rates. The rate of learning cannot be increased with lots of activities and toys. Babies can take in only so much. Too many activities and toys can confuse or bore the baby.

Weave activities into daily routines like feeding, bathing, and diapering. Adults do not need to have a set schedule of daily games. The number and types of games are not as important as the warmth and caring that adults show for babies.

A skillful caregiver knows how to use activities to meet babies' intellectual needs. Adults can use the following methods:

☐ Watch for signs of the baby's interest in certain experiences. To check for interest, show the baby how to use a toy, and then give him or her a turn. Repeat several times. If there is little or no interest, the toy or game is probably too advanced for the baby. Try it again in a few days or weeks.

☐ Let the baby begin most activities, then expand on them. For instance, the baby may be patting a high chair tray. Expand the activity by patting a different object (that makes a different sound). You may also pat the tray harder, softer, faster, or slower than the baby.

☐ Repeat games many times. Using games over many months helps the baby retain the skills each game helps build.

☐ Let babies try things on their own. This helps them learn to solve problems.

▶ Activities to Stimulate the Senses

Sensory stimulation involves using the five senses to learn about the environment. According to Piaget, babies use their senses as a major way of learning. Babies use their senses to learn from toys made for them, such as a crib mobile. They also use their senses to learn in other ways, such as by exploring the contents of a drawer.

4

5

6

1—*Resource: Play Throughout the House,* SAG.

2—*Discuss:* Describe the elements of an enriched environment.

3—*Discuss:* What do babies learn during a stroller ride? Discuss all areas of development.

4—*Note:* Too many activities also may overstimulate a baby, causing him or her to become fussy.

5—*Resource: Babies Need an Enriched Environment,* SAG.

6—*Discuss:* What kinds of objects could you place in a drawer for a child to safely explore?

For the baby to develop fully, all the senses (seeing, hearing, touching, tasting, and smelling) must be stimulated. One example of a sensory stimulation activity is to let the baby touch and feel a number of safe objects. This can be done while walking around the room or outdoors. Letting the baby touch the bark of a tree while talking to him or her helps to improve sensory development. See 10-16 for other ways to help children stimulate their sensory learning.

▶ Problem-Solving Activities

As babies use their senses to observe their world, they try to make sense of what they see, hear, feel, touch, and taste. In an enriched environment, babies learn how their world works as they explore on their own.

A number of games and activities can help babies begin to organize and understand their world. Playing peek-a-boo is one of the first

10-16   Sensory stimulation activities help babies learn about their environment.

Sensory Stimulation Activities

	Activity	Sense
1	 © John Shaw	**Mobiles** ☐ Place mobiles on crib and playpen. Keep them out of the baby's reach. Change the objects on the mobile often. Try to visualize them from the baby's point of view.	**Sight**
		Tracking Objects ☐ Hold an object like a yarn ball, small flashlight, or rattle about 12 inches from the baby's eyes. Move it in a short arc and gradually extend the arc to a half circle. The baby's eyes should track or follow the object.	**Sight**
	 © John Shaw	**Wind Chimes** ☐ Hold the baby near wind chimes blowing outdoors. Hearing wind chimes and seeing them move is interesting for babies.	**Hearing & Sight**
		Face Hoop ☐ Draw a face by decorating fabric with fabric scraps or paint. Insert the fabric between round embroidery hoops. Hang the face down or hold it for the baby to see. (The face hoop is not safe for the baby to mouth.)	**Sight**
2	 © John Shaw	**Sound Can** ☐ Place some large wooden beads or large spools of thread in a juice can. Tape on the lid. The baby can hear the objects move inside the can. Other baby-safe objects can be used, too.	**Hearing**

1—*Activity:* Collect pictures of different types of mobiles. Describe what a baby may learn from each.

2—*Activity:* Make a sound can. Share it with the class.

games babies love to play. Cover your eyes, or go out of sight, saying, "Where did (baby's name) go?" Baby waits expectantly for you to uncover your eyes, or come out of hiding, and say, "Peek-a-boo, I see you!" Babies learn to understand that the person is still there even though he or she can't be seen. This is an example of an object permanence activity.

Babies need to repeat games with many objects and with some changes in order to be sure this is the way something really works. There are many kinds of problem-solving activities. More activities are found in 10-17.

▶ Motor Activities

Movement is important for infants. Even before birth babies move. Although motor nerves are not fully developed for four or five years, coordination improves quickly after birth. (**Coordination** is the working together of muscles in movements such as walking.) As infants explore, motor activity helps mental development and coordination. As motor skills improve, babies feel better about their abilities.

Babies will engage in many motor activities on their own if they are free to move. However, they need to be encouraged. Babies use their large muscles to roll over, sit, crawl, stand, and walk. These are called **gross-motor skills.** An activity that encourages gross-motor skills is crawling in and out of boxes or cartons. **Fine-motor skills** refers to coordination in the small muscles, especially those in the fingers and hands, 10-18. By playing with blocks, children learn to set one block on top of another and gain coordination of their small muscles. See 10-19 for other activities for gross-motor and fine-motor games.

▶ Language Activities

Hearing spoken words is important for the child's language development. Babies learn language by hearing people talk. This is best done during baby's routine care. Adults can talk about the foods, toys, people, and routines that are part of the baby's world. Exact words are not as important to the infant as hearing language. While dressing a baby, for instance, the adult could make any of the following statements:

☐   "I'm putting on your green shirt."
☐   "Isn't this a pretty shirt?"
☐   "Are you ready for the shirt to go over your head?"
☐   "Here's a button, here's a button, and here's one."
☐   "Do you like green?"

Although exact words aren't important, words should be pronounced correctly. Changing pitch or singing also varies the sound.

Adults can encourage babies to talk, too. Often, the baby will babble in response. When the baby babbles, encouragement should be given such as, "That's right!"

Reading to children each day exposes them to new words and ideas. Even babies who can't understand what is being read benefit from being read books, magazines, and newspapers. Time spent reading and hearing words is important at all ages.

Language games can be worked into daily routines. This can be a special time of sharing for babies and adults, 10-20. Perhaps one of the earliest language action games babies enjoy is pat-a-cake. See 10-21 for this and other language games.

● **Social-Emotional Needs**

Babies have needs that must be met for healthy social-emotional development. During the first year, social and emotional development seems to center around the baby-adult interaction, the baby's developing self-awareness, and adults' ways of handling special problems.

▶ Baby-Adult Interaction

Each baby comes into the world with a unique temperament. Adults may respond positively or negatively toward the baby's temperament. Adults' feelings are conveyed mainly

3

4

1—*Discuss:* Why are motor activities important?

2—*Note:* This is learning by imitation.

3—*Discuss:* Do you think a caregiver should use baby talk with a baby? Explain.

4—*Discuss:* What are other benefits of reading to babies?

Problem-Solving Activities

Spatial Relationship Activities

Stacking

© John Shaw

Stacking

© John Shaw

Nesting

© John Shaw

☐ **Stacking and Nesting**
Find or purchase three cans or boxes that are different sizes. They must fit inside each other. These can be stacked by placing one on top of the other. They can also be nested by placing one inside the other. Show the baby how to stack and how to nest. (For young babies, the boxes should differ greatly in size. If there are many pieces, start with only the smallest, the middle-size, and the large pieces. After the baby can work with three pieces well, add others one at a time.)

☐ **Far and Near**
Hold a toy close to the baby's eyes. Move it back slowly and say, "There it goes." Move it forward slowly and say, "Here it comes." The game helps babies see size differences in near and far objects.

Object Permanence Activities

☐ **Where's the Object?**
Hide a favorite toy, starting with simple ways of hiding and moving. Advance to more complex ways as the baby masters each. During each game, let the baby watch you hide the toy. If the baby finds the toy, move on to the next step. (1) Partially hide the toy under a blanket. (2) Next, totally hide the toy under the blanket. (3) Wrap the toy in paper so that the shape of the object shows. (4) Place the toy in or under a box. (5) Place the toy in a box that is in another box.

☐ **Hide and Seek**
Hide from the baby, leaving some part of yourself visible. Let the baby find you. Once found, make the reunion happy, with lots of hugs and kisses. (This helps the baby overcome anxiety when left with others.) After partially hiding yourself during many games, hide yourself completely. Choose a hiding spot where the baby can find you easily.

Activities Using Objects as Tools

☐ **Pulling Strings**
Babies can learn to get an object by pulling a string in many ways. You may buy toys that are pulled on a string. You also may attach any toy or safe household object to a string for the baby to pull.

☐ **Making Sounds with Objects**
By hitting objects together, babies can learn to make different sounds. They will learn to vary the sounds by hitting softer or harder, or by changing the objects. Different objects to use include a pan with a spoon, a box with a spoon, a drum with a stick, and a block with a block.

10-17   Problem-solving activities help babies understand their world.

1

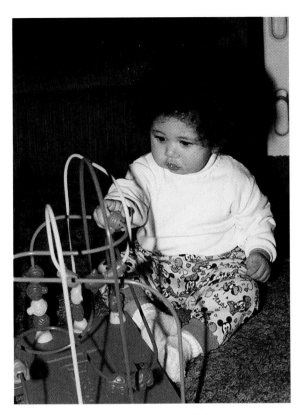

10-18   Using activity toys helps a baby improve fine-motor skills.

10-20   Language games can be part of fun times shared by babies and adults.

© Nancy P. Alexander

Gross-Motor and Fine-Motor Games

Gross-Motor Games

▮ ▮ ▮ ▮ ▮ ▮ ▮ ▮ ▮ ▮ ▮ ▮ ▮ ▮ ▮

☐ **Knock the Toy**
When a baby can stand by holding a playpen or crib railing, place a stuffed toy on the railing. Tell the baby to hold the railing with one hand and to knock the toy off with the other.

☐ **Cartons or Boxes**
Place a large carton or box on its side so that the baby can crawl into it. Let the baby crawl in and out of the carton.

☐ **Dance to the Music**
Tell the baby to dance to the music. You may want to dance with the baby.

Fine-Motor Games

▮ ▮ ▮ ▮ ▮ ▮ ▮ ▮ ▮ ▮ ▮ ▮ ▮ ▮ ▮

☐ **Cups**
A baby can improve fine-motor skills by playing with a plastic infant cup. When the baby can handle the hand-to-mouth movement, add a teaspoon of water to the cup. As the baby becomes more skilled, add more water.

☐ **Blocks**
Show the baby how to use blocks in different ways. Then let the baby try. Blocks can be stacked, hit together, or placed in a line and moved by pushing the last block.

10-19   Gross-motor and fine-motor games help babies' coordination and mental development.

through the way they hold, touch, and look at the baby. The baby reacts to adults' feelings and actions. For instance, if adults are tense or the baby's needs are not met, the baby becomes fussy and difficult. On the other hand, when adults are relaxed and the baby's needs are promptly met, the baby is quiet and cooperates.

Adults who have good relationships with babies seem to respect their temperaments. For instance, active babies will get into places they don't belong. They require more watching than less active children.

2

1—*Discuss:* List fine- and gross-motor skills babies may develop from this toy.

2—*Note:* Patience is an important factor when dealing with an active baby who gets into everything. An active baby also demands more of a caregiver's time and attention.

Language Games

☐ **Verbal Imitation**

Imitation of verbal (and even nonverbal) signals helps language development. Two stages are used during the baby's first year.

Stage 1 (0-6 months)—Imitate the baby's gestures and babbling. If you see a gesture or hear a sound, repeat it with a smile or laugh. See whether the baby repeats it. If the baby has not repeated the gesture or sound in return, repeat the sound. Once the baby catches on, the baby will imitate sounds after you.

Stage 2 (6-12 months)—In this stage, you can begin by making a gesture or sound. See whether the baby imitates it. If the baby has not repeated the gesture or sound in return, make the same gesture or sound again. The baby should catch on quickly.

☐ **Books**

Begin looking at books while the baby is still young. At first, talk about the pictures. As you talk, point to the pictures. Later, begin to read if the story is short. Go on to the next page as the baby loses interest in one page. Between 9 and 12 months, you can ask the baby to find certain pictures, such as cars, pets, or people.

☐ **Puppets**

You can make or buy a puppet to talk to the baby. At first, the baby will just look and listen. Later, he or she will talk to the puppet.

☐ **Action Rhymes**

Children can enjoy action rhymes toward the end of the first year. Action rhymes combine the rhythm of language with a few motor actions. An example follows:

Pat-a-Cake

Pat-a-cake, pat-a-cake, baker's man.
(Help baby clap hands on the words "pat-a-cake")
Bake me a cake as fast as you can.
Roll it, and pat it, and mark it with a "B."
(Help baby roll hands on the word "roll.")
Put it in the oven for baby and me.

10-21 Language games expose babies to words.

Babies feel loved because of physical contact with the adult, 10-22. Physical messages shape feelings between adults and babies. A single or seldom sent message does not determine the relationship. What makes the relationship is the total number of messages and the strength of the messages. Even the most loving adults can be hurried and tense. For a good relationship, the balance must be on the positive side.

Adults should realize that relationships with children are rather one-sided for many years. Babies may give some smiles and hugs, but adults must do most of the giving. This giving is important, though, because the feelings adults show for babies help to shape babies' self-concepts. Fostering good feelings in babies seems to increase the joy and love between babies and their caregivers.

1—*Activity:* Use one or more of these activities with children in observations, child care centers, or the classroom. Record results and report to the class.

Riegel Textile Corp.

10-22   The feeling of love and joy between a baby and an adult can be shared through physical contact.

▶ ## Helping Babies Develop Their Self-Awareness

Babies begin to develop self-awareness as they achieve goals. For instance, when a baby crawls to get a toy, the baby realizes that he or she can make things happen. Babies do not see themselves as separate individuals, however, until eight or nine months of age.

Adults can help self-awareness by using the baby's name as much as possible. Using the baby's name during happy times gives the baby positive feelings about his or her name. Happy times include reunions between adult and baby, such as after a nap or when the adult returns from work. The name also can be used during child care tasks or games like peek-a-boo.

Looking in mirrors also increases self-awareness. Babies enjoy seeing themselves in mirrors even before they know the images they see are their own. Calling the baby's image by name is helpful. Adults may also place babies in front of mirrors so they can watch themselves eat, dress, etc. Babies also enjoy having metal play mirrors as toys, 10-23. They like to point to their eyes, ears, nose, mouth, and toes. They also like finding these body parts in the mirror.

Toward the end of the first year, babies become possessive about some objects. This should be encouraged, because babies' understanding that some objects belong to them is part of self-awareness. Also, a baby must possess something before he or she can own it. Adults can help teach possession by making statements like "Here's Barbara's dress," or "Where are Keith's blocks?"

10-23   A metal baby mirror helps babies see themselves and begin to learn self-awareness.

© John Shaw

1—*Reflect:* List ways to develop a baby's self-awareness.

▶ Handling Special Problems

All babies have some problems. These may include feeding and sleeping problems, fear of strangers, or lots of crying. When problems arise, these tips may help.

☐ Decide if the problem is temporary. Wait a few days, unless the baby seems ill. Babies do have mood changes. Also, the problem may be because of a hurried or tense caregiver. In these cases, the problem will likely end as soon as the adult slows down or relaxes.

☐ If the problem continues, talk to an expert. Start with your pediatrician or a family doctor.

☐ Get help when needed. For instance, parents who have a fussy baby may need to use baby-sitters to rest or get away from home for a few hours.

☐ Give in to a baby's demands sometimes, if the results are not serious. Even babies have wills of their own, and letting them have their way sometimes isn't going to spoil or harm them. For instance, if a baby refuses to eat peas, try other vegetables with almost the same nutrients.

☐ Remain calm. This helps the baby and the adult.

Experienced caregivers tend to almost ignore many common, not-too-serious problems. Experience teaches that all babies are different and that most problems are solved in time.

● **Recognizing Developmental Delays**

As you read in chapter 1, a developmental delay simply means a child is behind typical children of his or her own age in one or more areas of growth and development. The more a child lags behind other children of the same age, the more serious the delay. Infancy is the best time to begin watching for delays and treating problems before they become too serious. If development seems to be much slower than the norms, parents should consult a doctor. Regular medical care is the best way to detect and treat problems. Knowing some typical infant behaviors may help parents to recognize delays, 10-24.

1—*Note:* It is important for a working parent to realize that a disruption at work can carry over to home. A baby may sense stress and become more fussy and demanding than usual.

2—*Note:* Emphasize that a stressed caregiver often causes a baby to become stressed and fussy.

3—*Reflect:* Why might this help to prevent child abuse?

Typical Infant Behaviors	
Age	**Behavior**
One Month	Raises head slightly when lying on stomach
	Can hold head up for a second or two when supported
	Briefly watches and follows moving person or object with eyes
	Makes throaty sounds
Two Months	Holds head erect but bobbing when supported in sitting position
	Responds to smiles with an occasional smile
	Vocalizes
Three Months	Lifts head and chest when lying on stomach
	Has strong body movements
	Has good head control—less bobbing—when supported in sitting position
	Recognizes bottle or breast (knows it is feeding time)
	Coos
	Chuckles
Four Months	Rolls from side to side
	Grasps objects held near hand and may reach for objects
	Follows moving objects with eyes easily from a sitting position
	Laughs aloud
	Plays
Six Months	Sits with very little support
	Rolls from back to stomach
	Transfers objects from mouth to hand and from hand to hand
	Babbles three or more sounds ("ma," "pa," and "be")
Nine Months	Sits without support and can change position without falling
	Plays with two objects at a time
	Can unwrap a block placed in a piece of cloth
	Repeats same babbling sounds ("ma-ma" and "ba-ba")
One Year	Pulls to standing and may take a step or two with support from an adult's hand or an object
	Picks things up with thumb and one finger
	Stacks two blocks
	Gives toy when asked
	Shows affection ("asking" to be picked up by holding arms up, kissing)
	May say two or three words

10-24   Knowing what typical infant behaviors are can help to recognize developmental delays.

Summary

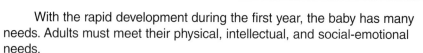

With the rapid development during the first year, the baby has many needs. Adults must meet their physical, intellectual, and social-emotional needs.

Only formula or breast milk is recommended for the first six months. After that, adults can introduce solid baby foods one at a time. Learning to drink from a cup and use a spoon is gradual. It requires the child to use a different set of throat and tongue muscles.

Babies outgrow their clothing quickly. Good consumer sense is important when buying baby clothes. It is important to read labels for care instructions and check for flame retardant and anti-static finishes. Clothing, including diapers, must be clean and free of detergent residue before wearing.

Other needs include bathing, sleeping, and playing. When tub bathing a baby, see that the water is comfortably warm and keep the child safe from slipping. Children should have their own sleep area away from distracting noises. Make sure there are no soft, fluffy products under the infants while they sleep. All play spaces for babies and young children should be safe, yet provide stimulating play.

In order to develop intellectually, children need an enriched environment. They need activities that will stimulate all of the senses. Problem-solving activities help them learn about the world around them. Activities that develop motor skills are encouraged. For language development to take place, it is important to talk to children and to encourage them to talk.

Babies' social-emotional needs center on their interaction with others and their growing self-awareness. Adults and those around them help babies develop their self-identity.

Different problems in feeding, sleeping, and crying may develop. Parents and caregivers need to try a number of methods to handle these problems calmly, yet effectively.

To Review

1

Write your answers on a separate sheet of paper.

1. Babies most basic needs are in the _____ (physical, intellectual, social) area.
2. Give three reasons for not starting solids before babies are six months of age unless advised by a baby's doctor.
3. Which statements about the weaning process are true?
   a. Weaning is best done gradually.
   b. Complete weaning prior to nine months has no harmful effects on the baby.
   c. Weaning is a physical and social-emotional process.

1—*Answers:* Answers to review questions can be found in the front section of this TAE.

4. True or false. Generally, SIDS occurs in babies between 10 and 12 months of age.
5. List three suggestions in planning sleep and play spaces for a baby.
6. True or false. Activities and games should be woven into child care routines.
7. The statement below is followed by three pairs of phrases. Choose one phrase from each pair that best completes the statement.
   Skillful caregivers can help babies learn by
   _____ a.   checking age charts and doing an activity when it's time
   _____ b.   watching for signs of each baby's interest in certain experiences
   _____ a.   repeating games many times over several months
   _____ b.   not repeating games because babies get bored with them
   _____ a.   showing babies exactly how to do activities so that the babies will not become confused
   _____ b.   letting babies try things for themselves
8. True or false. Learning to sit up is an example of a fine-motor skill.
9. True or false. Babies learn language by hearing people talk.
10. List two ways to help a baby learn to talk and understand words.
11. How can parents help their child develop self-awareness? List three ways.

To Do

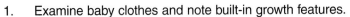

1. Examine baby clothes and note built-in growth features.
2. Examine infant's clothing. List the good features. Attach a hang tag to each item that lists its best features. Compare your lists in class.
3. Watch a caregiver bathe a baby in a tub, then practice the steps with a doll. (Remember to talk and play with the baby as you give the bath.)
4. Share with the class ways you have observed children solve their problems.
5. State how you have observed children react when playing games like peek-a-boo.
6. Brainstorm in class. List activities that promote small- and large-motor development.
7. Recall times that you observed children who were not ready to use a new skill or try a new activity. Discuss what they did and how they acted.
8. By talking as a group, list all the ways people make you feel valued and loved. Discuss whether a baby could or could not feel loved in each way.

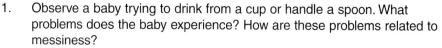

To Observe

1. Observe a baby trying to drink from a cup or handle a spoon. What problems does the baby experience? How are these problems related to messiness?
2. Observe several babies wearing different types of outfits. Describe the outfits and list the advantages or disadvantages of each.
3. Observe a baby (6- to 12-months-old) at home. If this were your baby and home, what childproofing would you need?
4. Observe a baby playing. What senses are being stimulated? Which motor and language skills are being developed?
5. Observe a baby playing. How does the parent or caregiver encourage a positive relationship?

To Think Critically

1. Some parents believe that feeding babies solids is the best way to ensure that they sleep throughout the night. How can this belief be harmful to babies?
2. In the text, playing "peek-a-boo" is described as a good game for developing object permanence in babies. Besides "peek-a-boo," what other games develop object permanence?
3. Adults need to respect babies' temperaments. What are some ways parents can respect the temperament of a happy baby? A shy baby? A fussy baby? An active baby? A quiet baby?

A parent provides for the developmental needs of a baby.

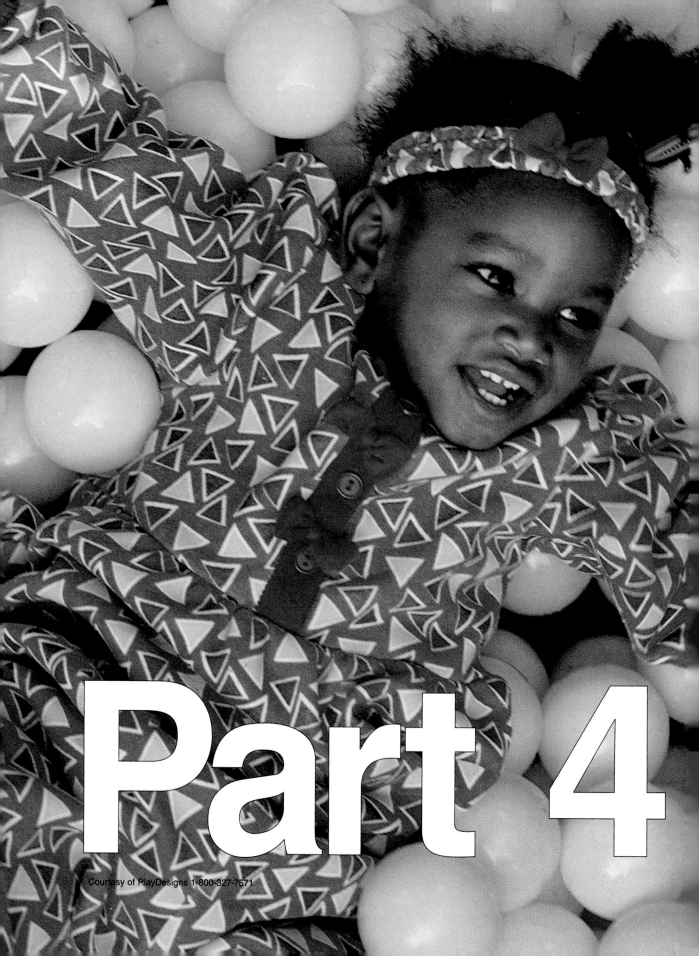

Part 4

Toddlers

Children between the ages of one and three are called toddlers. This name fits them, since toddlers "toddle" during almost all their waking minutes as they explore the world around them.

You will see how the one-year-old chubby baby develops into a slender three-year-old in **chapter 11.** During this time, toddlers become sure-footed as they practice jumping, hopping, throwing, and catching. Small-motor coordination improves some, also.

In **chapter 12,** you will see that toddlers truly begin to understand their environment. They learn about the properties of objects and what happens when they manipulate them. Because they learn to think before acting, toddlers plan new ways to achieve goals. Toddlers also become able communicators as they learn new words and speak in short sentences.

Chapter 13 discusses the other traits of toddlers—their desire for independence and sometimes negative expression of self-will. Although toddlers express their emotions in intense ways, their self-esteem is fragile and adults must protect it.

Chapter 14 will give examples of ways to assist toddlers' development. Adults need to help toddlers begin to think independently and practice self-care. They need to help children find a balance between their own will and the limits to self-will society expects.

Chapter 11

During the toddler years, changes in the body make many new skills possible.

Physical Development of the Toddler

After studying this chapter, you will be able to

☐ describe the physical changes that occur between the first and third years of life.

☐ identify the toddler's major gross-motor and fine-motor skills.

After studying this chapter, you will be able to define

eye-hand coordination
large-muscle development
muscle development
small-muscle development

As toddlers develop physically, their bodies mature. This helps them handle more complex tasks. Although toddlers do not grow as quickly as infants, they go through many important physical changes, 11-1.

Babies do not have much control over their muscles when they are first born. By the end of their first year, infants are just learning to control voluntary muscle movements. Both the gross-motor and fine-motor skills of toddlers improve. These skills improve so much that, by the end of their second year, toddlers can run, jump, throw, and feed themselves.

11-1 Toddlers change physically in many ways.

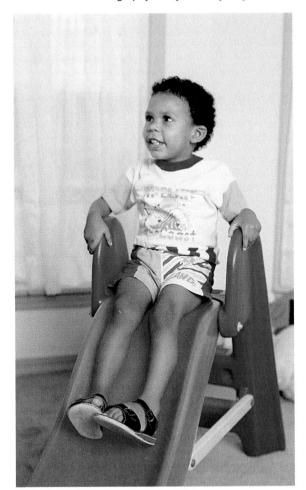

© John Shaw

Body Growth and Development

After the first year, babies continue to grow quickly. Their organ systems continue to mature, too. However, they do not grow as quickly as they did during their first year.

▶ Height and Weight

Toddlers grow at different rates. This is due to environment and heredity. What does heredity affect? Heredity affects a baby's height. It affects how fast the baby grows tall, too. Because genes determine height, they also influence weight. (Taller people usually weigh more than shorter people.) However, the environment (diet, exercise, health, and even emotions) affects a baby's weight, too. Because of these factors, toddlers sometimes grow at different rates than norms predict for their age.

Years One and Two

Body growth begins to slow after the first year. Babies gain about twice as much height in the first year as in their second year. Most babies triple their birth weight during the first year, then gain one-fourth of that during the second, 11-2. Some babies grow a little faster than these norms in their second year. (They may be "catching up" to norms after a premature birth or first-year illness.) Most girls reach 53 percent of their adult height by age two. Boys reach 50 percent of their adult height by age two, 11-3. Also, it often is true that a tall two-year-old will be a tall adult. Likewise, a short two-year-old may be a short adult.

After Year Two

After 24 months, children grow at a slower but steadier rate. They tend to gain two to three inches and about six pounds per year throughout childhood. (This rate of growth stops at about 11 years for girls and 13 years for boys.) Chart 11-4 shows the height and weight norms from 12 to 36 months.

1

2

3

1—*Reflect:* Think of a toddler you know. Which parent is he or she most like in build? Can you accurately predict at this age how tall a toddler might be as an adult? Why or why not?

2—*Math Activity:* Make these calculations for your own birth length and weight.

3—*Math Activity:* Calculate a child's approximate weight at the end of year one if he or she weighed nine pounds one ounce at birth. Calculate the child's approximate weight at the end of year two.

Growth from Birth to Age Two Years

Let's suppose Sarah was 20.5 inches and weighed seven pounds at birth. She is growing exactly by the norms. Based on her birth length and weight, we would calculate her two-year growth the following way:

First Year		Second Year	
Length/Height	**Birth**............................ 20.5″ **Add 9″** (based on norms) ...+ 9.0″ —————————— **Total Length** .... 29.5″ a 9″ increase	**Length/Height**	**12 months** .... 29.5″ **Add 1/2 of 9″** ....+ 4.5″ —————————— **Total height** .... 34.0″ a 4.5″ increase
Weight	**Birth** .... 7 lbs. **Triple birth weight** .... x 3 —————————— **Total** .... 21 lbs. a 14 lb. gain	**Weight**	**12 months** .... 21 lbs. **Add 1/4 of total weight at 12 months** .....+ 5.25 lbs. —————————— **Total weight** .... 26.25 lbs. a 5 lb. increase

11-2 Growth slows after the first year.

1

11-3 Most girls reach 53 percent of their adult height by age two. Boys reach 50 percent of their adult height by that age.

2

Fisher-Price

▶ Other Body Changes

The body proportions of a two-year-old are still different from those of an adult. At 24 months, the head is one-fourth of the total height. An adult's head is one-tenth of his or her height. A 24-month-old's chest and abdomen are about the

11-4 The height and weight of children from one to three years increase steadily.

Average Height and Weight from One to Three Years		
Age in Months	**Height**	**Weight**
12	30″	21 lbs.
18	32″	24.5 lbs.
24	34″	27 lbs.
30	36″	30 lbs.
36	38″	32 lbs.

1—Resource: Growth Slows and Slows, SAG.

2—Math Activity: Calculate a girl's adult height if she is 35 inches tall at age two. Calculate a boy's adult height if he is 36 inches tall at age two.

same size. By 30 months, the chest is larger than the abdomen. As the child matures, the difference between chest and abdomen size will become even greater.

Bones

As toddlers grow, their bones continue to become harder. The toddler still has a larger proportion of soft cartilage to hard bone. The toddler's bones are more flexible and less likely to break than an adult's. However, the softer bones are more prone to disease or deformation. The toddlers' fontanelles (gaps between the skull bones) are closed or almost closed. The toddler's spine becomes S-shaped rather than C-shaped. This makes standing and walking easier. Shortly after two years, babies have their full sets of deciduous teeth (often called baby teeth), 11-5.

The Brain

By the end of the second year, the brain is four-fifths of its adult weight. The brain now is closer to maturity than any other organ. The other body organs continue to mature, but they do so at a slower rate than the brain. (This is an example of the head-to-foot principle—development is completed from the brain down the spine.)

2

Fat Tissues

Fat tissues under the skin decrease rapidly between 9 and 30 months. The chubby baby becomes a slender child, 11-6. ***Muscle development*** (the lengthening and thickening of muscles) is slow during the toddler stage.

11-6   The toddler will slowly become slender because fat tissues under the skin are decreasing.

3

11-5   Soon after their second birthday, toddlers have their full set of deciduous teeth.

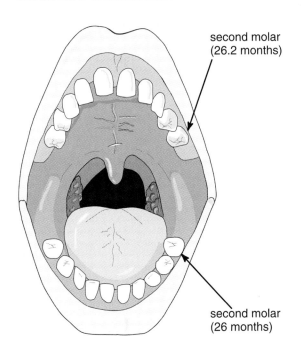

second molar
(26.2 months)

second molar
(26 months)

© John Shaw

1—*Discuss:* Are an adult's bones more or less likely to break than a toddler's? Why or why not?

2—*Discuss:* Why would this be true according to the head-to-foot principle?

3—*Activity:* Compare your baby pictures to a picture of yourself as a toddler. Observe how the fat tissues decreased.

● Motor Development

Toddlers improve the motor skills they developed as infants. However, they also learn lots of new skills. Motor skills develop as the child grows and develops. As the child practices new skills, motor development improves even more.

▶ Large-Muscle Development

Large-muscle development refers to the development of the trunk and arm and leg muscles. Movements such as crawling, walking, jumping, and running depend mainly on these large muscles. (These movements are examples of gross-motor skills.) During the first year, most babies developed these muscles at least to the point of standing and walking with support. After one year, babies master walking and begin learning other motor skills. Toddlers love to run, jump, and use other large muscles. When they are held in one place too long, they begin squirming, as if to say, "I want down!" (Squirming is an example of a large-muscle movement.)

▪ Walking

Babies may walk without support two or three months before or after the first birthday. Why do babies begin to walk at different ages? Some children are not physically ready to walk but want to so much that they fall when they try. Others who creep quickly may not walk early because creeping gets them where they want to be. Often, girls begin to walk before boys. Also, lighter babies may walk earlier than heavier babies.

Although some conditions are helpful, babies learn to walk in their own time and way. To do so, they need warm adult support, a positive reaction to the baby's attempts, and a safe area. Pushing a baby to walk early will not help. It may even delay walking and will surely frustrate both the baby and adult.

Beginning Walkers.   Regardless of age, all beginning walkers share some common traits. They stand with their feet wide apart, which gives them a wider base of support. They turn their feet

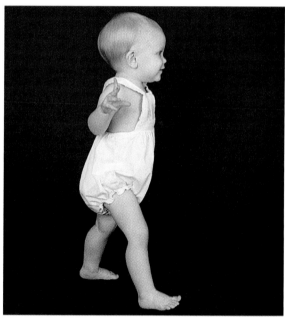

John Shaw

11-7   To maintain balance, toddlers first walk with a wide stance and knees flexed.

outward and slightly flex their knees, 11-7. Some children walk on their tiptoes. This is not because they want to stand taller (which they learn to do). Babies stand on their tiptoes because they have not learned to lower their heels yet. A baby's first steps often seem like staggers. The baby may step to the side or backwards. The baby also may take irregular steps, lurch forward, and weave. Because it is hard for babies to balance their large heads, they fall a lot.

A flat spine causes the toddler to tilt forward slightly when walking. As the toddler grows, this walking posture changes, 11-8. The lower back curve takes on the S-shape. As it does, the walk becomes more upright. This, plus improved ability to balance, helps the toddler to walk steadily. The toddler's stance also becomes more narrow, the feet straighter, and the knees less flexed.

Walking at Two.   At two years, a child's walk may look like a run, but it is not a run. Toddlers take about 170 steps per minute. Their stride is half the length of that of an adult. Can you

---

1—*Activity:* Inquire about the age at which you first walked without support. How close to average were you in this respect?

2—*Discuss:* What examples can you give of providing warm support and a positive reaction to baby's attempts to walk without support?

3—*Activity:* Observe a baby who is just beginning to walk with or without support. Describe his or her attempts and movements. Share with the class.

1

2

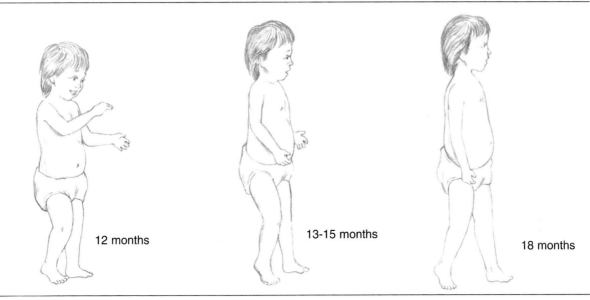

12 months

13-15 months

18 months

Thomas J. Roberts

11-8   Toddlers walk in a more upright way between 12 and 18 months of age.

imagine doubling your steps, taking 170 steps per minute, and having someone hold your hands above your head? No wonder walking tires young children before it tires adults.

Children must watch their foot placement while walking until almost three years of age. They must watch each step the same way you would if you were walking on stones across a creek.

Running

True running, not just a hurried walk, begins around two years of age. Two-year-olds are not skillful runners. This is due to their arm placement. They tend to hold their arms up or out. Running is also awkward because they cannot start or stop quickly.

Jumping

Stepping off low objects at about 18 months is the way children learn to jump. Before two years of age, children may step off a low object and remain suspended in air for a brief moment.

At two years, children can jump off of low objects with two feet. However, they move their arms back instead of helping the jump by swinging their arms forward, 11-9.

Climbing

Babies may begin to climb as soon as they can crawl or creep. Between 15 and 18 months, babies will climb onto furniture. They will walk up and down stairs with help. For toddlers, going up stairs is easier than coming down stairs. Toddlers do not change feet while climbing until after the second birthday.

When does climbing begin? There really isn't a set time. Climbing ability relates to the kinds of stairs the baby has nearby. Babies can climb more easily if the stairs are not too steep. Climbing also relates to courage. A courageous baby is likely to try climbing sooner than a timid baby.

Throwing and Catching

Infants begin throwing by accident. They forget to hold onto an object while swinging their

3

1—*Activity:* Working with a partner, practice walking at your normal pace. Have your partner keep time for one minute while you walk. How many steps did you take per minute? Compare results with other class members.

2—*Activity:* Observe a toddler who is running. Describe arm and leg movements and starting and stopping.

3—*Activity:* Visit a baby between one and two years old. Walk up and down stairs with him or her. Record and describe the motions the child used, comparing his or her motions up and down the stairs. Why do you think it is easier for the child to go up the stairs rather than down?

Thomas J. Roberts

11-9 At first, toddlers "jump" by stepping off low objects. Then they jump with both feet while pulling their arms back instead of swinging them forward.

Courtesy of PlayDesigns

11-10 Toddlers squat to pick up thrown objects until they are about two years old.

arms. They enjoy seeing the object move and hearing the sound it makes when it lands. Then, babies start to throw on purpose. Planned throwing begins around one year of age.

Year-old babies usually throw from a sitting position, such as from their high chair. After babies feel secure standing or walking, they throw from standing positions. Children under three are not skillful throwers. These children usually use a rigid throw and do not shift their weight. They also cannot release the ball at the right time, which sends the ball in almost any direction.

For almost a year after children begin to walk, they "catch" an object by squatting and picking it up, 11-10. Around two years of age, the child will bend at the waist to pick up the thrown object. Children two- to three-years-old may try to catch by standing in one position with arms extended and elbows stiff. For the child to catch it, the ball must be exactly on target. The child does not move toward the ball. In fact, many children close their eyes as the ball comes toward them.

Small-Muscle Development

Small-muscle development refers to the development of small muscles, especially those in the hands and fingers. The movements that depend on these muscles are called *fine-motor skills.* Fine-motor skills also depend on a child's level of eye-hand coordination. To have **eye-hand coordination,** children must coordinate what they see with the way they move their hands. As eye-hand coordination and small muscles improve, toddlers can handle more complex fine-motor skills.

By the end of the first year, babies can hold objects between the thumb and index finger. This helps them learn many new fine-motor skills. Between 12 and 18 months, toddlers can hold spoons in their fists. They can feed themselves and drink from cups. They may miss their mouths a little or spill food at first. With practice and better eye-hand coordination, however, toddlers become better at feeding themselves. They also can make marks on paper by holding a pencil or crayon in their fists. At this age, the toddler can

1

1—Activity: Practice throwing and catching a large ball with a toddler. Record the age of the child and how he or she picks up the ball. Record how the child catches the ball. Practice encouraging remarks. How does the child respond to these?

2—Discuss: What activities in your life depend on good eye-hand coordination?

Thomas J. Roberts

Photo provided by and reproduced with permission of Binney and Smith

11-11   A toddler can hold crayons with the thumb and fingers, but the grasp is much more awkward than a mature grasp.

remove a hat and shoes, insert rather large objects into holes, and turn pages of a book several at a time.

Between 18 months and two years, fine-motor skills improve even more. By this stage, toddlers can string large beads on cords. They can turn the pages of books one at a time. They can open doors by turning knobs. Most two-year-olds can hit pegs with a hammer. After two years, many children hold crayons or pencils with the thumb on one side and fingers on the other side, 11-11. They still cannot hold or write with a crayon or pencil the way an adult can.

By two years, most children show a definite hand preference. They still switch hands a lot. Their right hand tends to be used for drawing or throwing a ball and the left hand for holding a cup and eating. With each passing year until age seven or eight, more and more children use the right hand for most activities. At that time, 95 percent of all children are right-handed, 11-12. (This is the same percentage as found among adults.)

3

1—*Activity:* Practice this grasp on a thick crayon. Practice drawing or coloring using this grasp and your opposite hand. Describe the experience.

2—*Resource: Motor Skills Continue to Develop,* SAG.

3—*Resource: Motor Skills of a Toddler on the Go,* SAG.

11-12 These two children use different hands for the same task. By age seven or eight, however, 95 percent of all children are right-handed.

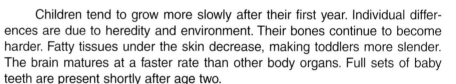

Summary

Children tend to grow more slowly after their first year. Individual differences are due to heredity and environment. Their bones continue to become harder. Fatty tissues under the skin decrease, making toddlers more slender. The brain matures at a faster rate than other body organs. Full sets of baby teeth are present shortly after age two.

Toddlers refine their walking, climbing, and throwing skills. Many new skills are emerging, such as running, jumping off objects, and catching objects. Their fine-motor skills depend on the child's level of eye-hand coordination. Most children begin to show a definite hand preference by their second year.

To Review

Write your answers on a separate sheet of paper.

1. A person's height and the rate of increase in height is mainly due to _____ (heredity, environment). A person's weight and the rate of increase in weight is mainly due to _____ (heredity, environment).
2. True or false. A baby's rate of growth slows after 12 months.
3. True or false. Most babies triple their birth weight by the time they are one year old.

1—*Activity:* Interview a left-handed person. What tasks are more difficult for this person because of equipment and teaching methods? How could our society help people who are left-handed?

2—*Answers:* Answers to review questions can be found in the front section of this TAE.

4. The fastest organ to develop is the
   a. heart
   b. brain
   c. liver
   d. lungs
5. True or false. Children are usually chubbier after their first year than before.
6. Give two possible reasons why babies might begin to walk at different ages.
7. Explain why toddlers may fall if they do not think about what they are doing as they walk.
8. Match the toddler's skills to the motor actions by putting the correct letter before the skill.
   Skills—
   _____ walking
   _____ running
   _____ jumping
   _____ climbing
   _____ throwing
   _____ catching
   Motor Actions—
   a. moves arms toward the back
   b. uses improper arm actions and cannot stop or start quickly
   c. stands without moving with arms extended stiffly
   d. begins each movement with the same foot rather than changing feet
   e. shows little or no weight shift
   f. steps forward, backward, and to either side
9. True or false. One-year-olds have well-developed eye-hand coordination.
10. True or false. Year-old babies can grasp objects between the thumb and index finger, so they hold flatware and crayons the same way adults hold them.

To Do

1. As a group or class project, write a one- or two-page brochure explaining toddlers' motor skills. Include information on the order (and approximate age) when toddlers learn motor skills. Also explain the motor actions used when walking, running, jumping, climbing, throwing, and catching. (Illustrations may help.) Have the teacher check your brochure, then make copies. Give copies to parents and adults at a program that serves toddlers, such as a child care program or nursery school.
2. Observe the motor skills (both large-muscle and small-muscle) of toddlers between 12 and 36 months of age. Note the kinds of movements they make and how they compare to adult movements. Share your findings with the class.

1—*Activity:* Prepare the brochure on the computer with graphics or clip art to add interest. Hospitals and medical centers may also be interested in providing distribution.

3. Play catch with a toddler. Use a soft rubber, foam, or cloth ball about six inches in diameter. Notice the skills that the toddler uses. How far can the toddler throw a ball? How straight is the aim? Does the toddler use an overhand or underhand throw? Is there a weight shift? How does the toddler stand to catch the ball? Does the toddler move toward the ball if the ball is a little off target? Does the toddler drop the ball? Describe your findings in class.

To Observe

1. Observe the height of several 24-month-olds. Do the taller toddlers have taller parents? Do the shorter toddlers have shorter parents?
2. Observe infants and toddlers. How do they look different?
3. Observe a toddler just beginning to walk and a toddler who is just three-years-old. How is their upright posture and walk different?
4. Observe a toddler while playing catch with a soft rubber ball. What does the toddler do with his/her arms and hands as you begin to toss the ball? What does the toddler watch—you or the ball? How does the toddler pick up a missed ball? How does the toddler throw the ball—overhand or underhand, with one or two hands? How close to you (the target) does the ball come?
5. Observe toddlers with materials that require fine-motor skills. How do they grip pencils, crayons, or markers? How messy is their self-feeding? Are breads and puzzle pieces hard to manage?

To Think Critically

1. Two-year-old Sarah has a shorter-than-average mother and a taller-than-average father. Her parents wonder whether Sarah will be a tall, average, or short adult. Can they predict her height? If so, how? Do you think such a prediction will be very accurate? Why or why not?
2. When toddlers walk or run, they usually hold their arms out. Why? In what situations might adults do this?
3. Why is "coloring within the lines" an impossible skill for toddlers?

Because toddlers have more control over their muscles, they can accomplish more difficult physical tasks.

Chapter 12

Intellectual Development of the Toddler

After studying this chapter, you will be able to:

☐ describe how and what toddlers learn.
☐ describe the sequence of language development.

After studying this chapter, you will be able to define the following terms:

articulation
communication
deferred imitation
grammar
language

Toddlers love to learn about the world around them.

In past chapters, you have read about how babies learn. Much of what babies learn begins in the newborn stage. By age one, their skills become much more advanced. Along with mental development, babies' motor skills improve as they grow into toddlers. Then toddlers begin to walk, and their physical and mental worlds expand because they can explore.

Toddlers are eager to learn. They are curious about anyone and anything, 12-1. They may not always work their hardest to learn what adults want them to learn. However, once they decide to solve a problem, they will stay with the task until they find a solution.

12-2   Playing with sand on the beach helps children learn through their senses and motor actions.

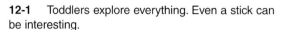

12-1   Toddlers explore everything. Even a stick can be interesting.

How and What Toddlers Learn

Through stages of development, Piaget has described how children's thinking changes as they mature. He called the first stage the *sensorimotor stage.* It includes children from birth to two years of age. As you read in chapter 8, children in this stage learn through their senses and motor actions, 12-2. From about a year to 18 months, says Piaget, children learn by discovering new ways to solve problems. Piaget states that the beginning of thought occurs from 18 months to about two years of age.

▶ Discovering New Ways to Solve Problems

At about a year to 18 months, children are busy exploring. They show lots of interest in new actions. They also love to repeat their actions.

1—*Activity:* Describe a toddler you know. How does curiosity help him or her learn more about the world? What questions does the toddler ask?

2—*Discuss:* What could a child learn from playing with a stick? A clothes hanger? A spoon?

3—*Discuss:* How could you help a toddler develop more sensory learning when playing with sand? What types of motor actions could increase sensory learning?

4—*Discuss:* Why is it an advantage for a toddler to repeat his or her actions? Compare this to learning to drive a car.

■ **Working Toward a Goal**

In this stage, children's actions involve reaching a goal. The goal may be obvious to an adult. For instance, a child may pull an object by its string in order to grasp it. Sometimes the goal may not be obvious. It may seem as if the child is only playing with or throwing objects. However, children play with objects to see how they work, 12-3. They want to know what happens to objects when they are rolled, shaken, thrown, or moved in other ways. Children are looking for the best ways to reach their goals. This is why children, when repeating their actions, change them in some way.

As toddlers learn more about objects and gain thinking skills, they can solve common problems themselves. Toddlers learn how to feed and dress themselves, 12-4. They know how to open doors and put objects in boxes and pails. They

12-3   Children learn by playing with different objects.

© John Shaw

12-4   Toddlers feel proud when they dress themselves. Elastic waists and wide neck holes make their task easier.

can find ways to grab out-of-reach objects. They solve their problems the best way they know how. To snatch a cookie on the kitchen table, a toddler may pull on the tablecloth until the cookie falls.

▶ **Beginning of Thought**

Around 18 months to two years of age, most children think about what they do before they do it. Because their thinking is not mature yet, they think in terms of actions. A 30-month-old child may answer the question, "What is a ball?" with the reply, "To play with," or "To roll."

1—*Discuss:* How do toddlers learn from rolling, shaking, throwing, or moving objects?

2—*Reflect:* Do you think a caregiver should do everything for a toddler, such as dressing him or her, because it saves time? Discuss why or why not.

3—*Discuss:* What would a child learn by playing with cups of different colors and sizes?

4—*Note:* Emphasize the adult's role as a self-esteem builder.

5—*Resource: Toddlers Are Scientists,* SAG.

Thinking and Imitation

Children also show they can think by imitating what someone else has done at an earlier time. The ability to recall someone's behavior and imitate it later is called **deferred imitation,** 12-5. (Deferred means postponed.)

Thinking and Goals

Thinking also shows in the child's way of reaching goals, 12-6. A child may want to reach a toy on a high playroom shelf (goal). He or she may have used a step stool in the bathroom but not in the playroom. The child thinks about the step stool and how it works in the bathroom. Then the child gets the step stool to reach the object. If the child cannot bring the step stool into the playroom, he or she may use another object as a stool. The child has thought through how to reach the goal.

Thinking and Hiding Games

Thinking is evident in hiding games, too. Children at this stage will search for objects they have not seen someone hide. This might happen when the adult pretends to hide a toy in one place but really hides it in another. The child knows the object still exists (object permanence) and thinks about where the adult could have hidden it.

12-6   Thinking is evident as this toddler tries to put eggs in a basket.

12-5   Feeding a doll the way adults feed babies is an example of deferred imitation.

© John Shaw

Thinking and Shape, Size, Color, and Texture

Toddlers begin to perceive differences in shape, size, color, and texture. They may confuse them but know they are different.

Thinking and Object Exploration

Toddlers also learn more about what will happen as they handle objects. They learn by throwing, rolling, shaking, or moving objects, 12-7. They learn that round objects roll and flat objects slide. They also learn that hard objects hit together will make a loud noise but soft objects hit together do not.

4

5

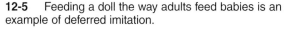

1—*Discuss:* What are some examples of deferred imitation?

2—*Discuss:* How could the idea of object permanence be reflected in a child's separation anxiety? (For example, a child may be less likely to cry when a parent leaves because he or she knows the parent will return.)

3—*Enrich:* Practice hiding an object with a toddler you know and report your results to the class.

4—*Enrich:* Provide examples of toddlers' perception of differences in size, shape, color, and texture. If necessary, experiment with children in a child care center. Report the results.

5—*Resource: Toddlers Learn by Throwing Objects,* SAG.

12-7 Toddlers often mouth objects. This is a common example of how a toddler manipulates objects to learn about them.

Thinking and Language

Finally, the way children think is observed through their use of language. **Language** is a symbol system in which words are used as labels for people, objects, and ideas. Unlike other symbol systems, such as pictures, words do not sound or look like the people and objects they represent.

In order to learn language, babies use two thinking skills. First, children must associate the word and the person or object. For instance, toddlers must understand that the word "milk" refers to a certain liquid, not water or juice. Second,

children must recall the word and its meaning when they hear the word or want to say it. Language requires high-level thinking skills.

● Language Abilities

As you read in chapter 8, babies begin to learn language as infants. Newborns will turn toward the sound of human speech just minutes after delivery. Babies react to differences in sounds during the first couple of months. Then they begin to babble these sounds at about six months. Toward the end of the first year, they understand many words and sentences. They may also say a few words.

Language is often used to distinguish infants from toddlers. Learning language is important for children's mental and social development.

▶ Learning Spoken Language

Spoken language develops at a faster rate between one and three years than at any other time in a person's life. However, learning to talk is hard and takes time. This is because speaking involves *articulation* (making the sounds of language) and learning the meanings of words.

■ Learning to Articulate

Babies can make all the sounds of any language. They learn the words and language of those around them through imitation. Learning to control the tongue, lip muscles, and vocal chords to form words takes practice. Babies do not pronounce sounds accurately each time.

Children who cannot make one sound will substitute another. For instance, they may use "d" for "th." A toddler may say "dat" instead of "that." Sometimes children can articulate the right sound in one place in a word but not in another. A toddler may have no problem with "m" at the beginning of a word such as "milk." However, the toddler may have trouble making the "m" sound in the middle of "hammer" or at the end of "broom."

Toddlers may also change the sound order of a word. They may say "perslip" to mean "slipper." They even may change an entire word, such

1—*Note:* This is a method of sensory learning (how it feels on the tongue).

2—*Activity:* Observe a toddler and record single-word requests he or she uses. Does the toddler appear to understand the request? Report to the class.

3—*Resource: Toys Are Tools for Thinking,* SAG.

4—*Discuss:* Have you observed a child who said many words you did not understand? How could you help the child learn to say the words correctly? Should you expect the child to catch on quickly when you help?

5—*Discuss:* What are typical sounds you have heard substituted for others?

as say "book" and mean "bird." Sometimes toddlers will drop a sound if they can't pronounce it. For example, they may say "seepy," instead of "sleepy."

A few children articulate most, if not all, sounds correctly from the beginning. Most children make substitutions. They tend to correct themselves in time. Adults should pronounce words correctly, even if the toddler's way of saying words sounds cute. Children need good examples to follow.

Learning Meanings

Learning the meanings of words is hard. To do so, the child must link certain features with a name. This is hard because many objects with different names share common features. For example, both lambs and ponies run outside and have four legs. Sometimes children confuse the meanings of words they hear. They may use a wrong name for an object, such as call a cow a "moo" or a stove "hot." Without meanings attached to spoken sounds, there would be no language. These meanings give the child two new tools—communication and a new way to think.

Communication is the skill needed to understand others and to be understood by them. Already, toddlers can understand many words and sentences. When they begin to say words, they want to be understood, 12-8.

As you read, language is part of the thinking process. In other words, people learn to think in words. As the child learns to talk, words go with actions. For instance, the toddler will say goodbye while waving. Later, children talk to themselves as they play or lie in bed. They then often whisper words. Finally, they think about words without saying them.

Meanings are attached to words (*vocabulary*) and to the order of words (*grammar*). Young children develop both vocabulary and grammar.

Vocabulary. Most children's vocabularies grow slowly until 18 months to two years of age. The fastest growth occurs around 30 months of age.

The norms on the number of vocabulary words children know at different ages vary. They depend on whether all spoken words are counted or whether only words used with correct meanings are counted. Then, too, children will often use words for awhile, drop them, and pick them up again months later. The size of the vocabulary can be different among children by three years of age.

Grammar. Grammar begins with single-word sentences and will often progress to simple sentences of a few words during the toddler years.

12-8 Toddlers can communicate their needs.

The Tool of Communication	
Reasons to Communicate	**Examples of Communication**
To achieve a goal	"Want cookie." (I want a cookie.) "Go bye-bye." (I want to ride in the car.) "No!" (I don't want _____.)
To identify an object	"See doggie." (I see a dog.) "Big!" (That is big.) "What dat?" (What is that?)
To create a bond with another person	"Mommy?" (Where are you mommy? I want you.) "Kiss." (I love you.) "Hurt." (Please help me.)

1—*Discuss:* Why should parents avoid speaking baby talk to toddlers?

2—*Note:* Reinforce the point that communication is a two-way process. If the toddler is asking a question, he or she expects an answer. The answer helps the toddler learn about the world.

Single Words. From one year until 18 months of age babies use one-word "sentences." A single word is often used by the toddler to mean different ideas at different times. A child may use "bye-bye" to identify a moving object (a car) and to make a request ("Let's go!")

To understand these meanings, the caregiver must note how that baby says the word, how the baby gestures, and what is happening at the time.

Children use words that stand for the people and objects they know and the actions they see. Children's first words are usually nouns and simple action verbs. Nouns may include words like "mama," "daddy," and "kitty." Action verbs may include "hi," "bye-bye," "run," and "fly." Next, the baby learns descriptive words (adjectives and adverbs), such as "big," "hot," "pretty," "loud," and "fast." Young children quickly learn words for love and affection, too, such as "hug."

Two or More Words. After 19 months, many children begin combining two or more words to form sentences. At the early stage of combining words, toddlers use only the most necessary words. By 24 to 30 months, many toddlers begin using three or more words in their sentences. When the child begins to use these multiple-word sentences, the words that are added fill in the gaps. "All gone milk," becomes "Milk is gone." By the time the child uses three-word sentences, the word order of simple statements often is correct. The child may say, "Bird is flying," instead of "Fly bird."

12-9 Toddlers talk about their world of activities.

1—*Resource: Toddlers Begin to Think, SAG.*

▶ Different Rates of Learning to Talk

Differences in the rate at which toddlers learn to talk can vary by several months. Many adults worry about a "slow" talker, only to see the baby become a nonstop talker a few months later. These toddlers are hearing sounds and learning meanings all along. When they begin to talk, they progress quickly.

A number of factors can affect language development. Learning to talk depends on the following:

☐ Hearing—A baby must hear human speech clearly in order to learn to talk without special training. Even ear infections can delay speech in toddlers.

☐ Interest—Some active toddlers are more interested in motor skills than in talking. (They often catch up to earlier talkers quickly.)

☐ Mental abilities—Because language is so closely related to thinking, a child with a mental disability is often slower to talk. On the other hand, early talking does not mean that a child is bright. Children of average and even below average mental abilities may talk at a young age simply by repeating what they hear.

☐ Sex of toddler—From the first year of life, girls tend to excel in verbal skills more than boys. Researchers do not know whether this is due to heredity or the environment. (For example, adults may talk to girl toddlers more than to boys.)

☐ Need for speech—Some children get what they need without saying anything. For instance, if a toddler receives milk by pointing, holding a cup, or crying, there is no need to learn to say, "I want milk."

☐ Interesting environment—Just as adults have more to say when they have new experiences, so do toddlers, 12-9.

In some cases, the rate of language development may lag far behind the norms. In these situations, the child should receive professional help. Each child needs the best opportunity to develop language. This is because language is important to mental and social-emotional development.

4

Summary

As toddlers explore and learn more about their world, they discover many new ways to solve problems. Through their actions, they find out what and how things work. You can see children begin to think by the way they work through problems to reach goals. Their language development is a good indication of the way toddler's think.

Language is one of the most difficult skills children must learn. Articulating sounds and learning meanings of words takes time and practice. The peak age of language development occurs between one and three years of age. Children first use single words of familiar people, objects, and actions before joining them into sentences.

A number of conditions can affect language development. These include hearing problems, interest in talking, and mental abilities. Girls tend to talk sooner than boys. Having a need for speech, along with an interesting environment, also affects when and how toddlers learn to talk.

1—*Note:* A child who has repeated ear infections without treatment might lag behind in his or her speech. The child also may have difficulty catching up if this is not remedied.

2—*Note:* This could be explained by referring to the diagram explaining how each area of growth simultaneously produces growth in the other areas of development.

3—*Note:* Avoid making assumptions about intelligence based on early talking.

4—*Discuss:* Can you think of an example of a child who gets what he or she wants without verbalizing requests? If you were the primary sitter for a toddler like this, how could you improve the situation without angering a parent?

To Review

Write your answers on a separate sheet of paper.

1. Which of the following statements describes toddlers' learnings?
   a. Toddlers have a real desire to learn about their world.
   b. Toddlers prefer to solve their own tasks, not the tasks adults plan for them.
   c. Toddlers will often try many times to solve their tasks.
   d. Toddlers learn using their past learnings and their increased motor skills.
   e. All the above statements are true.
2. True or false. Trying to see how something works helps toddlers in their mental development.
3. According to Piaget's developmental stages, problem solving is achieved by
   a. thinking on an abstract level
   b. trying out all possible answers physically
   c. thinking in terms of physical actions
   d. watching an adult and copying the adult's action
4. True or false. Learning to talk is a high-level thinking skill.
5. Give two reasons why language development is one of the most difficult skills toddlers learn.
6. Describe what the term *articulation* means.
7. Replacing one sound with another sound, such as saying "wed wabbit" instead of "red rabbit," is _____(common, uncommon) among toddlers.
8. True or false. Good language development is reinforced when adults repeat and encourage children's cute sayings, even when they are wrong.
9. In the following groups of words, which would the toddler probably learn to say first?
   a. happy
   a. bye-bye
   a. kitty

   b. daddy
   b. empty
   b. pretty
10. Describe three reasons why children may be late talkers.

1

To Do

1. Choose one student to read H.A. Rey's *Curious George* (Scholastic Book Services) to the class. Discuss how curiosity is a motivator and also can lead to trouble.
2. For one week record a toddler exploring his or her world for 30 minutes a day. While observing, note answers to the following questions: What senses were used? What activities interested the toddler most? How did the baby try to solve problems? What were some possible learnings?
3. Make a poster describing in words and/or drawings the toddler's learnings between 12 and 24 months.

To Observe

1. Observe a toddler playing with an object. Which senses did the toddler use? How did the toddler handle the object (shake, hit, or squeeze it)? What might have the toddler learned about the object (color, texture, rolls when dropped, soft when squeezed)?
2. Observe a toddler. List words the toddler says. Did the toddler seem to understand each word's meaning or incorrectly name some items? What type of words did the toddler mainly use (nouns, verbs, adjectives)?
3. Observe two or more toddlers of the same age. After listening to them talk, compare their vocabularies, articulation skills, and abilities to speak in sentences (versus words or phrases).

To Think Critically

1. Parents often think their toddlers throw objects to see how often they'll pick them up. Do you agree with this idea? Why or why not? What might a toddler learn from objects?
2. Why is imitation an important mental skill? What things do toddlers learn by imitation? What are some things you've learned by imitation? Why is deferred imitation a more advanced mental ability than imitating while seeing an action performed?
3. Why is it important for adults who talk to toddlers to pronounce words correctly, as opposed to "baby talking" to them?

Chapter 13

Social-Emotional Development of the Toddler

Many new emotions and interactions with people are part of the toddler stage.

After studying this chapter, you will be able to

☐ describe how toddlers develop self-will.

☐ explain the way toddlers extend their social relationships with others.

☐ describe how toddlers develop a sense of self-worth.

☐ identify how toddlers reveal their emotions.

After studying this chapter, you will be able to define

autonomy
egocentric
self-awareness
self-esteem
socialization
temper tantrum

Most babies begin life surrounded by people and objects that meet all their needs. Babies' needs are rather simple, so caregivers can meet most of them quickly. When their needs are met, babies become attached to their caregivers. They then learn to trust their world.

As babies become toddlers, two changes happen. First, toddlers find out more about their world and themselves as individuals. Second, toddlers find their world is not solely devoted to meeting their needs. Toddlers learn that caregivers are not always there when they want something, 13-1. However, if love and trust are established by the end of the first year, toddlers will reach out in this new world. They will learn about themselves and others. Toddlers will begin to meet their needs without depending on others. They will show emotions to others and learn how people respond to those emotions.

13-1 Toddlers often feel they should receive most, if not all, of a caregiver's attention.

© John Shaw

● Self-Awareness

By the first birthday, babies have rather highly developed physical and mental skills. They can move around by themselves and reach objects they want. They are beginning to talk, which also helps them get what they want. These fast-growing skills influence the toddlers' relationships with others. In turn, the way others react to them affects how toddlers feel about themselves. *Self-awareness* is how a person feels about himself or herself. This concept begins at birth and continues throughout life.

3

▶ Achieving Autonomy

Erikson stated that social-emotional development begins in infancy when the baby learns to trust or mistrust. As you read in chapter 8, babies whose needs are met develop a sense of trust. This sense of trust helps them as they enter the second stage, called "autonomy versus shame and doubt," 13-2. For most children, this stage begins sometime between the twelfth and eighteenth month. The stage is completed at about three years of age.

Autonomy is a form of self-control. A toddler seeks to develop his or her own will. Erikson explained autonomy as a child's feeling that he or she can do some tasks without help from others. Although toddlers want to be independent, they do depend on adults in many ways. During this stage, parents may wonder why their child suddenly turns negative and yells or kicks when told what to do. Their attitude changes because they are developing many new skills.

4

Toddlers want to test their new skills. In addition, they want to test them by themselves. While trying new skills and exploring new places, toddlers get into everything. They often want to do more for themselves than they are able to do. Adults may see danger in some of these actions, but the toddler won't always. Because much of the toddler's activities center on routines, many conflicts concern eating, sleeping, toileting, and dressing, 13-3.

5

Erikson's Stage of Autonomy versus Shame and Doubt

Basic Trust versus Basic Mistrust (First Year of Life)

Autonomy versus Shame and Doubt (Second Year of Life)

☐ Toddlers seek some autonomy so they can use their new skills and knowledge.

☐ Toddlers seek control over whether or not to rely on others as they see fit.

☐ Autonomy learned at this stage leads to self-pride.

☐ Failure to achieve autonomy leads to feelings of shame in front of others and self-doubt.

Initiative versus Guilt (Preschool Years)

Industry versus Inferiority (Middle Childhood)

13-2   Toddlers want to have the independence and freedom of self-direction. They begin to make decisions for themselves, but still need limits. They take pride in their new skills. To help toddlers establish their guided control, adults should encourage them to explore the world around them. If adults emphasize failures instead of successes, toddlers will feel ashamed and discouraged.

■   **Promoting a Toddler's Autonomy**

Adults may find it hard to help toddlers achieve autonomy while keeping them safe and preventing conflicts. Erikson feels that adults should firmly reassure the toddler. They do not need to give in to the child's will all the time. However, when they confront a child, they should stay calm. They also must assure the child that they still love him or her. This protects children from harm without making them feel ashamed or guilty. Chart 13-4 shows how to help the toddler in this stage.

© John Shaw

13-3   A conflict of wills between toddlers and adults often occurs during daily routines, such as at mealtime.

▶ Extending Social Relations

As children get older, their motor and mental abilities help them interact with others more. These interactions teach them new skills and attitudes, which help them get along with other people. The process of interacting with others is called ***socialization***.

Toddlers with a healthy attachment to caregivers have a safe base from which to meet people, 13-5. Although toddlers continue to look to their main caregivers for social interaction, they now spend more time with other adults. These adults include baby-sitters, relatives, and neighbors. Having more than one caregiver often helps toddlers adjust to others. This also helps children to expect differences among people. When children have positive experiences with many adults, they develop trusting relationships with them, 13-6.

1—*Discuss:* What might happen if the parent is permissive and gives in to the child all the time?

2—*Reflect:* Recall a time when you were younger and refused to eat a certain food. How did your caregiver react? Would you react in the same way to a youngster? Why or why not?

3—*Resource: Toddlers Are Being Socialized,* SAG.

How to Help a Toddler Develop Autonomy Rather Than Shame and Doubt	
Do...	**Do Not...**
☐ make sure toddler areas for play and care are safe (See chapter 21.). ☐ decide on some limits for the toddler. Follow through on the limits by seeing that the toddler does as told every time. ☐ permit the toddler to make a few decisions, such as whether to have more peas or play with a truck or doll. ☐ let the toddler make mistakes without scolding or criticizing. Toddlers will break items, spill liquid, and clutter the house even when they are trying to be good. ☐ let the child play in safe places with safe toys in his or her own way. Erikson sees play as the safe place where children develop autonomy. ☐ praise the toddler for becoming more autonomous.	☐ warn or threaten the toddler constantly. ☐ make everything off limits for the toddler. ☐ punish the toddler for something one time and not another. Let the toddler know what is off-limits beforehand. ☐ make all decisions for the toddler. ☐ make demands that are too rigid for a toddler to follow. ☐ scold and criticize every time the toddler makes a mistake. ☐ tell the child exactly how to play, such as "Put this block on top of this one." ☐ couple praise with criticism, such as "Put your shoes on. That's good, but they are on the wrong feet."

13-4   Adults should let toddlers explore and make mistakes within adult-set limits.

13-6   A warm relationship between this toddler and father teaches the child to trust adults.

13-5   Mothers often serve as the security base from which toddlers explore new experiences and new people.

© John Shaw

1—*Note:* It is important for a caregiver to be consistent. It is also important for two primary caregivers to be aware of each other's expectations and to strive for consistency.

2—*Discuss:* List other simple decisions a toddler can make.

3—*Note:* Expectations that are too high will produce tension and anxiety in a toddler, just as for an adult.

4—*Reflect:* Discuss a memorable mistake you made. What positive results occurred from making this mistake? When should adults intervene to prevent mistakes?

Getting Along with Other Children

During the second year, toddlers tend to interact more with other children. Their first interactions are brief. They often imitate each other's actions with a toy. Later, they talk as they play.

Toddlers are possessive about their toys and other belongings when they play. They have not learned how to share. Between the ages of 30 and 36 months, toddlers become good at keeping their possessions.

Some studies show that toddlers are not as *egocentric,* or self-centered, as experts once thought. Toddlers can share sometimes. They may return a snatched toy if the owner cries. They praise other children and show concern for someone who is hurt. When toddlers have loving relationships with their caregivers, they seem better able to show concern for other children.

Self-Esteem

Children become more aware of themselves as they approach their first birthday. They enjoy hearing their names and looking at themselves in the mirror. With the help of caring adults, children develop good feelings about themselves. Feeling good about yourself and what you can do is called *self-esteem.* People with high self-esteem believe they are worthwhile people, 13-7.

As you read in chapter 9, babies sense how others feel about them by the way they are spoken to and held. Toddlers must feel loved, even when they make mistakes or are difficult. If adults scold toddlers each time they do something wrong, toddlers will feel they are beyond being loved, 13-8.

When toddlers feel good about themselves, they seem to admire themselves and their growing control over their bodies, 13-9. They are confident and like to show off their physical feats for others. They will often clap for themselves and laugh with delight at their new skills.

Toddlers become more aware of their bodies and what their bodies can do. They can name some body parts and know that they can see, hear, touch, taste, and smell. They may not know the sensory organ that controls each sense. (For example, they may not know that eyes are used for seeing). Toddlers seem to have little awareness of their own weight. Toddlers will run and thrust themselves on the lap of adults. They also may run and cling to standing adults causing adults to lose their balance. They can feel pain, but do not always know where it is. Unless they

13-7   Toddlers build their self-esteem by completing simple tasks.

© John Shaw

13-8   Adults need to comfort toddlers who have made mistakes.

© Nancy P. Alexander

1—*Discuss:* Describe the socialization of a toddler you know. Have you seen him or her act in selfish ways? Loving and concerned ways? Describe each.

2—*Reflect:* Why is it important for you to have good self-esteem? Can you think of ways to improve yours? How is a toddler's development of self-esteem similar to yours?

3—*Discuss:* What might happen if tasks are too difficult for toddlers and expectations are too high? Discuss the meaning of age-appropriate.

4—*Discuss:* How can you let them know their actions are wrong without harming self-esteem?

13-9 Touching a mirror image is one way toddlers say to themselves, "I am special."

can see a cut, scrape, or burn, they cannot tell someone where it hurts. A toddler with a throat infection may even deny having a sore throat. More advanced body concepts develop later.

● Emotions

Toddlers' mental abilities seem to result in the following changes in emotions, which are different than those of adults or infants:

☐ Toddlers react to more stimuli than infants. They know about more people to love and more things and people to fear, 13-10.

☐ Toddlers can better sense emotions in others. Toddlers can detect fear in adults. They may even sense that something is wrong when adults are anxious. Toddlers respond to emotions in other children. They can imitate others' emotions, too.

☐ Toddlers' motor skills allow them more physical responses. For example, they can run or hide when fearful, or they can hit or

kick when angry. The toddler's ability to talk allows a verbal response. Even the single word "No!" shows feelings.

☐ Toddlers' abilities to imagine increase the number of negative emotions, such as fear of the dark and fear of monsters. Toddlers cannot totally separate what's real from what's pretend. Emotions caused by imagination are just as real as the feelings they may have when a prized toy is broken.

2

▶ Affection

Toddlers are still attached to their caregivers. They express affection for their caregivers by wanting to be near them. They seek caregivers

13-10 Toddlers sense more things to fear than do infants.

1—*Resource: Helping Toddlers Gain Self-Esteem,* SAG.

2—*Discuss:* What types of emotions do toddlers experience? Describe their actions.

1

when faced with a strange situation. This attachment seems to help other aspects of social-emotional development. This is because a toddler's affection for loving caregivers extends to other adults, children, and pets, 13-11.

▶ Fear

Many fears that began during infancy are evident after the first birthday. Fears increase quickly after age two because toddlers know about more things to fear. They know of more objects and situations that can hurt them. They can also imagine things that do not exist, such as monsters, 13-12. Toddlers also may fear animals, darkness, nightmares, "bad people," injury, gestures, and startling noises.

Instead of talking about their fears, toddlers tend to act them out in play. It is common to see a two-and-a-half-year-old who fears dogs barking and growling in play. Toddlers may imitate "bad people" seen on television or in books.

2

Adults should handle these fears in a matter-of-fact way. Never tease toddlers about

13-12   Toddlers fear monsters and unnatural creatures that exist in their minds.

their fears or push them into scary situations. To decrease toddlers' fears, adults may want to keep them from watching horror movies.

▶ Anxiety

Separation anxiety continues into the toddler stage and sometimes beyond, 13-13. Many toddlers overcome some of their separation anxieties if they feel a caregiver's love and know the caregiver will return. Increased language skill helps toddlers understand why parents sometimes leave. Parents must make sure their toddler receives good and loving care during separations.

Nightmares may begin around two years of age. These show other kinds of anxiety. Nightmares may stem from fear of being left alone, of getting hurt, or of angering adults. The details of the nightmare are unreal, often including unknown lands and monsters. If toddlers are content during the day, nightmares do not reveal a problem. The bad dreams are a way of dealing

13-11   Holding a pet helps toddlers learn to love and care for others.

© Nancy P. Alexander

1—Discuss: How do different toddlers show affection?

2—Reflect: How could you help a toddler act out fear?

3—Enrich: How does television viewing influence a toddler's fears?

4—Discuss: Is this situation positive or negative? Dave is the father of two-year-old Randy. Randy has cried every day for two weeks when his dad leaves the child care center. Dave decides to stay for a half hour and then sneak out.

5—Resource: Observation: Toddlers and Separation Anxiety, SAG.

with anxiety. For most children, nightmares decrease in time.

▶ Anger

Sudden emotional outbursts of anger, called **temper tantrums,** often appear during the second year of life. The child may lie down in the middle of the floor and kick and scream. Tantrums tend to happen when something doesn't go a toddler's way. Because this is often the case, temper tantrums are common for toddlers.

Temper tantrums attract attention. Often they are not directed at anyone. Because temper tantrums are done for attention, ignoring the toddler may cause him or her to stop. After the tantrum is over, give the toddler love and reassurance, 13-14. Remember that a toddler's anger is not directed toward others until the child is three years old.

13-13 Being separated from caring adults still causes anxiety in the toddler.

13-14 Toddlers often feel alone and even unloved after a temper tantrum.

© Nancy P. Alexander

1—*Discuss:* What are some positive ways to deal with nightmares?

2—*Discuss:* How do tantrums relate to autonomy?

3—*Discuss:* What are some causes of tantrums? Discuss some factors about shopping that often result in tantrums.

4—*Reflect:* How do you think a tantrum should be handled? Would you handle a tantrum the same for all children? Explain your answer.

5—*Resource: Temper Tantrums and Toddlers,* SAG.

Summary

The second period of social-emotional development begins when children develop wills of their own. Erikson called this period "autonomy versus shame and doubt." During this time, toddlers become independent. They don't always understand dangers their actions may cause. Because of this, many conflicts with caregivers occur.

Toddlers begin to interact with others besides their parents and caregivers. Through socialization, they learn to get along with others. Having positive experiences with others helps develop trusting relationships. Toddlers' interactions with other children are brief. They often imitate each other before they interact by talking. They are possessive with their toys and belongings, but can show concern for others, too.

The good feeling children develop about themselves is called *self-esteem.* Toddlers are becoming aware of their bodies but do not always know where they feel pain.

Toddlers experience a wider range of emotions now than when they were younger. They are still attached to their caregivers. Fears tend to intensify during this period, especially fears of monsters. Having nightmares is often a way to deal with anxieties. Being separated from their parents continues to concern them. Temper tantrums occur when events don't go the way the toddler wants. Ignoring the tantrum will make it end sooner.

1

2

3

To Review

Write your answers on a separate sheet of paper.

1. True or false. Toddlers find their world is solely devoted to meeting their needs.
2. True or false. Adults' reactions to toddlers affect how toddlers feel about themselves.
3. True or false. *Autonomy* means being able to do some things without the help of others.
4. Circle the correct statement in each pair.
   a. Autonomy often happens during new activities.
   a. Autonomy often happens during routines.
   b. Autonomy often involves working at the ability level.
   b. Autonomy often involves trying to work beyond the ability level.

1—*Reflect:* Do you think toddlers may have more trouble getting along with other children if their parents argue and fight often? Explain your reasons. What principle of development explains this?

2—*Reflect:* Do you think this would be worse if the parents are separated or divorced? Explain.

3—*Answers:* Answers to review questions can be found in the front section of this TAE.

5. List three ways adults can help the toddler develop autonomy rather than shame and doubt.
6. True or false. Adjusting to others is easier if the child has had only one main caregiver, such as the mother.
7. Which statement is true?
   Socialization is not aided by
   a. spending time with others
   b. baby-sitters and other caregivers
   c. insisting that toddlers play alone more often
   d. letting other children play with the toddler
8. Shaming toddlers for their mistakes (does, does not) affect their self-esteem.
9. Toddlers' sense of self-esteem is centered on their awareness of their _____ (physical, mental) abilities.
10. What four general changes in emotion occur during the toddler stage?
11. List three fears common to toddlers.
12. How should adults react to toddlers' temper tantrums?

To Do

1. Interview one or more parents about how their toddlers showed autonomy. (Most parents have amusing stories.) Ask how they give their toddlers freedom with some control.
2. We know that toddlers admire themselves in mirrors and enjoy their new abilities. Have a class discussion on how adults admire themselves and whether or not self-admiration is good.
3. Some refer to the toddler years as the "terrible twos." Write an essay explaining why people use this term to describe toddlers. Also discuss why this term is incorrect.
4. Observe toddlers in a group care situation. Note how toddlers show autonomy. Under what conditions did adults prevent toddlers from carrying through their goals? How did the toddlers react?
5. Role-play a situation in which a toddler fears the dark and monsters that loom in the closet. Have one student play the toddler and one (or two students) play the parent (or parents) coping with the toddler's fears.

1—*Activity:* Ask if they had trouble "letting go" of the child once he or she became autonomous.

To Observe

1. Observe two or three toddlers of the same age. How do they show their attachments to several people? How do the strengths of these attachments differ for a parent versus a baby-sitter?
2. Observe several toddlers playing together. Are they possessive about toys? How do they reclaim a special toy from another child? How does the child react once the toy is reclaimed by the first toddler? How do adults settle toddlers' disputes?
3. Observe several toddlers playing. Describe actions that would show positive self-esteem. Describe actions that would show the toddler doesn't feel good about him- or herself. What did the adults do to promote positive self-esteem in toddlers?
4. Observe a toddler showing affection, fear, anxiety, or anger. What seemed to trigger the emotion? Compare what you noted with your text.

To Think Critically

1. A conflict of wills between children and adults often occurs during routine care times such as meals and dressing. How much freedom should parents give toddlers? How much permissiveness might result in spoiled babies?
2. Why is it impossible to explain to toddlers that monsters and other unreal creatures exist only in their dreams or minds?
3. What are various means people use to seek attention? Why do toddlers use temper tantrums to get attention rather than other means?

Toddlers begin to meet their needs without depending on caregivers.

Chapter 14

Providing for the Toddler's Developmental Needs

Although toddlers still need care, they are learning to be independent.

After studying this chapter, you will be able to

☐ plan ways to meet toddlers' physical needs.

☐ stimulate toddlers' growing mental abilities.

☐ help toddlers adjust to their first social controls.

After studying this chapter, you will be able to define

contrariness
nutrient density
obedience
registered dietitians
ritual
self-assertion
self-restraint
sensory learnings
spatial
toilet training
training pants
transitional stage

Toddlers continue to develop quickly between their first and third birthdays. Toddlers still depend on adults to provide for their needs. During these years, however, toddlers begin learning some self-care skills, such as self-feeding, self-dressing, and toileting. They will even help with washing their hands and bathing.

At this age, intellectual abilities seem to blossom. Toddlers learn to use language to talk with others and to help them think. Toddlers learn many concepts through daily routines at home. They then practice these concepts in play.

Toddlers have many social-emotional needs. They try to do tasks on their own, but they find some too hard for their immature bodies and minds. Toddlers need loving adults who understand their wills. Adults need to allow some freedom. They need to praise toddlers when they master a new skill. They need to help toddlers when they can't manage a task.

● Physical Needs

Caregivers must meet toddlers' physical needs to keep them healthy and safe. Meeting physical needs also keeps toddlers mentally and socially fit. To meet toddlers' physical needs, adults must make sure toddlers are fed, clothed, cleaned, and rested. Adults also must guide toddlers' self-care skills, such as self-feeding, self-cleaning, and toileting. As toddlers learn self-care skills, they can meet their physical needs. Self-care skills also help toddlers advance in mental and social-emotional development.

▶ Feeding

During the toddler years, the eating experience changes. Toddlers graduate from a bottle and baby foods to table foods. Toddlers begin to feed themselves. In addition, toddlers often join the family for meals instead of eating at other times.

The Eating Style of Toddlers

Between 12 and 18 months, the toddler's appetite decreases. This is because the physical rate of growth slows. Toddlers gain only six to eight pounds between the ages of 12 and 30 months.

Toddlers want to feed themselves (*self-feed*), 14-1. They want to control their own eating. Now the child can learn to pick up food with fingers or a spoon. However, a toddler's fine-motor skills are not mature. Therefore, playing with food—including smearing it on the wall or dropping it on the floor—is part of self-feeding, 14-2.

When mishaps occur, parents must remember that the toddler is not being naughty. He or she is learning about the texture, color, and qualities of food. (See "Preventing Feeding Problems" for more information on this topic.) Self-feeding also helps the toddler show independence. Self-feeding helps the toddler's growing self-concept.

14-1 Toddlers handle spoons with an overhand palm grasp, not the thumb and finger grasp of the adult.

Gerber Products

1—*Discuss:* What daily routines do toddlers act out in their creative play? What precautions does a caregiver need to take to set a good example?

2—*Discuss:* How much is too much help? Does this differ from child to child? Explain your answer.

3—*Note:* Recall that growth in one developmental area will initiate growth in the other areas.

4—*Activity:* Practice various eating activities using the opposite hand. Discuss problems encountered. What could a caregiver do to help self-care in each situation?

5—*Reflect:* Recall a situation from your childhood when you spilled something. How did others react? How did you feel? How do you think a caregiver should react?

14-2 Toddlers are messy eaters because they are learning about food.

Basic Daily Diet for Toddlers

- ☐ Bread Group—6 servings total
- ☐ Vegetable Group—3 servings total
- ☐ Fruit Group—2 servings total
- ☐ Milk Group—2 servings total
- ☐ Meat Group—5 ounces total

14-3 Toddlers need a well-balanced diet to meet their growth and energy needs. This chart shows a 1,600 calorie diet. Toddlers who need fewer calories can eat smaller servings. It is important, however, for toddlers to have the equivalent of two cups of milk a day. Adults should check with a doctor to find out how many calories their child needs each day.

Meeting Nutritional Needs

Food intake always should meet a child's nutritional needs. Toddlers eat smaller amounts of food than infants or adults. Adults must give toddlers foods that are of high nutrient density. **Nutrient density** is the level of nutrients in a food in relation to the level of calories in the food. High nutrient density foods are high in vitamins and minerals needed for the body's growth and repair. These foods also do not have a high calorie content. Foods of low nutrient density mainly provide energy, not vitamins and minerals. They also have more calories. (These foods sometimes are said to contain *empty calories* because they are not nutritious.) Children who eat foods of low nutrient density often are too full to eat nutritious foods. This is unhealthy and may cause the child to gain too much weight.

Chart 14-3 gives the basic recommended intake for toddlers. Some toddlers have special food needs. A physician or registered dietitian should plan the diets for special cases. (**Registered dietitians** have special training in nutrition and diet. They meet the qualifications of the American Dietetic Association.) Adults should not give toddlers popcorn, nuts, or other small, hard foods because they may choke.

Toddlers often have odd food habits. They may settle on a diet of only a few foods for days or even weeks. They may skip a meal or two, then eat as though starved a few hours later. Although these habits may concern the adult, the habits should not harm the child. Most toddlers who are given good diets for meals and snacks will have their food needs met over time.

Preventing Feeding Problems

Sometimes toddlers develop feeding problems. Most stem from the toddler's stage of development—the slowing growth, growing motor and learning skills, and changing social needs. See 14-4 for some common feeding problems and suggestions to solve them. Toddlers work out most feeding problems in time with the help of patient adults.

▶ Clothing

Choosing the right clothes and shoes for toddlers is important. Proper clothing helps toddlers stay active, comfortable, and safe. It also stands up under the strain of constant movement and messy play.

Choosing Garments

Although toddlers grow more slowly than infants, they still outgrow their clothes quickly. Fit is important for the toddler. Clothes that are too

1

2

3

4

1—*Enrich:* Do research on nutrient density. Report to the class.
2—*Math Activity:* Using several labels from food items commonly consumed by toddlers, calculate the nutrient density of each. Provide recommendations for parents.
3—*Activity:* Prepare a brochure with information from the research and math calculations. Define nutrient density and empty calories. Summarize recommendations. Distribute the brochures to preschools and child care centers.
4—*Activity:* Invite a registered dietitian as a guest speaker. Emphasize careers, education, responsibilities, and work settings.

Feeding Problems of Toddlers

Problem—A toddler refuses to eat a meal or takes only a few bites.

Possible Solutions—
- ☐ Keep records of all the foods the toddler eats during the week. (The toddler may be getting enough of the needed foods)
- ☐ Break meals up by offering part of the meal early and the rest of the meal in two or three hours.
- ☐ Make snacks high in nutritional quality.
- ☐ Eat foods of high nutritional quality. Toddlers imitate adult food habits.
- ☐ Serve small portions and let the toddler ask for seconds. Too much food can be discouraging.
- ☐ Make mealtime pleasant even when the toddler refuses to eat.

Problem—A toddler refuses to eat new foods.

Possible Solutions—
- ☐ Offer a taste or two of new foods on a regular basis to help the toddler to accept them over time.
- ☐ Offer only one new food at a time.
- ☐ Serve a taste or two of a new food on a plate that also has favorite foods.
- ☐ Model proper food attitudes for toddlers. Saying, "Eat your spinach, it's good for you," may give the toddler the idea that spinach is a must but not good tasting.
- ☐ Try a new way of preparing foods. For example, toddlers usually like simple foods more than mixtures (casseroles). They like raw vegetables such as raw carrots more than cooked carrots. Toddlers prefer finger foods to foods eaten with flatware. They like less salty and spicy foods more than highly seasoned foods.
- ☐ Remain pleasant with the toddler. Force feeding and anger do not work.

Problem—A toddler shows lack of self-feeding skills and plays with food.

Possible Solutions—
- ☐ Give the toddler time to learn how to feed. (Most children cannot hold flatware in the mature way until five years of age or older.)
- ☐ Provide a comfortable setting for eating. The correct chair provides support (so that the child is not sliding down), is the correct height, and has a place for feet to touch rather than dangle.
- ☐ Provide suitable eating equipment, such as small plates (especially those with sides), small cups with handles and weighted bottoms, and baby or junior flatware (or small spoons and salad forks).
- ☐ Use a high chair or table and chair that can be cleaned easily. (Nearby floor and walls should also be easily cleaned.)
- ☐ Keep cleaning supplies handy during meals.
- ☐ When possible, prepare foods in easy to manage form, such as finger foods. (Runny foods, foods that must be cut, and foods that are hard to pick up, such as peas, will be messy for the toddler.)
- ☐ Praise the toddler for successes. Never laugh at mishaps.
- ☐ Prevent playing with food by staying near the toddler during eating time and removing food once the toddler is playing more than eating.
- ☐ Be firm in saying no when the toddler goes too far with playing. You may even say, "Balls are for throwing, food is for eating," or "I want the kitchen to stay clean; food on the floor is messy." If the toddler does not control the play, remove the food or the toddler. (Toddlers learn quickly when eating rules are fair and enforced.)

14-4   Feeding problems are common for toddlers.

1—*Activity:* List some nutritional snacks.

2—*Note:* Emphasize the importance of modeling.

3—*Enrich:* Role-play (in pairs) some of these feeding problems.

Typical Toddler Clothing Sizes

Sizes for Clothing	Height	Weight	
1T	29"-32"	23-27 lbs.	
2T	32½"-35"	28-31 lbs.	
3T	35½"-38"	32-36 lbs.	
4T	38½"-41"	37-40 lbs.	

14-5 Toddler clothes, like all clothing, should be purchased by size, not age.

tight will bind and restrict movement. Clothes that are too loose will be uncomfortable and perhaps unsafe. To check for fit, let toddlers try on garments. When it is not possible for the toddler to try on the garment, choose clothing by measurement, not age, 14-5.

Quality features include safety, comfortable fabric and construction, growth features, durability, attractive style, and easy care. See chart 14-6 for some examples of each of these features.

Some adults consider self-dressing features when choosing a toddler's clothes. Such features make dressing and undressing without help easier. However, toddlers are better at taking clothes off than putting them on. By 18 months, toddlers will help by extending arms and legs while being dressed. They will also unzip zippers and remove mittens, hats, socks, and untied shoes, 14-7. A few items are designed to teach self-dressing to children under three, 14-8. Adults should accept self-dressing efforts the toddler tries, even if the toddler dresses incorrectly.

Fitting Shoes

Because the bones and muscles of the foot are developing, shoe fit is important for proper growth and comfort. When children's shoes do not fit properly, they can cause permanent damage. Toddlers often outgrow their shoes before they wear them out. The average rate of foot growth for two-year-olds is one change in size

every three months. For children between the ages of two and three years, the rate is one change in size every four months.

The feet of the toddler are flat because the arch is relaxed. The flat-footed look disappears around age three. Going barefooted or wearing socks without shoes is good for the development of the arch. Shoes, even high-top shoes, do not provide support. High-top shoes are used because they are more difficult for the toddler to remove.

Toddlers need shoes to protect their feet from cold, dampness, and harmful objects. Shoes that fit properly have ½ inch of space between the large toe and shoe when the toddler stands. They also have a flexible sole and a snug-fitting heel.

▶ Rest and Sleep

Toddlers often sleep fewer hours and nap less than babies. Chart 14-9 shows the general trend in sleep patterns. The sleep needs of toddlers vary. Toddlers may sleep less when under stress and more than average when recovering from an illness.

How much sleep does a toddler need? Do not use ages to figure this. Instead, awaken toddlers at the same time each morning for about a week. Then note when they become sleepy. The amount of time between the average "sleepy time" and the same "getting up" time is close to the amount of sleep needed.

1—*Note:* If a toddler is unable to go on the shopping trip, take along a garment that fits properly to help sizing.

2—*Note:* This is important in developing autonomy and self-esteem.

3—*Note:* It is important for the child to try on the shoes and have a reputable salesperson check them carefully.

Important Features in Toddler Clothes				
Safety	**Comfort**	**Growth Features**	**Quality Construction**	**Easy Care**
☐ fire retardent (will burn, but smolders slowly rather than flames up when on fire) ☐ no loose buttons, fasteners, or trim ☐ belts, ties, sashes, and drawstrings fastened to the garment securely (Toddlers can trip, choke, or cut off circulation if these items are missused.) ☐ bright clothing (increases ability to see toddlers)	☐ made of light-weight and absorbent fabrics ☐ made of fabrics with stretch or ease qualities. Elastic encased or nonbinding. Fullness in pant legs to permit knee bending and stooping with ease. ☐ collars and sleeves that do not rub or bind ☐ coats,sweaters, and jackets that can fit over clothes without binding ☐ underwear that is not binding ☐ neck openings large enough for ease of dressing	☐ made of stretch fabrics ☐ dresses without definite waistlines ☐ pants and skirts with elastic or adjustable waistbands ☐ adjustable shoulder straps ☐ clothes with deep hems, large seams, and pleats or tucks that can be easily let out ☐ two-piece outfits	☐ reinforcement at points of strain such as seams, knees, pockets, and pocket edges ☐ stitches that are even and not too long ☐ seams that are flat, smooth, and finished ☐ securely attached fasteners and trims ☐ built-in growth features, such as deep hems ☐ plaids, stripes, and checks matched	☐ washable (especially machine washable with other colors) ☐ little or no ironing needed ☐ easy to mend

14-6   Toddlers' clothes need to have certain features.

Toddlers are more likely than babies to resist rest and sleep, even when they are tired. Bedtime problems stem partly from the toddlers' struggle for autonomy. Often adults become physically tired from coping with toddlers who resist sleep. Adults may even feel stress if bedtime becomes a battle of wills. These ideas may help solve problems.

☐ Accept that adults cannot force toddlers to sleep. Resistance often disappears after the toddler years.

☐ Have a definite hour for bedtime. Use a neutral sign, such as a clock (not a person), to signal the hour.

☐ Set up a nighttime (and even naptime) *ritual* or routine. The ritual should last about an hour a night. Include only restful activities, such as a warm bath, a drink of water, a story, song, or hug.

☐ Provide a comfortable place for sleep.

☐ Tell toddlers who do not want to sleep that they do not have to sleep, only stay in bed. Toddlers usually accept this.

1—*Enrich:* Do research on flame-retardant clothing. Report to the class.

2—*Discuss:* Why is it difficult to get a child to go to bed when preceding activities have been active?

American Association of Retired Persons
W.B. Doner and Company

14-7   Toddlers master how to remove shoes and clothing before learning to dress themselves.

14-8   Simple dressing aids, such as a mitten and zipper sewn in a cloth book, help teach toddlers self-dressing skills.

© John Shaw

Average Sleep of Toddlers		
Age	**Night**	**Naps**
9 to 12 months	12 to 14 hours	1 to 4 hours, morning and afternoon
13 to 18 months	10 to 12 hours	1 to 3 hours, afternoon
19 to 30 months	10 to 12 hours	1 to 3 hours afternoon
31 to 36 months	10 to 15 hours	Naps beginning to disappear*

*Two-thirds of two-year-olds take a nap; 10 percent of three-year-olds take a nap.

14-9   A toddler's sleep needs change over time.

☐   Comfort fearful toddlers. Tell them where you'll be while they sleep. Provide a night-light in their room. Place a stuffed animal in their bed. Tell fearful toddlers you are there to keep them safe and will check on them every 10 to 15 minutes. (Toddlers are often asleep after two or three check times, 14-10.)

☐   Comfort toddlers who awaken with nightmares. Do not ask them to tell you about their nightmares. It is best to forget them. (If they want to tell you about their nightmares, listen. Assure them that these are just bad dreams.)

☐   Return children who get up to their bed. Meet any real needs such as a drink for a child who is thirsty, but turn down nonessential requests. Be firm but calm.

☐   Keep the child away from active spots, such as where others are watching television or reading.

Adults' actions will determine whether toddlers learn the tricks to get what they want or learn that adults will insist on their staying in bed.

1—*Resource: Bedtime Rituals, SAG.*

14-10   Checking on toddlers helps them feel secure enough to get needed rest and sleep.

▶ Hygiene

One of the most important parts of hygiene for toddlers is bathing. Bathing is fun for most toddlers. Although toddlers can sit and stand easily, they are not safe when left alone while bathing. Toddlers seem to feel more secure being bathed in a child's tub. The tub can be placed inside a regular tub for easy bathing and less messy splashing, 14-11.

Toddlers may want to help bathe themselves. A mitt-type wipe is easy for them to use. (You can make one by sewing three edges of two washcloths together.) Most toddlers have fun trying to hold slippery soap. Some toddlers enjoy rinsing themselves with a hand-held shower.

1

14-11   Keeping children safe in the tub is extremely important. A secure toddler usually enjoys bathing and splashing in the water.

© John Shaw

1—*Discuss:* What should you do if the phone or doorbell rings while you are caring for a child who is in the bathtub?

14-12 Water play during the bath is fun.

Water Play

Toddlers also need some time for water play during the bath, 14-12. Toddlers not only have fun playing in water, but they learn a great deal, too. They learn that

☐ some toys float and some sink

☐ water power can push toys

☐ water can be held for a brief time in the cupped hand

☐ water makes all things wet

☐ they can make water splash, squirt, and drip

☐ the bottom of the tub can be seen through water

☐ soap makes bubbles

Many bath toys are sold for toddlers. Toys can also be made easily from household objects.

Dental Care

Dental care is also important for toddlers. They should begin having dental checkups at age two. A proper diet helps teeth stay healthy. However, cleaning teeth regularly is also needed. When the toddler is about 18 months of age, a caregiver can brush the toddler's teeth with a child-sized brush, 14-13. This can replace wiping the teeth. The toddler may "help" brush teeth around 30 months of age. (Adults should supervise brushing throughout the preschool years.)

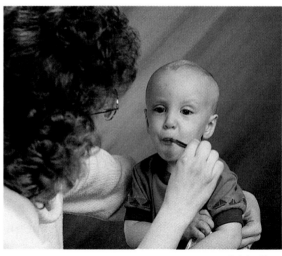

© John Shaw

14-13 An adult must brush the toddler's teeth.

▶ Toilet Training

Toilet training is one of the most discussed aspects of toddler training. **Toilet training** is the process by which adults help children control their excretory systems, namely bowel movements and urination. Over the years, adults have tried to train children at different times. They have tried training children early—before age one. They have let the child become self-trained. (The child chooses when to train.) They also have tried every time between these extremes.

These adults have found that two things are certain in toilet training. First, the timing of training varies from toddler to toddler. Second, many toddlers do not complete total training quickly. Training may take most of the toddler years and perhaps even more time to complete.

Physical and Emotional Factors

Toilet training involves factors like physical development, motor skills, and emotional readiness. The physical and motor skills involved are the following:

☐ Ability to feel a full bowel and bladder. Until about 15 months, children move their bowels and pass urine without knowing in advance or realizing they have done so.

☐ Ability to know what the sensation of needing to eliminate means in time to get to the potty.

☐ Ability to control muscles used for "holding in" or "letting go." These muscles, which are low in the body, are among the last to develop. (This is a good example of the head-to-tail development principle.) Nerves can control these muscles around 18 months of age. Children tend to learn to control bowel movements before they learn to control their bladders.

☐ Ability to walk (or often run) to the potty.

☐ Ability to remove or push down clothes. Several layers of clothes or a one-piece jumpsuit can be hard for the toddler to manage. Some fasteners make the task impossible.

For toilet training to work, emotional readiness must occur at the same time the child is physically developed. Toddlers must see the need to use the potty. Busy toddlers often do not want to sit the needed time. Saying no to toilet training is part of the self-will toddlers want to express. Toddlers also may need to master fears of falling in, the flushing water, and even the stools passed.

Procedure for Toilet Training

Caregivers have tried many methods for toilet training. Although many work, certain proven ideas help the toilet training process.

First, adults should realize that toilet training is not a one-way street. Adults cannot do the training for the toddler. Toddlers must be ready and help. Adults also should accept the fact that toddlers vary in age of complete control. The average age for complete day control is 28 months, but the normal range varies. There is no relationship between being a big or smart child and the age of training. A rule of thumb is that a child must be able to stay dry two or more hours before the child can begin to learn.

Even before toddlers are ready for training, adults can help them see what is expected. If an adult notes the child is eliminating, he or she should say something to make the child aware of it. When a diaper gets wet or soiled, the adult

should say to the child as he or she changes the diaper, "Try to tell me next time, that way we can use the toilet."

When the Toddler Is Ready

When the toddler is ready for toilet training, caregivers should borrow or buy a toilet training chair. Regular toilets are hard to use and sometimes scary. A toilet training chair designed for toddlers is the easiest to use, 14-14. "Chairs" that fit on standard commode seats also are made for toddlers. When standard commodes are used with or without toddler seats, place a sturdy platform in front of the stool. (Getting on a high stool is hard. Also, dangling legs for a few minutes hurts.) Show the child the potty that he or she will use. Some toddlers will sit on it with their clothes on to check it out. Bathroom light switches should be easy to reach. You also may want to use a night-light.

Easy-to-manage clothing is crucial. Many adults wait until warm weather for training because toddlers can wear fewer clothes. They can also wear elastic-waist shorts or pants, which are easy to manage.

14-14   Toilet training chairs are easy for toddlers to use.

© John Shaw

1~—*Discuss:* What types of fasteners make it easier for the toddler to learn self-care?

2—*Discuss:* Discuss experiences in toilet training with toddlers.

3—*Note:* If possible, have the child try out the seat in the store. Check for safety.

Once Training Begins

Once training begins, adults should encourage the toddler to use the toilet. However, they should not put requests in moral terms like, "Be good and use the potty." Take toddlers to the toilet at set times until they go on their own. Before and after meals, before and after sleep times, and every two hours are good times. Adults must remind children to use the toilet for many years after they are trained.

Adults need to accept success and failure in a matter-of-fact way. Toddlers need some praise, but too much adds to the pressure to achieve the next time. Adults should not let failures make children feel bad or little. They should stop training during illness or if a child shows signs of stress. Using diapers during sleep times or when away from home for long periods of time makes training less stressful.

Accidents

No matter how much care is taken, accidents will happen. Being prepared helps prevent accidents from causing too much stress for toddlers or adults. *Training pants* (pants with a multi-layered cotton fabric crotch) help lessen the mess of accidents. Keep household cleaning products on hand to clean accidents.

Toilet training helps children handle their elimination needs the way our society expects—cleanly, without help, and without fuss. Complete training is a long process.

▶ Indoor and Outdoor Spaces

Toddlers still enjoy being near adults and other children for most of their waking hours. However, between the second and third birthday many toddlers begin playing more on their own. They need a place where they can rest and sleep without being disturbed. Thus, many families plan indoor and outdoor play spaces and bedrooms for their toddlers.

Bedrooms and play spaces must be safe. (See chapter 21 for safety tips.) If possible, these areas should fit toddlers' needs for play, rest, and learning self-help skills. Open floor and yard spaces make it easy for the toddler to be active. A cozy chair, a fuzzy throw rug, a corner area, and a toddler's bed are examples of quiet places. Self-help features include low shelves for toys and low hooks for coats. They also include a sturdy footstool for climbing one step and light switches within reach.

Toddlers like furniture and room decorations chosen especially for them. Furniture designed for toddlers is often made smaller than other furniture. It also may be brightly painted. Choose bedspreads, window coverings, wallpaper, floor coverings, lamps, and night-lights the toddler will like. Wall hangings and pictures can be chosen with the toddler in mind, 14-15. Even a few of the toddler's toys or books on display can make the room or area special.

● Intellectual Needs

For the most part, toddlers learn during daily activities. They learn as they are eating, bathing, dressing, "helping" with household tasks, and running errands with adults. Adults

14-15   Bedroom furniture and decorations should be chosen with the toddler in mind.

1—*Discuss:* What are some signs of stress?

2—*Resource: Toilet Training,* SAG.

3—*Discuss:* What are some other self-help features?

4—*Note:* It is wise to choose furniture that will last many years without becoming outdated. Smaller, less expensive accessories that follow a theme can be replaced more often without high cost.

5—*Activity:* Find pictures of items to put in a child's room. Be practical.

should take advantage of everyday activities to help toddlers learn. Toddlers can learn during meals. They can talk with others at the table (language learnings). They can see, taste, smell, and feel foods of many colors, shapes, sizes, and textures (***sensory learnings***). They can make choices about the foods and amounts of each they want (decision making). Toddlers can handle finger foods and flatware (motor skills). They hear comments such as, "Food helps us grow and become strong," (a nutrition lesson). They even join in celebrations involving food, such as eating birthday cake (a social time).

▶ Learning through Activities

Many other activities help toddlers learn, 14-16. Bathing and dressing provide the means for language, sensory, health, and motor learnings. "Helping" with household tasks develops ***spatial*** (pertaining to space) concepts as toddlers put items in drawers or laundry in a basket. Vocabulary increases as toddlers learn the names of common objects found in the home and yard. Science becomes a part of everyday life as toddlers see how the vacuum cleaner picks up dirt, how air dries clothes, and how heat makes dough change into cookies.

▶ Learning through Play

Toddlers also learn as they play in a safe environment with many objects to explore. Play lets the toddler check and recheck learnings. A toddler may fill a plastic pail with the same toys many times to check how much space the toys need. Adults may play with toddlers sometimes, in a game of chase or catch. For the most part, however, they should let toddlers play on their own, stepping in only when toddlers need help. They may show a toddler how to put a piece in a hard puzzle or introduce new ideas to play.

Adults may need a few ideas for games to enrich a toddler's learnings. Use adult-planned games when they seem to fit the toddlers' interest and skills. These planned games should never be used at a given time each day or in a demanding

way. Adults should keep ideas in mind and use them only to enrich toddlers' learnings. This method is the best way to meet their intellectual needs.

3

▶ Sensory Stimulation Activities

The senses help toddlers learn about the qualities of objects. Through sight, they learn about an object's color and darkness or lightness. Touch teaches them if objects are rough or smooth. They use hearing and touch to find out if objects are hard or soft. Toddlers use taste to learn about sweet and sour. Using the senses helps toddlers form concepts about objects. For instance, they learn oranges are round, smooth, orange colored, sweet smelling, sweet tasting, hard outside and juicy inside.

4

Games can enrich what toddlers are learning on their own. As toddlers play games, adults should teach them by talking through the activity.

14-16   Helping to fill a pool with water teaches toddlers about science and their world.

1—*Activity:* Locate pictures of toddlers engaged in daily activities. Discuss the type of learning involved.

2—*Discuss:* What types of household tasks can involve children? What learning could occur? What could a child learn from playing with flour?

3—*Resource: Learning Happens in Everyday Experiences,* SAG.

4—*Activity:* Design a sensory experience for a toddler. List each of the senses and explain what a toddler could learn about each.

Sensory Stimulation Activities

Activity	Sense
Looking at objects	**Sight**

Looking at objects   **Sight**
Ask a child to look in a certain area (such as out of a window) and name something that he or she sees. When the child points to or names an object, say, "That's right, it's a _____." Then talk about the qualities of the object. You may include color, size, the sound it makes, and what it does. Talk about other times when the toddler has seen the object. Three or four objects at one time are enough for most toddlers.

Animal sounds   **Hearing**
Sing "Old MacDonald Had a Farm" and point to pictures of each animal as you sing. Start with a few of the toddler's favorite animals and gradually add others.

Recognizing objects by touch   **Touch**
Put three or four familiar objects in a paper bag or pillowcase. Pull an object out of the bag. Ask the toddler to name it. Then show the toddler how to feel the object using the fingers. As the toddler feels the object, the adult should describe the texture. For instance, a ball may feel "round and soft." Continue in the same way with the other objects. After feeling all the objects, put them back into the bag. Have the child identify each one by feeling without peeking.
Variations: (1) Place pictures or identical objects outside the bag. Have the toddler feel an object in the bag and point to the object or picture outside the bag. (2) Describe and name an object and have the toddler find it. You may say, "Put your hand in the bag and see if you can find the comb with all the points."

Recognizing objects by smell   **Smell**
Select three or four familiar objects that have distinct odors. Show the toddler how to smell by sniffing loudly. First, smell and talk about each object's odor. Then have the toddler close his or her eyes and identify each object by smelling it. If the toddler needs help, name two objects from which the toddler can choose. You may say, "Is this soap or a banana?"

Sweet and sour   **Taste**
Give the toddler a sugar cube and refer to it as *sweet.* Then have the toddler taste lemon juice mixed with water. Refer to it as *sour.* (Use equal parts of lemon juice and water. Pure lemon juice is too sour and can be hard on teeth.) Sweeten the lemon juice and water with sugar and serve as lemonade. Although the toddler may not understand, explain, "I am making this sour lemon juice sweeter with this sweet sugar. Now we have lemonade. It is sweet."
Variation: Give the toddler a small amount of salt to taste. Give the toddler a bite of a salty food, such as a salty cracker. Use the term *salty* to describe both flavors.

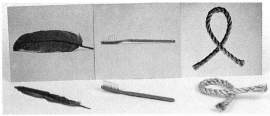
© John Shaw

14-17   Sensory stimulation activities help toddlers learn about the qualities of objects.

When a caregiver notices that a toddler hears a sound, the caregiver should stop briefly and listen. Then say, "Do you hear that? I hear a _____. Do you hear it, too?" Point in the direction of the sound. This helps stimulate the toddler's sense of hearing. As another activity, when cooking a food with a distinct odor, sniff loudly and tell the toddler what you smell. Say, "I smell chicken frying," or "I smell a cake baking." Later, ask the toddler, "What's cooking? What smells so good?" Variations of this include smelling and talking about other odors. Flowers, burning leaves, an outdoor barbecue, and the rain all have distinct smells. See 14-17 for other examples of sensory stimulation activities.

1—*Resource: Planned Activities for Sensory Stimulation,* SAG.

Problem-Solving Activities

Opening lids
Place a small object in a container with a snap-on lid. Show the toddler how it works. Then let the toddler try to open it. When the toddler has mastered one type of lid, try another. You may use screw-on lids and plugs. *(Do not* show toddlers or even older preschool children how safety caps work.)

Opening lids

© John Shaw

Stacking

© John Shaw

Stacking and nesting
If the toddler can nest and stack two or three objects as described in chapter 10, add a few more pieces for nesting and stacking. Rings can be sequenced also. The toddler should start with two or three rings. Slowly add the other rings as the toddler masters the game. (If there is very little difference in the size of the objects, the task becomes much more difficult. These objects can be saved for children who are a little older.)

Where am I?
Hide from a toddler who is involved in another activity. Call out. The toddler will look for you. Praise the toddler for finding you. (Of course, do not hide behind locked doors or other places where the toddler cannot search.)

Rolling cars
Place small cars or trucks on a board that is flat on the floor. Chair cushions, sturdy cardboard lids, or trays can be used as the board. Say, "The cars do not go." As you slowly raise the board on one end say, "Here they go." After the toddler has played with the cars in this way many times, ask, "Can you make the car go down the hill fast (slow)?" See if the toddler increases (decreases) the slope of the board.

Through the tunnel
Using a mailing tube with both ends removed, show the toddler how to roll objects through it. The toddler will learn how objects can go in one open end and come out the other open end. After much play, some toddlers may learn to vary the slope of the tube to control the speed of the object's roll.

14-18   Problem-solving activities encourage toddlers to try out their ideas.

▶ Problem-Solving Activities

Toddlers can solve many problems by trying out their ideas. They are not ready to solve problems just by thinking through likely answers. Many of the best problem-solving games involve motor actions, such as opening and closing containers, finding hidden objects, and watching how objects move.

Simple puzzles are another good problem-solving activity for children. Begin with a few pieces and work up to puzzles with five or six pieces. For toddlers, each puzzle piece should be an entire picture of an object, not a "jigsaw" piece. A knob on the puzzle piece helps fine-motor control. See 14-18 for other problem-solving activities.

▶ Motor Activities

Toddlers are developing motor skills quickly. Because most toddlers are always on the go, they need few planned motor

2

1—Discuss: Why is it important for a toddler to learn problem-solving activities?

2—Resource: Planned Activities for Problem Solving, SAG.

© John Shaw

14-19   The toddler develops most gross-motor skills in play.

© John Shaw

14-20   Hitting a peg with a hammer develops fine-motor skills and teaches cause and effect. Toddlers learn that the force and speed of pounding affects the peg's descent.

activities, 14-19. Some games can improve gross-motor skills whereas others improve fine-motor skills, 14-20.

Riding toys help children develop their large-motor skills. Toys that the toddler pushes with the feet or mounts and rides help develop gross-motor skills. Small, snap-together blocks that the child can use in an imaginative way help fine-finger control. See 14-21 for other suggestions for gross-motor and fine-motor games.

▶ Language Activities

There are ways to enhance the toddler's use of language. Early childhood programs that let children explore and play help language learning. Parents can organize their homes to promote language learning, too. Good feelings between the child and caregivers may also increase the child's verbal skills.

▪ Toddlers Need to Hear Language

The toddler's active world needs a background of language. Adults should talk during many games played with toddlers to improve toddlers'

skills. Adults and children should talk during daily routines, too. As adults do things, they should say what they are doing and what the toddler is doing.

Adults can begin talking in a conversational manner even before the child can take part. They can pause as though the child will answer. This is an example.

> Adult—"Aren't you hungry?"
> Pause about half a second.
> Imagined response from toddler—"Yes."
> Pause about half a second.
> Adult—"You surely are. Lunch smells good, doesn't it?"

As adults talk to toddlers, they should use all types of sentences. Using statements, questions, and exclamations helps the toddler hear the rise and fall of the voice. Adults can also help toddlers learn to make different sounds. For example, they can make sounds that go with toys, such as "rrr" for a siren.

▪ Clear and Simple Speech

Speech should be clear and simple. Most adults match their sentences to the child's level. For instance, new words are explained using

1—*Resource: Planned Motor Activities*, SAG.

2—*Discuss:* Contrast the type of response received from open-ended versus closed-ended questions. Which type helps most children with language development? Why?

Gross-Motor and Fine-Motor Games

Blocks

© John Shaw

Making a face

© John Shaw

Gross-Motor Games

Push and pull
Push and pull toys aid the motor skills of walking and crawling. Push toys seem to be easier because the toddler can see the toy's action without walking backward or looking back over the shoulder.

Fine-Motor Games

Pounding pegs
A hammer and peg set can help the child coordinate what is seen with the action. Toddlers should use both hands on the hammer to prevent getting the fingers hit.

Blocks
Building a tower with three to five blocks and knocking it down is fun for toddlers. As toddlers grow, they will build taller towers. Balancing the blocks in towers requires good fine-motor control. *Variation:* Push three or four blocks in a "train" while saying, "choo choo." Pushing blocks in a train requires much fine-motor control.

Making a face
Putting the eyes, nose, and mouth on a felt face can be much fun. The parts of the face are made out of felt with a hook-and-loop tape backing, such as Velcro. Because the pieces are rather small, the toddler should be supervised during play. *Variation:* Many other "pictures" can be made using felt pieces. For instance, the toddler can put wheels on cars or trains. They also can put flowers on stems.

14-21   Gross-motor and fine-motor games help toddlers improve their skills.

words that the child already knows. ("A bus is like a big car.") However, mispronouncing words is harmful, such as is talking beneath the child's level. Challenging children slightly helps their development.

Adults should model language for toddlers. However, they should be relaxed about toddlers' language errors. These examples show ways to model language.

☐ Toddler—"My wed (red) sooes (shoes)."
Adult—"Yes, these are your pretty red shoes."
Purpose is to correct pronunciation.

☐ Toddler—"I singed a song."
Adult—"You sang a song about a rainy day."
Purpose is to correct grammar.

☐ Toddler—"See the plane go."
Adult—"The plane flies fast."
Purpose is to introduce a new word.

☐ Toddler—"See the smoke."
Adult—"It does look like smoke." Sniff loudly. "It doesn't smell like smoke, though. We see fog. Fog is a cloud near the ground. Can you say, fog?"
Purpose is to correct meaning.

1

In each case, the adult corrects by expanding the sentence. Toddlers (and even older children) often feel defeated when adults only correct errors.

Choosing Books for Toddlers

"Reading" books and saying poems and rhymes helps toddlers develop language. These activities should begin early in the toddler years. When choosing books, look for the following features:

☐ Pictures must be colorful and simple. Young children's books are called picture books because pictures carry the story rather than words. Picture books may not even have words.

☐ The story should be about toddlers' favorite subjects. Subjects may include animals, toys, fun places to visit, cars and trucks, or home and family.

☐ Books should be durable. They should be sturdy and washable. Books made of cloth, vinyl, and heavy cardboard with a plastic coating are best, 14-22. You can make books by sewing a few plastic kitchen storage bags together. Then slip pictures mounted on heavy paper or cardboard into the bags. (These books have the added bonus of having pictures you can change.)

2

☐ Pages should be easy for the toddler to turn and keep open.

14-22   Toddler books must be sturdy and easy to clean.

© John Shaw

How Toddlers "Read."   Toddlers will not sit still and look at books for a long time. Young toddlers may enjoy glancing at a page and turning it. (Using the motor skill of turning the page is more fun than looking at the pictures.) Later, toddlers look at the pictures for a little longer, but they still may not want to hear the story. Adults can name one object and point to it. Then they can ask toddlers to point to the objects named. As language develops, toddlers can name objects in the pictures and even make some sounds of animals or other objects. The two-year-old often enjoys hearing the whole story, as long as it contains a short sentence or two for each picture page.

Reading to Toddlers.   Many older toddlers (and even older preschool children) insist on hearing the same story over and over. They often request the same story at bedtime. Routines, including favorite, repeated stories, help the toddler feel secure. The child knows what will happen in the story's beginning, middle, and end. Sometimes children will insist that not even a word be changed. The loving adult who reads daily to a child is likely to bring more security than the story itself.

Singing with Toddlers.   Songs that act out the meanings of words are helpful to toddlers. An example is "Here We Go 'Round the Mulberry Bush." This song lets toddlers sing and act out lines like, "This is the way we eat our soup," and "This is the way we wash our hands." Toddlers can sing many other verses, too. See 14-23 for other language games that are fun and encourage children to use language.

● Social-Emotional Needs

Toddlerhood is like the teenage years because the toddler is in a *transitional stage* (passing from one stage to another). Adults cannot treat toddlers as they do babies or as five-year-olds. Toddlers are somewhere in-between. They want to do things for themselves, but this desire exceeds what they are

1—Resource: Modeling Language for Toddlers, SAG.

2.—Activity: Read a children's book and decide on the recommended age level. Report to the class.

3—Discuss: What social-emotional benefit comes from reading with a toddler?

4—Activity: Visit the public library and find a children's book that involves singing. Report to the class.

5—Activity: Read or sing a children's book in class.

6—Resource: Planned Language Activities, SAG.

Language Games

Show Me
Young toddlers enjoy running around and pointing to objects. When an adult names objects for the toddler to touch, the toddler's language skills improve. Make statements like, "Show me the door." As the toddler touches the door, praise him or her with a statement like, "You're right. That's the door."

Follow Directions
Give the toddler simple directions using familiar objects. For example say, "Bring me the ball." Praise the toddler for following directions promptly. You may also play the game "Follow the Leader." Give simple directions such as, "Clap your hands," or "Pat your head."

Telephones
Listening to voices on a phone and talking into a phone can help language develop. Toddlers enjoy play phones. Some types have recorded voices that talk to the toddler. Talking on a real phone with adult supervision also is good language practice.

14-23   Adults and toddlers can enjoy language games.

able to do. Toddlers are trying to become persons, 14-24. They go back and forth between wanting to be totally independent and wanting to be totally dependent.

These changes in toddlers' wills confuse adults. Most adults find they have to give toddlers freedom at times and be firm at other times. Their actions depend on the toddlers' needs.

▶ Discipline

Toddlers do not have **self-restraint**. In other words, they cannot always control themselves. They also do not know all the rules of acceptable behavior. Adults must set limits for toddlers. Limits keep toddlers safe and show them how to become more socially acceptable.

▨ Balancing Self-Assertion and Obedience

Adults must help toddlers balance **self-assertion** (doing as one chooses) and **obedience** (acting within the limits set by others). The best way to do so is to meet toddlers' needs, not punish what they do wrong. Although each toddler has his or her own special needs, some needs are common.

Toddlers Need to Feel Loved.   Toddlers need to feel loved by caring adults. They seem to sense love that is shown to them physically and

directly. For instance, most toddlers respond to cuddling, loving words, and special times each day when attention is focused on them, 14-25. Toddlers do not seem to sense love shown in indirect ways, such as having cooked meals or clean clothes, although these are important.

5

Toddlers Want to Feel Lovable.   When toddlers are always made to feel they are "bad," they may grow to dislike themselves. Adults should label incorrect behavior as a mistake. They should not call the child bad, selfish, naughty, or mean. Harsh punishment may cause toddlers to feel they are "bad," too.

Toddlers Need Respect.   Toddlers are worthy of the same respect other people receive. Adults should not meet toddlers' mistakes with hurtful teasing or anger. Respecting toddlers helps them like themselves. It also serves as the model for the growing child's relationships with others.

6

Toddlers Need Understanding and Patient Guidance.   Toddlers need some freedom. Giving toddlers choices allows them to express their tastes. For example, adults can let toddlers choose between two green vegetables for lunch. A

1—*Activity:* Practice giving one-step commands. When this is mastered, try a simple two-step command to see if the child can follow it.

2—*Reflect:* Describe three transitions you have made during adolescence that are similar to transitions a toddler makes. How are they similar?

3—*Resource: Transition Stages Are Difficult,* SAG.

4—*Reflect:* Describe a toddler you know who is extremely assertive and strong-willed. How does he or she challenge a caregiver? How could you successfully handle each challenge?

5—*Reflect:* You visit a friend at home. His house is disorganized and messy, but he and his son are obviously having fun in their play. Comment on the situation.

6—*Reflect:* Reflect on the following saying: If a child lives with criticism, he learns to condemn; If a child lives with approval, he learns to like himself.

Cosco/Peterson

14-25 Special times spent with loving adults help toddlers to feel loved.

14-24 Toddlers often pull away from their parents because they want to gain independence.

toddler also may choose between self-control and adult-control. The adult may say, "You may color on the paper, or I'll have to put the crayons away." Toddlers seem more willing to accept a firm no when given choices at other times. Limits given in one situation will seldom carry over to similar cases. For instance, a toddler pulling books from a shelf may be told no as the adult pulls the hand from the books. The toddler may pause a moment, then reach for the books with the other hand. Adults must give limits for each case. They also must repeat limits again and again before they become part of the toddler's life.

Toddlers Need Consistency in Discipline. Consistency helps people feel secure. However, people also need flexible rules at times. Toddlers may need flexible rules when they are ill or when other problems occur. Once the situation is back to normal, rules should become consistent again. Of course, discipline changes as children grow. As they grow, children are often allowed more freedom.

Toddlers have good days and problem days, just like adults. When limits are set and discipline is firm yet kind, the toddler will begin to have good days more often. Good days are a sign that toddlers are getting better at balancing self-assertion and the need to obey, 14-26. Balancing the two is a skill they will need throughout life.

▶ Guidance: Helping Toddlers Control Their Emotions

Understanding toddlers' emotions is the first step in helping toddlers control them. To do so, caregivers must control their emotions,

1

1—*Note:* It is important to justify your limits by explaining your reasons and remaining firm.

2—*Discuss:* How would a special needs child influence a caregiver's rules and flexibility?

3—*Reflect:* Why is it so important for caregivers to control their emotions when dealing with children?

as well. Problems with toddlers often include contrariness, temper tantrums, and fears and anxieties.

Contrariness

By 18 months, many toddlers show definite signs of *contrariness*. They tend to oppose adults and even other toddlers. They replace yes with no, even when yes is what they really mean. "Me want" is replaced with "Don't want."

Let the Toddler Choose.   Certain methods often reduce contrariness. The simplest way is to let the toddler make some choices. As long as results are not harmful, allowing toddlers some freedom makes obeying easier.

14-26   Toddlers have many good days.

Mead Johnson Nutritional Division

Tell the Toddler in Advance.   Telling the toddler about changes about five minutes in advance helps reduce contrariness, too. This time allows the toddler to prepare emotionally for the change of activities, 14-27. Saying no is often a toddler's response to sudden changes. Once they say no, it is more difficult for them to back down. If toddlers say no when you tell them about a change, ignore the reply until the change happens. If children say no again, express toddlers' feelings. Adults can say, "You are really having fun in the sandbox, but we must eat now." If toddlers still resist, use calm actions, such as picking up toddlers.

1

Use Pretend Games.   Another way to reduce contrariness is to play a pretend game of obedience. The adult might say, "I'm going to wash my hands before you do." (Of course, after much scrubbing, the toddler wins.) Sometimes pretend games of obedience become rituals, such as a "chase" to the bedroom at naptime.

14-27   Telling toddlers what will happen next prepares them for a change of events.

2

© John Shaw

1—*Discuss:* Pretend you announce a change five minutes ahead then follow through with the new activity. If the child becomes upset, how could you get him or her to comply without force?

2—*Note:* This can help to prevent a tantrum.

Temper Tantrums

As toddlers discover the powers of self-assertion, they may have temper tantrums. Many two-year-olds have temper tantrums, but some do not. Toddlers who are lively, under stress (even the stress of being hungry), and cannot talk yet are prone to tantrums. The number and frequency of tantrums may be reduced by trying the following ideas:

☐ Reduce or avoid demands when the toddler is tired, hungry, or ill.

☐ Make requests in a pleasant tone of voice.

☐ Remove toys or play equipment that seems to frustrate the child.

☐ Have enough toys or ideas to prevent boredom.

☐ Offer help when the toddler seems to need it. (Waiting until the child shows frustration is often too late.)

☐ Give in on small demands. (Toddlers need to get their way sometimes.)

☐ Praise the toddler for signs of control.

Once a temper tantrum is underway, allow the tantrum to continue. It is a form of release for the child. Leaving the child alone (if at home or in a preschool program) often helps because tantrums are often performed for the audience. Toddlers have been known to follow adults from room to room, throwing the tantrum each time. If a tantrum occurs in public, the adult and child should go to a quiet place for the toddler to become calm.

Comforting the Child. Adults should acknowledge the feelings of toddlers and show comfort. The adult may say, "I know you really wanted to stay outside. I'm sorry you are so upset about coming in the house." After the tantrum, hugs often are helpful. When adults hold back this comfort, toddlers may feel unlovable.

Do not use spankings to punish for tantrums. If the adult expresses displeasure (or even anger) in a physical way, he or she is modeling that behavior for the toddler.

Tantrums, when handled calmly, often decrease during the preschool years. Also, adult calmness serves as a model for children of ways to deal with anger.

Fears and Anxieties

Adults should not dismiss children's fears and anxieties as silly. They should not tease children about them, either. They should handle the toddler's feelings in a matter-of-fact way.

Reducing Fear and Anxiety. Adults should show differences between real and pretend things in the toddlers' world. For example, adults should explain that dreams are not real. This will help reduce toddlers' fears of pretend things. Toddlers will often ask whether something is real or pretend. Toddlers will even ask about the same thing many times just to be certain.

Giving toddlers security also reduces fear. Night-lights, toys in bed, and familiar baby-sitters add security. Avoid situations that cause much fear or anxiety. However, some situations, such as going to the doctor, cannot be avoided, 14-28.

14-28 A warm and caring adult helps a child overcome fears.

Brian LaPeter—The Island Packet

1—Note: It is important to observe the child's emotional state and attitude to avoid confrontation.

2—Note: Make sure toys are age-appropriate.

3—Note: Letting a child choose one time and you choose the next time establishes a model of sharing and taking turns.

4—Activity: List positive and negative ways to handle tantrums. Explain your reasons for each.

5—Reflect: What fears do you have? How do you feel when someone teases you about them? How do you think you should treat a child's fears?

These should be explained in a simple, honest way. As they are explained, mention only fears that the toddler has already shown.

Overcoming Fear and Anxiety. For toddlers to overcome fears and anxieties, they need to see and talk about their fear in safe ways. Telling toddlers that other children have the same fear may comfort them. Gradual exposure to a feared subject may also help, 14-29. If the toddler is afraid of dogs, the adult may talk about dogs. Later, the adult may read the child a book about dogs or give the child a toy dog. After some time, the toddler may stand near a friendly dog behind a fence. This method is better for the toddler than suddenly exposing the child to fearful situations.

Toddlers should be praised for small steps toward overcoming fears. For instance, toddlers can be praised for only crying a little or for not running from the puppy behind the fence.

Most of the toddler's fears and anxieties will disappear with age. If parents handle fear and anxieties in understanding ways, toddlers will be better able to cope with present and future fears and anxieties.

▶ Planning Self-Awareness Activities

A person's self-awareness begins at birth and continues throughout life. The roots of self-awareness seem to form in the toddler years. Self-awareness grows mainly out of the toddler's daily contact with his or her world. A few planned activities may enhance self-awareness, 14-30.

14-30 A "Me Doll" helps toddlers understand that they are seeing themselves in a mirror.

© John Shaw

14-29 Through many experiences in water, this toddler enjoys rather than fears the water.

South Padre Island Convention and Visitors Bureau

1—*Activity:* Locate children's books that deal with fears and anxieties. Summarize the books to the class.

Self-Awareness Activities

Name the Parts of the Face
Place the toddler's hands on your face. Name aloud each part of your face as the child feels it. Ask the child to name the parts.

Mirrors
With the toddler on your lap, hold a mirror to reflect the toddler's face. Ask, "Who is that?" If the toddler does not answer say, "That is you." Say the toddler's name.

Dressing Up
Children under age three enjoy dressing up with old purses, hats, necklaces, and large flat shoes. To help the toddler play while dressing up, show the child one object. For example, show the toddler a hat and say, "Look at this pretty hat. I'm going to wear it." Place the hat on your head and talk about how pretty it is. Then say, "Do you want to wear a hat?" Place a hat on the toddler's head, saying how nice it looks. If the toddler enjoys this, try other items.

Pretend
Have a pretend tea party with a toddler. Talk about the pretend foods in much the same way you would talk about real food. If the toddler looks confused say, "How funny! We can pretend to have a party!"

A Book About Me
Take pictures of the toddler's daily activities. Place the pictures in a photo album or in plastic bags that are fastened together with string.

14-31   These activities enhance a toddler's sense of self.

14-32   As toddlers begin to understand their abilities, they become more confident and content.

© John Shaw

Examples of self-awareness activities include placing photographs of the toddler on the refrigerator or another viewing area at the child's height. Keeping a photo album of the child's early years is fun for all family members. The parents and child can sit together and talk about how the child has grown and how important the child is to the family. Measuring the child's height on a chart and keeping a running tally of his or her height also helps the child gain self-awareness. See 14-31 for other examples of self-awareness activities.

With help from loving adults and their increasing mental abilities, toddlers can smoothly leave the baby years behind. Toddlers emerge as happy, confident young children, 14-32.

1—*Resource: Planned Activities for Self-Awareness,* SAG.

Recognizing Developmental Delays

Toddlers with developmental delays may show some of the behaviors of infants as listed in Chapter 10. As you may have noted, infant development is judged mainly by gross-motor skills.

During the toddler years, gross-motor skills are still important behaviors to observe, but fine-motor skills and language become more important in indicating normal signs of development. Knowing some typical toddler behaviors may help parents recognize delays and bring their concerns to the attention of a doctor, 14-33.

Typical Toddler Behaviors	
Age	**Behavior**
15 Months	Raises head slightly when lying on stomach May walk without support Vocalizes with pitch changes (babbling sounds like a sentence) Uses 4 or 5 words Begins self-feeding
18 Months	Walks and may run some Climbs up or down one stair step Plays with pull toys Uses 5 to 10 words Likes being read to Marks with crayon on paper attached to a table (cannot hold paper and mark) Partially feeds self
2 Years	Turns pages (may turn 2 or 3 at a time) Kicks large ball Imitates some household work (feeding baby or washing dishes) Recognizes familiar objects in pictures Uses two or three words together ("juice gone")

14-33   Knowing what typical toddler behaviors are can help to recognize developmental delays.

Summary

Toddlers practice self-care skills like self-feeding, self-dressing, and toileting. These skills also help them advance in their mental and social-emotional development.

Toddlers eat table food and can feed themselves. Parents must provide high nutrient density foods for the child. A number of feeding problems can arise because of the toddlers' growing independence.

Clothing and shoes that fit and allow for growth are important. Other features to consider when purchasing clothing for toddlers include safety, comfort, fabric, attractive style, and ease of care.

The sleep and rest habits of toddlers have changed since infancy. Bedtime problems can develop, but if adults establish quiet nighttime rituals, bedtime is less stressful.

For bathing, place a small tub inside the regular tub. Toddlers help a little in their bathing and use this time for play. Having a proper diet and cleaning teeth regularly is part of good dental health. Dental checkups can begin at age two.

Before children can be toilet trained, their body must be physically ready. They also must see the need to go to the bathroom. This generally occurs sometime after age two. Children should not be shamed or punished when they have accidents. They need praise and encouragement.

Parents need to give toddlers some freedom while still setting limits for them. Contrariness and temper tantrums are typical problems at this age. Feelings of fears and anxieties should be handled in understanding ways. As toddlers become more aware of themselves and their abilities, they become more confident.

To Review

Write your answers on a separate sheet of paper.

1

1. True or false. Besides meeting food, clothing, rest, sleep, and hygiene needs, teaching self-care skills is part of meeting the physical needs of toddlers.
2. Which statements about feeding toddlers are true?
   a. Because toddlers are larger, their appetites increase.
   b. Toddlers want to feed themselves.
   c. Toddlers who play with their food are being naughty.
   d. Empty calorie foods, which provide energy, are all right for toddlers due to their high energy demands.
   e. Many of the toddler's feeding problems are worked out in time.

1—*Answers:* Answers to review questions can be found in the front section of this TAE.

3. Toddlers are better at (putting on, taking off) their clothes.
4. True or false. Shoes help toddlers walk by providing good support.
5. Give four suggestions that may help toddlers go to bed.
6. Toddlers feel the sensation of a full bladder or bowel at
   a. 9 months
   b. 15 months
   c. 18 months
   d. 24 months
7. True or false. Toilet training chairs do not make toilet training easier.
8. Intellectual needs are best met
   a. through planned activities
   b. when toddlers are involved with household activities on a day-to-day basis
   c. when needed concepts and skills are taught in a drill fashion
   d. when language is not part of most activities
9. Give two ways to reduce contrariness in toddlers.
10. Give three ways to reduce the number of temper tantrums in toddlers.
11. True or false. Toddlers become less fearful when quickly exposed to the feared situation again.

To Do

1. Prepare one week's menus for a toddler. Use chart 14-3 as a guide.
2. Prepare a poster or mobile of good finger foods for toddlers.
3. Borrow some toddler clothes from parents. Examine each garment for the features listed on chart 14-6. Make a list of the good features included. Compare your list with others in the class. Attach a hangtag for each clothing item listing its best features.
4. Invite two or three successful caregivers to share with the class hints that have helped them solve some toddler problems. The guests may include feeding problems, bathing and toothbrushing problems, toilet training, contrariness, temper tantrums, and fears/anxieties.
5. Gather or make the materials for some of the planned activities listed in the text or Teacher's Resource Guide. Then make a display, adding cards that explain how the materials are used. (You may do this alone or as a group.)
6. Try some planned activities while baby-sitting or as a helper in a toddlers' group-care program. Discuss with your class what did or did not work and possible reasons why.

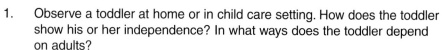

To Observe

1. Observe a toddler at home or in child care setting. How does the toddler show his or her independence? In what ways does the toddler depend on adults?
2. Observe a toddler in his or her bedroom or playroom. What decorations seem to have been chosen with a toddler in mind? What things seem to especially fit this toddler?
3. Observe a toddler playing. What type of learning(s) does the play activity involve (sensory problem solving, motor, language, and/or self-awareness)?
4. Observe a toddler while reading a story. Which features of the book did the toddler like? Was there anything about the book that didn't seem fit for toddlers? Explain.
5. Observe adults caring for toddlers who are having a hard day. What actions seem to work best? Why? What adult actions do not seem to work? Why?

To Think Critically

1. Examine some items used to teach self-dressing. Although these items teach some skills, how are they different from actual dressing? (Be specific about each item.)
2. Examine several pieces of equipment that can be used for problem solving, such as a jigsaw puzzle. What specific skills does a child have to have or develop in order to use the materials? (As you answer this question, visualize each step.)
3. What are some of the ways adults fail to respect toddlers? What might be the outcome if adults treated their friends in this way? How can they be respectful to toddlers? (Be specific.)

Toddlers often develop an attachment to a favorite toy.

Part 5

Preschoolers

Children grow and develop in significant ways between the ages of 3 and 5. The most obvious changes are physical. However, the maturation of the brain and the broadening of experiences allows children to master new physical and social tasks.

In **chapter 15,** you will see how striking changes in size and shape begin to occur at age three. By the end of the preschool period (at age five), children's bodies look much more like those of adults than those of babies. Children's motor skills also improve. This enables them to engage in activities that demand coordination and balance, such as biking. Fine-motor skills are improving, but they still lag behind gross-motor skills.

Chapter 16 will show you why preschoolers' expressions often amuse adults. Although these children use symbols, including language, in a more mature way, they cannot consistently use logic in reasoning.

In **chapter 17,** you will study how preschoolers develop independence as they try new activities and meet new adults and peers. These experiences lead to self-understanding.

Chapter 18 will give you many ideas about how to assist preschoolers. You will learn how to help them meet their nutritional needs as they choose the foods they eat. You will read about the types of clothing and furnishings that are pleasing and also foster a child's self-help abilities. You will learn activities that meet their intellectual needs and help them understand their social selves.

Chapter 15

Physical Development of the Preschooler

Preschoolers change physically to look more like adults and less like babies.

After studying this chapter, you will be able to

☐ describe the physical development that occurs in preschool children.

☐ describe preschool children's gross-motor and fine-motor skills.

After studying this chapter, you will be able to define

body rotation
internal organs
manipulate
preschool children
reaction time
static balance
weight shift

Preschool children are those between the ages of three and five. As you can imagine, they are becoming grown-up. The bodies of preschoolers continue to mature, which makes them able to handle harder tasks. They are changing in ways that make them more like adults and less like small children.

Toddlers have gained many gross-motor and fine-motor skills. However, they do not have as much control over their movements as they would like. In the preschool years, children improve their skills of walking, running, balancing, and self-dressing.

● Body Growth and Development

Preschool children grow even more slowly than toddlers. (If the growth rate did not slow, all people would be as big as giants!) Instead of growing much larger, the preschoolers' body proportions change and their organ systems mature.

The growth rate slows in almost the same way for all preschool children. This means that children who are larger than their peers at age three likely will be at age five.

▶ Height and Weight

Most preschool children grow steadily at about 2¹/₂ inches to 3 inches each year. On the average, girls are shorter than boys, but the difference is ¹/₂ inch or less, 15-1.

The rate of weight gain also slows during the preschool years. Preschoolers gain about three to five pounds per year. Seventy-five percent of the weight gained during the preschool ages is due to muscle development. Because boys have greater muscle development, even during the preschool years, they average a pound heavier than girls their age, 15-2.

Average Height from Three to Five Years		
Age in Years	Boys	Girls
3	38″	37.25″
3¹/₂	39.25″	39.25″
4	40.75″	40.50″
4¹/₂	42″	42″
5	43.25″	43″
5¹/₂	45″	44.50″

15-1 The height of children from three to five years increases rather steadily. Boys tend to be slightly taller than girls.

4

15-2 The weight of children from three to five years increases rather steadily. Boys tend to be slightly heavier than girls.

5

Average Weight from Three to Five Years		
Age in Years	Boys	Girls
3	32.25 lbs.	31.75 lbs.
3¹/₂	34.25 lbs.	34 lbs.
4	36.50 lbs.	36.25 lbs.
4¹/₂	38.50 lbs.	38.50 lbs.
5	41.50 lbs.	41 lbs.
5¹/₂	45.50 lbs.	44 lbs.

1—Discuss: Discuss ways that preschoolers are physically becoming more like adults.

2—Discuss: Classify these skills as fine- or gross-motor.

3—Resource: Average Heights and Weights of Preschoolers, SAG.

4—Discuss: Why are boys generally slightly taller than girls?

5—Discuss: Why are boys generally slightly heavier than girls?

▶Other Body Changes

As baby features begin to disappear, the preschooler's body proportions begin to look more like those of an adult, 15-3. The lower face grows more rapidly than the head. This helps the preschooler's face look more like an adult's. Until 30 months of age, the waist, hips, and chest measure almost the same. By age five the waist is smaller than the shoulders and hips. The trunk grows to allow more space for the *internal organs* (heart, lungs, liver, and others). As the trunk grows, the abdomen protrudes less. The legs grow rapidly, too. By 5½ years, most children's legs are about half the length of the body. This is the same as the adult's leg-to-body proportions.

▪ Bones

The bones continue to ossify and grow larger and longer. Deciduous (baby) teeth begin to fall out between ages four and five. Although permanent teeth may not erupt until the early school years, they are growing under the gums. Bone and teeth development can be harmed by malnutrition and other health problems during the preschool years. Bones, muscles, and joints are more prone to injury in preschool children than in older children.

15-3 These preschool girls have body proportions more like those of adults than babies.

South Padre Island Convention and Visitors Bureau

1—Math Activity: If a child's height at age five and one-half is 41 inches, determine his or her approximate leg length.

2—Discuss: Why are they more prone to injury?

© John Shaw

15-4 Eye-hand coordination becomes more refined in the preschool years.

● Motor Development

The motor development of preschoolers improves with body growth and development and with physical activity. Preschoolers have an increase in muscle development. Their eye-hand coordination becomes more refined, 15-4. Their *reaction time* (time required to react to a sight, sound, etc.) becomes shorter. Preschool children are able to perform many physical activities. Through play, preschool children's motor skills develop quickly, 15-5.

▶ Large-Muscle Development

As preschool children's large muscles develop, the children become stronger and more coordinated. Large-motor skills include walking, running, jumping, climbing, throwing and catching, balancing, hopping, and skipping, 15-6. Chart 15-7 shows the development and improvement of these large-motor skills.

Organs

Other organs are maturing, too. The heart rate slows and becomes steady. Blood pressure increases. Breathing slows and is deeper. Although the digestive tract is maturing, it lags behind the maturity of other organs. Therefore, the preschooler's digestive tract is more irritated by high fiber foods and seasonings than the adult's. The preschooler's brain continues to grow, too, but it grows at a slower rate than before.

Fat Tissues

Fat tissues continue to lessen slowly. At 5¹/₂ years the preschooler's fat tissues are less than half as thick as they were at age one.

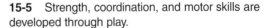

15-5   Strength, coordination, and motor skills are developed through play.

You will notice that preschoolers walk more smoothly than toddlers. The chart shows they like to try more challenging ways to walk. They run faster, and their arms and legs alternate in rhythm. Four-year-olds use a forward arm action to jump higher. With increased courage and better balance, climbing becomes easier. They can catch balls that are bounced better than those thrown by others. There are wide differences in their balancing skills. Three-year-olds begin hopping. Older preschoolers can hop and skip faster and for longer distances than younger preschoolers. Their actions become more advanced in all areas, 15-8.

Two new actions help the preschooler's throwing ability. One is body rotation and the other is weight shift. **Body rotation** is the action of turning the trunk of the body to one side when the hand on the other side is used to throw. **Weight shift** is the change of weight from the back foot to the front foot. Body rotation and weight shift may begin during the third year. They become much more refined by the end of the preschool period. These two changes improve a preschooler's throwing distance, speed, and accuracy.

▶ Small-Muscle Development

The preschoolers' ability to manipulate, or work with, the hands is still awkward. However, as preschoolers play with small objects, their small muscles develop and fine-motor skills improve. Improved eye-hand coordination also helps fine-motor skills. Chart 15-9 shows what to expect in the fine-motor skills of preschool children. (Remember that the ages at which children develop may vary. The order of development is almost the same for all children.)

© John Shaw

15-6 Balancing is an example of large-muscle development.

1

Preschoolers' Large-Motor Skill Development	
Walking	☐ Balance becomes better. ☐ Hold hands close to the body. ☐ Begin to swing arms in alternate rhythm of foot placement. ☐ Like to walk sideways, backward, and on tiptoes. ☐ Like to spin around and try to become dizzy, which help balance (three-year-olds).
Running	☐ Have short stops and starts. ☐ Can turn corners quickly. ☐ Begin to swing arms in alternate rhythm of foot placement. ☐ Increase speed a lot (five-years-old).
Jumping	☐ Have stronger muscles. ☐ Increase distance of broad jump (with girls often lagging behind boys). ☐ Increase height of hurdle jump (with boys and girls are almost equal).
Climbing	☐ Climb with more skill due to longer legs. ☐ Can alternate steps going up stairs (three-year-olds). ☐ Can alternate climbing down steps (four-year-olds).
Throwing and Catching	☐ Begin to turn body to one side (body rotation) when the hand on the other side is used to throw (three-year-olds). ☐ Begin to shift weight from back foot to front foot (three-year-olds). ☐ Can catch balls they bounce better than those thrown by others. ☐ Show increased strength, balance, and coordination and thus improve throwing distance, speed, and accuracy. ☐ Can catch ball with the arms to one side (between ages four and five).
Balancing	☐ Can walk heel-toe on a straight line without falling (three-year-olds). ☐ Can balance on one foot *(static balance)* for a few seconds (three-year-olds). Can do more static balance feats (four- and five-year-olds).
Hopping and Skipping	☐ Can hop on preferred foot (three-year-olds). ☐ Can hop faster and for longer distances (four- and five-year-olds). ☐ Can skip (between ages four and six). ☐ Can do rhythmic hopping (hopping on one foot and then the other without breaking the rhythmic pattern) and precision hopping (following a certain pathway) (some five-year-olds).

15-7   Compared to the toddler, the large-muscle movements of the preschool child are smoother and less awkward.

1—Activity: Practice playing ball with a preschooler. Record your observations. Report to the class.

2—Activity: Have a student demonstrate balancing on one foot. Emphasize the term static balance.

3—Activity: Go for a walk with a preschooler. Practice these large-motor skills. Record your observations and report to the class.

© Nancy P. Alexander

15-8 Floor blocks are prefect for large-muscle development.

Age Three

At age three, most children can feed themselves using a spoon and fork, but they are still rather messy. They can build towers from blocks, but the towers are crooked. Three-year-olds can draw straight lines and copy circles. They can unbutton buttons and pull up large zippers.

Age Four

By four years, movements are more steady. Four-year-olds may try to use a knife when they feed themselves. They are able to build straight towers and place blocks with steady hands, 15-10. Four-year-olds begin to cut along lines with scissors. (Scissors used at this age should have

Sequence of the Development of Fine-Motor Skills

Age	Skills	
Three Years	☐ Builds uneven tower of blocks. ☐ Pours water from a pitcher. ☐ Copies a circle (with some skill). ☐ Draws a straight line.	
Four Years	☐ Cuts on line with scissors. ☐ Washes hands. ☐ Copies a letter *t*. ☐ Makes a few letters.	
Five Years	☐ Folds paper along the diagonal. ☐ Copies a square and a triangle. ☐ Traces a diamond shape. ☐ Laces shoes and may tie them. ☐ Copies most letters.	

15-9 Fine-motor skills develop in a certain order.

1—Discuss: What could he build? How does this promote mental development? How could you promote social development with this activity?

2—Activity: Observe a preschooler's self-help skills in dressing. Discuss in class.

LEGO Dacta, the educational division of the LEGO Group

15-10   Small blocks, designed just large enough for preschool hands, aid small-muscle development.

rounded tips.) These children can brush their teeth, comb their hair, and wash their hands. They can also begin to lace, but probably not tie, their shoes.

Age Five

At age five, eye-hand coordination is greatly improved. Right- or left-hand preference is definite by this age. Five-year-olds use a spoon, fork, and knife to feed themselves. They can build towers and place other small toys with skill. They can make simple drawings freehand. Five-year-olds can fasten large buttons and work large zippers. They may even be able to tie shoelaces.

2

Summary

Preschoolers are beginning to look less like babies. Their face begins to look more like those of adults. Their height and weight gain is much slower than in their toddler years. The waist becomes smaller than shoulders and hips. Bones grow harder, larger, and longer. Deciduous teeth begin to fall out. Other organs and systems continue to mature.

Large muscles become more coordinated and stronger. Preschoolers are better able to walk, run, jump, climb, throw and catch, balance, and hop and skip.

As preschoolers manipulate small objects, their fine-motor skills improve. Better eye-hand coordination helps skills develop. Their fine-motor skills develop in a certain order that is similar for all children. Three-year-olds can build uneven towers of blocks. Five-year-olds may be able to lace and tie shoes. Hand preference is definite by age five.

3

To Review

Write your answers on a separate sheet of paper.

1.   True or false. Compared to the toddler years, the rate of growth speeds up during the preschool years.

4

1—Activity: Check catalogs for other types of small building blocks or tiles suitable for preschoolers.

2—Resource: Observation: Strength and Coordination Increase, SAG.

3—Activity: Obtain a child's baby picture and a picture at age four or five. Describe his or her physical differences.

4—Answers: Answers to review questions can be found in the front section of this TAE.

2. Preschool children's weight increases because of
   a. an increase in fat
   b. head (brain) growth
   c. muscle development
3. True or false. At the end of the preschool years, the child's legs equal about half the total body length.
4. One of the slowest maturing organs is the
   a. brain
   b. digestive tract
   c. heart
5. True or false. A four-year-old can cut on a line with scissors.
6. True or false. Fine-motor skills refer to how well a child can balance and jump.
7. True or false. Most five-year-olds can do rhythmic and precision hopping.
8. Match the preschool child's motor action to the skills by putting the letter (or letters) before the skill.
   Skills
   _____ walking
   _____ running
   _____ jumping
   _____ throwing
   _____ balancing
   Motor actions
   a. uses forward action of arms
   b. shows some body rotation and shifting of weight
   c. uses increased speed
   d. swings arms in alternate rhythm of feet placement
   e. can walk heel-toe on a straight line
9. List four fine-motor skills developed in the preschool period.
10. True or false. Most four-year-olds can tie their shoelaces.

To Do

1

1. Write a one- or two-page brochure about the motor skills of preschool children. Illustrations may help. Give copies to local programs serving preschool children for parents and other adults to use. (Ask your teacher to check the brochure before making copies.)
2. Observe the motor skills (both large-muscle and small-muscle) of children ages three, four, and five. Make a chart to record the advancing skills. The chart might look like this—

   Age of child _____
   Male/Female _____

1—Activity: Prepare the brochure using a computer. Provide copies for child care centers and medical facilities to distribute.

Motor Skill—
Hopping
  can hop _____
  distance hopped _____
  can hop rhythmically _____
  can hop with precision _____
Jumping
  length of broad jump _____
  height of hurdle jump _____
  forward movement of arms seen _____
Compare the skills of each age by using the average for each skill.
3. On index cards draw a circle, a square, a rectangle, a triangle with three equal sides (equilateral), and a diamond. Have children ages three, four, and five draw each of these shapes on a piece of paper. (Children should use a crayon or pencil.) Make a bulletin board of these drawings labeled with each child's age. Compare the drawings by age.
4. Informally compare the skills of three-year-olds and five-year-olds in handling scissors, pencils or crayons, and a paintbrush. What changes happen in this two-year period? Describe your findings in class.

To Observe

1. Observe a group of preschoolers playing. What motor skills have they developed? What motor skills need improvement?
2. Observe three-year-olds and five-year-olds doing fine-motor activities. What differences in the skill levels did you observe? Were there exceptions in either group?

To Think Critically

1. Why are the preschool years important ones for providing children with many opportunities for large-muscle development? (Think of this question in terms of all areas of growth and development—physical, mental, and social-emotional.)
2. If you were writing a magazine article about gift suggestions to aid in preschoolers' small-muscle development, what gifts would you suggest?
3. Why do preschoolers feel so grown-up? More specifically, what physical changes (appearance and skills) give them this idea?

Chapter 16

Intellectual Development of the Preschooler

After studying this chapter, you will be able to

☐ relate how new thinking skills emerge in preschool children.

☐ identify the major concepts learned at this stage of mental development.

☐ chart the increasing language skills of preschoolers.

After studying this chapter, you will be able to define

abstract
classification
collective monologue
egocentrism
internalized
intuitive substage
logical thinking concepts
mental images
monologue
preconceptual substage
preoperational stage

Preschool children are just beginning to think as adults do. There are still many problems with the ways they think.

What children have learned as infants and toddlers greatly expands during the preschool years. Because they have better motor skills, preschoolers look more carefully at objects, people, and events. They no longer rely only on their senses and motor actions to learn about their environment. The more mature brain gives preschool children longer attention spans. It also helps them to think and recall more.

Piaget has described the second major stage of mental development as the **preoperational stage**. This is the stage children reach before they acquire logical mental actions, which Piaget calls *operations*. These logical mental actions, or operations, require the mind to think through problems and act accordingly. They are what most people consider logical thinking. *Logical thinking* includes combining ideas or objects, placing them in order, and doing "if-then" thinking. Preschool children have not entered the logical thinking stage yet. Just as toddlers who are walking are prone to missteps, preschool children who are thinking are prone to thinking errors.

Piaget's Stages of Cognitive Development	
Stage 1	Sensorimotor Stage *(birth to 2 years)*
Stage 2	Preoperational Stage *(2 to 7 years)*
Substage i	Preconceptual *(2 to 4 years)*
Substage ii	Intuitive *(4 to 7 years)*
Stage 3	Concrete Operational Stage *(7 to 11 years)*
Stage 4	Formal Operational Stage *(11 years on)*

16-1 The preschool child functions in the preoperational stage.

4

How Preschool Children Learn

The preoperational stage occurs during the preschool years. It may include the first year or two of school. Chart 16-1 shows the two parts of the preoperational stage—the preconceptual and the intuitive substages. In the **preconceptual substage,** children, ages two to four, are developing some concepts. They are able to form a mental image of what they see around them. However, many of these concepts are incomplete or illogical. Children may see different members of the same group as identical, such as all collies as Lassie.

In the **intuitive substage,** children sometimes are able to grasp a problem's solution by how they feel about it. Through their intuition, they base their solutions on "feeling" their way through problems rather than on logic.

▶ Obstacles to Logical Thinking

Although preschool children mentally are more advanced than toddlers, they do not think logically yet for the following reasons:

☐ Preschool children, especially those under four, are *egocentric.* Piaget says this means they believe that everyone thinks the same way they do, 16-2. They view the world in relation to themselves. Children may offer others candy from their mouths. Because they are enjoying it, they think others would, too. If children say the slide is tall, they think an adult thinks it is tall, too. They do not think the taller adult may see the slide as small. Egocentrism, in this sense, does not mean that children are selfish or too concerned with themselves. **Egocentrism** is the term for the preschooler's belief that everyone thinks in the same way and has the same ideas as he or she does. The preschooler cannot even imagine other people might have different ideas.

5

1—*Activity:* Prepare a list of Piaget's preoperational activities on a blackboard, poster, or transparency. Have students add to the list. Label as three- to five-year-olds.

2—*Enrich:* Research Piaget's preoperational stage of mental (cognitive) development. Include information on the preconceptual and the intuitive substages. Report to the class.

3—*Activity:* In a large group, prepare a list of problems a preschooler could solve in the intuitive substage. Test these with four- and five-year-olds. Report to the class.

4—*Note:* Review this chart.

5—*Reflect:* Give examples of egocentrism in preschoolers.

© John Shaw

16-2   The three-year-old (left) is asked to describe what she believes is the older girl's view of the bear. She describes the bear's face. This is her view from her side of the table.

□   Preschoolers center their attention on only one part of an object or event. They do not see all parts at the same time, 16-3. The preoperational child sees the tall beaker and thinks tall means more. The child does not see that the tall beaker is also thinner, and thus it holds the same amount of liquid as one of the original glasses. The same thinking occurs when the child sees the liquid in the wide bowl and thinks "wide" means "more." To think of both height and width at the same time, the child must look at two or more aspects at once.

□   Preschool children tend to focus on single steps, stages, or events, rather than see the order of changes. Piaget says the focus is like seeing each frame of a film as a separate, unrelated picture rather than a running story. As shown in 16-4, if a pencil is held upright and falls, it passes from an original state (vertical) to a final state (horizontal). This happens through a series of angled states. Preoperational children, after watching the pencil fall, will draw only the first or the last state. How something happened or what something was like before a change took place does not enter their minds, 16-5.

□   Preschoolers cannot follow a line of reasoning back to where it starts. They cannot

1—*Reflect:* Describe each child's view. How could you help them understand each other better?

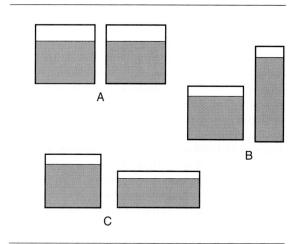

16-3   Preschool children know that the amount of liquid in the two equal-sized glasses is the same (A). When the liquid of one container is poured into a tall tube (B) or a wide bowl (C), preschool children incorrectly say the amount of liquid has changed.

retrace the steps to undo the task. For instance, adding two to three equals five. To reverse the problem, subtract two from five to equal three. Because the preschooler cannot see why subtracting can "undo" addition, Piaget says the preschooler cannot reverse (undo an action).

☐ Preschoolers link actions without using logic. Reasoning this way causes problems in logic. An example is when a mother makes coffee just before a father comes home from work each day. The child may conclude, "Coffee brings dad home." The preschooler links events to each other when they occur close together in time. A preschooler also links objects without using logic. For example, tell a child that a bug with eight legs is called a *spider*. Then show the child a daddy longlegs and say, "The daddy longlegs has

eight legs. What is the daddy longlegs?" The child will probably say, "It is big," "It is brown," or "It bites." The child was given the information, but cannot conclude that the daddy longlegs is a spider.

▶ New Abilities Emerge

Preschoolers can think in their heads better than before. They depend less on their actions. The preschoolers' thinking is marked by a number of new abilities—symbolic play, mental images, drawing, and language.

Symbolic Play

Preschool children play many pretend games. In play, they change something from the real world (including dreams) in some ways. The ideas in the pretend games may stand for anything the child wants. The preschooler chooses symbols to represent the pretend world and the child's role in it, 16-6. Because children make up their own symbols, such as a leaf for a plate, pretend play is a mental step beyond imitation.

16-4   When preschool children are asked to watch as a rod is dropped and then draw what they have seen, they draw only the first state or the last state. They do not draw any of the in-between states.

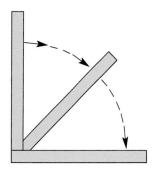

1—*Activity:* Try this experiment with preschoolers. Discuss the results.

2—*Resource: Preschoolers Lack Complete Logical Thought,* SAG.

3—*Resource: Observation: Using Symbols in Play,* SAG.

4—*Activity:* Try this experiment with preschoolers. Discuss the results.

16-5   When asked to recall catching a fish, this preschooler would focus on the fish in the water and the fish in the boat. He would not focus on the in-between stages of getting the fish into the boat.

Mental Images

Mental images are symbols of objects and past experiences that are stored in the mind. They are the pictures in the mind when words or experiences trigger the image. Unlike imitation and other play, mental images are private and ***internalized*** (thought about only). They are not exact copies of real objects and experiences. However, mental images do relate to the real world.

Drawing

Preschool children no longer scribble without any attempt to draw something. Now they try to depict their world through drawings, 16-7. Preschoolers intend their drawings to be realistic. They draw what they think is visually accurate, not what is. A side view of a goldfish drawing may show both eyes and even a smiling mouth. Drawing is a step between symbolic play and mental image. This is because preschool children often draw first, then decide what their pictures represent.

1—*Enrich:* Ask a preschooler to tell you about a recent experience like this one. Describe what he or she says and the steps the child omits.

2—*Activity:* Close your eyes and develop a mental image of an object. Report in class what you visualized. Discuss how it was internalized. Try this with a preschooler. Report to the class.

© Nancy P. Alexander

16-6   The young boy's hat and climbing frame may be anything he imagines.

Language

Spoken words are symbols used to represent something. The symbols used in language are the hardest of all symbols to understand. This is because words are **abstract** (do not relate to what they represent). The word *car* does not look, sound, or move like a car. Although words are abstract, they do help in talking. Once language abilities develop, the child can exchange ideas with others. Language also helps the thinking process. Thinking is faster when we think words.

● What Preschool Children Learn

Preschoolers have learned a lot by now. However, many errors and gaps still exist in a preschoolers' concepts. During these years, learning is exciting and stimulating.

▶ Concepts Children Learn

Children must learn many concepts. Concepts about the physical qualities of objects, logical thinking concepts, cause and effect, and human versus nonhuman qualities are some of what they must learn, 16-8.

Physical Qualities

Preschool children develop concepts about size, shape, color, texture, and other physical traits about objects and people. In order to develop concepts, they must be able to detect differences.

The preschool child's understanding of these concepts is limited. This is because the child may not note the object's most important features. The child must note a zebra's stripes to distinguish it from a horse. Second, because preschoolers tend to look at parts of an object,

16-7   This older preschool girl's drawing shows she is in an advanced stage of thinking. She uses rather realistic symbols to show her ideas in her drawing.

3

Wood Designs of Monroe, Inc.

1—*Discuss:* What could he imagine?

2—*Discuss:* If a car is defined as a vehicle with wheels that moves on a road, think of all the vehicles this might involve. Discuss why the word in its simplest form might confuse a

child. Think of other words, such as "dog," that would confuse a child.

3—*Reflect:* How could the other girl's picture differ according to theme and content? Why?

© Nancy P. Alexander

16-8 By playing house, children can learn about the physical qualities of objects and use logical thinking concepts.

they cannot always "see" the whole object. Preschool children were shown drawings such as those in 16-9. They recognized the parts but not the whole. (Nine-year-olds could see both.) The ability to see parts as well as the total figure is important for accurate perception.

Logical Thinking Concepts

Logical thinking concepts are not experienced through the senses. They are understood mentally. These concepts include classification, arranging by size, and understanding numbers, space, and time concepts. These are the hardest concepts for preschool children to understand.

Classifying Objects. *Classification* is the ability to mentally group objects by their similar qualities. Preschool children cannot see how objects are alike, so they cannot classify them into groups by traits, such as color or shape.

Arranging by Size. It is hard for preschool children to arrange objects by increasing or

16-9 Most preschool children will see only parts of these drawings. They do not see the faces in the whole drawings.

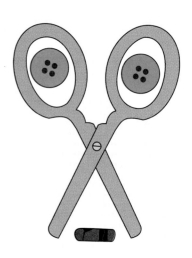

decreasing size, weight, or volume. For example, preschool children find it hard to place sticks of many different lengths in order by length.

Understanding Number Concepts. Many preschool children can count. However, counting does not show that they understand numbers. For instance, a preschool child may be able to count to five by saying the numbers in order but cannot find five apples drawn on a page. Number concepts may be hard for the child to grasp because people use many indefinite terms, such as *less, few, many,* and *some,* too.

Understanding Space Concepts.   Preschool children understand words like *up, down, left, right, under, over, here,* and *there.* However, they have problems with space concepts. They have problems knowing what is on the other side of a wall in their house until about age five. Preschool children draw what they think about space rather than what they see. Preschool children draw objects at right angles to the slope of a hill, 16-10.

Preschool children think of an object's or person's location in relation to themselves. Learning left and right from another's perspective is hard—especially if the person is facing them. Simple tasks, such as setting a table, help children grasp these concepts.

Understanding Time Concepts. Preschoolers can recall a recent past. Yesterday is recalled but a week or a year ago may be forgotten. Children link time to events, such as time to eat lunch. They cannot see time passing. There is no physical change in the days of the week. Morning, afternoon, and seasonal changes are gradual. For these reasons, time concepts are hard to understand. They are among the last concepts to develop.

Cause and Effect

Preschool children try to understand cause and effect, 16-11. Asking questions helps them to do this. Many cause and effect questions deal with natural events that may be too hard for young children to understand. Children ask questions

16-10   A preschool child often draws trees and other objects at right angles to the slope of a hill.

6

like, "What causes the rain?" and "What will happen to my dead fish?"

Although adults may give them scientific answers, these children seem to settle on their own ideas. They may believe that giants cause the rain. Children even reverse cause and effect. They

16-11   By pulling a wagon and checking on it often, this young girl is learning cause and effect in steering.

STEP 2 Corporation

1—*Activity:* Experiment with a group of preschoolers individually. Show each three groups of coins: ten pennies, two nickels, and one dime. Let each one choose which he or she wants. Remove that choice and let each choose again. Record and discuss.

2—*Activity:* Practice these indefinite terms with preschoolers individually or in small groups. Read a children's story emphasizing these terms.

4—*Discuss:* What other tasks could help them learn left and right?
5—*Discuss:* List some ways to help them learn time concepts.
6—*Activity:* Test this with preschoolers. Discuss results in class.

Barrier Free Environments, Inc., Raleigh, N.C.

6-12 Deaf children express their needs and feelings to others using sign language.

may say, "Because I am staying in bed, I am ill." Sometimes they give life and human qualities to nonhumans, such as plants, animals, and nonliving objects. For example, a preschooler may say, "My teddy bear likes my sandwich." As the child leaves the preoperational stage, he or she replaces these ideas with more mature concepts.

Language Abilities Increase

Some preschool children speak rather well. They use language to express their needs and feelings to others, 16-12. The age of three is an important time for language use.

Preschoolers' speech is as egocentric as their thinking. In other words, they talk but often do not communicate. *Egocentric speech* includes telling a story from the middle instead of the beginning. Children may also use pronouns without naming the person, such as, "She is eating."

Other types of egocentric speech include repeating words without speaking to anyone. Sometimes children talk to themselves (**monologue**) as though thinking aloud. Other times they engage in a **collective monologue** (talking to another person but not listening to what the other person has said). All children go through this stage of language development.

Egocentric speech disappears in time, making communication easier. Better articulation, a larger vocabulary, and advanced grammar also make communication easier.

1—*Resource: Fairy Tales and Children,* SAG.

2—*Discuss:* List examples of egocentric speech.

▶ Articulation of Preschool Children

Most toddlers have some problems making all the sounds in their spoken language. Most children substitute one sound for another for a period of time. In the English language children master sounds between ages three and eight. How fast preschool children master the sounds varies. However, the order in which they master them is about the same for most children. *Total mastery* means the child can articulate the sound in different positions within words. (Most sounds, but not all, are found in the beginning, middle, and end of words.) Chart 16-13 shows the sounds that most preschool children have mastered.

▶ Vocabulary of Preschool Children

Experts study vocabulary growth. They have found that children know about 900 words at age three, 1,500 words at age four, and 2,000 words at age five. Experts agree that words for concrete items (such as names for objects and people) are learned before words for abstract ideas (such as names for emotions). Also, preschool children often assign their own meanings to words. A three-year-old may use the terms *less* and *more* to mean more.

▶ Grammar of Preschool Children

Sentence structure becomes much more complex during the preschool period. During the beginning of this stage, preschool children do not seem to notice word order. Young children will respond to "Give doll the Mommy," as quickly as they do to "Give Mommy the doll." By five, children will not respond to, "Give doll the Mommy." Preschool children's use of grammar matures a great deal between ages three and five.

Grammar at Age Three

As shown in chart 16-14, three-year-olds begin to have some ideas about grammar rules. Once they learn the rules, they tend to apply them even to the exceptions. Three-year-olds may know that "ed" means past tense. Once they know the rule, they apply it to all verb forms. They may even say, "I eated." Adding "ed" to all verbs simply shows that the child has learned about this grammar rule. In time, the child will learn the exceptions to the rules.

Children may have a hard time with questions because the word order is switched. Three-year-olds use question words like *when* and *why,* but they do not switch the word order. A three-year-old may ask, "When Mary will come?"

Negatives are hardest for children. Once the child knows about negatives other than "no," they add extra negatives. Sentences like, "I don't never want no more spinach," are common at this age.

Grammar at Ages Four and Five

Four- and five-year-olds speak in longer sentences. They make their sentences longer by using clauses, conjunctions, and prepositions.

16-13   Ninety percent of all preschool children master these sounds by the given age.

Articulation Mastery of Preschool Children		
Age	**Sound**	**Word Examples**
3 years	m n p h w	monkey, hammer, broom nails, penny, lion pig, happy, cup hand, doghouse window, bowl
4 years	b k g f	boat, baby, tub cat, chicken, book girl, wagon, pig fork, telephone, knife
5 years	y ng d	yellow, onion fingers, ring dog, ladder, bed

3

4

1—*Enrich:* Research articulation of preschoolers. Report to the class.

2—*Reflect:* What actions could you take with a preschooler who constantly misuses terms like less, more, few, many, some, and none? What end results do you want to achieve with your actions?

3—*Discuss:* Do you think a primary caregiver with poor grammar would influence a preschooler's grammar? Explain.

4—*Note:* Review the list of commonly misused sounds. How do they relate to children you know?

Grammar of Three-Year-Olds	
Form Used in Speech	**Examples**
☐ The *ing* verb ending used.	☐ Rolling, falling
☐ Past tense for regular verbs (ed) used.	☐ Rolled, walked
☐ Past tense for some irregular verbs used.	☐ Sank, ate
☐ Verb "to be" used to link noun to adjective.	☐ Truck is red; I am good
☐ The *s* for making plural used.	☐ Cars, dolls
☐ The *s* for possessive used.	☐ Bob's, daddy's
☐ Articles used.	☐ A, the
☐ Prepositions referring to space used.	☐ On, in

16-14 Three-year-olds are learning many of the rules of grammar.

Instead of saying, "We played games. I had fun," the older preschool child says, "I had fun because we played games."

These children can also ask questions by switching the word order. They no longer simply put the question word at the beginning, such as "What the dog is eating?" Instead, they put the verb after the question word and say, "What is the dog eating?" By age five, many children can ask *tag questions* (questions that are asked by making a statement and then tagging on a yes or no to ask the question). An example of a tag question is, "The baby is small, yes?"

Grammar Problems

Older preschool children seem to have two problems with grammar. They have trouble with pronouns. They use objective case pronouns where subjective case is correct. The child may say, "Him and me went to town," instead of "He and I went to town." Pronouns may cause problems for children into the school years.

Children also continue to apply grammar rules to every case. They may say "eated" instead of "ate." Once the child learns the irregular form, he or she may even say "ated." A five-year-old may learn to use the plural form "feet" and ask, "May I go barefeeted?" The many irregular forms in the English language will trouble some children for years.

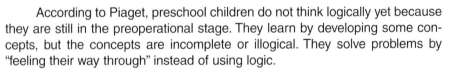

Summary

According to Piaget, preschool children do not think logically yet because they are still in the preoperational stage. They learn by developing some concepts, but the concepts are incomplete or illogical. They solve problems by "feeling their way through" instead of using logic.

Preschoolers are beginning to think in their heads rather than depend on actions. Through their new abilities, such as symbolic play, mental images, drawings, and language, they are better able to solve problems and communicate.

Children need to learn many concepts, such as size, shape, color, texture, and other qualities of objects and people. They also learn logical thinking concepts, such as classification, arranging in proper order, numbers, space, time, cause and effect, and human versus nonhuman qualities.

Age three is an important time in language development. Most children at this age are ready to express their needs and feelings to others. Communication is easier because they can now articulate better and their vocabulary has increased. Sentence structure and grammar rules tend to be difficult for many preschool children as well as older children.

1—*Activity:* Role-play this situation: a four-year-old child speaks with several grammatical errors and the caregiver responds. Do this with several groups in the class for alternative solutions.

2—*Discuss:* List other pronouns that are misused.

To Review

Write your answers on a separate sheet of paper.

1. Two children are playing together. They want to play different games. Each insists their game is best. This is an example of _____.
   a. egocentrism
   b. symbolic play
2. True or false. Preschool children tend to see the entire picture rather than concentrate on its parts.
3. True or false. It's difficult for preschoolers to subtract numbers because their concept of reversing is not fully developed.
4. A four-year-old begins a seven-hour car trip to his grandparents' home. Many times during the first hour, the child asks, "When will we get there?" The parents respond, "We will be there soon after lunchtime," thinking the statement will help their child understand. A few minutes later the child says, "Let's eat lunch." This is an example of _____.
   a. lack of ability in reversing the operation
   b. associating action without using logic
5. Complete each of the following sentences by placing the correct terms in the blanks.
   Terms
   a. symbolic play
   b. drawing
   c. mental images
   d. language
   Sentences
   _____ is a step between symbolic play and mental images.
   _____ is made up of the most abstract symbols.
   _____ are symbols stored in the mind.
   Through _____, children use ideas from their real world, dreams, and imagination.
6. Briefly describe the preschooler's ability to understand the following logical thinking concepts:
   a. classification
   b. ability to place objects in order
   c. space
   d. time
7. True or false. Preschool children tend to settle on their own ideas for answers to scientific questions.
8. True or false. Preschool children often talk to themselves.
9. True or false. Preschoolers learn words for emotions, such as love and hate, before they learn words for objects and people.

1—*Answers:* Answers to review questions can be found in the front section of this TAE.

2—*Reflect:* How could parents help a child understand this time concept?

10. Of the following sentence pairs, choose the sentence that a three-year-old is most likely to say.
   a.   "Mommy fixed my toy."
   b   "My toy was fixed by Mommy."
   a.   "I'm never going no more to your house!"
   b.   "I'm not ever going to your house again!"
   a.   "I like food. I like apples best."
   b.   "I like food, and I like apples best."

To Do

1. Watch a group of preschool children play a pretend game. What symbols were used? (Examples are material symbols, such as a block for a boat; sound symbols, such as sirens; and action symbols, such as pretending to eat.) In what ways were the symbols realistic? Discuss your findings with the class.
2. Draw or collect pictures of items that can be used in pretend play. Sort items into two groups. In one group, place purchased items that often stand for one thing in play, such as a doll. In another group place household items that can be many things in play, such as a box. Mount each group of pictures on a separate poster. Discuss with the class these two questions—
   a.   Are purchased items or household items more apt to be used in one way? Which are more likely to be used in many ways?
   b.   From which type of items do you think children mentally profit more—items that are often used in one way or items that are used in many ways?
3. Ask a preschool center director for permission to visit with children about their drawings. (Ask permission to borrow some of the drawings after the visit or to photograph them.) Ask the children to tell you about the drawings. (Say, "Tell me about your picture," rather than, "What is this?") Take notes on their responses. Using the borrowed drawings or the photos and your notes, share with the class the symbols used in the drawings. Look for ways in which the drawings were an attempt to show reality but were not visually accurate. Such ways might include being able to see four wheels as complete circles on a car.
4. Try the liquid task (as described in 16-3) with a three-year-old and a five-year-old. Discuss how people's eyes trick them. Can problems with perception arise in storing food leftovers, in packing luggage, and in other tasks? Think of examples where items are commercially packaged to look like a larger quantity. Why do some weight loss ideas suggest eating meals on smaller plates?

5. Try these logical concept tasks.
   a. Borrow a set of blocks in various colors and geometric shapes from a preschool center. Ask a three-year-old to group together blocks that are alike in some way. Repeat the task with a five-year-old. Were there differences in the ability of the children to classify blocks?
   b. Make or borrow a set of rods or dowels in different sizes. (Their lengths should vary at least 1/4 inch.) Ask children ages three, four, and five to put the sticks in order from longest to shortest. (You may show them one time.) Can the children place them in increasing or decreasing size?
6. Record the speech of preschool children in play. Listen to the tape and try to answer these questions.
   a. What sound substitutions did you hear?
   b. Did you hear complex sentences—both statements and questions? Give examples.
   c. What incorrect grammar did you hear?
   d. What concepts seemed to be correctly understood by the children? What, if any, incorrect ideas were expressed?

To Observe

1. Observe a group of three- and four-year-old children. As they play and talk, note what they do or say that shows they still do not think logically. Which concepts seem difficult for these children (time, classification, and cause and effect)?
2. Observe a group of preschoolers in a child care program. As children make up symbols, list them. Share these in class.
3. Observe a three- or four-year-old. Note errors in articulation and grammar. Compare your findings with charts 16-13 and 16-14.

To Think Critically

1. Why do adults sometimes confuse preschoolers' egocentrism with selfishness? Is there anything an adult can say or do that will help children develop a less egocentric point of view? If so, what?
2. How can a preschool teacher who has many dramatic play, art, and literature/language activities justify these as intellectual and not "just play" activities?
3. How is a collective monologue an egocentric behavior? Would selfish adults tend to engage in collective monologues? If so, how might an adult monologue differ from the definition of children's monologue?

Chapter 17

Social-Emotional Development of the Preschooler

Preschool children leave behind much of the temper tantrums of the toddler stage. They become happier and more confident, and they increase their circle of friends.

After studying this chapter, you will be able to

☐ analyze the problems preschoolers face as they develop initiative.

☐ explain the roles of adults and children in responsibility.

☐ describe how preschool children learn gender roles.

☐ discuss the growing importance of friends.

☐ describe how feelings and emotions change during the preschool years.

After studying this chapter, you will be able to define

emotional dependency
gender role learning
guilt
initiative
peers
repressed jealousy
sex typing
sexual stereotyping
siblings
stressors

Preschool children continue to relate socially with people outside the family circle. As they reach out, they learn more about themselves as individuals within adult and child social groups.

As preschoolers begin to take initiative and show responsibility, they also begin to learn to control their emotions. (**Initiative** is the ability to think or act without being urged.) They start to understand that temper tantrums and some other ways of showing feelings are not acceptable to adults. Preschoolers' emotions also become more complex as they understand more about their world.

● Developing Social Awareness

Children's social awareness grows during the preschool years. Their feelings about themselves and how they fit into social groups are beginning to emerge. They are becoming more dependable and can complete simple tasks in the home. Through better use of language and social skills, they start to make friends with other children.

▶ Taking the Initiative

Between ages three and six, children become even more independent. Because of their improved abilities and limitless energy, they have a strong desire to learn, explore, and do. These children want to experience many things. They may show never ending curiosity, talk a lot and loudly, move all the time, and even attack others to get what they want.

When children are in this stage, which Erikson calls "initiative versus guilt," they are eager to try new activities. Initiative motivates them to do so. Developing initiative is important because it sets the stage for ambitions later in life. Yet, initiative can lead to failures. Too many failures may lead to **guilt** (blaming yourself for something done wrong) and fear of trying new things, 17-1.

Erikson's Stage of Initiative versus Guilt
Basic Trust versus Basic Mistrust (year 1) **Autonomy versus Shame and Doubt** (year 2)
Initiative versus Guilt (preschool years) ☐ Preschool children have growing abilities, much energy, and desire to engage in activities. ☐ They begin trying things on their own (initiative). ☐ The sense of initiative learned at this stage leads to ambition and purpose. ☐ Too many failures and too many negative responses from adults lead to guilt and fear of trying new activities.
Industry versus Inferiority (middle childhood)

17-1 Showing initiative while avoiding guilt is a major social-emotional task of childhood.

When mistakes are made, the preschool child may feel that he or she is bad. When children feel too guilty, obedience becomes so important that they are afraid to try new things. This fear and guilt stifles initiative. To prevent guilty feelings, children must know that it's all right to make mistakes.

Children who are allowed to ask questions, experiment, and explore, develop initiative. However, this sometimes leads to actions that are dangerous or above their abilities. Adults need to step in and set limits.

▶ Showing Responsibility

During the preschool years, children often take the first steps toward becoming a dependable person, 17-2. They begin to show responsibility, a sign of being dependable. Learning to show responsibility takes time and calls for experience. Children will have many successes and failures before they learn responsibility.

3

4

1—*Reflect:* Write about three situations in which you took initiative.

2—*Reflect:* Write about a time in your life when initiative resulted in failure.

3—*Note:* Refer to the guilt versus initiative aspect of Erikson's theory.

4—*Note:* Refer to the negative aspects of permissive parenting. Emphasize the positive aspects of democratic parenting.

1

Wood Designs of Monroe, Inc.

17-2   As preschool children put their belongings in "cubbies," they are learning responsibility.

© John Shaw

17-3   Children learn to be dependable when they can help with real tasks in their world.

Adults help children become responsible by their examples and by giving children chances to learn. For this to occur, adults must select tasks the child can do. The child should have both the ability and the time to do each task. He or she also must be shown how to do tasks. Any requirements must be made clear. Adults must follow through with praise or other rewards for successes. They also must help after failures.

Preschool children are often given responsibility for household tasks, such as helping in the kitchen, putting toys away, and folding laundry. In preschool programs, children often are required to put away toys, books, and other materials. They help hand out snacks and care for plants and animals. Erikson believes children should take part in the routines of their world in real and important ways, 17-3.

▶ Learning Gender Roles

Learning about yourself is an important part of social awareness. This is because you learn how to fit into certain social groups (family, school, clubs, and others). In order to fit into any social group, people learn what is expected. *Gender*

role learning is knowing what behavior is expected of a male or a female.

Gender role is a major concept that children learn in the preschool years. Most children cannot identify whether they are a boy or girl until age two. By age three, gender role learning is beginning. They know there are physical differences between boys and girls. They are beginning to sense that boys and girls act differently in many situations.

▪ How Does Gender Role Develop?

Children learn their gender roles by how others treat them and how they see others in their male or female roles. Some families treat boys and girls differently (*sex typing*). There is a big difference in the clothing worn, toys received, and ways parents react to boys and girls. Other families do not distinguish between what a boy and girl can do, play with, or wear, 17-4.

Children most often identify with and imitate models of the same sex. They begin to think and behave as though the traits of another belong to them. They identify with and model themselves

1—*Discuss:* What other ways could you teach responsibility?

2—*Enrich:* Do research on children from birth to age five and gender roles. What environmental factors influence the development of gender roles? Report in class.

3—*Enrich:* Plan and conduct a debate on sex typing versus no sex typing.

4—*Reflect:* Do you think boys should play with dolls? Do you think girls should play with tractors? Do you think clothing should be distinguished as boys' or girls'? Explain.

17-4   Through clothing, games they play, and activities, many girls today are sex typed in a broader sense than they were in the past.

after family members. They also may model teachers and television, movie, and storybook characters.

Cultural Factors

Our society's view of male and female roles is not as clearly defined as it once was. Traditional gender roles see the male as more aggressive and the economic head of the family. The traditional gender role sees the female as the wife and mother who stays home. **Sexual stereotyping** is a statement or even a hint that men and women always do or should do certain tasks. You can find examples of sexual stereotyping in books, television shows, and in some people's conversation.

These traditional roles are changing with the increase in the number of women employed outside the home. Also, more men have been sharing household and child care duties. Some people believe that in order to thrive within today's lifestyle, roles must adapt to the situation. Both men and women may want to show assertive traits (such as sharing opinions) on the job. They both may want to show loving, gentle traits with their children.

Different cultures or groups hold different beliefs about gender roles. Some groups stress differences between male roles and female roles.

Others stress similarities between male and female roles.

▶ Extending Social Relations

Preschool children not only improve motor skills and knowledge through social activities, but they also increase their social learnings. These social learnings include sharing, controlling anger, thinking of other's feelings, and joint efforts, 17-5.

Adults Are Still Important

Preschoolers continue to depend on adults to meet many of their needs. Adults also serve as social models. They teach children by example. Besides responsibility and gender role, they also teach friendships, morals, self-control, manners, and much more.

Other Children Become More Important

Siblings (brothers and sisters) and peers are more important to preschool children than to toddlers, 17-6. (**Peers** are others near the same

17-5   Small acts of kindness grow into concern for others.

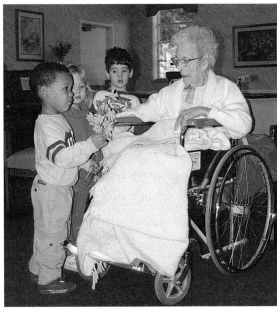

© Nancy P. Alexander

1—*Discuss:* What actions would you take if your child frequently modeled his or her negative actions after a television or storybook character?

2—*Discuss:* List and discuss examples of sexual stereotyping in children's television programs. What can a caregiver do about this influence on children?

3—*Reflect:* How do you think a child in a home where both parents work would be influenced? A child in a home where the father works and the mother stays home?

4—*Reflect:* How do the primary caregivers set the pace for the child's future?

5—*Discuss:* List benefits for both age groups.

17-6   Warm relationships with siblings are important to the preschool child.

age.) Preschool children's reactions to other children at this age are different. Some preschoolers have fun playing with other children, others do not.

Making Friends

The ease of making friends depends on a child's friendliness, ability to follow group rules, and lack of dependence on adults. Preschool children also prefer friends of the same sex, 17-7.

Preschool children have a rather self-centered view about friendships. They see friends as people who play with you, help you, and share their toys. Because of this self-centered view, usually two or three preschool children form a closed circle of friends. After all, if there are too many friends, a child may not get enough from a friend. (A toy may be shared with another child.) To protect their interests, preschool children will often call out, "You can't play with us." When a friend does not do as the child desires, feelings quickly change. Someone else becomes the child's best friend—at least for the moment.

Learnings from Play Groups

There are many learnings in the peer group. As preschoolers play together, play experiences become richer. Children get new ideas and can play games with more than one child. Children are taught how to behave with peers through group play. Peers are a society of equals. Children can simply refuse to play with a child who doesn't play fair. Children become less egocentric, or self-centered, in peer groups. They hear other children's points of view. Finally, children learn that friends are fun. A child can play with friends, sit and talk with friends, and celebrate with friends, 17-8.

17-7   Most preschool children prefer having friends of the same sex.

Carter's

1—*Reflect:* Describe a special sibling activity or relationship (your own or someone else's).

2—*Activity:* Observe children at play with peers or siblings. Note those who enjoy playing with others and those who prefer to play alone. Discuss their actions.

3—*Resource: Friends Are Important*, SAG.

4—*Resource: Learning from Play*, SAG.

5—*Resource: Observation: Children at Play*, SAG.

© John Shaw

17-8   Children enjoy having a birthday party with their friends.

Feeling and Controlling Emotions

Preschool children feel many emotions and express them in intense ways. They continue to react to the more common child-like stressors, such as adult no's, short separations from caring adults, and fear of monsters. (***Stressors*** are situations that cause stress.) Besides these stressors, preschool children will react to many more long-lasting and serious stressors. These may include illness, moving, death, adult quarrels, and divorce.

Preschool children feel many emotions and are expected to control many of their intense feelings. Controlling outward signs of emotions, such as crying, screaming, or hitting, helps children to become socially acceptable. However, if children control emotions without admitting their underlying feelings to themselves and others, they may become emotionally troubled. Children need to express feelings. Statements like, "I am angry," or, "I'm afraid you'll leave me the way you left Daddy," are healthy.

▶ Dependency

Preschool children often feel a conflict between their needs for dependence and independence. Like toddlers, three-year-olds most often show their dependency in emotional ways. ***Emotional dependency*** is the act of seeking attention, approval, comfort, and contact.

In emotional dependency, the child is often dependent only on one person. Unlike toddlers three-year-olds are more apt to accept comfort from strangers. However, three-year-olds still prefer a loved adult or a peer. By age five, children express more need for help in achieving a goal than emotional dependency. Older preschool children may ask the adult to button their coat or reach a toy off a high shelf. In most cases, the child really does need help. The child also may ask for help that is not needed. He or she may do this to check the adult's love or concern. In other words, emotional dependency is sometimes disguised as a way to earn attention and comfort.

▶ Fear and Anxiety

Many of the toddler's fears disappear by the preschool years. New fears and anxieties replace older ones. Boys often report a greater variety of fears as they grow older. Girls report more intense reactions to fears. Although fears are personal, the following are some common features of preschool fears:

☐   Fear of the known, such as vacuum cleaners, disappears. However, fear of the imagined, such as monsters and robbers, increases. Children often associate these fears with the dark.

2

3

4

1—*Reflect:* Discuss the major stressors in your life. How are these similar to those of preschoolers?

2—*Discuss:* Why is it important to encourage a child to label and discuss his or her feelings? Explain.

3—*Enrich:* Do a role play involving a caregiver and a child who constantly asks for help with tasks, even when he or she

is able to do the task. Why does the child request help? How should the caregiver react?

4—*Discuss:* What situations could cause fear of monsters and robbers?

Rebecca Lawrence

17-9   The fear of being hurt is a common emotion in the preschool years.

As you can see, these fears are due to the growing mind. Preschoolers understand many new concepts only a little. This creates fears and anxieties. A preschool child would not understand that only certain weather conditions cause tornadoes. On the positive side, some fears may help protect children from trying unsafe activities.

▶ Anger and Aggression

Anger and aggression begin around 10 months of age. They peak with displays of temper in the toddler years and continue in the preschool years. Children often use aggression to get their way or intentionally hurt another. They may even use them as a way to gain attention or affection. A little shove may be given in greeting. Of course, the child receiving such a greeting may not recognize it as a friendly sign. Fights can start from innocent behaviors.

Preschool children tend to hit or bite less and threaten or yell more. Increased language skills cause this change. However, boys tend to be more physical than girls, while girls tend to be more verbal.

☐ Fears of physical injuries become more common. Examples include the fear of death by fire, an auto accident, or drowning, and the fear of bites and stings of animals and insects, 17-9. These fears emerge as children know they can be hurt, 17-10.

☐ Fear of pain caused by medical and dental work occurs.

☐ Fear of a general nature is experienced. Children's fears grow from specific to general. For instance, fear of a tornado may spread to general fear of a thunderstorm or even a strong breeze.

17-10   Safety precautions may help lessen a preschool child's fear. Floating in an inner tube may help a child who fears water to feel more at ease in a pool.

1—*Reflect:* Provide examples when you (or a child you know) have been afraid to go to a medical or dental appointment. What helped or could have helped?

2—*Discuss:* Discuss beneficial aspects of fears.

3—*Reflect:* Why do you think boys tend to be more physical and girls tend to be more verbal? Provide two examples that prove or disprove this.

Anger and aggression seem to be directed more toward siblings and peers than toward adults. Preschool children appear to have learned that aggression toward adults, especially the physical type, is not acceptable. Also, anger and aggression are directed more at siblings and close friends than at casual peers.

Causes of Anger and Aggression

Sometimes objects cause a preschooler's anger. The child may blame a bike for a fall rather than his or her lack of skill.

Several conditions cause, or at least strengthen, anger and aggression. Having goals blocked can cause anger. One study shows that preschool children have 90 of their goals blocked each day. Preschool children who like to take charge are affected most by not getting what they want when they want it. The more carefree child often is not unhappy when goals are blocked, 17-11. This type of child simply changes the goal. If a toy is taken by another child, they find another toy.

17-11   Tears often follow feelings of anger when a goal is blocked. Adults need to be there for the upset child.

© Nancy P. Alexander

▶ Jealousy

Jealousy begins when people realize they must share with others the love, attention, possessions, and time once given only to them. Jealousy often develops when there are changes in the family.

The most common time for jealousy is when a new brother or sister is born. Now children must share their parents' love. Babies take a lot of time and energy. Children translate this as love. Children may feel there is more love for a baby and less for them.

Preschool children show fewer attachment behaviors than do toddlers, but attachment has not disappeared. In times of stress, preschool children may try to recapture the early attachment feelings. They may cry, cling, show signs of emotional dependence, and use behaviors such as toileting accidents.

Some preschool children may feel jealousy but ignore the feeling. ***Repressed jealousy*** is jealousy not directly expressed and even denied. Children may show jealousy by having nightmares or physical problems, such as upset stomachs, headaches, fevers, and change in appetite.

Unlike toddlers, preschool children are better able to understand when parents explain why, for example, the baby gets so much attention. Preschoolers are able to talk about some of their feelings. They can feel important by helping with a new baby. Preschoolers have more contacts outside the family with friends and people in preschool programs. This often makes it easier to adjust to a new family member or situation.

2

3

4

1—*Discuss:* List causes of anger in preschoolers. How do they act?

2—*Reflect:* Recall a time in your life, either past or present, when you were jealous of someone. Describe the situation, your feelings, and your actions.

3—*Discuss:* How do preschoolers act when they are jealous?

4—*Discuss:* How should a parent react to a jealous child? How should a child care teacher react to a jealous child?

Summary

Preschoolers who are allowed to try new activities develop a sense of initiative. If they have too many failures or no's from adults, they may feel guilty and fear trying new things on their own.

Adults need to help preschoolers become dependable. Gender roles are not as clearly defined as they once were. However, they are an important part of learning. Children learn gender roles by how others treat them and through their associations with others. They begin to identify with and model the thinking and behavior pattern of others. In this way, they learn family and workplace gender roles.

Preschool children increase their social learnings. They are still dependent on adults, but other children have become more important. Play experiences help preschoolers learn how to get along with others and develop friendships.

The preschoolers' emotions are becoming more complex. They want to be independent, but are still dependent on adults, especially for emotional support. Some of their old fears and anxieties have disappeared, but others have appeared. During the preschool years, anger and aggression surface. Also, family changes bring about feelings of jealousy. However, preschoolers are better able to talk out their feelings, which helps them adjust to the changes.

1

To Review

2

Write your answers on a separate sheet of paper.

1. True or false. When limits are given to preschool children, they will quit showing initiative and feel guilty.
2. True or false. When adults show preschoolers how to do something, they are teaching them about dependability and responsibility.
3. True or false. Preschoolers are too young to react to praise when they meet goals.
4. True or false. One of the best ways to teach responsibility is to have preschoolers place a mark on a checklist when they accomplish each task.
5. True or false. In gender role learning, children learn what is expected in the boy or girl role.
6. True or false. A preschool child identifies with and imitates only the father role model.

1—*Discuss:* How would a child care teacher be aware of family changes or disruptions? Is this important to know when dealing with a child? Explain your reasons.

2—*Answers:* Answers to review questions can be found in the front section of this TAE.

7. Preschool children tend to have a closed circle of friends because
    a.   too many friends overwhelm the child
    b.   children's games are usually played with only two or three children
    c.   children have an egocentric view of friendships
8. What can children learn from group play? List four learnings.
9. Which of the following fears are most common in preschool children:
    a.   loud sounds
    b.   monsters
    c.   physical injury and pain
    d.   flushing toilets and vacuum cleaners
    e.   teasing by other children
    f.   darkness
10. True or false. Anger in the preschool years is always a sign of frustration.
11. Preschool children direct their anger more at (known, unknown) children and adults.
12. True or false. Jealousy over a new baby is common.

To Do

1. Interview teachers of preschool children about how the indoor and outdoor space, equipment, and materials found in their programs do the following:
    a.   encourage children to take the initiative for their own learnings
    b.   lessen feelings of guilt about mistakes made when the initiative exceeds the child's skill
    c.   give children a way to show responsibility
2. Find some examples of sexual stereotyping in our society. Discuss how sexual stereotyping affects gender role learning.
3. Watch nursery school children at play. List some of the differences you noted in their play activities, what they talked about, and other interactions that related to their gender.
4. Draw a cartoon that shows preschool children's ideas of friendship.
5. Interview preschool children about something scary that happened to them. Have them draw a picture. Display these on a bulletin board.
6. Discuss the pros and cons of adults using fears for discipline purposes. How can adults teach dangers without starting fears in children?
7. Read about the development of phobias. Write a short report on your findings.

1—*Activity:* You may choose to write an essay.

2—*Activity:* Discuss pictures with each child, printing a few of the child's comments on the picture. This will provide a basis for parent communication.

3—*Activity:* Do you have any phobias? Describe.

To Observe

1. Observe a preschooler at home or in a group program. What tasks was the child asked to do? How did the adult explain the task? Was the child able to do it, and why or why not? Did the child seem to feel successful?

2. Observe preschoolers in a group program. What emotions were expressed? How did the adult handle the intense emotions? Did the adult help the children find more acceptable ways of expressing feelings?

1

To Think Critically

1. How have gender roles changed over the last two or three generations? Do you think learning gender roles is easier or more difficult for today's children than for children 50 or more years ago? Why?

2. How do you think preschoolers benefit from their interactions with the elderly? How do you think the elderly benefit from the interactions?

3. How might adults lessen the possibilities of jealousy in preschoolers? How can adults help preschoolers deal with their jealousies if they occur? How is uncontrolled jealousy harmful in the teen and adult years?

1—*Reflect:* What might you have done as the adult in charge? Explain.

Friends are important to preschoolers.

Chapter 18

As preschoolers grow, their physical, intellectual, and social-emotional needs change.

Providing for the Preschooler's Developmental Needs

After studying this chapter, you will be able to

☐ plan ways to meet the developmental needs of preschool children.

☐ help preschool children care for their own physical needs.

☐ stimulate preschool children's mental thinking.

☐ assist preschoolers in meeting their social and emotional needs.

After studying this chapter, you will be able to define

aggression
altruistic behavior
assertive
class
class complement
compare
contrast
convergent thinking
cooperation
divergent thinking
enuresis
passive observing
problem solving
properties
reversals
self-assertion
transformation

As you have seen, preschool children's motor, mental, and social skills develop at rapid rates. These skills help preschoolers meet their own needs. Preschoolers want to do things for themselves and for others. They like to use their motor skills to feed and dress themselves and to help with everyday tasks.

Mental thinking (as opposed to using physical actions to solve problems) is well underway in the preschool years. Preschoolers can mentally see objects and actions. They can even solve problems in mental ways. Concepts become more correct. Language helps preschoolers expand concepts. Language is also a sign of a preschooler's progress in learning concepts.

Social skills also grow in the preschool years. Preschool children's social world includes many new adults, close friends, peers, and perhaps younger siblings. Adults expect preschool children to become more independent, more responsible, and more in control of their feelings. Peers and siblings treat children more as equals. Peers do not give each other the special favors adults often do. A child will not always be given the first turn when playing with peers as he or she would when playing games with adults.

Preschool children are learning a whole way of life in which needs in one area of development affect needs in other areas. Thus, preschool children's changing physical, mental, and social needs demand a great deal of support and much time from caring adults.

● Physical Needs

Preschool children no longer completely depend on adults to meet all their physical needs. As the body matures, motor skills are refined, and the mind grows, preschoolers are better able to help care for themselves. At this age, children want to help meet their own needs. They want to help prepare meals and dress themselves, 18-1.

Children will take the initiative in learning how to meet their physical needs. However, adults must help. This is the first chance the child

© John Shaw

18-1 Children like to help make their own food and do other self-care tasks.

and adult have to work as a team and meet the child's physical needs.

▶ Meeting Nutritional Needs

To meet the preschool child's nutritional needs, adults must plan carefully. Children at this age grow at different rates. In addition, their growth and energy output varies from month to month. For preschool children, eating junk foods (foods low in nutritional value) may become more of a problem.

■ You Are What You Eat

The slogan, "You are what you eat," is correct. What you eat affects how you grow. Growth slows during the preschool years as compared to the first three years of life. However, a preschooler is not finished growing. In the preschool years, height increases about seven inches, and weight

1—*Discuss:* What signs of advances in mental thinking occur in preschoolers?

2—*Reflect:* Do you think adults often expect too much of older preschoolers? Explain your answer.

3—*Discuss:* What types of cooking activities are good for a preschooler's participation? How can children help in cooking

and meal-related activities?

4—*Note:* Relate this to autonomy and independence.

5—*Note:* Review initiative. Emphasize the importance of child-adult teamwork.

6—*Reflect:* Explain how it influences children when you eat junk food in their presence.

increases about 13 pounds. Other body systems must keep pace with skeletal growth. If the diet does not meet the body's needs, the body may conserve fuel needed for its own upkeep. This may slow the rate of growth. Children are also more prone to diseases when nutritional needs are not met. In addition, their recovery time is slower.

The preschool child is an active child, 18-2. Watch preschool children at play. Their bodies twist, turn, and bounce as they walk. Because preschool children don't sit still, their energy needs are high. Their energy must come from the foods they eat.

Proper nutrition is needed for brain growth, too. General alertness is affected by a person's daily diet. Diet also seems to affect emotions. When daily food needs are met, the child seems less irritable and restless.

Basic Food Choices

The daily basic food needs for most preschool children are given in 18-3. The menu may need to change to suit a child's growth rate, which varies from month to month. It may also need to change to suit differences in energy levels, health, and food preferences. When a child needs a special diet for health reasons, adults should consult a doctor or registered dietitian.

Children should eat snacks that provide nutrients as well as calories. Experts say children as well as adults should lessen their intake of sugar, salt, and animal fats. Why limit these items? Sugar can lead to tooth decay, obesity, and other health problems. Consuming too much animal fat and salt early in life may increase chances of high blood pressure in later years. This chance increases if high blood pressure exists in the family's health history. Snack foods are often high in sugar, salt, and animal fats.

Food Attitudes Are Learned

The food attitudes preschoolers learn may last a lifetime. Offering a variety of foods in a pleasant atmosphere helps preschoolers form good food attitudes.

Courtesy of PlayDesigns (800-327-7571)

18-2 Preschool children have high energy levels.

For the most part, people like variety in their lives. This includes what they eat. Some children and adults may go through phases where they want the same food(s) day after day for a time. Others eat or drink a few of the same foods daily but vary other foods.

There are many options within a food group. Children should be able to eat foods they like and still meet their nutritional needs, 18-3. Forcing children to eat foods they don't like can cause children negative feelings toward healthy foods, 18-4. Using food to reward or punish can also

---

1—*Discuss:* When you do not get enough to eat (or the right foods to eat), what happens to you mentally, emotionally, physically, and socially? Would children feel the same effects?

2—*Activity:* Bring to class different types of snack foods that preschoolers could consume. Analyze their nutritional value and summarize the results.

3—*Discuss:* Give examples of their high energy levels.

4—*Activity:* Divide into groups, each group studying one of the food groups. List as many options as you can for each group.

Basic Daily Diet for Preschool Children

- ☐ Bread Group — 6 servings total

- ☐ Vegetable Group — 3 servings total

- ☐ Fruit Group — 2 servings total

- ☐ Milk Group — 2 servings total

- ☐ Meat Group — 5 ounces total

18-3 Preschoolers need to eat healthful foods each day to meet their growth and energy needs. They should eat a variety of foods and may need fewer than 1,600 calories per day. The chart shows a 1,600 calorie diet. For fewer calories, preschoolers can eat smaller servings. They must, however, have the equivalent of two cups of milk a day.

18-4 Preschool children often reject foods if they feel forced to try them.

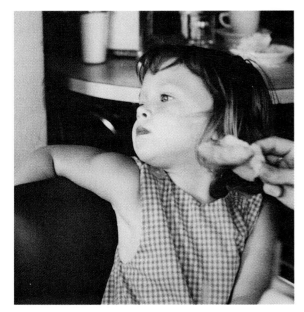

have a bad effect. (Adult: "You can't have dessert until you eat your peas!") Children who are rewarded and punished with food may learn to eat as a way of blackmail. (Child: "How many cookies do I get if I eat my peas?")

■ Preventing Eating Problems

Adults can prevent some eating problems in preschool children. Adults need to know that children and adults have different senses of taste (and smell). Many adults wonder why some children do not like spinach. There is an acid in spinach (oxalic acid) that leaves a bitter aftertaste in the mouths of children, but not adults. Children often prefer mild flavors and odors over strong flavors and odors. They do not tend to like foods that are too spicy, either. Children are influenced by other food tastes and qualities, as well.

Food That Looks Good. How food looks may influence whether children think they will like it. Children like attractive-looking foods. Foods of different sizes, shapes, colors, textures, and temperatures look better than foods that look the same. Plates should have some empty space. Full plates can give children the feeling of too much before they take one bite. (Children can have second helpings.) Children also enjoy foods prepared especially for them, 18-5. Special dishes, napkins, or centerpieces may make a good meal or snack even more special.

Separate Rather Than Combination Foods. Children often prefer foods that are eaten separately rather than foods that are combined. If children taste one food they do not like in a casserole, soup, or salad, they may reject the whole dish. They accept mixtures of fruits more easily than mixtures of vegetables. Children may eat what they choose to mix rather than adult-chosen mixtures. For instance, children may mix their own salads from several bowls of precut vegetables.

Room Temperature Foods. Children often prefer foods nearer room temperature to foods that are too hot or too cold. Most children do not care for hot drinks. Hot soups need to be cooled down,

2

3

4

1—Discuss: Compare this to adult requirements on the Food Guide Pyramid.

2—Discuss: Why shouldn't a caregiver use food as a reward or punishment?

3—Resource: Special Foods Are Fun, SAG.

4—Discuss: How does making these choices help children develop problem-solving abilities?

A

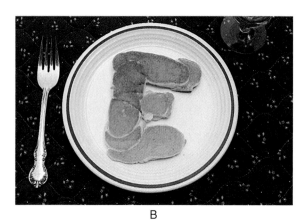

B

C   © John Shaw

18-5 Foods that look fun to eat also seem to taste better.

both for reasons of safety as well as acceptance. They eat cold foods slowly. There may be more of an ice cream cone on the outside than on the inside of a preschool child!

Foods Prepared in Different Ways. Children show likes and dislikes for ways to prepare food. A child who turns down cooked carrots may eat a crisp, raw carrot. A salad dressing or dip that is not too tangy may make almost any vegetable or fruit easy to eat.

New Foods in Small Amounts. Children will often take one bite or a small amount of a food just to see whether they like it. Give children new foods in small amounts (one slice or a tablespoon). Serve new foods with ample portions of foods children like to eat.

Easy-to-Eat Foods. Foods should be easy for preschoolers to eat. Bite-sized and finger foods are preferred over foods that are harder to eat. Most children at this age cannot cut food. They may not hold spoons and forks the right way. These problems make eating messier for preschoolers than it is for older children and adults, 18-6.

Making Meals Fun

Children enjoy helping to prepare food. By helping, children learn about colors, shapes, tastes, odors, textures, and appliance names (blender, oven). They learn food preparation terms (cut, boil, poach, bake) and food names. Cooking teaches math concepts (measurement, numbers, temperature, time, and shapes). It also introduces children to science as they see changes in foods (rising, baking, freezing, and boiling). As an added bonus, children often eat what they help prepare.

Children should enjoy eating with others. Meals should be a time to relax, share, and have fun. There should be a quiet time before and after meals. Enough time should be given for the meal itself, because eating with children takes time.

Setting an example of taking turns talking and other table manners allows children to learn at mealtimes. However, discipline

1

1—*Activity:* Ask preschoolers what foods they like to eat.

2—*Discuss:* List some ways to encourage children to eat fruits and vegetables.

3—*Discuss:* Summarize the learnings from cooking activities.

(especially punishment and scoldings) should not take place at the table. All talk should be pleasant.

An attractive room for eating helps, too. Dishes and flatware suited to the child's hands make mealtime easier and also lessens the chance of accidents. Preschool children may want to help make the table attractive by choosing the napkins, picking a flower from the garden for the table, or helping set the table.

Food becomes a part of many celebrations. Preschool children may look forward to helping prepare a special holiday dish or choosing their birthday menu. Trying different eating styles is fun, too. A restaurant, a cafeteria, a picnic, a clambake, or a cookout provides children with more food experiences, 18-7.

© Nancy P. Alexander

18-6   Preschool children still cannot hold a spoon or fork in an adult way.

18-7   Participating in a cookout can enhance a child's appetite and interest in food.

► ## Selecting the Right Clothes

Selecting the right clothes for preschool children is important. Clothes protect the child's body from harsh weather conditions and scrapes and cuts. Clothes are also important to a child's growing self-concept, 18-8.

Fit

Fit is an important feature of preschool children's clothes. Clothes must give the active child freedom to move. Fit children by size, not age. Sizes for children's clothes are often given as 1 through 6x. Hang tags and charts on children's sizes often give several measurements (chest, waist, hip, inseam, and others) rather than just height and weight. You may note some overlap of sizes such as Toddler Size 4 (4T) and Children Size 4 (4). Often the chest and waist measurements are the same in Toddler and Children sizes. However, Children sizes are often longer, and both the shoulders and back are wider than Toddler sizes. In addition to regular sizes, some clothes for children are sold in sizes to fit the slender child (called Slims or Superslims) and the heavier child (called Chubbies or Huskies).

2

3

4

1—*Discuss:* Why is soup hard for children to eat?

2—*Reflect:* How could a constant pattern of tension and yelling during meals affect a child?

3—*Note:* A plastic tablecloth or a washable rug can be placed under the high chair to catch spills. This will help eliminate tension at mealtime.

4—*Activity:* Consult the telephone book for children's restaurants. List special places you know.

© John Shaw

18-8 Cute clothes enhance the preschooler's self-concept.

Fabric and Construction Features

Preschool children's clothes must have most of the same quality fabric and construction features as toddler clothes. (Review the clothing section in chapter 14.) Preschool children grow mainly in the length of the arms and legs and the width of the shoulders. For these reasons their clothes should have the following growth features:

☐ wide hems that can be let out as arms and legs grow

☐ kimono or raglan sleeves that allow for increase in the width of the shoulders

☐ adjustable shoulder straps and waistbands that allow for both length and width increases

Also, because preschool children explore indoors and outdoors, their clothes need more safety features. Outdoor clothing worn after dark should have a trim of reflective tape that will reflect the light from cars or other vehicles. Hoods attached to coats and rainwear should easily detach if caught on large objects. (Children have suffered neck and back injuries from nondetachable hoods.) Floppy headwear can prevent children from seeing traffic or other hazards. Floppy or wide pantlegs and long shoelaces can cause tripping. Long, wide sleeves that are not gathered into a cuff; drawstring ties; long sashes and scarves; and extra large clothes are also dangerous.

Self-Dressing Features

By the end of the preschool years, many children can dress themselves with only a little help from adults. Of course, adults should always be near to help the child and to check the child's attempts. Chart 18-9 shows the features that aid self-dressing. In addition to self-dressing features in garments, special toys can help children learn to button, snap, zipper, etc., 18-10. These give children extra dressing practice.

Shoes and Socks

Most preschool children grow one shoe size every four months. By the preschool years, children may have more than one style of shoe. Along with size, check for certain features in each style, 18-11. When you buy bigger shoes, you may also need to buy bigger socks. Sock size corresponds to shoe size. Socks should be $1/2$ inch longer than the longest toe.

Clothes and Self-Concept

Preschool children are well on their way to developing a unique personality. Clothes are one way to express their personality. Preschool children show off their clothes and talk about clothes worn by others. Children may make comments about pockets or trim.

1—*Activity:* Find pictures of unsuitable preschooler's clothing. Explain to the class.

2—*Resource: Evaluating Preschoolers' Garments,* SAG.

Self-Dressing Features	
Feature	**Reasons for Feature**
☐ Large openings, especially for slipover garments.	☐ Children are not skilled in pulling clothes just right to squeeze through small openings. Children do not like (and may fear) having tight neck openings pulled over their face and ears.
☐ Easy-to-recognize fronts and backs of garments like labels, threads, or tape sewn inside.	☐ Children cannot easily hold a garment by the shoulder seams or waist to find the back and front. Children can learn to place slipover garments with the label face down before putting arms in sleeve openings. They can also learn to place the label of step-in clothes (pants and skirts) next to the body before stepping into the garment. Children may need help with wrap dresses, skirts, and jumpsuits.
☐ Front rather than back openings, such as front buttons and attached belts that hook in front.	☐ Back closures are hard for children to reach and cannot be seen.
☐ Elastic in waistbands and in sleeves (at wrist).	☐ Elastic is easier to manage than are buttons, hooks, snaps, and zippers.
☐ Easy-to-work fasteners. These include zippers with large pull tabs; smooth, flat buttons at least the size of a nickel; and shank or sew-through buttons sewn with elastic thread for a little give. Easy-to-work fasteners also include gripper snaps the size of a dime that do not fit too tightly together and "Velcro" hook and loop tape fasteners.	☐ Children do not have the small-muscle skills needed to work small, tight-fitting fasteners.

18-9   Self-dressing features help preschool children learn to dress themselves.

Preschool children should make some choices about their clothes. Perhaps they can choose the color they want from similar outfits. If the outfit is to be sewn, a child could choose between two pattern views or among a few trims. Not only will children enjoy clothes they have chosen, but they also learn to make decisions.

4

1—*Note:* A picture on the front of a garment will easily distinguish the front from the back.

2—*Note:* Elastic should be soft and stretchy for comfort.

3—*Note:* Emphasize the importance of autonomy.

4—*Activity:* Observe a group of preschool children. What themes do you notice in their dress? What special colors are common among boys? among girls?

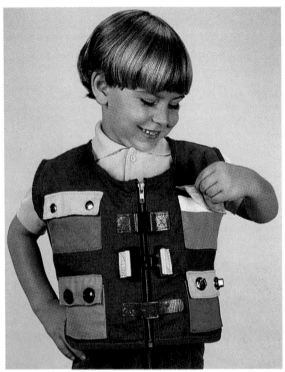

Lakeshore Learning Materials; Carson, Calif.

18-10 Many toys make learning to dress fun for preschoolers.

▶ Handling Sleep and Toileting Problems

The routines of meeting sleep and toileting needs are often in place by the end of the toddler years. Some children are still having problems in these areas. Most children will have a few problems from time to time.

Sleep needs are individual. They will even vary from time to time. Most children give up all daytime naps during the preschool years. However, they will still need 10 or more hours of sleep at night. If bedtime rules have been enforced in the toddler years, most preschool children accept them. The bedtime ritual is still wanted (and needed). Fears of the dark and monsters still exist, but many preschool children develop their own routines that help ease such stress. (Locking windows or having a doll watch over their sleep may comfort the child.)

Toileting accidents occur once in a while with most preschool children. Daytime accidents are most often caused by waiting too long to visit the bathroom. Adults may need to remind these children as well as early school age children to go to the bathroom. Remind children after

18-11 Shoe fit includes more than the right length and width.

Style and Fit for Children's Shoes	
Style	**Fitting Features**
Activity shoes	☐ Flexible soles that are 1/4-inch to 3/8-inch thick to absorb the pounding of walking, running, and jumping.
Sneakers and athletic shoes	☐ Arch support in correct position. Check fit with the socks to be worn with the shoes. The socks are often bulky, requiring larger shoes.
Sandals	☐ Adjustable straps and buckles that do not press into the foot.
Dress shoes	☐ As flexible a sole as possible. (Thin soles of dress shoes do not absorb pounding. For this reason, dress shoes should only be worn for short periods of time.)

1—*Enrich:* Look through catalogs or store advertisements to locate pictures of toys that teach self-help in dressing. Did you have any toys that taught you these skills?

2—*Note:* Fit and comfort are not necessarily determined by cost.

3—*Discuss:* What other methods have you tried to get a preschooler to go to bed?

awakening in the morning or from naps. In addition, reminding them before going outside, and before and after meals helps prevent accidents.

Time seems to be the major cure for bedtime accidents. Most children are not night trained until at least age three. Any instance of involuntary (by "accident") urination of a child over three years of age is called **enuresis**. Sometimes, people use the term to apply to bed-wetting when the child no longer has daytime accidents. There may be many causes of bedtime accidents in the late preschool years (and even in the school years). Some problems include deep sleeping, fear of getting up in a dark house, and too much liquid before bedtime. In a few cases, physical problems may be the cause. Most children outgrow these problems within a few years. For those who do not, medical or other trained help may be needed.

© John Shaw

18-12   Storage space helps when adults try to teach children to care for their own things.

▶ Providing Needed Space and Furnishings

Unlike babies and toddlers who want to be in the almost steady company of adults, preschool children want to be on their own more. Often preschool children have more toys and belongings than younger children. They need to be able to safely reach and return many of their own things. Adults must plan carefully for storage and furnishings.

Preschool children want a little space to call their own. This may be anything from one or more rooms to a chest or drawer. Even when a bedroom is shared with another child, a screen, a storage cabinet, or a curtain can divide the room. This allows some private space for times when children want or need to be alone.

▶ Learning Responsibility

Preschool children can learn self-help skills and become responsible for the care of their belongings. However, they need some storage space that is easy for them to use, 18-12. A pegboard wall with holders for equipment helps children store toys neatly and keep them in sight. A window can be flanked with storage shelves. A

window seat or desk can be used in front of the window. Strips of hook and loop tape tacked to a wall of the closet or other places can hold lightweight toys. Storage ideas are limited only by the imagination.

Plan storage so that preschool children can help themselves. Lower clothes hooks and rods for a child's use. Place often-used toys and items near where they will be used and within the child's reach. There can be some order to their clothes and toys—one that the child can understand and follow.

● Intellectual Needs

Adults must help preschool children meet their intellectual needs. As they did during the toddler years, adults direct children's attention to things to do and problems to solve. Preschool children may be enrolled in special programs. However, the home and neighborhood play groups are still the most important places for

2

1—*Discuss:* Why is it important for a preschooler to have space to call his or her own?

2—*Discuss:* List all types of storage plans that can be used for preschoolers to help them learn self-help and responsibility.

The First Years

18-13 Many learnings come from everyday tasks, such as shopping.

learning. Preschool children's mental abilities can and do develop any time and any place. Think about how much a child can learn from a simple shopping trip, 18-13. While shopping, the child can

☐ observe properties of items. (**Properties** of items describes the qualities of objects such as color, size, shape, and texture. Properties can be evaluated with the senses.)

☐ classify items (an item is found in certain types of stores, such as food in grocery stores, and in certain places in a store, such as fresh fruits in the produce section).

☐ learn number skills (you buy a certain number of items in a store)

☐ learn language skills as items are named

18-14 Observation activities help children learn to compare and contrast.

Observation Activities

Magnifying objects

Show the child a simple magnifying glass. Help the child look at a leaf, penny, fingernail, design, piece of food, or other small object. Use a pencil to point to details you want the child to see. Later, ask the child to describe the objects shown.

Alike and different

Gather pairs of objects or pictures that are exactly alike. Mix up the objects and have the child put the ones that are alike together. Books can be made where detachable pieces can be matched to those that are attached to the page.

© John Shaw

Variation: Have the child explain how some items are the same in some ways and different in others. Examples of objects to compare include a fork and a spoon, a poodle and a collie, an apple and an orange, two different hats, or two different coins.

Shape sorting

Shape sorters have holes that fit various shapes, such as square, circle, and pentagon. Have the child match an object with the hole through which it will drop. As children master simple shape sorters more advanced ones can be used.

Variation: (1) Use precut shapes of paper, plastic, or wood to make other shapes, designs, or pictures. Ask older children to name shapes and explain how they recognized each shape. (2) Cut shapes out of one-half-inch sponges. Using a clothespin, dip in tempera paint, and stamp on paper. (3) Using a pegboard and rubber bands make shapes.

1—*Note:* Talk about textures, sizes, shapes, and colors.

2—*Note:* Have the child help locate items.

3—*Note:* Practice counting as you go through the store.

▶ Learning Through Observing

Children must learn to really observe by seeing, hearing, touching, smelling, and tasting. During the preschool years, children should be able to see details. They then can **compare** (see how objects or people are alike) and **contrast** (see how objects or people are different). Games and activities can improve these skills. As an example, give a child a magnifying glass. Help the child look at a leaf, penny, fingernail, piece of food, or other small object. Use a pencil to point to details you want the child to see. Later, ask the child to describe the objects he or she saw. See 18-14 for other suggestions for observation activities.

▪ Television Viewing

Children also observe by watching television. Attractive characters, animation, movement, repetition, and many sounds used on children's television programs and many commercials cause children to observe. However, **passive observing** (attending without responding) is not the same as learning. Most television shows do not require responses from children. Even if a show encourages a child to respond, the child may not.

Children need more time to digest an idea than the few seconds a television image may provide. Caring and teaching adults are more important to children's learning than any television program. Thus, television should not be used as a baby-sitter. However, when a quality program is viewed with a sharing adult who builds on the concepts, then a learning boost will likely occur.

▶ Learning Through Problem Solving

Problem solving is a broad term. It most often includes noting a problem, observing and questioning what you see, and solving the problem. Almost from birth, babies are action problem solvers as they physically try to make items work. By the preschool years, they use mental and action problem-solving skills.

Mental problem solving depends on basic skills described in chapter 16. These basic skills are classifying; reversing; and arranging objects according to increasing or decreasing size, weight, or volume. Knowing about transformations is another basic skill. **Transformation** is the sequence of changes by which one state is changed to another. For example, a caterpillar is transformed into a butterfly. Heat transforms ice to water. Understanding transformation is logically difficult for preschool children.

4

▪ How Adults Can Help Preschoolers Solve Problems

Preschool children, especially three- and four-year-olds, find it hard to sort and classify items. Adults can help them solve these problems. Adults can help children sort any number of household items. These items could be laundry, toys, flatware, and groceries. To turn a shopping trip into a lesson, adults might say, "Lets put together all the food that came in boxes and then put all the canned food together. Now lets put the fresh fruits and vegetables together."

5

Helping Children Classify Items.   Adults can help children classify items. After showing the child small blocks that may be classified by color or shape, the adult can ask, "Are any of these alike in some way?" The child may respond by saying that some of the objects are red, smooth, or round. When the child singles out a common property, the adult might say, "Would you like to find all the round pieces and put them in this box? Then we'll put all the other blocks that are not round in the other box." When classifying items, there are only two groups. The **class** is a group of items that are alike in some way. The **class complement** is all those that do not belong to the class. See 18-15 for other sorting and classifying activities.

Helping Children Put Items in Order.   Preschool children have trouble putting items in order. Many activities can help children with this concept Children may line up from shortest to

1—*Resource: Planned Observation Activities for Preschoolers,* SAG.

2—*Discuss:* Describe a child who is engaged in passive learning. How is it different from active learning?

3—*Reflect:* Watch a television program with a preschooler. What could you discuss? Why would this be more beneficial

than having the preschooler watch alone?

4—*Activity:* Read a book to the class, such as "The Very Hungry Caterpillar." Discuss what this book teaches.

5—*Discuss:* How can children learn about sorting and classifying from a shopping trip? How could the trip help to develop self-help skills?

Sorting and Classifying Activities

Button sort
Use an egg carton or other sectioned container, and sort buttons into three or more groups. You may have the child sort according to color, size, way sewn on, or shape. (Buttons can be sorted using pieces of paper or boxes if sectioned containers are not handy.)

Variation: Sort many other objects for fun and even as a household task. Flatware, laundry, toys, and groceries can all be sorted.

Make a book
Children can cut or tear pictures from newspapers, catalogs, and magazines. The pictures can be mounted by groups, such as fruit, cars, dogs, and toys. (The child should decide on the groups.)

Does it belong?
After the child can easily classify, bring out another object and put it with the class. Ask the child, "Does this belong?" The child should explain why it does or does not belong.

© John Shaw

18-15 Sorting and classifying activities enhance children's problem-solving skills.

18-16 After looking at a book, preschoolers often enjoy telling the events in order.

Fisher-Price, Inc.

tallest or from tallest to shortest. The keys on the piano are ordered by pitch from high to low or low to high. Children can see and hear this. In retelling a story, events must be put in order, 18-16. The number system is a series.

Adults can help preschoolers learn to put items in order through games and activities. However, they should keep two points in mind. First, restrict the number of items to be put in order to five or fewer. Second, make the differences in the items easy to notice. As an activity, adults could read to children about the fabled Three Bears. After reading the story, talk about the sizes of each bear, their chairs, beds, etc. See 18-17 for other activities.

Helping Children with Reversals. Before the child can mentally handle *reversals* (mentally doing and undoing an action), they need to perform some physical reversals. Reversals must be

1—*Activity:* Read a story to a preschooler and ask him or her to retell the story.

2—*Activity:* Read "The Three Bears" (or another story with size gradations) to a group of preschoolers. Discuss the story with the group after reading, emphasizing sizes of the bears and other objects in the story.

Activities for Putting Objects in Order

Make yourself little
Help a child act out different sizes with his or her body. Show how to make yourself little (by crouching down), bigger (by standing), and biggest (by stretching).

Little, bigger, biggest
Gather three boxes—one small, one large, and one even larger. Place the boxes in front of the child so that the smallest box is to the child's left, the medium box is in front of the child, and the largest box is to the child's right. Ask the child to find the little box, then the bigger box, then the biggest. If the child makes a mistake and does not correct it, try nesting the boxes to compare sizes for him or her. To vary the game, you may reverse the box order or use four or five boxes that vary in size.

The Three Billy Goats Gruff
Read this story to a child. A copy with illustrations will help the child better see the sizes of the goats. After reading the story, talk about the sizes of the goats that crossed the bridge.

Ordering blocks
Cover three blocks of wood with different grades of sandpaper. Have the child put the blocks in order from least rough to roughest by rubbing them. Then ask the child to put the blocks in order using only sight. For a variation, the child may stack items in order of weight and size.

18-17   These activities enhance children's concepts of order.

experienced—not taught. An example might be letting the child pour water from one container into a different size container, 18-18. See 18-19 for other reversal activities.

Helping Children with Transformation.   As a transformation activity, the adult and child could look in the family photo album or other pictures of the child. Point out the changes in size, hair length, and motor skill abilities like sitting, crawling, standing, and running. See 18-20 for other transformation activities.

▶ Learning Through Symbolizing

Intellectual needs also are met as the child begins to think in terms of symbols or signs. There are a number of ways children think in these terms.

The way in which children pretend is a form of symbolism. Through play children take on the representation of another person or object, 18-21. They need many chances to

18-18   Children learn reversal skills through their play activities.

© John Shaw

1—*Activity:* Try some of these activities with preschoolers. Report to the class.

2—*Resource: Problem-Solving Games: A Step Toward Logic,* SAG.

Reversal Activities

Tower of blocks

Help a child build a tower with blocks. Have the child take the stack of blocks down, one by one, to reverse the order of building.

Lacing cards

Make or buy lacing cards. To make one, draw a picture on cardboard, then punch holes in the cardboard over the outline. Use a shoestring to lace through the holes and create the picture's outline. Children can lace, undo, and relace the card.

Water and sand play

Gather two containers of different sizes and put some water in one. Let the child pour the water from one container into the other and then back. To vary the game, use sand.

18-19   These activities help teach children about reversals.

pretend to be other people and objects. Many children begin pretending around their first birthday, but pretending does not reach a peak until the preschool years.

For the most part, children need only a little help in pretending. For example, adults can have the child pretend to be any person or thing. If they suggest an underwater diver, they may see the preschooler putting on their pretend deep sea fish-ing outfit. Soon they will be diving after lost treasures, being careful not to be attacked by sharks.

■ **Using Symbols in Art**

Children use symbols when they paint, color, or do other art work. Younger children make their art products first and then sometimes decide what they represent. As children mature, the idea comes before the product is made. As is true of all

18-20   These activities help children grasp the concept of transformation.

Transformation Activities

Growing plants

Help a child plant a fast-growing seed, such as a bean. You also may put a sweet potato in water. Look at it each day. Talk about the changes you see. Taking pictures also can help the child see the progress.

I am growing

Look at the family photo album or other pictures of the child. Point out changes in size, hair length, and motor-skill abilities like sitting and standing.

Cooking

Ask the child to help you cook. Point out changes that happen. Baked goods increase in size in the oven. Liquids freeze to make ice. Gelatin liquids become firm. Sugar dissolves. Eggs boil and become firm.

Making new colors

Gather paints, crayons, or colored water. Show a child how to make a new color by combining two different ones. Let the child combine different colors.

1—*Activity:* Try some of these activities with preschoolers. Report to the class.

2—*Activity:* Try some of these activities with preschoolers. Report to the class.

3—*Reflect:* Describe pretend activities that you have experienced with preschoolers. What are some new pretend activities that you could try? Do these activities differ for different children? Explain.

Helping Children through Symbolizing

I'm a monster!
Begin by asking the child, "How do you think monsters look? How do you think they move? What sounds do you think they make? Show me." (Pretending to be a monster may help children overcome the fear of monsters.)
Variation: Have the child pretend to be any person or thing.

Pantomime
Have the child act out an action. The adult may suggest one, or the child may choose one. Have others try to guess what the action is.

Ballet
Ballet is acting out a story or idea through dance. Play some music and let the children act out something in the form of dance. The child can choose what to be and how to dance it. You may need to give a few ideas to get the child started.

18-21 These activities help meet children's intellectual needs.

representations, the child decides on the symbol, not the adult.

Using objects such as building blocks, clay pieces, dolls, and many other objects to represent who or what they want is a form of symbolism. Children's play materials may or may not be like the real world, but they symbolize the real world for them, 18-22.

Using Symbols in Language

Spoken words are the main kinds of abstract symbols. One of the issues of early childhood education is whether children should be taught to read and do simple math problems at an early age. Many experts feel most preschool children need more time to deal with their world using less abstract forms of symbols. They question early reading and math for these reasons.

☐ Young children must arrive at their own meanings and develop their own skills. Repeating without meaning is not real

learning. Adults need to provide materials, ask questions, and present problems for children to solve.

☐ Problem solving in the real world gives a practical reason for learning. By setting the table, the child may see the need for counting forks. However, the child may not see the need to count objects in a picture shown by an adult.

3

☐ **Divergent thinking** (coming up with different possible ideas) is more often developed through rich, everyday experiences. On the other hand, **convergent thinking** (coming up with only one right answer or way to do a task) is more often seen in formal lessons. Answers to many of life's problems require divergent minds.

☐ Children need time to deal with their real world.

☐ Some children feel stress as a result of formal lessons. If young children see learning as fun, this attitude may carry over to the years ahead.

4

18-22 Children use play materials to symbolize their real world.

Fisher-Price, Inc.

1—*Activity:* Try some of these activities with preschoolers. Report to the class.
2—*Resource: Observation: Let's Pretend,* SAG.

3—*Note:* Emphasize the importance of practical problem-solving activities.

4—*Discuss:* Why would a child become stressed if he or she was instructed in reading or math too early?

Gross-Motor Games
Getting objects While the baby is watching, roll or move any toy or safe object out of the baby's reach. Encourage the baby to get the object. As the baby's motor skills improve, increase the distance between the baby and the object.
Knock off the toy When a baby can stand by holding on to a playpen or crib railing, place a stuffed toy on the railing. Encourage the baby to hold on to the railing with one hand and knock the toy off with the other.
Splashing in water Splashing in a tub or pool helps the baby improve motor skills. Adults must watch babies at all times when children are in or near the water. The adult can hold the baby and encourage the baby to splash and kick.
Cartons Place a large carton on its side so the baby can crawl into it. Let the baby crawl in and out of the carton.

18-23 Gross-motor games promote children's physical skills.

18-24 Puzzles and other small objects help children develop fine-motor skills.

© Nancy P. Alexander

Unless the child sees the mental link between a real object and its symbol (such as a real cat and the word *cat)*, the symbol means nothing. When learning is meaningless (and too difficult), it is stressful, not fun.

▶ Learning Through Motor Skills

As children move and do things, they not only become more skillful in physical ways but in mental ways. Children learn as they move their bodies in space. They learn as they do things with their hands.

Because preschool children are in almost constant motion, they learn many gross-motor skills through play and play activities. However, a few planned activities may be fun and help mental development as well. For example, adults can help children plan an obstacle course of tables, chairs, and sturdy boxes. Have the child go under, around, through, and/or on top of the obstacles. Other suggestions for games and activities that promote gross-motor skills are found in 18-23.

Fine-motor skills should be enjoyed, too. Some of the best items are art materials, puzzles, small wooden beads to string, pegboards, and lacing cards. Small construction toys, such as plastic snap-together blocks and other building materials, also promote fine-motor skills, 18-24.

1—*Activity: Try some of these activities with preschoolers. Report to the class.*

2—*Resource: Vocabulary Grows from Everyday Activities,* SAG.

3—*Discuss:* How would this obstacle course help a child learn vocabulary?

Courtesy of Kimberly-Clark

18-25   Looking through a window screen on a quiet, rainy day gives preschool children time to talk with their mother.

▶ Learning Through Language

Preschool children learn language from what they hear—the articulation of sounds, vocabulary, and grammar. For this reason, adults must be the best language models they can be.

Preschool children need many daily chances to talk with adults and older children, 18-25. When preschool children play only with age mates or younger children, they do not learn as quickly as they do by talking with adults. For this reason, only and firstborn children are often better in language than younger siblings.

Language needs to be a part of all activities. When it is used only to give orders, language learnings are not expanded. When activities and speech are combined, children's concepts and skills grow.

▨ Television and Reading

Adults should limit the amount of television children watch. Although children can hear speech on television programs, it is one-way speech. This is because the child hears but does not respond. Children's shows that urge children

to respond ask for one- or two-word responses. Studies show that children who watch less than five hours of television per week do much better in school. (Some children watch five or more hours per day.)

Reading to children every day increases language learnings. Books take us beyond the day-to-day world. Reading helps to expand concepts. It also helps children see books and reading as important.

● Social-Emotional Needs

During the preschool years, children's personalities seem to blossom and become more stable, 18-26. Preschoolers begin to learn more about themselves. Questions, such as "Who am I?" and "What can I do on my own?" are more fully answered in the preschool years. Through successes and mistakes, preschoolers test their skills. They begin to see themselves as boys or girls with role differences.

1—Reflect: Do you learn better when an action or activity accompanies a lecture? Give an example. How does this relate to preschoolers?

2—Discuss: What are advantages of reading to children? Discuss in terms of all areas of development.

1

Adults need to meet the social-emotional needs of preschool children. Lots of reasons for limits or requirements must be given and often repeated. Firmness and fairness must be the adult's rule if the child's self-concept is to remain healthy.

▶ Discipline: Helping with Initiative and Mistakes

Preschool children define themselves in terms of what they can do. In order to find out what they can do, almost all children try many activities. (In other words, they show initiative.) Active preschool children are curious. They do many things on impulse without thinking about the results of their actions. In trying new things, preschool children go beyond their abilities and make mistakes. These mistakes are self-defeating because preschool children see almost everything as within their control. Too many mistakes may bring on guilt.

2

When children are successful, they need to hear positive statements from adults. Children need adults to tell them what they are like. This gives children a feeling of self-worth.

Children learn more by their own attempts than by having adults do for them or tell them what to do. Preschoolers learn from both suc-

cesses and mistakes. Thus, children must be given some freedom to try. Adults must accept the fact that children will try things even when told no. Some preschool children decide the pleasure of doing something is worth the punishment. Children can even dream up new activities not presently covered by the rules.

◻ Limits

Preschool children should be given reasonable limits. They need limits for safety purposes and to prepare them for the real world. These rules should be spelled out. When children fail to obey, they need to be disciplined in a loving, yet firm, way.

◻ Honest Communication

Parents and other adults need to communicate honestly when guiding and disciplining children. Being honest helps children build trusting relationships. It also helps children realize they should be truthful.

Children need to be aware that adults, too, make mistakes. Children learn this when they hear adults say, "I goofed!" or "I'm sorry." They begin to understand that all people make mistakes. They also start to see that making mistakes doesn't make them bad.

▶ Sharing Responsibility

Preschool children see tasks as new skills to learn, fun, and a way to please others, 18-27. Adults can help them become more dependable and able to handle more responsibilities.

Some adults offer few, if any, opportunities for children to help. These adults may see preschool children as not having the desire to help. The child may stop in the middle of a task to play. Perhaps the adult thinks children lack the ability. The child may break a dish. A few adults think of children as servants who should perform tasks upon demand and to adult standards. Most,

18-26 Laughter and looks of confidence are signs of a healthy self-concept in preschoolers.

© Nancy P. Alexander

1—*Reflect:* Describe the importance of firmness and fairness in your life. Why is this especially important to a child?

2—*Enrich:* Tomi is a curious five-year-old who likes to do tasks on his own. While you are on the phone, he climbs onto the kitchen cabinet to reach a box of cereal. On his way down he breaks his mother's favorite vase. Give him a posi-

tive statement, but at the same time discourage him from doing something like this again.

3—*Enrich:* Role-play a situation in which a caregiver has to discipline a preschooler. Make sure you discipline in a loving and firm way as well as teach him or her that this is not acceptable behavior.

4—*Reflect:* Describe a situation in which you learned honesty through modeling.

5—*Note:* Emphasize that it is important for adults to laugh at themselves when they make mistakes, but to tell children they did something wrong and will not do it again.

Courtesy of Park Seed Company

18-27   Helping others is a fun way to learn and to please.

however, agree that family life and school life are made better when both adults and children help each other.

The following suggestions will help children share responsibility:

☐ children may suggest tasks but adults must decide which tasks are safe and within children's grasp, 18-28

☐ physical conditions should help children perform tasks. Low hooks or clothes rods, a place for each item, and a sturdy stool for reaching a cabinet are examples of helps.

☐ adults can talk about tasks planned for the day, and they can tell children what they should do. Young preschoolers often help the adult do a task, but five-year-olds can work alone on some tasks.

☐ adults should not expect perfection. The finished task should remain as it is, or the task can be explained again for the child to do over. (When adults redo tasks, children feel failure.)

☐ adults can make some tasks seem more fun by creating a game. Blocks can be hauled to the "lumber yard" (the shelf).

☐ at times, adults should respect children's priorities. There may be no harm in letting a child do a job 10 minutes later.

Children need to be rewarded for tasks completed. Adults must decide whether work is done for love only (and thus should not involve pay) or work should have pay (with money or other wants fulfilled). Some adults compromise on this issue. They expect certain jobs to be done without pay. Then they may consider other jobs—those elected by the child—to be beyond the call of duty. The extra jobs may involve pay. Whether adults pay or do not pay, children need to be thanked and skills need to be praised.

3

18-28   A child should be given a pet to care for only if the parent thinks the child can handle the responsibility.

© John Shaw

1—*Reflect:* How do you feel when you help someone?

2—*Reflect:* Describe a situation in which you have worked together with an adult to perform a task. How did you help each other? Did you accomplish more by working together?

3—*Resource: Helping with Tasks,* SAG.

© John Shaw

18-29 Toys or books on careers help children think about what they want to be when they grow up.

▶ Aiding Gender Role Learning

Due to changes in our society today, many parents and other adults are questioning the more rigid gender roles of the past. As is true with all personal priorities, parents need to be informed about the issues and make decisions. How adults feel about gender roles are made known to children in many ways. The roles adults allow or encourage their children to try and the day-to-day attitudes adults convey all affect children.

Preschool children learn their gender roles mainly through observing adults of the same sex. They learn as they help their same-sex parent with household tasks and with errands. Seeing parents and other adults at work also shows children adult gender roles. Toys and books related to jobs allow children to learn about many gender roles, 18-29.

▶ Providing Time for Friendships

Living in a social world involves balancing between **self-assertion** (insisting on one's rights) and **cooperation** (joint effort). Because preschool children must learn to see from another person's point of view, the balance between a child's will and the wills of others takes a long time, often years.

Seeing differences in people helps children learn to see from another's point of view. The process begins in the infant and toddler years. At this time, children expand their social world beyond parents to include other family members. Friendships with peers help children see even more differences in people, 18-30. Friction, which almost always occurs in play groups, shows children in a direct way that others see

18-30 Friendships help children really understand others.

© Nancy P. Alexander

1—*Discuss:* How does creative play help a child investigate careers?

2—*Discuss:* What are some ways you could help a child learn a variety of gender roles? Do you think this would confuse the child? Discuss your reasons.

3—*Discuss:* Why is it important for a child to learn both self-assertion and cooperation? How can this learning help the child in future years?

4—*Discuss:* What are some skills that children learn through friendships?

issues in different ways. In peer groups, children also witness **altruistic behavior** (concern for others). This helps children learn that others are important, too.

Friendship is a way to learn from others. Preschool children's ideas are expanded through play. In play groups children also have fun times, which are an important part of their lives, 18-31.

Helping Children's Social Relations

Adults can help children's social relations by giving them time to play with friends. These friends may be neighborhood playmates. They also may be friends from church, preschool, or special interest groups (such as swimming or dance class). Adults should allow children to interact with each other and not interfere with little conflicts (except for safety reasons).

Reducing Conflicts

Adults can reduce the conflicts of preschoolers in these ways:

☐ Teach children that they do not always have to share, any more than adults do. Sometimes adults expect children to share all their toys, even with casual friends. Adults are not expected to share all their belongings with even close friends.

☐ Model concern for the hurt rather than shame the person doing the wrong. Children learn more when adults show real concern for the hurt or wronged child while ignoring the child who was in the wrong. They see that care is given to children who are harmed.

☐ Explain feelings of both children wanting the same toy or wanting to do the same thing. Often toys are given up rather quickly when the adult says, "Maria needs to play with the car for a little while, but when she's ready to give it up she'll let you know."

▶ Helping Children with Emotional Control

Emotions are intense in the preschool years. The growing minds of preschool children broaden their emotions. They also help children control how they express their emotions. People cannot control feelings. They must, however, learn to control how they express feelings. Better control of expression is a major task of the preschool years.

Adults can help children control how they express feelings by setting an example. Children imitate control, or the lack of control, seen in adults. They also imitate other children and television and movie roles.

Adults need to explain to children that it is all right to feel sad, angry, hurt, and happy. They should also tell children it is all right to express some emotions. ("It is all right to cry when we feel sad." "We laugh when we're happy." You should tell Tabitha, "It makes me mad when you take my toys. Give them back.") However, children need to hear that people must not hurt others even when they are wronged. ("Hitting hurts," or "You make others feel sad when you call them names.") Adults should talk about how all people have to work to control their feelings. There are many books on this topic, 18-32.

18-31   Through play, these children are expanding their ideas about Mardi Gras celebration.

1—*Discuss:* How can you teach a child altruistic behavior?

2—*Example:* "Sophia, you could put away your new doll when Aaron comes, but can you help me decide which toys we will leave out for you to share with him?"

3—*Example:* "I can see you are upset that Charlie kicked your leg. Let's look at your leg and see if I can do something that will make it feel better."

4—*Example:* "Jose is our guest today, and he would like to ride your tricycle for a while. Could he ride your bike, and when he gets ready to play with something else you can have it back?"

5—*Enrich:* Practice using "I" statements with a partner. Develop an "I" statement for a situation with a preschooler. Report to the class.

© John Shaw

18-32 Preschool children can get ideas from books about how to express their feelings in more positive ways.

Dependency

Knowing when and how to help preschoolers can be hard. Preschool children need to become more independent. Other times they do not want to let go of help from adults. Sometimes they are not able to handle tasks on their own. Other times they do not want or need the help adults offer.

Adults can help by loving and respecting children. This gives children a secure base from which to try things on their own. When children ask for help, adults should be willing to help. Adults need to judge how much help children need. (Adults must avoid being too helpful or protective.) Physically arrange the house with low hooks, stools, and other aids that make tasks more manageable for children. Adults should plan tasks for preschoolers that are within their abilities. Children need praise when they try tasks on their own.

Fear and Anxiety

Some fear and anxiety helps protect people. However, too much may be harmful. The following ideas may help keep children's fears and anxieties in check:

☐ Accept the expressed fears and anxieties of children. (Never make fun of them.)

☐ Assure children that you will help keep them safe. (Never threaten to leave a child, even in a playful way.)

☐ Model courage. Children learn fears from adults.

☐ Handle one fear at a time. Repeat reasons why children should not be afraid. Small steps taken slowly in dealing with fears and anxieties may help.

☐ See a doctor if fears seem too prolonged or too intense.

Anger and Aggression

Handling children's anger and aggression is not only draining but often stirs up angry feelings in adults. Adults should note the difference in anger (a feeling) and *aggression* (an attempt to hurt or an act of hurting someone). They should not try to stop anger in children. Instead, they need to help children try to manage anger in ways other than aggression. Look for reasons why the child feels angry. Does the child want attention? Is he or she frustrated in reaching a goal? Is he or she looking for revenge? Understanding motives makes finding ways to manage anger easier.

Competitive situations between peers should be reduced. Enough toys should be supplied so that children do not have to wait too long for a turn, 18-33. Play should be de-escalated. Some games that begin on a rather low key become aggressive. Other games can calm children or encourage cooperation. Watch peer play groups closely. Adults can stop aggression before it occurs (and the child gets some satisfaction from the act). If children need discipline, adults should punish them in nonphysical ways. However, a child should know when adults disapprove of aggressive acts. Likewise, adults need to praise cooperation.

Spanking. Studies show that punishment by aggression (spanking), especially for a child's aggressive act, increases aggression in preschool children. Spanking increases the

---

1—*Note:* Emphasize that even if the adult is busy it is important to help and cooperate with the child. It may mean rearranging a schedule.

2—*Example:* "I see you are afraid of my dog. Let's play with this stuffed dog and see how soft he is. We can read this dog a story. Then we can take the stuffed dog outside to see my dog in the cage."

3—*Enrich:* Use the dictionary for definitions of anger and aggression. Give some examples of actions that could occur for each. Why should a caregiver avoid stopping anger but should stop aggression?

4—*Discuss:* How can understanding that the child wants attention help you deal with the anger?

5—*Discuss:* Why does it work better to praise cooperation than to punish aggression?

child's anger. This produces a negative, aggressive response from the child. Furthermore, adults are serving as models of aggression—the exact behavior they wish to stop.

Modeling Aggression.   Children see aggression modeled in many ways including adults' acts, peers' acts, and television programs. All studies show that children learn to be more aggressive by example.

Even letting a child hit a pillow or kick a tree trunk sends the message that aggression is all right. Instead, teach children that it is all right to feel angry, but acts of anger must be controlled.

Society tries to teach an attitude of being ***assertive*** (speaking out, standing up for your rights, and defending yourself), but not being hurtful to others. Trying to find the line between assertiveness and aggression can be most difficult for preschool children. (It can even be difficult for adults at times.) Because of this, preschoolers may act in an aggressive way when they are trying to be assertive.

4

Jealousy over a New Baby
Preschool children need help in accepting a new baby. Parents should tell the child about the new baby before the event. They should sound

18-33   If preschoolers have enough to do and plenty of space, acts of aggression are reduced.

© Nancy P. Alexander

1—*Enrich:* Do research on spanking. Have students read different books and articles and summarize their opinions and reasons. Report to the class.

2—*Reflect:* Do you believe in spanking a child? Why or why not?

3—*Note:* Emphasize the difference between the feeling and the act.

4—*Reflect:* How can you teach a child to be assertive without being aggressive?

pleased, but not overly excited, because children may think new babies are more important than they are.

The new baby should be described in realistic ways in terms of the work involved and other facts. Some preschool children are led to believe that the new baby will be an instant, able playmate. If possible, seeing a friend's new baby can help. The child should be involved in plans for the new baby.

Preschool children seem to be happier when they can stay in their own home or near their own home and visit their mother in the hospital (even by telephone or closed circuit television). They do not prefer to be sent to stay with friends or relatives for several days. (A preschool child can imagine only so much, and separations from loved ones are always difficult.)

When the Baby Arrives. Older children need time alone with parents after the new baby arrives. A little time spent with a preschool child says, "I love you, too." Showering an older child with gifts does not make up for time and may be seen as a bribe.

Older children should be allowed to help with the new baby. Adults should sincerely thank those extra feet and hands that help so much, 18-34. However, adults should avoid talking about how grown up older children are. Older children may want to be babies at times. Some children enjoy pretending to care for a baby with a doll. Preschoolers enjoy being told or shown with photos how they were once cared for in the same ways.

© John Shaw

18-34 There are many ways in which an older child can help with a new baby.

● Recognizing Developmental Delays

Preschool children with delays may show some of the behaviors of toddlers as listed in Chapter 14. Because preschoolers are becoming more social, these behaviors as well as gross and fine motor skills and language are observed. If preschool children are attending child care or preschool programs, their teachers are often good judges of developmental delays. Parents should consult with preschool teachers on a regular basis and also observe their own children "working" and playing with other children of the same age. Knowing some typical preschool behaviors may help parents identify delays and bring their concerns to experts, 18-35.

Typical Preschooler Behaviors	
Age	**Behavior**
Three years	Walks up stairs Stands a second on one foot Rides tricycle Opens a door Verbalizes the need to use a toilet Feeds self
Four years	Hops in place (no real forward movement) Throws ball Catches bounced ball Copies circle Knows colors (red, yellow, blue, orange, green, purple) Uses simple sentences with "heard" grammar Washes hands without help Plays with other children
Five years	Walks backward heel-toe Runs on tiptoe Recognizes his or her own printed name Tries to write a few letters Begins to cut foods with a table knife Recognizes some coins Answers greetings ("Hi" or "How are you?") Draws rectangles and triangles Laces shoe

18-35   Knowing what typical preschooler behaviors are can help to recognize developmental delays.

Summary

Preschool children are active and need to eat nutritious meals and snacks. They learn attitudes about food likes and dislikes from others. Preschool children like food that is easy to eat and looks attractive.

Clothing must fit properly and allow room for the child to move and grow. When selecting clothing for children, adults should look for safety features and those that promote self-dressing. Adults should allow preschool children to make some choices about their clothes.

Bedtime rules and rituals continue to be important. Toileting accidents sometimes occur. Children need to be reminded at times to use the bathroom.

Preschoolers need some space to call their own. Their area should feature storage space that is easy for them to use.

Adults need to offer opportunities for children to learn. They need to provide materials, encourage observation, and present problems for children to solve.

When guiding and disciplining preschoolers, adults must set limits. When children fail to obey the rules, reasonable actions by a loving, but firm, adult should be taken.

Adults should give children responsibilities that suit their age and ability. They need to be rewarded for completing their responsibilities.

Children learn gender roles at this age. Books and toys help children have a wider view of gender roles in various work situations.

Adults should see that children have friends to play with and not interfere with their small conflicts. By playing with others, children learn different points of view and ways that others think and behave.

When children have fears and anxieties, adults should never make fun of them. Modeling courage and handling one fear at a time is helpful.

Adults can teach children about anger and control. Adults also need to help children learn how to express their feelings without hurting others.

Jealousy over a new baby can be lessened if the preschool child is prepared in advance. Spending time alone with the preschool child and having the child help with the baby will ease feelings of jealousy.

To Review

Write your answers on a separate sheet of paper.

1

1. Which statements are true about a preschool child's diet? (You may choose more than one.)
    a.   The preschool child has a steady growth pattern and the same food needs from month to month.
    b.   The preschool child needs food to meet his or her high energy output.
    c.   Eating junk food can be more of a problem for preschool children than for toddlers.
    d.   Preschool children should be told to eat their vegetables or give up their dessert because vegetables are good for them.
    e.   Preschool children and adults like foods prepared and served the same way.
2. True or false. Forcing children to eat a food they don't like does little or nothing to help them learn to like that food.
3. Garments should have the following features that allow for growth:
    a.   short zippers
    b.   narrow hems
    c.   raglan sleeves
    d.   wide shoulders
    e.   adjustable shoulder straps
4. What clothing features could cause accidents? List three.
5. True or false. By the end of the preschool years, children can dress themselves with little help from adults.

6. When shopping for children's clothing, which features would best encourage self-dressing? Choose one or more features that help children dress themselves.
   a. "Velcro" hook and loop fasteners
   b. garments that are close to the neck and pull over the head
   c. zippers with large pull tabs
   d. pictures or designs marking the back or front
   e. back openings
   f. elastic waistbands
7. List two ways adults can help children have fewer toileting accidents.
8. True or false. Preschool children are too old to learn through motor games.
9. The best resources to help preschoolers learn language skills are (other children, adults).
10. Adults (should, should not) redo tasks that preschool children have done below their standards.
11. List two things that adults can do to make children's mistakes less self-defeating.
12. True or false. Gender roles are learned mainly by example.
13. Describe two ways to reduce conflict among preschoolers.
14. True or false. The way adults control their emotions does not affect children's emotional control.

To Do

1. Name some examples of junk foods. (Read the ingredients listed.) Why are these foods called junk foods? Using chart 18-3 as a guide, plan several nutritious snacks.
2. Borrow some clothes designed for preschool children from department stores or from parents. Examine each garment for self-help features listed in 18-9.
3. Visit some homes that have bedrooms and/or playrooms designed for preschool children. (Or look at rooms in furniture stores or magazines.) How was storage planned? How did the design meet the child's desire to be more independent through self-help?
4. Make or gather the materials for one or more of the examples of planned activities for children. Use the planned activity while baby-sitting or as a helper in a child care program. Discuss with your class what did or did not work and possible reasons.
5. Think of some ordinary events or objects, such as Halloween costumes; a tall slide; and a large, playful dog. Describe how the situation may appear to a preschool child.
6. Read about phobias and discuss the readings. How can adults teach dangers without making children fearful?

7. Role-play a situation in which a child is angry and hits a friend. Have one person be an adult who is supervising the children. Discuss some good discipline methods.

8. Interview several parents about how their older children showed jealousy toward a new sibling. How did the parents handle the jealousy?

9. Discuss how an older child must feel when a parent makes these types of statements about a new baby.
    a. "We got this baby just for you."
    b. "You'll have so much fun with your brother (or sister)."
    c. "Look, _____ (name of baby) loves you."
    d. "_____ (name of baby) brought you this gift."
    e. "We expect you to be our big boy (or girl) now."

To Observe

1. Observe preschoolers in a child care program eating lunch or a snack. What foods are they provided? Did they seem to like the foods or reject some? Why do you think a certain food was rejected? How did the adult encourage eating?

2. Observe preschoolers in a group program. How do their space and furnishings meet preschoolers' needs? Which features could or should be used in the home?

3. Observe preschoolers playing in a group program. Which materials help them solve problems (classify, put things in order, and symbolize)? Which materials help their motor skills?

4. Observe two or more preschoolers playing. What examples did you see of self-assertion? What conflicts occurred? Why did these conflicts occur? How were they resolved? What examples did you see of cooperation? Why do you think the children were cooperative (ages of children or enough play materials)?

To Think Critically

1.   Your text states that food attitudes learned in the preschool years may last a lifetime. What is meant by a food attitude? What food attitudes do you have that perhaps began as early as the preschool years?
2.   What types of clothing did you like or did not like as a preschooler? How did your clothing tastes reflect your personality? To what extent should parents permit or encourage their preschoolers to make clothing choices?
3.   How can adults support preschoolers' learnings through friendship? When should adults "back off" and allow children to learn how to make friends and resolve conflicts with friends?

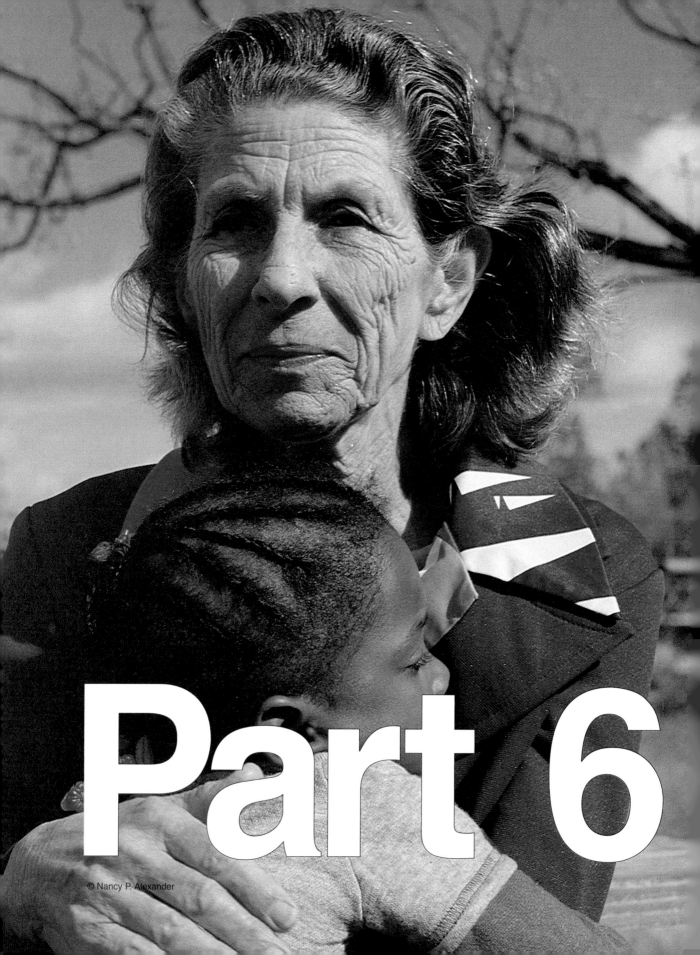

Part 6

Guiding and Caring for Children

All children need help growing and developing. Parents are not the only people who guide and care for them. Many other adults in child-related careers care for children, too. Guiding and caring for newborns, infants, toddlers, preschoolers, and school-age children is an exciting experience. Adults in child-related careers need stamina to care for newborns and keep up with toddlers. They need patience to answer toddlers' countless "why" questions. Adults also need the ability to encourage children to master their physical and social worlds in the preschool and school years.

In **chapter 19,** you will study school-age children. Physical development slows, and most children's gross-motor skills become graceful and strong. Fine-motor skills improve, too. Intellectually, school-age children are becoming logical and express themselves competently. During these years, children also learn formally in school. They depend less on parents and make more decisions. Friendships and groups become important for their social development.

In **chapter 20,** you will learn how children expand and refine their learnings through play. You will find many suggested activities and materials for providing important experiences children will enjoy.

Chapter 21 will help you become more aware of the risks to children's health and safety. You will also learn many ways to protect children.

Selecting quality group programs is a hard task. In **chapter 22,** you will study various child care programs and the qualities that make some programs better for children than others.

Finally, **chapter 23** will review child-related careers. You will also learn how to determine whether any one of these careers is right for you.

Chapter 19

School-Age Children

After studying this chapter, you will be able to

☐ describe the physical development of school-age children.

☐ describe the intellectual development of school-age children.

☐ describe the social-emotional development of school-age children.

☐ explain how adults and parents can help school-age children meet their developmental needs.

After studying this chapter, you will be able to define

auditory
concrete
concrete operational stage
conservation
deductive reasoning
flexibility
formal operations
growth pains
growth spurt
hierarchal classification
inductive reasoning
middle childhood
orthopedic
permanent teeth
precision
psychological security
scapegoating
school-age children
scientific reasoning
shortcomings
six-year molars

School-age children grow and develop, becoming more and more like adults.

During the years between ages 6 and 12, **school-age children** progress from dependent first-graders to independent almost-teens. Their motor, mental, and social skills develop quickly during this time, which is called the school-age years or **middle childhood**.

The school-age years are filled with fun, adventure, school, friends, family, and other events. Disappointments, challenges, and hard work are also part of this scene.

Many physical changes happen in children during the school-age years. Their large- and small-motor skills improve. Older children become skillful at tasks like model building and handi-crafts.

School-age children begin to think more log-ically and rely less on perception. This helps them learn new skills. Soon, they can articulate all English sounds. Their vocabulary continues to grow. Self-evaluation becomes more common during the school-age years. Children judge them-selves in relation to others. They deepen their social relations with adults and peers.

Adults are still an important part of school-age children's lives. Guiding and directing them during these crucial years are important tasks.

● Physical Development of School-Age Children

Middle childhood is a period of many changes in the body. Although these changes sometimes seem awkward as they happen, they help school-age children become more coordinated.

▶ Body Growth and Development

The slow, steady growth rate continues in school-age children. Toward the end of middle childhood, some children—mainly girls—begin a growth spurt and other body changes of the pre-teen and teen years. (A **growth spurt** is a rapid period of growth, usually linked with adoles-cence.) During these years, body proportions change and organ systems mature.

▓ Height and Weight

School-age children's height increases more steadily than their weight. This is because, for the most part, genes determine height. (Height is not easily affected by the environment, except by long-term conditions like malnutrition or certain illnesses.)

Weight somewhat parallels height. Taller children tend to be heavier and shorter children tend to be lighter. The environment also influences weight because of factors like nutrition, illness, activity, and stress.

Boys are taller and heavier than girls until the ages of 10 or 11. At this time, most females enter a growth spurt. Many girls are taller than boys at this age. Children are often sensitive to the size difference, especially if they are becoming interested in the opposite sex. In reality, the aver-age difference only adds up to about one inch at age 12. The difference shows up mainly in a boy who matures slowly and a girl who matures quickly. Most boys catch up in growth during the early teen years.

▓ Body Proportions

During middle childhood, body proportions become even more like those of an adult. A child's waist and head begin to look more in proportion to the body. Their arms and legs grow longer, which gives them a lower center of gravity and better balance, 19-1. During these years, the trunk grows until it is two times as long and two times as wide as it was at birth. The abdomen protrudes even less than it did in the preschool years because of the longer trunk.

▓ Bone Growth

The bones continue to ossify and grow larger and longer. The most significant bone growth is in the teeth. School-age children con-stantly lose baby teeth and grow permanent ones. Girls often lose and replace teeth before boys do.

The first two teeth, often the bottom front teeth, fall out during the late preschool years. The last of the 20 baby teeth, the cuspids (shown in chapter 7) fall out around age 12. (The tooth fairy is busy during these years!)

3

4

1—*Discuss:* Summarize the changes in a school-age child's life.

2—*Reflect:* When did your growth spurt(s) occur? Describe some of the changes and feelings associated with the changes.

3—*Enrich:* Sam and Heidi are both 10 years old. Sam weighs 100 pounds and is five feet tall. Heidi weighs 80 pounds and is four feet six inches tall. Explain these height

and weight differences. Why does the environment have more influence on weight than on height?

4—*Activity:* Prepare a bulletin board illustrating the physical differences of school-age children. Locate pictures for each age between 6 and 12 to illustrate these differences.

© John Shaw

19-1 School-age children develop more adult-like proportions. These new proportions make many tasks easier than they were in the preschool years.

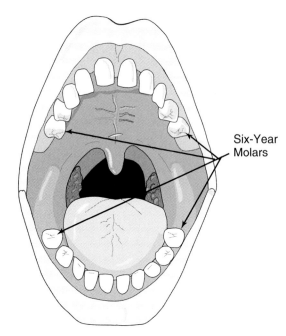

Six-Year Molars

19-2 Six-year molars are the first permanent teeth.

Unlike baby teeth, **permanent teeth** are intended to last a lifetime. They are harder and less sharp than baby teeth. The first set of permanent teeth to come in are called **six-year molars**. They do not replace any lost teeth. Their name tells at what age they usually erupt in a child. They grow behind the second set of deciduous (baby) molars, 19-2. The next permanent teeth replace lost baby teeth. The permanent teeth change the look of the lower part of the face, 19-3.

Muscle Growth

Muscles grow and become more firmly attached to bones during middle childhood. However, the muscles are not mature and are easily injured. Bone and muscle (**orthopedic**) defects are the most common defects of this age.

The skeleton grows more quickly than the muscles. The lag in muscle growth gives a loose-jointed, somewhat awkward look. Children of this age cannot completely keep their muscles from moving. This makes sitting still almost impossible!

School-age children may complain of aches and pains. These muscle aches are called growth pains. **Growth pains** are caused by muscles trying to catch up with skeleton size.

▶ Motor Development

School-age children enjoy almost all large-motor activities. They seem to have a surplus of energy.

Large- and Small-Motor Skills Improve

Motor skills improve during middle childhood. Children ages six to eight enjoy active games that use their large muscles. They are more developed in large-muscle coordination than in small-muscle coordination. For this reason, they enjoy running, jumping, climbing, and playing simple games like tag and catch.

Children ages 9 through 12 begin to develop interests in more specific motor skills. This is due to increased mental ability as well as

1—*Enrich:* Do research on orthopedic defects during the school-age period. Add a career component with research on orthopedic doctors. Report to the class.

2—*Reflect:* Did you have growth pains? Describe them. When did you grow out of them? Did you have a specific remedy for them?

Marcia Hillman Hart

19-3   Permanent teeth, which look almost too large for the child's face for a time, change the look of the lower jaw. Young school-age children's teeth are in many stages of growth.

improved large-muscle coordination. They tend to prefer organized sports, skating, or bicycling rather than running or jumping, 19-4.

Motor skills become better in middle childhood for the following reasons:

☐   faster reaction time. *Reaction time* is the time required to respond to a stimulus like a thrown ball.

☐   improved precision. **Precision** includes balance, steadiness, and skill in aiming at a target.

☐   greater speed and improved strength.

☐   improved flexibility. **Flexibility** is the ability to move, bend, and stretch easily.

Older school-age children have highly developed fine-motor skills. Improved skill helps them with art activities, craft work, writing, playing musical instruments, self-dressing, and other tasks that need small-muscle precision. These skills seem to increase steadily during the school years. Improvement in writing ability is shown in 19-5.

2

1—*Discuss:* Give other examples in which reaction time is faster.

2—*Activity:* Divide the class into groups. Arrange for each group to visit a different elementary class of children in the school-age years. Observe the following: recess activities,

large- and fine-motor skills, physical characteristics, art and music experiences, and socialization skills. Report results to the class.

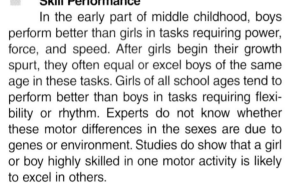

19-4 Older school-age children enjoy sports, such as baseball.

Skill Performance

In the early part of middle childhood, boys perform better than girls in tasks requiring power, force, and speed. After girls begin their growth spurt, they often equal or excel boys of the same age in these tasks. Girls of all school ages tend to perform better than boys in tasks requiring flexibility or rhythm. Experts do not know whether these motor differences in the sexes are due to genes or environment. Studies do show that a girl or boy highly skilled in one motor activity is likely to excel in others.

Providing for School-Age Children's Physical Needs

Although most school-age children have outgrown the need for direct physical care, they still have many needs that adults must meet. As children begin to think for themselves and as peers become more important, meeting needs becomes more complex. Having a warm coat is not as important to school-age children as having a coat that fits in with what everyone else is wearing.

▶ Encouraging Health and Safety Practices

Good health habits, such as diet and exercise, strongly influence how school-age children develop physically. Health habits affect their weight, posture, complexion, hair, and energy levels. Adults must promote safe living habits.

A Healthful Diet

Eating right helps the body meet the school-age child's growth needs and increased energy demands. Proper diets help school-age children resist infections. School-age children also need to store some nutrients for the rapid growth of their teen years. Chart 19-6 gives a daily food plan for school-age children. Adults should adjust the food plan to meet the child's own needs.

19-5 Fine-motor skills increase each year, as seen in writing attempts.

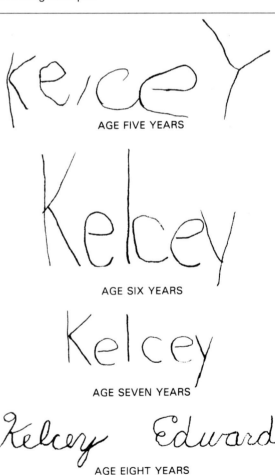

AGE FIVE YEARS

AGE SIX YEARS

AGE SEVEN YEARS

AGE EIGHT YEARS

1—*Resource: Sports, Games, and Physical Qualities,* SAG.

2—*Discuss:* Why is appearance more important than warmth or comfort? Does this influence show more in boys or in girls?

3—*Activity:* Obtain copies of signatures for each of these ages and compare with 19-5.

Daily Food Plan for School-Age Children

☐ Bread Group—6 servings total

☐ Vegetable Group—3 servings total

☐ Fruit Group—2 servings total

☐ Milk Group—2 servings total

☐ Meat Group—5 ounces total

19-6   School-age children need a well-balanced diet to meet their growth and energy needs. This chart shows a 2,200 calorie diet, which is right for most children.

When children start school, adults can no longer guide their diet because they often eat lunch at school. Some schools publish their weekly menus to help parents plan the other meals and snacks of the day. However, at times children may not eat what is on their lunch plate. Even children who carry their lunches to school may give or throw away some of their food. Parents and school staff should urge children to eat a proper diet while away from home, 19-7.

Snacking is often unsupervised. By this age many children buy snacks with their spending money. These often include junk foods. Children who eat too much junk food can lose their appetite for nourishing food. Junk food can also increase tooth decay and cause obesity. (Obese children can have serious social adjustment problems by nine years of age.)

Adults can promote healthy snacking by keeping nutritious, ready-to-eat snacks on hand. Examples are cheese cubes, fresh fruit, and carrot or celery sticks. Adults can urge children to prepare their own nutritious snacks, too. Because school-age children like to eat, they often enjoy cooking. Many good cookbooks are written for this age group. They contain simple recipes that children can prepare on their own.

Exercise and Other Good Health Practices

In addition to providing nutritious food and promoting a good diet, adults can promote other health practices. School-age children need moderate exercise daily or at least three to four times a week. Exercise is the major contributor to physical fitness. Adults must see that children spend time being active and not sitting in front of the television or computer.

Children also need between eight and nine hours of sleep a night. School-age children need sleep on a regular basis. If they don't sleep enough, they are unable to concentrate and do quality work. They also become irritable.

Safety Practices

Safety rules need to be modeled and practiced. For example, adults must insist on seat belts and bicycle helmets, 19-8. Adults need to keep the home safe from potential hazards. Most home accidents are due to falls and fire. Other dangers include those from poisoning, drowning, firearms, and electricity.

19-7   Nutritious foods can be popular, too.

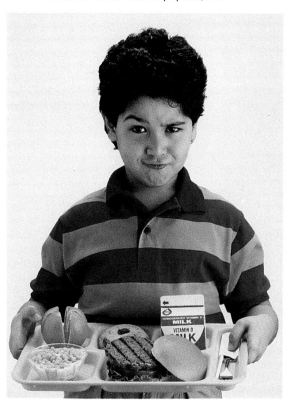

Protein Technologies International PROPLUS®

1—*Discuss:* If the diet provided too many calories, which foods would you serve in smaller portions?

2—*Activity:* Obtain a weekly or monthly lunch menu for elementary and middle school students. Working in groups, plan breakfast and dinner for five days for a family with school-age children. Share plans with the class.

3—*Reflect:* Do you think children should carry their lunches to school on a regular or occasional basis? Explain your reasons.

4—*Enrich:* Do research on obesity in children. Emphasize physical, mental, social, and emotional implications. Report to the class.

Selecting the Right Clothing

Like children of all ages, school-age children need clothing that fits and is well constructed. School-age children are active, so clothing should have growth features and withstand stress and strain. Most school-age children have developed self-dressing skills except for a hard-to-reach button or a specially tied bow. Younger school-age children may still need to have some self-dressing features. Shoe and sock sizes change on the average of every six months for children ages 6 to 12.

Children of this age develop their own preferences for color and style. They are concerned about how peers view them. The right clothing and shoes help make children feel part of the group, 19-9. If clothing and shoes are too different from what others wear, children may feel rejected. Compliments on clothing help boost children's self-confidence.

Speigel, Inc.

19-9   School-age children want to dress in much the same way as their peers.

19-8   Bicycle helmets keep children safe as they ride.

▶ Providing Needed Space and Furnishings

School-age children need and want an area of their own. Adults should think about these features when planning a space for school-age children.

☐ Space that may be used for many purposes—playing, working on hobbies, studying, daydreaming, sleeping, and dressing—is best. Children often want space for their friends to visit for the afternoon or even overnight.

☐ Storage space is needed for clothes and shoes, play and hobby equipment, and books. Display areas for photos, pennants, collections, hobbies, and keepsakes are often prized.

☐ Attractive space is important to school-age children. They like to choose their own color schemes and accessories, 19-10.

☐ Easy-to-clean rooms help children who are just learning home care skills.

☐ Furniture and accessories the child can use as a teen and young adult may be a wise investment.

19-10   School-age children prefer bedrooms planned with their tastes in mind.

● Intellectual Development of School-Age Children

Thinking mentally involves thinking with symbols rather than having contact with the real object or event. School-age children can think using even more abstract symbols than preschoolers.

Between ages 7 to 11, children's thinking depends more on logic and less on perception. Piaget has called this third stage of mental abilities the ***concrete operational stage,*** 19-11. The term ***concrete*** means that logic is based on what the child has at some time experienced.

Piaget called the last stages of mental abilities formal operations (ages 11 and older). In ***formal operations,*** a person can reason more abstractly.

The difference between concrete and formal operations can be seen in how a child plays a checker or chess game. A child at the concrete operational stage can play checkers or chess by the rules. The child makes each move based on what is on the board at that time. He or she does not think in terms of the next three to five moves. Older players in the formal operational stage can think ahead and plan strategies. A person in formal operations plans game strategy by thinking, "What if my opponent does such and such, then what will be my options?"

1—*Discuss:* What interests show in this room?

2—*Resource: A School-Age Child's Bedroom,* SAG.

3—*Resource: "I Do and I Understand,"* SAG.

Piaget's Stages of Cognitive Development	
Stage 1:	Sensorimotor Stage (Birth to 2 years)
Stage 2:	Preoperational Stage (2 to 7 years)
Stage 3:	Concrete Operational Stage (7 to 11 years)
Stage 4:	Formal Operational Stage (11 years on)

19-11 The school-age child functions in the concrete operational stage.

▶ How School-Age Children Think

School-age children are in the stage between *preoperational thinking* (before logic) and reasoning on a more abstract level. They are slowly using more advanced thinking skills.

▦ Seeing from the Viewpoint of Others

School-age children begin to see that others have ideas that differ from their own. Realizing that others have different ideas leads to doubt and the need to find the right answer. School-age children work to prove or deny answers by using logic.

Piaget believed that contact with peers is the greatest help in freeing children from egocentric thinking. For real communication with others, the person must recognize the point of view of others and notice how it compares with their own ideas.

▦ Focusing on More Than One Part

During the school years, the child comes to focus on more than one aspect of something at a time. This means the child can see more than one change in an object at one time. Think of Piaget's water task with a tall, thin glass and a short, wide glass. The child now sees that the greater width in the first glass makes up for the greater height in the other glass. Because the child can note both width and height changes at the same time, it is easier to understand how the same amount of liquid looks taller in a thinner glass.

1—*Activity:* Interview school-age children to discover if they are influenced more by their family or their peers. Report to the class.

▦ Noting Transformations

School-age children can mentally put together a series of events to see changes in an object. When they watch a liquid being poured from one glass to another, they see the liquid in the first glass, then going through the air and on into the second glass. Once the transformation is noted, children know the liquid in the second glass is the same as the liquid in the first glass. They know this even though the glasses are different shapes.

Being able to note transformations helps children understand other concepts. For instance, school-age children can accept the fact that their parents were once babies. They can believe that a tree grew from a seed. They understand that water can turn to ice,19-12.

▦ Using Reversibility Logic

School-age children are better able to understand reversibility logic. As you read earlier, reversibility is the ability to follow a line of reasoning back to where it started. They can carry out a task in reverse order. There is the understanding that if something is put back the way it was to

19-12 Playing in the snow helps children understand that snow becomes water when it melts.

2—*Enrich:* Do research on transformations. Design a transformation experiment to use with school-age children. Test the experiment. Report to the class. (Activity books may be used).

begin with, it will be the same. The child who flattens a clay ball knows that the clay can be made into a ball again. (In math, this concept is carried out in subtraction.)

Another part of reversibility is knowing that one change, such as in height, makes for another change, such as in width. The child knows the clay can be bigger in diameter because it is flatter. (In math, this concept is carried out in division.)

Using Deductive and Inductive Reasoning

The school-age child uses deductive reasoning. **Deductive reasoning** is reasoning from the general to the specific. It is a general statement that all fish live in water. One type of fish is a guppy. If a child knows both of these facts, he or she can use deductive reasoning to conclude that guppies live in water, 19-13.

Older school-age children may begin to use inductive reasoning. **Inductive reasoning** is reasoning from specific facts to general conclusions. Inductive reasoning is called **scientific reasoning** because it is the form of logic commonly used by scientists. Inductive reasoning is most often found in children over 11 years of age. These children can weigh several ideas they have tested and draw a conclusion. A child may know that people make ice cubes by putting

19-13 School-age children begin to use deductive reasoning to form their own concepts about the world around them.

water in a freezer. The child may put fruit juice in the freezer and find that it becomes solid, too. After trying other liquids, such as soft drinks or milk, the child may use inductive reasoning to conclude that cold temperatures change liquids into solids.

▶ What School-Age Children Learn

Because school-age children are beginning to use logic in their thought processes, they are able to learn many new things. Logic helps them learn school subjects like language arts, reading, math, geography, science, and the arts. School-age children's concepts are clearly more advanced than preschool children's concepts. However, they still have trouble grasping some concepts, such as events in history, scientific logic, and value systems.

Physical Knowledge Concepts

As you recall, physical knowledge concepts include concepts about size, shape, color, texture, and other qualities of objects and people. These concepts become more advanced in school-age children because their perception has matured, 19-14. Their senses mature, making sight, sound, smell, and feeling more accurate. The brain, too, processes what is seen and heard in more defined ways.

Perception. *Perception* in school-age children changes in many ways.

☐ They do more in-depth exploring of their world. By age nine a child uses the eyes or fingertips to trace the outline of an object rather than glancing at it quickly.

☐ Children learn what information to act upon and what to ignore as they examine an object. If the child is identifying geometric shapes, the color of the shapes is ignored.

☐ They learn to correctly pair *visual* (seen) and **auditory** (heard) stimuli, such as written letters and their sounds or written music notes and their pitches.

3

4

5

1—*Discuss:* What are some other examples of reversibility?

2—*Discuss:* What are some other examples of deductive reasoning?

3—*Discuss:* What are some other examples of inductive reasoning?

4—*Discuss:* Give some specific examples of physical knowledge concepts.

5—*Discuss:* What are some examples of learning to pair stimuli?

© John Shaw

19-14A Parquetry (or attribute) blocks, blocks in geometric shapes, are used for making designs.

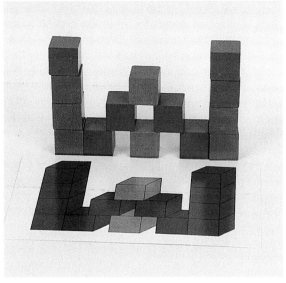

© John Shaw

19-14B Design cubes, like parquetry blocks, are arranged in designs. Both help children develop visual perception.

Memory. School-age children have an improved *memory*, which helps them learn. They are beginning to see the need for remembering. Children also develop methods to help them remember. Such methods include singing the alphabet or learning a rhyme about the number of days in the months of a year.

Logic. *Logic* allows school-age children to form better, more accurate physical knowledge concepts. The ability to use logic helps children master the concept of conservation. **Conservation** means that changing the shape, direction, or position of an object or objects does not alter the quantity. This concept must be understood before children can form accurate physical knowledge concepts related to length, mass, weight, or volume. Understanding some of these concepts begins at around age 6. Other conservation tasks cannot be solved until age 11.

Perception, memory, and logic work together to help the child develop physical knowledge concepts. With increased physical knowledge, the child is better able to give more meaning to words, drawings, and other symbols.

Logical Thinking Concepts

The ability to mentally understand relationships among objects becomes well developed in the middle childhood years. School-age children better understand classification, order, numbers, space, distance, time, and speed. These logical thinking concepts become more accurate as children replace perceptual thinking with logic.

Classification. As you read in chapter 16, *classification* is the grouping of objects into a class and its complement. As school-age children classify, the property (shape, color, way used) that defines the class remains stable. School-age children do not group by shape and switch to color in the process. School-age children also include all objects that meet the property for that class. By middle childhood, children fully understand the class and the complement, 19-15.

School-age children learn hierarchal classification. **Hierarchal classification** is having classes within other classes. The large class of animals can be broken down into subgroup classes like birds and fish.

1

2

1—*Reflect:* In what ways do you depend on your memory?

2—*Enrich:* Do research on conservation. Report to the class.

3—*Discuss:* What are some other examples of hierarchies?

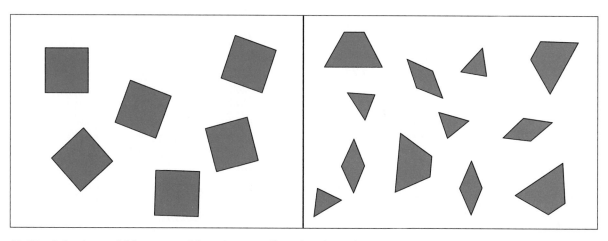

19-15   School-age children group things that are alike—the class of squares. They also place the complement (other shapes) in a random way.

Order.   School-age children can show relationships among objects by putting them in order. This involves putting in order the objects' differences. These differences might include those seen (color, shape, size), heard (pitch, loudness), and felt (texture and temperature). Other differences involve time or order of events. Series are used in daily life, such as in calendars and the chemical elements.

Number.   During the last part of the preschool stage and the early part of middle childhood, children learn many basic concepts about number. They need to learn number concepts like greater than, less than, equal to, and others. Some of these basic ideas must be grasped before children can understand math, 19-16.

Children also learn that groups are changed in number if more objects are put with the group (adding). They also learn that the number changes if objects are taken away from the group (subtracting).

Space.   School-age children have many correct ideas about space. They can tell whether objects are open or closed and whether they are far or near. They can also see the relationship of two or more objects. They understand such concepts as close to, connected, behind, in front of,

above, below, left, or right. They know, too, that distant objects like a flying jet do not get smaller.

Distance, Time, and Speed.   Children who are younger than age eight have problems grasping distance, time, and speed. They mainly have trouble understanding the ways these concepts relate. Time and distance are often confused. The young, school-age child may say that walking some place is far, but that running makes it near.

19-16   Many materials are available for teaching number concepts. Because math is a logical concept, children need to wait until the late preschool and early school-age years to work with math symbols.

© John Shaw

2

1—*Discuss:* List other ways that school-age children learn and apply order.

2—*Activity:* Look through a toy catalog to identify toys or games that would teach number concepts.

Children often learn clock time and calendar time in the first or second grade. However, they do not understand time and age well at age 10 or 11. The time of historical events seems difficult to grasp until the teen years. Stories written for children often reflect their understandings of time. Stories for the young child often begin with "Once upon a time." Stories for school-age children give hints about seasons or years. Books for late childhood years mention exact times.

Cause and Effect Relationships.   School-age children begin to resolve many cause and effect relationships. As children become less egocentric, they begin to understand that humans do not cause natural happenings. They begin to have more of a scientific approach to their thinking.

The earlier belief that nonliving objects have lifelike qualities is given up for scientific answers. However, natural matter (sun and stars, oceans, mountains) that are thought of as powerful may be seen as lifelike by older children.

▶ Language Is Mastered

Around six or seven years of age, children's speech becomes more social. They want to talk with their friends and with adults. The speech of school-age children is not as involved or intellectual, however, as many adult conversations.

▪ Vocabulary

Speaking vocabulary continues to grow in middle childhood. Children of this age give more exact definitions than do younger children. If you asked children to define the word *orange*, preschool children would often say, "You eat it." School-age children would give a more exact definition, such as, "It is a color or a fruit." Definitions of words are often used as part of tests given to children during the school years, 19-17. A reading vocabulary develops during these years. A spelling/writing vocabulary also develops. Reading helps the speaking vocabulary grow.

▪ Articulation

Articulation of all English sounds is often mastered by age eight. Children who have the most articulation problems at the end of the preschool years often continue to have speech handicaps in the school years. Speech problems are also related to reading problems. This is because children need to say sounds in exact ways in order to understand and pronounce what they read.

▪ Grammar

Around age nine, children have mastered their grammar. They use their own set of grammar rules to make plurals, use pronouns, and show tense. These rules may or may not be those accepted by grammar experts. Changing grammar habits after this age requires relearning.

Middle childhood is also the age of having fun with words. Children learn different word rhymes, raps, and chants, 19-18. Name-calling can even become a word contest that may turn a

19-17   Defining words is part of many tests for school-age children.

Teaching Resources

1—*Discuss:* Why do children learn time concepts better when they begin school?

2—*Activity:* Interview elementary school teachers to find out how they attempt to correct articulation problems. Report to the class.

3—*Discuss:* What are some common grammar problems of school-age children? How do they learn proper and improper grammar?

4—*Reflect:* Do you think an avid reader would score higher on these tests? Explain your answer.

Spiegel, Inc.

19-18   Saying jump rope rhymes is one way school-age children play with words.

fight into laughter. Humor is expressed more in words during the middle childhood years. Children come to enjoy many kinds of jokes, riddles, and simple puns.

● Helping School-Age Children Meet Their Intellectual Needs

School-age children need time to play, enjoy hobbies, be with peers, and daydream. They also have intellectual needs to meet. School meets many mental needs of children. However, home is an important learning environment. Children need a rich out-of-school world, a world of things to do and see. Even day-to-day activities can be rich in learning experiences.

▶ Guiding Intellectual Growth

Adults can help school-age children meet their intellectual needs in many ways. For example, adults can—

☐   provide opportunities for children to participate in activities that require effort over longer periods of time. Such activities might include learning to play an instrument or being involved in sports. It might include the beginning of a hobby, such as stamp collecting, model building, or other projects.

2

☐   allow children to choose the activities they find most rewarding.

☐   encourage children to learn. However, adults should not overuse rewards and praise. The feeling of doing a good job is often the best reward.

☐   show an interest in and support the school's program.

3

☐   show interest in their own activities. Adults whose skills and satisfactions grew over long periods of time are children's best models.

Adults can enrich children's language in many ways. Sharing ideas and experiences with children can be mutually rewarding. Reading to children and listening to them read is helpful. Adults can encourage children to express themselves correctly. Children learn the language they hear, speak, and read.

4

There are many language games that are fun as well as helpful. Individual word puzzles of all types are available, too. These include crossword puzzles, word finds, and scrambled words.

▪ Preparing the Child to Enter School

Between late August and September each year, several million five- and six-year-olds enter

---

1—*Resource: Children's Humor: A Reflection of Mental and Language Development,* SAG.

2—*Reflect:* What types of hobbies did you have while you were growing up? How did they help your intellectual development?

3—*Discuss:* What happens when an adult overuses rewards?

4—*Discuss:* How can reading with a child help him or her to articulate and use grammar correctly?

school. Many older children also enter new schools because their families have moved. Starting school is exciting and perhaps scary for many children.

Entering school is a new developmental task for children. They must deal with new people—both children and adults. They also must deal with new concepts and skills and with a different daily structure, 19-19. School-age children spend 44 percent of their waking hours at school.

Adults need to help children make the transition from home to school as enjoyable as possible. Stress may accompany the new hours and routines. Adults need to realize that children may manage anxiety at school, but they may show anxiety and stress at home. Extra patience is needed during the adjustment time. This is a poor time to add new learnings or tasks, such as music lessons or a new pet, to a child's life.

Adults can help children have a good basis for their school experiences in many ways. For example, they can—

☐ develop a secure and trusting relationship with their children

☐ allow children to have more independence by letting go to some extent

☐ teach children to accept the authority of adults other than parents

☐ help children overcome separation anxiety

School also means getting along with peers for many hours. Children sit next to, line up by, work with, eat with, and share with other children. Unlike the preschool play groups, where children choose their own friends and play when they want, school relationships are more teacher directed. Children who are adaptable and who have had contacts with others find it easier to adjust than those who haven't had this opportunity.

Getting the Child to School. Adults need to make transportation plans clear to children. Younger children who walk or catch a bus need instructions. Some adults or older children who

© John Shaw

19-19 The people, concepts, and schedules of elementary school are different from those of the preschooler's world.

are known to the child should be nearby. Children should be reminded not to talk to or go with strangers. They should know their full name, parent's names, address, and phone number.

School should be viewed as a natural course of events—everyone goes to school. Adults should create a normal routine for the first few days of school. Overdoing photos, sounding anxious, getting the child ready too early (or too late), or serving a special breakfast are not ways to make school a matter-of-fact event.

Adults should say goodbyes at the bus stop, on the school yard, or at the classroom door. These goodbyes should be warm but not clingy. The teary-eyed child often regains control soon after the adult is out of sight, 19-20.

If the first days go well, children look forward to school. Experiences that are not good may lead to situations where the child wants to avoid school and will use every excuse to stay at home.

Reinforcing School Tasks

School children need daily encouragement and help. Adults must continue working with and

---

1—*Reflect:* How could you help your child manage his or her first years of school? What would be some signs of the child's stress?

2—*Discuss:* List what you could do to prepare your child for school before he or she begins kindergarten.

3—*Reflect:* Try to recall (or ask a parent) your feelings and experiences associated with starting school. How could you help a child with this transition?

19-20   Saying goodbye in the schoolyard helps children enter the classroom in a composed, positive state.

helping their children. Help is not effective if given only a few days after the teacher shares negative reports with parents. The schools and parents and other adults close to children have the same goal. They all want to give children the best possible education. Children are best helped when all those concerned work as a team.

Adults have a number of responsibilities concerning their children's schooling. Among these are the following:

☐   See that children attend school regularly and follow the rules.

☐   Take an interest in what children are learning.

☐   Talk with children about school work, look at their papers, and stay in close contact with the school.

Adults and children need to plan a quiet place for study. Space with a desk or table for doing work like writing is important. Many children also enjoy a place to stretch out while reading.

A certain amount of time needs to be set aside for doing homework. This amount varies with the age of the child. Elementary school children need time to play and perhaps have a snack or evening meal before doing homework. Homework should be done before watching television or other activities. School-age children who do not have homework can use the set time for reading or being read to, drawing, or doing other activities that complement school tasks. Adults may supervise a cooking project to reinforce fractions.

Adults can ensure that children follow through on any activities that the school sends home with the child. They need to supervise but not do children's homework for them. In the elementary school, homework most often is assigned to reinforce skills learned in class. Doing children's homework makes them rely on adults to solve their tasks. It also prevents the child from getting needed practice. (If homework is often too difficult, adults should talk to the teacher.)

Guiding Television Viewing.   It is up to parents to limit television viewing and leisure activities on school nights. Several studies show that as hours of television viewing increase, grades drop at the same rate. Children who do not watch as much television tend to concentrate better and use their imaginations more. Also, school-age children who learn to budget their work and leisure times develop proper, lifelong work and play habits.

Television can be a useful tool for learning and entertainment. However, adults must limit the number of hours the set runs while children are in the home. It can replace many other worthwhile activities, especially involvement with others and hands-on activities.

1—*Discuss:* Why is it necessary that all adults who are part of the child's life work together as a team?

2—*Discuss:* What happens when parents do not respect school attendance and rules?

3—*Discuss:* What happens when parents are not interested in their child's school work and do not communicate with teachers or other school personnel?

4—*Discuss:* What happens when parents are not concerned about children's homework? What happens when parents do homework for children?

Social-Emotional Development of School-Age Children

A whole new social experience begins in middle childhood. Children need to make many new adjustments. School-age children have to be much more independent. They are concerned about what others think of them. Getting along with age-mates is fun, but sometimes difficult. They find that mastering skills needed in order to fit into society can be stressful.

In many ways, social development becomes the most important aspect of development in middle childhood. The peer group becomes more and more important as children progress through the school years. Relationships with peers affect all aspects of development. School-age children's physical skills are often judged by whether they have the skills needed for playing sports and games with peers. Through their school activities, they make daily judgments of their own learnings compared with those of their peers. Peer groups also act as a source of socialization. Each group teaches their own rules of conduct needed for acceptance.

▶ Self-Concept

School-age children take a close look at themselves, 19-21. They become keenly aware of their **shortcomings** (areas where a person wants or needs to improve) and failures. Self-evaluation becomes more complex for these reasons.

☐ School-age children almost totally become concerned with what others think of them. Peers can judge harshly. Adults cannot often change how peers judge each other.

☐ Abilities in reading, mathematics, music, computer literacy, and other skills are more difficult for them to measure. Earlier, they could tell how they compared with other children in their motor skills like playing baseball. Now it is much harder to compare because their school studies are more abstract.

☐ School-age children are generally evaluated in comparison to other children's skills. School grades are earned more in comparison to other children's work than in comparison to the child's own previous work.

▶ Showing Social Awareness

During middle childhood, children begin to show a greater awareness of what is going on around them. School-age children develop a sense of work and industry as they learn some of the skills needed to become ready for adult life. Social relationships grow and become more complicated.

■ Sense of Work and Being Industrious

In the school years, children want to satisfy themselves while being acceptable to society. The play of earlier years is replaced with more meaningful work (at least by adult standards). However, play is still important in middle childhood.

19-21 School-age children often spend much time alone thinking about themselves.

© John Shaw

1—*Discuss:* How can a parent help with peer group adjustments? What kind of advice can they give?

2—*Discuss:* If a child is having a great deal of difficulty with peer adjustments, what helpful resources are available?

3—*Reflect:* Do you think this is a fair evaluation? Explain your reasons.

4—*Discuss:* Why is play still important in middle childhood?

Children learn the proper attitude toward work at this time. Those with a sense of industry see work as the way to learn new ideas and skills and to perform in worthwhile ways. These children also see work as a way to win approval from others. Parents, teachers, and peers encourage the learning of skills. Even social organizations like 4-H, Boy Scouts, or Girl Scouts make learning skills the route to success and higher status, 19-22.

School-age children like to learn to do things with and for others. They are learning and practicing cooperation as they enjoy the interaction with others.

Working and being industrious increases children's feelings of self-worth and responsibility. They see that what they do makes a difference. There is also a greater sense of independence.

Peers Become Important

Adults become less important as children spend more time with peers. Children in the elementary school years like to hang around in groups. The nature of friendships changes as children mature.

Close friendships are beginning to develop in the early school years. By age eight, there is more separation of sexes. Peer groups are informal and are made up of children who live near each other. Groups are often within walking or cycling distance. The groups change as families move in and out of the neighborhood.

In this stage, children often see a friend as someone who helps them. They seldom think in terms of how they can help the friend. Give and take does occur, but it serves the individual rather than the mutual interest of friends.

19-22   Youth organizations, such as cheerleading groups, encourage and recognize children for their hard work and skills.

1—*Discuss:* What social organizations are available for school-age children in your community? What benefits does each organization offer?

2—*Resource: Industry Is Important in the School Years,* SAG.

3—*Discuss:* How can parents encourage supervised peer group activities?

Between the ages of 9 and 11, more close friendships form. Boys choose boys for friends, and girls choose girls for friends. Children also show dislike for the opposite sex. However, girls may become interested in boys around age 11, 19-23. Similar interests and tastes determine friendships more often than physical nearness. Some formal groups, such as team sport groups, form at this time, also. The nature of these friendships becomes one of cooperation and helping each other in order to achieve group goals.

Peer Groups Serve a Purpose.   Peer groups are important to children and may serve the following purposes:

☐ Belonging to a peer group gives children a feeling of sharing and loyalty. Special friends may huddle, talk, giggle, argue, and fight as they share times together. Children feel a sense of security and self-worth when working or playing with others in their group.

☐ Peer groups reinforce self-concept. School-

19-23   Toward the end of the elementary school years, girls show more interest in boys than boys do in girls.

Spiegel, Inc.

age children are highly concerned about how they appear to others. In peer groups, children tag others with labels, such as captain of the team or the last one chosen. These labels make children aware of how others feel about them. Once they absorb these peer attitudes, children react to themselves as others have reacted to them.

☐ Peer groups provide emotional support. Adults cannot provide the comfort that children feel when they realize others their age share similar feelings. Their group members understand how they feel.

☐ Peer groups share information with each other. Children learn from their peers as they work on group projects. They not only want to be part of the group, but they want to be the best in the group. This makes children want to learn all they can from their peers.

☐ Through their peer groups, they learn how to deal with rules and get along with others. Even the earlier play groups become more organized as children participate in games with rules. These groups teach children that social relationships involve rules and that rules help groups work as teams. Peer group codes contain more rules about what not to do than what to do. Children learn consequences of what can happen, such as being removed from the group, if rules are broken.

☐ Peer groups help school-age children become more self-controlling and less dependent on adults. The peer group serves as a sifter for thinking through adult-taught priorities. Peers help children decide what priorities to keep and what priorities to throw away. As children consider priorities, they learn to conform to others at times and stand firm in their own beliefs at other times.

1—*Discuss:* How is peer group support different from family support? Are both necessary during the school-age years? Explain your reasons.

2—*Reflect:* Describe the value of working on group projects in school. How does this apply to the school-age child?

3—*Resource: Peers Are Important,* SAG.

▶ Controlling Emotions

By the time they enter school, children show patterns of emotional behavior. These patterns are fairly well-established. Their emotional development and personality continue to merge. Thus, the emotions felt by school-age children affect all of their behavior, which influences their personality.

Love

All school-age children need love. They show love to adults and age mates who care for them and accept them as they are. School-age children do not seek relationships where they must give too much in return. They do care for others who share common interests.

The need for love is shown in school-age children's great desire to be accepted by others—adults and peers. These children, however, do not express their love as openly (with hugs and kisses) as younger children. School-age children show love for adults by kindness and doing activities with them. They show affection for peers by wanting to be with them and sharing secrets. They also show affection by staying in touch through the telephone and notes and giving small presents, 19-24.

19-24 The telephone is a big part of older school-age children's lives. They like to keep in close touch with friends.

Spiegel, Inc.

School-age children who do not feel loved have a narrowed emotional range. They experience little or no joy, grief, or guilt. Thinking abilities are hurt because these unloved children cannot concentrate. These children often turn to antisocial behavior, such as hostile acts.

Fear and Anxiety

Some of a child's earlier fears and worries become less threatening. There is a greater separation of fantasy and reality. Thus, fear of the dark disappears after age seven. Fear of the supernatural declines by age 9 or 10. Fears of physical harm, such as disease, injury, and death, continue from the preschool years into the school years. School-age children's fears and worries also center around the future, embarrassment, and people and their actions, 19-25.

Fears and worries of middle childhood often do not disappear with age. Some studies report that over half of the school-age children's fears and worries persist into adult years.

Anger and Aggression

The form of anger and aggression changes with age. School-age children do not display their anger physically as much as younger children. They are better able to control their bodies and to express themselves verbally. By this time, they know what is and is not acceptable. Therefore, children in middle childhood show their anger in less direct ways. For example, anger may be expressed in the forms of disrespect, sulkiness, and *scapegoating* (blaming others for your own mistakes). School-age children also show anger by gossiping, plotting, and even imagining the downfall of their enemies. Withdrawal from a situation, such as quitting or using less ability, may be another sign of anger.

As children grow older, they become angry about different things. Like preschool children, school-age children are angered when their wants are denied and their possessions are threatened. However, unlike preschool children, school-age children are also angered by what they see as wrongs to others. In later years, anger at social wrongs may be turned into positive social action.

1—Discuss: How do school-age children show love?

2—Discuss: What types of antisocial behavior are promoted by not feeling loved?

3—Discuss: What types of fears are typical for school-age children?

4—Discuss: Is expressing anger a negative behavior?

5—Discuss: Give some examples of scapegoating. How could a parent discourage this in a positive way?

6—Reflect: If you were a fifth-grade teacher, how would you handle a student who constantly hit and kicked other children when he or she became angry?

Fears and Anxieties in Middle Childhood	
Types of Fears/Anxieties	**Examples**
The future	☐ any new situation, such as a new school or new neighborhood ☐ the world in general, such as war, pollution, and economic changes
Embarrassment	☐ school failure ☐ unchosen for a team sport, part in a play, or other event ☐ mistake made in a game, recital, or other performance ☐ poor personal appearance ☐ physical examinations and fear of changing clothes in a locker room or public place ☐ personal handicaps
People and their actions	☐ family quarrels ☐ divorce/disagreement of parents ☐ fear that custodial parent may leave ☐ kidnappers and child enticers ☐ abuse ☐ unfriendly school gangs

19-25 The major fears and worries of middle childhood are the future, embarrassment, and people and their actions.

● Helping School-Age Children with Their Social-Emotional Needs

Although the peer group becomes a more major part of school-age children's social lives, adults are still important. Adults need to help children in their activities and school work. Parents often help meet the costs of children's training or participation. They arrange for children to get safely to and from the site of activities. Adults give children support and encouragement in their emotional development.

School-age children enjoy just being with adults. Elementary school children are still interested in doing things with and for their families, 19-26. These children also enjoy being with other adults, such as teachers and youth leaders.

▶ Guiding and Modeling Behavior

Adults model values and attitudes about almost all aspects of life. School-age children watch and listen to important adults in their lives. They pattern many of their thoughts and actions after these adults. School-age children still need a certain amount of guidance.

■ Balance Dependence with Independence

School-age children often question adults' guidance. Yet, school-age children need adults to listen to them and, at times, to advise and set limits. Adults must learn the balance between letting go and being there for children. This is not easy. Adults do not know whether they should protect children from problems with friends or let them cope on their own. Adults may be torn between trying to enforce their teachings and allowing children to make some of their own decisions.

1—*Reflect:* Describe a family you know (or an ideal family) with school-age children who support and encourage each other positively in social, emotional, and intellectual development. How do they interact with each other?

2—*Reflect:* Describe a role model you had when you were a school-age child.

© John Shaw

19-26   Taking part in family activities is still important to school-age children.

adults must focus on what children can do rather than on their faults. They should set reasonable standards. When standards are too high, children feel they can't reach them and won't try. If standards are set too low, children may not work up to their potential. Even small successes help children feel good about their work, which increases their self-esteem.

Adults can help by encouraging children to succeed in school. Children do better in school when they have loving, caring parents who want them to do well than when parents show little or no concern.

Expand Children's Horizons

Adults should plan activities that can develop children's physical, mental, and social skills. By the school years, children begin to develop more unevenly. A child who has developed advanced reading skills may lag in motor skills. Children still have a wide range of talents,

2

Extend Gender Role

Adults help extend the gender role development in the school years. Mothers and other female adults close to school-age girls affect girls' feminine gender role learnings, 19-27. These learnings include goals in the world of work. Fathers and other male adults close to school-age boys affect boys' masculine gender role learnings. Fathers and other adult males who model warmth and sureness in their masculine roles directly affect femininity in girls. Warm, masculine-type models also help girls in their teens relate well to males in their age group. The same is true for female adults and their affect on school-age boys' learning.

Encourage Work and Industry

In middle childhood, children develop attitudes that prepare them for adult work. In order to help them develop positive feelings about work,

19-27   This school-age girl may wear a bright bow and necklace because she has seen a female role model, like her mother, do the same.

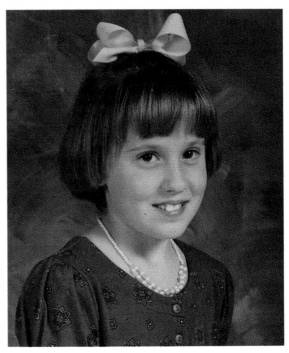

3

1—Discuss: How does the school-age child develop attitudes about gender role from adults in his or her life?

2—Discuss: How does self-esteem relate to motivation and positive attitudes toward work?

3—Reflect: Do you think this girl would be influenced more by her peers or her mother? Explain.

so they could achieve in many fields. On the other hand, children should not be expected to excel in all areas. Adults need to encourage children to test and expand their abilities.

Adults can suggest hobbies where children can succeed, 19-28. Children enjoy the steps involved in hobbies, such as making and finding objects. They like to display their new learnings.

Keep Family Communication Open

It's important that parents and children talk and express their feelings openly. If good communication patterns are established during middle childhood years, later teen/parent relationships will be much better.

During the early school years, children view their parents as the greatest in every way. By age 9 or 10, they begin to see their parents' mistakes. Relationships between parents and children become somewhat strained. However, good communication can help ease the strain.

19-28   Hobbies, like insect collecting, can be a fun learning experience.

© Nancy P. Alexander

To communicate clearly, adults must talk to children honestly and openly. They need to explain why they feel a certain way and show willingness to listen to their children's feelings. Parents may be upset because their child went to a friend's home after school without telling them. They should explain that they become worried when they do not know where their child is. They also should let the child have input on how they can avoid the problem in the future.

Listening.   Listening is an important part of communication. Parents may pick up on children's emotions by listening to their comments. A child may say, "You always pick on me!" Parents can use such comments as a chance to ask children what is on their mind. They may learn that certain actions bother their children. Parents also may clear up misunderstandings at these times.

When children realize their parents will listen, they are more likely to come to their parents with problems. Children may be having problems with friendships or school. Children often look to parents in these situations. Giving advice and assuring children helps them bounce back from problems. Children see their parents as people who weathered some of the same problems.

Throughout the school years parents are still admired. This is true even though children feel that parents create many of their problems. Open communication allows children to build strong bonds with their parents that will last into adulthood.

▶ Enjoying Family Ties

School-age children think of their families as home base. They not only think of home as a place for food, clothing, and shelter, but also for psychological security. **Psychological security** is a feeling that someone cares and will help when needed.

The family provides a balance between letting go and holding on in the school years. In this role, the family provides security for trying new skills. They also need to be available when children need support.

1—*Activity:* Interview school-age children to find out what types of hobbies and interests they have. What are some tasks they do not do very well?

2—*Discuss:* Why is it important to develop good communication skills during the school-age years?

3—*Reflect:* Describe your hobbies as a school-age child. Were they valuable experiences?

4—*Discuss:* What topics are important for parents and school-age children to discuss openly?

5—*Discuss:* Give examples of psychological security.

Family activities can extend the skills children learn in school-age peer groups. In addition to direct help, parents can help by organizing the child's schedule, seeing that needed equipment is ready (washing uniforms, buying ballet slippers), and driving children to and from activities.

School-age children enjoy just being with their family. They want to learn home care skills. Children are pleased when they are old enough and skilled enough to do many things they were not allowed to do in the preschool years. Children also enjoy family times. They enjoy family meals, weekend outings, yearly vacations, and family celebrations, 19-29. The special plans and surprises are all part of taking a major role in family rituals. School-age children may even think about how they will continue these customs when they are adults.

▶ Providing Time for Friendships

Children need time to be with friends, 19-30. Some adults have so many other plans for children that they don't have a chance to form friendships. Making friends welcome in the home and encouraging peer activities is important, 19-31. Parents must understand that children will like best friends almost as much as the family and will want to include them in family outings.

19-30   School-age children need to have fun times with friends.

Because the peer group is so important, fears of rejection are real in middle childhood. Every child, at one time or another, feels rejected by peers. You often hear school-age children say, "Nobody likes me," or "I can never do anything

3

4

19-31   Parents who encourage children to spend time in their yard or home with peers help friendships form.

19-29   Family outings strengthen family ties.

1—*Discuss:* How can children help to get their equipment ready? Why is their help important for children themselves? Families?

2—*Reflect:* Describe your family activities and rituals. Why are these activities important to you?

3—*Reflect:* What types of activities would you provide for a school-age child of your own?

4—*Resource: School-age Children Want to Be Accepted,* SAG.

right!" Such statements from a child who is usually accepted are best ignored. However, adults do need to help when children experience general rejection, especially if the rejection lasts over a week. How to help depends on the child, but these ideas often work.

- ☐ Try to discover the problem behind the rejection. The problem may be the child's physical appearance. The problem may also be the lack of certain skills—physical or athletic skills, academic skills, or social skills.

- ☐ Give children direct help in overcoming the problem. The child may need a weight-loss diet or grooming tools and lessons. The child may also need coaching in a new skill or step-by-step suggestions on how to make friends.

- ☐ Plan games and activities where there is not so much pressure on a child's own skills. Play dodge ball rather than softball.

▮ Loss of Friendship

Children also need help when they lose their best friends through conflict, new interest, or moving away. School-age children can suffer great pain, even depression, from such a breakup. Depression can cause a decrease in eating, sleeping, working, or playing.

Adults can help in many cases. Children may talk to adults about the loss of a friend. Adults should choose words carefully when they discuss the breakup. For instance, they should not say, "It's not as bad as you think. You'll feel better soon." Many children will tune out well-meaning adults at this point. Instead, adults should try to talk about the emotions felt without mention of getting over them.

Adults need to stay neutral if the breakup was caused by conflict. Joining a child's anger or hurt places all the blame for the breakup on the former friend. It may also say to the child, "You made a poor friendship choice."

Adults can prepare children in advance for breaks in friendships. Preparation should begin in the preschool or early school years. It can include talking about why people become friends and sometimes end friendships. Adults can also tell children about some of their friendships and break-ups (or read stories about loss of friends and the hurt it causes). Preparation can also include encouraging children to play with more than one child so that the loss of one friend will not be too crushing.

▶ Helping Children Control Their Emotions

Adults should continue to guide and help children control their emotions in middle childhood. Adults should explain that all people have strong feelings. They should talk about some of their emotions, too. School-age children may also be helped when they read about the struggles of other children and adults to control feelings. Adults can also point out that a person controls his or her emotions out of respect for others.

Children need to see parents model control of their own behavior. Children learn by the way adults handle frustration and anger over discipline problems. Parents should talk about the child's problem. If they use nonphysical means to let the child know he or she has done wrong, they model acceptable ways of behavior. These are better methods than physical punishment, which shows loss of control.

Control of emotions can be helped in indirect ways, too. Physical exercise and creative tasks help children control their anger. Children show less fear of the physical world as they gain skills and knowledge. Fear of water is overcome when a person learns to swim well. As children improve skills, they develop healthy self-concepts. Having healthy self-concepts helps children overcome many social fears because children are not as worried about being embarrassed or rejected.

1—*Resource: Helping Children Deal with Rejection*, SAG.

2—*Enrich:* Working in pairs, practice discussing these situations with a school-age child.

3—*Enrich:* Do research on childhood depression. Report to the class.

4—*Note:* When adults talk about their emotions and how they deal with them, children can understand their actions better.

5—*Note:* This could be compared to redirecting, which is used to distract the child or to help forget a disappointment.

▶ Helping Children Improve Their Self-Concept

Children's feelings about their self-worth are influenced by how others, who are important in their lives, treat them. Parents and other adults who provide love, appreciation, and encouragement form the base for a positive self-image.

Every child has special talents and abilities. Parents and adults need to praise and encourage those traits. They can offer positive feedback for what the child is doing well. Saying, "You did a good job," is an important message for children to hear.

Parents need to communicate their love and acceptance to their children. School-age children still seek parental affection and approval. Children need to know that they are important to their family.

Adults should discipline children privately, not in front of their peers or others. If criticism must be given, the act should be criticized and not the child. In this way, they learn that what they have done was wrong but that they can still be trusted and loved as a person.

Parents and adults need to help school-age children continue to build their courage and self-image. They need to help them learn to believe in their own abilities. By their love, praise, and support, they can help school-age children in their struggle for self-esteem.

● Recognizing Developmental Delays

Although it is hoped that children's developmental delays have been recognized and successfully treated prior to the school years, many school-age children have delays. Some of these children's delays were identified at younger ages, but these children have not yet caught up with their peers. Unfortunately, some children's developmental delays may not be recognized until the school years.

Many teachers are excellent judges of developmental delays in physical, intellectual, and social-emotional areas. Most teachers have had some training in child development. Also, because they teach so many children, teachers are often more experienced than parents in recognizing children who are "typical" and children who are delayed.

Parents are usually informed of delays during the formal parent-teacher conferences or sometimes through more informal contacts with adults such as teachers, coaches, or scout leaders. Although developmental delays are not the only reason children fail to achieve in school, parents should note the achievement of their children. Parents who note that their children do not seem to be achieving should contact their children's teachers as soon as possible. Through the sharing of information about children's home and school life, problems can be more accurately identified and actions planned.

1

1—*Enrich:* Ask a teacher how he or she recognizes developmental delays in children.

Summary

School-age children's physical development continues slowly and steadily. They go through many body changes that seem to make the body appear awkward. Permanent teeth are coming in and changing the look of the face. Motor skills become better because of faster reaction time, precision, and improved flexibility. Their fine-motor skills begin to be highly developed.

Having a healthy diet and exercising are good health habits to encourage. Parents and adults need to emphasize good safety habits and basic rules of safety in the home.

School-age children are beginning to think more logically. They are beginning to realize that others have ideas different from their own. Being able to see more than one change in an object has improved their logic. They can mentally put together changes in an object and can join a series of events to see a transformation. School-age children are able to use reversibility skills. Deductive and inductive reasoning is becoming more accurate. Their understanding of physical knowledge and logical thinking concepts is getting better. They have mastered most of the rules of language, including grammar and articulation.

Parents and adults need to provide activities that will help the school-age child grow mentally. Common experiences can help children learn. Helping children prepare for school and creating an environment that encourages learning is important.

Children show greater social awareness during middle childhood. Adult and peer relationships deepen. Peer groups are important. Children's feelings about themselves are reinforced by how peers treat them. Their sense of work and industry increases as they develop attitudes that prepare them for adult work. The major emotions of love, fear and anxiety, and anger and aggression are fairly well set and affect their behavior.

Parents and adults can encourage their school-age children to take part in peer activities and help them get along with friends. Activities that challenge their physical, mental, and social skills can be planned. Adults can model emotional control when dealing with discipline problems. Creating an atmosphere of open communication builds strong bonds between adults and children. By their love, respect, and guidance, adults can help children maintain a strong self-concept.

To Review

Write your answers on a separate sheet of paper.

1. True or false. Boys are taller and heavier than girls throughout all of middle childhood.
2. True or false. The first permanent teeth to erupt replace lost baby teeth.
3. List four reasons why school-age children need an adequate diet.
4. Upon hearing another person's point of view, a child in the concrete operational stage thinks their own ideas are (always right, possibly wrong).
5. True or false. When noting change in an object, school-age children begin to take in more than one aspect of the change at the same time.
6. Give two examples of deductive reasoning.
7. List three reasons why entering school for the first time is stressful.
8. (Physical, Mental, Social) development is the most critical aspect of development in middle childhood.
9. Children can learn proper work attitudes when adults encourage them (to just get by, to do their best) in everything.
10. List six purposes of the peer group.
11. Which of the following statements are true? (You may choose more than one.)
    a. School-age children need adults to make most decisions for them.
    b. Adults need to encourage children to be independent.
    c. Adults affect the gender role learnings of children, even in the school years.
    d. Because peer influence is so great during the school years, it matters little what attitudes or priorities adults convey by their actions or words.
    e. Family activities like vacations should stop during middle childhood because children need and want to be with peers.

To Do

1. Make a collage of pictures of children from ages six through twelve. What physical changes do you notice?

2. Observe the play of six- and seven-year-olds and of eleven- and twelve-year-olds. How does their play differ in terms of motor skills?

3. Make a poster called "Qualities Needed In Motor Skills." Divide the poster into five areas. Label the qualities as reaction time, precision, speed, strength, and flexibility. Find pictures or draw sketches of activities that fit each quality. Basketball requires precision.

4. Make a list of gross-motor and fine-motor activities. Ask a class of fourth or fifth grade students to check their three favorite activities. Tabulate the results. Were gross-motor or fine-motor activities chosen most often?

5. In a class or panel discussion, consider these questions.
   a. What are some words that describe adults who readily see from the viewpoint of others? (One term could be *open minded*.) What are some words that describe those adults who have problems in seeing from the viewpoint of others?
   b. What skills are needed to see from the viewpoint of others? What are the reasons school-age children can only begin to develop the skill of seeing from the viewpoint of others?
   c. Give some incidents in which not seeing from the viewpoint of others has led to serious situations and in which it has led to funny situations.

6. Make a list of all the ways you could classify students in your class.

7. Ask an elementary school librarian or town librarian to show you some school-age children's books whose authors use puns and word play effectively. You might start by reading through the writings of Dr. Seuss and Shel Silverstein. After selecting a book, you may
   a. share some examples of the author's plays on words with your class
   b. read the book to school-age children (or one child) and share their reactions to the story with your class

8. Discuss how the world of work and home-care tasks have changed during the last two or three decades. (Your high school counselor and a family and consumer sciences teacher are good resource people.) Discuss how they have changed the skills important in adult years. How have the needed adult skills changed the knowledge and skills needed by school-age children? What courses have been added to the school curriculum in the last thirty years?

To Observe

1. Observe school-age children eating their school lunches and choosing snack foods. How nutritious are the foods they eat (not just buy)? What problems do you see with their diets in terms of sugars, fats, etc.? What physical problems, if any, can you observe?
2. Observe school-age children playing a table game like checkers, chess, or cards. What evidence of the use of logic (strategy) do you see? How would this be different for a five-year-old attempting to play the game?
3. Observe a group of school-age children. What "rules" are being set for acceptance in the group? Which aspects of development are being the most critically judged by peers (body appearance, physical skills, intellectual abilities, or socialization skills)? Explain your answer. What is happening to children on the fringe of the group?
4. Observe school-age children in the classroom. Which emotion or emotions seem the hardest to control? Give examples of how displays of anger, aggression, fear, or anxiety may be a way of saying, "I need love." Explain your answer.

To Think Critically

1. How do you think girls who mature early feel when they are taller and more mature looking than their classmates or when they excel in skill performance over these same peers?
2. Some parents give their kindergartners a "crash course" (often a few weeks or even a few days before school starts) in learning the alphabet, naming colors, counting, and writing their names. Do you think this is harmful to children? Why or why not? Is it truly helpful to children? Why or why not?
3. Why do you think school-age peers judge each other so harshly? What societal factors do you think contribute to this behavior?

Chapter 20

Teaching Through Play

After studying this chapter, you will be able to

☐ describe the importance of play and play activities in children's lives.

☐ explain how adults can help children learn through play, art, music, science, and books.

After studying this chapter, you will be able to define

active-physical play
imitative-imaginative play
language-logic play
manipulative-constructive play
manipulative stage
melody percussion instruments
percussion instruments
play therapy
prop box
representation stage
rhythm instruments
scribbling
transparencies
visual arts

In play, children learn important facts and skills they will need in later life.

Children are curious. They want to explore new objects, places, and people. Children also are eager learners. They ask countless questions as they strive for self-direction. Children express their learnings in many ways, such as through play, art, and music.

Learning and expressing are closely related. Learnings are reflected in the way children express themselves. Their expressions expand and refine their learnings, 20-1.

Children need adults to help them learn and to invite self-expression. Adults can see what the child is ready to do. They can provide the time, space, and materials for activities. They can give children ideas, if needed. For the most part, children learn more from their senses and actions than from being told. Adults need to provide play experiences that teach children instead of experiences that simply amuse them.

Children and Their World of Play

Through play, children interact with the world of people and objects. Play can even take the form of ideas, such as word play and problem-solving games. Play is a self-chosen activity that children do for its own sake. Most of all, play is fun.

▶ Importance of Play

Until recently, experts had not studied the value of play. They had not given it an important place in a person's life. Play—even for children—was not accepted in early history because children were expected to work. In the more recent past play was seen as something children and adults did in their spare time. Today, experts know that play is important.

Play and Physical Development

One reason play is important is that it helps a child's physical development. Play improves muscles and nerves. Activities help the heart and lung systems. Active children who play often are more likely to maintain a proper weight. Play also improves balance and coordination, 20-2. Active children and adults tend to feel healthier than those who are not active.

Play and Mental Development

Children learn through play. In turn, children's play reflects what they have learned. Play helps children learn concepts about their physical world. Play also brings children in contact with objects. Children can cause objects to do many things. They observe the results of actions. Children soon see how objects differ. They also learn how objects are made and about their physical limits.

Relationship Concepts. Through play, children learn relationship concepts. Number concepts form as the child sees that more blocks mean a higher tower or a longer train. In filling a sand pail, children see that small objects fit inside,

20-1 While playing in the sand, a child can express what he or she knows as well as learn more about the nature of sand.

4

Rebecca Lawrence

1—*Discuss:* Define the word *facilitate.* Why is it good to facilitate children's learning? Give examples of ways to facilitate learning.

2—*Reflect:* A child development specialist once stated, "Play is children's work." Write your reactions to this statement.

3—*Resource: Learning through Play,* SAG.

4—*Enrich:* List or locate household objects that would be suitable for sand play.

Fisher-Price, Inc.

20-2   A toy can help eye-hand coordination.

but a beach ball will not fit. Other relationship concepts also develop.

Symbol Systems.   Symbol systems are used in play, too. In symbol-type play, the child selects the most important aspects of an experience. For example, when playing with dolls, a child mostly feeds, bathes, changes clothes, and rocks them. When pretending to be a wild animal, a child may make loud sounds and pretend attacks.

Language.   Play helps children learn language. For the infant, the sound of peek-a-boo comes to signal the return of a person. The older child learns many words while playing with others. Children also try out new rhythm and sound patterns in language. Infants begin with babbling sounds. Older children try rhymes, jingles, and other forms of language sound patterns.

Humor and Creative Thinking.   Humor is mental play. When a child makes a harmless "mistake," such as drawing a dog with wings, the child is showing humor. Play also improves creative thinking. Through play, children try new ideas. For this reason, children who play the most are more apt to become artists and scientists as adults.

In play, children also learn that they can make mistakes. Because they do not feel pressure, children enjoy learning lessons through play.

Play and Social-Emotional Development

Children become aware of others through play. Through this greater awareness, they develop trusting relationships. Babies play games only with people they trust, such as parents and other caregivers. Parents who play with their children during the childhood years seem to be close to them in later years.

Play also teaches children the concepts of rights and properties, sharing, and settling disputes. In play, children learn to detect others' feelings. Children who play well with others seem to have the most friends, 20-3.

Children work out many of their problems in play. They also use playtime to make things happen their own way. Preschool children often feel limited in what they can do or make happen. By playing dinosaurs, they can identify with the dinosaur's size and strength and make up for their own weaknesses.

20-3   Playing as a group helps social development.

Del Monte Corp.

▶ Stages of Play

Children's play reflects changes that take place in their physical, mental, and social-emotional development. In a real way, play pulls together all aspects of development.

Children go through stages of play as they grow. These stages build on each other. Babies do not begin to play in advanced stages. Once children reach a higher stage of play, however, they can play in earlier stages, too. When older children play with younger children, the stage of play most often fits the younger children. When children play with new objects, the stage of play also becomes less advanced.

Stages of play are described in terms of the child's play with objects and with people. Chart 20-4 shows stages of play with objects and people and how these two areas compare to each other. Because experts do not agree totally on these stages, the chart shows only one way to view the stages of play.

▶ Types of Play

There are many types of play. One way to think about play is by its stages. Another way to think about play is by the basic skills involved. Types of skills involved in play include active-physical play, manipulative-constructive play, imitative-imaginative play, and language-logic play.

Active-Physical Play

In *active-physical play,* children use gross-motor skills. These skills use the large muscles for movements like walking, running, hopping, jumping, twisting, bending, skipping, galloping, catching, throwing, balancing, pushing, pulling, and rocking.

Through active-physical play, children learn about the space around them. They also learn about objects in this space and the movement of the body. Names for movements and positions in space take on meaning. These names include *forward, backward, big, little, fast, slow, under, over, up, down, behind, in front of, through, beside,* and *between.*

Through play, children improve and test many physical skills. They learn how strong they are by pushing, pulling, lifting, and carrying. Children learn to spring to lift their body and catch themselves on impact. Upward movement is a skill they often need. Catching themselves the right way when they land protects the body from injury. Play also improves their balance and reaction time. Reaction time improves as the body matures and the child practices. Children need balance for almost every large-muscle movement, 20-5.

2

Active-physical play helps children become more graceful. Grace improves when the large-muscle skills are developed and are coordinated with each other. Grace is pleasing to see. It also helps a person engage in many more fun activities.

3

Manipulative-Constructive Play

Manipulative-constructive play involves small-muscle skills. Small-muscle skills develop after the basic large-muscle movements. Writing, a fine-motor skill, develops after walking develops. However, small-muscle skills develop early in life. Crawling babies can pick up small objects (such as gravel and paper) on a carpet. They then can carefully put them in the mouth, ear, and nose. Eye-hand coordination also is involved in manipulative-constructive play.

Many toys and materials promote fine-motor skills. These include jigsaw puzzles, blocks and construction materials, beads for stringing, pegs and pegboards, art tools, woodworking tools, and cooking tools. Toys that promote fine-motor skills are made for little, unskilled hands as well as for more skilled hands, 20-6.

4

Besides small-muscle skills, manipulative-constructive play helps a child's ability to mentally picture objects. It also helps children make abstract models of what they see, 20-7.

Imitative-Imaginative Play

In *imitative-imaginative play,* children pretend to be persons other than themselves or objects. They carry out this play verbally and/or in actions. There are three stages of imitative-imaginative play—imitative play, dramatic play, and socio-dramatic play.

1—*Discuss:* Why would experts disagree?

2—*Activity:* Locate pictures of active-physical play. Identify physical skills each activity would improve.

3—*Activity:* Locate pictures of activities that promote grace. Share in class.

4—*Activity:* Wear gloves and play with some of the toys listed with the opposite hand. Discuss problems encountered and learning from each.

Stages of Play		
Age	**Play with Objects**	**Play with People**
From a few months to school age	☐ Practice play—Babies explore objects by picking them up and by tracking them with their eyes. Play activities are repeated.	☐ Solitary play—Babies ignore other children who are nearby. Sometimes babies treat others as objects to be pushed or walked on, to be poked in the eyes or nose, or to have hair pulled. ☐ Onlooker play—Toddlers watch others play but do not join in their play. ☐ Parallel play—Children play near other children and often play with the same or almost the same toys. They note that others have interests and skills much like their own. However, there is no real interaction among children.
From age 3 through elementary grades	☐ Symbolic play—Children engage in fantasy play. They pretend they are someone else. Also, they project mental images on objects. A stick can become a horse.	☐ Associative play—Two or more children play at a common activity. The children share ideas. However, the play is not well organized. For instance, one child may decide to run a food store and another may be a mother, but the mother never shops at the food store.
Peaks at age 9 or 10	☐ Rule play—Children make rules to govern their games or carefully follow the rules already established.	☐ Cooperative play—Two or more children share common goals and play complementary roles, such as chaser and the chased.

20-4 The stages of play can be described in terms of how children play with objects and how they interact with peers in play situations.

1

1—*Reflect:* Why would a child be more likely to conform to a rule he or she helped establish? Relate this idea to rules in your life.

Wood Designs of Monroe, Inc.

20-5 Balance, which children need for most activities, develops slowly.

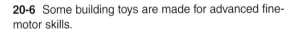

20-6 Some building toys are made for advanced fine-motor skills.

LEGO Dacta, the educational division of the LEGO Group

1—*Activity:* Look through catalogs to locate Dacta sets for different levels of fine-motor skills. If possible, obtain or borrow sets for analysis.

2—*Discuss:* Give examples of imitative play and symbolic thought.

Playskool, Inc.

20-7 Making structures with blocks and other building toys improves a child's mental image of the real objects.

Imitative Play. Imitative play begins at about two years of age, or just as children begin to use symbolic thought, 20-8. Symbolic thought allows the child to let one thing stand for another. A stack of books may become a space ship.

Dramatic Play. The second stage, dramatic play, begins at around three or four years of age. Dramatic play involves role playing with more than one child. Each child's role, however, is independent of the others'. Three children may be space creatures, but each child plays the game in his or her own way.

Socio-Dramatic Play. In the last stage, socio-dramatic play, a group of five- to seven-year-olds plays with a theme. They assign roles to each child. Instead of just being space people, the children may look for new planets. In this form of play, each child has a special role, 20-9.

3—*Discuss:* Is this example characteristic of parallel play or cooperative play? Why?

4—*Discuss:* Is this example characteristic of parallel play or cooperative play? Why?

2

3

4

Angeles Group

20-8 For toddlers and young preschoolers, symbolic play is simple. Often, they use only one object and one action to symbolize the real object or event.

Imitative-imaginative play has great value. Children learn to imagine or picture themselves as if they are other people and objects. This kind of play helps memory because children must recall events in play. It also helps language because children must listen and speak during play. There is much freedom in expression, too, as children try to bridge the gap between what they know and do not know. Children can use their bodies to extend their language. For example, a child may say, "I'm a barber," while using the fingers to snip.

Children also can try out many roles in play. In this way, children get some feel for others' real-life roles. Children join in holiday and other rituals as they act out roles, 20-10. Children also can express fears, resentments, and even hostile feelings in ways that are socially approved. **Play therapy,** using play as a way to help children with their problems, is used by trained counselors.

Language-Logic Play

Language-logic play is the form of mental play most often seen in school-age children. There are many different types of language and word games. Some language games include those in which children compete using vocabulary skills. Other language games include humor that is based on language, such as puns. Logic games require much thought about one's actions. Children must think ahead and plan strategies for sports and table games, 20-11. Logic games also include object puzzles and word problems.

▶ Adult Role in Children's Play

Adults have a major role in children's play. They must provide time, space, and materials. They need to allow for a great deal of free expression. Their attitude toward play influences how a child views an activity. Adults can promote creativity by what they do and say. Adults should provide play experiences that are important to children. To help children learn through play, adults need to allow freedom to play, allow time to explore, display the right attitude toward play, and select toys with care.

20-9 As older children play house, they take on specific roles of adults. Symbolic play is much more advanced than in the earlier years.

Angeles Group

1—*Discuss:* Review the benefits of imitative-imaginative play. Discuss each.

2—*Enrich:* Do research on play therapy as a career. Present information to the class.

3—*Activity:* Provide examples of language-logic games, or examine catalogs for examples. Discuss the benefits of each.

4—*Enrich:* Divide into groups. Have each group develop a positive and negative play environment, emphasizing adult attitudes, environment, and communication.

Allow Freedom to Play

During play, children should be allowed as much freedom as possible, 20-12. Children's play can be restricted by toys that suggest something specific to do, such as jigsaw puzzles. Adults restrict play by setting many rules for safety or other reasons. Peers, too, restrict play by telling each other what and how to play. Although play can never be totally free, adults should help keep restrictions to a limit.

Allow Time to Explore

Adults should give children time to explore materials on their own. Adults can observe play and, at times, add ideas or materials. Children should decide whether to use them. One example of how to add ideas and materials is modeling an action, such as pretending to eat make-believe food. Adults also can increase a child's language

© Nancy P. Alexander

20-11   Because school-age children have logic skills, they can plan strategy for board games and even play with adults.

2

skills by adding to a child's growl. They may say, "Growl! I am a tiger looking at you with my big, green eyes." Adults also can explain new concepts. They can describe airplanes as objects that go quickly down a special road called a runway so they can fly in the air. They can use blocks and a toy plane to explain. Adults need to change toys or add new toys from time to time.

3

Display the Right Attitude Toward Play

Adults need to see the importance of play and express that feeling to children. Think of the attitude an adult expresses to a child when the adult says, "Can't you see I'm busy? Go away and play." Toys and play need to be seen as important, too.

4

Select Toys with Care

Adults should select toys with care. Toys should be safe and fun. (See chapter 21 for more details about toy safety.) In addition, because all children are different, they like different types of toys. Many infants and toddlers like texture toys, squeeze toys, and toys that make sounds. Preschool children like toys for large-muscle play (balls, pedal toys, climbing toys) and small-muscle play (puzzles, beads, pegs). They also like construction toys. They need role-playing toys, too. These include floor blocks, dress-up

5

20-10   The mood and meaning of holidays are captured through role-playing.

Libby, McNeill and Libby, Inc.

1—*Discuss:* What other ways can adults promote language skills and pretending?

2—*Activity:* Check catalogs for board games for school-age children. Note recommended ages. Report in class.

3—*Note:* Relate this to the previous idea that adults who play with their children seem to be close in later years.

4—*Discuss:* Why is it a good idea to rotate toys frequently?

5—*Enrich:* Look through parenting magazines for ideas on playing with children. Report to the class.

20-12   Looking at fossils through a magnifying glass is an interesting way to learn and play without restrictions.

clothes, puppets, toy cars, trucks, planes, animals, and people. They also can use prop boxes for role-playing. A **prop box** is a collection of real objects placed in a box to fit different roles, such as store clerk or nurse. Games with rules are popular with school-age children.

Toys should be planned for different play settings, such as indoors, outdoors, and travel. Travel toys must be chosen with much thought. These toys must be held in children's hands or laps. They must be safe in a moving car. They cannot make too much noise for a small space or distract the driver. Toys must be able to withstand the heat or cold of a closed car. Some toys and games are designed for travel. These toys include cassette tapes of songs and stories, magnetic game boards, and games where older players spot certain items, such as license plates and road signs, while moving.

Children's toy collections need to be balanced. Children need different types of toys to aid all aspects of development. Adults need to avoid giving too many toys that "perform." These toys do not allow much involvement. Children can use toys like building blocks, art supplies, and balls in many ways, 20-13.

Adults must be wise when purchasing toys. They should keep in mind that children usually have too many toys. These toys are expensive. In addition, children learn a lot from making toys. Sometimes they spend as much time making toys as they do playing with them. Making toys also teaches children to save and recycle useful items often thrown away.

1

2

1—*Enrich:* Consult developmental scales for children from birth through age five. List toy suggestions for each characteristic, or find pictures of toys that would facilitate each stage of development. Share with the class.

2—*Activity:* Develop a collage of toys, games, and activities appropriate for traveling.

3—*Activity:* Consult craft magazines or preschool activity books for toys that can be made with children. Plan ways for children to help.

Landfield Co., Rig-A-Jig

20-13   A child can use this building set to make other toys.

Providing Enrichment Activities for Children

Adults can provide many learning experiences that enrich children's lives. They can encourage creativity by the type of play they provide and the ways they value these activities. Experiences in art, music, science, and literature help children learn aesthetic, creative, and scientific concepts. Having rich and fulfilling experiences in these areas also reinforces other basic learnings and helps children develop.

Art

Art is important in children's lives. This includes the *visual arts* of painting, constructing, and photography. Visual arts help children in many areas of development. For example, fine-motor skills improve as children handle brushes, scissors, and crayons.

The arts increase intellectual learnings, too. Sensory experiences help children expand their concepts of color, line, shape, form, texture, and size. Because children create what they know, visual arts cause children to think about their world. Children then record their ideas in their finished products.

1—*Discuss:* Describe what a child learns from finger painting.

2—*Discuss:* Summarize the benefits of art experiences. Why is it important to allow a child freedom of expression?

Finally, art helps children develop in social-emotional areas. Children make choices about what they want to do and how they want to do an art activity. Art helps them to express feelings, too. Taking pride in their art and knowing that others accept their products helps their self-concept, 20-14.

2

Stages of Development in Visual Arts.

Experts study the stages of children's development by watching children use art materials and by looking at their finished products. A child's total development determines how he or she uses crayons, paints, clay, and other art materials. At first, children play with the art materials. They then use the materials to represent objects, experiences, and feelings. For these reasons, development is divided into the manipulative stage and the representation stage.

Manipulative Stage.   In the *manipulative stage,* children play with art materials rather than use them to create artwork. Early in

20-14   Children express their feelings through art.

3

3—*Note:* An art therapist has training in analyzing these feelings and helping children with emotional problems.

this stage, children under two years of age enjoy art for motor reasons. They cover paper with marks and pinch, pat, and even eat clay.

Soon the child begins to see what happens as a result of certain actions. At about 24 to 30 months, children begin the second step in this stage, called *scribbling*. **Scribbling** consists of dots, straight and

1

20-15   Human figure drawing begins with the head (A). Later, the child adds single lines to show trunk, arms, legs, fingers, and feet (B). Next, the child uses double lines for body thickness (C). Finally, the child adds detail to clothing (D).

A

C

B

D

1—*Discuss:* Compare these drawings.

20-16 A baseline of ground or water is the first way children show spatial relationships among objects.

curved lines, loops, spirals, and imperfect circles. Scribbling is important because the child must make the eyes and hands work together.

About 30 to 42 months the third step in the manipulative stage occurs. The child begins to use basic shapes, such as crosses, rectangles (including squares), and ovals (including circles). They combine shapes in drawings, too. Many of these shapes are lost in the layers and layers of crayon marks and paint.

In the transition step between the manipulative stage and the representation stage, children ages 42 to 60 months create their first symbols. Because the child often decides what the symbol is after it is made, the symbol may or may not be named. The face is often the first and favorite symbol seen in children's drawings. Even when children draw a body, it appears to be an afterthought. Children add lines to draw arms, hands, body, and legs. They use circles for feet or shoes, 20-15. The head remains the largest part of children's drawings for years. Although drawings contain symbols, there are no spatial relations among objects. Symbols seem to float.

Representation Stage.   Most five- or six-year-old children have reached the ***representation stage.*** In this stage, children create symbols that represent objects, experiences, and feelings. Adults can see that a child has entered this stage when the child decides what the symbol is before creating it. ("I'm going to draw a tree.") Another signal is that the child shows spatial relations among objects. In a simple spatial relationship, the child shows what is on the ground by using a baseline. (A *baseline* is a line of grass, dirt, or water drawn near the bottom of the paper. The baseline also can be the lower edge of the paper itself.) The sky often appears as a strip of color across the top of the paper. "Air" is between the objects on the baseline and the sky, 20-16. A child may draw two or more baselines, which show objects at varying distances. The objects closest to the child always are drawn on the baseline closest to the lower edge of the paper.

Other spatial relations in the representative stage include folding over. *Folding over* is showing a spatial idea by drawing objects perpendicular to the baseline, even when it means drawing objects upside down, 20-17. Some children draw a mixture of side view and top view in one drawing. A child may draw a table and chairs with

20-17 Children often show objects that are across from each other by drawing objects at right angles to a baseline. This results in upside-down objects.

1—*Activity:* Divide into groups. Have students prepare posters for the four age groups explaining or illustrating the steps in the manipulative stage for play dough, clay, easel painting, and drawing.

2—*Enrich:* View drawings of preschoolers. Compare these with text information.

3—*Activity:* Have students illustrate the baseline information.

chairs showing from the side view, but with the whole top of the table showing.

In an effort to depict what they know about objects rather than what is visually true, children's symbols often have certain features. Many times they *exaggerate* (or increase) size to show importance. A child may exaggerate the size of his or her parent in a drawing.

Children often draw symbols pictured as transparencies. **Transparencies** are pictures that show the inside and outside of an object at the same time, much like an X ray. A drawing of a house may have windows on it, but it may show people and furniture inside the house as well. In other types of transparencies, children mix the profile and side views of an object. For instance, a profile view of a person may show two eyes.

20-19   School-age children begin to include visual depth in their drawings.

After age seven or eight, representation becomes more exact. Children draw a more detailed human face that shows expression, 20-18. Visual depth also becomes a part of these more advanced drawings, 20-19. Children draw the perspective of objects as they see it, not as they think it should look. By nine or ten years of age, children can draw objects from their perspective and from the perspective of others.

■ The Adult's Role in Stimulating Art Experiences

Adults can stimulate art experiences by introducing children to artistic skills and to art activities suited to their stages of development. Adults should provide art materials that allow children to explore and enrich their art skills. Adults can encourage children in their artwork in many ways.

In introducing children to art activities, adults should provide children with the right environment and supplies, 20-20. They must show children how to use artistic tools, such as scissors and paint brushes. Once children understand how to use tools, adults should let children do their own work. They should not make models for children to copy or add to the child's work. Children's work reflects their skill in handling tools and their way of seeing the world. See chart 20-21 for suggested art activities.

20-18   School-age children add many details to the human face.

1—*Enrich:* Compare actual drawings of six-year-olds and four-year-olds. Describe the differences.

2—*Reflect:* Describe an early art experience you can remember. Were you free to create your own work or was it structured for you? Explain the importance of allowing a child freedom to create his or her art product.

Environment and Supplies for the Visual Arts

The Environment

Space	☐ Find a place to draw, paint, model clay, cut and paste. The space must be easy to clean, such as a kitchen, playroom, or outside.
Storage	☐ Use a large cardboard box to store supplies. You may decorate the box with the child's favorite artwork.
Display	☐ Hang pictures on the refrigerator with magnets, mount on a bulletin board, or display in a picture frame. Change artwork frequently.
Keeping artwork	☐ Select a few products and store them in scrapbooks or photo albums.

The Supplies

Paper
☐ Buy newsprint and construction paper, shelf paper, and paper bags.

Crayons
☐ Buy large crayons (suited for small hands) in the eight basic colors. (For young children, nontoxic, washable crayons are best.)

Paint
☐ Buy dry tempera that is mixed with water for brush painting and with liquid starch for finger painting.

Pudding Finger Paint
Prepare instant vanilla pudding to which a few drops of food coloring has been added.

Scissors
☐ Buy quality child-sized scissors. Scissors are available for left-handed and right-handed children. Depending on a child's age, select either blunt or pointed styles.

Paint brushes
☐ Buy three or four brushes with short handles and bristles that are about one inch wide.

Paste
☐ Buy white paste or glue that works on paper and cloth. You also may make your own paste.

Flour Paste
1   cup flour
1/2 cup water
   Combine flour and water. Mix well until creamy. Store in covered container.

Clay
☐ Buy plasticine (clay that remains soft due to oil) or play dough. You also may make play dough.

Peanut Butter Play Dough
2   cups peanut butter
1   cup flour
1   cup confectioner's sugar
   Combine and mix.

Play Dough

2	cups flour	2	tablespoons salad oil
1	cup salt	4	teaspoons cream of tartar
2	cups water		food coloring

Combine and cook until mixture thickens into a soft ball. When cool enough to handle, knead. Store in an airtight container.

Collage materials
☐ Collect alphabet cereal, pasta, dried beans or peas, seeds, boxes, cloth, yarn, ribbon, paper, flowers, leaves, twigs, straws, and other objects that children can glue to a flat surface.

Art smock and cleanup supplies
☐ Use an old, long-sleeved man's shirt. Cut sleeves to child's wrist length and put on backwards. Button only the top button. Use a vinyl piece to cover work table.

20-20   The right environment and supplies enhance art learnings.

1—*Discuss:* Why is it important to save a child's artwork? Why is it desirable to let a child choose items to be displayed?

2—*Note:* Stress the importance of safety.

3—*Note:* Stress the importance of not eating this substance.

4—*Note:* Provide enough materials to let children select what they want to use.

Art Activities

Squeeze bag art

Use a self-locking, clear food storage bag. Put a few tablespoons of finger paint inside. Smooth the bag until paint covers the inside of the bag with a solid film. Press air out, lock the bag, and seal the bag with tape. Place the bag on a flat surface. The child can draw on it with fingers. To renew drawing surface, rub the bag lightly with your hand.

Deodorant bottle pens

Gather deodorant bottles that have rings and balls. Remove the rings and balls. Fill bottles with tempera paint mixed with water, then replace the rings and balls. (Do not use starch in tempera.) Children can roll paint on paper to make designs.

20-21 Children enjoy art activities like these.

Adults should encourage children by showing interest in their artwork. They can help children try new techniques by saying that they have confidence in the children. Adults can show interest by joining children in art activities. (However, adults should never compete.) They also can display children's artwork, which increases self-esteem.

Reacting to Children's Art

When children show adults their artwork, what should adults say? A good response is to ask the child to tell them about the work. Adults can say, "Can you tell me about your drawing (painting, clay project, or other)?" This is a better response than asking, "What is it?" When children don't know what they should draw or color and ask for ideas, adults can suggest three ideas. The child then can choose the one or ones that appeal the most. This may even inspire more creative thinking, and the child may come up with his or her own idea.

Music

Sounds in many pitches, rhythmic patterns, and degrees of loudness are the parts of music. These parts surround people from birth. Not only do children hear sounds, but they respond by paying attention, moving, and making sounds. Thus, musical development is like all other development. Those children who have had a rich world of sound and movement will have a good background for later learnings and pleasure.

For young children, there is a oneness between movement and music. Even toddlers move to music without being prompted by adults. Because young children need chances to move, music can be a fun way to support this need.

Benefits of Music Experiences

Music provides chances for sensory and expressive experiences. Listening to music is the basis of all musical learning. As children become more attuned to the sounds around them, they learn to translate the sounds in musical ways. They may say that sounds have high or low pitch; even or uneven rhythm. Also, listening to the sounds of music can improve children's listening skills in general.

Making music is fun. Even babies invent ways to make sounds. They shake or hit objects and make sounds with their voices and hands. When children are able to care for musical instruments, adults should encourage them in learning to play.

Many instruments require more finger strength and skill than young children have. For these reasons, the first instruments children use are often percussion instruments. The tone of a **percussion instrument** is produced when a child strikes some part of the instrument. Percussion instruments without a definite pitch, such as drums, are called **rhythm instruments. Melody percussion instruments,** such as xylophones, produce various pitches when certain bars are struck, 20-22. By using these instruments, young children see how sounds are made, play rhythmic patterns, and perhaps play simple melodies.

Singing seems to make children feel good. They often sing or chant to tell what they are doing. ("Feed . . . ing ba . . . by.") They use the

1—*Resource: Development through the Visual Arts,* SAG.

2—*Enrich:* Introduce this section by playing tapes of children's music that could encourage a child to dance and sing. Explain the value of music.

3—*Reflect:* Describe how listening to musical sounds could improve a child's general listening skills.

Lakeshore Learning Materials; Carson, Calif.

20-22   Rhythm instruments are the best instruments for young children.

same words for singing as they do for speaking. Thus, singing helps language learnings.

Although young children do enjoy singing, they often cannot sing a tune. They are not able to match their voice pitch to the notes of the music. Until young children find a singing voice, they simply talk in a sustained hum they call singing. When the singing voice is found, the range is often limited to about six tones (from middle C to A). By practicing and listening, children can develop singing skills over time.

Preschool children also may have problems singing with other voices or with musical instruments. In order to sing with others, children must hear their own voice, the voices of other singers or instruments, and the unison sound.

3

The Adult's Role in Guiding Music Experiences

To guide music experiences, the adult must introduce children to music activities suited to their interests. These areas include listening, singing, playing instruments, and moving to music, 20-23. In addition to providing activities, adults can provide an environment that is rich in sound. They can model enthusiasm and appreciate a variety of music.

Perhaps the adult's most difficult role is listening to and praising children's musical attempts. Children need adult encouragement if they are to practice enough to gain musical skills. Especially during the school years parents and other adults may listen to many less-than-perfect performances. However, with loving acceptance children can become skilled musicians or, at least, learn to appreciate music.

4

Science

Children are born scientists. They wonder and seek answers. The raw materials of science surround children in their homes, in their yards, and in their preschools and schools.

What Is Science?

To children, science is wondering about the world and everything in it. Before they can wonder, children must progress through a few steps. They must be aware, then focus on an object or happening by ignoring other things, and then observe, 20-24.

Science is part of everyday life. Children experience science when they catch a cricket, put it in a jar, and watch it. They experience science when they watch water freeze and see snow melt. Children can learn about science when they ask, "Why do I need to eat my green beans?" or, "How do clouds move?"

5

1—*Reflect:* Why are rhythm instruments good for young children? Describe your favorite rhythm instruments when you were a preschooler.

2—*Reflect:* How does singing make you feel? How would these feelings also apply to children? What do children learn from singing?

3—*Activity:* Participate in a singing activity with a group of young children. Record your observations (including their ages). Report to the class.

4—*Reflect:* How would you encourage a child's musical attempts?

5—*Reflect:* Provide two answers for each question.

Music Activities

Hearing sounds
Play tapes that feature sounds in nature and sounds that manufactured products make. Talk about the tones heard in terms of sound qualities like *high-low, loud-soft, near-far,* and *continuous-discontinuous.* Also talk about the direction of the sound.

Story sounds
Read stories that mention sounds. Ask children to make the sounds mentioned in the story using their voices, their bodies, or objects.

Matching sounds
Play different tones on the piano or on bells. Ask the child to match his or her voice to the pitch. (Notes should be between middle C and one octave above middle C.) For a variation, match rhythms by tapping a simple rhythmic pattern and having the child echo the pattern. After the children echo several patterns, ask a child to play a pattern and you echo.

Finding the Sound
Have children pretend to be kittens or other animals that make a sound. Have the kittens hide while mother cat (one of the children) pretends to be asleep. After the kittens have hidden, the mother cat awakens and meows a call to her kittens. Kittens meow in response, and the mother cat must find the kittens by following the sounds. For a variation have the children point in the direction of a sound that they hear. You may also have children locate a loudly ticking clock or metronome.

1

20-23 Music activities provide sensory and expressive experiences.

Science is appreciating beauty. Most children are awed by the world of living and nonliving matter. They are eager to share what they find with others, 20-25.

Science is caring for the world. For the most part, children translate beauty into caring. However, because of their young minds, children may

Lakeshore Learning Materials; Carson, Calif.

20-24 All scientists—both children and adults—observe in order to learn.

not know that living things can be hurt or even killed. They may not understand that resources like water, land, and air can be damaged. They may not realize that people can spoil beauty when they are not careful.

How Adults Can Encourage Science Activities
Adults should encourage children to wonder, to appreciate the beauty of their world, and to focus on science in everyday life. Adults can call attention to the beauty of many science concepts. These include light coming through a prism, colors on butterflies' wings, the smell of roses, and the songs of birds. Adults also can read books on nature. They can visit zoos, gardens, and forests with children.

© Nancy P. Alexander

20-25   Children like to share special objects they find in nature.

(Some places have special children's tours.) Adults also can help children make collections of beautiful things, such as seeds, rocks, and shells.

Children usually explore and ask questions without being led by adults. However, adults can use some methods to help children explore. They can ask children to name the sense(s) used in learning about many objects—a bell, a rainbow, the rain, foods, a frog, or any other object. Adults can encourage children to classify objects. Adults may ask, "How are these two objects alike? How are they different?" Adults also should ask many questions to encourage children to test ideas. Adults may ask, "What goes through a sifter?" "What do magnets pick up?" "Which objects float?" "What would happen if. . . ?"

Lessons on care must begin early. Adults can begin by giving children tasks in caring for living things from the toddler years on, 20-26. (The task must match the child's age.) Adults also should model care. This includes saving energy in the home and asking young children to help turn

off lights and running water. Families also should help with cleanup work around the home and in their community.

■ Focus of Science Activities

Science activities should focus on what children see and question around them. Science should never be a magic show. Instead, adults should explain science so that children can learn about the world, 20-27. For this reason, the topics and their order may differ from child to child. Generally speaking, topics should focus on children's questions and play activities.

Children should focus on substances (physical matter of things). As children play, they handle liquid, granular, and solid substances. Activities should focus on the properties of substances. An adult may ask, "What is water like?" See 20-28. Other activities should focus on what objects can be made from (or with) a substance or how the substance is used.

Children can overcome some fears with science facts. Children often fear thunderstorms. By the early school years, children can understand the causes of thunder and lightning with adults' help. Adults can explain that thunder is a loud noise caused by lightning, which rapidly heats the air causing the air to expand. (To demonstrate the sound, blow up a paper bag, hold the

3

4

20-26   Children must learn to care for the treasures of nature, such as animals, early in life.

3—*Enrich:* Using several substances, develop questions to use with children.

4—*Discuss:* What does a child learn from caring for an animal?

1—*Enrich:* Take a group of children on a nature hike. Provide each child with a small bag for collecting interesting objects. Have the children prepare a collage or picture from their materials.

2—*Enrich:* Develop more questions to encourage children to explore and ask questions.

1994 Stanley Rowin

20-27 An adult could turn this play activity into a science lesson by talking to these boys about communication and sound waves.

20-28 Children need to have many firsthand experiences with substances like water.

© John Shaw

neck of the bag tightly, and hit the bag with the other hand. As the air expands and breaks the bag, there is a pop.) Lightning is a flash in the sky caused by energy (electricity) being released. (In a dark room, you can create "lightning" [static electricity] by rubbing two inflated balloons on your clothes, then holding the balloons close to each other. A spark jumps between the two balloons much as lightning does within a cloud or between a cloud and the ground.)

Children should focus on fun activities that can involve many learnings, 20-29. For example, cooking is one of the best ways to learn many science concepts, and both preparing and eating food is fun.

▶ Books and Literature

Books and literature open up a world of magic and new ideas for children. What child is not enchanted with stories? Books and literature are important learning tools.

20-29 Cooking activities can help children learn about science.

© John Shaw

Benefits to Children

Books enrich life and help children appreciate beauty. Books answer children's endless questions and cause children to want to learn. Through quality stories and poems, children hear the rhythm of language, the rise and fall of the voice, and tongue-tickling phrases.

Reading to children helps them improve their spoken language. Language development improves when adults read to children often. Children then may make up their own stories and poems at an early age, 20-30. A young child made up this poem while watching water flow from a water hose. "Water drip, water fall, running down my outside wall." (Keith, age three)

Children who have learned to love books can express themselves through dramatic play, art, music, and other experiences, 20-31. They are able to express themselves and their feelings in many forms.

Children like to hear stories about others their own age and about people and things with which they are familiar. They better understand themselves by hearing stories that draw on their backgrounds.

Selecting Books and Literature for Children

In order for books and other literature to stretch the mind and stir creativity, adults must choose them with care. A children's librarian can help adults make good choices.

Books need to be on the child's level. Babies and toddlers enjoy hearing nursery rhymes. Toddlers and preschool children enjoy picture books with quality pictures. First picture books need only simple captions (or perhaps no caption at all). Later picture books have simple plots. In picture books the pictures tell the story. Books for older children have more involved plots and more word descriptions.

Children should experience books with delight. Story time should help children relax. Adults should hold children as they read or seat children close to them. They also should read in interesting ways, using inflections and different voices. Children should be able to see pictures

clearly. Adults can encourage remarks or laughter as they read.

Adults can plan some follow-up activities after reading a story or poem. These activities do not have to immediately follow the story. However, they should occur while the book is still fresh in the child's mind. Follow-up activities include talking about the story, finding details in

20-30   Children who are read to often use their rich source of background material for original works.

Disappearing Candy on Halloween
Once there was a jack-o'-lantern who sat in a windowsill and thought, "I'll never get to go somewhere. All I do is sit on a dumb windowsill on Halloween night while kids get to go trick-or-treating. Then they get candy. All I get is lighted with a match!" But the jack-o'-lantern was wrong. That night, a little girl picked up the jack-o'-lantern and put candy in him. Every once in a while there would be a "Crunch! Crunch!" Then the neighbors would say, "You are getting sleepy." When the girl got tired of trick-or-treating, she went home. She decided to eat her candy. Then she reached inside the jack-o'-lantern and pulled out nothing. She picked up jack-o'-lantern and stared with her eyes as big as saucers. She asked, "What has happened to my candy?" She began trick-or-treating again. Meanwhile back at the house, jack-o'-lantern thought, "Well, I guess Halloween is not so bad as long as you are patient and have bushels of candy."

—Kelcey, age seven

The Sad Pumpkin
Once there was a pumpkin. He hated any pie. One day someone gave him some pie and he began to cry. The cook asked, "Why are you crying?" He said, "Because I hate this pie." And when the cook heard this, she too began to cry. The maid came in, and when she saw the mess she said, "What's the meaning of this? I really cannot guess."And when the maid heard, she too began to cry. When the wise man came in, he gave a big, long sigh. He said, "This pumpkin hates it 'cause it's pumpkin pie."

—Keith, age seven

1—*Discuss:* Summarize the benefits of reading to children.

2—*Activity:* Visit a local library to examine children's books. If possible, arrange a presentation by the children's librarian.

3—*Activity:* Check out children's books from the library. Classify each according to the age level. Share with the class.

4—*Activity:* Select a favorite children's book. Explain why it is a favorite. Report to the class.

20-31 Children enjoy drawing their favorite stories.

the pictures, and relating the book to the child's own experiences. Other activities include drawing a picture or making a three-dimensional model. Children also can do activities discussed in the book, such as going to the airport. This makes the story or poem more meaningful to them.

1—*Activity:* Locate a simple story that would be suitable for a child to draw. Share with the class.

2—*Activity:* Consult preschool activity books for ideas on pre- and postactivities for specific children's books.

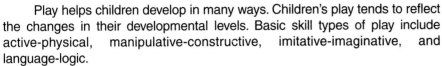

Summary

Play helps children develop in many ways. Children's play tends to reflect the changes in their developmental levels. Basic skill types of play include active-physical, manipulative-constructive, imitative-imaginative, and language-logic.

Adults need to allow children freedom to play and time to explore. Their attitude should reflect the importance of play. Adults should choose safe and fun toys. Selections also should be based on the age of the child and type of play settings. Children can make many toys from objects found at home.

Adults should promote learning experiences in art, music, science, and through books and literature. Children can learn many skills that enrich their lives through these activities.

Children go through the manipulative and representative stages as their art skills develop. Adults need to provide the right environment and supplies to help children with their art activities. They should be supportive and show interest in their children's artwork.

At an early age children move to the sound of music. Most children enjoy singing and making music. Adults can introduce music activities and provide an environment that is rich in sound and movement.

Children's exploring and observing leads to many questions about science concepts. Adults can encourage children's curiosity about the world and help them seek answers to their questions.

Children who have stories and poems read to them increase their language development and self-expression. Adults should choose books and literature with the child's age and interests in mind. Follow-up activities help to reinforce learnings.

1—*Enrich:* Do research on how regular reading influences children's enjoyment of reading in later years. Report to the class.

To Review

Write your answers on a separate sheet of paper.

1

1. Play helps children with
   a. physical development
   b. mental development
   c. physical and social-emotional development
   d. all of the above
2. Match the type of play with the basic skills.
   Types of play
   _____ active-physical play
   _____ manipulative-constructive play
   _____ imitative-imaginative play
   _____ language-logic play
   Skills
   a. symbolizing skills
   b. small-muscle skills
   c. large-muscle skills
   d. high-level mental skills
3. True or false. Different types of skills develop through different types of play.
4. True or false. Visual arts are mainly important for social-emotional reasons.
5. True or false. Scribbling does not have any value in the child's art development.
6. True or false. When children use a baseline in their artwork, they are showing spatial relationships.
7. True or false. Children use transparency symbols in their artwork when they are between two and three years of age.
8. Listening to the sounds of music (can, cannot) improve children's listening skills in general.
9. True or false. Rhythm instruments are often the first musical instruments children use.
10. True or false. Children's science learnings are mainly made up of special activities planned for children.
11. True or false. Children's spoken language reflects what has been read to them.
12. Explain how books can help children appreciate beauty.

To Do

1. Make a bulletin board that reads "Science Is. . . (Wondering, Appreciating Beauty, Caring for Our World, and Part of Everyday Life)."
2. Observe two children of different ages at play. Try to place the children in the stage of play with objects and the stage of play with people. Explain your reasons for placing the child in the stages.
3. Display children's visual arts products. Label the products with the correct stage and any other descriptive term, such as "Representation Stage—Transparency."
4. Help an older preschool or school-age child make a simple musical instrument. One good source is the book *Music and Instruments for Children to Make* (Book 1 and Book 2) by John and Martha Faulhaber Hawkinson. Your music teacher may have more resources.
5. Select and read a book to a child. Use a follow-up activity with the story. Report how the child responded to the class.

To Observe

1. Observe children of different ages at play. Using Chart 20-4 as a reference, identify the stage of play you are observing. Explain your answer. Also identify the type or types of play involved.
2. Observe a teacher encouraging children's creative development in visual arts or music. How is the teacher guiding the children's development? How are the children reacting? What skills are children developing? Are the children learning to enjoy the experiences? Explain your answer.
3. Observe children as they select books in a preschool center. Listen to the children talk with each other about the books. Describe the types of books that interest young children. (Note subject matter; illustrations; novelty items, such as "pop-up" pictures; or fun language, such as rhymes.)

To Think Critically

1. If you watch a group of children have free choice play over a period of time, you will note they show preferences for active-physical play, manipulative-constructive play, imitative-imaginative play, and language-logic play. What connections do you see between the children's personalities and their play choices? Which type of play did you prefer as a child? Do you see any connection between preferred play as a young child and your preferences for study, leisure, or work activities now? Explain.
2. The text states that "a child's total development determines how he or she uses crayons, paints, clay, and other materials." Make a collection of children's creative art work. How is the child's physical, intellectual, and social-emotional development reflected in each work of art?
3. Why is play one of the best ways to learn? Can you still learn through play? Give some examples.

Chapter 21

Children need special care
to stay healthy and safe.

Protecting Children's Health and Safety

**After studying this chapter,
you will be able to**

☐   explain ways to protect children from diseases and illnesses.

☐   create a safe environment for young children and teach simple safety practices.

☐   discuss the steps in preparing a child for medical care in the doctor's office, in the hospital, and at home.

**After studying this chapter,
you will be able to define**

active immunity
allergen
allergy
antibodies
antigen
childhood diseases
childproofing
contagious disease
dental caries
diagnosis
first aid
hospitalization
immunity
immunization
inoculation
lethal
orthodontist
passive immunity
restraint systems
symptoms
terminally ill
vaccination
veterinarians

Today's advances in health and safety are greater than ever before. However, growing up is still risky business. Each day, infants and children face the risks of illness, injury, and even death. Sometimes people can control these risks, other times they cannot. Children can avoid many risks altogether. Adults are responsible for children's health and safety more than any other aspect of child development.

● Protecting Children from Disease and Illness

How can a disease, an injury, or an abnormal condition affect a child? Any one may cause pain, lifelong damage to physical health, and low self-esteem. When health problems are prevented, detected early, or treated properly, children have a better chance of leading a healthy life.

▶ Nutrition, Rest, Cleanliness, and Exercise

What are a person's basic needs? For good health, a person must meet his or her needs for good nutrition, rest, cleanliness, and exercise. People must meet these basic needs throughout life. However, paying careful attention to them may be more important in childhood than at any other time.

Basic health care is important because it helps children grow and develop properly. In turn, good health provides children energy for their daily activities. When a disease or injury occurs, children who are otherwise healthy tend to recover quickly and completely. Also, neglecting health needs for long periods of time causes health problems that medical science cannot repair.

Adults need to help children meet their basic physical needs early in life. In addition, adults must model good health practices. These actions positively affect children's health. They also may help children develop good, lifelong health care habits.

▶ Medical and Dental Care

The goal of health care is to keep children well. To do so, doctors examine children regularly, not just when they are sick. Earlier chapters discuss well-baby checkups. These checkups may find possible health problems before they become serious. They even may prevent problems altogether.

Doctors check children's growth and development. They protect children from certain diseases. They also note eating, sleeping, and playing habits. Doctors answer parents' questions about their child's development. Because well-baby checkups are so important, doctors suggest a schedule for regular visits. The schedule varies slightly among doctors, but the following is often used:

- □ birth to six months of age—one visit per month
- □ six months to one year of age—one visit every two months
- □ one to two years of age—one visit every three months
- □ two to six years of age—one visit every six months
- □ six to 18 years—one visit per year

Dental care by dentists should begin after children have most of their primary teeth. Most children have these teeth between two and three years of age. Dentists clean teeth. They inspect and X ray teeth for **dental caries** (decayed places in teeth) and repair damaged teeth. They also teach children how to care for their teeth. A dentist who specializes in general dentistry may refer a child to an orthodontist. An **orthodontist** is a dentist who specializes in correcting irregular teeth. For example, an orthodontist may make crooked teeth straight. When teeth are straight, a pretty smile is not the only benefit. Straight teeth allow people to chew food properly and decrease the chance of tooth and gum disease, 21-1.

1—*Vocabulary:* Use a dictionary to define the term *proactive.* In which aspects of child care is this important?

2—*Enrich:* Do research on government-sponsored health care plans. Compare information. Could these programs help to ensure basic health care for all children? What types of programs are implemented in other countries?

3—*Note:* Stress the importance of parental modeling throughout a child's life.

4—*Enrich:* Interview a dentist. Ask about the recommended age for first visit and how to prepare a child.

3

4

American Association of Orthodontists

21-1 Even teeth that look right at first glance may need straightening for good dental health.

► Immunization

People who have *immunity* to a disease have or will quickly develop antibodies when exposed to the disease. *Antibodies* are agents that prevent a person from having a disease. (A person does not develop immunity to some diseases.)

The newborn may be immune to several diseases because the mother's antibodies entered the baby's blood through the placenta.

(Infants who are breast-fed also receive antibodies from the mother through the first few feedings.) This type of immunity is called *passive immunity.* Passive immunity only provides immunity to diseases for which the mother has antibodies. Also, it does not last after the first few months of life.

Further protection can prevent children from having some diseases. Doctors call this type of protection either *vaccination, inoculation,* or *immunization.* All these terms have the same meaning. Regardless of the term used, a child receives an injection or drops that contain an antigen. An *antigen* is made from the substance that causes a disease. The substance is changed so that the antigen does not cause a reaction as serious as the disease itself. The child reacts by developing *active immunity,* which means his or her body produces its own antibodies. Many times, a child needs more than one treatment (or *primary dose*) to develop full immunity.

Vaccinations prevent some serious diseases. These diseases once caused serious illness and death among children. They include tetanus, diphtheria, pertussis (whooping cough), polio, measles, rubella (German measles), mumps, and chicken pox.

Infants should begin receiving immunizations at birth. Most doctors agree immunizations that begin at birth give children the most protection from disease. Immunizations should protect the baby without competing with antibodies received from the mother. The immunization schedule in chart 21-2 is based on current knowledge.

Children's doctors keep records of immunizations. Doctors check these records before giving more doses. Schools and camps also require them as official records. Parents should keep a record, too, for their own information.

► Medical Attention During Illness

Sometimes children need special medical attention. Many childhood illnesses end quickly without cause for worry. However, many

1—*Reflect:* Describe a childhood vaccination you recall (or ask a parent). Describe any adverse reactions.

2—*Enrich:* Do research on these diseases. Report to the class.

3—*Enrich:* Contact college admissions offices to learn about vaccinations schools require before acceptance.

4—*Vocabulary:* Define the term *symptom.* Choose several common communicable diseases and list symptoms for each.

Recommended Childhood Immunizations		
Recommended Age	Immunization	Comment
Birth	Hep B-1	
1-2 months	Hep B-2	
2 months	DTP, Hib, OPV	DTP and OPV can be initiated as early as four weeks after birth in areas of high endemicity or during outbreaks.
4 months	DTP, Hib, OPV	A two-month interval (minimum of six weeks) recommended for OPV.
6 months	DTP, (Hib)	
6-18 months	Hep B-3, OPV	
12-15 months	Hib, MMR	MMR should be given at 12 months of age in high-risk areas. If indicated, tuberculin testing may be done at the same visit.
12-18 months	Var	Var may be administered to susceptible children at any visit after the first birthday. Unimmunized children who do not have a reliable history of chickenpox should be immunized at the 11- to 12-year visit; susceptible children 13 years of age or older should receive two doses, at least one month apart.
15-18 months	DTaP or DTP	The fourth dose of diphtheria-tetanus-pertussis vaccine should be given 6 to 12 months after the third dose of DTP. It may be given as early as 12 months of age, provided that the interval between doses three and four is at least 6 months and DTP is given. DTaP is not currently licensed for use in children younger than 15 months.
4-6 years	DTaP or DTP, OPV	DTaP or DTP and OPV should be given at or before school entry. DTP or DTaP should not be given at or after the seventh birthday.
11-12 years	MMR	MMR should be given at entry to middle school or junior high school, unless two doses were given after the first birthday.
14-16 years	Td	Repeat every 10 years throughout life.

Vaccine Abbreviations

- ☐   HepB = hepatitis B virus vaccine
- ☐   DTP = diphtheria and tetanus toxoids and pertussis vaccine
- ☐   DTaP = diphtheria and tetanus toxoids and acellular pertussis vaccine
- ☐   Hib = *Haemophilus influenzae* type b conjugate vaccine
- ☐   OPV = oral poliovirus vaccine
- ☐   MMR = live measles, mumps, and rubella viruses vaccine
- ☐   Td = adult tetanus toxoid (full dose) and diphtheria toxoid (reduced dose) for children age seven and older and for adults
- ☐   Var = Varicella vaccine

21-2   This schedule recommends that infants start their immunization program at birth.

symptoms (signs of an illness or injury) may reveal a need for prompt medical help. Chart 21-3 lists some major symptoms for which adults should consult a doctor. Even if they notice vague symptoms, adults should call a doctor if the child's behavior seems abnormal.

In order to understand a child's condition, doctors need specific information. The adult should think of questions the doctor may ask, such as the following:

☐   What are all the child's symptoms? (Give exact information, such as, "Louisa has vomited five times in the last two hours. Each time she has lost about one cup of fluid.")

☐   How long have you noted the symptoms?

☐   Has the child recently been exposed to a **contagious disease** (disease that can be caught from another person)?

☐   Have you treated the child's illness in any way? When? Have you given the child food or liquid? When? Does the child take any medication regularly?

Symptoms Indicating Possible Illness	
Area of Concern	**Symptom**
Appetite	☐ more than one feeding refused
Blood	☐ large amount lost in bleeding ☐ bleeding will not stop
Body movement	☐ convulsions ☐ immobility in any part of the body ☐ shaking ☐ stiffness of the body
Bones and muscles	☐ swelling ☐ pain ☐ difficulty in movement
Brain	☐ dizziness ☐ visual problems ☐ acts strange or looks different ☐ unconsciousness
Breathing	☐ hoarse or noisy ☐ difficulty in breathing ☐ slow or rapid ☐ continued coughing, sneezing, or wheezing
Color	☐ flushed or pale
Digestive system	☐ vomits all or large part of feeding ☐ vomits between feeding ☐ forceful vomiting as opposed to spitting up foods ☐ abdominal pain or tenderness ☐ vomits for several hours with inability to retain fluids ☐ sudden increase or decrease in number of bowel movements ☐ stools unusual in color, odor, or consistency (continued)

21-3   When certain symptoms appear, children may need medical help.

1—*Note:* Stress the importance of noting frequency, intensity, and amounts.

2—*Discuss:* Which of these symptoms would require immediate medical attention?

3—*Discuss:* List examples of contagious diseases.

☐ Do you know whether the child is allergic to any medication? (A new doctor will not know about a child's allergies.)

☐ What is the name and phone number of your pharmacy? (The doctor may phone in a prescription.)

Adults need to write down all this information before calling a doctor, except in extreme emergencies.

Adults should also take notepaper to the phone to write the doctor's instructions. They should ask the doctor questions like the following:

☐ Is there anything I should know about giving medication or other treatments? What other measures should I take (keep the child lightly covered? warmly covered? in bed?)?

☐ When may I expect an improvement?

☐ What changes would merit another call or office visit? Adults should repeat the instructions for the doctor to be sure they are correct.

Symptoms Indicating Possible Illness (continued)	
Area of Concern	**Symptom**
Eyes	☐ irritated or red ☐ sensitive to light ☐ blurred vision
Fever	☐ rectal temperature of 101° F or above ☐ mild fever that lasts several days
General behavior	☐ unusually quiet, irritable, or drowsy ☐ looks strange after a fall or other accident ☐ already ill, there is a rise in fever or new symptoms appear
Nose	☐ nasal discharge (note color, amount, and consistency)
Pain	☐ sharp screaming ☐ ear rubbing, head rolling, or drawing of legs toward abdomen
Skin	☐ dry or hot ☐ excessive perspiration ☐ rash or hives
Throat	☐ sore ☐ red ☐ choking
Urine	☐ change in amount ☐ change in color or odor

1—*Activity:* List information that should be available for a substitute caregiver in case of emergency.

Childhood Diseases and Allergies

Adults who care for children should be aware of diseases that are often contracted during childhood. These are called *childhood diseases*, 21-4. Most of childhood diseases are contagious. Until immunizations were developed for prevention and modern drugs were found effective for treatment, many children died or were left impaired by some of these diseases. Even today, many children suffer negative effects and even die of these diseases. This can occur when adults are not aware of the diseases and their symptoms and do not follow medical advice for prevention or treatment.

Childhood Diseases				
Condition	**Cause**	**Symptoms**	**Medical Advice**	**Protection**
Bronchitis	reaction of air tubes in the chest	cough after a cold that lasts for more than 2 weeks	yes	none
Chicken pox	virus	fever runny nose cough rash (pimples, blisters, and scabs)	yes see Reye's Syndrome keep child away from others for 6 days after rash begins	vaccine
Colds	virus	runny nose scratchy throat coughing sneezing watery eyes	yes, if child develops rash or looks and/or acts very ill — see Reye's Syndrome	none
Conjunctivitis	virus and bacteria	watery eyes mucus in eyes red/pink color "whites" of eyes eyelid redness	yes keep child away from others for 24 hours after treatment is begun	none
Diaper rash	secondary infection may be caused by bacteria or yeast	redness, scaling, and pimples or sores in diaper area	yes if infected, keep away from other children for 24 hours after treatment is begun	none
Diphtheria	bacteria	headache fever severe soar throat with exudate over tonsils and throat cough bloody nasal discharge	yes keep child away from others about 2 weeks after fever begins; throat cultures must be clear	vaccination (continued)

21-4 Childhood diseases can be serious illnesses in the early years.

1—*Reflect:* What childhood diseases have you had?

2—*Enrich:* Ask a doctor to discuss childhood diseases.

Childhood Diseases (continued)				
Condiition	**Cause**	**Symptoms**	**Medical Advice**	**Protection**
Earaches	bacteria and virus	fever pain difficulty in hearing drainage from ear	yes	none
Haemophilus influenza type b (Hib)	bacteria	fever lethargy (tired) vomiting poor appetite earache breathing and swallowing difficulties cough purple area on skin near eyes	yes keep child away from others until fever is gone or until physician determines	vaccine
Hepatitis B	virus	fever jaundice (yellowing of skin and "whites" of eyes) loss of appetite nausea joint pain rash	yes keep child away from others until fever is gone and skin rash is dry	vaccine
Impetigo	bacteria	red, cracking, oozing blister-like pimples often seen on the face	yes keep child away from others for 24 hours after treatment is begun	none
Measles	virus	fever cough runny nose watery eyes rash (brownish red and blotchy that begins on face and neck and spreads downward) white spots in mouth	yes keep away from other other chldren for 6 days after rash begins	vaccine
Meningitis	virus and bacteria	fever lethargy (tired) poor appetite vomiting irritable (fussy) headache stiff neck	yes, emergency medical advice physicians will determine when child may have contact with others	vaccines (Hib-type b and meningo-coccal) (continued)

Childhood Diseases (continued)				
Condiition	**Cause**	**Symptoms**	**Medical Advice**	**Protection**

Mumps	virus	fever
		swelling of one or
		  more salivary
		  glands
		earache; headache
			yes
			
			keep child away from
			  others for 9 days after
			  onset of swelling
				vaccine

**Pertussis
(whooping
cough)**
	bacteria	runny nose
		coughing spells
		vomiting
			yes
			keep child away from
			  others for 3 weeks
			  after cough begins
				vaccine

Polio myelitis	virus	fever; vomiting
		irritable (fussy)
		headache
		stiffness of neck
		  and back
		paralysis in some
		  cases
			yes
			physician will determine
			  when child may have
			  contact with others
				vaccine

**Reye's
Syndrome**
	virus (often
	  within 3 to 5
	  days after
	  other viral
	  infections)
		vomiting
		sudden fever
		mental confusion
		lethargy (tired)
		  and drowsiness
		irritability (fussy)
		body rigidity; coma
			yes, emergency
			  medical advice
				aspirin has been
				  linked to onset
				  in over 90% of
				  cases; thus give
				  <u>no</u> medications
				  containing
				  aspirin

**Roseola
infantum**
	virus	fever
		rash follows fever
		(seen in chldren
		  under 2 years as
		  suggested in the
		  name "infantum")
			yes
			
			keep child away from
			  others until fever is
			  gone
				none

Rubella	virus	red rash
		enlarged lymph
		  nodes
		joint pain
			yes
			
			keep child away from
			  others for 6 days after
			  rash begins
				vaccine

**Scarlet fever
(scarlatina)**
	bacteria	fever
		rash that causes
		  skin to peel
			yes
			keep child away from
			  others for 24 hours after
			  treatment has begun
				none

**Streptococcus
(strep throat)**
	bacteria (same
	  bacteria that
	  causes scarlet
	  fever; thus strep
	  throat is some-
	  times called the
	  scarlet fever of
	  the throat)
		sore throat
		skin infections
			yes
			
			keep child away from
			  others for 24 hours
			  after treatment has
			  begun
				none

Allergies affect over one-fourth of all children and are the greatest cause of chronic long-term health problems in young children. An **allergy** results when a child's immune system is very sensitive and reacts when the child comes into contact with an **allergen**. An allergen is a substance that causes an allergic reaction, 21-5. Common symptoms of allergies include: frequent "colds" and ear infections, chronic congestion ("stuffy nose"), headaches, frequent nosebleeds, dark circles under the eyes, wheezing, skin rashes, frequent upsets to the stomach, and irritability (fussiness). Allergies may be life-threatening, but more often make the child "feel bad." Allergies are treated by removing or limiting contact with the substance (not having a pet or staying inside as much as possible when the pollen count is high), using drugs for allergies (antihistamines, decongestants, and bronchodilators), and receiving injections for some allergens (called "desensitization therapy").

● Accident Prevention

Accidents claim the lives of more children than any of the major killer diseases of childhood. Children depend on adults to protect them. Adults can do so in two ways. First, adults can create a safe environment by removing dangerous objects, preventing unsafe situations, and taking safety measures. Second, adults can model and teach safety practices.

▶ How Do Accidents Happen?

Several factors lead to an increased accident rate among children. Children are energetic and curious. By toddlerhood, their motor skills and curiosity are at a high level.

Accidents happen more often when adults do not supervise children carefully. For example, accidents often happen in large families, when older children supervise younger ones. They also happen in late afternoon and early evening, when adults are busy making dinner and doing other tasks. When adults are ill or are preoccupied, accidents are likely, too.

Types of Allergens		
Allergies	**Agent**	**Symptoms**
Ingestants	☐ Foods (often milk, citrus fruits, chocolate, wheat and eggs) and drugs (medicines taken by mouth)	☐ Digestive upsets ☐ Respiratory problems
Inhalants	☐ Pollens, molds, dust, and animal dander	☐ Respiratory problems
Contractants	☐ Soaps, cosmetics, fibers in clothing, carpets, drapes, and upholstery, plants, and drugs (applied to skin)	☐ Hives and rashes
Injectables	☐ Insect bites and stings, thorns, and drugs (that are injected)	☐ Respiratory problems ☐ Digestive problems ☐ Hives and rashes

21-5 Children may suffer from one or more of these types of allergies.

1—*Reflect:* Have you experienced an allergy? What were the symptoms?

2—*Enrich:* Ask a doctor to discuss allergies.

3—*Discuss:* Compare safety precautions in a child care center and in a home situation.

4—*Resource: Adults Model Health Practices,* SAG.

5—*Resource: Supervision Decreases Accidents,* SAG.

More accidents happen before children learn safety practices. Adults can prevent many accidents by removing hazards, taking safety measures, and making children aware of the need for safety.

Creating a Safe Environment

Creating a safe environment is crucial for preschool children. These children often cannot make sound safety judgments. Children may not understand why they must be careful. They may be too busy reaching their goals to remember warnings. Adults must do all they can to keep the environment safe for children. In such an environment, accidents are reduced and children can play without being too concerned about safety. Older children can help protect themselves.

Anticipating Possible Hazards

Creating an environment free from all risks is impossible. Even if it were possible, doing so would not teach children to face and cope with risks. However, risks must not be too great, or serious accidents may happen. To prevent serious accidents, adults must look for possible hazards.

Children's developmental changes lead to certain types of accidents. Babies face hazards at birth. These hazards multiply as babies' motor skills, curiosity, and independence increase. Chart 21-6 shows accidents that are likely to occur during stages of development. Adults must watch each baby's development carefully. As they see growth stages occur, the adult must take certain safety measures. A child who can crawl up one step or onto any low object can climb an entire flight of steep stairs. Falls are common when babies first climb. However, an adult can keep the child safe by blocking off stairs before a child can climb a whole flight.

Helping Children Meet Goals in a Safe Way

Adults should help children meet their goals in safe ways. Young children learn about the world by climbing and putting objects in their mouth. Adults need to provide children with safe environments rather than change their goals. When babies want to climb, let them climb up and down a carpeted step or off and on a chair. This environment is safe for them to explore, even if they take small tumbles. In addition, it helps children meet their goals. Also, it teaches them to cope with possible dangers when the risks are not great. Adults should block off a steep staircase, however, because this poses a great risk for the child.

Childproofing the Environment

Adults must note dangerous objects in children's worlds. Moving objects out of a child's reach or preventing a dangerous situation is called *childproofing* the environment.

To childproof, adults must move around where children move. They must be at least one step ahead of a child's development. If they are not, the child could be hurt. A child who stands for the first time by grasping a tablecloth may pull off hot soup. Adults also must childproof every part of the environment—inside the home and vehicle as well as outside. They also need to check that the child's belongings are safe, including baby supplies and toys. Adults must choose pets carefully, too.

Indoor Safety

The indoor environment is often the greatest hazard to a child. See 21-7 for some unsafe indoor items, situations, and suggested childproofing measures.

Poisoning. Poisonings of children under age five account for more than half of all accidental poisonings in homes each year. Children at this age like to examine objects. When attractively packaged household products and medications catch their attention, they often swallow products that look (or even taste) like candy.

If adults take safety measures, children are less likely to become victims of poison. Adults need to learn which products are dangerous, 21-8. They must read all product labels and heed

1—*Activity:* Divide into groups representing various ages. As a group, list necessary safety precautions and describe to the class. Why is it important to provide the child with as much freedom as possible without neglecting safety?

2—*Discuss:* Why is it important for a child to have a safe environment to explore rather than a nonsafe environment with a caregiver frequently cautioning him or her?

3—*Activity:* List ways to childproof, including safety equipment parents can purchase.

4—*Resource: Childproofing Is Essential,* SAG.

Accidents Children Are Likely to Experience		
Age of Child	**Child's Traits Leading to Possible Accidents**	**Major Accidents**
Birth through 3 months	☐ skin is much more sensitive to heat than adult's skin ☐ wiggles and rolls off flat surfaces but cannot move away from danger ☐ puts objects into mouth and swallows them	☐ bath scalding ☐ falls ☐ injuries from swallowing small objects ☐ drowning ☐ strangling on cords or smothering from items like dry cleaning bags or balloons
4 through 6 months	☐ skin is more sensitive to heat than adults' skin ☐ moves by rolling over and may crawl or creep ☐ grasps any object and places it in the eyes, ears, nose, or mouth ☐ hits objects, including breakable ones	☐ bath scalding and burns from hot water faucet ☐ falls ☐ injuries caused by swallowing small objects or putting them into eyes, ears, or nose ☐ injuries from broken objects like glass or plastics
6 through 12 months	☐ sits alone ☐ grabs anything in sight ☐ looks for objects hidden or fallen out of sight (around 10 months) ☐ puts objects in eyes, ears, nose, or mouth ☐ hits, pokes, and pushes objects ☐ may walk with or without help	☐ falls from stairs or high places ☐ injuries caused by pulling on cords of kitchen appliances, pulling or grasping containers filled with hot foods or beverages ☐ burns from open heaters and floor furnaces ☐ injuries caused by swallowing small objects or putting them into ears, eyes, or nose ☐ injuries from dangerous objects like knives, sharp-edged furniture, breakable objects, and electrical outlets
1-2 years	☐ walks ☐ climbs ☐ throws objects ☐ pulls open drawers and doors ☐ takes items apart ☐ puts objects in mouth	☐ falls on stairs, in tubs or pools, and off high objects like crib railings or tables ☐ burns from grabbing handles of pots on stove ☐ poisoning from medication and cleaning agents ☐ injuries from dangerous objects like knives, electrical outlets, breakable objects, toys with small parts, and sharp-edged objects inside and outside ☐ injuries caused by being on driveways and roads and in outside storage areas

(continued)

21-6   As children develop, the type of accidents most likely to occur change.

1—*Note:* Turning down the water temperature on the hot water heater is recommended.

2—*Note:* Safely dispose of plastic bags immediately.

Accidents Children Are Likely to Experience (continued)		
Age of Child	**Child's Traits Leading to Possible Accidents**	**Major Accidents**
2 through 3 years	☐ can rotate forearm to turn doorknob ☐ likes to climb on objects ☐ likes to play with and in water ☐ fascinated by fire ☐ moves at fast speed ☐ does not like to be restrained ☐ likes ride-on toys	☐ injuries caused by getting into almost anything that is not locked or equipped with special devices ☐ injuries caused by falls from high places, jumps onto dangerous surfaces like concrete, falls off ride-on toys and swings ☐ burns from cigarette lighters, matches, and open flames ☐ injuries caused by playing in driveways and roads and darting across streets ☐ injuries caused by swallowing small objects or putting them into eyes, ears, and nose
3 to 6 years	☐ explores neighborhood ☐ plays rougher games ☐ plays with other children ☐ tries to use tools and equipment of the home	☐ poisoning from medicines and household products ☐ injuries from using home, shop, and garden tools ☐ injuries related to action games, bicycles, and rough play ☐ various injuries from interesting hazards like old refrigerators, deep holes, trash heaps, and construction sites ☐ drowning ☐ burns from electrical outlets, appliances, and open flames ☐ traffic injuries
6 to 12 years	☐ participates in sports ☐ likely to try stunts on a dare ☐ in traffic as a pedestrian or on bicycle ☐ interested in firearms and fireworks ☐ uses tools in home and yard care	☐ sports-related injuries ☐ drowning ☐ firearm and fireworks accidents ☐ traffic injuries

Indoor Dangers		
Danger	**Reason for Danger**	**Childproofing Measures**
Beverages Alcoholic	☐ Alcohol is a drug that acts as a depressant.	☐ Keep locked or out of children's reach.
Carbonated	☐ Unopened carbonated beverages are under pressure. They can explode, breaking the glass bottle.	☐ Keep glass bottles out of reach, or buy soft drinks in plastic bottles or cans.
Cords Drapery and venetian	☐ Double cords can wrap around neck, causing strangulation.	☐ Knot the looped cords to prevent slipping over a child's head.
Small appliance	☐ Child can pull appliance down using cord. Playing with cord can result in electrocution.	☐ Drape cords behind appliances while in use. Put cords away when appliances are not in use. Keep small appliances out of children's reach.
Table lamp	☐ Child can pull lamp down. Playing with cord can result in electrocution.	☐ Wrap the cord around the back table leg.
Curtains	☐ Child can suffocate if curtain is wrapped around head.	☐ Keep out of baby's and young child's reach. If buying window coverings, consider short curtains, blinds, or shutters.
Doors Swinging	☐ Some doors lead to unsafe areas. Others are used often by children, and children may accidentally lock themselves in a room.	☐ Keep doors to unsafe areas locked or secured with a safety device.
Sliding Glass	☐ Child may walk into or through glass. Fingers can be pinched by door.	☐ Block off door if seldom used, or put decals on glass at the child's eye level. Place a doorstop high on the doorjamb.
Electrical outlets	☐ Child can be electrocuted by putting objects or fingers in outlets.	☐ Cap unused outlets with safety devices or seal them with electrical tape. Place heavy furniture in front of some outlets that are never used or have cords plugged in them rather permanently.
Fans	☐ Fingers can be cut by twirling fan blades.	☐ Place window screening between fan blades and grills. Keep fans out of children's reach.
Firearms	☐ Child may decide to play with gun and accidentally fire it.	☐ Lock firearms and ammunition in separate places. Keep key out of reach.
Fireplaces, open heaters, registers, and floor furnaces	☐ Getting too close can cause burns.	☐ Place guards in front of fireplaces and open heaters as well as around registers and floor furnaces.
Furniture	☐ Unstable furniture can fall on child. Furniture with sharp edges can cause cuts and bruises.	☐ Remove unsteady furniture like plant holders, when possible. Pad sharp edges of furniture. Remove or keep out of reach furniture with glass components.

(continued)

21-7   Children can find many dangerous items indoors.

1—*Note:* Avoid long cords on blinds, draperies, appliances, or telephones.

2—*Activity:* Check your classroom for safety hazards. Develop an improvement plan.

Indoor Dangers (continued)		
Danger	**Reason for Danger**	**Childproofing Measures**
Hot liquids and foods	☐ These can cause burns if spilled on child.	☐ Keep hot liquids and foods out of children's reach. Turn pot handles toward wall. Keep cords behind small appliances being used. Avoid using hanging tablecloths, which children can pull down and spill hot liquids and foods.
Insects, spiders, and rodents	☐ These can bite and spread disease.	☐ Have all pests exterminated. (Be careful not to allow children into areas that have been sprayed for pests until sprays have been cleaned off of surfaces. Also, keep traps out of children's reach.)
Matches and lighters	☐ Children like to play with these. They can burn themselves or even start fires.	☐ Keep all matches and cigarette lighters out of sight and reach.
Rugs, area and throw	☐ Children can slip on or trip over loose rugs.	☐ Use nonskid mats, or put rubber guards under rugs.
Stairs	☐ Small children may fall down stairs.	☐ Place safety gates at the top and bottom of off-limit stairs.
Tools	☐ Many tools are heavy or sharp. Used improperly, they can cause many injuries.	☐ Lock dangerous tools out of children's reach.
Tubs	☐ Child may slip or drown in tub.	☐ Use nonskid mats or apply adhesive rubber appliques on the bottom of the tub. Never leave children alone in a tub or any other body of water.
Waste baskets and garbage cans	☐ Children can get into garbage and find many harmful objects.	☐ Never place anything in trash or garbage containers within a child's reach that would harm him or her. Tie knots in plastic can liners. Put can lids inside cans and stuff papers on top before throwing away. Place broken glass in a sturdy container before throwing away. Do not throw away unused medication. (Flush unused portions, instead.)
Water, hot	☐ Water that comes out of the faucet at too high a temperature can scald a child.	☐ Set hot water heaters at no more than 120°F. Paint hot water faucets with a little red fingernail polish to help small children remember which is hot. When bathing a child in a sink or tub, run a little cold water last to cool the faucet.
Windows	☐ A child can fall through or out of windows.	☐ Use tight-fitting screens or locks that child cannot remove. Equip windows above the first floor with locked screens and safety bars.

Poisons Cause Accidents			
Cleaning Products	**Garage and Garden Products**	**Medications**	**Personal Products**

air fresheners
ammonia
bleach
cleaners
dishwasher and dish-
  washing products
disinfectant
drain opener
floor wax
furniture polish
laundry products
lye
metal polish
oven cleaner
rust remover
spot remover
toilet bowl cleaner
water softener
	antifreeze
	caustic lime
	fertilizer
	gasoline, kerosene,
	  lighter fluid, oil, and
	  other petroleum
	  products
	paint
	pesticide
	putty
	strychnine
	varnish
	weed killer
		amphetamines
		antibiotics
		anticonvulsants
		antidepressants and
		  tranquilizers
		antidiarrheals
		aspirin and
		  acetaminophen
		camphor
		cold preparations
		iron, vitamins with iron
		oil of wintergreen
		sleeping pills
		vitamins
			aftershave
			deodorant
			hair coloring products
			hair remover
			lotion
			mouthwash
			nail polish and polish
			  remover
			perfume
			permanent wave
			  solution
			powder, talcum (baby
			  and body powder)
			rubbing alcohol
			shampoo
			soap

21-8   Many substances are poisonous.

warnings. Store household products above floor level (rather than under sinks) to keep them away from crawling babies. Lock up household products when children can walk and climb. (Reach is almost without limits when children can climb.) If adults must leave an unsafe product unattended, they must store the product in a safe, out-of-reach place. Do not leave the product unattended, even for a minute.

Products must be kept in their original containers with labels intact. Never transfer poisons to food or drink containers (such as a box, jar, or bottle). Do not put a safe substance in a container that originally held a poisonous product, such as water in a bleach bottle. A child seeing water used from a bleach bottle may think the contents of bleach bottles are safe. Keep medication in childproof containers. Store household products in safety containers. Adults must carefully check containers after each use, because the container may be difficult to close or faulty.

Do not keep products that are **lethal** (deadly) in the house. The risks are too great. One teaspoon of oil of wintergreen contains six grams of salicylates. This equals the amount in 20 adult aspirin.

Medication is safer when adults take the following safety measures:

- ☐ Flush old medication down the toilet.
- ☐ Replace childproof caps carefully after use.
- ☐ Lock medication in a cabinet or in a small chest or suitcase.
- ☐ Never give a child medication in the dark.
- ☐ Never refer to medication as candy.
- ☐ Do not give medication in baby bottles or juice glasses.
- ☐ Do not take medication (even vitamins) in front of young children.
- ☐ When carrying medication, store a limited amount in a childproof container and keep it in a purse or pocket.

2

3

4

1—*Enrich:* Obtain a chart listing poisonous substances and methods of treatment. Display this in a child care center.

2—*Activity:* Inspect your home kitchen and bathroom for dangerous household products that are easily accessible to children. Reorganize them according to safety guidelines.

3—*Discuss:* Why is it unsafe to keep old medication? Why should a caregiver flush rather than throw away this medication?

4—*Discuss:* Why is this an important safety measure?

Outdoor Safety

Adults must check that outdoor areas are safe for children, too. Common unsafe objects in the outdoor area include rocks, broken glass, ruts, holes, and bumps. Nails and other sharp objects can puncture children. Areas may turn slippery and unsafe when wet.

If the outdoor area has pools, ponds, wells, or deep holes, adults should be sure they are enclosed by a fence the child cannot climb. The areas also should be closed and safely locked or covered to provide complete safety. Remove doors and trunk lids from old refrigerators, freezers, stoves, and cars if they are near children's playing areas. This prevents children from getting trapped inside.

Plant Safety.   Outside plant life presents a special safety problem. Many plants, flowers, vegetables, shrubs, and trees are poisonous or have poisonous parts. When children eat a plant leaf, it is not always obvious to an adult. Children do not hold an empty bottle or gag and cry, signs they would show after swallowing drain cleaner. However, many plants are dangerous when eaten. Some plants, because of their chemical makeup, harm the digestive tract in ways similar to eating ground glass. Other beautiful plants are deadly. One leaf of a poinsettia can kill a child. Chart 21-9 lists some poisonous plants. Children need close supervision when playing outside, especially in wooded areas, gardens, and greenhouses. Indoors, remove poisonous houseplants when children are near.

Safe Play Areas.   Making sure children will not wander out of a safe area provided for their play is a great task. Yards are best enclosed with fences. Gates should be locked or equipped with childproof safety devices that keep children from opening them. For example, attach a screen door latch on the outside of the gate. Adults also may fit a gate with a bolt from the inside to the outside where the nut is attached. Because they require an adult to reach over a gate to unlock it, these devices are out of a child's reach.

When young children are playing in driveways or carports with pull/push toys or riding toys, adults should watch them closely. An extension ladder laid across the driveway a few feet from the street can help remind a child to turn around. Adults can replace the extension ladder with a stop sign for older preschoolers. Remember, ladders and signs are only reminders, not safety devices. Children still need close supervision.

Traffic Safety

Car accidents are the number one cause of death for infants and children. Experts say protecting children with proper restraint systems could reduce that rate by 90 percent. ***Restraint systems*** include car seats, harnesses, and other devices that hold children safely in place during accidents or sudden stops and turns. Approved restraints have passed crash tests and suit infants and children. A few of these seats are approved for air travel, too.

Many adults feel they can hold babies and protect them during an auto crash. Not only do loose objects fly about in a collision or hard stop, but the weight of an object is greatly increased. For instance, in a crash at 30 miles per hour, a baby who weighs 10 pounds moves forward with a force of 300 pounds. Such force is impossible for an adult to hold. At the same speed, an adult who weighs 125 pounds is thrown forward with a force of between one and two tons. A baby who is riding on an adult's lap is apt to be crushed in a car crash. A baby sharing a seat belt with an adult is in equal danger, even when the car is moving slowly.

Car beds and infant feeding seats offer no crash protection. They should not be used in a moving car. Regular seat belts do not protect children under age five for the following reasons:

- ☐   Young children can slip through a regular seat belt because they do not have long, heavy legs to anchor them.

- ☐   Regular seat belts can ride up to a child's abdomen, where there are no bones to protect the child. The standard shoulder harnesses can move across a child's face or neck, which is unsafe.

Poisonous Plants

amaryllis	cowbane	johnsongrass	pokeberry
angel's-trumpet	croton	larkspur	poppy
apricot (pit)	crown imperial	lily	poison ivy (oak, sumac,
arborvitae	cyclamen	lily of the valley	hemlock)
autumn crocus	daffodil	lobelia	potato (leaves)
azalea	daphne	love-in-a-mist	privet
barberry	datura	mahonia	rhododendron
belladonna	death camas	may apple (mandrake)	rhubarb (leaves)
bittersweet	dieffenbachia (dumb	milkweed	rosary pea
black locust	cane)	mimosa	sago palm
bloodroot	dogbane (Indian hemp)	mistletoe	sedum
bluebonnet	elderberry	monkeypod (raintree)	snowdrop
boxwood	four-o'clock	monkshood	snowflake
bracken	foxglove	moonseed	snow-on-the-mountain
buckeye	gelsemium	mountain laurel	sorghum
buttercup	golden chain	mushroom (some	staggerbush
caladium	grape hyacinth	species)	star-of-Bethlehem
camellia	holly	narcissus	stinging nettle
cassava	horsetail	night-blooming cereus	strawberry bush
(root, bitter variety)	hyacinth	nightshade	sudan grass
castor bean	hydrangea	oak	tansy
century plant	iris	oleander	tobacco
cherry (pit)	ivy	pansy	tulip
cherry tree	jack-in-the-pulpit	peach (pit)	tung tree
chinaberry	Japanese plum	peony	varnish tree
Christ's-thorn	Japanese yew	periwinkle	wandering Jew
clematis	jasmine	pheasant's-eye	water hemlock
columbine	jequirity bean	pimpernel	wormseed
corn cockle	Jerusalem cherry	poinsettia	yew
cotton	jimson weed	poison berry	yucca

21-9 This chart lists some poisonous plants. Some plants (or parts of them) contain moderate poisons. Others contain poisons that are deadly.

☐ Young children need a harness designed for their size and body proportions to protect their necks. Compared to adults, babies' neck muscles are weak and their heads heavier in proportion to their total weight.

For auto safety, adults should place children in *certified* (tested and approved) restraint systems. These are required by law in all states. Adults may buy new ones in many stores or car dealerships. In some towns and cities, adults may rent or borrow restraint systems.

Proper Use of Restraint Systems. In order to protect a child, restraint systems must be selected that fit the child's age and weight and the car in which the child will be riding, 21-10. Safety seats that meet the Department of Transportation's (DOT) requirements have a label which reads: "This child restraint system conforms to all applicable Federal motor vehicle standards." The stamp of manufacturing should be after January 1, 1981. Child safety seats for use in both cars and airplanes also carry the Federal Aviation Agency (FAA) stamp. In all 50 states and the District of Columbia, the law says all small children must ride in safety seats.

2

3

1—*Note:* Point out common poisonous plants.

2—*Enrich:* Do research on child and adult restraint laws in your state. Report to the class.

3—*Discuss:* When would it be an advantage to rent or borrow restraint systems?

Selecting Child Restraint Systems				
	Infants	**Toddlers to 4-year-olds**	**4-year-olds to 8-year-olds**	**8-year-olds to 12-year-olds**
Age and weight	birth to 9-12 months	9-12 months to 4 years	4 years to 8 years	8 years to 12 years
	20 lbs or less	20 to 40 lbs	40 lbs to 70 lbs	70 lbs and heavier
Type and location of seat	rear facing infant or convertible (toddler) seat in back seat	forward facing convertible (toddler) seat in back seat	booster seat with car's lap/ shoulder belts or shield type booster seat in back seat	back seat of car with lap/shoulder belts
Please note:	Car seats are attached to the car by the vehicle seat belts. Child is secured by the child car seat harness.			

21-10 Children are not properly restrained unless they are snugly restrained in the correct type of seat which is securely fastened by the vehicle seat belts in the back seat of the car.

1

Before starting the car, an adult must buckle a child into a restraint system properly. Each buckle, strap, and shield exists for a purpose. The child is not protected unless the adult uses the restraint correctly, 21-11. If a child restraint system is not being used, the sitting child must be buckled firmly with the regular seat belt. The child should be in the center back seat. (This is the safest place for a child who is not properly restrained. However, it in no way matches the safety of proper equipment.)

2

All restraint systems are designed for the back seat of the car. Placing children in the back seat is becoming even more important due to passenger-side air bags that are being installed in many models of cars. Many adults do not understand what causes deaths or serious injuries to infants and any child under 12 years of age riding in vehicles in which passenger-side air bags inflate during a crash. Air bags are designed to work with lap/shoulder belts to protect teens and adults. In almost all cases involving injuries and deaths to infants, the rear-facing safety seat was so close to the dashboard that the air bag hit the safety seat with such force that it broke the back

of the car seat and caused brain injury. Injured toddlers and older children facing forward were often unbuckled or not wearing the shoulder portion of the safety belt. In other cases, these children were simply too close to the dashboard because they were playing with something on the dashboard or because they slid or flexed forward during pre-crash braking. Neck and head injuries often occur when the body is closer than 12 inches to the dashboard at the time the air bag is triggered.

Many adults who have a sports car or a pick-up truck without a back seat wonder what they should do. Adults need to realize these are not safe vehicles for children. The best thing you can do for infants is to have the passenger-side air bag turned off and properly use the rear-facing seat. For pre-teen children in forward-facing seats, use the air bag but move the front car seat back as far as possible and do not allow children to lean toward the dashboard.

Adults should make sure that car doors are locked at all times. They should never allow passengers—especially children—to ride in the following ways:

1—*Note:* Stress the importance of safety restraints appropriate for a child's height and weight.

2—*Note:* Stress the importance of reading and following manufacturers' directions.

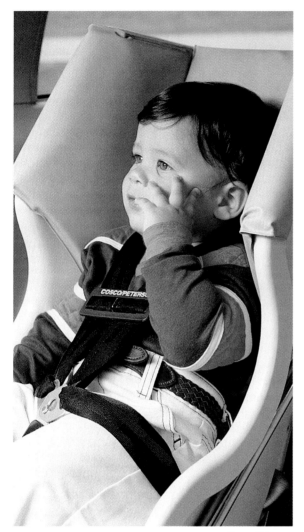

Cosco Peterson

21-11   For a restraint system to work it must be buckled correctly.

- [ ] Children should never ride with any part of the body hanging out an open window.
- [ ] Children should never ride in cargo areas of cars, vans, or trucks.
- [ ] Children should never kneel on the floor board of the front seat.
- [ ] Children should never sit on an adult's lap in the front or back seats.
- [ ] Children should never share a seat belt with another child or with an adult.

Adults should set an example by always wearing a seat belt and driving safely. They should stop the car for a while when children tire or need attention. Travel toys and games can make long trips more pleasant.

Children who have always used restraint systems and have seen adults use them do not refuse to wear them. They do not know there is a choice. Adults must teach children who have not used these systems to stay in them. Studies find that children behave better in cars when restrained than when not restrained. Perhaps restraint systems cause children to feel less car motion (which is tiring) and enable them to see out the windows better. Restraint systems also allow children less motion and less ability to misbehave.

Street Safety.   Young children on foot or riding tricycles and bicycles are another traffic concern. These children are not able to see ahead or react with caution to moving traffic. Traffic safety skills are not completely mastered until about age 11. Children first must know that traffic, which is fun to watch, can be unsafe. Traffic safety skills depend on perceptual judgments of space, speed, direction, and distance. In addition, these perceptions must interact. A child's brain and body must react quickly and correctly.

Scoldings and warnings will not solve these safety problems. Rather, adults must set limits for play areas, supervise children closely, model safe behavior, and teach safety. (Teaching safety is discussed later in this chapter.)

Baby Items and Toy Safety

Children's products cause many injuries each year. The number of injuries could be reduced if adults chose baby items and toys carefully. Also, adults must realize that even safe items and toys become dangerous when children misuse them. Supervision and safety lessons are crucial.

Selecting safe baby items and toys is important. Some safety features are now required by law. The slats in cribs and playpens must be spaced no more than 2 3/8 inches apart. The law requires paint on baby items and toys to be nontoxic. Remember that items and toys made

1—*Activity:* Practice buckling different types of child restraint seats.

2—*Reflect:* How would van rules differ from car rules? Do you think adults who drive vans allow children more freedom? Explain.

3—*Note:* Review games and activities that can be used in a car.

1

prior to the law, in addition to handmade items, may not meet these standards. Some new toys must carry warnings, such as "Not Intended for Children Under Three Years of Age." Other items, such as lawn darts, cannot be sold in toy departments or toy stores because they are dangerous for children to use.

2

When selecting baby items and toys, adults should read labels and examine items for safety features carefully. Safety features are especially important on baby items, 21-12. Check toys for durability. Also, think about whether the toy suits a child's age and skill level, 21-13.

3

Adults also should think about how much supervision a child needs when he or she uses the item. Can an adult watch a child as he or she uses an electrical toy? Can toys meant for older children be kept away from younger siblings?

Adults also need to think about the space needed to use and store equipment. For instance, is there a safe place to ride a bicycle? Is there a place to store outdoor toys when they are not in use? Are there places to store toys to prevent accident-causing clutter?

Baby items and toys should be checked often, too, for the following:

- ☐ sharp points; jagged edges; and small, loose parts
- ☐ rust on outdoor equipment, which weakens the structure
- ☐ stuffed toys and dolls that must be repaired and cleaned
- ☐ electrical parts that need to be replaced (This is an adult's task, not a child's.)

Adults can add a few safety devices to baby items and toys, too. If a toy chest is not properly ventilated, drill a few air holes. Place a piece of adhesive tape around the wheel edge of skates to slow them. To remind children not to hold the chains of a swing too low (and thus be thrown off balance), mark chains with tape on the proper holding place.

4

Pet Safety

Because pets can bite, transmit diseases, and cause allergic responses, adults must choose them carefully. Adults should choose breeds of animals that are less apt to bite. Dogs that are one year and older and cats that are nine months and older have developed immunity to many diseases. These animals make better children's pets than puppies and kittens. If children show an allergy to a pet, adults must keep the animal away from them.

Veterinarians (animal doctors) should see pets on a regular basis. The veterinarian will advise on regular care of the animals. A sick pet should be examined at once.

Children should learn how to treat a pet. Adults should not expect young children to care for a pet. Children in the lower elementary grades can learn some pet care duties from adults. Adults also must remind children to wash their hands after each time they handle a pet.

▶ Safety Devices and Safety Measures

To help prevent possible accidents, adults must be a step ahead of children. They must childproof the child's environment before he or she is able to get into trouble. Adults cannot wait until a child opens a door that leads to a steep flight of stairs. Behind the first opened door, danger may be present. Adults should never rely on norms or past experiences to tell them when to childproof. Children develop at different rates, even within the same family. Also, some children explore more than others.

Safety devices can help prevent accidents. These include electrical outlet covers and safety latches on cabinets and drawers that only an adult's hand pressure can release. Using safety knobs that fit over standard knobs that require an adult's grip to open them are also important, 21-14. Although these devices are helpful, they do not take the place of careful supervision. Fire and smoke detectors need to be installed. Fire extinguishers must be ready for use.

Medical emergencies arise from both illnesses and accidents. Adults need to recognize symptoms requiring emergency treatment, 21-15. Adults must also take proper action. These steps include:

1—*Activity:* Check catalogs. Do any toys carry these warnings?

2—*Note:* Review the meaning of age-appropriate.

3—*Discuss:* How could a parent childproof when several children of varying ages play in the same space?

4—*Resource: Toys Should Not Hurt*, SAG.

5—*Activity:* Develop a checklist for pet selection.

6—*Note:* Stress the importance of individual differences in developing rules and safety precautions.

Safety Standards for Baby Items	
Item	**Safety Standards**
Baby vehicle (carriage or stroller)	☐ Should be pretested for balance and weight distribution. ☐ Safety brake can be quickly set. ☐ Protective bumpers should pad.
Car seats	☐ Must be listed as meeting federal standards. ☐ Should be tested for strength and performance in crashes. ☐ Proper installation required. (A given car seat may not fit all cars.)
Crib	☐ Slats must not be more than $2^3/_8$ inches apart. ☐ Height of crib side from bottom of mattress to top of railing no less than 26 inches. ☐ Child has outgrown crib when side rail is less than three-fourths of child's height. ☐ Children 35 inches and taller must be removed from portable cribs. ☐ Latch on drop sides should be releasable only on outside and require a double kick. (This prevents young children and large dogs from tripping the latch.) ☐ Crib sides should lock at maximum height. ☐ Paint should be lead free. ☐ Teething rails are preferred. ☐ Crib should not have horizontal bars inside, because a baby can climb on them. ☐ Bumper pads with 6 or more ties are the safest. They are not recommended until the baby can raise the head and should be removed once the baby can stand.
Crib mattress	☐ When rail is in lowest position, the top of the mattress support and the top of the rail should be no less than 9 inches for standard crib and 5 inches for portable crib. ☐ Mattress should be covered with durable plastic with air vents. ☐ Torn mattress covers should be discarded. ☐ Mattress should fit snugly in crib. Space between crib and mattress should be smaller than two adult fingers held together.
High chair	☐ Wide-spread legs improve stability. ☐ Tray should lock in place. ☐ Crotch snap and wrap-around seat straps are needed. ☐ Nonskid rubber mats (available for bathtubs) placed on seat help prevent baby from sliding.
Playpen	☐ Slats should be no more than $2^3/_8$ inches apart. ☐ If playpen has mesh netting, the weave should be smaller than tiny baby buttons and pierced earrings. ☐ Floor should not collapse. ☐ Hinges on folding models should lock tightly.
Vaporizer	☐ Has Underwriters' Laboratories (UL) seal. ☐ Cold water models are safer than steam models.

21-12   Baby items must meet these standards to keep children safe.

1—*Note:* It is important to check the safety of a car seat before or after purchasing a different car.

2—*Note:* It is important to determine this when using old baby furniture.

3—*Activity:* Check catalogs for bumper pads. Check the number of ties on each.

4—*Note:* Discuss the safety standards on this list.

Safe Toys for Infants, Toddlers, and Older Children	
Safety Features	**Safety Measures**
For Infants and Toddlers	
Size should be larger than the child's two fists	Even large toys can break, exposing small parts.The law bans small parts in new toys intended for children under age three. Older and handmade toys may still have small parts.
Nonbreakable	Toys that break may expose small parts or break into small pieces. Toys made of glass or brittle plastic are the most unsafe.
No sharp edges or points	The law bans new toys with sharp edges or points intended for children under age eight. Broken toys often have sharp edges. Wires with sharp points are often inside stuffed toys.
Nontoxic	Painted toys should be labeled nontoxic. Avoid all painted toys for children who put playthings in their mouth.
No long cords or strings	Toys with long cords or strings should not be used with infants and young children who can wrap them around the neck.
Nonflammable, flame retardant, or flame resistant	Dolls and stuffed toys should be made of materials not likely to ignite.
Washable and hygienic materials	Dolls and stuffed toys must be clean when bought and must be easy to keep clean.
For Older Children	
Safe electric toys	Electric toys must meet requirements for maximum surface temperatures, electrical wiring, and display of warning labels. Electrical toys that heat are intended for children over age eight.
Noise at acceptable levels	The law requires a label on toys that produce a noise above a certain level. The label warns, "Do not fire closer than one foot to the ear. Do not use indoors." Toys making sounds that can result in hearing damage are banned.
Items used for age intended	Chemistry sets, hobby sets, balloons, and games and toys with small parts are extremely dangerous if misused or left within the reach of younger children.
Sturdy, safe, large equipment	Space between moving parts is wide enough not to pinch or crush fingers. Bolt ends would be covered with plastic end caps. Swing seats should be lightweight and have smooth, rolled edges. All swing sets, gyms, and other large equipment should be anchored firmly to the ground.
Safe tricycles and bicycles	Tricycles and bicycles should have proper assembly. Seats should be adjusted to rider's height. Pedals should have skid-resistant surfaces. Reflectors (at least two inches in diameter) should be used on bicycles.

21-13   When selecting toys for infants, toddlers, and older children, adults should note special safety features.

KinderGard

21-14   Safety devices help protect children from many dangers.

Symptoms Requiring Emergency Treatment

Seek emergency treatment when a child:
- ☐ looks or acts very ill or seems to be getting worse quickly
- ☐ acts very confused
- ☐ breathes so fast or hard that is interferes with making sounds or drinking
- ☐ has uneven pupils
- ☐ has a high fever (for infants under 4 months a rectal fever of 101°F or higher; for children over 4 months a fever of 105° or higher)
- ☐ has forceful vomiting (for infants under 4 months - once; for children over 4 months - continuous vomiting)
- ☐ has severe headache or neck pain or stiffness
- ☐ has a seizure for the first time or has a seizure that lasts more than 15 minutes
- ☐ has a blood-red or purple rash NOT associated with an injury
- ☐ has hives or welts that appear rapidly
- ☐ has a stomach ache that causes screaming or doubling up or has a stomach ache after a blow to the stomach region
- ☐ has bleeding that does not respond to first aid
- ☐ has black or blood-mixed stools
- ☐ has not urinated for 8 hours
- ☐ has continuous clear drainage from the nose after a head injury
- ☐ has a fracture (broken bone)

21-15   Adults who note these symptoms should seek emergency medical treatment for the child.

21-16   A few first aid supplies are needed to treat minor mishaps.

First Aid Items

- ☐ adhesive bandages (various sizes)
- ☐ adhesive tape
- ☐ antiseptic for cuts and scratches
- ☐ calamine lotion (for insect bites)
- ☐ gauze bandages and squares
- ☐ scissors
- ☐ syrup of ipecac (used to induce vomiting for **some, but not all,** poisonings)
- ☐ first aid chart or book (for quick reference)

1—*Activity:* Develop a basic first aid supply kit.

- ☐ Apply first aid. ***First aid*** is treatment for an illness or accident that is given immediately before professional medical help. Training in first aid can be most helpful to parents and is required as part of teacher training. First aid supplies, including a first aid chart or book, should be kept current and nearby as well, 21-16.

- ☐ Call the Emergency Medical System. Adults need to keep emergency phone numbers updated and quickly available, 24-17. When emergency situations occur

Emergency Phone Numbers

Local emergency number
(if you have one): 555-1243

Ambulance: 555-7820

Dentist: 555-6473

Doctor: 555-7654

Drugstore: 555-8901

Fire department: 555-8041

Hospital: 555-7302

Neighbors: Mrs. Rodriguez 555-4060
Mr. Peterson 555-3867

Police department: 555-8938

Poison control center: 555-8392

Relatives: Grace Taylor (Grandma) 555-2323
Mr. and Mrs. Mason (Uncle Dan
and Aunt Dianne) 555-3374

Taxi: 555-4222

21-17 Posting the correct emergency phone numbers near the telephone saves time in a crisis.

while the child is in a child care program or in school, one teacher must read and follow the parent's decisions found on the Emergency Medical Form; stay with the child until a parent arrives; and complete an incident report.

☐ Continue first aid until professional help arrives and then do not interfere with the assistance.

Sometimes emergency situations occur due to fire, explosion, or weather situations. In these cases, parents or teachers should conduct evacuation or safety plans that have been practiced with young children and should reassure children who are frightened. A parent or teacher should

have a flashlight and first aid kit next to the evacuation door(s) or in the safety area for easy access. (A tote bag filled with these supplies makes it easy to carry while helping children.) Training in first aid can help parents handle children's emergencies before medical help arrives.

▶ Safety Lessons

Teaching safety is an ongoing process that begins almost at birth and continues for life. The first lessons occur in the home and yard. They expand to include the total environment, such as school safety, water safety, traffic safety, and job safety.

Adults are models for children. A child will absorb the adult's approach to everyday actions and safety measures, such as buckling seat belts and looking before crossing streets. Adults may even exaggerate behavior to make safety measures clearer for the child. They may stop, look, and say, "I don't see a car coming, so we can cross now," before walking across a street.

Adults should carefully explain the boundaries of play. They must show as well as tell children what they can and cannot do. Such warnings are helpful only if they are stated in positive ways. An adult may say, "Grass is for playing, and streets are for cars and trucks." Warnings stated in negative ways may tempt children to act in unsafe ways. Also, overly repeated warnings lose their meanings.

All warnings should be coupled with reasons, or the child may think a given action is all right if the adult is not watching. For instance, adults should explain the importance of safety devices like seat belts, crash helmets, and life jackets. They should also explain how to use the devices properly, 21-18.

Adults need to insist on obedience. Children want and need to be protected. Parents require obedience when they take action against wrong doings instead of simply threatening children. Taking action does not call for physical punishment. It can mean making the child stay in the bedroom or come inside for a short time. Insisting on obedience is a way of saying, "I care about you."

1—*Enrich:* Examine infant and child first aid books in groups. List positive and negative factors about each book. Emphasize ease of use. Where should the book be located? Report to the class.

2—*Enrich:* Arrange for an emergency technician who is skilled in handling infants and children to speak in class.

3—*Discuss:* Why is it important to demonstrate these safety

precautions to a child during a walk rather than just tell him or her?

4—*Reflect:* Describe an overly repeated warning in your life that lost its meaning. How does this apply to children?

5—*Enrich:* Role-play (in pairs) situations in which an adult states a safety rule, explains the reason for the rule, and informs the child that he or she cares.

Louisiana Department of Wildlife and Fisheries

21-18   Safety devices protect a person's life.

Practice Safety Measures. Adults should practice safety measures with children. These measures might include a fire drill or a safe walk to school. Adults can also read books or stories on safety to children. They can watch special segments on safety in children's television programs. To support the safety lessons, adults can have children talk about, act out, or draw the safety actions.

● Preparing a Child for Routine and Hospital Care

Medical care should be part of children's lives, either on a routine basis or when problems arise. Going to the doctor or dentist can be stressful for both child and adult. There are ways to ease the stress.

▶ Preparing Children for Routine Care

Depending on their age, children react in different ways to routine care. Children under two often cry while being examined. (They may begin crying when undressed and placed on cold scales.) Two- and three-year-olds often cry.

They may also hide from, kick, or push the doctor. (Hiding, kicking, and pushing are attempts to get rid of those who are checking or treating them.) Older children are better able to understand what going to the doctor means. These children are apt to become anxious ahead of time. They may become more anxious in the car or walking in the office. They often cry or kick during routines that are not comfortable. Many children are more relaxed about procedures that are painless. Following the visit, older children may act bossy. This may help reduce the feelings of powerlessness they felt during the visit.

Adults can lessen some of the stress of routine care in several ways. First, they can select a capable and caring doctor or dentist. Adults should feel free to ask the doctor questions. They should also feel the doctor answers these questions completely and clearly. The doctor and dentist should appeal to the child, too. Children often like doctors and dentists who greet them in a friendly way and by name. They also like caregivers who notice something personal, such as a child's new haircut or pretty dress. Talking to the child during the checkup and remaining calm, even if the child doesn't, are other positive qualities. Colorful waiting rooms and examination rooms also appeal to children, 21-19.

Adults should bring books and toys to appointments to make waiting more pleasant. They should also bring a change of clothes, if needed. They should ask before giving a child candy or gum, which changes the color of the mouth and throat. This may make *diagnosis* (identifying the disease) more difficult. Adults should arrive at the appointment with information and prepared questions.

If a child feels sick, adults can reassure the child that it is all right to feel sick. Pain or other sick feelings or reactions may frighten a child. Adults can explain a little about procedures and relate them as much as possible to everyday life. They may use such phrases as, "X rays are pictures," and, "The dentist will look at your teeth." Too many explanations, such as, "The doctor will use a large machine to make the X ray," can add to a child's fear.

2

3

1—*Discuss:* How can television programs teach safety measures? Why is it important to watch these safety programs with a child?

2—*Discuss:* Summarize ways to lessen the stress of routine medical or dental care.

3—*Discuss:* How can adults affect the child's attitude, both positively and negatively?

© John Shaw

21-19 Waiting rooms that appeal to children make medical care less stressful.

Helping the Child During the Examination

During the actual examination, the following will help the child feel more comfortable:

☐ Adults should stay with the child and stand where the child can see them. (Dentists, however, usually prefer that adults stay in the waiting room.)

☐ Use a soft, soothing voice. A child may stop crying to hear whispered words.

☐ Hold the child, if the doctor asks.

☐ Do not tell the child a procedure will not hurt if, in fact, it will. Instead, tell the child, "It will be all right," or "Soon it will be over." If the child cries, reassure him or her that crying is all right. Say, "I know this hurts, but it will stop hurting in a little bit."

☐ Do not distract a baby or child by making noises, such as jingling keys. Such sounds interfere with a doctor's ability to hear internal sounds. Some babies and children cry louder when the adult tries to distract them. (Perhaps they feel the distraction means the procedure will be painful.)

☐ Above all, never threaten a child with a doctor's visit or shot. These threats add to a child's anxiety during a visit. They also are meaningless because shots are never given as punishment. Such threats are not fair to the child or to medical caregivers.

▶ Preparing Children for Hospital Care

Hospital care is often a special problem for both parents and children. Parents see hospitals as places where people experience separation from loved ones, pain, and even death. Hospitals may also seem large and *impersonal* (not concerned about the child as a person). Parents tend to feel they are no longer in charge of their child's care once they enter the hospital. Also, doctors or nurses often ask parents to assist during painful treatments. This can be almost unbearable for some parents.

Parents or other adults may also feel guilty about the cause for needed hospital care. They may feel they could have prevented a fall if they had been watching more carefully. They may think, "I should have known that cough was bad."

Children may also fear **hospitalization** (being cared for in a hospital). Children from ages one to four often fear separation from parents. Older children are concerned about what doctors will do to their bodies. Children react to actual tests and treatments in much the same way they react to office visits. However, reactions to hospital care can be more intense. This is because new people are caring for the child. Also, the child may endure more frequent, unfamiliar, and probably more painful tests and procedures. Hospital stays are longer than office visits and the surroundings are unfamiliar, too. Children may think of hospital care as punishment.

Easing the Stress of Hospital Care

There are several ways to ease the stress of hospital care for parent and child. Adults should start by finding out as much as possible about the stay. Then they will be better prepared to help the child. If possible, they should tell the child about

---

1—*Activity:* Make a list of desirable toys, games, and furnishings for a children's waiting room.

2—*Discuss:* Why is this important?

3—*Reflect:* Describe instances you have observed when an older person has threatened a child with a doctor visit or a shot. How do you think this affects a child?

4—*Discuss:* Do you think a parent should stay with a child constantly during a hospital stay? Explain your reasons.

the stay ahead of time. The talk should focus on good points (time in the hospital will help the child feel better). However, adults should never say, "It won't hurt." The child learns to trust adults when they are honest.

A doctor's kit and some books may help children solve some of their fears, 21-20. Some hospitals have playrooms where children can act out hospital care. (The rooms also provide art activities, games, and books.)

An arranged tour of the hospital's children's area makes the child feel more comfortable. The nurse who will care for the child should give the tour, if possible. Children need to develop friendships with those they'll be seeing most often, 21-21. This helps hospitals seem less threatening.

Parents should plan to room in with babies and young children when possible. Many hospitals help parents by providing a bed or reclining chair, food service, phone, television, and magazines. Members of service groups may help parents by doing such things as serving snacks and shopping for small purchases. They may also volunteer to sit with the child for a while so the parent can take a break.

During the Hospital Stay

While in the hospital, parents can help care for nonmedical needs like feeding, bathing, and toileting. They should go with the child for tests

21-20   Toy medical kits and books about hospitals may ease children's fears about medical care.

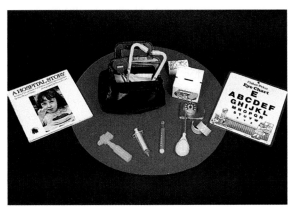

© John Shaw

© John Shaw

21-21   A warm feeling between a child and a nurse makes hospital care easier.

3

and treatments when allowed. In some hospitals, parents go with the child to surgery and stay with the child until he or she is unconscious. Parents may also be present in the recovery room as the child awakens.

Children need items that remind them of home and comfort them during their stay, 21-22. Adults should bring some of the child's toys, pajamas, or other items to the hospital. If the child can have visitors or phone calls, adults can arrange for friends, adults, and siblings to stay in contact.

Older children may want to keep a scrapbook or box to help them remember their stay. The book or box might include pictures, hospital bracelets, covers to disposable thermometers, and syringes without needles.

1—*Discuss:* Why is it inadvisable to tell a child that a procedure will not hurt if it may, in fact, be painful?

2—*Enrich:* Obtain (or borrow) several toy medical kits. Role-play ways to use them to ease children's fears.

3—*Discuss:* Describe a desirable children's nurse. Describe undesirable characteristics of a nurse.

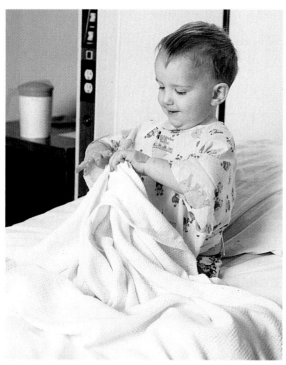

© John Shaw

21-22   Items from home, like a favorite blanket, make a child's hospital stay more comfortable.

Children can show hospital items when telling others about their stay. Talking about a hospital stay, like talking about any other experience, is good for children.

Caring for an Ill or Injured Child

Parents and adults who work with children need to care for ill or injured children at some time, 21-23. Children experience many scrapes as they learn what their bodies can and cannot do. Young children, especially those under age seven or eight, have many common illnesses, such as colds and digestive upsets. Adults often handle such small problems. Doctors expect adults to follow through with care for more complex problems.

1—*Resource: Taking Fear Out of Hospital Care,* SAG.

© John Shaw

21-23   If adults know some simple first aid steps, they can treat many minor accidents at home.

There are several common conditions that adults must frequently treat in children. See 21-24 for practices doctors recommend. Adults should use a current first aid chart or book to give first aid for major injuries.

▶ Giving Medication and Proper Care

For many illnesses, adults are expected to give medication. They should use accurate measuring devices, 21-25. A medically defined teaspoon contains exactly 5cc of liquid, but a household teaspoon varies from $^1/_2$ teaspoon (2.5 cc) to $1^1/_2$ teaspoons (7.5 cc) of liquid. The amount also may vary depending on who pours the medication. Incorrect dosages may prevent infections from clearing up (from too little medication). They may also cause a child to be poisoned (from too much medication).

Adults should give medication to children in ways that make it easy for them to take. Babies may suck medication through a nursing nipple with ring attached. Some may take medication from a syringe (without a needle) inserted far back at the side of the mouth. Older children often receive medication from medical measuring devices. (The same device is used both to

Caring for Children's Health Problems	
Problem/Procedure	**Doctors Recommend**
Diarrhea (water stools)	Dilute milk or formula. Give child electrolyte solutions, such as a sugar-water mixture. The first solids given are ripe, mashed banana, scraped apple, and rice cereal. Return to regular diet after 24 hours of normal stools. Call doctor if other symptoms appear or if diarrhea does not ease in 24 hours.
Fever—Temperature above normal—98.6°F oral, 99.6°F rectal, 97.6°F auxiliary (in the armpit)	Keep child cool with minimum clothing and coverings, but do not let child shiver. (Shivering increases temperature.) Give the child cool fluids—the more the better. Give fever-reducing drugs as prescribed by doctor. Sponge bathe by wiping the child's back, arms, and legs in lukewarm water or equal parts of water and rubbing alcohol. Call physician if fever is high, if other symptoms appear, or if the fever remains (even if mild) after three days.
Runny nose	Use a nasal aspirator (a rubber syringe) and suck mucus out of nose. Place saltwater drops made by combining 1/4 teaspoon salt in four ounces of water in the nose five times per day. Using the drops causes sneezing and clears the passages. Use a cool air humidifier in the child's bedroom. Call the doctor if other symptoms appear.
Scrapes and scratches	Wash with soap and water and rinse well. If desired, apply an antiseptic made for scrapes or cuts. Cover with an adhesive strip bandage or a small piece of gauze held with adhesive tape if the wound is in an area open to dirt or further injury. Consult the doctor if the wound is deep or puncture-like or if the wound does not heal as it should.
Vomiting (does not include spitting up a little breast milk or formula)	Do not feed or even give water for four hours after the last time the child vomited. After four hours, offer one ounce of fluid (except milk) and repeat every four hours. If there is not more vomiting, feed simple foods for the next 48 hours, such as crackers, gelatin, broth, rice, and applesauce. Do not feed the child any milk products. Call the doctor if other symptoms appear or if vomiting does not ease after four hours.

21-24   Doctors often expect adults to care for these health problems.

measure and give medication.) Before children can swallow tablets, they can be crushed (and mixed with sugar or a bite of food, if bitter) and taken from a spoon. An older child can learn to swallow a tablet by tipping the head back. This action causes the tablet to sink in the back of the throat. Children also can learn to swallow a capsule by bending forward. This causes the lightweight capsule to float toward the back of the throat.

Keeping an active child in bed is a challenge for most parents. As children begin to feel well, they do not want to stay in bed. Quiet games, books, television, music, and paper and crayons can help children pass the time. Visits from adults (and other children, if the illness is not contagious) also help.

When children are ill or injured, they need a little extra attention. Babies and young children often need lots of holding and rocking.

3

1—*Activity:* Check catalogs and store ads for different types of child thermometers. List prices for each. Demonstrate the use of each on a doll.

2—*Enrich:* Consult a pharmacist for information on different devices used to give a child medication.

3—*Resource: Ill Children Need Quiet Activities,* SAG.

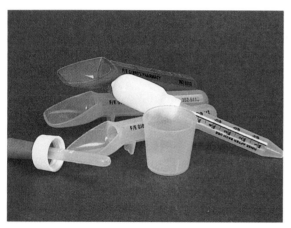

© John Shaw

21-25 Adults should buy medical measuring devices and use them to give liquid medication.

Older children may need their illness or injury and the treatment explained to them. Most children enjoy little surprises, too. These might include a small gift; a special dish, if food is all right; new bed clothing; or a get well card. Above all, adults should appear cheerful and confident because anxious parents can cause children to worry.

● Caring for a Terminally Ill Child

Despite great advances, medical science cannot cure every illness. Among those who are *terminally ill* (have diseases that will result in their deaths) are children. Terminal illness in children include some birth defects, such as heart and liver diseases and cystic fibrosis. Other diseases, such as AIDS and forms of cancer, are also terminal illnesses.

A family facing the death of a family member, especially a child, is facing one of the most profound emotional experiences people ever encounter. Often the child's family feels this period more keenly than the ill child. They feel a sense of loss before the death occurs. They show this by going through the stages of coping with

death. Families show denial. ("The doctors are wrong.") They may try bargaining with God. ("Just let my child live and I will . . .") Families feel depressed thinking about the loss and its impact. Finally, they accept the fact that the child will die. Although family members feel sad, they usually want to appear cheerful for the ill child's sake or for the sake of others. They also want to remain hopeful.

▶ Helping the Ill Child Cope

Besides trying to cope with their own feelings, family members must help and seek help for the ill child. How a child perceives his or her condition depends to a great extent upon his or her age. Children begin to understand death in the preschool years, but their understanding is rather limited until school age. What and how much should a family tell a child? That is a personal decision best made after the family discusses the child's case with professionals and among themselves.

Parents need to find out how much the sick child wants or needs to understand about his or her illness. Older children often realize what may happen. They may fear possible tests and treatments, the separation that death brings, and being left alone. Ill children may be concerned about their parents' feelings of loss. Families must allow sick children to do all they can physically tolerate and as much as possible for themselves.

▶ Helping the Family Cope

Family members need the help of professionals during this time of crisis. Many hospitals that treat terminally ill children hire professionals like medical staff, religious leaders, and social workers to help the family. Parent support groups are also available. Members often provide much comfort because they have gone through or are going through the same problems.

The family needs the help of friends at this time, too. Friends should learn as much as they can about the disease and its treatments. This will help them better understand what family

1—*Discuss:* Why is it important for parents of terminally ill children to have outside sources for their own recreation and communication?

2—*Enrich:* Contact local hospitals for information on special programs for terminally ill children, such as the Make A Wish Foundation. Report to the class.

members share with them. The role of friends can be described best as a role of listening rather than advising. Certainly friends should express their concern and sorrow, but they should carefully think through their words. For example, saying, "I understand how you feel," may prompt a hurt response, such as, "How could you? Your child is healthy!"

If possible, friends should offer their help. They should think through the family's needs, then suggest a concrete way to assist them. For instance, a friend may offer to cook the family dinner one night or drive a healthy child to an after-school activity. Such offers are easier for the family to accept than the vague offer of, "Let me know if there is anything I can do." Most of all, friends must remember that family members will need their support during the weeks and months after the ill child's death.

2

Summary

Protecting and maintaining children's health and safety is one of the major responsibilities of adults. In addition to teaching and modeling good health practices, adults need to provide a safe and healthy environment.

In order to monitor growth and development, adults should have children checked by health care professionals on a regular basis. Getting children vaccinated will protect them from many diseases. Children need prompt medical attention when they show certain or prolonged symptoms of illness.

Adults need to anticipate and remove possible hazards in their home. Childproofing the environment will help prevent many accidents.

Preparing children for routine or hospital care will help lessen their fear and anxiety. Ill or injured children should be treated as doctors recommend. Families experience severe emotional stress when a child is terminally ill. Caring friends and others can help family members at this time.

To Review

Write your answers on a separate sheet of paper.

1. True or false. Good nutrition serves as a physical support when accident or injury occurs.
2. List the two best ways for adults to prevent accidents.
    a. Warn or threaten a child.
    b. Create a safe environment.
    c. Prevent the child from doing dangerous acts.
    d. Let the child learn lessons from dangerous experiences.
    e. Teach safety.
    f. Remove all unsafe items from the home and yard.
3. True or false. The type of accidents a child commonly has changes with the child's age.
4. Why does the time of day affect the number of accidents children have?

1—*Reflect:* If you were the parent of a terminally ill child, what support systems and services would you utilize? Explain.

2—*Discuss:* How could you help a family with a terminally ill child?

3—*Answers:* Answers to review questions can be found in the front section of this TAE.

5. Poisonings of children under the age of five account for what percent of all accidental poisonings in homes each year?
   a. 10
   b. 25
   c. 50
   d. 75
   e. 85
6. True or false. Poisonings from plants are harder to detect than poisonings from household products.
7. Which of the following is the number one cause of death for infants and children?
   a. plant poisonings
   b. household poisonings
   c. household falls such as on stairs
   d. car accidents
   e. diseases
8. Explain why holding a child on your lap or sharing a seat belt in a car is unsafe for the child.
9. List four ways an adult can lessen the stress of routine medical care for a child.
10. Give three reasons why hospitals are stressful for the parents of sick children.
11. True or false. Teaspoons from household flatware are suitable for measuring liquid medication.
12. List two guidelines for helping the family of a terminally ill child.

To Do

1. Select a safety book to read to children ages three to five. Read the book to a child or a group of children. As a follow-up lesson, have children dramatize a safety practice, draw a safety practice, or do another activity.
2. Go shopping to purchase the latest inexpensive safety devices, or write companies for brochures on their devices. Demonstrate how each device works. (You may invite parents of young children.)
3. Check children's toys and outdoor equipment at a local preschool or child care center for safety. Make suggestions for discarding, repairing, or reusing equipment.
4. Borrow or purchase a few toys used with children under age three. Examine the toys for safety features. Do any features of the toys appear to be unsafe? Explain.
5. In class, interview a state highway patrol officer or local city police officer about children's restraint systems. You may ask the following questions:

    a.   What are the statistics on traffic injuries to infants and young children in your state or city?

    b.   What percentage of adults wear seat belts?

    c.   Why are restraint devices important?

    d.   What are the local laws regarding the use of restraint systems for children? For adults?

    Give the officer your list of questions in advance so he or she can prepare answers.

6. Select a way to prevent an accident that can be illustrated on a poster. Display the posters in school.

7. Ask a local hospital administrator to give your class a tour of the hospital's children's section.

8. Look at one or two rooms of your home and list ways to childproof them.

9. Make a list of emergency telephone numbers for your home. Place a list near each telephone. (Use chart 21-17 as a guide for the numbers needed.)

10. Invite a support team from a hospital to discuss how they help families cope with the death of children.

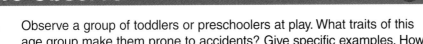

To Observe

1. Observe a group of toddlers or preschoolers at play. What traits of this age group make them prone to accidents? Give specific examples. How did adult actions or the environment prevent or lessen potential accidents?

2. Observe toddlers or preschoolers in a doctor's waiting room. What environmental factors lessened children's stress? Did any environmental factors increase the stress? How did parents increase or decrease stress in children?

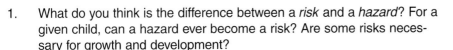

To Think Critically

1. What do you think is the difference between a *risk* and a *hazard*? For a given child, can a hazard ever become a risk? Are some risks necessary for growth and development?

2. If a young childless couple were choosing a car they hoped to keep five years, what car advice would be helpful if you knew they were planning on starting a family? Be specific.

3. Why might a person sometimes be fearful of medical procedures or hospitalization? How are the causes of these fears perhaps similar to those of young children? How are the causes perhaps different? What harm do you think occurs when parents or other adults threaten medical procedures when disciplining children? Is this abuse?

Chapter 22

Child Care in Group Settings

After studying this chapter, you will be able to

☐ trace the history of the major types of group programs for young children.

☐ describe what to look for when choosing a quality program.

☐ discuss the effects of group care on children's development.

☐ describe ways to help children adjust to group care.

After studying this chapter, you will be able to define

Casa dei Bambini
child care programs
developmentally appropriate practices (DAP)
developmentally inappropriate practices (DIP)
family child care
field trips
finger plays
for-profit program
group child care
Head Start
hidden added costs
hidden cost credits
Infant Schools
in-home child care
kindergarten
Montessori schools
not-for-profit programs
nursery school
private programs
public programs
regulations
work-related child care programs

Good group settings can enhance physical, mental, and social-emotional growth.

Why do some parents enroll their children in group programs? Some may work outside the home and need child care while they are gone. Others may need relief from caring for children full time because of health (or other) reasons. Still others may use group care to challenge their children mentally and physically.

Programs for young children have not always been common. Today, the picture has changed. In the last three decades, the number of group programs has increased. Why? One reason is the public's growing concern about the lack of quality education for children. Another reason is the growing numbers of parents in the workforce. Yet another reason is that quality group programs can affect children in many positive ways.

Along with the increased numbers of children enrolled in group settings, the types of programs have grown. There has been a trend toward meeting the needs of even younger children through infant/toddler programs. There is also a trend toward reaching children with special needs, such as children who are disabled or gifted.

Types of Group Programs

There are all kinds of group programs for children, including child care, kindergartens, nursery schools, and Head Start programs, 22-1. Descriptions of how these programs differ follow.

▶ Child Care Programs

The term *child care programs* often refers to programs that operate to care for children for extended hours, usually between 9 and 12 hours a day. Child care programs provide basic care for children when parents are not available. More and more child care programs are providing education as well as care services for children. These programs offer services for children from infanthood to preschool age. They even may serve school-age children after school and during school holidays.

22-1 Group programs vary from those that only care for basic needs to those that provide many special activities to enhance development.

■ Historical Overview

In Europe in the late 1700s and early 1800s, child care programs were called *Infant Schools*. Despite the name, these programs served poor children from toddlerhood to ages five or six when they entered the work force.

By the middle of the nineteenth century, child care for children of poor parents existed in urban areas of the United States. Many of these programs included parent programs to teach home and child care to adults. Federal funds aided child care programs during the Great Depression of 1929 and World War II.

After World War II, child care programs declined until the 1960s. At that time, women entered the workforce in great numbers. Some experts fear that, in the next 10 years, quality child care programs will not exist for children needing care. The number of children needing care due to working parents is increasing faster than quality child care places.

■ Types of Child Care Programs

There are three types of child care programs—in-home care, family child care, and group child care. Each type has its merits and drawbacks, 22-2. *In-home child care* is care provided by a person hired to care for children in the family's home. For example, homes with

1—*Discuss:* Summarize reasons that parents enroll children in group programs.

2—*Discuss:* Summarize reasons for the recent increase in the number of group programs.

3—*Discuss:* Summarize aspects of child care programs.

Types of Child Care Services and Their Advantages and Disadvantages		
Type of Care	**Advantages**	**Disadvantages**
In-home—A person is hired to care for children in the home.	☐ The children receive all of the caregiver's attention. ☐ Chances of health and safety problems are small. ☐ Children can be cared for when they are ill. ☐ Children are not taken outdoors in inclement weather or early hours. ☐ Children stay in the home atmosphere.	☐ Quality care can be a problem. ☐ Adults must make alternative plans if the caregiver cannot work. ☐ Adults must pay social security employer taxes. ☐ Education activities are rarely offered unless the person hired is well trained and does not have major housekeeping duties.
Family child care—A small number of children are cared for in another person's home.	☐ A good selection of family child care services may exist. ☐ Usually all children receive the attention they need. ☐ This type of program suits after-school care. ☐ Hours of operation often are flexible and meet parents' needs. ☐ Children from the same family who are different ages may be cared for appropriately. ☐ Children stay in a home-like atmosphere.	☐ Quality care may not be given in all family child care programs. ☐ Most family child care programs are not licensed. ☐ Parents must make alternative plans if the caregiver cannot work. ☐ Children must leave the house each day. ☐ Children may not be allowed to attend the program if they are sick. ☐ Education activities may not be offered.
Group child care—A fairly large number of children are enrolled in a center.	☐ Caregivers emphasize cooperative play and social living. ☐ Centers often are licensed so quality may be ensured. ☐ The center director makes any alternative plans needed. ☐ The center may provide special services, such as an educational program. ☐ Facilities and equipment are designed for children. ☐ Education activities are often offered.	☐ Parents often are concerned about their children's health and safety. ☐ The day may involve too many structured activities, especially for younger children. ☐ A home atmosphere is usually missing. ☐ Every child may not receive the attention he or she needs. ☐ Hours and days of operation are not flexible. ☐ Often payment is expected in advance and even for days when the child is absent. ☐ Often ill or injured children cannot attend the center. ☐ Children must leave their home each day. ☐ Some centers are costly.

22-2   Each type of child care service has its advantages and disadvantages.

1—*Discuss:* What would you do if your regular in-home care-giver canceled at the last minute?

2—*Note:* This often causes frustration and stress.

nannies would have child care called "in-home child care." *Family child care* is care of a small number of children in another person's home. Often, family child care is found in homes in which a parent of young children cares for other children in addition to the parent's own children. Some state laws limit the total number of children cared for in family child care to five or six children, including the parent's own children. *Group child care* is care provided in centers (not homes) and is also called "center child care." Centers are staffed by more than one adult, depending on the number of children served. Many centers serve 20 or fewer children who are cared for in one or two rooms. However, some centers enroll several hundred children who are cared for in one or two rooms. Other centers enroll several hundred children who are placed in age-groups and cared for in a building with many rooms that resemble a school. State laws set the standard for all aspects of center care (building requirements, staff, program, etc.).

Most child care programs are *for-profit, privately-owned programs.* (Individuals or family corporations may own them.) A few for-profit child care programs have grown into large chains. Other child care programs are not for profit. These may be funded by parents as cooperatives and by religious and service groups, such as churches. Others are funded by businesses, such as colleges, industries, hospitals, and branches of the armed services, for their employees. Programs funded by businesses are often called *work-related child care programs.*

For many years, child care programs mainly served preschool children. A current trend is to serve age groups beyond the preschool years. Today, infant/toddler programs are growing rapidly. Infant/toddler child care programs serve children from birth to age three. Quality programs with an adult-child ratio of one to four are hard to find. Programs with special housing and safety practices are also hard to find, 22-3. Such quality programs tend to cost more than child care programs serving preschool children. The costs of child care to families will continue to increase because over half of mothers return to work before the child reaches age one.

A second trend in child care programs is school-age child care (also called after-school care). These programs serve children who are in preschool programs and kindergartens located in schools when school is not in session. School-age child care programs may operate with preschool programs. However, more school-age child care programs are operated separately. They often are sponsored by religious groups, civic organizations, and schools themselves. In these programs, children usually receive a snack, participate in activities, and receive help with homework. School-age child care programs will continue to increase because parents realize the risks of leaving children home alone before and after school and on school holidays.

► Kindergartens

Kindergarten programs are publicly and privately operated for four- and five-year-old children. In the United States, kindergartens are part of each state's public education system. They serve as an entrance to school education. Kindergartens give children the chance to play and develop through various activities.

■ Background of Kindergartens

Kindergartens were founded as private programs in Germany. (*Private programs* are programs owned by individuals, churches, or other nongovernment groups.) The programs enrolled children from ages three through seven and provided teaching suggestions for mothers with younger children. The word kindergarten

22-3   Quality infant/toddler programs are in demand.

Environments, Inc.

1—*Activity:* Check the telephone book for a listing of child care programs. Call and inquire about cost per week.

2—*Enrich:* Investigate state laws regarding the adult-child ratio. How does this vary in other states?

3—*Discuss:* What are some reasons for the high cost of infant-toddler programs?

4—*Activity:* Which of the child care programs listed in your telephone book offer after-school care? How much do they charge?

5—*Discuss:* What risks are involved in leaving children home alone after school?

means "children's garden." Founder Friedrich Froebel chose the name because he thought of young children as tender plants, not small adults.

Froebel felt that a school for young children should be different from a school for older children, 22-4. He planned many children's activities that we see today in kindergartens and other programs for young children. Examples include activities with building blocks, beads, art materials, sand, math concepts, animals and plants, stories, and music. Another example is *finger plays,* or poems and rhymes that are acted out with the hands. These activities were unlike the drill methods used in other schools of Froebel's time. In fact, Froebel's statement that "play is the highest level of child development" was scorned by many of his time.

22-4 Kindergartens allow more time for play and creativity than schools for older children.

© John Shaw

1—*Reflect:* Do you think the emphasis in kindergarten should be to teach reading and other abstract learnings? If no, what should be emphasized? Explain your answer.

2—*Discuss:* Describe some of the major goals of nursery schools in your community.

Kindergartens came to the United States with German immigrants in the mid-1800s. Soon, English-speaking groups began to adopt the kindergartens. People began to see the good effects of kindergarten programs on the lives of young children. Because of this, public schools began to include them as part of public education.

Over the years, kindergartens have changed some to meet children's needs, 22-5. Some people have expressed concern about efforts in some programs to teach reading and other abstract learnings. Many feel this causes too much stress on children. The challenge of kindergartens is to fit the needs of children today and lead slowly toward children's next years in school.

▶ Nursery Schools

Nursery school is the term that applies to a program for children under age five. Nursery schools provide education as well as physical care for children. Most nursery schools are privately owned, but a few operate in public schools.

The Origin of Nursery Schools

Nursery schools began in England in the early 1900s. They were designed to help children who lived in slums and whose needs were not being met by their family. When nursery schools came to the United States, child development was becoming a science. The schools opened as laboratory schools directed by staffs of research and teaching hospitals and colleges. The schools studied children. They also trained mothers and teachers to care for and teach children.

Today's Programs

The activities of nursery schools build on life within the family. Thus, most activities are first-hand experiences. Children play in a setting rich with materials, equipment, other children, and loving and well-trained adults, 22-6.

Some nursery schools still study children and provide career training. These laboratory nursery schools operate in colleges, universities,

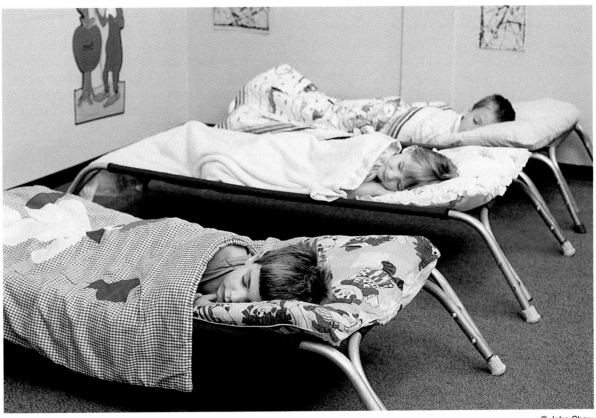

© John Shaw

22-5   Kindergarten children have special needs to meet.

and some high schools across the nation. However, more nursery schools are owned by individuals. Some nursery schools have programs such as those offered in laboratory settings. Others are called *nursery schools,* but they only meet children's physical needs.

▶ Montessori Schools

Montessori schools, named for their founder, Maria Montessori, opened in Rome, Italy, in the early 1900s. Montessori was a medical doctor who had worked quite successfully with then called *mentally handicapped* children. Because of

22-6   Nursery schools offer many rich play activities.

4

1—*Discuss:* What types of needs should be met?

2—*Activity:* Are any of the nursery schools listed in the phone book laboratory schools? What types of laboratory connections do they include?

3—*Reflect:* Would you select a nursery school that mainly stresses physical skills? Explain your answer.

4—*Reflect:* Why is it important to have creative and caring nursery school teachers?

her success, she planned an all-day program for slum children between ages two and one-half and seven. She named her school the **Casa dei Bambini,** which means "children's house."

Montessori believed that children are different from adults and from each other. She also felt that children can absorb and learn from their world as they work at tasks. (Montessori did not like Froebel's ideas about the child's need for play. She believed the child works for work's sake and not to complete a task, as does the adult.) Her philosophy continues to be taught in Montessori schools.

Montessori classrooms are made up of a mix of children from a three-year age span. Children within this span are not separated by age or grade. They are free to move about the classroom, work with other children, and use any materials they understand, 22-7. Teachers trained in Montessori methods guide the children's use of materials. However, they do not teach in the

sense of telling children what is right. In this way, Montessori schools strive to make each child more in charge of his or her own learnings.

Activities center on sensory learnings as children learn to see, hear, touch, taste, and smell the world around them. Daily living activities, such as preparing food and washing hands, also are a major part of the program. Children join in language and other activities, too.

▶ Head Start

In the 1960s, Americans became concerned with the effects of poverty in America. Studies showed how important the early years were to a child's development. **Head Start** was launched in 1965 as a federal program for children from families with low incomes. These children seemed to need more food, medical care, and help with learning. At first, Head Start was much like other programs for young children

22-7   Low, open shelves allow children to be more in charge of their own learnings.

American Montessori Society/Montessori Greenhouse School

1—*Note:* This encourages self-help.

2—*Discuss:* Summarize Maria Montessori's classroom philosophy.

from middle-class families. Soon, staff designed new activities and new ways to teach just for these children, 22-8.

Parents and families are an important part of planning and operating local Head Start programs. Community involvement is also important. Although activities are designed to strengthen learning, they also are designed to meet special needs of low-income children. Activities help children build self-esteem. They focus on helping children and their families work together to solve problems. In addition, these activities often relate to the child's ethnic background and culture.

● Choosing a Group Program

Group life cannot replace the teachings of home life. However, when quality group life is used to support and enrich home life, children can grow in many ways.

22-8   Children in Head Start programs are encouraged to engage in a lot of dramatic play. This helps them develop concepts needed for later school learnings like reading.

© Nancy P. Alexander

Children learn values away from home as well as in the home. Adults need to look for programs that promote their beliefs and values.

Adults should choose programs that meet the needs of each family. Because family needs differ, a program may or may not meet those needs. There should be a special match between family and program. However, families should consider a few basic guidelines when choosing a group program for children.

▶ Regulations

Regulations are standards that govern a group program. Regulations cover housing, equipment, staff, services, and business operations. Some regulations, such as fire safety, apply to all programs. Other regulations apply only to private programs. Still other regulations apply only to public programs. (*Public programs* are funded by federal or state monies. Examples include public schools and Head Start programs.)

Children should attend programs that meet regulations. However, regulations are minimum standards. Compare this idea to passing a test. Some students pass with high grades, others barely pass, and many others fall between these groups. In the same way, a poor-quality program may meet regulations and still be of low quality.

Also, some regulations are easier to check than others. If a fence is required around the outside play area, this is easy to check. On the other hand, a warm and loving staff is much harder to evaluate.

Finally, some regulations are simply on record with little or no enforcement. For instance, there are many regulations that cover family child care. However, homes are seldom checked to see if they meet all regulations.

▶ Housing and Equipment

The type of housing and equipment varies with a program's goals. However, the housing should be healthy and safe. There should be enough space for comfort and activities.

Furniture, equipment, and materials should meet the needs of the children in the program, 22-9. The housing and equipment should convey the message "It's nice here!"

► Staff

Children have many needs. For this reason, they must be cared for in small groups with enough adults looking after them. Regulations state the maximum number of children who may be cared for as a group. Regulations also state the number of adults who must be on duty at all times. The number of children who can be cared for as a group often are the following:

☐ between five and eight infants

☐ between 12 and 16 two- and three-year-olds

☐ between 16 and 22 four- and five-year-olds.

One teacher and one other adult are required for each of these small groups. Other staff are required to prepare meals, clean, and perform special duties.

Children need adults who are in good physical and mental health and help them feel secure. Children must feel loved and wanted. To feel loved, children must know that what they do matters to others. They need to have others hug them, comfort them, and listen to and talk with them. Children even need adults to say no or scold them when needed, 22-10.

Adults also must guide children in their care. Children need adults to help them develop during their early years. In order to meet children's needs, adults must apply their knowledge of child development at different stages of growth. Adults who care for infants must cuddle and accept dependent babies because this helps the infants develop. Adults who work with toddlers must encourage them to explore and learn. Adults who serve preschool children must welcome their curiosity, questions, and energy.

Staff members must also work well with adults. Staff must work well with each other. Staff and parents must talk and share for the sake of each child.

22-9   Housing and equipment in a good program provide plenty of space; neat, cheery surroundings; and activities suited to a child's development.

LEGO-Dacta, the educational division of the LEGO Group

22-10   Staff members must care deeply for the children they teach.

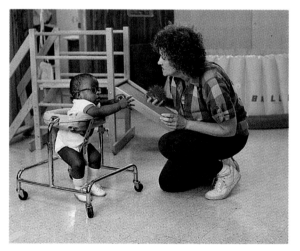

© John Shaw

1—*Discuss:* What are your state's regulations?

2—*Reflect:* Do children sense that staff members care deeply for them? If yes, how?

3—*Enrich:* Each student should select one of the child care programs listed in the telephone book. Call to determine

required qualifications for their director and employees. Report to the class. Is this the only factor you would consider when selecting a child care center?

▶ Program Activities

Program activities vary with the goals of early childhood programs. Goals should be determined in keeping with ***developmentally appropriate practices (DAP)***. (DAP is a term originally used in 1986 by the National Association for the Education of Young Children, an organization concerned with young children and their families.) DAP is child care and education that uses knowledge about:

☐ child development

☐ the strengths, needs, and interests of each child within the group

☐ the social and cultural contexts in which children in a given program live

DAP is used to contrast with ***developmentally inappropriate practices (DIP).*** DAP are not easy to rate for a specific program's practices can be seen on a scale from very appropriate to very inappropriate. For example, based on knowledge of child development, young children need to move about a great deal rather than sit still. To judge whether a certain program is developmentally appropriate or inappropriate on this practice, you would have to consider the age of the children as well as how long, how often, and for what reasons they are asked to sit still. For example, asking children to sit "rather still" for a 15-minute story would likely be considered as a DIP for two-year-olds, but as DAP for five-year-olds. However, if a given five-year-old had a short-attention span, 15 minutes would likely be too long and thus a DIP for this child. Besides story time, you might want to consider all the other times children are asked to "sit still." In choosing "the right" program for a child, parents should know the major DAP that make for quality (good) early childhood programs, 22-11.

Contrasting Developmentally Appropriate and Inappropriate Practices		
	DAP	**DIP**
Program Goals	Goals are planned for physical, mental, and social development. Children are seen as individuals who differ developmentally and will grow and change at their own rates. Children are also seen as having their own unique styles of learning and their own interests.	Goals are planned mainly for mental development. Although children may differ developmentally at time of program entrance, they should achieve age-norms by the end of the program. Children's unique styles of learning and interests are not seen as important; children must conform to group instruction.
Housing/ Materials	Room is arranged with learning or activity centers (art, book, science, manipulative, block, etc.) throughout. Materials are mainly play materials. Most materials have no right or wrong answers (dramatic play props, art materials, sand, and water) and many materials invite children to play together in small groups.	Room is often arranged with tables with an assigned place for each child facing the teacher's desk. Materials are often workbooks or duplicated sheets for teaching beginning reading and arithmetic. Drill software is often used on computers. (continued)

22-11   Programs with DAP are based on child development and on what is known about each child. In contrast, programs with DIP are based on teacher expectations for the group of children, and these expectations are often directed mainly toward early reading and arithmetic achievement.

1—*Activity:* List examples of DAP and DIP activities.

Contrasting Developmentally Appropriate and Inappropriate Practices (continued)		
	DAP	**DIP**
Curriculum Content	Children's activities help them develop gross and fine motor skills, literacy skills, social and scientific concepts, and creative abilities.	Children's learnings are mainly focused on developing reading and arithmetic skills. All other activities are not seen as important.
Assessment	Teachers access children mainly through observations and note what they observe about each child in anecdotal records, check sheets, etc. Teachers also collect samples of children's work (art work, photos of children's block structures, and videos of children in many types of activities). Often a portfolio (much like a scrapbook) is kept which includes the teacher's observation for each child records and the samples of work and is shared with the parent(s).	Teachers give "paper and pencil" tests and even end-of-the-year standardized tests. Scores that compare each child with the norms (how the typical child does) are shared with the child's parent(s).
Teaching Methods	Teachers permit children to work on their own or in small groups as much as possible. Through the teacher's constant observations, he or she decides when the children need a little help or when the housing or materials need changing.	Teachers do a great deal of group "telling." Drill methods are often used for learning (the alphabet, counting, etc.)
Guidance of Children	For a given child, teachers encourage self-control based on his or her stage of development. Teachers help children achieve self-control through simple explanations ("Hitting hurts."), modeling the desired behavior, and redirecting ("Chairs are for sitting. You may climb on the _____.") Teachers use positive comments when children use self-control.	Teachers expect all children to "sit still and listen" most of the day. When they do not conform, they are often punished (time-out chair, etc.). Treats are sometimes given as a "bribe" to keep children doing what teachers expect.

Generally, a DAP program helps children grow in all areas of development and builds confidence. It gives children the feeling that they can handle tasks themselves.

DAP programs use day-to-day routines to help children learn. In these programs, eating serves more purposes than curbing hunger. Snacks and meals offer a time to learn about foods and styles of eating. Eating also offers the chance to talk with others, 22-12. Self-care is also part of daily routines. Children want to become independent by learning to take care of themselves. Many programs encourage self-help skills.

Special activities are often planned, too, as ways to help children develop. These program activities often include

☐ language learnings. Language skills are improved by talking, listening, and looking at good books, 22-13.

☐ math learnings. Math skills are developed by counting, matching shapes in puzzles, and seeing who is taller.

☐ social learnings. Social learnings increase as children try new roles and help each other, 22-14. Celebrating holidays and birthdays are fun social events, too.

1—*Discuss:* How could a child care center extend a child's language learnings beyond the learning offered in the home?

22-12   Snack time is a time for sharing with others.

22-14   As children help each other, they learn important ways to say, "I care about you."

22-15   Dramatic play is a way to "try on" real life.

☐   science learnings. Learning about living and nonliving worlds is most exciting for young children. Children learn through activities with pets, plants, food, and others.

☐   creative fun. Children enjoy expressing themselves through art, dramatic play, and music, 22-15.

22-13   Listening to a storyteller read good books out loud helps children learn language.

© Nancy P. Alexander

1—*Note:* It also helps them to enjoy books.

☐   motor skills. Gross-motor skills are developed through active play, especially outdoor play. Fine-motor skills are improved as children play with many materials (art materials, puzzles, and building materials) as well as materials designed for the purpose of helping fine-motor skills, 22-16.

Many good programs utilize people who are not on staff as a way to help children learn. Many times, people in the community (including parents) are willing to share their special skills with children. When parents share skills, the self-concepts of both parents and children improve. Staff can plan community **field trips** (outings that take children to places off the program's property) to provide first-hand learnings, 22-17.

22-17   Children enjoy field trips to interesting places.

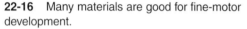

22-16   Many materials are good for fine-motor development.

Fisher-Price, Inc.

▶ Other Considerations

Some families have needs that can better be met in programs having some special services. These might include transportation to and from the program, extended hours, or programs for exceptional children, 22-18. Programs with special services are not always conveniently located. If several families have the same needs, they may be able to persuade programs to add these services. Work-related child care programs are good examples of how businesses have met the special needs of their employees.

Good programs for young children cost money. Costs of programs are rising due to increased costs of staff salaries, buildings, equipment, and supplies. Costs of programs vary with the type of program, days and hours of care, age-group served, and location.

Families may or may not have to pay all of a program's costs. For-profit programs earn most, if not all, of their income by charging families. (**For-profit programs** are programs that are set up to make money.) These programs cost families the most money. Not-for-profit programs often are funded mainly by nonfamily sources, such as the

1—*Discuss:* What types of field trips would be beneficial?

2—*Discuss:* What types of materials encourage fine-motor development?

3—*Discuss:* What can children learn from a trip to the zoo?

4—*Activity:* Check the telephone book for child care programs that serve exceptional children. What types of special needs do they serve? Report to the class.

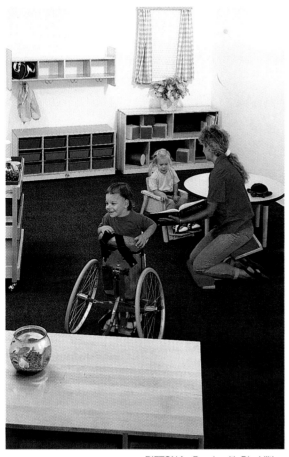

RIFTON for People with Disabilities

22-18   Programs for exceptional children offer needed services for these children.

22-19   Families must decide whether they can afford programs with such extras as swimming lessons.

state and federal government and service groups. (**Not-for-profit programs** are child care programs in which income only covers costs.) Often families either do not pay any of the costs or pay only a small fraction of the total costs. Not-for-profit programs that are operated as cooperatives (co-ops) are funded by families. In co-ops, parents help keep some of the costs down by offering their time and services.

Families must decide what they can afford and try to get the best program for their money, 22-19. Often families spend 10 percent of their total gross income to meet child care costs. Besides the direct costs, families need to look at the costs in terms of **hidden added costs**. These are costs that add to the direct costs.

Examples are costs of transportation, supplies, and disposable diapers. Families must also consider **hidden cost credits**. These are credits that lower direct costs of child care. They include money that may be added from a second income. They also include money saved in the cost of utilities, food for at-home care, and child care tax credits.

▶ Quality of Group Programs

Only high quality programs can have good effects on children. However, adults cannot judge a program by simply meeting the staff or checking the indoor and outdoor areas. Also, they cannot judge a program by noting the papers that say the program is meeting standards, 22-20. The only way to be sure of a program's quality is to observe the day-to-day activities.

Families need to quickly recognize programs that are not safe for children. The following are signs of poor programs:

☐   programs that people cannot visit without asking (Programs should welcome parents' visits at any time.)

☐   programs with staff who are not trained to work with young children

☐   programs that do not take special interest in children's needs (Programs with large groups of children and few adults are more likely to have this problem.)

2

3

4

1—*Enrich:* Plan and implement a field trip to a child care center for exceptional children. What did students learn?

2—*Resource: Local Child Care Facilities,* SAG.

3—*Reflect:* Would you become suspicious if a program did not allow visitors without prior approval? Explain your answer.

4—*Discuss:* Why would this be undesirable?

Landscape Structures, Inc.

22-20   Having nice outdoor areas for play is only one standard of a quality program.

1   ☐   programs that push children to perform above their abilities and cause them stress

Adults need to remember that children are defenseless clients of programs they attend. That is, young children cannot measure the quality of a program for themselves or take action if the quality is not good. Children depend on families to find quality programs for them, 22-21.

2   See 22-22 for a checklist to use when evaluating a child care facility. As children often spend a great deal of their early life in child care, adults must see that the staff and care facilities meet the needs and values of their family.

● Effects of Group Care on Children

Families are concerned with the effects group care has on children. Experts have studied these effects on children's health, mental development, and social development.

22-21   Children need to have adults find the best programs for them.

▶ Effects on Health

There has been some concern over the health of young children enrolled in group programs. Studies do not agree on the number of common illnesses in enrolled children versus children not enrolled. However, there seems to be no increase in serious illness in children who attend programs that follow good health practices. Families should consult their doctors about what is best for their children.

▶ Effects on Mental Development

Group programs do not seem to have either a positive or negative effect on the mental development of children from middle-class homes. As a whole, group programs offer more activities in certain areas than do most homes. Programs like Head Start can help the mental development of children from low-income families. If gains from such programs are to remain stable, however, there must be home and school follow-up for many years.

▶ Effects on Social Development

Since the early 1900s, there has been concern that group programs weaken bonds between children and families. Many recent studies do not

1—*Discuss:* Why would this be undesirable?

2—*Resource: Finding a Quality Group Program,* SAG.

3—*Enrich:* What types of health requirements do local child care centers have?

4—*Discuss:* Why is it difficult to evaluate gains from programs like Head Start?

Child Care Program Checklist

Overall Evaluation

_____ Does the program meet regulations?

   _____ The child care center is licensed.

   _____ The family child care home is registered.

   _____ The licensed center is accredited.

Safety

_____ Does the inside and outside appear safe?

   _____ The outside area is fenced.

   _____ Both the inside and outside areas are childproofed.

   _____ Equipment and materials are in good condition.

_____ Is the center or home clean and orderly?

_____ Is at least one staff member trained in first aid?

_____ Are parents required to complete health records and emergency forms?

_____ Has the facility been inspected by the fire department and health department?

Equipment and Materials

_____ Is the equipment the right size for children?

_____ Is the furniture the right size for children?

_____ Are the equipment and materials the right types for the children's ages and special needs?

_____ Is there a variety of equipment and materials?

_____ Is there enough equipment and materials for all children in the program?

_____ Do the materials invite a child to play?

_____ Are there shelves for the equipment and materials when they are not in use?

_____ Is there enough space for children to play?

Group Size and Number of Staff

_____ Are different age groups of children cared for separately?

_____ Are there eight or fewer infants in one group?

_____ Are there 22 or fewer preschool children in one group?

_____ Are there two adults with children at all times?

_____ Does the program employ additional staff to cook and clean?

(continued)

22-22   Adults need to carefully check out prospective programs for children.

find the child-family bond damaged because of care in group programs. One example is a recent two-year study of children between three and one-half months and two and one-half years. The study found that constant, daylong separation of children from families did not change the importance of family in the child's life.

Some studies do show that children are more aggressive as a result of group programs. Contact with peers tends to increase aggression in children because they must stand up for themselves. On the positive side, children may learn needed coping skills that will help them in the future, 22-23.

3

1—_Discuss:_ Why is this important?

2—_Note:_ Go over this list carefully.

3—_Resource: Good Programs Help Children Grow,_ SAG.

Child Care Program Checklist (continued)

Staff

_____ Are the staff members warm and loving with the children?

_____ Staff kneel to a child's level to speak with them.

_____ Staff look at children when they speak with them.

_____ Staff smile often.

_____ Staff use pleasant voices.

_____ Staff seem calm and unhurried.

_____ Do staff members provide appropriate activities for physical, mental, and social-emotional development?

_____ Do staff members welcome parents at any time and talk with the parents as they pick up and drop off students every day?

_____ Are routines (eating, toileting, napping, and putting on outside clothes) handled pleasantly?

_____ Is self-care encouraged when appropriate?

_____ Are some special activities planned each day?

_____ Have staff members passed criminal records checks?

Special Services

_____ Is transportation provided?

_____ Can parents arrange for extended care?

_____ Does the program enroll special needs children?

_____ Does the program have ways to serve mildly ill children?

Costs

_____ Is the cost reasonable compared with programs offering similar services?

_____ Are there hidden costs, such as an extra charge for supplies?

_____ Can the program costs be reduced for low-income families, for families with several children enrolled, or for parents who can provide services like volunteer time?

_____ Is the payment plan workable?

● Helping Children Adjust to Group Care

The change from home care to group care is a time of adjustment for children who are six months of age and older. These children often have separation anxiety, 22-24. Even school-age children may feel a bit uneasy for the first few days away from home.

Adults need to make the adjustment seem casual. Adults can make a child anxious by talking too much about the change. Adults may be anxious, too, but must do their best to stay calm and confident. Adults should also show they are sure of

22-23 In group programs, children must learn to share with others.

© John Shaw

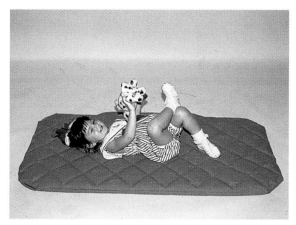

Angeles Group

22-24   A favorite toy often eases the stress of nap time away from home.

the child's ability to adjust. They may say, "I know there are many new boys and girls, but you will make new friends. Everyone is new for a while."

About a month before enrolling a child in a group program, the adult should explain what the program is like. He or she may explain there will be other children, toys, and activities. They should also visit the program, if possible.

Some children do not adjust to group care, even after a few weeks. In these cases, adults should either try other programs or help the child adjust. They may allow children to play with other children in a friend's home, 22-25. Later, these children may stay in group care for shorter periods of time. This might include temporary care in group programs. Once children adjust, they often accept group programs more easily.

2

22-25   Children who have trouble adjusting to group programs may need to spend time with one or two other children before they feel at ease.

Summary

There are large numbers of group programs for children throughout the country. Some are called *child care programs.* Others are called *kindergartens, nursery schools, Montessori schools,* and *Head Start programs.* They all have a history of meeting particular needs of children and families.

Because many children spend a great portion of their life in group programs, adults must choose them carefully. Adults need to pay attention to the kinds of facilities, number and qualities of staff, program activities, costs, and special services. Getting involved in programs helps to find out whether or not a program is of high quality.

Studies show that children in group programs do not seem to have any more serious illnesses than those not attending programs. Children's mental development does not seem to be positively or negatively affected through group programs. However, group programs often offer more activities that provide needed help in these areas. According to one study, being in a group

1—*Discuss:* List ways adults can ease separation anxiety for children who are entering group care for the first time. How can adults help children adjust to group care?

2—*Discuss:* How can adults help children who do not adjust to group care after an extended period of time?

program does not change the importance of the family in the child's life. The interaction with others may make children more aggressive and yet better able to stand up for themselves. This is a worthwhile coping skill for their future.

Adults need to help children adjust to group care. Visits to the program by the adult and child are recommended. If children are not adjusting easily to group care, adults might try other programs. Adults may shorten the time children spend in group care. Having others play with children in their own homes or in the home of a friend is helpful, too.

To Review

Write your answers on a separate sheet of paper.

1

1. Group programs for children are growing both in _____ and _____.
2. True or false. Montessori programs began in the United States.
3. Match the names of the types of group programs with their descriptions. (You may use each name more than once.)
   a. child care programs
   b. kindergartens
   c. nursery schools
   d. Montessori schools
   e. Head Start programs
   _____ businesses may operate these for their employees' children
   _____ based on the methods used to help mentally handicapped children
   _____ the oldest types of group programs
   _____ funded by government monies to help children from low-income families overcome some of their problems
   _____ based on the idea "play is the highest level of child development"
   _____ stresses that children absorb from their world as they work at tasks
   _____ have served as a laboratory setting for the study of children
   _____ today, most are operated on a for-profit basis
   _____ have a focus on sensory learnings and daily living tasks
   _____ part of the public education system in the United States
4. List five guidelines for choosing a quality child care program.
5. True or false. In a child care cooperative, families share the costs of operation.
6. There are direct costs as well as hidden added costs in sending a child to a child care program. Name two hidden costs.
7. True or false. Children in group care seem to be at a higher health risk for serious illnesses than children who stay at home.
8. Suggest three ways families can help their young children adjust to group care.

1—*Answers:* Answers to review questions can be found in the front section of this TAE.

To Do

1.   Visit two or three group programs for young children in your area. Discuss in class how their goals and services differ.
2.   Interview families about child care services in your area. Share your findings in class.
3.   Examine a licensing manual in your state. Review the standards that family and group child care programs must meet. Also scan the state fire and health department regulations.
4.   Compile a directory of child care programs in your area. The directory can include the program's name, owner, address, phone number, admission requirements, hours operated, and comments on special services or licensing. Copies of this directory could be placed in physicians' offices, the Chamber of Commerce, and other places where parents may read it.

To Observe

1.   Observe activities in two types of group programs for children. How were the programs similar? What differences did you note?
2.   After carefully studying chart 22-22, observe a child care program. Use the checklist to rate the program. Explain why you would or would not enroll a child in this program.

To Think Critically

1.   Today there are many types of early childhood programs. What factors should parents consider in choosing a program? Which factor or factors do you consider most important? Why?
2.   If you and your spouse had preschooler(s) and were trying to decide whether to be a single- or dual-career couple at this time, what factors should enter into your decision making? Be specific. What is the most important factor to consider? Why?
3.   As a kindergarten teacher, you have some children who have been in preschool programs and others who have never attended any preschool program. What differences might you notice in these two groups of children, especially during the first few weeks of school?

Chapter 23

Careers in Child-Related Fields

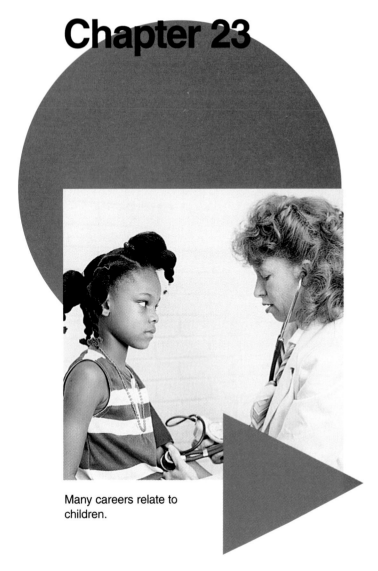

Many careers relate to children.

After studying this chapter, you will be able to

☐ describe careers in child-related fields.

☐ explain how personal and professional qualifications affect your career choice.

☐ describe how to find a job.

☐ explain several ways to get involved in child-related careers.

After studying this chapter, you will be able to define

career burnout
consultants
direct intervention
entrepreneur
formal leadership
informal leaders
licensing personnel
lifestyle
personal qualifications
personal references
professional qualifications
resume

You live in a world of change. No one can be sure of all the concerns people will face in coming years. However, today's trends can guide you to explore promising career options. For example, the widespread effort to improve children's quality of life is one trend that makes child-related work a good career choice.

In the past, parents reared their children with little or no outside help. Members of the extended family helped with the task. They used agencies like schools and hospitals much less often than we do today. In fact, stepping outside the family for help was sometimes seen as a family failure. Over the years, family life has changed greatly. The support of an extended family is not as common. Many times, this is because families move often, adding distance between the family and other relatives. Parents of preschool and school-age children often work outside the home.

In addition to these trends, many people believe a child has the right to a quality life. This belief has increased the demand for child-related services. Careers in child-related fields have grown out of these demands for services. The demands are growing daily.

● Types of Careers in Child-Related Fields

One way to describe child-related careers is in terms of the amount of contact with children. In some careers, adults work with children directly, 23-1. (This is called *direct intervention.*) People in such careers include school teachers and pediatricians. In other careers, adults serve as

23-1 Teaching is one career that involves direct intervention with children.

© John Shaw

1—*Note:* Review extended family. Do you think your parents would babysit your first child while you worked? Explain.

2—*Discuss:* What societal factors have contributed to the increased need for child care?

3—*Vocabulary:* Define intervention. Why is this often used with young children?

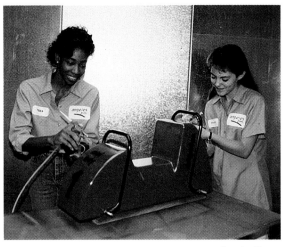

Angeles Group

23-2   Product development and sales are booming child-related careers.

consultants. **Consultants** share their knowledge about children with other adults. For example, college child development professors may serve as consultants to teachers who work with children. In other careers, professionals develop and sell products for children, 23-2. These adults use their knowledge of children to design and sell toys, clothing, furniture, and educational products.

Careers in child-related fields also include general career fields. Six areas to consider are health and protective services; care and education; entertainment; design; advertising, marketing, and management; and research and consulting.

▶ Health and Protective Services

Demand for children's physical and mental health services has increased. Adults in these services have good health care backgrounds. They also know about children's health needs. These careers include the following:

☐ pediatricians—doctors who specialize in the care of children

☐ pediatric dentists—dentists who specialize in the care of children, 23-3

☐ pediatric and school nurses—nurses who specialize in the care of children

☐ child psychologists—professionals who specialize in the emotional and mental health of children

☐ dietitians—specialists in nutrition who may plan the diets of healthy children and children with special food needs

☐ school food service personnel—people who plan school menus and prepare and serve food to meet children's needs

In addition, adults with careers in protective services work to find injustices to children and to correct poor situations. Positions include juvenile officers and judges, child welfare workers, and licensing personnel. (**Licensing personnel** check the quality of services for children, such as the quality of child care centers.) Jobs in protective services are increasing as society becomes more concerned about the rights and needs of children.

▶ Care and Education

More young children are enrolled in group settings than ever before. Private programs are growing in number. Government agencies on both federal and state levels are committed to

23-3   Caring for children's teeth and gums is one of the many careers in health and protective services.

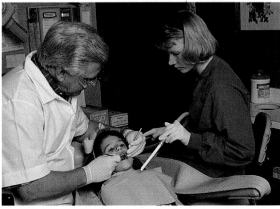

© John Shaw

1—*Note:* Refer to the child care career ladder.

2—*Resource: Contact with Children in Child-Related Careers,* SAG.

3—*Discuss:* Discuss how dietitians might address children's special food.

4—*Discuss:* What types of injustices toward children might require protective services? List protective services careers.

children's education, 23-4. Public support can be seen in the growth of public school kindergartens and programs for even younger children. Support also is growing in services for exceptional children, Head Start programs, and other programs to help children of low-income families.

The following care and education careers can be found in both public and private settings:

☐ child care personnel—people who care for infants, toddlers, and preschool children. They may care for school-age children before and after school and on holidays.

☐ teachers and teachers' assistants—professionals who teach and assist teachers in public and private school programs.

☐ special education teachers—teachers who work with children with disabilities or with learning disabilities. Many specialize in one or two types of learning problems.

☐ administrators—directors of child care and education programs as well as principals and supervisors of school programs.

23-4   Teachers with special knowledge are needed in education careers.

© John Shaw

© Nancy P. Alexander

23-5   Teachers who can provide instruction in two or more languages are in demand as society seeks to meet the needs of diverse cultural groups.

☐ children's librarians—specialized librarians who work in school libraries or in children's sections of other libraries. They often read stories to children and design programs to help children learn to read for fun.

☐ high school teachers and college professors—professionals who are involved in many fields concerning children's health, education, and welfare.

☐ child and youth leaders—people who work with children in religious programs and youth organizations like scouting groups, recreational programs, and camps.

☐ recreational instructors—professionals who guide or teach children in such areas as music, art, sports, and hobbies.

These careers are growing in numbers. Some predict the United States will encounter a child care crisis in the near future. People say the cause will be the lack of child care programs and teachers. Teachers, now in high demand, most likely will be in the future, 23-5. The demand for teachers with special skills, such as computer teachers, is even higher.

1—*Enrich:* Do research on college minors that would make an early childhood or elementary education teacher more marketable. Report to the class.

2—*Discuss:* Which languages would be most beneficial?

3—*Activity:* List youth organizations in your community or county. What services and activities do they provide?

4—*Activity:* List recreational activities available in your community. Where are these offered?

▶ Entertainment

The growth of careers in children's entertainment is rather recent. Entertainment planned for children did not exist until people began to see children as a different audience than adults. Earlier, children's entertainment was limited to plays, books, and a few games.

In recent years, entertainment in general has become a big business. Children's entertainment also has expanded greatly. Many new children's television programs, movies, and live programs have been produced. A wider variety of children's books and games are available. People in entertainment careers include producers, directors, writers, actors, and musicians, 23-6.

▶ Design

As people began to see children differently from adults, they began to design items with children in mind. Children's items are designed to better meet their needs for physical, mental, and social-emotional development. The knowledge of children affects the design of clothing, buildings, furniture, and toys, 23-7. Designers of these items must understand child development. They also must have artistic talent and knowledge of design.

▶ Advertising, Marketing, and Management

With the number of products for children increasing, people who understand children's needs are becoming an important part of many businesses. Careers in advertising and marketing are growing. Another growing career choice is managing businesses that produce and sell children's products. People must be sensitive to children's needs. Career positions are available in large corporations, agencies, firms, and smaller businesses, 23-8.

▶ Research and Consulting

Research on children is being conducted in fields like health, education, entertainment, design, and business. Research studies provide knowledge that people need to serve children best. The field of research is growing so quickly that a massive amount of information is now available. For instance, over 100,000 research studies on children's education are published each year. The challenge is passing on this information to those in education careers.

23-6   Clowns have entertained children for years.

© Nancy P. Alexander

1—*Activity:* List children's entertainment in your community. How do they benefit or not benefit children?

2—*Activity:* Look through catalogs for products of children's designers. Discuss themes, colors, and appeals.

3—*Discuss:* List personal qualities a clown must possess. What benefits would a clown provide for children?

Hasbro, Inc.

23-7   Children need products like toys designed for them.

In the business world, sales clerks in children's stores or departments have daily contact with children.

© John Shaw

23-8   In the business world, sales clerks in children's stores or departments have daily contact with children.

Consultants work in teams on behalf of children. They are the link between researchers and others in child-related careers, 23-9. Consultants relay information to those in direct intervention, product development, and sales. Some adults consult on a daily basis. Child development experts who provide state and federal lawmakers with information are an example. Other adults work as consultants when called on for written or oral input. With knowledge increasing daily, consultant careers will become more in demand.

▶ Entrepreneurship

The careers just discussed and others related to children offer many chances for self-employment. A person who creates and owns his or her own business is called an ***entrepreneur.*** The most common child-related businesses that entrepreneurs start are in in-home child care. However, some operate child care centers as well. Many other careers work well for

1—*Discuss:* What businesses or state organizations might utilize the services of children's consultants?

© Nancy P. Alexander

23-9 Consultants interpret research findings to others involved in child-related careers.

self- employment. These include child photography, recreational instruction, private medical practice, and writing for and about children.

Self-employed people must have many skills other than those related to their specialty. For example, owners of child care centers must know much more than how to teach and care for children. They must be able to manage money. They must charge clients enough to pay for supplies, rent, salaries, and other expenses involved in running a center. They must find ways to advertise their center. Owners must be sure their center complies with laws that apply to child care centers. They also may serve as managers to child care workers, receptionists, and other workers.

Many people find owning their own businesses rewarding, 23-10. They like having the freedom to run their business the way they see

23-10 Owning a business is hard work, but many people find it rewarding.

© John Shaw

1—*Discuss:* What child care-related entrepreneurships are located in your community?

2—*Activity:* List qualities most successful entrepreneurs possess.

3—*Enrich:* Interview an entrepreneur. What type of training does he or she recommend? What personal qualities does the entrepreneur possess that influenced his or her success? What are advantages and disadvantages of this entrepreneur's job?

best. They also like the variety of being able to fill different roles, such as teacher, manager, and budget director. There are drawbacks, however. Entrepreneurs may have to use their personal money if the business goes into debt. Entrepreneurs must make their own decisions about the business and live with them. Another drawback is that many owners work longer hours and have fewer vacations than they would if they were employed by others.

If you have the skills, knowledge, and energy, you may enjoy starting and running your own business. Self-employment in child-related fields can be satisfying and profitable. Creativity, knowledge, and hard work can make your business both rewarding and profitable.

● Heading Toward a Career

More and more people are interested in child development and ways to meet children's needs. Adults in both families and child-related careers are most important in the lives of children. If you choose to work with children, you must be qualified to meet children's needs in the best ways. You also must be prepared to find and secure a job.

▶ Personal Qualifications

Personal qualifications are all the traits you possess that you do not learn in career training. Personal traits are harder to define and measure than learnings that result from career training. For this reason, little research has been done on personal qualifications. Thus, only general traits are discussed.

▪ Concern for Children
The most important personal qualification is a deep concern for children, 23-11. Sometimes, in the effort to perform well, people lose sight of the most important concern of all—the child. If you work directly or indirectly with children, you must always make decisions based on what is best for the child.

Many other qualities are almost as important as concern for children. The importance of having the qualities depends on how closely you work with children. You need to be kind and patient with children and their families. You must be able to cope with children's noise and activity. You should enjoy children's physical, mental, and social worlds. This includes children's games, songs, stories, and even humor. You need to feel comfortable helping young children with physical needs. This might include helping with toileting or dressing. It might mean letting a child show you a scraped knee or loose tooth.

Finally, you must be able to accept physical closeness from young children. Children want to touch adults' clothing, jewelry, and hair. Sometimes they may do so with paint, dirt, or food on their hands. Children need adults who will hold their hands, hug them, and let them sit on their lap.

23-11   People who work with children should be concerned about their safety and welfare.

© John Shaw

Flexibility

In working with children, it is important to remain open to new ideas. Flexibility is important, too, because children can be unpredictable. Research shows that the constant changes required in working with children often cause people to have career burnout. *Career burnout* is a state in which a person becomes emotionally tired of a career. It even may lead to health problems from stress.

Leadership Skills

No matter what kind of career you choose, at some time you will need to be a leader. Sometimes people take a formal leadership role. The mayor of your town and a manager of a store practice *formal leadership.* These people have been chosen by others to lead a group. There are times when people must take an informal leadership role. *Informal leaders* lead or guide others even though they are not officially chosen to lead. People may be informal leaders within an organized group as well as outside of one.

Leadership involves motivating others to complete tasks or goals. People need many qualities to fulfill this role. Leaders must communicate well with others. They must have a positive outlook and help others stay positive, too. Leaders need to handle responsibility. This means following through to complete started tasks, accepting blame for mistakes, and keeping promises. Leaders need to be good decision makers who are confident in their choices. They should know how to set goals that will help the group fulfill its purpose. They must be able to delegate responsibilities to others. (When people *delegate* they give responsibilities to others.) It also means making sure others can handle the responsibility and finish the task.

Leadership ability is especially important when working with children. Children look up to all adults. Even if you are a volunteer helper in a center, children look to you as a leader. Therefore, you must be self-confident. Your confidence will help children feel secure. You need to be able to set limits and be firm with children. Children are not self-disciplined yet and need

your help to meet goals. Being able to listen patiently is important, too. Children may need to try several times before they say something in ways adults understand.

Like other personal qualities, leadership qualities are a part of your whole life, not just your working hours. Some people seem to have more natural leadership ability than others. You can improve your ability through practice. Even babysitting gives you practice at making decisions and being responsible. Being a member or an officer of a school club gives you practice, too. For example, an excellent way to develop leadership skills is through your school's chapter of Future Homemakers of America (FHA). One of FHA's purposes is to provide opportunities for making decisions and assuming responsibility. FHA also encourages students and teachers to go through the following steps to make wise choices:

- ☐ identify concerns
- ☐ set a goal
- ☐ form a plan
- ☐ act
- ☐ follow up

▶ Professional Qualifications

Professional qualifications are the physical, mental, and social-emotional skills you need to perform in a career, 23-12. People most often learn these skills by training. Training might include classes in high school or college as well as on-the-job training. However, you will need an aptitude for learning these skills. (*Aptitude* is a potential for learning a subject.) For instance, before you may study to become a pediatrician, you need a college degree in certain areas (often premedicine). You need to score at a certain level on tests that measure your background knowledge. You also might need to submit references, interview with faculty at medical school, and pass physical examinations.

Child development is the basic science for understanding children. If you want to have a career in a child-related field, you must know

1—*Vocabulary:* Describe career burnout. What are some factors that contribute to it?

2—*Activity:* Develop a leadership checklist.

3—*Reflect:* Why is it important for a leader to delegate duties?

4—*Enrich:* Develop a leadership action plan for yourself. How can you develop better leadership skills through school participation, studies, activities, and community participation?

5—*Reflect:* How does aptitude enter into your career training program?

© John Shaw

23-12   Professional qualifications help this teacher meet both the regular and special needs of the children she serves.

about child development. Because physical, mental, and social-emotional development are related, you study all aspects of child development. However, professional training for a career often stresses one aspect of development more than others. For example, pediatricians deal more with physical aspects of development. They still must be aware of how other aspects of development affect a child's health.

In addition to learning about child development, you will become specialized in your career area. For instance, teachers must have specialized knowledge in the following and other areas:

☐ ways children learn

☐ what to teach and in what order to teach certain facts and skills

☐ the best methods and materials for teaching the facts and skills

☐ ways to evaluate children's knowledge

For some careers, people must learn specialties within a specialty. Specialties require in-depth learnings. Pediatric opthamologists are children's eye physicians. These adults learn general medicine. Then they learn to treat diseases of the eye. Finally, they learn to care for children's eye problems. Because so few adults have specialties within specialties, these adults often serve as researchers or consultants. They may only directly handle the most difficult cases.

The training needed for a job is affected by the level of a job. There are many levels of positions within the field of child care. The career ladder in 23-13 shows some of these levels. Teachers' assistants and some associate teachers do not need college degrees. They may have had some training in high school, vocational classes, community college, or college. Supervisors generally have at least bachelor's degrees in child development, early childhood education, or related areas. Many supervisors and most directors have master's degrees in a specialized area of child development. Consultants may have more than one master's degree or a doctoral degree.

2

3

Job Training

The amount of training a job requires depends on the level of responsibility a career demands. Teachers have greater professional responsibilities than teachers' assistants. Some careers require study in schools and colleges and supervised work in the career field. People may earn professional qualifications for other careers, such as entertainment, through on-the-job training.

4

In addition to basic career training, adults in child-related careers are expected to keep up with the latest knowledge and practices in their field. Keeping up in a child-related career may require more classroom study, seminar attendance, or

1—*Discuss:* Why is flexibility important for a teacher?

2—*Discuss:* How does position on the career ladder influence salary?

3—*Resource: Meeting Professional Qualifications,* SAG.

4—*Discuss:* What types of child care careers require on-the-job training?

23-13 People are needed at various levels in the field of child care.

independent study. It also may involve on-the-job training in a different setting. In addition, it may involve exchanging knowledge and practices among those working in the many child-related careers.

▶ Job Search Skills

Being qualified is one part of finding a child-related career. Another part is looking for and securing a job. Finding a job you want is hard work. There are many steps involved.

■ Step One

First, determine what kind of job you want. A teacher may help you decide what kind of child-related career suits you best, 23-14. Once you decide, you can look in the right places for jobs in that field. If you want to be a camp counselor, you may look for job ads in local newspapers. You also may call local park districts, schools, or churches to find out whether they offer such programs. Once you find out where the camps are located, call to ask who handles hiring counselors and how to apply.

To apply for jobs, you may need to write a resume. A **resume** is a short, written history of your education, work experience, and other qualifications for employment. Prospective employers will look at your resume to understand more about your experience. It will help them decide whether or not you are qualified for a job.

■ Step Two

Next, you will need to set up a job interview. Some places allow you to set up an interview over the phone. Others prefer a written letter requesting an interview, 23-15.

23-14 A teacher or career counselor can help students decide what child-related career they wish to pursue.

1603 Green Street
Southland, Wisconsin 66732
April 15, XXXX

Ms. Anna Martinez
Program Director
Big Lake Day Camp
Rural Route 3
Southland Township, Wisconsin 66732

Dear Ms. Martinez:

I am interested in working as a counselor-in-training at Big Lake this summer. My counselor at Southland High School, Mr. O'Brien, suggested I write you.

Although this job will be a good learning experience for me, I have much to offer you as an employee. I have taken three child development classes in high school. In two of the classes, I worked four hours per week in the school child care center. I planned many activities for children, including plays, crafts, games, and snacks. I enjoy being with children and helping them. In fact, I hope to open my own child care center when I graduate from college.

May we meet for an interview? I will call your office next week to see whether we can schedule an appointment. If you would like to speak with me sooner, or if you have any questions, please call me at 555-7472. Thank you for your time and consideration.

Sincerely,

Willa Holtz

Willa Holtz

23-15   People often use written letters to request a job interview.

1—*Activity:* Write an application letter for a child care-related job. Use the computer. Share your letter with the class and critique. Make necessary changes.

Step Three

1

At some point, often just before the interview, you will fill out a job application. The application asks for such information as your name, address, social security number, educational background, and past jobs. It often asks for personal references. ***Personal references*** are people who know you well enough to discuss how you are qualified for a job. Employers may call personal references to find out more about you before making a hiring decision. People usually can't use relatives for personal references. However, you may use past employers and former teachers.

Step Four

At the interview, you need to put your best foot forward. Your personal appearance should be neat. As a rule, jeans do not make a good impression at interviews. Clean, neat dress pants, dresses, or suits are appropriate (depending on the type of job you want). Good posture, a pleasant smile, and good eye contact are also important in an interview.

You may want to rehearse the interview with someone before you go. This will help you prepare answers to some of the questions interviewers often ask. Examples of questions include the following:

- ☐ Why are you interested in this job?
- ☐ Why did you choose a child-related career?
- ☐ Where do you see yourself professionally in five years?
- ☐ List your strengths and weaknesses.

2

Sometimes you will be asked to interview a second or third time before an employer makes a decision.

Step Five

Unless you are told differently, the employer will probably contact you within two weeks. If the employer offers you a job, respond promptly and politely as to whether or not you accept. If you are not hired, it is still important to be polite and friendly. The employer may consider you for a future position.

3

1—*Activity:* Obtain a blank copy of a job application. Fill out the application using these points as a guide.

2—*Enrich:* Role-play either the role of interviewer or interviewee. Draw a slip of paper describing a specific job, then participate in a formal interview. Dress properly, and conduct the interview as you would in real life. Interviews may be taped.

● Make a Wise Career Choice by Getting Involved

Careers in child-related fields are increasing. There is a demand for competent adults who can meet children's needs. You can begin thinking about careers and basic preparation now. Many adults say they became interested in their career during their school years.

In order to make any wise career choice, you must get involved. There are many ways to get involved in child-related careers. The following ways can be used as starting points.

▶ Study Children's Development

First, study and observe children's development. Take courses and read books on children's development. Observe children in group programs, with their families, and at play with friends.

▶ Involve Yourself with Children

Next, get involved with children and children's products. Baby-sitting is an excellent way to learn about children, 23-16. Another way is working as a volunteer assistant in a child care center, children's religion class, or summer camp. Getting involved with professionals is helpful, too. You may be able to serve as an assistant in a business. Some people find volunteer positions. Others find paid positions that help them learn and earn money.

▶ Join Professional Organizations

Joining organizations that are concerned about children and their families also will help prepare you. You may want to join one or more of the following organizations:

- ☐ Future Homemakers of America
- ☐ National Association for the Education of Young Children
- ☐ Association for Childhood Education International

3—*Discuss:* List specific polite behaviors.

4—*Reflect:* List ways to become involved with children in your community. Which ones would you select? Why?

© John Shaw

23-16   Baby-sitting is one of the best ways to earn experience caring for children.

Professional organizations publish journals or magazines that keep members informed on current child care issues. They also publish other materials to help members understand children and child-related careers. Almost all organizations have meetings that help members find out the latest news and share ideas with others.

Joining professional organizations also helps you show your interest in child care to others. For instance, your membership may help you show school officials the need for high school classes in child development. Organizations may give you the chance to work toward quality child care programs. Joining a group says to parents and the public in general, "I am joining with others in an effort to provide the best for our children."

▶ Consider the Future

As you consider your future, talk with guidance counselors and professionals about the qualifications needed for certain careers. Also ask about the employment opportunities. Find out how many positions presently are open or are expected to open in that field. You also need to evaluate your own interests and personal qualifications. In addition, consider your ability to acquire the needed professional qualifications.

▶ Make Wise Career Moves

Finally, begin to work toward entering the career. This may include taking certain background courses, earning better grades, or increasing needed skills. It also may mean applying to schools or colleges or to businesses. You may need to begin saving money needed for training or apply for loans or scholarships.

Choosing a career is serious. Careers are more than what you do for so many hours a day. To a great extent, careers influence many aspects of your lifestyle. (**Lifestyle** is the typical way of life for a person, group, or culture.) Careers often affect where you live, who you meet, what your income is, and what you consider to be important.

2
3

4

Summary

Careers in child-related fields continue to grow. This is because of changes in family life. This trend, along with efforts to improve the quality of children's lives, will likely result in a continuing growth of child-related careers.

Adults may work with children in a number of career areas. These include health and protective services; care and education; entertainment, design, advertising, marketing, and management; research and consulting; and entrepreneurial services.

People need a basic knowledge of child development to understand children. Personal and professional qualifications are required to enter a child-related field. After becoming qualified for a child-related job, you must use organized, efficient job search skills to find a job.

Those wishing to enter the field should study and observe children. Getting involved with them through baby-sitting and joining organizations or other activities helps to identify and clarify interests. Judgments need to be made about personal qualifications and the ability to get the needed advanced education and training. People need to understand, too, that the chosen career affects many aspects of an individual's lifestyle.

To Review

Write your answers on a separate sheet of paper.

1

1. In general, careers in child-related fields are _____ (increasing, decreasing) in number.
2. True or false. All people in child-related careers work directly with children.
3. _____ often do not work directly with children. Instead, they share their knowledge about children with other adults.
4. Name three items that people can design and sell for children.
5. Match the specific career with the career area by placing a letter or letters in each blank.
   Career areas
   _____ health and protective services
   _____ care and education
   _____ entertainment
   _____ design
   _____ advertising, marketing, and management
   _____ research and consulting
   Specific careers
   a.   child welfare case worker
   b.   music teacher
   c.   speaker at an in-service meeting for teachers
   d.   school librarian

    e.   pediatrician

    f.   architect of school buildings

    g.   dietitian in a summer camp for overweight children

    h.   director of a children's holiday television special

    i.   4-H sponsor

    j.   juvenile judge

    k.   person who tests children's skills in walking balance beams and writes a report on the findings

    l.   manager in an advertising agency promoting a product for children

6. True or false. An owner of a child care center must be able to manage money.

7. The most important personal qualification for working in a child-related field is
   a. patience
   b. high level of intelligence
   c. good physical health
   d. deep concern for children
   e. desire to work hard

8. List three personal qualities needed by adults working directly with children.

9. Professional qualifications are mainly (taught, not taught).

10. True or false. Professional qualifications for all careers in child-related fields require study in schools and colleges.

11. All adults involved in careers in child-related fields must have a basic knowledge of _____ in order to be effective.

To Do

1. Make a list of careers in child-related fields that are available in your area.

2. As a class or group project, compile a list of questions concerning careers in child-related fields that you could use to find out more about a career. You could ask when the person first became interested in the field, why he or she became interested, and the personal and professional qualifications for those entering the same field. Interview one or more people involved in careers in child-related fields.

3. As an individual project, list some of your personal traits. Put them in order from weak to strong. Ask yourself how your traits match the desired personal qualifications of those entering careers in child-related fields.

4. Using information given by your school guidance counselor, prepare a chart of child-related occupations. List the occupation, pretraining needed, formal training needed, and on-the-job training needed.

5. Hold some mock interviews for jobs in child-related fields. Invite one or two employers (such as a child care director or a toy store owner) to conduct the interviews. A few days before, choose four or five students to be interviewed. (Discuss some general interview procedures and possible questions with these students before the interviews.) After the interviews, have the employers share constructive comments on the strengths and weaknesses of the students during the interviews.

6. As a class, sponsor a baby-sitting clinic. (Find resources at the library or through government agencies.) Invite other students to attend.

To Observe

1. Observe people working in a child-related career field. What skills do they use? What aspects of the child's development (physical, mental, and/or social and emotional) do they especially need to know for this career?

2. Observe your friends as they become involved with children in different settings. What skills are they developing? Would these skills be helpful in parenting?

To Think Critically

1. Why would it be good to take one or more courses in child development almost regardless of career choice?

2. If you wanted to inquire about particular careers in child-related fields, how would you proceed? What questions would you need to have answered?

3. Why is it wise to get involved in child-related fields even before completing secondary school? How can early involvement even help you *after* you complete your training or education for the career?

Many people find child-related careers to be interesting and rewarding.

Part 7

Special Concerns

Children: The Early Years closes with challenges related to children's growth and development. Part 7 addresses situations that some children and families experience.

Every family has problems and challenges. A few children and families have problems so severe that they challenge the health of children and the strength of families. In **chapter 24,** you will study both ordinary challenges and more severe problems. You will also learn some ways to confront these concerns and problems.

In **chapter 25,** you will learn more about children who develop in exceptional ways. Because these children have special needs as they grow and develop, adults must use special techniques in areas where children need more attention. Adults must also foster all facets of a child's growth and development.

Chapter 24

Concerns of Children and Families

After studying this chapter, you will be able to

☐ describe four sibling relationships and explain how a child's birth order affects development.

☐ describe how parental employment affects children.

☐ explain how stress from family moves can hurt children and how to lessen the effects.

☐ describe ways adults can help children handle divorce, remarriage, and death.

☐ point out problems single parents and teenage parents face.

☐ describe ways to protect children from neglect and abuse.

☐ list resources available for children in crisis.

Siblings and families are the main force in shaping a child's physical, intellectual, and social-emotional growth.

After studying this chapter, you will be able to define

child abuse
child neglect
children in self-care
educational neglect
emotional neglect
experimental children
latchkey children
medical neglect
middle children
mobile
moral neglect
physical abuse

physical neglect
psychological abuse
psychological neglect
quality time
role guilt
role strain
separate identities
sexual abuse
singletons
social isolation
verbal abuse

Family life is complex these days. Sometimes stressful events occur that cause tensions and problems that affect family life. These problems affect children.

Children need to grow up in a strong family. When divorce, remarriage, or death upsets the family, adults need to help children cope. When the family must relocate, adults must reassure children that they will soon feel secure in their new environment.

Some parents must balance family and work issues. Single and teenage parents face additional challenges when raising and supporting children.

Child abuse and neglect cause serious emotional and psychological problems for children. Many carry the problems with them all their life. Adults must protect children from abuse.

The types of relationships children have with their family play an important role in their development. Sibling relationships are especially important because children learn a lot by playing and living with siblings.

● Sibling Relationships

In most families, children grow up with siblings (brothers and sisters). Today, the average American family has two children. This means most children interact with at least one sibling.

▶ Sibling Interactions

Siblings influence each other's lives in many ways. They play the roles of playmates, teachers, learners, protectors, and rivals. Sibling relationships teach children about social give-and-take.

▪ Playmates

Brothers and sisters are built-in playmates for each other. In play, siblings learn to set goals and cooperate. Siblings also share hours of fun, 24-1. Brothers and sisters remember these fun times throughout their adult years.

▪ Teachers and Learners

Older children often act like teachers while younger siblings play the part of eager learners. As teachers, siblings explain, define, describe, show, and select examples. Most brothers and sisters show interest in their sibling's efforts. They help them reach their goals as well.

Older siblings also model social skills. These social skills include learning gender roles. Younger siblings learn gender roles faster than firstborns and only children. Having a sibling also helps children learn the difference between good and bad social behavior. From a child's point of view, a sibling shows good social behavior if he or she plays nicely, helps with chores, and doesn't tattle. Children consider being pesty or bossy to be bad social behavior.

▪ Protectors

If you have ever seen an older child run to a younger sibling's defense, you know that siblings protect each other. Siblings protect each other most often in the following situations:

☐ when siblings have an age gap of three or more years

☐ when siblings come from large families

3

24-1 Siblings often share in the happiness of celebrations.

4

© John Shaw

1—*Vocabulary:* Provide a definition for *dysfunction.* List problems that could cause a family to be dysfunctional.

2—*Reflect:* What evidence of this have you seen or experienced?

3—*Discuss:* What are some advantages for younger siblings?

4—*Reflect:* What celebrations have you shared or observed?

☐ when children are unsupervised outside, on the way to and from school, or with a baby-sitter

☐ when peers attack a younger sibling in a physical or verbal way

Older children can help adults watch younger brothers and sisters (although adults never should leave children alone). As a bonus, older children who help parents care for siblings are better prepared for parenthood and child-related careers, 24-2.

Rivals

Two or more children in a family compete in both physical and verbal ways. Younger children and boys fight physical battles more often than older children and girls. Younger children plead, whine, and sulk. Older children often command, boss, and call each other names.

Why does rivalry occur? Children may compete for the love and attention of parents and friends for several reasons. They may be jealous of siblings who seem more capable than they are.

24-2   Caring for a brother or sister prepares children for future parenthood.

© John Shaw

They also may not be able to see a situation from another's point of view. To young children, fair means equal instead of meeting another child's special needs.

Adults cannot prevent rivalry, but they can lessen it by giving all their children lots of love. Each child needs positive feedback. Parents must not compare one child to another. Children are different, and comparing them usually makes one child resent the other and feel angry toward parents.

Space.   Parents need to control the space children use. Children need space for their belongings. High shelves keep toddlers away from older children's toys and books. Adults should teach children to share, but they should not expect them to share 100 percent of the time. Children should share in the same ways adults share—sometimes, but not in all cases. Also, children should have some time to play without siblings. Playing alone and with friends is healthy. Siblings, especially younger ones, can pester children when they always are around.

Fights.   Adults should ignore fights unless children are in physical danger or property may be damaged. If adults settle each dispute, children may feel rewarded with the adults' attention. If the fight must be stopped, adults should tell children to stop without adding a threat. If the command does not work, adults should separate the children.

Family Togetherness.   Parents should stress the importance of family togetherness and support. Families should take part in some activities everyone enjoys. Adults must teach children to take pleasure in another's good fortune. Adults should explain that although family members get angry at each other, they still love each other. Above all, adults should praise loving behavior, 24-3.

▶ Birth Order and Development

To some degree, the order of children's birth affects their social roles and personalities. Facts about birth order cannot be applied to all children.

24-3 Adults should praise children who work together to accomplish a task.

Personality traits also depend on the sex of the siblings, the number of older and younger siblings, the attitudes of parents, and a family's culture. Larger age gaps between a child and the next older sibling reduce the effects of birth order.

Only Children. About 10 percent of married couples have one child. This figure has doubled since the 1950s. More women in the workforce and more women having children later in life are some reasons for this increase.

Many myths surround only children. Some believe only children are lonely, spoiled, selfish, less bright, dependent on parents, and different. Only children seldom live up to these cliches. Like all children, only children are distinct persons with their own personalities. However, they usually are not lonely if playmates are a part of their life. In fact, they learn to spend time alone as well as with others. Only children often are less selfish or jeal-

ous than other children. This is because they are less threatened by the loss of attention or possessions. Only children usually have high intelligence quotients (IQs). For example, all but one of the first astronauts were only children. See 24-4 for a list of some traits of only children.

Firstborn Children. You will see in 24-4 that firstborns have many of the same traits as only children. This is partly because most firstborns are only children for a little while (except siblings from a multiple birth). Like only children, firstborns often are bright. They often teach younger siblings, and teaching benefits their intellect. Firstborns are also mentally creative because siblings look to them for ideas.

Like only children, firstborns often are called *experimental children*. Parents must try untested ideas on them. Because they are experimental children, they are not always treated the same way in similar situations. Also, they are punished more severely and rewarded more than children born later. New parents often are more anxious and not as sure of their parenting skills as are parents of more than one child.

Firstborn children often are not as popular with other children as are only and later-born children. Those who are firstborn tend to use high-power social tactics like bossing, threats, and physical force to protect younger siblings. These social tactics do not make them popular with peers.

Middle Children. Birth order findings seem to best fit families with four or fewer children. For this reason, the term *middle children* refers to the second child in a family of three siblings. The term also refers to both the second and third children in families of four siblings. Findings on middle children, shown in 24-4, do not fit large families (five or more siblings) or families who have multiple-birth siblings, such as twins.

Middle children seem to have lower IQs than those of only and firstborn children but higher than those of youngest children. When children are spaced closer than three years, adults tend to spend less time with middle children. Adults

2

3

1—*Discuss:* What can parents do to improve the social skills of an only child?

2—*Vocabulary:* Define experimental children. List their characteristics.

3—*Discuss:* List positive and negative characteristics of firstborn children. Discuss typical parenting styles.

Traits Affected by Birth Order

Only Children
high intelligence quotient
achiever
perfectionist
high self-esteem
relaxed
not jealous
unselfish
socially outgoing
leader as adult

Firstborns
highest intelligence quotient
achiever (stays in school most years)
creative
lots of zeal and drive
ambitious
anxious
conservative
mature
conformist
wants company in times of stress
angry and irritable at times
not popular
leader as adult

Middle Children
slightly lower intelligence quotient than only
    children and firstborns
less highly driven
attracted to nonacademic areas like sports or
    the arts
cheerful
easygoing
relaxed
patient
adaptable
gentle
tactful
outgoing
popular
charming
see themselves as less skillful than older siblings
feel lost in the middle at times

Youngest Children
lowest intelligence quotient as compared with only
    children and older siblings
underachiever
seek pleasure
relaxed
secure
calm
kindhearted
popular
negotiator
good companion
need to feel loved and cherished as an adult

24-4   Birth order can affect a child's mental and social-emotional development.

spend more time with these children when the age gap is three or more years. This is especially true when the second child is a boy and the first is a girl. The amount of time an adult spends with children seems to affect intelligence most in middle-class families.

Socially, middle children seem to adjust easily to new situations. When other children are born, middle children do not feel as displaced as firstborns. This may be because they always have shared their parents. They've even shared hand-me-down clothes and toys. On the negative side, they may feel caught in the middle. Some middle children feel they must constantly compete with older siblings. A middle child may also feel that a younger child steals attention as the family baby.

Youngest Children.   As shown in chart 24-4, youngest children do better socially than mentally.

1—*Note:* Review traits on this list.

© Nancy P. Alexander

24-5   Youngest children receive plenty of attention from older siblings.

Their IQs are usually less than those of their siblings. This may be because they rarely play the role of teacher with siblings.

Youngest children are often relaxed and cheerful. Parents usually are comfortable with their parenting skills by the time this child is born. Youngest children deal with more personalities from the time they are infants than do older siblings. Plus, they are used to receiving attention and care from older siblings, 24-5.

On the negative side, parents may "baby" the youngest because they know he or she is their last child. Siblings tend to take care of the youngest child, too. These factors may cause the youngest to be more dependent and less mature. Youngest children are more likely to resort to sulking, tattling, teasing, and fighting.

A Child's Identity.   Birth order does not need to affect a child's later success. Adults can avoid the pitfalls of birth order by focusing on the child, not the child's place in the family. Comments referring to birth order can create bad side effects, such as

dependency. ("She's just a baby.") Other comments may cause stress. ("You're the oldest so you should know better.")

Adults also need to treat each child fairly. Unfair treatment includes showing favoritism and forgetting to praise children. Spoiling the youngest and expecting too much from those who are firstborn and only children is also unfair treatment. Adults need to promote their children's best traits. Adults also need to help children overcome the negative effects of birth order. If adults treat children as individuals, children will develop their own identities.

▶ Children of Multiple Births

Many people ask whether multiple-birth children are different from **singletons** (children born one at a time.) In many ways they are. Parents must meet twice as many needs at once. In meeting these needs, tasks, time, and costs often double or triple. Most parents soon realize they need extra help, especially right after birth.

1

2

3

1—*Discuss:* Give other examples of negative comments.

2—*Reflect:* What actions and comments should parents avoid?

3—*Enrich:* Divide into groups based on birth order (only, first-born, middle, and youngest children). Discuss feelings about parenting styles and traits based on birth order. Report to the class.

Multiple birth children react to the world differently than singletons. This is because they spend a lot of time with each other, go through the same grades in school together, and may look alike. For these reasons, children of multiple births share perhaps the closest of all human relationships. Their relationship even may be closer than that of parent and child, 24-6. These siblings have few problems remaining close. Instead, they have problems developing **separate identities** (feelings of being a distinct person.) Those who have the most problems are identical children and same-sex, look-alike fraternal children. If adults think of multiple-birth siblings as distinct children rather than as a unit, the children's identity problem will decrease.

When fostering these separate identities, adults need to preserve the siblings' special bond. Identical children share more than the same birthday. They share a common genetic makeup. There are many stories of how identical children, even when raised thousands of miles apart, have many of the same health problems, interests, and careers. Being more alike than different is often normal for them. Adults should allow children to choose how much alike or different they wish to

be. In this way, separateness and closeness will be worked out by these brothers and sisters just as it is by other siblings.

● Parental Employment

Today, many parents work outside the home. Some families need or want two incomes. Many see careers outside the home as rewarding. Over 50 percent of all mothers work outside the home during some or all of their children's childhood years. In families with children between ages 6 and 17, 60 percent of mothers work. About 52 percent of mothers of preschool-age children work.

Many single parents, whether mothers or fathers, are forced to work in order to support their children. In families maintained by women, 70 percent of women who have school-age children under age 18 work. About 46 percent of mothers of preschool-age children work. In families maintained by men, 82 percent of men with children ages 6 to 17 work. About 79 percent of men with children under age 6 work.

Not all parents work outside the home. Some have family businesses, such as farms and stores. More and more people are running businesses from home. Many home-based workers have computers, modems, video teleconferencing, and faxes in their home office. This equipment allows them to conduct business without leaving home. When families are involved, working at home takes special planning. Parents must set aside time and space to complete work tasks in an efficient way.

▶ Effects on Children

How does a parent's job affect a child's development? Research shows that babies have fewer adjustment problems if mothers return to work before they are three months old or after age two. Babies develop strong attachments to their caregivers between 3 and 24 months. Another awkward time to enter the workforce is when children are ages 11 through 13. At this time, children

24-6   Twins and other multiple-birth children often have very close relationships.

1—*Discuss:* Give examples of how siblings and twins develop separate identities.

2—*Enrich:* Make copies of a research study involving twins who were separated shortly after birth. Note their differences and similarities? What causes the similarities and differences?

3—*Discuss:* How can parents help twins develop separate identities?

4—*Note:* Discuss the statistics.

5—*Reflect:* How would you feel about operating a home business and caring for your child at home? List four adjustments you would need to make.

are coping with many changes in their life. Dealing with a parent returning to work may be too much.

Some studies show that today's children receive as much attention from their working parents as yesterday's children did from their full-time mothers. This may be true. Working parents use more time-saving home appliances today, so keeping a home doesn't require as much of their time. Also, working parents may try to make up for the hours away from home by spending meaningful time with their children each day, 24-7.

Children of parents who work enjoy some advantages over those with a parent who stays home. Children with working parents tend to miss fewer days of school. They usually enjoy meaningful and well-planned free time with parents. They also help with household chores and learn home care skills. These children may live in homes with more structured times and more clearly stated rules. In this environment, children

24-8   Spending more time with a father can be a positive aspect of having a working mother.

often show more positive self-esteem. Another advantage of working parents is that children interact more with others and spend more time with other adults and children, 24-8.

When both parents work, children think in broader terms about gender roles. Children who grow up in these homes do not think of women only as homemakers and men only as wage earners. They see their father prepare dinner and their mother arrive home from a day at work.

24-7   Working mothers enjoy spending special time with children after being away from them all day.

© John Shaw

▶ Effects on Parents

Working does affect the emotional state of parents. Sometimes, working brings happiness. Often it brings **role strain,** a feeling of having too many jobs to do at one time. Working may also cause a parent to feel role guilt. **Role guilt** is a feeling of not doing the best job at work or at home because of role strain. When parents are happy with either working full time or staying home, then children seem to adjust well, 24-9. However, if either the mother or father is unhappy, it creates family stress.

Most parents do have some problems as a result of their work. They cannot always find time to relax. They may have trouble making child care arrangements. Some parents end up spoiling

1—*Discuss:* Why could this special time be difficult for a working mother to schedule regularly?

2—*Reflect:* How are children's attitudes about gender roles affected by parents who work outside the home?

3—*Discuss:* Give examples of role strain and role guilt. How do these lead to family stress?

Photo courtesy of Washington Hospital Center, Washington, D.C.;
Photographer Jim Douglass

24-9 When parents are happy with their work, they tend to enjoy parenting more, also.

children as they try to make up for time away from home. Parents often feel guilty for not being able to attend some school functions that occur during work hours.

▶ Balancing Family and Work

By planning carefully, parents can lessen the stress of parenting while holding a job. Working parents need to budget their time carefully. Letting some minor tasks slide may be necessary. They should plan family time, which is essential, in their daily schedules. Parents need to give their children some **quality time** (a time when parents are totally attentive to their children) each day. Also, parents should check on the next day's clothes, lunch, and homework before children go to bed. This helps avoid stressful morning panic.

What do working parents do if a child is sick, the sitter is ill, or the child care center is closed? Parents must think about this in advance. If a child must stay alone after school, parents must talk about safety measures before problems occur.

Working parents should meet and talk with teachers. They should attend events important to their children or carefully explain why they can't. Likewise, parents should include their children in their work life. They can set up a visit to their work

site, explain their job, and share stories about their day at work.

Working parents still need to set limits for their children. Parents cannot make up for time away from the family by letting children do what they want to do. As with other children, children of working parents want and need guidance.

Parents who return to work after a time spent with children need to recognize and accept the feelings of their children. Children show feelings in many ways. Two- through four-year-olds may *regress* (act less mature than before) for a few weeks after the parent returns to work. Sick children may want a parent to stay home. Children usually express their feelings during the early evening hours (when everyone is tired and hungry). Children often want to share their entire day at this time. However, parents may need to relax a few minutes after long hours at work. After spending a few minutes alone, parents can devote their complete attention to the family.

▶ Children in Self-Care

In the 1800s, society began to recognize the problems of children of working parents. These children wore their house keys around their neck. They stayed home alone after school or for a portion of a day and cared for themselves until a parent returned from work. During World War II, they were called **latchkey children**. Today, they are called **children in self-care**.

It is estimated that between 25 and 33 percent of all children below the teen years are in self-care. The numbers increase when the statistic includes teenagers. More children are in self-care for the following reasons:

☐   more working mothers

☐   the high costs of child care

☐   the decrease in the number of families who have grandparents or other adults in the home

☐   the decrease in family size resulting in fewer older children to care for younger ones

☐   the lack of before- and after-school programs designed for the school-age child

Effects of Self-Care

Positive Effects on Children
- ☐ Children can show initiative and industry. (This is especially true for 8- through 13-year-old children who are old enough to understand rules and less prone to peer pressure than teens.)
- ☐ Older siblings receive child care experience.

Negative Effects on Children
- ☐ Minor emergencies can become life threatening. For instance, a young child may open a window "to let the fire out."
- ☐ Children are at greater risk for sexual abuse from older siblings and adults.
- ☐ Children may have increased feelings of being separated from or rejected by parents (who are at work) and friends (with whom they cannot play). This may lead to emotional or social problems.
- ☐ Feelings of anxiety may be especially strong for 8- through 13-year-old children who fear burglaries.
- ☐ Children may be overexposed to television and have no guidance while watching.
- ☐ Lack of adult guidance may lead to a child's poor food choices and improper nutrition.
- ☐ Academic achievement may drop due to excessive television viewing. Also, parents may not be able to help children with homework until they return from work; then both children and parents are tired.
- ☐ Children have increased risks of exposure to alcohol and other drugs.

Positive Effects for Parents
- ☐ Child care costs are reduced.
- ☐ With careful planning for the self-care situation, the adult-child relationship may be close, and children may more quickly learn self-care and how to be more responsible.

Negative Effects for Parents
- ☐ Parents have many feelings of guilt and concern.
- ☐ Loss of work productivity occurs while checking or refereeing children over the telephone. This is especially true during after-school hours.

Positive Effects for the Community
- ☐ Community leaders may challenge people to consider the needs of children and their families, such as low-cost child care programs and after-school programs.
- ☐ Challenges people to provide training for parents and children who must rely on self-care.

Negative Effects for the Community
- ☐ There is a greater risk of accidents, including home fires.
- ☐ Rates of vandalism, arson, shoplifting, and vagrancy may rise.

24-10   Self-care has both positive and negative effects.

Children, their parents, and the community all are affected by self-care. Some of these effects are positive and some are negative, as shown in 24-10. There are ways parents can decrease risks and increase the positive effects. First, parents should plan for self-care by taking the following steps:

- ☐   establish a routine for children to follow

1—*Note:* Discuss the positive and negative effects of self-care.

2—*Enrich:* Plan and conduct a debate on effects of self-care. Have each student read one magazine article for background information.

☐ keep a list of telephone numbers near the phone, and teach younger children how to place calls

☐ give children safety tips. These can include not telling others they are alone and locking doors. Parents also should explain what to do in case of fire or if strangers come to the door. Another good safety policy is requiring children to ask permission to leave the house or ask friends in.

☐ teach children which equipment and appliances they may use and how to use them

Parents of children in self-care may acquire a pet to reduce fear or loneliness. Parents can also enroll children in after-school programs like Boy or Girl Scouts. They can also work for better, low-cost child care programs. Some religious groups already provide such programs. Child care block grants provide federal funds for school-based child care. More work can be done to provide safe, realistic alternatives to self-care.

● Coping with Family Moves

The United States is a *mobile* society. This means that families today move a great deal. Earlier in history, more people lived in extended families. Today, more than one-fifth of the population moves each year. On the average, each person moves 14 times in a lifetime.

Although a few people enjoy moving, most feel some stress. Usually the stress lasts only a few weeks or months. However, for others, it may last a couple of years. Stress lessens when

☐ moves do not occur too often

☐ no added stress is present, such as death or divorce

☐ parents are pleased about the move

☐ children have siblings who can act as playmates until they make new friends

☐ school-age children move at the beginning or end of a school term

☐ school-age children have good grades

☐ children have special skills or interests (sports, hobbies) that help provide some stability

Stress occurs because moving is a change. People need time to adjust to a new town or city, a school, a job, and people. Moving can cause loneliness. Children may feel unsure about the past if they move often. They may ask, "Did this happen, or did I dream it?" "Did I know this person when we lived in our old town?" "Where was my bedroom when we lived in our old house?"

Adults can reduce the stress of moving for children. Pointing out the positive reasons for moving is a good way to start. They may let children know that the family will have more income and that they will go to better schools. Moving can enable children to widen their interests, make more friends, and learn more about different people. However, adults need to be honest about the move. They need to mention the bad as well as

24-11 Young children may need to act out moving as a way to prepare for the real move.

© John Shaw

1—*Activity:* Develop your own safety plan for self-care. Compare in class.

2—*Resource: Planning Ahead for Self-Care,* SAG.

3—*Vocabulary:* Define mobility. How does it apply to society today? Compare to other societies.

4—*Discuss:* Summarize ways to lessen stress from a move. Add individual comments.

the good. For example, the family will miss old friends and their house. Adults should also explain each step that will be happening as they move. Children will ask many questions. They may even want to act out certain events, 24-11.

If possible, parents should take children with them to see the new home and school before the move. Otherwise, a few pictures of the new area may help make the change easier.

Children should help with packing. It is often best to pack preschool children's items last. A few favorite toys should be placed in the car or in luggage carried with the family.

Adults need to plan more time to be with children both before and after the move. Children need a few special treats and family times to help them feel secure.

● Coping with Death

Death is a basic part of life, and even young children need to learn to come to terms with it. One-fifth of all children lose a parent before they finish elementary school. Many more face death of a close friend, relative, or even a pet during childhood.

Children gradually begin to understand death. At about six or seven months, the baby has separations from caring adults. These separations, most of which are brief, are the earliest times of loss in a child's life. Early separation may set the stage for later responses to separation, loss, and even death. Until age three or four, children have little, if any, understanding of death. Preschool children's concepts of death are limited. They try to learn the physical facts of death. They find many facts difficult to believe, and thus, they question the facts. Some concepts that give children trouble include the following:

☐   Life can stop.

☐   Death is forever.

☐   People and pets cannot come back to life, even if they really want to.

Preschool children usually do not explore religious beliefs about death. However, they may repeat statements they have heard others say.

© John Shaw

24-12   When children lose a loved one—even a pet—they must find ways to express their grief.

Adults should teach children to express grief, 24-12. Toddlers and preschool children may act in what may seem to be improper ways during a time of death or during its rituals. This is because they do not know how to express their grief. Experts say that, when it comes to the issue of death, the feelings of preschool children and adults are very much alike. Both children and adults feel anger, protest, sadness, and loneliness. Both want to be in close contact with others during times of death. Adults need to be honest about the loss and their feelings. They need to allow children to talk about death and grieve in their own ways, even through pretend play. In time, most children come to terms with their loss and the stress lessens. Through their experiences, they learn more about death and grief.

▶ Helping Children Cope with Grief

Usually, adults do not talk about death with children unless a person or a pet dies. If a child asks about death, adults should answer all questions honestly. Many books suggest ways to explain death to a child. Adults need to help children understand and deal with death and grief, 24-13.

If a family member or close friend is terminally ill, adults should prepare the child for the upcoming death. Simple, truthful statements are best. An adult may say, "You know that Grandma is very sick. The nurses and doctors are trying to help, but Grandma is getting sicker. She may die soon." Adults should not tell children that a sick person is on vacation.

When Death Occurs

When death occurs, adults should explain at the child's level what has happened. They should say what they believe to be true about death. Children become worried if they feel that adults are keeping facts from them or avoiding their questions. Adults should explain death well enough so that children do not expect the person (or pet) to return. An adult may say, "Father is dead. This means that he doesn't move or breathe any more." Adults should not tell children that a deceased person is sleeping. They also should explain religious beliefs simply. Children need to know that they have not caused the death. (For example, they may think that they caused the death because they had a fight with the person.)

24-13 Carefully chosen books may help answer some questions about death.

© John Shaw

Adults should be prepared to answer questions and repeat facts for a long time after a death. At first, a child may seem to understand that Mother has died. However, a week later the child may ask, "When is Mommy coming home?"

As children begin to understand death, they may become afraid that a parent will die. Parents can reassure their children that they will probably live a long time. However, they should never promise children they won't die. If a parent should die after such a promise, the child may feel betrayed and develop a lack of trust in others.

Adults also should help children express their grief. They should let children know it is all right to be sad and cry. Adults should set an example by not trying to hide their own sadness. Adults should give children time to experience sadness and loss. For this reason, a pet that has died should not be replaced too soon.

Parents need to make a decision about whether the child should be included in rituals like the funeral. The decision depends on the child's age and maturity, the child's wishes, and the family's beliefs. Some feel that seeing open coffins makes death more real. Others feel this is too traumatic for the child. An adult should explain rituals in advance if the child is to participate in them.

● Coping with Divorce

In the United States, many couples divorce. Approximately one-half of couples between the ages of 20 and 34 will divorce. About one-fourth of couples between the ages of 45 and 54 will divorce. The divorce rate is even higher for teens who marry. About three-fifths of all teen marriages end in separation and divorce.

▶ Causes of Divorce

Why do so may people divorce? Many factors contribute to the high rate of divorce. The mobile society in which we live causes people of dissimilar backgrounds to meet and marry.

Sometimes couples with dissimilar backgrounds have problems when they marry. Being pregnant before marriage as well as marrying before age 20 increases chances of divorce. Statistics show that living together prior to marriage does not reduce a couple's chance of divorce.

Financial problems and other stresses, such as job or child care demands, can cause marital problems. Working women in troubled marriages feel more economic independence and may be more likely to request a divorce.

Society contributes to divorce by emphasizing the importance of personal happiness in marriage. If couples are unhappy, they are more likely to divorce and escape an unhappy situation than try to work out their problems. Society also places less stigma on divorce and remarriage today.

▶ Effects of Divorce

The sting of divorce affects couples and children. Adults have to work through problems like overcoming negative feelings and adjusting to a new lifestyle. They often have a continual relationship with the former spouse and in-laws if they have children.

Children of divorce are affected during the separation process and often for years following the divorce. Even children who were infants when their parents divorced deal with the issue in their school years.

It is hard to predict the impact of divorce on children. The child's age affects how children cope as well as the child's gender, 24-14. Divorce usually confuses young children. They do not understand the divorce process or final decision, but they know one parent is not living with the family. Personalities of children affect how they cope, too. Some children are more positive than others and have fewer coping problems.

The family's standard of living often changes after a divorce. The income of single mothers drops about 73 percent, but the income of single fathers rises by about 42 percent. Almost 90 percent of all children live with their divorced mother, which often means their standard of living drops. This affects all family members.

▶ Coping with the Effects

Parents seeking to divorce may find professional counseling helpful. Counselors or members of support groups can discuss the effects of divorce on parents and children. Parents may need help coping with their personal feelings and meeting their children's new needs. The couple will have new stresses, such as changes in residence, jobs, income, or roles.

3

Adults should not discuss problems of the marriage or divorce with children. Children cannot understand these complex issues. Because they cannot help solve the problems of marriage, they should not be burdened with them. However, adults should give children honest answers. They may say something like, "Your dad (or mom) and I once were happy together. We no longer are happy living together, so we have decided never to live together again. We both love you, and we will always love you. We will always take care of you." Parents may need to repeat this message many times. They should not explain why they are unhappy. It is more important to reassure children that both parents will continue to love and care for them.

4

When children are in their late teen years, parents may explain more about the marriage failure. Even then, it is best for parents to state their feelings rather than discuss the flaws of the other parent. A parent might say, "I was very hurt," or, "I felt misunderstood."

Once custody plans are firm, parents should tell children about them (if they are old enough to understand). Custody battles can hurt children. For this reason, parents should shelter children from the details of custody decisions. Parents can explain the custody plan and that both parents feel it is best for the family. They should not discuss other details with children.

▪ Family Members Need Support

Children also need neutral people to support them. These people can help children express their sadness or anger in acceptable ways. Support people also can help children cope with loneliness and a new lifestyle. They can serve as needed role models, too.

1—*Reflect:* How does divorce affect couples and children? Give examples.

2—*Discuss:* How does divorce affect a mother's standard of living? A father's? Children?

3—*Reflect:* How does counseling affect family members?

4—*Reflect:* Do you think this is typical? Explain your reasons. Describe an ideal situation.

Effects of Divorce on Children	
Age	**Common Behaviors and Feelings**
2½	whine cry cling show regressive behaviors, such as increased bedwetting act fretful have no appetite
4	whine cry hit or bite other children mistrust other adults feel they caused the divorce
5-6	cling are aggressive toward children show anxiety are moody seem restless are least affected, perhaps because of peers and teachers
school-age children	feel rejected by absent parent may feel lonely fear abandonment drop in school achievement shift the balance between family and friends too much in one or the other direction show anger at one parent for divorce become the confidant of custodial parent and thus have too much adult-type pressure
Gender	**Common Behaviors and Feelings**
Boys	act oblivious and inattentive have a drop in school achievement act more aggressively have more problems during the process of the divorce and for the first two years after the divorce do better if they have a positive relationship with the father
Girls	feel grief and frustration cry withdraw blame themselves are more troubled a year after the divorce than at the time of the divorce

24-14   The effects divorce has on a child depend on the child's age and gender.

1—*Discuss:* Why is it important for nursery, child care, and school personnel to know about a divorce? How could these people help a child?

2—*Discuss:* Discuss the effects of divorce on children according to age and gender.

Both parents and children may need a support system for many years. Long-term effects occur more often if there are prolonged tensions in the relationships or other major problems. Children have more problems if they are girls, if their parents divorced during their school-age years, or if their parents suffer role strain. Mothers often experience more role strain because they usually have primary custody in addition to less income. Studies show that 44 percent of divorced mothers report more conflicts with their children. An equal percentage of divorced fathers report a better relationship. Role strain can be reduced with understanding of causes, with support when needed, and with some loving apologies for unnecessary conflicts.

24-15   The number of men who are single parents is increasing.

© John Shaw

Single Parenting

One out of every five children is raised in a single-parent family. Women head 90 percent of single-parent families. Ten percent of men are single parents, and that number is increasing, 24-15. In some cases, single parenting is a transition between divorce and remarriage.

4
5

▶ Problems Single Parents Face

Single parents and their children face many problems that are the same as those of other families. However, some problems are unique to the single-parent family or are felt more keenly by them.

Financial problems are often the greatest problems the single parent faces. Two out of every 5 families headed by single parents have incomes below the poverty level. This figure compares with 1 out of 16 families headed by two parents. Single mothers have more financial problems than single fathers. The average income of single mothers is about one-third that of families headed by two parents. Single fathers have incomes that are close to three-fourths that of families with two parents.

6

Men and women report different types of problems as single parents. Fathers report more problems with housework and the physical aspects of child care, such as cooking and buying clothes. Mothers say their biggest problems are disciplining children and not earning enough money.

Many times, emotional problems trouble families headed by single parents. In cases in which two-parent families become single-parent families, family life is disrupted. Anger and grief are present in both divorce and death situations. Single parents also feel more *social isolation,* or feelings of being alone. They may have no one to talk to about problems and feelings. The person also may feel depressed, fearful, and unhealthy.

1—*Discuss:* List three circumstances in which children are likely to have more problems during or after a divorce.

2—*Reflect:* How can role strain after a divorce be reduced?

3—*Reflect:* Why do you think the number of male single parents is increasing?

4—*Discuss:* Summarize the statistics on single parenting.

5—*Enrich:* Do research on statistics in your state.

6—*Discuss:* Summarize financial problems.

Helping Children Cope

Besides coping with their own feelings, single parents must deal with their children's problems. Parents are the base from which children grow. When death or divorce end a two-parent family, children feel the loss of a relationship and a role model. In cases of divorce, children may feel they caused the problems or that their parents may "divorce" them too. Children's daily life patterns also change as one parent takes over the duties two parents once shared.

Children react to changes. The problems in children's behavior are not caused by the number of parents. They are caused by stress. The way a child reacts depends on his or her age and personality, 24-16. Although most single-parent homes become stable in two years, a few long-term effects may continue. In homes where fathers are absent, boys may rebel or do poorly in school. Teenage girls may become overly aggressive or shy around boys.

Single-parent families need support. Family members may need outside help with problems like finances, child care, and housework. Adults may need to talk about their feelings and reactions with other adults. Some single parents find support or social groups, such as Parents Without Partners, helpful. Parents should not use children as their sole source of friendship.

Children in single-parent families need special care and support. They need time to work out their feelings. Adults should allow children to express their feelings through actions and words. (Books on the topic may be helpful.) However, a parent should be careful not to express hostile feelings about the other parent to children. They never should ask children to choose sides or relay messages between divorced parents.

24-16   The way children react to divorce or death often depends on their age.

Children's Reactions to Loss of a Parent Through Death or Divorce	
Two- and Three-Year-Olds whine cry cling have sleep problems have bed accidents may regress (This occurs most often at a time of day when the absent parent was often with the child.) **Four-Year-Olds** whine cry hit others feel they caused the divorce (and sometimes the death) **Five-Year-Olds** feel anxious act aggressively want physical contact with others feel abandoned deny the loss and even pretend parents will be together again have problems in creative play	**School-Age Children** deny loss feel bitter (blame parent whom they think is responsible) feel angry feel deprived fear future feel lonely show antisocial behavior, such as lying or stealing have more headaches and stomachaches. have school problems, such as not being able to pay attention show premature detachment. Reject parent who is gone and those qualities they shared with the father. (For instance, if the father has athletic ability, the child may reject sports.) daydream more

1—*Discuss:* What fears may surface in a child during and after a divorce?

2—*Reflect:* Why do you think children react differently depending on their age?

3—*Enrich:* Report on sources of support for divorced parents and their children. Use the phone book; call for information.

4—*Enrich:* Check the library for children's books on the subject of divorce. Share with the class.

5—*Reflect:* Why should adults never ask children to take sides?

Children need to know that their parents still love them. Parents should explain that a divorce is not the child's fault. They should not expect children to handle the divorce in an adult way. Children may feel stress if they are expected to act too maturely for their age. On the other hand, these children still need consistent, firm discipline.

When the family structure changes, parents should tell teachers and other adults who work with children. These adults can help children cope if they are aware of the home situation.

Remarriage and Stepparenting

Three-fourths of all divorced people remarry within five years of becoming divorced. Many widowed parents remarry, and parents who have not been married may marry, too.

The younger people are at the time of divorce, the more likely they are to remarry. Other factors that influence the potential for remarriage include how long the first marriage lasted and whether the divorced person has children. Women under age 30 who have young children are the most likely to remarry.

In most cases, one stepparent enters a single-parent family that has been working together as a family. (In more than half the cases, stepfathers enter into a single-parent family headed by the mother.) A new living arrangement changes all daily living patterns. Single parents often are proud that they can run a household by themselves. After remarriage, they may have problems sharing the parenting roles with a spouse.

▶ Preparing for Family Changes

Parents should prepare to blend their households by speaking to a family counselor. Social workers or clergy may conduct such sessions. Older children may want to take part in some of the sessions.

All children (beyond infancy) need to be prepared for the new marriage and family life. Children should be told by their parent that the parent and new spouse love each other and they want the marriage to work out well for everyone. Telling children that the new marriage will work or that it's going to be better or fun is not an honest approach.

Children also need to know that other children face similar problems. Stepchildren may not know what to call a new stepparent. They may not know whom to invite to school or other special functions. Books on blended families may help children adjust, 24-17.

Perhaps one of the most difficult tasks for the stepparent is knowing how much to discipline stepchildren. Disciplining stepchildren is more difficult than disciplining biological children. Stepparents are often afraid to punish because they want their stepchildren to like them.

It is usually not easy for children to adjust to a new family. The adjustment is even harder if children of the stepparents live in the same household. However, when new family relationships work out, the family ties are worth the effort.

Teens as Parents

The United States has the highest teenage birthrate of all industrialized, democratic nations. The overall percentage of children born to unwed

24-17   Books on blended families help children realize that other families have similar problems.

© John Shaw

mothers of all ages has not risen much recently. However, the percentage of children born to unwed teens has more than doubled. Until the l960s, most unwed teen mothers married quickly. Today, only about one in four marries before the birth of her baby. Few unwed mothers choose adoptive families to parent their babies. Thus, most teenage girls who choose to give birth and keep their babies become single mothers.

Teen parenting is a risk. Becoming a teenage parent does not have any advantages over having children between the ages of 20 and 34. The risks affect many aspects of the teen's life, and it is impossible to reverse the consequences. See chart 24-18 for the consequences of teen parenting. Many of these problems relate to health, financial concerns, and lifestyle changes.

▶ ## Health Risks for the Teen Mother and Baby

Teenagers' bodies are still growing and developing—only babies growing in the womb and infants develop more quickly. Because of all these physical changes, proper nutrition is crucial for a teenager. When a teenager is pregnant, the baby depends on the mother for nutrition. This depletes the mother's body of nutrients. Poor nutrition before or during pregnancy puts the mother and her baby at risk.

In earlier chapters, you read about the health risks associated with smoking, STDs, and pregnancy. Smoking rates are declining for some of the population. However, they are increasing for teens. More teens have STDs, too, and they are rarely treated before an unplanned pregnancy. Teenage mothers' risk of STDs is high. One reason is that most teens become pregnant by men between the ages of 22 and 25. These men usually have had multiple partners, which often makes them carriers of STDs.

The lack of medical care is another health risk for teen mothers. All mothers-to-be need early and continuous prenatal care and additional care for about two months after delivery. Only half of all teens receive care in the first three months of pregnancy. Teen mothers-to-be may take this risk because they

- ☐ do not think they are pregnant
- ☐ feel their parents will be upset
- ☐ are afraid the relationship with the baby's father will end
- ☐ lack money for medical care or do not know where to go for help
- ☐ cannot find transportation to a medical facility
- ☐ feel medical care is not necessary
- ☐ are afraid of medical procedures

Both mother and baby are affected by these risks. Even with good health care, teen mothers experience other health risks. These include longer labors and more C-section deliveries than older mothers.

The *mortality* (death) rate for babies of teens is high. Many of the babies who survive have low birth weights. These small babies have higher rates of SIDS and grow slowly throughout childhood. Studies show that they have more learning problems in school and more social problems with peers.

Health risks increase even more for both mother and baby if the teen mother is under age 15 or if she has had more than one pregnancy in the teen years. One-fourth of all teenage girls have a repeat pregnancy before age 20.

▶ ## Financial Concerns

Prenatal care and deliveries are expensive. Most teens are not covered by maternity insurance. Health problems add to the costs for mother and baby. The added expense of a baby is a real burden for teens who are already financially strapped. Parents must pay for a baby's food, clothing, equipment, and perhaps child care. These costs increase as babies become children and children become teenagers.

Some teens turn to their parents for help. This usually is stressful for them and their parents. Over one-third of the teens require public assistance in the form of Medicaid, Aid to Families with Dependent Children (AFDC), and food stamps.

1—*Reflect:* List four of your life goals. Write how each goal would be affected if you found out you were going to become a parent.

2—*Discuss:* Summarize the effects of poor nutrition.

3—*Discuss:* Summarize health risks for teen mothers.

4—*Enrich:* Do research on Medicaid, AFDC, and food stamps. Report to the class.

Consequences of Teen Parenting

Consequences for teen mothers

☐ Health risks are greater for younger teen mothers and for all teen mothers who don't receive quality prenatal care.

☐ Eighty percent of women who become mothers at age 17 or younger and 50 percent of women who become mothers at age 18 or 19 never complete high school.

☐ Teen mothers lack entry-level skills for the job market. Their income is usually 50 percent below that of mothers who have their first child in their twenties.

☐ Teen parents who marry are at high risk for divorce. Statistics show that
    —one in five marriages end in divorce after the first year
    —one in three marriages end in divorce after two years
    —three in five marriages end in divorce after six years

☐ Teen mothers report major marital problems. These problems include the following:
    —more sexual activity than they desire
    —loneliness (Many times a husband maintains his social life while the teen mother assumes more child care responsibility. Also, most teen mothers lose touch with girlfriends.)
    —lack of support (Many times, older men who father many babies are not interested in marriage or parenting. The teen mother may not receive companionship, parenting support, or child support.)

Consequences for teen fathers

☐ Teen fathers have poor school performance and many times drop out of high school.

☐ Teen fathers often lack education and training. For these reasons they usually cannot earn adequate incomes to support their family.

☐ Unmarried teen fathers report not being able to see their babies when they wish. Married teen fathers report problems with the child's maternal grandparents.

☐ Teen fathers show lower self-esteem than other teens because of less education and more income problems.

Consequences for children of teen parents

☐ Babies of teen parents have high mortality (death) rates if their mothers are age 15 or younger. This death rate is twice as high as that for babies of mothers between ages 20 and 34.

☐ Babies of teen parents are at greater risk for birth defects.

☐ Children of teens have lower achievement in school because of
    —having birth defects
    —being born too soon or too small
    —having less family income

☐ Children of teens are at a higher risk of being abused because of
    —having birth defects
    —being born too soon or too small
    —having parents who do not know when a child is ready to do or learn a task (A study shows that a group of teen parents thought babies could be toilet trained at six months of age.)
    —crying when parents want to sleep, study, socialize, or when parents are depressed

Consequences for society

☐ Often extra child care and the need for more income burdens the grandparents of the teens' child.

☐ Teen parents lose productive income because of their lower-income jobs or unemployment.

☐ Society pays the costs of assistance programs to teen parents.

☐ Society pays for assistance to children and loss of productive income in the next generation if children do not overcome their problems.

☐ Societies may be more violent if children are abused.

☐ The numbers and the problems faced by single-parent, divorced, and remarried families may increase.

24-18   The risks of teenage parenting affects parents, children, and society in general.

1—*Activity:* Divide the class into four groups. Have each group study one of the consequences of teen parenting. Discuss and report to the class.

Sadly, these financial problems can continue into adulthood. Studies show teens who become parents usually have financial problems all their lives. Eight out of 10 teen mothers who are age 17 or under never finish high school. Teen fathers may drop out of school to get a job. Teens do not have entry-level skills because of their lack of education. This means they usually qualify for only low-paying jobs. Even teens who do finish high school rarely complete college, and this also keeps them from earning adequate pay. College graduates earn almost twice as much in income over the course of their lifetime than high school graduates.

Teen parents find education difficult or impossible for the following reasons:

- [ ] Teen parents cannot afford child care while they attend classes or study.
- [ ] Teen parents feel out of place in a traditional program because they are older than other students.
- [ ] The need for a job, even a low-paying one, may override teen parents' hopes of completing an education.
- [ ] Teen parents' time to study is limited, 24-19.

Over half of all teen families live in poverty. Living and growing up in poverty causes problems that adversely affect the lives of teenage parents and their children.

© Nancy P. Alexander

24-20 Teen parenthood has changed this teen father's lifestyle in major ways.

© Nancy P. Alexander

24-19 Even healthy, happy babies take so much care that teen mothers find little time to study.

▶ **Lifestyle Changes**

When teenagers become parents, their life changes in dramatic ways. They may find themselves in an unhappy marriage. They may encounter problems living with their baby in their parents' home. Most have financial pressures, 24-20. Most teen parents also socialize less often with friends because they have more responsibility. Teen parents usually lead stressful lives.

Life with Mom and Dad

Teen parents who continue to live with their parents report additional friction at home. Many parents of teens may act differently because they are unhappy that the teens became parents so soon. They may insist that one of the baby's parents stay out of their lives. Grandparents of the baby often feel more stress because they are juggling child care, work, and other family obligations. They may need more money to help their child and grandchild. They also may feel stressed because they are coping with a crying baby or a curious toddler later in life.

1—*Reflect:* Why would college completion be difficult for a teen parent?

2—*Activity:* Interview a young mother. What daily demands does she face? How much time does she have for herself? How does she deal with school responsibilities? Report to the class.

3—*Discuss:* How would teen parenthood affect his life?

4—*Discuss:* Summarize problems for teen parents who continue to live with parents.

Social Life Changes

Before pregnancy, a teen's life focuses on school, social activities, and family, 24-21. Once a teen becomes a parent, life changes. Now the teen focuses on the medical aspects of pregnancy, the costs of a baby, and ways to meet the baby's needs. Teen parents have little time to study or spend with friends because baby care takes too much time. Baby expenses leave little or no money to spend on nonessential items.

Many teen mothers say they feel isolated. Although friends usually stand by teen mothers, they may not maintain the same social contact. This often happens during the pregnancy and after the baby is born. This leads to depression and frustration.

Family Violence. Teen frustrations may initiate family violence. Spouse abuse may occur in unhappy marriages. Children of teens are at high risk for abuse. Teens' needs do not mesh with their children's needs. Teen parents rarely have enough support in parenting tasks. They often do not know about child development and may expect children to reach unreasonable goals. The parents' frustration with a child's "lack of progress" often leads to child abuse.

Parenting is a choice teens cannot reverse. The responsibility of parenthood affects almost every aspect of a teenager's life. The added risks make early parenting a real hardship.

Although teenage parents face challenges, many overcome them and have positive experiences as young parents. However, this only happens through hard work and effort. Each parent must be determined to do all he or she can to help their baby and their family. They must also have people they can turn to for help. They need emotional and maybe even financial support to help them overcome their problems. For many, finishing school or getting a high-paying job is not possible and may never be.

24-21 Teen parents usually do not have extra time or money, which means they often miss out on good times with friends.

© John Shaw

● Child Neglect and Abuse

When adults cannot handle stress or do not know how to care for children, they threaten children's health and welfare. Adults who abuse children cause them physical, mental, and emotional harm. Untold numbers of children suffer because of neglect or abuse by parents, friends, relatives, or child care workers.

Why would an adult hurt a child? Sometimes child neglect and abuse relates to drug and alcohol use. Other times it happens because an adult has severe personal or emotional problems, is immature, or cannot control emotions.

▶ Neglect

Child neglect refers to an act of omission (failing to do something legally expected) by parents or adults that causes harm to a child. Neglect does not involve violence. Each state has its own definition of "neglect," but neglect most often involves adults not providing for the child's needs

1—Reflect: How would your social contacts change?

2—Discuss: How would extra-curricular activities be affected?

3—Discuss: Why are children of teens at high risk for child abuse?

4—Reflect: If you were a teen parent, how would you work to overcome the negatives? Explain.

5—Discuss: Recall cases of child abuse from newspapers or news broadcasts. Discuss.

6—Reflect: How would drug and alcohol use or emotional problems contribute to child abuse?

and proper level of care with respect to food, clothing, shelter, hygiene, medical attention, or supervision. There are several types of neglect. These include:

☐ *Physical neglect* is when adults fail to provide for a child's basic survival needs, such as clothing, food, shelter, and supervision, to the extent that the failure can be a hazard to the child's health or safety. (As you read in Chapter 10, a particular kind of physical neglect involving failure to feed a baby or small child sufficiently is called "the failure to thrive syndrome.")

☐ *Educational neglect* is failure to conform to state legal requirements regarding school attendance.

☐ *Medical neglect* is failure to seek treatment for a serious health problem or accident that could endanger the child.

☐ *Moral neglect* is failure to teach the child right from wrong in terms of general social values, such as stealing is wrong.

☐ *Psychological* or *emotional neglect* is failure to help children develop psychologically or emotionally.

Neglect most often occurs when parents do not know how to care for their children. Neglect may also happen when parents are under so much stress themselves that they cannot focus on their children's needs.

▶ Abuse

Child abuse refers to an act of commission (committing or doing an act) by parents or adults that harms or threatens to harm the physical or mental health or welfare of a child. Thus, abuse, unlike neglect, is intended to harm a child. Specific definitions of the types of child abuse include:

☐ *Physical abuse*, even if it is done in the name of discipline, is violence which results in injuries. Physical abuse is also called "battered child syndrome."

☐ *Sexual abuse* is any sexual act of an adult with a child. Some states define sexual

abuse as any sexual act between a child and anyone who is at least five years older than the child.

☐ *Psychological/verbal abuse* is any act in which an adult makes excessive demands, harasses, or verbally threatens the child resulting in a negative self-image or disturbed behavior on the part of the child.

Abuse statistics are alarming. Almost 85 percent of all abuse is physical. In two-thirds of the cases, abused children are under age three. One-half are under six months. Abusive adults may beat, bruise, burn, and/or cut children. They may break a child's bones and teeth. Physical abuse is the second most common way children die (only accidents kill more children each year). Verbal abuse accompanies almost all cases of physical abuse. This verbal abuse also occurs alone.

Experts believe that between 30 and 46 percent of all children are sexually abused before the age of 18. They also estimate that one-third of all girls and one-sixth of all boys are abused. The number of abused children is hard to define because many abuse cases are never reported. In addition, the definition of sexual abuse differs from state to state. Chart 24-22 explains some of the myths and realities of this form of abuse.

Physical harm is just one result of abuse and neglect. Some children die from their injuries. Abuse victims usually have other long-term problems. They may neglect and abuse other children. They may also have a poor self-concept and feelings of anxiety, shame, guilt, and depression.

Adults should learn all they can about child abuse and neglect. They must know the signs of abuse and the reality of the problem. Adults need to be active in its prevention and in the care of involved children.

▶ Who Is Abused?

All children in a family may be abused. However, in many cases only one child is. Some children are more likely to be the victims of abuse. Those who are small, have birth defects, or are

---

1—*Enrich:* Develop a list of ways to relieve stress. Extend this list for parents.

2—*Vocabulary:* Define abuse. Give examples.

3—*Discuss:* Summarize abuse statistics.

4—*Discuss:* Why would abuse statistics be somewhat inaccurate?

5—*Enrich:* Why are abusers sometimes unsuspected?

6—*Discuss:* How can you help prevent child abuse?

Myths and Realities of Sexual Abuse	
Myth	**Reality**
☐ Sexual abuse is rare.	☐ Sexual abuse occurs frequently and takes many forms, such as pornography and incest.
☐ The offender is an unknown, dangerous person.	☐ In 85 percent of the cases, the offender is a known person, such as a relative or friend.
☐ The incident occurs suddenly, such as when an adult is momentarily out of the room.	☐ The abuse usually is repeated over and over again and may occur for several years.
☐ Child sexual abuse usually is a violent attack.	☐ More often, child sexual abuse is subtle "force." The offender may call it a "new game."
☐ Children often make up stories of sexual abuse.	☐ Children rarely make up stories of sexual abuse. In fact, they are often reluctant to tell about sexual abuse because they fear the offender or feel guilty for being involved.
☐ Children who recant stories of sexual abuse were lying about the first report.	☐ The abuser may have pressured children to change their story.

24-22   Adults need to know the realities of sexual abuse in order to help children and prevent and treat this serious problem.

sickly are more likely to be abused than healthy children. Abuse may be triggered by the fact that unhealthy children have more needs, require more care, and develop more slowly than healthy children. They also tend to cry a lot, which may make coping harder for some parents. Children who look like or have traits similar to those of disliked relatives also may be abused. In addition, as children get older, clashes and arguments may ignite tempers and result in abuse.

Sexual abuse within the home most often occurs in blended families or families where parents do not watch children closely. Parents can lessen the chances of sexual abuse inside or outside the home by telling children about appropriate touching. Parents must urge children to tell if someone touches them in a wrong way. (Many children's books discuss this subject.) Watching children closely for signs of abuse or differences in behavior also is crucial.

▶ Who Neglects and Abuses Children?

Abusive parents come from all levels of income, intelligence, and education. Neglect may occur when parents only think of their own needs or are too poor to meet their children's needs. Generally, abusive parents do not have obvious signs of problems that others can see easily. Abusive parents may seem nice, quiet, and kind when they are at work or around friends. Yet, a closer look shows that most of them have one or more of the following traits:

☐ they believe in using physical force to punish children. Cultures with strong beliefs against striking children (or adults) have few cases of abuse.

☐ they were abused as children.

☐ they have low self-images.

1—*Discuss:* Discuss the myth-reality list. Include additional myths and realities, if possible.

2—*Reflect:* Describe a time when you cared for a child who cried constantly. If you had a child like this, how would you handle the crying? What could you do if you felt you were losing control?

3—*Enrich:* Do research on signs of sexual abuse, physical abuse, mental or emotional abuse, and neglect. Report to the class.

4—*Discuss:* How do modeling and cultural beliefs promote child abuse?

☐ they feel alone. In fact, they often are estranged from their relatives and do not have close friends.

☐ they are under stress. They have problems at the workplace or with an unhappy family life. They also may feel they cannot cope with their duties, including child care.

☐ they have set goals for their children that are too high. (Some even expect infant motor skills, such as walking, to develop too soon.)

Some families have become so troubled that members use violence to express anger or resolve conflicts. Sadly, this behavior becomes a pattern that is repeated over and over again. Children of abusive parents may model the same behaviors when they are parents. In this way abusive behavior is often passed down from grandparent to parent, from parent to child, generation after generation. However, this abusive cycle can be broken. If children, parents, and society do not accept this type of behavior, realize its dangers, and get help, then the cycle of abusive behavior can be stopped.

▶ How Can Adults Protect Children from Neglect and Abuse?

Some social changes may help curb the problems of neglect and abuse. These include the following:

☐ societal rejections of violence and aggression

☐ better economic security for families

☐ wide-spread education in child development and parenting

☐ efforts to reduce premature births and birth defects

☐ adequate child care facilities

☐ education of children about abuse and ways to protect themselves

☐ adult education on how to spot child abuse and steps to take when abuse is suspected

Some common signs of neglected and abused children are listed in 24-23. Adults who notice these signs and suspect abuse or neglect must report the case to a proper agency. There are many child abuse hot lines adults can call to report suspected abuse. The hot lines are listed in local phone directories as well as in national directories of toll-free numbers. When parents are feeling out of control and think they may abuse a child, they can call a national organization called Parents Anonymous. Members of this group form local chapters, and they can provide support services any time.

Failure to report suspected abuse is a criminal offense in many states. To report a case, the adult must call the local office of the Department of Children and Family Services. Working within the state's child abuse law, a caseworker will check on the situation. The reporter's name and information is confidential. If there is evidence of abuse, the case worker will take steps to help the child. Adults may also call other groups to report cases.

Adults must stop abuse by reporting suspected cases or stopping abusive cycles. Children must not be allowed to go through life being either neglected or abused. They need to receive help as soon as possible in order to ease the harm and heal the wounds that are caused by neglect and abuse.

● Resources for Children in Crises

Many resources are available to help children in crises. Some of the resources directly assist children and their families. Other resources provide information, registries, referrals to local support groups, and even counseling.

1—*Reflect:* Select two of these social changes. Explain two ways you could become an advocate for each.

2—*Enrich:* Check the local phone directory for child abuse hot lines. Call and request information on reporting procedures.

3—*Activity:* Check the local phone directory for Parents Anonymous. Call for information about services provided.

4—*Note:* Define the term *mandatory reporter.* All child care workers and teachers are legally responsible to report suspected child abuse.

5—*Discuss:* What happens if an adult suspects child abuse but does not report it?

6—*Resource: Traits of Child Abusers,* SAG.

Signs of Child Nelect and Abuse

Anyone who suspects child abuse or neglect should report it to proper authorities so that the child can receive help. In fact, the law in most states requires a person to report suspected abuse or neglect. The following signs will help you identify children who need help.

Neglect

A child may be physically neglected when he or she
- [ ] is malnourished
- [ ] fails to receive needed health care without a parental objection
- [ ] fails to receive proper hygiene (is not washed or bathed, has poor oral hygiene, has ungroomed skin, nails, and hair)
- [ ] has insufficient clothing or clothing that is dirty or unmended
- [ ] lives in filthy conditions and/or inadequate shelter

A child may suffer mental or educational neglect when he or she
- [ ] lacks moral training
- [ ] lacks constructive discipline
- [ ] fails to receive positive examples from adults
- [ ] fails to have adequate supervision
- [ ] is left alone for hours
- [ ] fails to attend school regularly because of parents
- [ ] fails to receive parent stimulation toward learning or education that suits the child's ability
- [ ] fails to be able to take part in wholesome recreational activities

A child may be emotionally neglected if he or she
- [ ] experiences constant friction in the home
- [ ] is denied normal experiences that produce feelings of being wanted, loved, protected, and worth
- [ ] is rejected through indifference
- [ ] is overly rejected, such as through abandonment

(continued)

24-23   People must know the signs of neglect and abuse so they can help children with these problems.

Some of these resources are departments and agencies of federal, state, or local government. Other resources are national private agencies funded by membership dues and contributions. Still other resources are the work of religious groups, hospitals and medical associa-tions, mental health centers, crises intervention centers, law enforcement agencies, legal associ-ations, counseling services, schools, and civic/volunteer organizations. You can use your telephone book or local library to find them.

2

1—*Activity:* Divide into groups to study neglect and abuse. Have groups give examples of each sign of neglect and abuse. Report to the class.

2—*Activity:* Summarize resources for children in crises. Which of these are available in your community or county?

Signs of Child Nelect and Abuse (continued)

Abuse

A child may be physically abused if he or she

☐ seems fearful or quiet around parents but has no close feeling for them

☐ is wary of physical contact initiated by an adult

☐ has little or no reaction to pain and seems much less afraid than most children the same age

☐ has unexplained injuries or shows evidence of repeated injuries, such as having bruises in various stages of healing or repeated fractures

☐ is dressed inappropriately. One example is an injured child dressed in pajamas who was reportedly injured on a bicycle or a child dressed in a turtleneck in the summer to cover bruises

☐ has long bones that, when x-rayed, show a history of past injuries

☐ has injuries not reported on previous health records

☐ has parents who have taken the child to many hospitals and doctors without appropriate explanation

☐ has parents who refuse further diagnostic studies of their child's injuries

☐ has parents who show detachment or see the child as bad or "different" during medical treatment

☐ has parents who give too many minute details about the cause of injury

☐ tries to protect parents when they are questioned about the child's injuries

A child may suffer verbal abuse if he or she

☐ has a low self-concept

☐ is either too quiet and polite or uses harsh and improper language when dealing with others, especially those who are smaller or younger

☐ expresses long-term feelings of damage and isolation

A child may be sexually abused if he or she

☐ has extreme and sudden changes in behavior, such as loss of appetite or sudden drop in grades

☐ has nightmares and other sleep problems

☐ regresses to younger behaviors, such as renewed thumb sucking

☐ has torn or stained underwear

☐ has infections (with symptoms like bleeding or other discharges and itching) or swollen genitals

☐ fears a person or shows an intense dislike at being left alone with that person

☐ has a sexually transmitted disease or pregnancy

☐ has unusual interest in or knowledge of sexual matters

Summary

Children's lives are influenced by their siblings. They learn by interacting with them. Children's birth order tends to affect their social roles and personalities. Multiple birth children strive to develop their separate identities.

When both parents work outside the home, all family members must cooperate to care for the home and plan time to spend together. How children adjust depends on how much time they spend with their children each day, when they enter the work force again, and how they feel about working.

Families in the United States tend to move a great deal. Moves can be less stressful for children if parents feel positive about the move and help their children get used to the new place.

It is hard for children to understand the concept of death and to deal with grief. Adults should answer children's questions truthfully and at the child's level of understanding.

There are many causes of divorce. The effects of divorce can have lasting effects. Parents need to help their children who are faced with these new stresses. When the family structure changes, such as through remarriage, families must adapt to these changes. Children need to be prepared for the new marriage and the changes this will create.

When teenagers become pregnant and have children, they are faced with many risks and problems. Because of the high risk nature of teenage relationships, many marriages end in divorce. Some teenage family structures survive through dedicated work and much effort.

Child abuse and neglect is a growing problem and one that must be stopped for the health and well-being of the children. Some social changes have been suggested that will help protect children from neglect and abuse. There are many observable signs of abuse and neglect and others that are not easily observed. By reporting suspected cases of abuse or neglect, children and adults can get the help they need.

To Review

Write your answers on a separate sheet of paper.

1. List the four main types of sibling interactions.
2. True or false. Only children are spoiled.
3. True or false. A parent should not allow multiple-birth children to wear identical outfits.
4. Name four possible advantages that children whose parents work outside the home have over those whose parents do not.
5. True or false. Most children readily adapt and look forward to family moves.
6. List the three physical concepts about death that children must learn.
7. True or false. Most teenage parents stay together for the sake of the baby and work out their financial problems.

8. Name two positive effects and two negative effects self-care may have on children.
9. True or false. Parents should give children a detailed explanation about why their marriage has failed so they can better accept it.
10. Explain the difference between child abuse and child neglect.
11. True or false. In an abusive family, certain children are more likely to be abused than others.
12. True or false. An abusive parent often acts mentally ill outside the home.

To Do

1. Make a bulletin board or poster with names and pictures of high achievers, such as political leaders or astronauts. Under each name, write the person's birth order. Are most of the people firstborn, only children, or born in other places in the family?
2. Interview teachers in your school to determine whether or not they are firstborn children who taught their younger siblings.
3. Write a fiction story entitled, "The Joys and Trials of . . ." (Being a Middle Child, Being an Only Child, Moving to a New Place, Being a Teenage Parent).
4. Ask an elementary school librarian for books on children and divorce and/or children in blended families. Give the bibliographical information, the age for which the book was written, and a few statements giving the main ideas the book conveys.
5. Read information about children in self-care and report on what you read.
6. Invite a resource person from one of the local social service agencies to speak on available services for children and their parents when parents have problems.
7. Discuss some statements people make about death that may confuse preschool children about death's reality. Look up the word *euphemism* in the dictionary. Are many of our culture's statements about death euphemisms? Explain.

To Observe

1. Observe older siblings with their younger siblings. In what ways, either directly or indirectly, do older siblings influence their younger brothers and sisters?
2. Observe a family in which the parent or parents work outside the home. What advantages do you see for the child or children? What disadvantages do you see? Do you feel the parent or parents show any role strain? Explain.
3. Observe a child who has recently experienced the stress of a move, death, or a family divorce. What seems to be the child's greatest stressor? (For example, if there was a divorce, does the main stressor seem to be missing the noncustodial parent or fearing being left by the custodial parent?) How is the child coping? How are parents, teachers, friends of the family, peers, or others helping the child cope?

To Think Critically

1. A young couple is trying to decide whether to have another child as a companion to their only child. Although they do not want another child, they have heard that only children are often spoiled and friendless. Are only children often spoiled and friendless? Under what conditions could they be spoiled? Friendless? What could happen to a child wanted only to serve as a companion to an older child?
2. Do you think role strain is solely caused by demands in a person's life or also by personality? Explain. What are some specific ways parents can lessen role strain?
3. In general, why are family moves, deaths, and divorces all difficult for children? What factors can affect children's adjustment to these situations?

Chapter 25

Children with Developmental Differences

After studying this chapter, you will be able to

☐ define the term exceptional children.

☐ explain why exceptional and other children are more alike than different.

☐ describe some of the common forms of exceptionality in children.

☐ outline steps people can take to help children with special needs.

After studying this chapter, you will be able to define

aggressive behavior
attention-deficit disorder (ADD)
attention-deficit hyperactivity disorder (ADHD)
behavioral disorders
borderline
chronic
correctable
developmental dyscalculia
dyslexia
exceptional children
gifted and talented children
hearing impaired
hyperactivity
Individualized Education Plan (IEP)
Individualized Family Service Plan (IFSP)
IQ tests
learning disabilities
legally blind
mental disability
profound
spatial orientation
speech impaired
visually impaired
withdrawn behavior

Children with developmental differences need special help.

Exceptional children develop differently than children who develop at an average pace. How does their development differ? An exceptional child's development can be faster than average or delayed. He or she may have exceptional abilities in seeing, hearing, motor skills, speech, thinking, and social behavior.

You can describe exceptional development in four ways. First, a child can be exceptional in one area or more than one area. (One child may be exceptional in art only. Another may be exceptional in art and music.) Second, a child's exceptional skills are measured by a test that shows a talent or problem. (A doctor tests a child's hearing and scores his or her abilities.) Third, the test results report the degree of a talent or problem. Words like **borderline** and **profound** describe a child's exceptional talents or problems. *Borderline* means an exceptional problem or ability is mild whereas *profound* means the problem or ability is severe. Fourth, an exceptional problem (not an ability) may be described as **chronic** or **correctable.** *Chronic* means the problem may exist for a long time, perhaps a lifetime. (A child who is missing a limb will have the problem for a lifetime.) Some problems may be *correctable,* which means they may be overcome. (A child may overcome a speech problem.)

A child's exceptional ability does not always predict success in life. Gifted children may go far, or they may not use their talents. Children with problems may make up for their problems and do well in life, or they may not.

© John Shaw

25-1 Exceptional children have the same basic needs as other children.

● Children Are More Alike Than Different

Exceptional and nonexceptional children are more alike than different. All children have the same needs. They need physical care, adults to rely on, and love, 25-1. In addition, exceptional children need special care.

Children also are more alike than different because they go through the same stages of development. However, exceptional and nonexceptional children develop at different speeds. For instance, children who are **hearing impaired** (have a hearing loss) learn to talk the same way all children do, except they learn more slowly. Children who are very bright develop just like other children, but at a faster pace. The development of children with mental disabilities is the same as for all children, except it is delayed.

In addition to speed, exceptional and nonexceptional children develop their abilities to different degrees. A child who is physically disabled may learn to walk but not to jump rope. A child who is bright may attain high-level thinking skills, unlike children of average intelligence.

3

4

1—*Discuss:* Explain the four ways to describe exceptional development.

2—*Reflect:* Do you think exceptional abilities determine a person's success in life? Explain.

3—*Vocabulary:* Define hearing impaired. Describe the special needs of a person who is hearing impaired.

4—*Discuss:* List similarities and differences between children who are and are not exceptional.

Exceptional and nonexceptional children also are alike in all ways but the exceptional area(s) of development, 25-2. A child who is physically disabled may be an average student, like others his or her age. A child who is hearing impaired may be just as good as his or her friends in sports. Many exceptional children work extra hard in the areas where they are the same as others. This helps them make up for their differences. In many cases the child is disabled in one area but gifted in another.

Children Who Are Exceptional

As you have read, the development of exceptional children differs from that of other children. When children develop faster than average, they often are described as *gifted* and *talented*. When children's development is delayed, they often are described as *disabled* or *impaired.*

Observations and/or tests are used to identify children who are exceptional. Some observations are simple, such as noting a child who uses a wheelchair. Some are more complex, such as determining whether the child has behavioral disorders. Medical examinations are given by experts in their field, such as eye and hearing tests. One test that is frequently used for determining mental exceptionalities is the IQ test.

IQ stands for "intelligence quotient." *IQ tests* are measures of how quickly a person can learn, of how able a person is to reason using words and numbers, and of how easily a person can find

25-2 Exceptional and nonexceptional children are more alike than different.

Courtesy of GameTime, Fort Payne, Alabama, U.S.A.

1—*Enrich:* Research instances in which people with disabilities have made special efforts to excel. Report to the class.

solutions to problems. Thus, IQ tests measure what is called "intelligence." As you have learned in math, a quotient is the answer to a division problem. Years ago, when children answered IQ test questions, they would be given a score called the "mental age." (The mental age meant that a given child performed like the typical child of that age. This means that a child with a mental age of six performed like a six-year-old, but could be actually a 4-year-old, 5-year-old, etc.) The mental age was divided by the chronological age (child's actual age). This division yielded a quotient which was multiplied by 100 and called an "IQ." If the child's mental age and actual age were the same or nearly the same, the child had an average IQ of 100 or nearly 100. If the mental age was a year or more older than the actual age, the child had an above-average IQ. If the child had a mental age a year or more younger than the actual age, the IQ was below average. Today, a special chart is used to compare the mental age with the chronological age rather than using the division problem to determine the IQ.

Intelligence tests are more accurate when given by the expert to one person at a time. Although intelligence tests can be given to preschool children, the results are more accurate when given in middle childhood and later (at about nine years and older). Intelligence tests for infants and toddlers are not accurate because these very young children are too difficult to test. They cannot sit still to take the test, and they do not have the needed skills to understand what to do or how to respond to the tester. IQ is more accurate when children have the ability to remember, reason, understand and respond verbally, make patterns, and work puzzles.

▶ ## Children Who Are Gifted and Talented

Almost every child has a talent he or she can do better than anyone else. A child might read, swim, or jump rope better than other children. Because all children have gifts, the words *gifted* and *talented* are hard to define.

Gifted and talented children are defined as children who can or who do show high performance in one or more of the following areas:

- ☐ general mental ability (the child shows above average intelligence)
- ☐ specific academic aptitude (the child excels in one or more subject areas)
- ☐ creative or productive thinking (the child writes or invents)
- ☐ leadership ability (the child plans or organizes)
- ☐ high skill in visual or performing arts (the child excels in art, music, or dance)
- ☐ high psychomotor ability (the child excels in sports)

Some children seem to be gifted or talented in almost all areas. Others are talented in one or two areas only, 25-3.

Statistics on gifted and talented children show that about 16 out of every 100 children are above average. About 3 of the 16 are gifted. About three to five percent of all school-age children—some two to five million children—qualify for special school programs.

2

25-3   This boy is gifted in the area of art. Giving children extra attention in their gifted areas helps them advance their talents.

3

Mississippi Dept. of Econ. and Comm. Dev.

1—*Reflect:* Describe your talents.

2—*Vocabulary:* Define the terms *gifted* and *talented*. Does your school have a program for students who are gifted and talented? Describe specific teaching techniques and activities used in these classes.

3—*Discuss:* What special instruction and activities should be provided for this boy?

1

Why are some children gifted? Giftedness seems to be due partly to genes. Certain talents seem to run in families. For instance, musical ability ran in the Mozart family. Giftedness also is due to an environment that encourages a child to pursue his or her gifts. Again, the father of Wolfgang Amadeus Mozart encouraged his son to play music at a young age.

Just as all children are unique, so are gifted and talented children. However, gifted and talented children often have some shared traits that set them apart from their peers, 25-4. Experts use test scores; art products; or judged performances in music, dance, or sports to see if a child is gifted and talented.

▶ Children with Physical Disabilities

There are many types of physical disabilities. Some children are *visually impaired* (have problems seeing). Some of these problems can be corrected with glasses. Other vision problems are so severe that they make a person unable to see. Some children who are *legally blind* do not have any vision. Others may see light, colors, shadow forms, or even large pictures. Children who are visually impaired may squint, hold objects close to their face, and rub their eyes. Having poor *distance judgment* (missing steps and bumping into objects) is a sign, too. *Self stimulation play* (making rocking movements or noises) is another sign.

2

People who are hearing impaired have hearing loss that ranges from hard of hearing to deafness. Hearing aids can help some of these people use their sense of hearing to learn and communicate. Others who are deaf have such severe hearing loss that even hearing aids cannot help. Children with hearing problems may not respond to sounds, may not make speech sounds correctly, or may not talk. Many children who are hearing impaired also touch more than other children and watch other peoples' faces and mouths closely.

There are many other kinds of physical disabilities in addition to vision and hearing problems. These include missing limbs; bone, joint, and muscle diseases; and damage to the brain or nervous system, 25-5. All of these problems cause delays in gross-motor development.

▶ Speech Disorders

The speech of children with speech disorders is different than average-sounding speech. Children who are *speech impaired* speak in ways that draw attention, are not easily understood, or cause the speaker to have a poor self-concept. Children who are speech impaired can have problems in one of the following three areas:

- ☐ articulation. Children may use one sound for another, distort sounds, or leave out or add sounds in words.

- ☐ voice problems. Children's voices may be too high or too low in pitch, too loud or too quiet, nasal, or husky.

- ☐ rhythm problems. Children may repeat sounds or words, be unable to get speech out, or speak rapidly.

▶ Children with Mental Disabilities

A child with a *mental disability* is often defined as a child whose intellectual abilities, when compared with the average, are a year or more delayed. Mental disabilities may vary from mild to severe. There are many causes of mental disabilities. They include gene disorders, prenatal and birth problems, and injuries and infections to the brain after birth. The lack of basic experiences in the environment also may cause mental disabilities. As is true of all children, those who are mentally disabled are all different. These children often share the following signs:

- ☐ delays in motor skills
- ☐ smaller vocabularies and shorter sentence lengths
- ☐ a grasp of simple, but not highly complex ideas
- ☐ attempts to avoid tasks they cannot do easily
- ☐ short attention spans
- ☐ fondness for repetition
- ☐ problems making choices

1—*Reflect:* Explain factors that contribute to giftedness.

2—*Vocabulary:* Define the terms *visually impaired* and *legally blind.* List characteristics of each. How can each be detected?

3—*Enrich:* Do research on types of physical disabilities. How are these disabilities treated? Report to the class.

4—*Discuss:* Describe signs of mental disabilities.

Traits of a Gifted and Talented Child	
Traits	**Examples**
The child uses advanced vocabulary at an early age.	At age two a child says, "I see a kitten in the backyard and he's climbing our fence," instead of just saying, "I see a kitten."
At age two or three a child may learn to read on his or her own.	Most gifted children do not read at an early age. This may be because they see no need to read. However, those who do read learn on their own.
The child is quite observant and curious.	As a toddler the child remembers where all the toys are stored on the shelf. At age two and three the child begins to ask many questions that begin with what, where, how, and why. They may ask, "How does the water get out of the bathtub?" "Where does the water go?" "Why does water go down?"
The child remembers many details.	The child can recall many past experiences with details that adults may have forgotten.
The child has a long attention span.	At age one the child may look at a book for five minutes. Other children may just glance at the book. By school age the child may spend hours on a project and even be totally unaware of other events.
The child understands complex ideas.	Children who are gifted want to learn so much that the topics that interest them change often.
The child develops critical thinking skills and makes careful judgments.	Children who are gifted note when something seems illogical. For instance, seeing water drops form on the outside of a glass, the child may ask, "How does the water get there? It did not rain on the glass." Children who are gifted also are more critical of themselves. They may say, "I should have done better. That was a silly mistake."
The child shows talents early.	A child gifted in visual arts may draw facial expressions like sadness or surprise at a young age. At this same time friends are drawing circles for the eyes and nose and a curved line for the mouth.
The child does not like repetition.	A child who is gifted likes the new and unsolved. The child may become bored when asked to do 50 basic math problems.

25-4   All gifted children are different. They also share some common traits.

1—*Discuss:* Discuss the traits and examples of people who are gifted and talented.

© John Shaw

25-5 Children with physical disabilities like to take part in many of the same activities as other children.

and spelling. They may find it hard to connect words with their written forms. These children may reverse words and letters when they read or write them. They may confuse the order of letters in words or read words backwards. More boys than girls have dyslexia. ***Developmental dyscalculia*** is another learning disability that affects a child's mathematical abilities. The problem is usually caused by injury to different parts of the brain.

Learning disabled children have average and often above-average intelligence. However, they function at lower levels due to their disabilities.

Causes of Learning Disabilities

What causes a child to be learning disabled? Studies show learning disabilities are not caused because parents do not help children learn. They also show they are not caused because children are spoiled, lazy, stubborn, or mentally disabled. Learning disabilities seem to be caused by physical problems. For example, dyslexia is associated with a disorder of the body's central nervous system. Other causes include problems before birth, such as lack of oxygen for the fetus. Problems during birth itself also may cause learning disabilities. Other causes are accidents, high fevers, and breathing or nutritional problems after birth.

In the past, learning disabilities were rarely noted before the school years. This is because a disability often shows up when formal learning begins. Some children can cover up their disability, even in the lower grades. They may memorize words in a reading text rather than really read them. The signs shown in 25-6 seem to be common for many children. However, the differences are that a child with a learning disability thinks in a disordered way. This happens at the same time his or her peers are ready to learn and think more clearly. Learning problems are part of the everyday life of a child with a learning disability.

Greater awareness of learning disabilities has made it possible to help these children. Also, more testing programs and more preschool programs have detected learning disabilities at an earlier age.

▶ ## Learning Disabilities

Learning disabilities are defined as problems in one or more areas of spoken or written language, mathematics, and spatial orientation. (***Spatial orientation*** is the ability to see the relationship of your body to objects in space.)

Some learning disabilities include dyslexia and developmental dyscalculia. ***Dyslexia*** is a disability that affects a child's ability to read. Children with dyslexia also have problems writing

| Basic Traits of Children with Learning Disabilities or Disorders ||
Traits	Examples
Brain messages are jumbled even though the sense organs are normal	☐ Reads the word *on* as *no*. ☐ Writes *24* for *42*. ☐ Says *aminal* for *animal*. ☐ Says *breakfast* instead of *lunch*. ☐ May stop in the middle of a sentence and start a new idea. May think someone asked, "How old are you?" when they really asked, "How are you?"
Poor spatial orientation	☐ Has problems doing tasks that involve spatial concepts like up and down, left and right, top and bottom, and above and below. ☐ Doesn't see items that are in the line of vision. ☐ Gets lost often. ☐ Has problems writing on a line. ☐ Has problems with jigsaw puzzles.
Seems awkward or clumsy	☐ Has trouble tying shoes or buttoning small buttons. ☐ Is poor at sports. ☐ Trips or loses balance because of misjudging distance. ☐ Has poor timing. ☐ Cannot coordinate several tasks at one time.
Has a short attention span	☐ Cannot listen to a story or finish a project.
Is overactive	☐ Is always moving, to the point of bothering others, because of overactivity.
Acts disorderly	☐ Needs more attention than most children of the same age and receives the attention by misbehaving. ☐ May misbehave to convince others that the behavior is bad instead of unintelligent.
Is inflexible	☐ Becomes upset when any routine changes. ☐ Becomes anxious in new places or around new people. ☐ Rejects objects that are different (for example, won't eat a cracker that is broken instead of round). ☐ Demands that others cater to his or her needs even when it is not possible.

25-6   In general children with learning disabilities or disorders cannot think clearly. The problems they face as they try to learn differ.

1—*Discuss:* Discuss the traits and examples.

▶ Behavioral Disorders

Behavioral disorders are problems that surface in a person's behavior. Disorders are often marked by extremes of behaviors. As with all other forms of exceptionality, disorders that affect behavior occur in all degrees of severity. Causes of a disorder are often a puzzle. In some cases, stress seems to be the cause, especially when stress is severe and constant. Disorders that affect behavior may be due to injuries to the brain and other physical reasons. Experts are in the early stages of solving the puzzle of disorders. There are several common behavioral disorders.

Aggressive behavior is an outward behavioral disorder. Children with this disorder name-call, fight, and bully without being provoked into such actions.

Withdrawn behavior occurs when children do not relate well with other people. They may resist change and panic when changes occur. They often have poor self-concepts and do not always think realistically.

Two related disorders have to do with the ability to pay attention. People must use attention and memory to learn and retain information and to solve problems. To pay attention, a person has to focus one or more of the senses upon a certain aspect of the environment (listen to a recording) and to ignore irrelevant information (a humming fan).

Although all people sometimes become distracted, some people are highly distractible. Two disorders that involve attention are: *attention-deficit hyperactivity disorder (ADHD),* which involves the lack of attention and *hyperactivity* (extremely active behavior) that is more than a normal high energy level, and *attention-deficit disorder (ADD),* which involves the lack of attention, but does not include hyperactive behaviors, 25-7. ADD is sometimes called "hypo-activity disorder."

ADHD and ADD are difficult to diagnose. Diagnosis in children is based upon observations rather than upon medical tests. Similar symptoms appear in childhood anxiety and depression. Although the problems with lack of attention and learning disabilities are different, they often occur in the same children.

1—*Resource: A More In-Depth View,* SAG.

Traits of Children with Attention Disorders

Attention-Deficit Hyperactivity Disorder

Are inattentive; easily distracted; forgetful

Act as if "driven"

Are fidgety (may run, climb, or move in other ways constantly; get out of their chairs or their places in group settings)

Constantly change activities often without completing anything

Do sloppy and incomplete work

Speak out in class

Will not wait for their turns

Have frequent and intense emotional outbursts (fight, have self-imposed isolation, defiant, and can't take criticism)

Are clumsy and accident prone

Have excessive activity in sleep

Attention-Deficit Disorder

Are inattentive; easily distracted; forgetful

Act disinterested ("tune-out") or daydream

Fail to finish a task or play activity

Appear not to listen

Cannot organize work

25-7 Children who cannot "pay attention" are often diagnosed with attention disorders. Some are also hyperactive.

Some researchers state that 10 percent of all children have either ADHD or ADD, but others claim that the numbers are much lower. Hyperactivity is often misdiagnosed; some experts say that only one to three percent of children who are labeled hyperactive are truly hyperactive in a medical sense. Hyperactivity is present, however, in 75 percent of the cases involving attention disorders. Attention disorders affect boys four to five times more often than girls.

Several techniques are being tried to help children with attention disorders. These include:

☐ Restricting stimuli (having fewer items to see, hear, etc., at the same time)

☐ Establishing a routine to be strictly followed

☐ Giving clear instructions

☐ Using praise and rewards

☐ Providing experiences that are challenging but manageable

☐ Having physical activities

☐ Watching diet especially food coloring

☐ Giving medications such as Ritalin which calms hyperactivity

Ritalin and other medications, when carefully monitored by doctors, have proved valuable in some cases. Giving medications without careful observations has been criticized for several reasons, however. First, it is often the first treatment tried. Second, Ritalin has side effects such as depression of children's appetite and growth, sleeplessness, listlessness, and even a stupor-like-state. Third, frustrated teachers and parents may use Ritalin as a way to "control" children who do not need the drug but who have high energy levels.

● Exceptional Children Need Special Help

Family members often are shocked when they learn for the first time that their child is exceptional. This news is even more shocking when this exceptional quality is a disability. Sometimes families face this when a child is born. Other times, the problem may not be noticed until the child does not make average progress in language or school work. For still other parents, an accident or illness disables a child. Even giftedness or talent shocks parents because the active minds or special talents of these children often baffle adults.

▶ How Many Children Are Exceptional?

One child out of every 10 children is exceptional. The percentage of children involved varies with the type of exceptionality. About 3.5 percent of all children have speech disorders. However, deafness affects far fewer children (about .075

percent of all children).

Anywhere from 3 to 45 percent of all children have learning disabilities, depending on the way the term *learning disabilities* is defined. Public Law 94-142, Public Law 99-457, and other laws require that all exceptional children receive a free and appropriate public education. It is important that enough government money exists to assist children who need lots of special help. For this reason, the term *special needs* must not be defined too broadly or funds would be too scarce to go around.

2

▶ What Kinds of Help Do Exceptional Children Need?

All exceptional children need special help. Parents generally start to seek help through a pediatrician. The doctor can refer the child for needed tests, 25-8. Once testing is complete, doctors can explain the child's strengths and weaknesses to parents and discuss ways to help the child.

Laws require public schools to educate

3

25-8 Experts use tests to pinpoint each child's disability or gift.

1—*Reflect:* How might discovering that a child is exceptional affect a parent?

2—*Discuss:* What legal provisions are made for children with special needs?

3—*Enrich:* Do research on tests used to detect disabilities or giftedness.

exceptional children between the ages of 3 and 17, 25-9. Laws also require an Individualized Education Plan (IEP) to be designed for each exceptional student. (An **Individualized Education Plan (IEP)** is an educational plan that is tailored to the special needs of an exceptional child.) Parents, teachers, and school administrators design the plan together and agree to carry it out. Parents also meet with their child's teachers on a regular basis, 25-10. The child also is retested on a regular basis.

States may, but are not required to, provide services for exceptional children who are younger than three years of age. Laws require an **Individualized Family Service Plan (IFSP)** be written if these services are provided. Unlike the IEP, which focuses on the child's needs, the IFSP focuses on the entire family's needs. The IFSP is

© John Shaw

25-10   Parents help plan their exceptional child's education.

written to coordinate all needed services for each family that are related to the infant's or toddler's development.

Members of the family often join support groups. Many of these groups are national with local chapters. At the national level, these groups provide family members with the latest information on exceptional children. National groups also seek money for research and assistance for families who need costly training or equipment. At the local level, groups support the goals of the national groups. They also provide helpful contacts and services among those with similar needs.

25-9   Special programs that meet the needs of children are available through public funds.

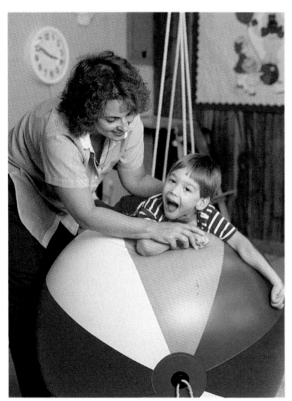

© John Shaw

Summary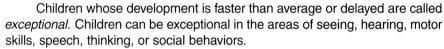

Children whose development is faster than average or delayed are called *exceptional.* Children can be exceptional in the areas of seeing, hearing, motor skills, speech, thinking, or social behaviors.

All children, whether exceptional or nonexceptional, are more alike than different. All children have the same basic needs. Children who are exceptional need special help in some areas.

Children who are gifted and talented often show high performance in one or more areas. These areas include mental ability, specific academic aptitude, and creative or productive thinking. Other areas of high performance may be in leadership, visual or performing arts, or psychomotor abilities. Gifted children tend to show their talents early and share some of the same traits, such as an early use of vocabulary and a memory for details. Gifts and talents may be due partly to heredity. They also seem to be due to the environment in which children are encouraged to practice and cultivate their talents.

Children who have problems in their developmental areas are sometimes described as *disabled* or *impaired.* Sometimes a condition is described as a *disorder.* The most common types include physical disabilities, speech impairments, mental disabilities, learning disabilities, and disorders that affect behavior.

Tests can help identify the strengths and the weaknesses of a child with a disability. Federal funds help these children in their education. When problems are indicated, an Individualized Education Plan is written for the child. This plan sets up a program of education that would best meet the special needs of that child.

Children with disabilities, as well as children with gifts and talents, can be a challenge for parents. Support groups are a great help because they provide helpful contacts and services with others in similar circumstances.

To Review

Write your answers on a separate sheet of paper.

1. Exceptionalities (are, are not) seen in degrees and (may, may not) last a lifetime.
2. True or false. Some forms of exceptionality are hard to define.
3. For exceptional children, the _____ of development and/or the _____ of development will differ from that of other children.
4. Name three types (areas) of gifts and talents.

5. Match the following traits seen in exceptional children with the type of exceptionality that best fits.

   Traits

   _____ asks many complex questions at a young age

   _____ watches others' faces very closely

   _____ uses one sound for another sound

   _____ shows poor distance judgment

   _____ writes *saw* for *was*

   _____ likes repetition

   _____ can't identify right and left

   _____ uses a large vocabulary

   _____ hits without being provoked

   _____ has many interests

   _____ has a poor self-concept

   _____ at an early age plays a musical instrument with much skill

   _____ has delayed motor skills and finds complex ideas hard to grasp

   Types of exceptionality

   a. children with gifts and talents
   b. children with vision impairments
   c. children with hearing impairments
   d. children who are speech impaired
   e. children with mental disabilities
   f. children with learning disabilities
   g. children with behavioral disorders

6. Name three signs of a possible learning disability in children.

7. Order from 1 to 5 the steps to help an exceptional child.

   _____ testing

   _____ writing an IEP

   _____ referral for testing

   _____ finding a suitable program to help the child

   _____ retesting and writing a new IEP from time to time

To Do

1. Invite a resource person from an agency dealing with disabled children to discuss one disability in depth.
2. Invite two or more parents of children with disabilities to discuss their children's disabilities, how they help their children, and what support groups are helpful.

3. Read a biography or autobiography of a person with gifts and talents. Report to your class on the traits that were seen at an early age.
4. Read a biography or autobiography of a person with disabilities. Report to your class on how this person compensated for the disability.
5. Observe a program serving exceptional children. How does the program differ from a regular classroom in terms of the housing and equipment, class size, staff to child ratio, subjects taught, teaching methods, and other factors? How is it the same as a regular classroom?

To Observe

1. Observe a classroom for children with disabilities or a classroom in which children with disabilities have been mainstreamed. Explain how all of the children are more alike than different.
2. Observe exceptional children in a group setting. List all the ways you note that the children received special help.
3. Observe an exceptional child in any setting. What special challenges do you think the parent of this child would face?

To Think Critically

1. Do you know exceptional children? What makes them exceptional?
2. What types of problems do families face when they have exceptional?
3. What is the overall goal of the special help given to exceptional children? Does this differ from the overall goal for children who are not exceptional?

1—*Enrich:* Do research on careers involving children with developmental differences. Report to the class.

Appendix

First Aid Procedures

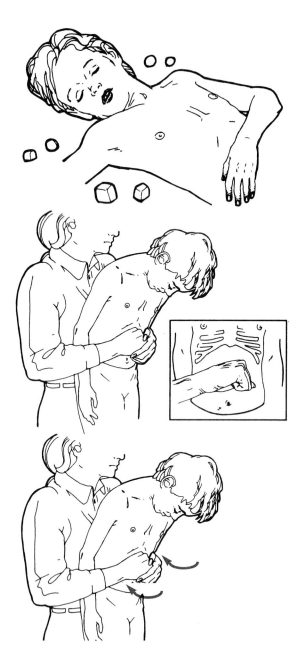

● Choking Abdominal Thrust (Heimlich Maneuver)

▶ **Call for Help!**

- ☐ Do not slap the child on the back.
- ☐ Do not hold the child upside down.
- ☐ Do not probe the child's throat with your fingers.

1   Recognize choking.

A child found unconscious, not breathing, and not showing signs of other injury is most likely choking. Bluish lips and fingernails also are signs of choking. DO NOTHING if the child is talking, breathing, or pink.

2   Pick child up from rear around the waist.

Place fist of one hand above navel but well below rib cage, as pictured. Cover fist with other hand. (For a very small child use two fingers from each hand.)

3   Pull upward with both hands quickly but gently three to four times.

Repeat if necessary to dislodge the object from the windpipe. (For a very small child lessen the force of thrusts.)

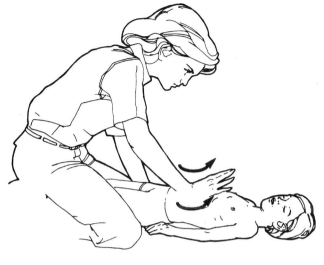

4   If the child is too big to pick up, kneel over the child as shown.

Place hands above navel well below rib cage. Press upward into the stomach with three to four quick thrusts. Repeat if necessary.

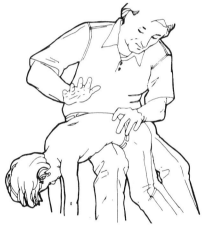

5   If all else fails, use back blows.

Drape a small child or infant over your arm or thigh so the child's head is down. The child's abdomen should be against your arm or thigh. Strike child sharply three to four times between the shoulder blades.

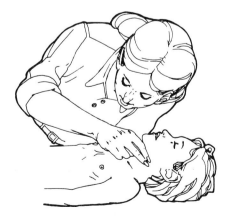

6   Watch breathing and check pulse.

Be prepared to give mouth-to-mouth breathing and chest compressions.

● Bleeding

▶ Call for Help!

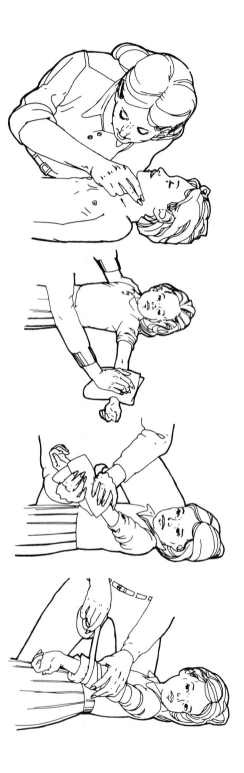

1 Make sure child is breathing and has a pulse.

If the child is not breathing or does not have a pulse in the neck, take steps to clear the airway or administer CPR before you stop the bleeding.

2 Apply direct pressure on bleeding wound with clean cloth.

3 Keep pressure on.

Elevate limb above the heart (unless limb is broken).

4 Bandage firmly but not tightly when bleeding is controlled.

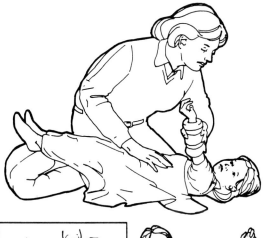

5 Treat for shock.

Elevate the child's feet. Keep the child warm.

If bleeding continues. . .

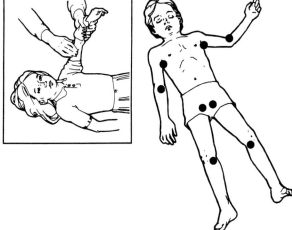

6 Find the pressure point between the bleeding wound and the heart.

Press firmly with other hand as you continue to place direct pressure on the wound (see picture).

7 Use a tourniquet **AS A LAST RESORT ONLY.**

Wrap a piece of cloth above the wound between the wound and the heart. Twist a stick around ties to stop the flow of blood to the wound. Hold or tie the cloth. NOTE THE TIME.

These pages are adapted from *Emergency Medical Treatment: Children,* by Stephen Vogel, M.D. and David Manhoff. The book includes procedures for 11 emergency situations commonly encountered with children. Obtain copies by writing to EMT Inc., Box 983, Wilmette, IL.

Glossary

A

abstinence: choosing not to have sexual intercourse. 3

abstract: words that do not relate to what they represent. 16

Acquired Immunodeficiency Syndrome (AIDS): a virus that attacks the body's immune system. 5

active immunity: immunity in which a person's body produces its own antibodies. 21

active vocabulary: the words used in talking or writing. 8

active-physical play: games and activities involving gross-motor skills, such as walking, running, hopping, jumping, twisting, bending, skipping, galloping, catching, throwing, balancing, pushing, pulling, and rocking. 20

adoption: the process by which a child of one pair of parents (or parent) legally becomes the child of other parents (or parent). 2

adoption agency: a state-funded or private agency licensed by the state to handle adoptions. 2

adrenaline: a hormone that prepares the body to cope with stress. 5

afterbirth: the placenta that is expelled through continued contractions following the birth of a baby. 5

age norms: average ages for children to reach certain points of development, such as talking, walking, or cutting teeth. 7

age of viability: the seventh month of pregnancy; the age at which the fetus could survive with special help if it were born. 4

age-appropriate behaviors: proper or normal ways to express emotions at certain ages. 9

aggression: an attempt to hurt or an act of hurting someone. 18

aggressive behavior: name-calling, fighting, or bullying without being provoked into such actions. 25

allergen: a substance that causes an allergic reaction. 21

allergy: result when a person's immune system is very sensitive and reacts when the person comes into contact with an allergen. 21

altruistic behavior: concern for others. 18

amniocentesis: a test in which a needle is inserted through the woman's abdomen into the amniotic sac and a sample of the fluid is removed for cell study. 5

amnion: a fluid-filled sac that surrounds the baby in the uterus. 4

anemia: a low level of oxygen-carrying substances in the blood. 6

antibodies: agents that prevent a person from having a disease. 21

antigen: an agent contained in a vaccination made from the substance that causes a disease. The substance is changed so that it does not cause a reaction as serious as the disease itself. 21

anxiety: fear of a possible future event. 9

Apgar test: a test that checks the baby's chance of survival. 6

articulate: to make the sounds of a language. 12

artificial insemination: when sperm is introduced into the uterus by a medical procedure rather than by sexual relations. 3

assertive: the act of speaking out, standing up for your rights, and defending yourself. 18

attachment: closeness between people that remains over a period of time. 9

attachment behaviors: actions one person demonstrates to another person to show closeness to that person. Actions include staying close to, clinging to, or following a person. 9

attention-deficit disorder (ADD): a disorder that involves the lack of attention, but does not include hyperactive behaviors. 25

attention-deficit hyperactivity disorder (ADHD): a disorder that involves the lack of attention and hyperactivity (extremely active behavior) that is more than a normal high energy level. 25

auditory: referring to the sense of hearing. 19

authoritarian: parenting style in which the main objective is to make children completely obedient. 2

autonomy: a form of self-control in which a person seeks to do his or her will. 13

B

babble: to make a series of vowel sounds with consonant sounds slowly added to form syllables, such as be, da, gi. 8

behavioral disorders: problems that surface in a person's behavior. 25

birth control methods: methods couples use to control the conception of children. 3

birth defect: a physical or biochemical defect that is present at birth and may be inherited or caused by environmental factors. 5

birthing room: a room used for both labor and delivery. 5

blended families: families that merge when one single parent marries another person or when two single parents marry. 2

body proportions: the relative size of body parts. 7

body rotation: the action of turning the trunk of the body to one side when the hand of the other side is used to throw. 15

bonding: developing an attachment or feeling of affection. 5

borderline: a term used to define a mild exceptional ability. 25

Brazelton scale: a test used to determine whether a baby is normal in these four behavioral areas: interaction with the environment, motor processes, control of physical state, and response to stress. 6

breech birth: a birth in which the baby comes out in a buttocks-first position rather than a head-first position. 5

C

career burnout: a state in which a person becomes emotionally tired of a career. 23

cartilage: soft, gristle-like tissue that is structural, such as bones, but more flexible. Cartilage is the tissue found in the tip of your nose. 4

Casa dei Bambini: an all-day program for slum children between ages two and one-half and seven that Maria Montessori set up in the early 1900s. 22

cell: the smallest unit of life that is able to reproduce itself. 4

Certified Nurse Midwives (CNM): nurses who have special training in delivering babies during normal pregnancies. 5

Cesarean section: a birth process in which the mother's abdomen and uterus are surgically opened and the baby is removed. 5

character: an inward force that guides a person's conduct and helps people make choices that meet acceptable standards of right and wrong. 1

child abuse: the act of one person physically hurting another person's body, using harsh language when talking to or about a person, and having inappropriate sexual contact with the person. 24

child care programs: programs that operate to care for children for extended hours, usually between 9 and 12 hours a day. 22

child-centered society: a society that sees children as important and works for their good. 1

child development: the scientific study of children from conception to adolescence. 1

childhood diseases: diseases that are often contracted during childhood. 21

child neglect: a failure to properly meet the needs of children. 24

childproofing: moving objects out of a child's reach or preventing a dangerous situation. 21

children in self-care (latchkey children): children who are at home alone after school or for a portion of the day and must care for themselves during that time. 24

chorion: membrane that surrounds the baby in the uterus. 4

chorionic villus sampling (CVS): a procedure for finding abnormalities in the unborn by testing a small sample of the chorion, which later develops into the placenta. 5

chromosomes: thread-like structures that carry genes in living cells. 4

chronic: term meaning something, such as a talent or problem, may exist for a long time, perhaps a lifetime. 25

class: a group of items that are alike in some way. 18

class complement: in classifying, anything that does not belong to the class. 18

classification: the ability to mentally group objects by their similar traits. 16

closed adoption: an adoption in which the identity of the birthparents and of the adopting family are not revealed to each other. 2

cognition: the act or process of knowing or understanding. 8

colic: a condition in which a baby has intense abdominal pain caused by allergies, tension, swallowing air when sucking, and hunger. 6

collective monologue: talking to another person but not listening to what the other person has said. 16

communication: the skill needed to understand others and to be understood by them. 12

compare: to see how things are alike or different. 18

concept: an idea formed by combining what a person knows about a person, object, place, quality, or event. 8

conception: the union of the ovum and sperm. 4

concrete: based on actual experience. 19

concrete operational stage: Piaget's third stage of mental development. In this stage, children begin to think logically, but logic is based on what the child has experienced at some time. 19

conservation: the concept that changing an object's shape, direction, or position does not alter the quantities of the object. 19

consultants: adults who share their knowledge, such as knowledge about children, with other adults. 23

contagious disease: a disease that can be caught from another person. 21

contrariness: the tendency to oppose almost everything that others say. 14

contrast: to see how objects and people are different. 18

convergent thinking: coming up with only one right answer or way to do a task. 18

coo: a light, happy sound babies begin to use to communicate between six and eight weeks after birth. 8

cooperation: joint effort. 18

coordination: the working together of muscles in movements like walking. 10

cradle cap: scaling of skin on the newborn's scalp. 6

crawling: moving by pulling with the arms but not lifting the abdomen from the floor. 7

creeping: moving by using the hands and knees or the hands and feet. 7

cruising: walking with the support of an adult. 7

culture: the way of life for a group of people, including language, attitudes, values, rituals, and skills. 1

D

deciduous teeth: the first set of teeth in a person, later replaced by permanent teeth. Also called nonpermanent, baby, and milk teeth. 7

deductive reasoning: reasoning from the general to the specific. 19

deferred imitation: the ability to recall someone's behavior and imitate it. 12

democratic: a parenting style in which parents set some rules but allow children some freedom. 2

dental caries: decayed places in teeth. 21

dependence: when one person relies on another person to meet his or her needs. 9

depressants: substances that slow the functions of organs and the nervous system. 10

depth perception: the ability to tell how far away something is. 8

development: the process of growth through many stages, such as infancy, childhood, adolescence, and adulthood. 1

developmental acceleration: when a child is performing like an older child. 1

developmental delay: when a child is performing like a younger child. 1

developmental dyscalculia: a learning disability that affects a child's mathematical abilities, usually caused by injury to different parts of the brain. 25

developmental tasks: skills that should be mastered at a certain stage in life, such as crawling, self-feeding, and dressing. 1

developmentally appropriate practices (DAP): child care and education that uses knowledge about child development; the strengths, needs, and interests of each child within the group, and the social and cultural contexts in which children in a given program live. 22

developmentally inappropriate practices (DIP): child care and education that do not use knowledge about child development, focus mainly on the group instead of each child. 22

diabetes: a disease caused by the body's inability to utilize sugar. This happens when the body does not produce or use insulin properly. 5

diagnosis: identifying the disease causing a person's illness. 21

dilation: the first stage of labor, during which the cervix opens wider. 5

direct intervention: working directly with children. 23

direct observation: watching children in their natural environments. 1

discipline: using different methods and techniques to help teach children self-control. 2

disposition: a person's general mood, such as a tendency to be cheerful most of the time or a tendency to be moody most of the time. 9

divergent thinking: coming up with different possible ideas. 18

dominant: a trait that shows up in a person even if only one gene in a gene pair is for that trait. 4

dyslexia: a disability that affects a person's ability to read. 25

E

eclampsia: a metabolic disorder that affects blood, causing swelling; formerly called toxemia. 5

educational neglect: failure to conform to state legal requirements regarding school attendance. 24

egocentric: self-centered. 13

egocentrism: the belief that everyone thinks in the same way and has the same ideas as one person. 16

embryonic stage: the second stage of prenatal development, which lasts about six weeks. 4

emotional dependency: the act of seeking attention, approval, comfort, and contact. 17

emotional neglect: failure to help children develop emotionally. 24

emotions: thoughts and feelings that cause changes in the body. 9

enriched environment: an environment with many objects, sounds, etc., that gives a person a chance to learn. 10

entrepreneur: a person who creates and owns his or her own business. 23

enuresis: any instance of involuntary (by "accident") urination of a child over three years of age. 18

environment: a factor that influences growth and development and includes all the conditions and situations that affect a child. 1

episiotomy: an incision made from the vagina to the anus to prevent tearing during the delivery of a baby. 5

exceptional children: children whose development is either faster than average or delayed. 25

experimental children: a name sometimes used to describe firstborn children because parents often try new, untested ideas on them. 24

expulsion: forcing out. 5

extended family: several generations of one family living together, including an older couple, their children, in-laws, and grandchildren. 2

eye-hand coordination: the ability to coordinate what a person sees with the way he or she moves his or her hands. 11

F

failure to thrive: a failure to grow, which is diagnosed as a drop in growth percentiles over time. 7

fallopian tube: a hollow tube connected to the uterus with finger-like projections reaching toward the ovary. 4

false labor: irregular contractions that happen in some women before true labor begins. 5

family child care: care of a small number of children in another person's home. 22

family culture: the beliefs and traditions of a family. 2

family history: stories of a family's past. 2

family life cycle: the stages or changes through which families go through the years. 2

family planning: deciding on the number and spacing of children a couple will have. 3

fertility counseling: determining the reasons for sterility and the fertility options available. 3

fetal alcohol effect (FAE): a condition in infants that is less severe than fetal alcohol syndrome. It occurs when mothers drink excessively during pregnancy. 5

fetal alcohol syndrome (FAS): a condition in infants that occurs when mothers drink heavily or excessively during their pregnancy. 5

fetal stage: the third stage of pregnancy, lasting from about nine weeks after conception until birth. 4

fetus: a term used to describe a baby in the fetal stage of development. 4

field trips: outings that take children to places off a child care program's property. 22

Fifth disease: a disease that causes dangerous anemia in the unborn anytime during pregnancy. 5

fine-motor skills: coordination in the small muscles, especially those in the fingers and hands. 10

finger plays: poems and rhymes that are acted out with the hands. 22

first aid: treatment for an illness or accident that is given immediately, before professional medical help. 21

flexibility: the ability to move, bend, and stretch easily. 19

forceps: steel tongs that fit the shape of a baby's head. They are used to gently pull or turn the baby during delivery. 5

foregone income: earnings given up by a parent or parents when a parent stays home to raise a child. 3

formal leadership: leadership used by elected or appointed officials and managers in organized groups. 23

formal operations: Piaget's last stages of mental abilities in which a person (age eleven or older) can reason more abstractly. 19

for-profit programs: programs that are set up to make money. 22

foster homes: families who take care of, but do not adopt, children who cannot live with their natural parents. 2

fraternal twins: children who develop from two different ova in the same pregnancy and have different genetic makeups. 4

G

gender role learning: knowing what behavior is expected of a male or a female. 17

genes: bead-like structures that are strung together to form chromosomes. They determine the various traits of a person. 4

germ cells: the sperm and ovum. 4

germinal stage: the first stage of prenatal development, which lasts about two weeks. 4

GIFT (gamet intra-fallopian transfer): a procedure in which the sperm is introduced into the woman's fallopian tubes, where several ova have also been placed surgically. 3

gifted and talented children: children who can or who do show high performance areas of general mental ability, specific academic aptitude, creative or productive thinking, leadership ability, performing arts, or psychomotor ability. 25

grammar: meanings given to the order of words. 12

gross-motor skills: the ability to use large muscles to roll over, sit, crawl, stand, and walk. 10

group child care: care provided in centers, also called "center child care." 22

growth pains: pains caused by muscles trying to catch up with skeleton size. 19

growth spurt: a rapid period of growth, usually linked with adolescence. 19

guidance: all of a person's actions and words around children, which affect the way children think and act. 2

guilt: blaming yourself for something done wrong. 17

H

Head Start: a federal program that was launched in 1965 for children from low-income families who need more food, medical care, and help with learning. 22

hearing impaired: having hearing loss that ranges from being hard of hearing to being deaf. 25

heredity: a factor that influences growth and development and includes all the traits from blood relatives that are passed down to a child. 1

hidden added costs: costs that add to the direct costs, such as costs of transportation, supplies, and disposable diapers. 22

hidden cost credits: credits that lower the direct costs of child care. 22

hierarchical classification: having classes within other classes. 19

hospitalization: being cared for in a hospital. 21

hyperactivity: an extremely active behavior in which a person is overactive, restless, and has a short attention span. 25

I

identical twins: children who develop from one fertilized ovum and have the same genetic makeup. 4

illegal market adoption: an adoption in which people pay money that exceeds medical and legal costs to an agency, independent source, or natural parents to adopt a child. 2

imitating: copying the actions of someone else. 8

imitative-imaginative play: play in which children pretend to be persons or objects other than themselves. 20

immunity: having agents that prevent a person from developing a disease. 21

immunization: an injection or drops that are given to a person to provide immunity from a certain disease. 21

independent adoption: an adoption in which a person, such as a lawyer or physician, works out the details between the natural and adoptive parents. In some independent adoptions, no one works out these details. 2

indirect costs: resources spent on something other than actual expenses that could have been used to meet other goals. 3

indirect observation: observation done by asking questions of parents, teachers, or children. Also includes observing products children make, such as artwork or stories children dictate or write. 1

individual life cycle: a description of how people change through the years as they go through various stages. 1

Individualized Education Plan (IEP): an educational plan that is tailored to the special needs of an exceptional child. 25

Individualized Family Service Plan (IFSP): a plan that focuses on the entire family's needs and is written to coordinate all needed services for each family that are related to the infant's or toddler's development. 25

induction: a technique in which parents discipline by reasoning and explaining. 2

inductive reasoning: reasoning from specific facts to general conclusions. 19

Infant Schools: child care programs in Europe in the late 1700s and early 1800s that served poor children from toddlerhood to ages five or six. 22

infertile: unable to reproduce. 3

inflections: changes of pitch. 8

informal leaders: people who lead or guide others even though they are not officially chosen to lead. 23

in-home child care: care provided by a person hired to care for children in the family's home. 22

initiate: to begin. 9

initiative: the ability to think or act without being urged. 17

inoculation: an injection or drops that are given to a person to provide immunity from a certain disease. 21

intellectual development: how a person learns, what a person learns, and how a person expresses what he or she knows through language. 8

intensive care nursery: immediate care for babies born with problems, such as heart, digestive tract, spine, or brain defects. 6

internal organs: body parts like the heart, lungs, and liver. 15

internalized: something that only is thought about and not shared with others. 16

intolerance: a negative reaction caused by eating a food. 10

intuitive substage: a substage of the preoperational stage in which children can solve many problems correctly. However, they rely on imagining how they would act out the solution rather than relying on logic. 16

In vitro fertilization: a procedure in which the mother's ovum or ova are surgically removed and fertilized with the husband's sperm in a laboratory dish, then implanted in the mother's uterus. 3

involuntary infertility: the inability to reproduce after one year of trying to become pregnant. 3

IQ tests: measures of how quickly a person can learn, of how able a person is to reason using words and numbers, and of how easily a person can find solutions to problems. 25

J

joint custody: an agreement between divorced parents in which both parents are involved in decisions that affect their children's life. 2

K

kindergartens: programs publicly and privately operated for four- and five-year-old children; serves as an entrance to school education. 22

L

labor: the process that moves the baby out of the mother's body. 5

Lamaze method: a type of delivery in which the pregnant woman uses breathing patterns to keep her mind off pain rather than using drugs. 5

language: a symbol system in which words are used as labels for people, objects, and ideas. 12

language-logic play: a form of mental play common in school-age children that may involve play with words such as word puzzles or puns, strategies, or problem solving. 20

large-motor skills: the use and control of large muscles that help babies to crawl and walk. 7

large-muscle development: the development of the trunk and arm and leg muscles. 11

latchkey: term describing children who are at home alone after school or for a portion of the day and must care for themselves during that time. 24

learning disabilities: problems in one or more areas of spoken or written language, mathematics, and spatial orientation. 25

Leboyer method: a method of delivery that focuses on making the baby as comfortable as possible during and immediately after delivery. 5

legally blind: having no vision or only having the ability to see light, colors, shadow forms, or outlines of large objects. 25

lethal: deadly. 21

licensing personnel: people who check the quality of services for children, such as the quality of child care centers. 23

lifestyle: the typical way of life for a person, group, or culture. 23

lightening: a change in the baby's position in which the uterus settles downward and forward and the baby descends lower into the pelvis. 5

locomotion: the ability to move from place to place. 7

logical thinking concepts: concepts not directly experienced through the senses; concepts developed through thought. 16

love-withdrawal: a discipline technique in which parents threaten children or suggest some form of parent/child separation. 2

Lyme disease: a disease spread by the deer tick that can cause heart defects in the unborn and result in premature birth or stillbirth. 5

M

manipulate: to handle objects in various ways, such as by rolling, shaking, or bending. 15

manipulative-constructive play: activities and games that involve fine-motor skills, such as painting and stringing beads. 20

manipulative stage: a stage in which children play with art materials rather than use them to create artwork. 20

maternity leave: time off from work taken by a mother-to-be before and after the baby is born. 3

medical neglect: failure to seek treatment for a serious health problem or accident that could endanger the child. 24

melody percussion instruments: instruments, such as xylophones, that produce various pitches when certain bars are struck. 20

mental disability: the condition of a person whose intellectual abilities are a year or more delayed than average. 25

mental images: symbols of objects and past experiences that are stored in the mind. 16

middle childhood: the period of development from ages six to twelve. 19

middle children: the term referring to the second child in a family of three siblings or both the second and third children in families of four siblings. 24

mobile: in a state of moving or relocating frequently. 24

monologue: talking to oneself. 16

monotone: sounds all in a single pitch. 8

Montessori schools: schools that encourage children to learn as they work at tasks. Children are allowed to roam freely and participate in whatever tasks they wish. 22

moral neglect: failure to teach the child right from wrong in terms of general social values. 24

mortality: death. 24

motor development: the use and control of muscles that direct body movements. 7

multiple pregnancy: two or more babies developing in the same pregnancy. 4

muscle development: the lengthening and thickening of muscles. 11

N

natural childbirth: a method of delivery in which the pregnant woman has the birth process explained to reduce fear. Instead of using drugs, she also is taught breathing and relaxation techniques to reduce pain and assist delivery. 5

neonatal intensive care units (NICUs): heated, completely enclosed beds for newborns that need intensive care. 6

neonate: medical term for the baby from birth to the age of one month. 6

neonatology: a branch of medicine concerned with the care, development, and diseases of newborn infants. 6

not-for-profit programs: child care programs in which income only covers costs. 22

nursery school: a public or private program for children under age five that provides education as well as physical care for children. 22

nurturance: all aspects of child care, such as feeding, dressing, bathing, and meeting emotional and social needs. 2

nutrient density: the level of nutrients in a food in relation to the level of calories in the food. 14

nutrients: substances in food that give people energy and help them grow. 10

O

obedience: acting within the limits set by others. 14

obese: extremely overweight. 5

object concept: the ability to understand an object. 8

object constancy: the ability to learn that objects remain the same even if they seem different. 8

object identity: the ability to learn that an object stays the same from one time to the next. 8

object permanence: the ability to learn that people, objects, and places still exist even when they are no longer seen, felt, or heard. 8

obstetricians: doctors who specialize in pregnancy and birth. 5

open adoption: an adoption that involves some degree of communication between birthparent(s) and adoptive family. The *openness* of the adoption refers to how much information is exchanged and how much contact occurs between the birthparent(s) and the adoptive family.

orthodontist: a dentist who specializes in correcting irregular teeth. 21

orthopedic: referring to bone and muscle. 19

ossification: hardening of bones caused by the depositing of the minerals calcium and phosphorus. 7

ovum: the egg or female sex cell. 4

P

passive immunity: the newborn's immunity to diseases brought about by antibodies passed to the infant from the mother through the placenta. 21

passive observing: watching another's actions without responding. 18

passive vocabulary: the words a person understands but does not say. 8

paternity leave: a usually unpaid leave taken by the father for a certain period of time after a child's birth. 3

pediatrician: a doctor that cares for infants and children. 6

peers: children who are around the same age, but not brothers and sisters. 17

perception: organizing information that comes through the senses. 8

perceptual learning: the process of developing perception. 8

percussion instrument: musical instruments that produced a tone when some part of the instrument is struck. 20

permanent teeth: teeth harder and less sharp than baby teeth that are intended to last a lifetime. 19

permissive: a parenting style in which parents give children almost no guidelines or rules so children make their own decisions about right and wrong. 2

personal qualifications: all the traits a person possesses that he or she does not learn in career training. 23

personal references: people who know you well enough to discuss how you are qualified for a job. 23

phenylketonuria (PKU): a disease that can cause mental retardation if left untreated by diet. 6

physical abuse: violence which results in injuries. 24.

physical neglect: when adults fail to provide for a child's basic survival needs, such as clothing, food, shelter, and supervision, to the extent that the failure can be a hazard to the child's health or safety. 24

placenta: an organ filled with blood vessels that nourishes the baby in the uterus. 4

play therapy: using play as a way to help children with their problems. 20

postnatal care (postpartum care): the care the mother receives during the six to eight weeks following the birth of her baby. 5

postpartum blues: a down feeling caused by hormone changes some women experience within a few days after delivery. 5

power-assertion: a discipline technique in which parents use or threaten to use some form of physical punishment. 2

precision: ability to perform motor skills accurately; includes balance, steadiness, and skill in aiming at a target. 19

preconceptual substage: a substage of the preoperational stage in which children are developing some concepts, but many concepts are incomplete or not logical. 16

premature: babies born too soon or small. 5

prenatal development: the development that takes place between conception and birth. 4

preoperational stage: the second of Piaget's developmental stages in which children have begun to do some mental thinking rather than solving all problems by acting. However, the thinking is not truly logical yet. 16

preschool children: children between the ages of three and five. 15

principles of growth and development: statements of the general patterns in which growth and development take place in people. 1

private programs: programs owned by individuals, churches, or other nongovernment groups. 22

problem solving: noting a problem, observing and questioning what you see, and solving the problem. 18

professional qualifications: the physical, mental, and social-emotional skills you need to perform in a career. 23

prop box: a collection of real objects placed in a box to fit different roles; used by children in role-playing. 20

properties: the qualities of objects, such as color, size, shape, and texture, that can be evaluated with the senses. 18

psychological abuse: any act in which an adult makes excessive demands, harasses, or threatens the child resulting in a negative self-image or disturbed behavior on the part of the child. 24

psychological neglect: failure to help children develop psychologically. 24

psychological security: a feeling that someone cares and will help when needed. 19

public programs: child care programs funded by federal or state monies. 22

Q

quality time: a time when parents are totally attentive to their children. 24

quickening: the movements of the fetus that the mother can feel. 4

R

reaction time: the time required to respond to a stimulus, such as the time it takes to react to a thrown ball. 15

recessive: a trait that does not show if only one gene is present. 4

reduplication babbling: repeating the same syllable over and over again, such as saying da-da-da-da. 8

reflexes: automatic, unlearned behaviors. 6

registered dietitians: people who have special training in nutrition and diet and meet the qualifications of the American Dietetic Association. 14

regulations: standards that govern a group program. 22

representation stage: a stage in which children create symbols that represent objects, experiences, and feelings. 20

repressed jealousy: jealousy not directly expressed and even denied. 17

restraint systems: car seats, harnesses, and other devices that hold children safely in place during accidents or sudden stops and turns. 21

resume: a short, written history of a person's education, work experience, and other qualifications for employment. 23

reversals: mentally doing and undoing an action. 18

Rh factor: a protein substance found in the red blood cells of about eighty-five percent of the population. 5

rhythm instruments: percussion instruments without a definite pitch, such as drums. 20

ritual: a pattern of activities repeated at a regular time, such as a bedtime ritual including a bath, a drink of water, a story, and a hug. 14

role guilt: a feeling of not doing the best job at work or at home due to role strain. 24

role strain: a feeling of having too many jobs at one time. 24

rooming-in: an arrangement in which the baby is placed in a bassinet in the room with the mother after birth. 5

rooting reflex: the instinct in babies to search for food. When you touch a newborn's cheeks or skin around the mouth, the head turns and the mouth moves. 6

Rubella: three-day measles; formerly called German measles. 5

S

scapegoating: blaming others for one's own mistakes. 19

school-age children: children between the ages of six and twelve. 19

scientific reasoning: the form of logic commonly used by scientists. 19

scribbling: the second step in the manipulative stage; writing that consists of dots, straight and curved lines, loops, spirals, and imperfect circles. 20

self-assertion: doing as you choose rather than doing what others want; insisting on your rights. 14

self-awareness: how a person feels about himself or herself. 13

self-esteem: the belief in yourself as a worthwhile person. 13

self-restraint: the ability to control yourself. 14

sensorimotor stage: the first of Piaget's stages of development. In this stage, children use their senses and motor skills to learn and communicate with others. 8

sensory learnings: the ability to see, taste, smell, and feel foods of many colors, shapes, sizes, and textures. 14

sensory stimulation: using the five senses to learn about the environment. 10

separate identities: feelings of being a distinct person. 24

separation anxiety: anxiety most common in babies caused by the fear that loved ones who leave them will not return. 9

sequence: order. 7

sequenced steps: the steps in growth and development following one another in a certain order. 1

sex typing: treating boys and girls differently. 17

sexual abuse: any sexual act of an adult with a child. (Some states define sexual abuse is any sexual act between a child and anyone who is at least five years older than the child.) 24

sexual stereotyping: a statement or even a hint that men and women always do or should do certain tasks. 17

sexually transmitted diseases (STDs): infectious diseases transmitted primarily through sexual intercourse. 5

shortcomings: areas where a person wants or needs to improve. 19

show: a small amount of blood in the mucous when the mucous plug in the cervix becomes loose, signaling that labor is imminent. 5

siblings: brothers and sisters. 9

single-parent families: families headed by one adult resulting from the death of one parent, divorce (and separation and desertion), births outside of marriage, and adoption of children by single persons. 2

singletons: children born one at a time, as opposed to twins or other children of multiple births. 24

skeletal system: the portion of the body made up of hard, structural tissue; the bones and teeth. 7

small-motor skills: the use and control of the small muscles of the hands and fingers. 7

small-muscle development: the development of small muscles, especially those in the hands and fingers. 11

social-emotional development: development of a person involving disposition, interaction with people and social groups, and emotions. 9

social isolation: feelings of being alone. 24

socialization: the process of interacting with others. 13

solids: foods other than breast milk that may or may not be in solid form. 10

sonogram: the picture of the fetus the ultrasound test produces. 5

spatial: pertaining to space. 14

spatial orientation: the ability to see the relationship of your body to objects in space. 25

speech impaired: having speech so different from others that it calls attention to itself, is not easily understood, or causes the speaker to have a poor self-concept. 25

sperm: the male sex cell. 4

spontaneous abortion: the expulsion of the baby from the mother's body before it can survive. 5

static balance: the ability to balance on one foot. 15

step-families: families that merge when one single parent marries another person or when two single parents marry. 2

sterile: the condition that prevents couples from conceiving by natural methods. 3

stillborn: babies born dead. 5

stimulants: substances that speed up the functions of organs like the heart and nervous system. 10

stimuli: an agent, such as light or sound, that directly influences the activity of the sense organs. 8

stressors: situations that cause stress. 17

surrogate mother: a woman who bears and sometimes both conceives and bears a child for a couple. 3

symptoms: signs of an illness or injury. 21

T

teachable moment: a time when a person can learn a new task because the body is physically ready, caregivers encourage and support, and the child feels a strong desire to learn. 1

teething: the appearance of teeth as they come up through the gums. 7

temper tantrums: sudden emotional outbursts of anger. 13

temperament: the tendency to react in a certain way, such as in a cheery way or a moody way. 9

terminally ill: having a disease that will result in death. 21

toilet training: the process by which adults help children control their excretory systems, namely bowel movements and urination. 14

toxemia: a metabolic disorder that affects blood, causing swelling. 5

Toxoplasmosis: infection caused by a parasite that can damage an unborn's nervous system. 5

training pants: pants with a multilayered cotton fabric crotch that help lessen the mess of accidents during toilet training. 14

transformation: the sequence of changes by which one state is changed to another. 18

transitional stage: a stage of development in which a person is passing from one stage to another. 14

transparencies: pictures that show the inside and outside of an object at the same time, much like an X ray. 20

two-parent family: the type of family that exists in most societies, consisting of a father, a mother, and their biological child or children. 2

U

ultrasound: a test in which sound waves bounce off the fetus to produce an image of the fetus inside the womb. 5

umbilical cord: the cord that connects the baby to the placenta. 4

uterus: the organ in which the baby develops and is protected until birth. 4

V

vaccination: an injection or drops that are given to a person to provide immunity from a certain disease. 21

verbal abuse: any act in which an adult makes excessive demands, harasses, or verbally threatens the child resulting in a negative self-image or disturbed behavior on the part of the child. 24

veterinarians: animal doctors. 21

visual arts: physical forms of art, such as painting, constructing, and photography. 20

visually impaired: having vision problems ranging from those that can be corrected with glasses to blindness. 25

vocabulary: the words a person understands and uses. 8

voluntary grasping: the ability that replaces the grasping reflex and uses arm, hand, and finger control. 7

W

weaning: the gradual process of taking a baby off the bottle or breast. 10

weight shift: the change of weight from the back foot to the front foot. 15

well-baby checkups: checkups doctors give when a baby or child appears healthy. 21

withdrawn behavior: behaviors that show a separation from the rest of society, such as not relating well to other people, not wanting changes to occur, and poor self-concept. 25

work-related child care programs: child care programs funded by businesses for their employees. 22

Z

zygote: the fertilized egg cell. 4

Index

● Photo Credits

▶ Chapter Opening Photos

Blanco, Joe / Blanco Photography, chapter 15

Carter's, Photography by Bruce Plotkin, chapter 8

Fisher-Price, chapters 7, 9, 16

Sears, Roebuck, and Company, chapter 5

Shaw, John, chapters 3, 12, 13, 14, 17, 18, 19, 20, 23, 25

▶ Photo Contributors to *Children: The Early Years*

Alexander, Nancy P.
P.O. Box 18008, Shreveport, LA 71138-1008
(318) 686-6613

American Association of Retired Persons
W.B. Doner and Company
400 E. Pratt Street, Baltimore, MD 21202
(410) 347-1600

American Montessori Society/Montessori Greenhouse School
17583 Oak, Fountain Valley, CA 92708
(714) 968-0107

Angeles Group, Inc.
9 Capper Drive, Dailey Industrial Park
Pacific, MO 63069
(314) 257-0533

Binney and Smith, Inc.
1100 Church Lane, P.O. Box 431, Easton, PA 18044-0431
(610) 253-6271

Evenflo Products Company
771 North Freedom Street, P.O. Box 1206
Ravenna, OH 44266-1206
(216) 296-3465

Fisher-Price, Inc.
636 Girard Avenue, East Aurora, NY 14052
(716) 687-3000

GameTime
P.O. Box 121, 150 GameTime Drive, Fort Payne, AL 35967
(256) 845-5610

Geo. W. Park Seed Company, Inc.
Cokesbury Road, Greenwood, SC 29647-0001
(864) 223-8555

Hart, Marcia Hillman
435 Buchanan Street, NW, Washington, DC 20011
(202) 722-2997

Kimberly-Clark Corporation
401 North Lake Street, P.O. Box 349, Neenah, WI 54957-0349
(920) 721-2841

Lakeshore Learning Materials
2695 E. Dominguez Street, P.O. Box 6261
Carson, CA 90749
(310) 537-8600

Landscape Structures, Inc.
P.O. Box 198, 601 7th Street South
Delano, MN 55328
(612) 972-3391

Pitsco LEGO Dacta
915 E Jefferson, Pittsburg, KS 66762

March of Dimes Birth Defects Foundation
National Office, 1275 Mamaroneck Avenue
White Plains, NY 10605
(914) 428-7100